Vos igitur, doctrinae et sapientiae fillii, perquirite in hoc libro colligendo nostram dispersam intentionem quam in diversis locis proposuimus et quod occultatum est a nobis in uno logo, manifestum fecimus illud in alio, ut sapientibus vobis patefiat.

—*Cornelius Agrippa*
De Occulta Philosophia, L. III Cap. LXV

The Forbidden Alchemies of Frater PVN

The Forbidden Alchemies of Frater PVN

Bill Siebert
Master, Forbidden Alchemies
also known as
Otz-PTN-GDO, Alobar Greywalker

Edited by Sam Webster
Reflections by Don Karr & Cliff Pollick

Concrescent Press

The Forbidden Alchemies of Frater PVN

Bill Siebert

Master, Forbidden Alchemies
also known as
Otz-PTN-690, La-Baj-AL
ASht ChOzar SSaratu 1103,
and Alobar Greywalker

Copyright 2021 Concrescent LLC

All rights reserved. Except for brief quotations in a review, the book, or parts thereof, including the cover art and interior illustrations, must not be reproduced in any work without permission in writing from the publisher. For information contact Concrescent Press, Richmond CA, USA

www.Concrescent.net
ConcrescentLLC@gmail.com

ISBN: 978-1-9583590-3-4

Library of Congress Control Number: 2021951984

List of Exclusions:

"PVN–416, some recollections", Art pp. 26, 163, 164, 165, 168, 169, 170, 171, © Don Karr
"Meeting and Knowing William Andrew David Siebert" © Cliff Pollick
Appendix pp. 186-194 © Work of the Chariot Trust

Paperback version of the 2nd Edition with corrections and new content.

In memoriam

William Andrew David Siebert

also known as
Frater PVN
OTz PTN-690
La-Baj-AL
ASht Ch0zar S*Saratu* 1103
and
Alobar Greywalker

May 27, 1945—July 2020

Greetings and a Warning

Not For Everyone

Herein lie the Forbidden Alchemies of Frater PVN. In these Alchemies are treated the use of sex for magic, drugs for illumination, and rituals for entering into dangerous realms. If any of these things offend you, put this book down.

This work is a collection of the rare chapbook editions of PVN's work mostly from the 1980s, reset and expanded with supplementary material, most of which has seen only limited distribution. With death of the author, his friends gathered their files to produce this volume.

None of what is herein is politically correct, socially approved or within the bounds of dogma; anyone's dogma. Enter at your own risk, apply what you learn at your own discretion. The views expressed in this work are solely of the authors and are not be attributed to the publisher.

We have preserved Frater PVN's idiosyncratic typography and grammar to convey the character of his writing. Commentary, except for a few clarifying remarks in the footnotes, will be reserved to the end.

Come meet Frater PVN as we did, on his own terms.

—the Publisher

Acknowledgments

A memorial work is best the product of many hands and this book is no different. Special thanks go to Denny Sargent of the Horus/Maat Lodge who found several articles and an autobiography in their archives. Also to Louis Martinie of Black Moon Publishing and the Cincinnati Journal of Ceremonial Magick & Archive which preserved many short essays from Frater PVN and granted us permission to raid their files for the selections reset herein. This work would be diminished without their contributions.

Particular thanks to the Work of the Chariot Trust for permission to reprint the appendix to *Nine-Fold Flowering of Alchemies within The Eleven-Star Working* introducing various traditional configurations of the Tree of Life.

Don Karr and Cliff Pollick provided personal essays describing their experiences of Frater PVN, especially about the time he was writing the contents of this book. To this I added a short text on my meeting Bill and his importance to me. Together, it is hoped that we provide enough of a portrait of Frater PVN that the man is not lost in his writings.

Thanks are due to Tina Beachy and Barbara Cormack for reading the proofs and making suggestions before readying the book press. Any remaining errors are mine.

—*Editor*

Herein...

Greetings and a Warning... xv
Brief introductions by Frater PVN.. xxiii

OF SEX & ALCHEMY
ChRySTAL Workings thru the Astral Mirror (Vol. I)...................... 1
ChRySTAL Visions thru the Astral Mirror (Vol. II).................... 27
The Chalice of Ecstasy 53
Trident of Set-3 prongs and Initiation....................................... 77
The Priesthood is a Condition of a Soul on Fire with Love 83
HGA and Kallas 86
Notes on VIII° Sexual Elixirs 87
Notes on Experiments Regarding the XI° Triune Elixir 90
Network Visions.. 99
Comment AL 2... 101
A True Account of the Eden Captivity 105
Early & Explicit Channelings 117
Of Shin, Teth, & Set.. 139
An Introductory Note of Explanation to the [Preceding] Pages .. 159
Spacemarks.. 181
The Rose of ChARON 187
Nine-Fold Flowering of Alchemies within The Eleven-Star....... 203
Further Notes on the Eleven Star Working.............................. 225
Eleven Star Ritual II.. 229
The Alchemy of Immortality 233
Doxology: a Vision of a Gnostic Mass..................................... 257
A Sex Magickian's Alchemical Guide to Quartz Crystals........... 273

OF CHAOS & ORDER
Math of the ChRySTAL HUMM 299
Muldalahara Chakra & the Orders 311
Roles & Nurturing within the Hive or Powerzone 315
Apologia Discordia 319
A Modest Proposal for a Superstructure to Unite the Order...... 325
Brief History of the Order... 331
Epistle to the Priest-Sovereigns of Thelema 347
The Chthonic-Auranian OTO: Origins, Purpose, & Structure ... 359
Gelfling Initiation.. 367

OF THE MISKATONIC ALCHEMICAL EXPEDITION
Miskatonic Alchemical Expedition 379
Regarding the on-Going Work of our MAE. 381
A Foray into the World of ASht Ch0zar S*Saratu* '.' 1103. 403

OF THE WORK
The Phoenix Cycle & The BAJ Material 417
Liber Set-Horus 447
Magickal Calling Cards 449

THOSE WHO KNEW HIM
The Publisher's introduction. 459
About the Author in His own Words. 465
Frater PVN's autobiography to the Horus/Maat Lodge. 469
PVN, ס-416, etc., some recollections 475
On Meeting and Knowing William Andrew David Siebert 509

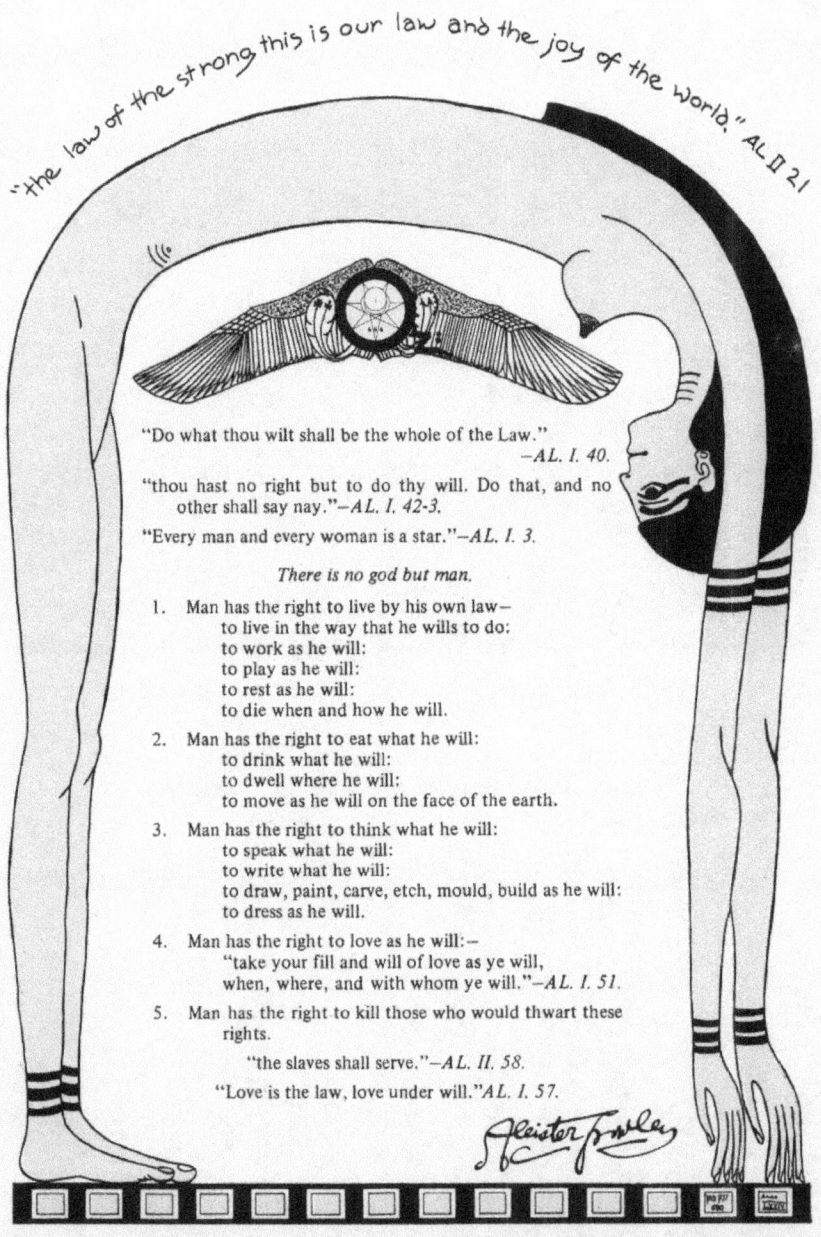

Brief introductions by Frater PVN of several of the works herein

Liber Oz sub figura LXXVII
Liber Oz is a brief political & magickal statement of the Law of Thelema suitable for mass distribution. Many Thelemites personalize Liber Oz to use as a 'calling card'. Liber Oz is well-suited for promulgating the Law of Thelema.

This version (left) of Liber Oz is more elaborate than Crowley's original card. Text has been newly typeset and is bordered with an Egyptian motif (inspired by the Stele of Revealing) in green, gold, & black. Liber Oz is printed on 3-1/2 x 5" coated cardstock, suitable for use as a domestic postcard in the USA. Artwork by Frater OTz PTN is based on a similar design by Alan Holub. One of the nicest versions we have seen so far.

OF SEX & ALCHEMY
ChRySTAL Workings thru the Astral Mirror
"Being the first volume in a series of excerpts from the Magickal Record of a certain Frater P., who must remain anonymous at the present time."

Raw unexpurgated diary material containing sexually explicit dreams, visions, & phantasies. Lovecraftian nightmare & horror made enjoyable by through the sexually libertine vision of a Thelemic Alchemist. First published work which gives glimpses into PVN's own unique branch of magick.

Rose of Charon
This Alchemical poem was penned as an intermediate 'thesis' during PVN's early experimentations with Liber HHH. Heavily influenced by his work with Typhonian magicks of Kenneth Grant and his personal explorations of certain ramifications of the formula of the XI°.

With explanatory notes of obscure references to the Trident of SET and the Quadriga Sexualis. Includes the life cycle of the mythical Set Beast, or Hound of Tindalos which is said to inhabit the esoteric nervous system of PVN.

Nine-Fold Flowering of Alchemies within the ELEVEN-STAR
"The Eleven-Star is an experiment to reify the spirit of the A∴A∴ within a pattern of inter-locking & over-lapping inter-dependent Alchemickal Powerzones, one for each of the 10 Sephira, both Dayside & Nightside, & the (oft mis-understood) Gateway at Death."

This essay contains one alchemist's view of this anarchistic magickal Order. Detailed outline of 3 Branches of Sexual Alchemy:
1. The Solitary Sanctuary of the VIII°
2. The Sovereign Sanctuary of the IX°
3. The Secret Sanctuary of the XI°

While not intended as a practical handbook, this essay does a tentative job of comparing & contrasting 2 of the major aspects of XI° sexual magick (which PVN poetically refers to as Sodom & Gomorrah).

An appendix gives a detailed skeleton for a practical alchemical experiment in recombinant genetics which shows how the various aspects of sexual alchemy are used to create a new form of humanity. Warning: explicit sexual details may offend &/or titillate some readers.

The Alchemy of Immortality:
VAMPIRES and the Alchemy of Blood
PVN resurrects the Vampire legends & examines them in the light of Holy Blood, Holy Grail, & the vampire novels of Chelsea Quinn Yarbro. This essay is a modest attempt to do for Vampires what Margaret Murray & Gerald Gardner did for Witches. This essay links Vampires to the Alchemies of Atlantis and to the mythology of the Dying God. It postulates that Jesus Christ was a Vampire & a member of this sacred priestcraft. Glimpses into a Lovecraftian & Machiavellian Universe by a Thelemic Alchemist who is a notorious sexually libidinous Xenophile.

Builds on work of 9-Fold Alchemy essay and reveals even more practical applications for sex magick. Includes a list of suggested readings and an appendix which states the modus operandi of sexual alchemy in words which even the novice can understand.

DOXOLOGY & Vision of a Gnostic Mass

A Thelemic Doxology by PVN dedicated to Jack Parsons with extended commentary to help elucidate the role of Babalon, Therion, & Prometheus within the microcosm of the initiate. Astral vision of a Gnostic Mass based upon the Trident of SET. First published work hinting at possible application of this practical Alchemical tool.

OF CHAOS & ORDER
Math of the ChRySTAL HUMM

Charter & Statement of Purpose for this Powerzone. Contains a mathematical model for accessing the trans-dimensional Gateway at 10^{-33} Meters and a preliminary outline of the 3 primary branches of the Alchemical Priestcraft.

Apologia Discordia

The Latin title of this essay translates as "In Defense of Disagreement". Apologia Discordia was originally penned by B.S. in violent reaction to certain non-constructive criticisms which he received at the start of his magickal career. The original essay was never published. Frater PVN has re-worked the original ms. to tone-down B.S.'s indignation & violent reaction to rejection while preserving the spunk & thrust of the original.

Brief History of the Order

A non-standard History of the OTO & the A∴A∴ based upon information given to Frater PVN while on a personal vision quest to the fountainhead of the Order. Text of this essay is designed to transcend history and tradition rather than clarify or justify them. This controversial document has been withdrawn from circulation for further editing at the request of several members of the OTO.

of Sex
&
Alchemy

Chrystal Workings thru the Astral Mirror

Being the first volume in a series of excerpts from the Magickal Record of a certain Frater P. who must, at this time, remain anonymous...

Do what thou wilt shall be the whole of the Law.

Introduction

The magickal system used by P. to achieve the visions noted within these pages is complex and not easily put into words. What is written of the 'mechanics' of his rituals are true, insofar as it is possible to convey Truth in linear form. Those who seek the linear truth of reason are warned to avoid any temptation to utilize P.'s system of magick, for it will surely lead to their speedy demise. This pamphlet is presented to these folks for their mindless entertainment only.

Anyone who is serious in his/her pursuit of High Magick should consider these workings as 'suggestive' rather than as literally True, for each must develop his/her own system of Magicks which is best suited to unlock the patterns of initiation from within. Study of the systems of other magickians will make the task much easier, but no magickian can produce new and innovative work by following slavishly in the footsteps of another. We each have a unique nervous system; we each bring to our magick a unique set of talents and aspirations; we must each create the future in unique ways.

At the moment there is not much in print on P.'s system of magick. He prefers to discuss his magicks face-to-face rather than through the linear & clinical medium of the printed word. But he has begrudgingly conceded that since he has neither the time nor the temperament to put up with chelas, he will do the necessary work to put his magickal system into print. PVN is concerned with neither grammar nor spelling; nor does he place great value on linear organization of material. All items in this series will be but strands within the fabric of the pattern of his magicks. A list of suggested readings will be issued sometime in the future. For information on obtaining other items in this series, please contact the publisher.

Love is the law, love under will.

yrs for the Great Work,
B.S.
(editor of P.'s material)

Here begins excerpt from Diary for Friday, 12 November, 1982 e.v.
I did a free-float before taking a nap & utilized the crystal to assist me in regaining entrance to a dream of the night before last (Tuesday night). I was asleep & had forgotten that I was asleep, so the dream was not under my conscious control. For the most part, the dream was forgotten, but there was a section in which I was being bitten & clawed by two small dogs. I awoke from the nap & remembered O-Shinnah's warning about avoiding those parts of the astral which were guided by dogs. According to her, these regions of the astral have temporary rifts between the planes & any who traverse these rifts are in dire peril of being stranded away from their bodies if/when the rifts close. These dogs are most probably the Hounds of Tindalos who guard the angles of the alien dimensions which impinge upon our space/time continuum. These hounds have harried me in dreams ever since I was a small child. I was determined to get back to my dream & deal with these hounds once & for all.

Using VIII Degree & my crystal as a focus I was able to get back to the general region of the astral where I had encountered these two small dogs. I met a young woman there (most probably a spirit guide) [who had assumed the outward form of M_____] who agreed to assist me in my quest for the two dogs. We performed the ritual of XI Degree (el. rub.) & I passed from her temple in trance to another place upon the astral where I saw myself retreating from the two small dogs (I am somewhat used to these convolutions in time, but it is still amusing to watch myself exiting the astral stage just as I am entering from another angle). This time the dogs did not attack me, for they knew that I was consciously dreaming.

As I approached them, they dissolved into a pool of ichor with glitters. I stretched the web of glittery goo into a triangular archway & peered through the rift. The background of the astral stage (a street scene which looked like any large city in Eastern USA, circa 1982) was totally invisible when viewed thru the archway of astral dog entrails. I moved the archway around & peered through it at various angles. I finally found a rift in the black background. The rift formed a very unusual angle which was very difficult to look at (the angle was too alien to be fully comprehended). I wedged the archway (which was quite rigid) into the rift in order to hold it open & then I stepped through.

On the other side of the rift I saw a hand with seven fingers. On each finger was a ring. Each ring had a precious stone of a different colour. There was one stone for each of the primary colours of light (red, blue, green), one stone for each of the primary colours of pigment (cyan, magenta, and yellow) and one very gaudy clear glass stone which looked to be of very little value. The long slender hand offered me the cheap glass ring, which I accepted. I then felt a quaking & I fell back through the ichor archway into the astral region of New York City clutching the ring. I opened my hand & I saw that the clear glass stone was now jet black. In fact it was so black & so cold that it seemed to draw-in all energy rather than reflect it. It was not the least bit shiny & it seemed to grow & absorb surrounding light the more I looked at it.

I purchased a small pouch at one of the many curiosity shops which abound in this region of the astral, & hung the ring (within the pouch) around my neck.

I then focused my energies on the web of energy which permeates my crystal & used it to draw me back into my physical body.

Back in bed, I lie awake with my crystal resting on my heart & my hand clutched to an invisible pouch which hangs around my neck. I am safely returned to my physical body, but my pretty bauble remains (for now) upon the astral.

Here begins excerpt from entry for Sunday, 14 November, 1982 e.v.
Saturday night I did my evening free-float at bedtime. I found myself upon that portion of the astral which I have identified with New York City. I feel a weight about my neck. It is the pouch containing the gem of night. I open the pouch & the darkness radiates outward threatening to engulf the maya of the astral. I seal the pouch & seek the company of the priestcraft of the Night.

I manage to procure two priestesses & one priest along with a suitable temple. We set-up to perform a modification of the Mass of the Mirror (see Outside the Circles of Time by Kenneth Grant for details) with me as a gynandrous priest/(ess). As I began to drift into the state of neither/neither (from the ministrations of both priestesses and the priest), I open up the pouch & remove the dark crystal ring. The darkness does not envelop the astral temple, but it does cause the mirror above me to turn absolutely black. Meanwhile, I am still aware of my physical vehicle which performs VIII° magick while clutching the quartz crystal to its heart. As the point of climax threatens to engulf me, I look into the black mirror above me & project through the gateways of sleep visible in the mirror and into the absolute void.

Upon waking on Sunday morning, I had a vague memory of being in some sort of public dancehall or brothel. I focused upon the memory & used my crystal to re-gain entrance to the astral. As my focus improved, I utilized VIII° Karezza to formulate the black crystal of Night within the astral pouch around my neck. [I return to the dream]

Upon the stage is a middle aged woman of very powerful charisma. She danced to her own internal music while clad only in myriad crystals. The crystals are woven about her with very thin threads, leaving most of her body exposed. Hanging (suspended in air) about a foot below her crotch—between her legs—is a fist-sized Herkimer diamond.

At first I assumed it was supported by threads from her garment of tiny gems, but then I noticed a single thin thread which linked the huge gem to her vagina. I instinctively know that on the other end of the thread [deep within her womb] I will find a similar sized black gemstone.

She beckons me closer & I mount the stage. She dances around & over me for a time & I find myself totally entranced.

I awake to a sharp pressure at the basal point of my spine. I am within the net of jewels pressed against the priestess while her Herkimer diamond is pressed to my coccyx. She draws in her breath & the Herkimer is sucked upward into her vagina. I am drawn up by the attraction from the vagina and pressed upward from the force of the Herkimer pressing on my tailbone. I momentarily blacked-out.

When I again became aware of my surroundings, I am within a black hole (astronomical, not anatomical). The universe of stars shine all around me, but I know that it would be fruitless to attempt to egress through the Vagina of Nuit, for a black hole absorbs all & allows exit to nothing.

There is an alien pathway (through an odd twist in time & space) which leads me deeper into the blackness of the dark star. There is much light behind me, but none shines through the stygian blackness ahead of me. I sense (but cannot see) the three-headed dog at my left side & another (unknown) 'presence' at my right side.

I travel onward in silence and without thought for quite some time. Eventually I come to a well-lit cave which opens outward into a large open marble palace bathed in yellow light.

Picture a marble floor as big as Manhattan island (only round), surrounded by pillars of inestimable height, and crowned by a roof as high as the heavens. Through the open archways I can see the cold blue snow & the black night sky which perpetually surrounds this place [how I know this I do not know, for I do not remember being here before]. In the center of the palatial room sits one of the elder gods upon a short pillar of rough (red veined yellow) rock. His(her?) long nose is rimmed in tentacles. The massive trunk of her(his?) body seems oddly incongruous with the small leather-like bat wings perched upon his(her?) shoulders. The hands each have seven fingers.

13 of these fingers are each adorned with a different colored gemstone ring. As he(she?) puts her(his?) fingers together I see the pattern of the colors & perceive the energy fields which surrounded them. On the left hand is six rings, the fingers arranged in a circle such that the colored stones form a color-wheel with red, blue, and green stones separated by magenta, cyan, and yellow. The other hand is the same, only the seventh finger (which bore a black stone) is held within the ring of six. As I look upon these rings, their energy causes my mind to spin.

When my mind clears, I know where I have seen this place before. I had caught the slightest glimpse of this place & this being when I had traversed the gateway of Tindalos Hound Ichor which led between the twisted planes (see previous entry). I am even now wearing the 14th ring upon a string around my neck. (My ring is now clearly a brilliant crystal, and not the stygian blackness which it emanated while it was upon the astral). I now seem to 'remember' that I had not been 'given' this ring of clear crystal/utter blackness but had snatched it just as I had dashed back to the astral through my self-created gateway.

My instinctive reaction to this 'memory' is to return the ring with an apology for my un-remembered kleptomania, when I am reminded of the verse from the *De Vermis Mysteriis* of Ludwig Prinn, which states clearly:

"Never accept a gift from a necromancer or demon. Steal it, buy it, earn it; but never accept it as a gift or legacy."

Since I am now definitely within the reality which Lovecraft knew far better than I, I put aside my native honesty & seek an escape route.

My self-created gateway is not sealed, but it is guarded by beings which hurt my eyes if I try to look at them too closely. I cannot return through the black-hole, for that pathway was most assuredly set-up as a trap for me & is therefore a one-way street.

I then remembered that I am not only 'here' (which I intuitively feel to be on the Plateau of Leng), but also back on the astral counterpart of New York City, acting as the priest/(ess) in a Mass of the Mirror. I focus my attention on the reality of my astral sexual being & feel the tug of orgasmic flow. As I began to dematerialize from the plateau of Leng, I reach out & snatch the black ring from the finger of the elder god.

I awake in the New York City brothel where I began my meditations 8 hours before. I am stretched out upon the bed/altar, being ministered to by the two priestess-acolytes & the priest. The black stone is around my neck & I hold the clear crystal in my hand. The elder god glares at us through the upper mirror, but he(she?) dares not traverse this gateway un-invited.

I take a brief nap upon this altar. All is dark. I have the impression of being in the Scottish Highlands (but I see/smell nothing). I overhear a conversation between two men.

The first says that a tax must be levied to support the empire. The second responds by saying that these people were freemen & would resist any taxes, for they were not part of the empire & would gain no benefit from the tax. The first sighs & says that an unpopular tax would (of course) result in an up-rising. If the freemen win, the empire would be in their hands; if they lost, they would become slaves to the will of the empire. The voices were again silent as I drift into a light sleep.

I awake from my morning crystal free-float. I am back home again. The New York City brothel/temple has been left on the astral. Neither stone which I have thus far won from the elder god has yet managed to materialize into concrete reality on Malkuth. These gems seem to be potent tools upon the astral & beyond, but I have not yet found a way to earth their reality on Malkuth or to fully comprehend their use. They do seem to tie into the two pearls (black & white) which have been used by me for HHH meditation & which appeared to me in my working which involved the riddle of the pyramid & the entombed Masters of the Temple.

DREAM WORKING: *Recorded 18 Nov. '82;*
Did my evening VIII° free-float with quartz after reading several more chapters of Outside the Circles of Time.

I project into my temple in astral New York City via my quartz crystal. I am working with a new priestess (professional) within a large round room. Over the bed is positioned a clear crystal mirror angled towards the North wall, which is a huge adamantine black mirror.

The priestess climaxes through my oral administrations & my consciousness merges with hers as I am sucked-up through her vagina at the point of her orgasm. United, we look at the clear mirror & project our blank mind onto the clear scrying stone.

Within the clear reflection of the mirror of light is contained the image of the black mirror upon the North wall, over our head. Within the blackness, a sigil forms. It is not unlike the sigil of Aossic, but it is distinctly different. It begins to waver—not through lack of focus, but because it has a life of its own.

It rotates 120 degrees widdershins & transmutes into a human skull with ram's horns—it is UM-UR-'ATWIEL—333, the guardian of the abyss who has been my friend & guide for years. Dangling from each horn & affixed in the cranial suture are the three rings of primary pigment (chroma) [cyan, magenta, yellow] while the three rings of primary light (spectrum) (red, green, blue) are within his mouth & eyesockets.

He smiles & I/we are drawn up into the mirror (I having been absorbed within my astral priestess). I am wearing my black & clear crystal rings. I know not if I am on the astral, or up in the 'real world'. Usually, I am able to use the color of my rings to determine my locus, but since I did not consciously place the rings upon my fore-fingers, I am unable to ascertain whether the rings are glowing with their astral light or with their true colors (as they do glow upon the other side of the abyss).

The dis-embodied head of my guide is facing me, but receding quickly down a corridor of uttermost blackness. I follow it as I utilize my rings of power to 'see' the walls of the passageway.

The tunnel is round & not very straight. Its curvature is very complex (not a simple curve or spiral) & I sense that if I but had some outside reference point, I would be able to sense my passage through far more than three dimensions.

The walls themselves are convoluted & rugose with waves of texture in both the longitudinal & circumferential dimensions. There is a complex pattern of different textures, each having a different wavelength, a different amplitude, and a different pattern of texture. Where several wave patterns meet or cross, coherent images can be briefly seen.

The pattern of these coherent images seems to make up a series of vignettes, similar to the hallway of Tarot Trumps which lies on the causeway of initiation under the great pyramid, but these vignettes seem to be living patterns rather than archetypes. They appear to be 'snapshots' at (random?) points of time which encapsulate history of life & culture upon the material plane.

There are three spirals of vignettes which wind deosil in the direction which I am traveling.

I pause to test an hypothesis.

I turn around & walk in the direction from whence I came. The three patterns of vignettes disappear & three other patterns emerge as a widdershins spiral which run the opposite direction in time.

All six patterns tell the evolutionary history of the universe. Each pattern tells the same story through the cultural 'eyes' of a different race. Three of these races travel 'forward' in time, while the other three travels 'backwards in time' (subjectively speaking).

I terminate my brief experiment & rush to catch-up to my guide. I use my large quartz crystal as my 'movie camera' to record the passing images, since I must focus my attentions on my path rather than on the scenery. The tunnel branches into a complex maze of translucent tunnels (6 of them—one for each strand of the pattern).

UM-UR-ATWIEL is nowhere to be found. I search the maze for any sign of his passage. I find a clear place in one of the tunnel walls. It is a window or a mirror (it seems to behave as both & yet neither). My guide is now 'outside' the pattern of tunnels, within the 'nest' of strands of the pattern.

I center myself before the mirror/window (both physically & within the core of my being). I begin the ritual of the Bornless One & make the Sign of the Opening of the Veil.

The mirror/window turns to black quicksilver & the rings on my fingers change color (the black stone turns clear & the clear stone turns black). My quartz (which hangs suspended around my neck on the knot in the end of my (still attached) umbilical cord) remains clear & pulsating with a life all its own.

I make the Sign of the Enterer as I fall/project through the window which is not a window (but a portal of some kind??).

I am 'outside'.

My guide is as large as a small planet. The pattern of colored tubes surround him like glowing worms or writhing eels. At one end of the maze is a black hole, into which the strands of light merge & disappear. At the other end of the maze is a star, out of which a single ray of clear white light fragments into three of the colored tubes. Between these three strands, I am barely able to discern three other strands, which are formulated not from the light of the star, but through the effect which its absence has upon the blackness of space itself. These strands which are formulated from the darkness are the three strands of negative time which (now that I look more closely at the black hole) emanate from the black hole itself (rather than disappearing into it) & disperse into the blackness of shadow which exists between the quanta of light coming from the star.

I approach my guide. As I get closer to him, his size diminishes (or does mine increase?). We are once again face to face & we are once again within the palace which exists upon the stark plane of endless night.

Eleven pylons uphold the structure of the palace. We are centered under its roof. The roof is a flat disk, containing all the physical matter in the universe. It is spinning at relativistic velocity (i.e., approaching the speed of light), propelled by the rotating sephira atop each of the pylons. Beneath the center of this disk, the tidal forces create a place outside of time. This is the palace which some (but not I) call DIS. Upon its floor is inscribed the pattern which was given to me over 9 years ago in a ritual to Ithaqa [Ithaca] the Windwalker (who is also known as Hastur)—a ritual which culminated in a blood sacrifice (bloody rabbit) brought to my magic circle by the hands of a nonmagical friend who knew not that blood was required for the rite being performed. [See the end of this diary entry for details of that ritual.]

I know this palace of my vision (of this waking dream), even as I recognize the glyph upon the floor—it is my true home. I know that I could choose to fuse with mine angel & the world would cease to be. The disk of matter would cease to spin. The strands of matter would cease their dance. Brahma would once again dream the dreamless sleep.

But although I am sometimes very weary of this world & its illusions, I am not yet ready for sleep. My angel and I embrace rather than merge. He kisses me & the ruby ring within his mouth is transferred to my mouth.

I flow back through the window which is not a window. I am now a pulsation of energy which traverses the pattern upon the walls of the maze rather than walks within its corridors. I traverse the path which depicts the exploits & history of the race whose spectrum matches the clear red of my newly acquired ruby ring. I sing with the energy which courses through my being. I feel much but remember no coherent images of my travels. My quartz remembers our travels, but it speaks to me in the language of crystals, not in any human tongue.

I fall backwards through the black mirror & am reflected by the clear mirror back into the ajna of my astral priestess. She convulses & I am expelled from her womb—newly born, yet very old. I rub the slime which covers my body into my quartz crystal, which I use to draw my spirit back into my body by touching my crown, my third eye, my throat, & my heart. I consume the ichor which remains. My newly-acquired ring is now tied to a lock of my hair. I remove the ring from my hair & I see that the clear red ruby ring has transformed to an opalescent aquamarine of mottled cyan color.

As I gaze at the ring, I feel a gentle tug from the free-end of my umbilical cord & as I blink my eyes, I am back in my human body sitting at my word processor, putting this tale down in a form which is intelligible to others. I now end this tale in order that I might go back to the start of this tale in order to edit my free-form narrative into intelligible paragraphs, adding details from the memories within my quartz, and appending a more complete description of my ritual to Ithaqa of a nearly a decade ago. Thanks to the magical crystals within my computer & their complimentary allies within my magnetic disk storage system, I will be able to complete my editing without the necessity of re-typing my narrative or using a scissors & paste to put my text in order.

ADDENDUM: some of my remembrances of the ritual of Ithaqa.
On the outer, a warmish winter afternoon was transformed into the icy coldness of the innermost ring of Dante's hell. Over the course of 4 hours, the temperature had dropped from 50° (Fahrenheit) to 10°. By midnight, the temperature had fallen to nearly 30 below zero with high winds, a vicious ice storm & a blizzard of snow. Such weather changes are extreme, even for Ithaca's unpredictable winters!

On the inner, I received a ritual and the image of a pattern.

I am no artist & I am no painter, yet I labored over a drawing of that pattern for days. Then I photo-copied that pattern and made-up a set of small stickers to be used by me over the years.

The Necronomicon ritual was also used by me over the ensuing years as an aid to opening the trans-dimensional gateways within me to access that part of me who did channel the Al Azif from beyond the Abyss. The main invocation which I received as a result of that ritual so long ago is as follows:

Thou that knowest the Gate, and the Guardian thereof
—who is Yog-Sothoth;

Thou that knowest the Great Old Ones, & the servitors thereof
—among whom are the Voormis, the Gugs, and the Gaunts of the Night;

Thou that knowest the Unmapped Lands, & the names thereof
—among which are N'Kai, Carcosa, and Far Kadath;

Thou do I call forth! Thou that hast seen the Walker on the Wind;
Thou that hast heard the Howler in the Dark;
Thou that hast spoken the Name of the Unspeakable One;
Thou do I call forth!
Thou that knowest the Place of Hidden R'yleh;
Thou that boldest the Secret of Far Kadath;
Thou that keepest the Key to the Door of Yhe;
Thou do I call forth!

Thou that wast He who did write the Al-Azif;
Thou do I call forth from the Shadows!

Him that hath came is returned; Him do I call forth again!
Him that hath set down the secrets is silenced;
Him do I bid speak again!

Him that abideth neither in darkness nor in light;

HIM DO I CALL FORTH FROM THE SHADOWS!

By the Five Pointed Star of Mnar,—and those who made it;
By the Sign of Kish,—and those who obey it;
By the Race of Yith,—and those who created it;
By the Assent of the Eider Gods,
By the Command of Nodens — Lord of the Great Abyss,
By the Inneffable Name which cannot be spoken;

LET HIM COME FORTH!

Intone 3 times, standing erect with feet shod, while facing the Nameless City (SE).[1]

The pattern which showed itself to me during that ritual so long ago began simply as a series of geometrical arcs which interpenetrated at peculiar angles. Over the weeks it took me to construct & concretize this glyph of the Universe, I began to attribute the Gods and Places of the Lovecraftian mythos to it.

Once I had an accurate representation of the glyph which had etched itself onto my mind & once I had worked-out the proper attributions of God-names & Sacred Tunnels (10% inspiration & 90% research via the glossaries of Lin Carter), I reproduced the glyph via photomechanical methods to freeze the actuality of this potent tool. Even today I have copies of this pattern, which is my Seal upon the Inner.

The overall pattern of the seal is a complex series of inter-penetrating threes. All the God-names are written in a slightly modified form of the Enochian alphabet, with letters from the alphabet of the Magi <described in this text within these angular brackets> symbolizing attributes of a particular locus.

---

1   Action taken from original typescript—Ed.

In the center is a complex pattern composed of the tri-lobed aspects of AZAThOTh interpenetrating YOG-SOThOTh (the two sets of triplicities which, while sometimes appearing chaotic & destructive, actually govern the laws of probability & energy transfer within the Universe—see also the two sets of triple strands in this vision) (along with two symbols for alpha & omega). NyARLATh-O-TEP & UBU-SAThYA are the Messengers whose tendrils oscillate from this center outward to the next set of triplicities.

The only triangle composed of straight lines symbolizes the three elements of:
  Fire: (Cthugha) <B> (RED)
  Water: (Cthulhu) <G> (GREEN)
  AIR: (Hastur) <V> (BLUE)

Between this triangle & the outer-most curved triangle lie the three sub-elements, each ruled by a pair of deities as follows:
  Fire/Water: Chaugnar-Faugn & Hydra (MAGENTA)
  Water/Air: Dagon & Ithaqa (CYAN)
  Air/Fire: Lloigor & Yig (YELLOW)

Between this triangle & the outer 3 circles are three regions (all governed by I) ruled as follows (labeling pattern changes from convex to concave at this point):
  Fire/Water: 'UMR AT-TAWIL
  Water/Air: Shub-Neggurath
  Air/Fire: Tsathoggua

Surrounding this triangular pattern are the three circles or cycles of Tunnels within the Earth (which are symbolic of the three veils of negative existence, the AIN, the AIN SOPH, and the AIN SOPH AUR) which proceed outward as follows:
  C'N-YAN
  (red-litten) YOTH
  (black-litten) N'CAI

[all orthography above is transliterated back to English from the Enochian, so is limited by the letters available in Enochian. For proper use, the names of power should be adjusted to reflect the 'flavor' of whatever alphabet with which the Magickian chooses to work.]

DREAM WORKING: Recorded 24 Nov. '82
I have just done some meditating upon the bookshop owner (original dream not reproduced here). I definitely know him from somewhere or somewhen. I now shall use my crystal to re-enter the dream.

    I am in the coffeeshop & I am looking very hard at the bookshop proprietor. The nimbus which surrounds his head is blinding. I take my black pearl from its pouch around my neck & use it to absorb all the light from the room. All is dark, but the bookseller's face is still brilliantly enshrouded with light. All action freezes. All the actors within the coffeeshop become statues, except for the bookseller & I. He smiles at me & nods his head. He beckons me to approach him. He extends his hand. It is incredibly old—not quite human. It triggers memories within me. The hand is very lizard-like, yet very gentle (in a very powerful way). There are no rings on any of the fingers, yet I can perceive a set of rings which somehow 'belong' on his fingers. The bookseller does not wear the rings of Power, but he somehow 'has access' to them whenever he needs them.

    The black stone materializes on the thumb of his six fingered hand. It is far blacker & far older than the black stone which I wear about my neck. The universe fades into utter blackness—all is void save his face, which is still luminous, but can now be discerned within the cloud of light which surrounds him. The face is definitely Atlantean. He is one of the Old Race which guided the transition between lizards and humans as the dominant species upon the earth. He is the guardian of forbidden knowledge whose library transcends Time, Space, and Alternity so that it can never be plundered by those who are not yet ready. The name Chozzar comes to my mind, but I lack the certainty to test him with my supposition. The ring evaporates from off his finger.

    We are back in the coffeeshop. He asks me to put away my black stone. I do so, & the 'people' come back to life as the light is no longer being trapped within my ring.

    I then accompany him to his bookshop, which is empty, but not locked. He goes behind the counter & asks to see my sigil. I show him my card with the OTz PTN sigil engraved upon it. He smiles & says it is very nice but far too young to gain admittance to his shop. He asks if I have any other sigils. I reach into the pouch wherein I keep my black & clear stones & pull-out the map of the Universe given me during the Ithaqa Working (see page above) & hand it to him. His smile broadens as he fondles & smells the sigil.

He tells me that this sigil should be my seal for working upon the inner, for it is older than Time itself. He asks me where I found it & I recounted its history to him. He smiles again as he nods his head & tells me that although the sigil is far beyond my earned grade, he will honor it because he honors 'they who did give me the seal'.

He then draws a 'map' upon the back of the sigil, which I cannot see (for to stare into that dimension makes my stomach turn & my eyesight go all blurry). He tells me that this 'map' will guide me to three places which I will undoubtedly find 'useful' in my quest.

I ask him for details on the places & he smiles broadly at me & begins to laugh. Tears roll down his face as he struggles to compose himself. He shakes his head in wonder as he looks to the heavens. He then becomes very serious & states that if I really know so little of my quest or of the sigil which has been allied to my destiny, then how do I expect to carry out my duties.

I reply that I am but a simple pilgrim seeking wonders beyond the edges of the known Universe. He scowls at me & takes me to a large tome. He bids me to read the tome.

I look at the pages, but they are total gibberish to me. I strain to 'look' at them differently. I remove the clear crystal from my neck pouch & cast a 'different' light upon the text. The text is now seen to be composed of diagrams, which seem to twist off their pages & lead me to places which I cannot quite reach. The shopkeeper stares at me in wonderment. He asks if I have any other gems. I reach deep into the pouch where I thought I had a ruby. It is not there, but I do have a stone which is not quite visible. I take it out of the pouch & show it to him. He smiles & tells me that the ruby is nice, but as yet it useless for it is uncharged. He extends his hand & the ruby ring materializes as my stomach flips with nausea. (I almost saw where that ring came from, but my mind refuses to remember how to access that place!).

In the red light from the Atlantean's ruby, the page changes from mathematical diagrams to a map of a large city. The perimeter of the city forms a large equilateral triangle. The center of the city exists on two separate levels, connected by some sort of crystalline astral bridge.

Instinctively I know that the center of the city contains the 'University' complex which I have visited many times over the years. The Atlantean smiles & points to three buildings which are marked prominently on the map.

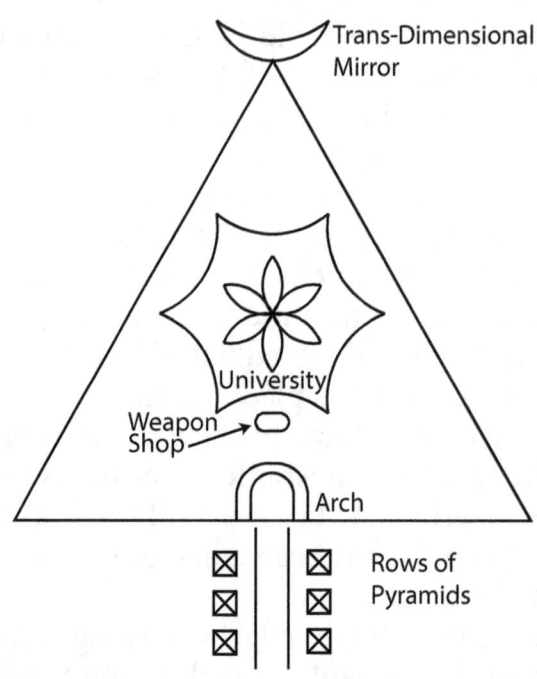

Centered upon the south edge of the city is a large archway which leads to the desert of the pyramids. I remember entering this gate in a vision some time ago. I was out in the desert listening to the mumblings of the Masters of the Temple, who had each imprisoned themselves in his/her own unique pyramid of solitude because they feared to recognize the validity of the other Masters who also lived within the City.

Again, the Atlantean points to the map. The North point of the pyramid contains the trans- dimensional mirror which leads to places beyond. I recognize the mirror from the same vision as the pyramids. When the black & white jewels are balanced, the aspirant may attempt passage through the mirror. If the aspirant passes the test, he/she is never seen or heard from again, for the gateway is a one-way street; if the aspirant fails, he or she is projected down the Tree to his/her 'earned' grade & must begin the climb again.

The third building is near the lower University, but not actually within its precincts. I have never seen it before. Outside is a simple wooden sign with a complex design. There is a golden Horus head in profile (facing right) with a barbed violet arrow shooting down out of its eye. Below the Horus head is a blue-black claw clenching a lightning bolt of forked white fire. Between the head & the claw are two crossed

Peacock feathers. At their crossing point there is a scale suspended from the feathers. The pans of the scale contain sigils which I cannot see clearly, but they are clearly out of balance. The lightning bolt from below supports the heavy pan on the left, while the arrow from above adds weight to the lighter pan on the right. Through the action of the lightning & the arrow, the pans are effectively balanced.

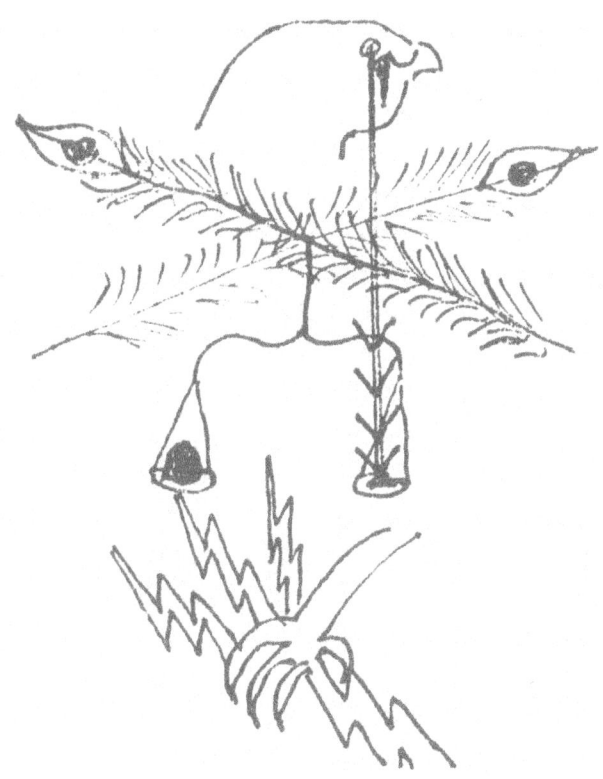

I ask about this shop & he smiles and asks to see my sword. Instinctively I reach for my samurai sword, which is stored always with me, yet rarely visible. I am startled by my actions as I am unable to comprehend how I am able to 'reach' through that impossible angle to pluck-forth the sword.

He smiles as he looks at the workmanship of the blade. He asks if I have ever met any of the other Shadow Knights. I reply that none whom I have ever met will admit to knowing of the organization. He laughs again & commends me for my fine sense of humor. I am perplexed but say nothing.

He tells me that the 'shop' marked upon this map is an 'extension' of The Weapons Shop (in one of its many guises) as it can be perceived upon this plane. It is accessible only to those whose Will is in accord with the concept of 'dynamic & assisted balance'. It is not run by or for the Shadow Knights, but it is accessible to them, so long as they do not turn too black.

The coin which the shopkeepers accept is the coin of karma. They are (somehow) able to 'convert' 'positive' (?) karma into weapons. These weapons can be used only in ways which further the purpose of they who 'sponsor' the Weapons Shop. Knights may use their weapons for: personal defense, adjustment to create an 'atmosphere' of balance, and to assist in the implementation of Universal Will. Other uses may or may not be possible, depending upon the 'karmic considerations' involved.

The Atlantean 'puts-away' his ruby ring, and closes the large book. We walk back to the front of his store & he shows me to the door with a smile. As I leave, I turn to the Atlantean mage & inquire timidly if his name is Chozzar. He laughs so loud that the astral landscape quakes.

The shop folds in upon itself & is gone completely. It is as if it had never existed in that place. Bewildered, I return to the coffeeshop, putting the preceding events aside as I rejoin my friends.

Here begins excerpt from diary entry for Tuesday, 14 December, 1982 e.v.
I begin the ritual with my meditation based upon HHH.

I am in the Tunnel beneath the Path of Tav. All is dark. I pick-up two rocks from the Tunnel floor as my physical body lights the Malkuth candle & picks up my healing crystal & my Atlantean crystal.

Astrally, I proceed in the direction of Yesod. At Yesod I bathe the two stones in the fountain formed from the streams flowing from Tiphareth, Hod & Netsach. My physical body lights the Yesod Candle from the Malkuth candle & rinses the two crystals in a bowl of sea water.

Astrally I proceed upwards via the two outer Paths to Hod & Netzach, crossing over via the Blasted Tower & circulating back down to Malkuth. When the flow of energy is strong & I can begin to feel my kundalini stirring, I shoot up the Middle Pillar to Tiphareth via the Arrow Star of Art & shower the energy downward & outward to Hod & Netzach.

I see/feel/experience as much as I am able on each of the Paths. My physical body lights the candles at Hod, Netzach, & Tiphareth. My internal energies are very stirred-up. I feel a churning in my gut—both from the rising kundalini & from my fears/hesitations on the operation at hand.

I calm myself & use the emerald under my tongue to process the energies in a harmonious manner. In about 5 minutes I am ready to proceed.

I shoot out astrally to Geburah and Chesed from Tiphareth & cross my energies over the Tree via the Path of Lust. When the field is stable, I use my body to light the candles at Geburah & Chesed & then astrally drop down the side paths to Hod & Netzach.

I circulate the current through these central 5 Sephira, dipping through the lower paths as necessary to balance out the flow. When I am convinced that all is harmonious, I proceed to the next stage. (for me, clocks are forbidden in the Temple. Subjectively, the ritual has thus far taken about 3 hours, but I know that less than 3/4 hours has passed in mundane time.)

I place my dream crystal on another copy of my map of the abyss to focus my energies. I project through the map & I am walking amongst the necropolis of pyramids which lies South of the sacred city. I locate my pyramid & focus all my energies on opening up myself to the energies from outside of myself.

The image of the Necropolis begins to fade, and an image of an oak grove is superimposed over the image of the pyramids. When my pyramid is transformed into an oak tree, I go inside & merge with that aspect of myself who lives/works/plays in this oak Tree (& who is also sometimes imprisoned within this pyramid).

I/We continue to focus on the more open reality of this oak grove. When most of the pyramids are fully transformed into trees with open doorways, I transport myself to the portal of the sacred city. I look back & the image of the pyramids/trees flicker back & forth like two competing mirages, flickering in the hot air above the desert.

Between the two rows of pyramids/oaks are my own footsteps, the footsteps of a camel VVVVV. I turn my attention higher in the city and I use my map to transport myself to the supernal transport device located at the Northern edge of the city. I still fear to use this transport device, even though I knew the task of this ritual would be much easier if I could approach the ritual from Kether. I guess I fear the tasks/obligations of higher grades as well as the penalty for assuming an office beyond my abilities.

When I enter the square at the Northern edge of the City, it is night & the sky is filled with stars so bright & alive it is impossible to describe to one who has never left Malkuth. The transport mirror stands on a low stone platform at the center of the square. It is opalescent like a pearl.

Based on what I learned from Rudy, I lick the mirror to clean it. The cloudiness comes off in my mouth. It is sweet & slightly nauseating, but not totally repulsive. I lick the entire mirror clean & I stand back. The mirror was concave when I began the operation, but now it is a convex sphere.

Within the sphere is a bloated corpse. It leers out at me & beckons me to join it within the sphere. I know the corpse is me & it is my fate to rot in this place if I undertake the high office pertaining to Kether without proper preparation. I re-focus my attention back to my physical body.

I am in a cold sweat & my heart is palpitating. I recirculate the energy through the lower 7 Sephira & focus on the emerald within my mouth to even-out my energies. I meditate upon my two crystals & I mentally merge their polarities. I re-focus my energies back to the sacred city. I know that I am as ready as I can be at this time, but it is not sufficient for the task at hand. I project to an alternative reality.

I am in a fancy hotel. The walls are made of smooth polished stone which appears to be marble. Black & white are blended in hypnotic streaks. The floor is a black & white tweed rug. Everyone's clothing (but mine!) is a balanced blend of black & white. All the guests are very bizarre looking (like the beings depicted in Star Wars), but are all dressed in very formal garb. I am dressed in a bright mosaic of rainbow colors.

There are many elevators. I know that if I approach the elevators, I will be expelled from the building. I see a door marked EMPLOYEES ONLY which I go through. Within I find an electrical panel box. I throw the switches which channel energy from Chokmah & Binah down to the sacred city on the Northern end of the Abyss. My physical body lights the candles for Chokmah & Binah. My astral form sneaks out of the fancy hotel before I am discovered.

I use my map to project to the weapons shop in the sacred city. The shopkeeper knows why I am there & what I need for my task. He is not permitted to give or sell me the tools I need, but he is willing to loan them to me. I give him my Atlantean crystal for safekeeping & put on the sacred beads of Kether & take the bowl of crystals with me out of the shop. I use the map to return to the city of the pyramids.

I have no trouble locating Frater 333. He has torn apart his pyramid with his bare hands. He is standing in its ruins. He is hip deep in boiling blood & the flesh falls from his legs like wet paper. He is casting blocks of stone from his pyramid outward at all who pass close to him, but he does not move from the ruin he has created, even though he must be in great pain. I focus my attention into my physical body.

I use the method of preparing the healing circle as taught by Oh Shinnah. I light the candles deosil from the East, asking each direction to ward & protect the healing circle from all outside influences. Each candle is lit from the previous candle. Once the circle of light is formulated, I lay the four small crystals within the square of candles (also at the Quarters), deosil from the East. All the crystals are double terminated (or nearly so) but I focus on the kinds of energy needed for this operation.

In my system, the East is the place of the Twins who represent the active & passive balance of the well-developed child. I invite this energy into the healing circle.

In the South is the force & Fire of Hadit. I direct the major point of the Southern crystal outwards in this direction to drain off Frater 333's excess (& perverted) Martial energies.

To the West is Babalon. Again, I use the crystal to drain out this energy, for my intuition leads me to believe that a good deal of his difficulties comes from viewing women in an imbalanced fashion—i.e., as objects &/or tools, but not as revered teachers, or equals.

To the North is Nuit, the Star Goddess. I point this crystal inward to invoke these energies in to heal & to fill the void within Frater 333. The four crystals are ringed with salt. I place my healing crystal over the chest of the small lead figure which I am using to represent Frater 333 & re-focus back to the city of Pyramids.

I am standing within the ruins of Frater 333's pyramid. It is no longer a prison or a temple—It is a place of self-torture. He is lying on his back & is glaring at me. I have a large crystal rod with which I manipulate his energies. He mellows out some, but he still hates/fears me. There is a look of total disassociation & madness in his eyes. I am knee deep in boiling blood, but it does not burn me. I calm myself & focus on that other reality. The ruined pyramid begins to shimmer & as the image grows more & more unstable, I focus harder upon Frater 333 so that I do not lose him during the transition.

The boiling blood turns to mud & then to rich humus. The stone ruin gradually turns to the remains of a lightning blasted oak tree. The tree is broken & old, but it is not dead. Frater 333 looks at me in total disbelief. He begins to stand-up, but he is unable, for both his legs are badly broken & gangrenous. A small crowd of well-meaning people from adjacent trees gathers to offer their best wishes for his speedy recovery. Frater 333 wants them to re-build his tree/house for him, but they politely refuse. They say that it is not permitted. They offer to loan him tools, and offer to give him materials & advice, but they tell him that the reconstruction must be done by him.

An old druid comes out of nowhere & the crowd disperses. This is not the druid whom I know, but he looks very similar to him. He gives Frater 333 unguents to speed the healing of his legs & gives him fertilizers to speed the recovery of his Tree.

He tells Frater 333 that the damage is severe, but not that difficult to mend, so long as Frater 333 is willing to assist rather than hamper the healing process. The druid gives Frater 333 a list of dietary restrictions. He is told to follow the diet so that his excrement will nourish the Tree rather than poisoning it. Frater 333 goes to sleep & looks peaceful for the first time since I have known him. I look up & the druid is gone.

In the distance I can see the beacon lights from 9 of the Sephiroth. I know that the meditation is nearing its end & I will have to leave Frater 333 in order to return to my body. I need to post a guardian so that Frater 333's consciousness will remain in the oak grove and not return to the city of the pyramids.

I leave the oak grove & use my map to project back to the Weapons' shop. I place the healing crystal into the bowl of sea water (it hisses when it hits the water!), return the beads of Kether and pick-up my Atlantean crystal. Its coolness gives me energy & renews my vigor. My concentration drifts back into my body.

Back in my physical body, I extinguish the candles around the four crystals (deosil from East) without disturbing the four crystals or the ring of salt. I move my consciousness down the Tree extinguishing the Sephirothic candles one by one as I go. I hold my dream crystal in my left hand & my Atlantean crystal in my right. My emerald (still in my mouth) processes energy.

When I am renewed & refreshed, I place a glass candle holder over the supine lead figure (which represents Frater 333) without disturbing the crystals or the ring of salt.

Upon this candle holder I place the fetish of UM-UR'ATWIEL & light the candle within it. This will burn all night & will give peace & anesthesia to Frater 333 while he sleeps & will permit the healing process to begin & continue.

The ritual is completed. I go to sleep invigorated by my work, but very tired. I know that my dreams will not be nightmares & I know that I have not inadvertently drunk any of Frater 333's poison into myself. All crystals used in the rite are either safely in salt water or are still affixed to the ring of salt which surrounds the images of Frater 333.

Here begins an excerpt from diary entry for Wednesday, 15 December, 1982 e.v.
Had quite a time with the Frater 333 ritual last night. Outline was same as I wrote-up yesterday, but with some changes in the astral details.

When I arrived at the Weapons Shop, I was advised not to borrow the beads of Kether. The shopkeeper told me that I had no real need for them at this stage of the ritual & I should save such power objects for those times when I needed them—unless I was willing to take-on the responsibilities of the Office of Ipsissimus full-time. I hastily declined the offer & transported myself back to the Necropolis of the Pyramids.

Frater 333's pyramid was no longer filled with boiling blood & Frater 333 was nowhere to be seen. The ruins were still a mess, but the desert sands seemed to mute the devastation & perhaps to convey a feeling that a gentle healing was in progress.

I located my pyramid & leaned my forehead on the sigil embossed on one of its stones. I merged with the pyramid & 'fell' into the pyramid, which was transformed into my Oak Tree. My attire was now appropriate for the Druidic grove of oaks. I left my tree to locate Frater 333.

I found him tending a small garden behind his Tree. He was now ambulatory, but with difficulty. His Oak was looking much better, but it still had a long way to go before it would be a serviceable dwelling.

Frater 333's garden was in the form of a Tree of Life, with appropriate herbs growing along each Path & an appropriate Tree or bush at each Sephiroth. Frater 333's eyes were a wonder to behold. They looked very 'saintly' (i.e., serene, composed, focused yet slightly distant, warm & loving) rather than the intense beady little rat eyes which I saw just the other day.

We talked about his recuperation in an effort to pin-point any difficulties which still needed work. As we talked, we took a stroll through his garden/map of the Tree of Life. Based on intuition & upon what I saw in his garden, I began to question him on his philosophy regarding the functions of the various sets of Paths: I saw that he was having difficulties reconciling the horizontal Paths with the Vertical Paths of the Middle Pillar & the difficulties worsened above Tiphareth.

It did not surprise me to discover these discrepancies. I then led him on an HHH meditation through the Tree in an attempt to pin-point any serious problems. It is fascinating how alike I am to Frater 333, yet how different. We both have very similar causes of dis-ease, yet our outward symptoms differ greatly.

The horizontal Paths serve the function of balance within the individual. The vertical & angular Paths which intersect the Middle Pillar serve as vehicles for aspiration towards higher consciousness &/or the descent of Higher Consciousness into the individual.

The vertical Paths on the two outer Pillars serve the function of balancing karma between the individual & the rest of the Universe. The trick with the horizontal Paths is that all interactions need to be reciprocal, otherwise one easily loses balance.

When one moves upwards from Tiphareth, one is balancing the energies of The Lover and The Star with those of The Priestess. This is extraordinarily difficult.

Lust is a necessary aid at this stage of the journey to assist in this delicate balancing act. An adept who is able to wear the mask of a whore is able to assist the aspirant in balancing the subtle interplay of forces necessary to reach the supernals. But it is very easy to become de-railed during this operation.

It is possible for the aspirant to use the whore for animal pleasure rather than for balance & thereby lose sight of the goal. The aspirant may use the whore in such a way that he/she is unable to see that the whore is but a mask worn by the adept who is also The Lover & The High Priestess.

If the aspirant fools him/her-self into believing that he/she is superior to s/he who wears the mask of whore, overbalance can result in the aspirant shooting over to Geburah or Chesed (depending on whether the aspirant attempts to degrade or rescue the whore) & then down the Tree via The Wheel of Fortune or The Hanged Man. Balance must then be gained via the Blasted Tower before any further sexual magick is possible.

The mask & the function of the horizontal paths are most easily balanced by reciprocal workings. Balance is most easily maintained on the Path of Lust if each aspirant/adept in a IX Degree working is a whore to the needs of the other. In theory, this is simple & straightforward, yet it is often quite difficult in practice.

Frater 333 & I then worked HHH together (as a meditative exercise) in such a way as to maximize the interplay of the horizontal & vertical paths. We kept balance & deliberately circulated energy down the outer Paths to make the energy flow easier & more productively.

Most of all, we practiced the chakra game on each other & on ourselves so that we could map the forces at work in our bodies at any given moment. I gave him the astral form of the healing crystal before I ended the session.

Back in my body, I placed the physical crystal in salt water for the night. Tonight, I shall modify the end of the ritual by removing the guardianship of UM-UR'ATWIEL from the Oh Shinnah healing altar. I shall not sleep in my temple, but move downstairs so that I will be able to focus more fully on the Atlantean material which has been brewing within me for some time now.

[*editor's (BS) note:* P. began to work with the 'character' of Frater 333 as a result of a manifestation which came through a fellow magickian during a rather intense alchemical experiment which caught him off-guard. However, the rituals above are best viewed as exercises by which P. deals with aspects within himself which are in serious need of balance, rather than as rituals designed to 'heal' another human being.]

Here ends the first volume of astral & dream workings extracted from Frater P.'s Magickal Diaries. Volumes II & III are now in preparation & should be ready early in 1984.

ChRySTAL Visions thru the Astral Mirror

Being Volume II in a series of narratives from the on-going Magickal Record of Frater P., in which he candidly discusses his divers Al-Chymical Experiments employing VIII° Sex Magick, ChRySTAL Vision, Conscious Dreaming, and Astral Projection

Do what thou wilt shall be the whole of the Law.

Introduction

The response to Frater PVN's first volume of Astral & Dream Workings has been overwhelming. Many people have written to tell is how much they enjoy PVN's 'un-polished' diary entries compared to the grave formality & 'seriousness' which characterizes so many of the standard texts on Sex Magick & Alchemy.

Many of you have asked for more volumes from PVN's on-going Magickal Record. We have convinced PVN to interrupt work on latest project to edit the series of diaries which you are now holding. It is with great pleasure that we are able to bring you Volume II of his Diaries so much sooner than expected.

The 'disclaimers' regarding literal use of PVN's material which appeared in Volume I also hold true for this volume. The Astral Plane is very personal. Each aspirant is counseled to make h-is/er own contacts on the inner & develop a personalized system of magick before undertaking to duplicate or expand on the experiments of other magickians.

The material in this booklet should be thought of as 'suggestive' & as an 'indication' of what may be accomplished by anyone who has the inspiration & fortitude to locate his/her own inner gateways & explore those regions which remain elusively 'outside' the realms delineated in standard texts. It is to these intrepid explorers of internal realities that this present volume is dedicated.

Frater PVN is none other than Frater PVN who is the author of many essays on Sexual Alchemy and Thelemic Politics. We have encouraged PVN to supplement his dream & astral material with outlines & fragmentary essays (also from his daily magickal record) to give readers an inkling of where he gets his inspiration, & how he begins to work his ideas into viable essays. We have always found that creativity in its 'raw' state is often exciting to behold, especially when all the 'loose ends' are left dangling, 'as an exercise for the student'.

Some readers have asked us to recommend texts or guidebooks to help them learn to work with dreams via crystals. After doing a bit of research on our own, & consulting with PVN, we have come to the conclusion that alchemical techniques which can only be 'hinted-at' in books, must be 'learned' by each seeker on an individual basis— thru internal hermetic exploration, &/or thru working in conjunction with others who already practice astral projection, sex magick, and crystal shamanism.

After much careful consideration, PVN feels that he has now reached that stage of development where it is now his Will to pass-on advice, guidance, & initiation to self-motivated seekers—utilizing techniques which he has found efficacious in his own work. For now, he can offer counseling via crystal skrying, Tarot readings, etc. Those with more advanced &/or personal needs will be able to work with PVN to design special programs.

Love is the law, love under will.

Yrs. for the Great Work,
Bill Siebert
(for Boleskine House)

Fragment from 15 Dec.'82
During dreams last night I did manage some Atlantean work. This universe seems to have a propensity towards being a closed circle with endless repetitions unless one exercises free will in order to break the cycle of inevitability.

The fall of Atlantis is in our collective past, yet it is also in our future unless we do something to avoid it. For all intents & purposes, this point in time is Atlantis. We are faced with both nuclear destruction & invasion from outer space (the invaders are being invoked by the fearful who want 'our star brothers' to come & put an end to the threat of nuclear destruction).

We could simply play-out one of the various destruction scenarios, or we could break out of the cycle altogether through the use of collective individual responsibility.

Atlantis & crystals are almost synonymous terms. Therein lies a key. Now I must locate the appropriate lock.

Using free association, I link together the crystal shamans (Oh Shinnah, myself, Rudy, etc.), the Space program (Carl Sagan, Timothy Leary), the OTO (both the individual Branches & united Above the Abyss), and computers. Crystals underlying the whole. The Atlantean crystal has been fragmented (so I am told) by the destructive end of the previous cycle. We all have a piece of it (probably within our trans-temporal esoteric nervous system). We need to give up exclusive rights to our individual pieces in order that we all may gain unrestricted access to the whole. Space travel to remove some of the eggs from our very fragile basket. Sex magick for personal development & an end to jealous ridiculousness & territorial stupidity.

Excerpts from Diary entry for Wednesday, 29 December, 1982 e.v.
I have just completed a two-day mini-working which I shall call the chocolate cream cheese pie Working. Rich foods at bedtime plunge my blood sugar down to a level where I am able to access information with little or no dream overlays to hinder the information flow. During neither night did I manage to reach the state of pure information transfer, but the dreams were quite interesting, although quite fragmented.

Night one gave me partial remembrance of a (series?) of vacations which I do not think belong to this life (at least not yet). I went to Boston & spent much time at the beaches on the ocean. While at the sea, I relaxed & was able to release the sorrows within me. I understood my purpose & my role in the formulation of the future. Other Shadow Knights were on the beach also. The whole resort was a kind of rest area for those whose main work is accomplished in their dreams. I tried to remember as much as possible, but the memories are only vague shadows. Binah brings remembrance, but my waking life is not able to comprehend such remembrances yet. All I have is a vague nostalgia for a vacation I do not remember having taken.

On the second night I was more able to extract concrete information from the dreams & bring the information back to my waking consciousness. I was in a region of astral New York City which I did not recognize. It was a high-class neighborhood with many opulent food carts along a sidewalk in front of movie theaters. The theaters were walled shut, but I knew I could enter them through the cracks in the mortar.

I selected a movie about zombies, and oozed into the theater. In the movie house, I met a doctor who had spent years investigating death & immortality by sleeping in graveyards within a sensory deprivation tank. His findings were of no surprise to me, even though I have never done such research personally.

There are aspects of bodily function which need the symbiotic relationship of a fully conscious 'soul', but there are also certain bodily functions (certain aspects of healing & regeneration) which require that the 'soul' leave the body so the 'lower' functions of the body can regenerate without interference.

During disease & old age, the soul must leave the body, or the body will weaken & die. Most people in our society do not know how to cope with such experiences & some lose their way while out of body. This is one of the myriad origins of the comatose state. The doctor told me that most people believe that death-mimicking coma is a nightmare of the past (when medical science was unable to detect faint heartbeat, respiration, etc.), but he assured me that it is every bit as common today as it was two centuries ago.

Now, however, the doctors have been able to mask the symptoms through prompt embalming to kill the body so the soul cannot return to embarrass them. With proper medical supervision during coma (refrigeration, blood pumps to keep the brain nourished, etc.) there is no reason why a body cannot heal itself of any disease while the soul goes off on a long astral trip (several years would not be extraordinary).

But most people are not that attached to their bodies. When the body is very ill, the soul simply leaves on a journey to find a new body in its formative stages. The ensuing nine months of sensory deprivation, coupled with the trauma of birth & the total un-coordination of the new body causes severe mental imbalance & total amnesia. But such problems are by no means mandatory.

With the proper training, a soul should be able to 'commute' between the old sick body & the new fetal body during the crucial nine months. If the soul is actually out of body at the moment of birth, but close enough to observe/participate in the birth, it should be possible to retain complete awareness & full memory. Whether this is desirable is yet another question.

Also some vague memories of entering an underground parking garage with a demon's maw as an entrance. The ramp spiraled down (deosil) with a shaft of light, flame, & smoke as the central core of the helix. I extended my leather wings & rode the air currents down into the pit at the center of the earth. I think this is where the Boston/Binah vacation memories began the first night, but it is difficult to assess clearly.

Time for bed. I will write more when my energy level is higher. I will work more with my father tonight. If he needs a new home for his soul, perhaps I can in some way ease the transition.[1]

Excerpt from diary entry dated Thursday, 30 December, 1982 e.v.
More strange/wonderful/bizarre dreams last night {without the use of chocolate cream cheese pie or other entheogens}. The dream is fragmented, but seemingly connected in a way which still escapes me. I have pieces of a holographic image, but not enough fragments to give the image very clear resolution. I am fairly certain that as I tell my tale, I will begin to perceive more fragments & be able to sort things out as I type.

I entered the parking garage with the demon's maw entrance which I remembered from the Boston/Binah dream. The central column of the helical ramp was medley of forces involved in an on-going dance which

---

[1] PVN's father was sick at the time of this working and was beginning his transition out of this life. PVN has never been emotionally close to his father, but he is very much aware of the presence of his father within his own nervous system.

transcended both time & space. From below, fire & smoke pushed upwards, while from above, clear light & gentle breezes pushed downwards. Eddy currents & counterflows were the rule rather than the exception.

I spread my leather wings & became a flying lizard with ape-like features. I coasted upon the wind as I spiraled downward. The parking ramp became a series of grottos & tunnels whose entrances were arranged in a spiral about the central shaft of light fire wind & smoke.

At each tunnel entrance there was one or more beings. Some were human, but most were not. Some of these beings would occasionally jump out into the central column & sprout wings such as my own. As they flew/glided in the wind & smoke, they would all gradually transform themselves into a being such as myself – a mammalian lizard with large leather wings attached to the shoulder blades, powerful clawed forearms with opposing thumbs, large kangaroo-like tail, rather feral head, but with no visible hair. Most (like myself) were exaggerated androgynes with swollen breasts oozing milk from large hard nipples complimented with stout purple veined cocks perpetually on the verge of orgasmic explosion. Below pendulous testicles lurked a cavernous vagina, which dripped sweet smelling juices into the air, bathing the whole central column in a fog of holy dew.

I observed my fellows with only mild curiosity, fixing most of my attention upon the caves & tunnels. Occasionally one of my fellows would land at the lip of a cave & I would see him/her transform into a being which looked much like one of the beings already upon the ledge.

As I flew/coasted along, I felt drawn to one particular cave. It looked 'interesting' in a way which I cannot begin to explain. I circled it a bit & then landed. A human came from the mouth of the cave & greeted me with great formality. I instinctively returned the greeting & was transformed into a teenage girl.

Memories a bit hazy at this point. I remember walking through endless miles of caverns, guided by an old man dressed as a monk, with flowing white hair & a beard. He held a sphere (about the size of a tangerine) which gave off blue light which had a slight reddish tinge to it.

The light was quite pure, but it was not sufficiently bright to allow me to see clearly. We did not go in a straight path, for we needed to pick up various items which had been stashed within the cavern system over the aeons. By the time we finally emerged on the surface, I had my arms full of various pieces of armor, weapons, scrolls, and implements which had no meaning for me.

My guide remained totally silent & carried naught but the blue sphere. When we reached the surface, my guide motioned me to leave the cave & join the group of people in a valley below us. He stayed within the cave & I did not see him again.

Somehow I found myself amongst a group of people watching the sky. I had no memories of the earlier portion of my dream or of any other lives. Most of the people around me seemed to be peasants of some kind. All were dressed in colorful clothing as if going to a festival. Technology was in evidence, but not prominent. A light bi-plane circled overhead.

Suddenly a large dragon flew over the ridge of hills & began pursuing the biplane. I unsheathed my lance & threw it up in the air (like a spear). The lance zoomed upwards for several hundred meters, but my timing was off. It struck the tail of the biplane rather than the dragon.

The lance fell back to earth & I went off to locate the lance so that I could do battle with the dragon. I was dressed in light alloy armor & I was somehow amused/confused that I was a girl. Somehow I knew that I had once been other than a girl, but I couldn't trace the memory very clearly.

The dragon had landed in one of the towers of the University & I followed it without my lance. I took one of the short axes from one of the decorative suits of armor in the hallway, by breaking the shaft of the weapon to free it from the restraining bolt. I charged into the room which had sheltered the dragon. The dragon had transformed itself into a huge eyeball with tentacles. As I slashed at the eye I sang:

Hail unto thee who art Ra in thy falling,
Even unto thee who art Ra in thy destruction;
Vengeance is mine for the maidens whom thou has slain,
Death to the all-seeing eye of the God!

As I sang the song, something in me was vaguely uncomfortable with the content. I somehow felt I was reciting a parody of something else, but I could not place the context or the memory.

I was suddenly overcome with a very powerful urge to engage in sex. This bewildered me somewhat (I think I was virginal). I was very distrustful of the peasant men I saw as I felt they were not very gentle or caring about the feelings of a warrior lass such as me. I bathed the ichor of the Eye of Ra from off my body in a secluded pool & wandered naked up to an old oak grove frequented by druids & faeries.

I located a band of gentle druids who initiated me into the magicks of sex & learned from them how to ride the winds of eternity. They warned me never to ride the winds near the dark caves, or the spirits of the darkness would steal my soul forever. I did not mock their warnings, lest I offend them, but I could not heed the warnings either. I loved to play amidst the windy caves near the top of the old dark mountains where no other souls dared venture. The more I played in these winds, the more I began to remember of other lives beyond this peaceful valley. If the truth be known, I was very bored when I was not astral tripping after sexual union.

One day I finally screwed up my courage enough to fly my astral self directly into the darkest & most foreboding of the caves. As I flew, I left my memories in various caches along within the tunnel as a trail to aid my return. But as I traveled, I found other memories, left there by another (perhaps even myself!) & I hungrily devoured them as I flew. By the time I reached the column of fire, wind, air, and light, I had all but forgotten my life amidst the peasants & druids of the quiet valley. But I knew a little about the many tunnels which branched outward from this spiral helix & of the central core of duality. I leapt off the edge of the path into the void of flame & smoke as I shed the last remnants of my soul-stuff. My demon body quickly formed around my central void & I became (once again) one of those androgenous monsters who fly & glide between the fabrics of reality.

Somehow I made it back to the tunnel entrance where I entered the maze. I shed my androgenous mammalian-lizard body & reformed myself into my 'usual' astral form. I left via the maw of the parking ramp & found myself in astral New York, near my astral temple in the red light district. I went to my temple & committed the memories of this dream to my dream crystal, to be stored there until my physical self was ready & willing to commit this vision to paper.

[end of dream]

Very bizarre! When I began this diary entry I had nothing more than vague fragments about flying in the parking garage, being some sort of a dragon slaying female, & the battle with the giant eyeball. Somehow I am developing a set of skills which allows me to 'record' my dreams far more lucidly than I can consciously remember.

Excerpt from entry for 19 January, 1983 e.v.
The last two nights I have had a series of (seemingly) inter-connected dreams which I feel belong to the Boston Dream cycle. It is not easy to explain exactly what I mean by the Boston dream cycle, but I shall do my best to clarify.

Those dreams which I remember as being powerful, initiatory, or memorable are (for the most part) not isolated dreams, but part of a larger group or family of dreams. For the sake of categorization, I have broken the overall set of 'magickal' dreams into subsets, even though I fully realize that they are all part of the same major set. Thus I have my 'Lovecraftian' dreams, my 'Pyramids in the Abyss' Dreams, my 'Druidic grove' dreams, my 'University Beyond the Abyss' dreams, my 'Astral New York City' dreams, etc., etc., which all seem to over-lap or impinge on one another sooner or later.

I have never really spent much time in Boston, so I really don't understand why I can name this dream cycle with such certainty. It is reminiscent of the great city which houses my University, just on the Kether side of the Abyss. It is a large city, but with a friendly feel to it (much like Ithaca), with lots going on in the way of Arts, Science, tourism, etc. I usually go to this city as an invited guest, or as a tourist at a nice hotel. I am always welcome & I always have a good time. The sea is always in the background, but I rarely go to the beach.

Of the dream from night before last, there is not much to say. I was staying with Paul & Liz (but Liz was very different from her usual self. It was a weekend party at a secluded house. In some ways it reminds me of the place in which they held their wedding reception, but much more massive. I met a woman there who really knocked me off my feet. Not many details, but very strong nostalgic feelings, as though I were remembering a sweet memory from a youth I never had (at least not yet in this lifetime anyway).

Last night was more substantial. In some ways it felt like I was back in the same dream, but on an entirely different level.

I was at the magickal convention which I dreamed of the night before my letter from Miracle. I was speaking with an old Sufi woman about Anne & the process of creating one's own soul. She spoke in words, while I spaced out & went into a trance in which I saw the process on a molecular level, devoid of most of the maya/ego/self-centeredness which makes the process so difficult for those who are unable to remember the theoretical mechanics behind the individual problem. The old woman stopped talking & I returned to an awareness of my surroundings.

She smiled & reminded me that one could not know one's office—indeed, could not have an office!—until the process of creating a center had been undertaken & had been successful insofar as was possible before entering service to the race. It was then & only then that one would be able to see the various offices as enticements rather than simply as burdensome chores.

She then named several of the Offices which she saw me as capable of fulfilling. Some of them I could not hear clearly. She smiled when I looked puzzled & nodded her head at me & said that I would learn when the time was ripe.

She then took a small box (about 1.56" on a side) from beneath her robe & handed it to me. She bid me to open it & accept the bauble which it contained.

I opened the box & was immediately sucked into the black maelstrom of force from the void within the box.

During the next phase of the dream, I had no recollection of the previous portion of the dream, or of any reality beyond the one in which I found myself.

I was some sort of quasi-human spirit guide to an old black priest. When the man was about to die, I gave him a shimmering black & silver chasuble in which he was to sing his own Requiem Mass. This was (of course) against the rules.

I was placed in a state of suspended animation until the end of the world. When I awoke, everyone who had ever lived was being revived at once. All were getting into groups behind their individual patron saints – all the English behind Saint George, all the Irish behind Saint Patrick, all the hookers behind Saint Floradora, etc., etc.

Somehow I managed to stray away from those who had not yet formed a group in order to watch the parade. When nobody was looking, I ducked-out completely.

I went 'behind' the scenes via a tunnel used by electricians & janitors. I stealthfully peered down a grate within the dark tunnel & spied on some aliens who were in some sort of a control room. One of them saw me & pushed up & over the grate & attempted to paralyze me with the stingers on its tentacles.

I opened a small box which I had always carried {the box given to me by the old Sufi woman in the previous dream sequence} & a brilliant white light blinded & confused the alien while I made my escape.

Further along down the tunnel I was met by three guards (humans, with ray guns) & they attempted to take me prisoner. After a skirmish in which I temporarily stunned two of them, I left the tunnel & made an attempt to escape from this reality altogether.

I began to remember that I did not belong here, but was only here to observe & to learn, rather than become caught-up in local politics. I changed myself into a rocket ship & took off.

I then created a simulacrum of myself to act as a decoy, should they manage to trace me.

They did manage to find me. All of a sudden, there were two aliens on the bridge with my decoy. They wore the outward form of humans, but there was definitely something 'snakey' and unsavory about them. They seemed fooled by the simulacrum.

Since my true being was the rocket ship itself, I was around the aliens while they 'questioned' my decoy (whom they believed to be me).

I did not understand the politics of this reality very well at all. Seems there was some advanced races which were 'staging' an end of the world for a primitive human race & the advanced didn't want me messing things up.

They started to search the flight control computer for information after my simulacrum dissolved during a rather intense set of questioning which caused it remember that it did not really exist. At first they could not get the box open, but when they did, they regretted it immediately.

The cabin of the spacecraft was filled with brilliant white light. I was drawn to the light, so I folded myself into the box & took the box with me. As I was the plane which contained the two aliens, they were forced through the vortex with me.

I was back with the old Sufi woman, only she was now young & very sexually provocative. I held the small box on my palm & was in the process of extracting a very massive ring, encrusted with jewels from the box.

The ring itself was composed of two Ureas serpents, intertwined & holding a round disk in their mouths. The disk was enameled metal, depicting the Necronomicon sigil. Locked to the rim of the disk was a spider-web like wheel whose spokes held precious stones which cast colored shadows upon the face of the disk.

The wheel could be aligned in many ways in relationship to the enameled disk beneath. As I rotated the wheel, the whole ring seemed to transmute into an entirely different design.

The original design was not lost, but somehow 'covered-up' as though a hologram of another ring had been projected over the design of the first ring.

In one orientation, the ring looked very much like a signet ring bearing the seal of the OTO; in another it looked like one of the emblems of the Shadow Knights; in yet another it bore the Papal insignia. As I spun the dial I recognized dozens of insignia and failed to recognize hundreds.

I asked the young Sufi woman if the ring actually carried the authority of any of the organizations which it could seemingly mimic. She looked at me with a crafty glimmer in her eyes as she told me that all true initiates would be able to see my ring was but a counterfeit if the real ring of Power for that particular organization were manifest & in the hands of the rightful ruler of that sect, but that if the rightful ruler were not in a position of power or if the Ring of Power was not then manifest on the outer, then none could be certain that my claims to office were invalid.

I became more puzzled than ever & the Sufi just laughed at me. I asked what was the purpose of a magic ring which did not represent real power. She told me that the power was very real, but was diffused so that it could be used to focus the empowerment of whomever wore the ring for whatever purpose was necessary.

With the aid of this ring, anyone could manifest any valid magickal current for as long as was necessary to reify the true contacts with the Fountainhead of the Current, but the ring could never be mis-used by those who did not comprehend that the leadership of a Magickal Order was an office appointed by the gods & not a bauble to be passed-on to a favorite nephew or son.

As I continued to play with the ring, I recognized the facial expressions of the two serpents whose inter-twined bodies formed the band of the ring. They were the two aliens who had tracked me down in the alternate reality of the previous dream sequence.

As I played with the ring, I noticed that the serpent beings were still alive & that through their motions, the ring was fully adjustable to fit any sized finger – in fact it expanded from a circle so tiny it could hold-tight to a human hair to a circle well over three inches in diameter (3.141593″ is a better approximation).

I held the ring up so the Sufi could see the huge maximum diameter of the ring. She smiled & said that since I had discovered the trick of expanding the ring, she would show me how to potentize the ring for any/all magickal Currents.

She slipped the ring over my cock & balls, tweaked it tight, and led me from the main convention room into a temple or shrine. The room was dimly lit by the light of alcohol braziers perched upon the heads of two huge stone Cobras. Between the Cobras was a Roman style couch with lion claw feet holding crystal spheres covered in blue satin with gold trim.

She led me to the couch, laid me down & mounted upon me. The bezel of the ring pressed into her clitoris as she drew me inside of her. The twin serpents seemed to bend over the couch as I passed into the neither-neither state – the flames from atop their heads illuminating the dome of polished anthracite which formed the ceiling of the room.

As the Sufi danced & gyrated upon the shaft of my penis, I could feel the wheel of precious stones moving with relation to the enameled disk. As different aspects came into conjunction & were anointed with the elixirs of the priestess, an electric tingle passed through me from the base of my anal chakra to the crown of my head.

The two stone serpents were now entwined over the couch (their two heads being merged into one) & the flames at their head lept upward each time the electric jolt reached my crown chakra. At each flash of the serpent flame, I saw images projected into the curved black mirror above me. The images were superimposed one over the other so fast that I could neither separate them into coherent vignettes, nor serialize them into a linear story.

When both of our bodies were covered with sweet smelling sweat, hounds came out from the inter-dimensional angles at the corners of the room & began to lick the sweat from our bodies as we continued the opus.

Tentacles came from the mirror & consumed the dogs as we both came to a mutual orgasm which caused the whole universe to project from the spinning cock ring up through my spine & out into the mirror & then then collapse back into me via the open crown chakra. As the images surged through me back down into the ring, I became lost within my own nervous system. My external senses of awareness closed down completely & I fell into the ring along with the images.

I awoke. I was fully clothed. I was standing with an old Sufi woman on a dirty street in New York City talking with her about the changing role of the priesthood in this AEon. She smiled at me and handed me a small box. I had a very strong sense of Deja-vu as I began to lift the lid, but could not quite pin the feeling down.

The box contained an invisible ring which seemed to change and shift as I moved it. It was too big to fit my finger. The old woman laughed at me and said that I would grow to fit the ring when I was ready to undertake its responsibilities. She passed her hands over my eyes & I remembered the whole of this dream as I have recorded it. When she removed her hands, I was alone, hanging in a void, playing with my two crystals – the dark & the clear.

Excerpt from Diary entry of 21 February, 1983 e.v.
Went back to bed after last entry (I am fighting off a cold) & spent much time thinking about my letter to Frater ___. As I lay between sleep & mundane reality, I began to feel a presence of power flow about me like a warm & welcome shroud. I was very aware of a nostalgic longing for the mystical reality in which there is no separation between myself & the rest of the Universe.

I invoked the god-form of PAN(NH) as used by me during my second successful practice of Liber Astarte. PAN(NH) is the ultimate vessel of the Universe. S/He contains the body of Nuit within H-is/er round belly. My merge with the godform was not complete, but it did give me a perspective from which to view the Universe.

I saw the body of NUIT from the outside. Within the continuous arch of her body was the absolute void of which interstellar space is but the palest shadow. But the void was not empty, for it contained the myriad twinkles of the sisterhood of Stars. [I realize as I write this that a void which is not empty is contradictory in this mundane reality of Malkuth, but from the viewpoint of my vision, there was no contradiction.] I was reminded of Crowley's Star Sponge vision & briefly wished he were with me in the flesh so that we could compare & contrast our individual perspectives.

In the center of the Void was a gigantic Star which appeared to be the pivot point of the Universe. I knew instinctively that it was the fountainhead of the Order which lies beyond Da"ath. As I watched, the Star went Nova & spewed its star-stuff throughout the Multiverse.

It was as if the Hadit point of the Order had experienced the ultimate orgasm which destroyed its individuality completely. The star-stuff expanded outward to embrace the Universe & to Unite with the body of NUIT. As each of the little stars passed through the cloud of star-stuff, it absorbed as much of it as it was able. As each of the stars absorbed the ejaculation from the Hadit-point, it became self-aware.[2]

I saw that each of the stars were alive & that each moved independently of the others, yet in their motion was harmony. Because of the infusion of the jism from the Hadit point, each believed itself to be the center of the Universe. Each star was correct, yet each was also in error – for each Star is indeed the center of its own Universe, but insofar as each Star is unable to perceive other Stars as also being the center of the Universe, it is also in error. For the Stars themselves are not stationary centers, but in constant motion. The dynamic pattern formed from the interaction of all the Stars in the Universe is the true center of the Body of NUIT.

I saw that the stars were not equal in their self-awareness, nor were they equal in their ability to perceive their place within the pattern of the whole. All contained the seed of initiation from the Hadit-point, yet most seemed uninterested in nurturing the growth of this seed.

From my perspective, I saw that the dance of the Stars was an initiatory pattern which nurtured that aspect of the essence of the Fountainhead of the Order which exists within each of the Stars.

But I also saw all dances as transitory. Each dance of interaction was capable of initiation, yet no one dance could fully embrace the totality of the Universal experience. I saw/perceived many intertwining themes repeat themselves endlessly as the spiral dances of the Stars sought to reify the Fountainhead of the Order within the personal experience of each & every individual Star.

But as I looked closer & closer I saw that the Stars were not alone in the Universe. Most stars had one or more dark companions, whose Will was to follow an intricate orbit about the parent Star. Such dark companions sometimes impeded the orbital dance of the parent stars,

---

2   Before I get too much further in this little account of my vision, I should point out that all that I write is allegory and analogy. What I 'saw' took place in a realm which is beyond time & space and is therefore very difficult to speak of directly using the mundane languages of this planet which were designed to speak of sensory reality. When I speak of stars or planets or comets, I should not be construed to be speaking of astronomical reality. I simply utilize what images I can to convey a certain 'feeling' for what I perceived. I do not wish to quibble over linear details of my words, for my words are not my vision.

for their dance was not yet graceful enough to fully compliment the dance of the stars. It was in those systems where the orbits of the planets were free-est that the stars were least impeded.

When a parent star grew old & finally went nova, it would spew out its star-stuff to those in orbit around it in a microcosmic reenactment of the primal orgasm. Some of the dark planets would then become stars on their own, while others would choose another star to follow. I also saw certain comets which were attached but loosely to a particular star; they spent much of their time in a complex orbit among various stars in the same neighborhood.

But here my attempts to communicate this vision begin to break down, for most of these comets were also stars in their own right, whose dance took them through the orbital plane of several other stars.

When these comets were in close proximity to another star, they shone as brightly as the brightest of them, but when they were far from any of their companion stars, they took on the appearance of the coldest planet.

Perhaps in this phase they might be likened to the Hermits spoken of in Liber AL vel Legis. It seemed to be the purpose of these wandering stars to disrupt the orbital patterns of those overly inert planets who seem to hinder the dance of the stars.

From where I stood, it seemed to me that those stellar systems which were visited most frequently by the cometary wanderers were the systems with the highest concentration of the life essence from the primal orgasm. In some way which I cannot put into words, these wandering stars regenerated the stable stars so that they could keep up the pace of their intricate dance for far longer before they would grow old & go nova.

These wandering stars had no planets of their own (nor did they desire any), but they did travel in the company of other wandering stars, which were neither stars nor planets in any conventional sense of the word. It is the function of these wandering stars to induce planets into Starhood by unconventional methods.

My perspective shifted once again & I was able to see that each & every star, planet & comet was involved in a complex dance within the body of NUIT. The center of the circle is nowhere found, yet it could easily be deduced from the intricate dance of Universal Will.

Each dancer is aware of the pattern insofar as s/he is in tune with the dance. When the dancer becomes the pattern, s/he is in tune with the Dance. When the dancer becomes the pattern, s/he becomes the embodiment of the Hadit-point of the Universe & becomes a direct link to the Fountainhead of the Order for those who have lost their step in the dance.

But the dance of each dancer is unique.

One may follow a particular dancer for a while to attune oneself with the dance, but as one becomes attuned with the dance, one ceases to follow any particular dancer, for each dancer must learn to follow the pattern composed of all the dancers, rather than any particular dancer (no matter how skilled any particular dancer may be). Once a dancer is able to discern the overall pattern, and is able to follow it, it then becomes his/her duty to assist in its on-going evolution, rather than simply following it by rote.

Each star, planet & comet contains a unique blend of the essence from the primal orgasm & therefore each dance is a uniquely valid expression of the Pattern which re-creates the fountainhead of the Order within each dancer, each according to h-is/er ability to receive, perceive & create the Pattern within as well as without the individual.

My perspective shifted back into the dance itself. As I fell back into my body, I came to a realization that I am indeed one of the wandering stars. I follow the dance insofar as I am able & I follow the dancers whenever I lose my step. I shine when I am in the company of those who shine & I keep my light well hidden (sometimes even from myself!) when I am amidst the company of those who are not yet aware that they are stars.

Excerpt from my Diary entry of 22 February, 1983 e.v.
Very very strange dreams last night. While they were in progress, I felt like I was in a terrifying nightmare, but once I awoke, I was able to see that my dreams were simply a very intense learning experience. I spent about an hour after I awoke in revery & dream reconstruction. Very useful techniques for getting through the Malkuth overlays of really intense dreams. I shall reconstruct the dreams as best as I can while feeling free to cut thru the maya of the dream images where possible to reveal glimpses of the fabric of the experience insofar as I am able.

Sometime during sleep my dream crystal migrated from my left hand to under my body. When I awoke from the dream, my crystal was wedged firmly into the base of my spine causing mild displeasure, but very intense kundalini activity throughout the lower chakras (from solar plexus on down). My body was filled with adrenalin (flight rather than fight) & I was covered in a cold sweat, which I worked to absorb back into my body during my dream reconstruction/revery & then cleansed off that which I was unable to re-absorb with a post-revery bath/shower.

As usual, I had projected into sleep via VIII° orgasm. I was wandering amidst the theater district in Astral NYC & I came upon a used bookshop. Anne was with me during this first segment of the dream. As we went into the shop, we saw some members of the Tibetan Secret Police capture a political refugee & haul him off to be crucified. I was slightly puzzled because I had not realized that crucifixion was commonly used for political activists in Tibet.

Once in the store I located a four-volume set of books which would answer all my questions about Tibet & crucifixion. I cannot remember the title of the set, but it seemed to be some sort of magical encyclopedia which could answer all questions. At first the type in the book was totally incomprehensible, but as I stared at the page, I began to make out many variations on the verb to crucify. I began to read the text aloud (it seemed to be in some sort of barbarous tongue with some Latin marginalia) and...

The bookstore vanished & along with it vanished Anne & all memories of anything outside of the reality in which I had found myself. I was in a very old house which was decaying around me. Each time I looked into a mirror, I would see myself looking older & more decayed. I knew that I was not aging or rotting, but that the mirrors were somehow causing this illusion (very much like one of the scenes in the movie Poltergeist).

As I began to look more deeply into the mirror, I saw another being revealed in its depths. He (it was definitely a he) was wrapping my reflection in old white cotton & moldy cobwebs. As he wrapped me up, he mumbled a chant of illusion, fascination, and death.

He had three sisters, each of whom had long since died, but yet who lived on in the mirror. He had wrapped them up long years before. When he saw that I could see him, he smiled & drew his oldest sister in front of my reflection, so that I would have to look through her in order to see my own reflection. As I looked I became terrified for my mortal self. The corpse flesh dropped loosely from her face & a worm was crawling out of her half-eaten eye. As she smiled & beckoned to me, maggots and cockroaches fell from her mouth. I was totally repulsed & tried to run, but instead I fell through the mirror.

Again no memory of anything which had transpired previously in the dream or in any other reality.

I had been captured by a band of young thugs in their teens & early twenties. Some of them looked punk while others looked like 1950's street hoods.

One of them would torture me lightly & then promise even more tortures, describing them in detail. I would go all to pieces & become a sobbing hulk lying in the fetal position at his feet. I was terrified of him. This seemed to please him, so I acted more & more terrified of him, even when I was not very fearful, for by pleasing him, he would not torture me directly.

At one point in the dream, he had me totally hysterical & he was so overcome with his own power that he took down his pants & fucked the fold in my leg behind my knee. His semen spread all over me & I remembered who I was & that this was but a dream.

I was about to act when I heard a little voice within me to accept the gift of semen & to use it to follow this man back to where he had come from.

I awoke in my bed with my heart beating very fast. I was terrified.

After much meditation & calming myself down I remembered all of the dream & went back into it as an observer looking for clues, using my dream crystal anointed with the cold sweat from my body as a focus.

The four books are a key. I believe that they are written in Enochian, but that they are also blank. That is to say, the four books correspond to the four Enochian elemental realities, but that they contain invokations &/or evokations which we write into them via our unexpressed needs for balance. When I looked into the book, I was looking for information about political martyrdom, ascent of the Tree via the pillar of Severity & the symbols of Tiphareth. Within the mirror were the three Fates & their brother (about whom not very much is recorded). The sister who had terrified me so much was Atropos, the inescapable one, whose magickal weapon is the scissors for she breaks the thread of life. Here was my link to my former master!

I return to the mirror. My brother is nowhere to be seen. My other two sisters are very prominent in their roles of weaving & spinning the thread of my life about the image of myself which dwells in the mirror. I see them clearly and know them to be called (in English) Destiny & Chance. My third sister once again dances between my image & myself, thus severing the thread woven by Clotho & Lachesis.

I step forward & embrace Atropos. In so doing, I reach behind her & touch the end of the thread she has broken. As I merge with the thread, Atropos becomes younger & younger. She is still a corpse, but a very sexually arousing corpse. The maggots have made her cunt all sweet & runny & the worms have loosened up her ass for my cock. As we couple, we dance & my brother (now visible) does weave a spell around us both.

I am now on board the plane with my former Master. He does not know me, for I am wearing the body of a woman. The plane explodes & I leave the plane to follow the scent of he whom I follow.

I am back in the bookshop in Astral NYC. I recognize the shopkeeper as Chozar, the Atlantean mage from the Age of Lizard-men who became the prototype for Choronzon. He smiles at me in greeting. I am holding one of the four volumes of The Book of Universal Dance.

The volume I hold is bound in black leather & has a rose incised on the front cover. The leather rose has thorns of stainless steel. One of the thorns has pricked my finger & the book is now smeared with my blood.

I know I am on the Astral Plane. Therefore, this text has taken on the attributes of Yesod. This text is the text of Knowledge, which relates to Swords, but here in Yesod, swords relate most easily to Cruelty & Despair through the influences of Mars in Gemini.

I put down the book, for I know that it is not for me to attain this book from this Place. Were I in Tiphareth, this book would be a real prize, but from here, it is a bit too 'interesting' (as in the old Chinese curse "May you lead an interesting life") for my present stage of development. Perhaps one day, but certainly not now... and I especially have no desire to take a book such as this back with me to Malkuth!

I enter the sleaziest men's room I can find & wipe the crud from the mirror. My sisters welcome me as I gain entrance to their world with the blood from my finger. Beyond the mirror, I have no reflection. Thus there are no weavings of the fates to bind me nor to cut me off from my task. I refresh myself at the Fountainhead & return to my body which sits before the computer keyboard. Here ends this dream research for today.

Excerpt from my Diary entry dated 3 March, 1983 e.v.
Only fragments of dream memories. The one part which sticks in my mind had to do with a written 'test' I was taking in which I had to evaluate both my strong points & my flaws. As I wrote, I saw that my flaws & my strong points were one & the same. It is all a matter of how I am able to use them.

The dream also began a series of adventures with a woman whom I met in the dream. She was so different from me that I had a very difficult time suspending judgement long enough to learn from her. It was difficult, but very instructive.

There was also a retromingence in Time in which the TV stars of M*A*S*H were re-assigned to World War II, once they had completed their task of humanizing the Korean War.[3] {I was told by my mother that the final episode of the M*A*S*H TV series was aired this past Monday evening after running for 11 years—I suspect there is a lot of strong feelings for this show on the astral at this time}.

Somehow the Kundalini Serpent within each Adept must be induced to bend back upon itself in order that the AL-Chemyst will gain the ability to re-vivify the past without being compelled to relive the errors of the Past.

As A. O. Spare and Kenneth Grant point out, nostalgia is a key—nostalgia for that which has not yet come to pass. Thanks to the re-searchers in the field of Quantum Chromo-dynamics, it is now possible to deduce, explore & mathematically map such a multi-Dimensioned Kundalini Serpent.

The Ouroboros serpent can be seen as far more than a simple concept which aspires to becoming a closed circle through the swallowing of its own tail. This representation of the Fire Serpent can also be viewed as an infinite regression of spirals which continually fold back on themselves by traversing Time in both directions (Future to Past as well as Past to Future).

The Ouroboros Serpent is the summation of these recursive spirals over all Time & all Space. Each separate unit within this complex

---

3   BS note: Frater PVN has not watched TV on a regular basis since the summer of 1963—hence the rather oblique reference to the final episode of M*A*S*H.

series of spirals is able to act either independently &/or as a cohesive part of the Macrocosmic Risen Kundalini even though the microcosmic units of this Grand spiral are separated by Time &/or Space.

The Serpent constantly overlaps its own coils, refining its essence through self-digestion & through a formula which is not unlike that of the Phoenix.

With these ideas in mind (but not yet worked out in an articulate manner), I performed my morning VIII° in the post-orgasmic swirl, I managed to latch onto a concrete dream object. It was a book.

The book intrigued me for it contained that which I perceive as a non-atomic quantum discontinuity within the fabric of Space/Time (i.e., a total non-linear discontinuity which existed upon a Macrocosmic scale rather than upon a sub-atomic scale).

While the book seemed to be real in-&- of-itself, I was also able to perceive it as an allegorical representation of a Truth which I was not able to apprehend directly in its pristine simplicity.

As I looked more deeply into the book, I saw that it was written in two very different kinds of language (far [more] different from each other than any two human scripts). Although I had never seen either script before & was unable to translate either of them (in the usual sense of the meaning of translate), I was able to intuit much from what I was able to see during my brief glimpse of the book.

The title of the book is the Book of Oblivion {I have a feeling that Oblivion is a person (or perhaps an Office) as well as a state of being aspired to by those who tire of the Wheel}.

The first portion of the text was written in a cursive script as might be designed by an organic creature & reproduced mechanically via a typewriter of some sort. As I stared at various pages of the book, I somehow knew that It was an ongoing magickal diary interspersed with a series of guidelines for aspirants. The writer of the text was an advanced adept.

Near the end of the first portion, the 'tone' of the writing became hesitant, apparently because the great adept became aware that all of his(her?) initiations were but the faintest shadow of true Initiation. Then came the quantum leap.

The text changed from an organically derived cursive to a series of non-Euclidean alien symbols which intertwined over themselves all over the page in a decidedly disquieting non-linear fashion.

The only way I am able to describe the text is to say that it looked vaguely mathematical, yet alive in a non-organic sort of way. It 'sort of' moved (without moving) in a way which I found profoundly disturbing. I have seen texts which exhibited this kind of 'motion' at other 'places' (away from Malkuth), yet I have no conscious recollection of seeing any quite like this one.

I am amazed that I was able to glean as much from this book as I did, for I only glimpsed it for an instant as I fell back into my body after the not-very-exciting orgasm.

Here begins M.R. entry dated SUNDAY, the 6th Day of MARCH, 1983 e.v.
Took Shroom Tea on Friday night with Anne. I was pleasantly surprised at how nice it was. Lately (i.e., over the past year or so), the intensity of a lot of my Shroom experiences has been less than pleasant. I seem to be becoming more in line with my Will & I seem to be able to allocate my time such that my Magick & my Malkuth are both being worked on together, rather than one being at the expense of the other.

Other aspects of myself (from other Times &/or from other Dimensions) were with me during various phases of the trip. No full manifestations of other entities, but lots of activity just beneath the surface. I saw lots of activity within Anne, but every time I worked to help bring it to the surface, she lost Trust in herself (&/or the experience) and her ego mask went rigid over the Window of her face so I could no longer see beyond Anne. I suspect that if we had both been tripping harder, perhaps I would have been able to get through.

I think I was somewhat hampered by 'Lust of Result' in that I was trying too hard for a full-blown manifestation of Higher Consciousness. Ever since the UT manifestation, I have sought to be a 'midwife' to assist such experiences whenever & wherever I can. I have learned a lot, but sometimes I can still be a bit too expectant & 'helpful' – i.e., my helpfulness is really a hindrance.

Anne pointed out an interesting connection for me. Every Man & Every Woman is a Star. The Star Trump is related to the Hebrew letter He, which means window. Thus every Man & Woman are Windows for that which lies beyond.

Lucifer was strong within me again during the Trip. The first-Born Son of God as Lightbearer. He who is off on his own in order to solve the problems inherent in the First creation. He who seeks to change the laws of nature. Sometime I must sit down & write-up Lucifer's autobiography. So many people see Lucifer as being against God, while he is really the head of God's Research & Development team with Carte Blanche (from old Long of Nose himself) to experiment with the Universe as a whole in order to seek ways of improving it. In a lot of ways, Lucifer is an 'art critic' much like Jonathan Hoag (in the story by Robert Heinlein).

I need to get back to the concentrative & distillation phases of alchemy. Mushroom tea is nice, but I am unable to make it as strong as the alcoholic elixir. I need to trip heavy now that I am on better terms with myself.

During the trip, I came to a better realization of why Lovecraft would not eat seafood. He had a 'contact' (Cthulhu) who was of aquatic origin. It is next to impossible to sort out the spatial or temporal relationships among various inner-plane contacts. That is to say, Lovecraft had no way of knowing which Planet or which Time Cthulhu was 'from'. Therefore, Cthulhu may have evolved in earth's future from that which is now considered to be seafood. Therefore: why risk eating that which may be a necessary evolutionary link for your contact. The reverse is also standard practice—i.e., the Great spider which I sometime commune with does not now eat monkeys, even though they used to be a staple of her diet before we made contact with one another.

Thus ends Volume II of ChRySTAL Visions thru the Astral Mirror. While these tales can be entertaining & instructive even to those with no serious interest in magick, I have been asked to provide a few 'clues' for those who would like to pursue these adventures on a more serious level.

PVN's system of Magick is a rather unique synthesis of Thelema, Science Fantasy & 'homegrown' American Shamanism, which can best be understood by those who are well versed in the writings of Aleister Crowley, Kenneth Grant, Austin O. Spare and Howard P. Lovecraft.

Crowley's writings are a maze of inter-connected essays, books, poetry, and plays which span over 50 very prolific years. Even a partial bibliography of the man's work would fill a book. PVN advises those new to Magick to read whatever comes to hand, while keeping good notes & re-reading to synthesize as new material becomes available. In some ways, reading Crowley is like learning a new language & culture without benefit of any comprehensive books on grammar or syntax. The Tree of

Life provides the basic dictionary. Beyond that, the student is on his own.

Kenneth Grant takes an entirely different approach. His books are meticulous, well thought out, and progress in logical sequence from his earliest (Magical Revival) to his latest (Outside the Circles of Time).

To those who would like to gain some insights into the historical development of Frater PVN's personal system of magick, I would recommend a careful perusal of his older magickal records, many of which are on file at the Magickal Archives of Bate Cabal in Cincinnati.

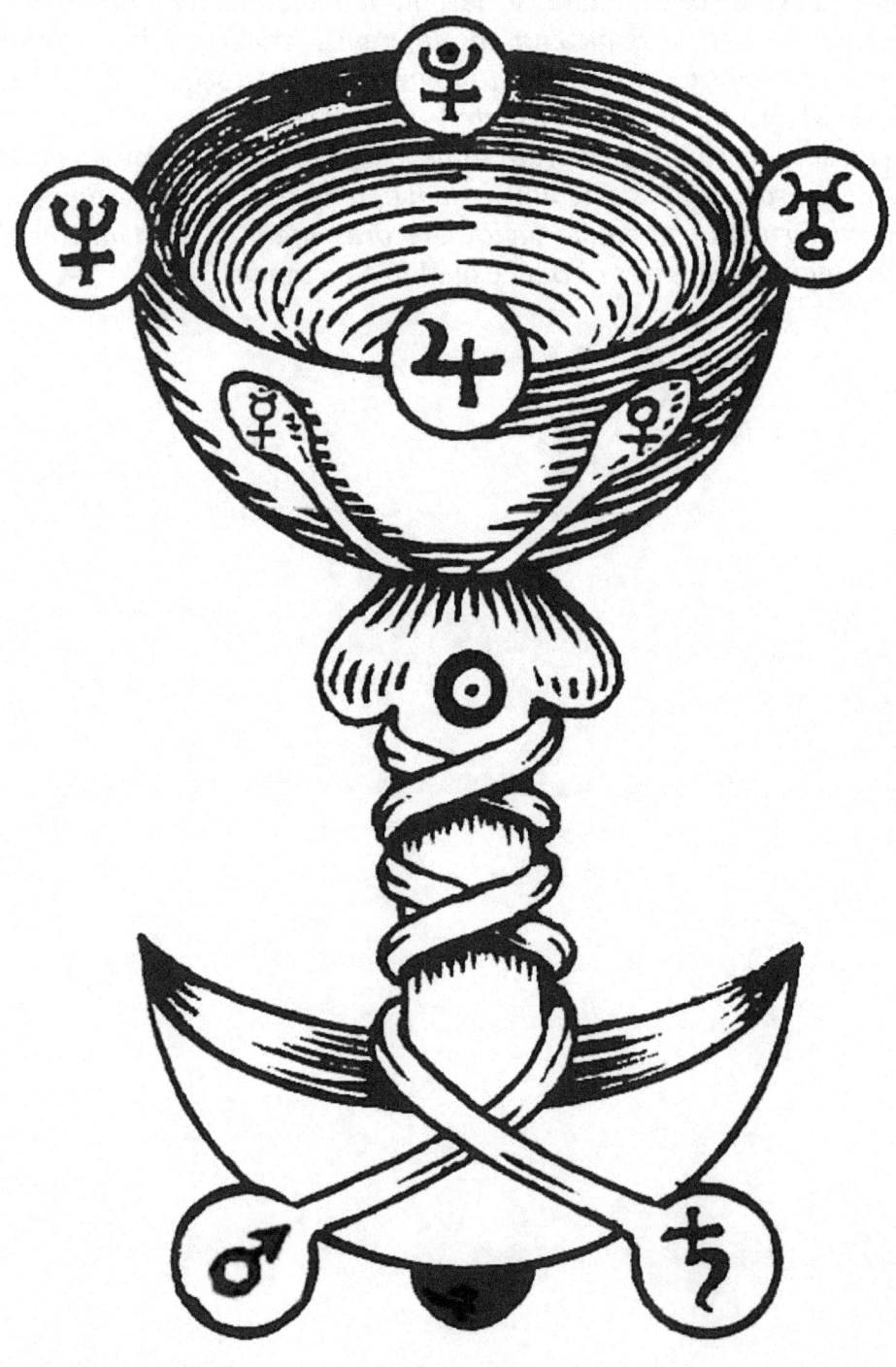

"The Chalice of Ecstasy" (1984)
showing the merger of the Cup of Babalon and the Perfected Tree—*D. Karr from Frater PVN's sketch*

The Chalice of Ecstasy

Being a Formula of Open-ended Initiation Suited for this Æon based upon a merger of the Tree of Perfection with the Cup of Babalon under the Auspices of Jupiter, promulgated by Frater PVN (Alobar), Master of Forbidden Alchemies by no Authority, other than his own.

During 3 different opera during the first pentad of Arachnæ of this year (May 16-21, 1984 e.v.) the fleeting images which usually follow VIII° orgasm were 'blacked-out' by an overwhelming vision which began with Don Karr's Tree of Perfection. In earlier work with his Tree, there had been a strong tendency for it to 'evolve' gradually (yet purpose- fully) into the Jovian Tree of expansion (Kether = Pluto, Chokmah = Uranus, Neptune = Binah, Daäth = Jupiter, Chesed = Venus, Geburah = Mercury, Tiphereth = Sol, Netzach = Mars, Hod = Saturn, Yesod = Luna), with an ensuing melt-down of the Paths into marbleized colored wax matrix as Jupiter went 'Nova' and became a star. The meltdown of the Paths 'imbedded' the Sephiroth into the 'backdrop' of the Universal continuity, while interconnecting each sphere to every other sphere by all the Paths.

But in these 3 opera, the transition was abrupt & without any hint of progression (like switching energy states by means of a quantum leap). What happened next was common to all 3 visions, but the detail of resolution of the vision has improved with repetition.

First: Jove/Daäth goes 'nova' & becomes a self-luminous body. Its color is Royal blue rayed with filaments of fine orangey gold which emanate as fine spider-webbed strands from the center of the Sphere & progressively become twisted snake-like pseudopods which extend beyond the boundary of the Sphere of Daäth to touch the marbleized back-drop of Paths (very lightly, like a spider testing her web for distant thrummings).

Second: The sun turns brilliant lemon-yellow with a network of royal purple strands (much like Jove's strands, but much finer in texture). Luna becomes a grail-shaped crescent of electric ultra-violet. Saturn becomes so black it looks more like a void than a color. Mars becomes a bright blood-red. Venus becomes an iridescent Kelly green while Mercury becomes a rich glowing psychedelic pumpkin orange.

Third: The Tree then begins to fold over itself & take on a palpable three-dimensionality. The upper 4 Sephiroth fold outward, so that the plane which defines them lies perpendicular to the axis of the Tree. Each of these 4 spheres becomes an iridescent narcotic gemstone on the rim of a celestial chalice. Kether becomes a brilliant white star (Sothis), Uranus becomes a 'justified' higher vibration of Mercury (feminine emphatic androgyne whose anus has been filled with the semen of his children) & becomes a shining pearl [i.e., Uranus who ate his children becomes your-anus who receives the seed of his children in joy]. The sterile mother at Binah becomes the three-pronged transmitter of the energies of the Trident of Set. Each of her prongs is tipped with a jewel (ruby, emerald & a royal blue stone) of the same crystalline composition.

Sol becomes the point at which the bowl of the chalice joins the stem. Venus & Mercury become twin serpents which emanate from Sol (like distended sperm) & encircle the inner surface of the bowl 3-1/2 times between Sol & the rim of the cup. Looking down on the rim, Mercury spirals deosil & touches the rim twixt Jove & Uranus; Venus spirals widdershins & meets the rim twixt Sothis & Neptune. Sol then elongates into a pillar of yellow fire with a surface network of royal purple 'veins' which distends downward to touch the Lunar Crescent. The Lunar Crescent then moves up thru the Sun & into the bowl of the chalice, where it atomizes into a vaporous electrical dew, the color of the light transmitted by a Wratten 18A filter (infra-red + ultra-violet, with no visible light transmitted). Saturn & Mars move inward to stand beside the pillar of fire like the red & black testicles of the Maha-Lingam. The marbleized paths become the shell of the body of the chalice—providing passive background support & communication among all of the Sephiroth.

The rim of the chalice then begins to vibrate (like a wet finger rubbed along the rim of a crystal goblet filled with fine wine) as a 'mating call' to those who would drink from the cup of initiation. The black Saturnian testicle represents the in-drawing of sexual power during periods of silence, while the red Martial testicle represents the outward surge of spontaneous orgasm during periods of speech. The golden phallus transmits both of these energies to the cup of Babalon, where it is structured & directed by the twin haploid lion-serpents (Mercury & Venus) within the menstruum of the trans-Abysmal

Lunar 'fluid', called Purpura of Ghee—a specialized form of Azoth. The royal road (purple network on the solar Maha-Lingam) absorbs a portion of the Purpura of Ghee for the education & enlightenment of the red and black testicles (whose Office is to wear masks of imbalance upon the outer).

Who (Hu?) is to drink from this chalice of ecstasy? Certainly not he who channeled its contents thru the Spheres of the outer Order. Certainly not she who refined the elixir by means of the feminine & masculine principles of Alchemy and concentrated it within the cup of Babalon. We are often warned of the dire consequences if the Whore of Babalon drinks from her own cup. Who is to drink from this Chalice? Is it reserved for the Gods alone, or are there also certain classes of mere mortals who may safely imbibe its contents as well?

The Whore of Babalon shares her cup with all, for she knows that no man may taste of its hidden delights save thru the purity of his heart & the transparency of his soul. The contents of her cup is the Elixir of Immortality of the Gods, yet it may be drunk by anyone who is Fool enough to actively seek initiation.

The rim Sephiroth are transmitters/emitters of energy and modes of specialization. Drink from each in turn, or all at once. The serpent's channel, temper, & sculpt the energy of the cup in accord with Will. Their venom is deadly, while their kiss is ecstasy. The aspirant is the Dove who descends upon the cup from beyond the microcosm of the Alchemist. He (the dove being active in approach to the Cup is masculine, while the cup of the Chalice is Feminine) bears the host (the army of his un-tempered desires & un-tested aspirations) as a token 'payment' for a taste of the dew of immortality. The host transforms the cup even as the Dove is transformed by her, for initiation is rarely one-way...

More details gained while in half-awake state after a phone call awoke me this morning (23 May,'84). I was drifting back to sleep when images of the Chalice of Ecstasy worked their way into my consciousness. I saw that the black & red scrotal Sephiroth were concentrations derived from the Jachin/Boaz pillars of the old Tree. The black sphere of Saturn embodies the essence of Jachin (God makes him firm) as the outer symbol for the formula of karezza. In this formula, the male ejaculatory current is reversed & repeated stimulation causes a Saturnian in-drawing of vital essence from the trans-Abyssal cup to nourish the Will. The red sphere of Mars is the embodiment of Boaz (eagerness, strength) which represents the spontaneous & automotive orgasm which is beyond the conscious control of the Alchemist. Together they symbolize the formula of IT (the un-manifest & manifest phallus)—see Crowley's comments on The Book of Lies.

I then began to see the Chalice on other levels. The Chalice of Ecstasy is the fruit of the Tree of initiation which is also a map of the esoteric nervous system of the Magus. To those 'outside' of the Magus's Universe, the Chalice appears very feminine & passive (for they are unable to perceive the dynamic Yin/Yang inner workings of the scrotum & Lingam). The aspirant is the male dove who comes to drink the nectar of transformation. Thus, the members of the outer Order are men, while the aspirants to the inner Order are women.

Those who have attained to the inner Order embody both the Masculine virtues of the Outer Order, & the Feminine virtues of the Second Order. The members of the trans-Abyssal Third Order seek always for further initiation. They work continuously to integrate new initiations into the fabric of their beings. They are ever ready to offer what they have to those aspirants who desire to drink of their Cup. The members of the Third Order are divine gynanders—those feminine emphatic androgynes who embody the quintessence of the Alchemical Marriage. The substance of their Chalice is their uniqueness which sets each of them apart from other members of the Third Order. The contents of the Chalice are a distillation of Azoth—the Universal Solvent. The body of the Alchemist must be inert to the actions of the Purpura of Ghee, else it will dissolve in ecstasy & cease to manifest as a unique entity. However, the Alchemist seeks always to expose h-im/er-self to the Azoth of other Chalices in the hope that s/he may attain dissolution. The dynamic balance of the testicles of Jachin & Boaz are crucial to this on-going task.

The developing symbolism in these visions is wondrous to me, yet its practical application seems so obvious to me that I feel I must be missing something. But, in the interest of completeness, allow me to belabor the obvious.

The lower 2 spheres are a specialized application of the energies of Mars & Saturn to the task of Sexual Alchemy using the formulæ of IT & Solvæ et Coagula. The Golden phallus of Tiphareth is the ego of the Alchemist made firm thru divine inspiration & nourished by the absorption of a portion of the elixir thru the purple nerve-net over its external surface. The body of the chalice is the pyramid of the Master, turned inside-out to offer the dew of immortality to all, rather than secreting it away like a black brother. The twin lion-serpents (Mercury & Venus) are the active (initiate) masculine & feminine components of the Alchemist which act as independent self-motivated agents of the aspiring Ego (the Star in its go-ing). The supernals (including Daäth) delineate the specialized nature of the cup of initiation which the Magus offers to the world (i.e., h-is/er specialized Magickal Current), while the Chalice is filled with the Universal solvent which initiates all who dare to imbibe it. The Chalice is the glyph for both the Wand & the Cup. Its rim is studded with the four elements and is thus the embodiment of the integrated Magickian. The Chalice is both the Tree of Life & the Cup of Babalon. It is the 3rd Order's symbol for that which is called the Rosy-Cross by the Second Order. Aspirants to the Third Order are warned never to drink from the Cup of Babalon, yet the Magi of the Third Order subsist almost exclusively upon its contents.

Because of the universal nature of the Chalice's elixir, an aspirant will rarely become a Master in the image of his initiator. The contents of the Chalice is the precursor to information (DNA, initiation into a specific Magickal Current, etc.), rather than information itself. Purpura of Ghee is infinitely transmutable by the Will of the aspirant in his journey from student to Ipsissimus, and is (in this Æon) not influenceable by the Will of the initiator.

This is a radical departure from previous Æons in which the Master dictated & controlled the development of initiation within the body/soul of the Aspirant. In the previous Æon, the formula for the Master was the pyramid, symbolizing the containment & the metering-out of the elixir of immortality. The primary vice of Masters who work the formula of the pyramid is Simony—the restriction of initiation for personal gain (acquisition of wealth; consolidation of power over others who possess contrary world-views; centralization & control-over prophesy/inspiration; and the promulgation of unimpeachable dogma). The restriction of initiation to pre-defined channels profits the power elite at the expense of the Magickal Current itself. Corruption of the Alchemical Chalice is the universal result of misapplication of the formula of the Pyramid. A sure sign of such corruption is the silencing of those who question authority (censorship of non-traditional views, excommunication of heretics or removing them from positions of authority, or {in extreme cases} torture & murder of those who dare to ignore the promulgations of the power elite.

Those whose Will is to work with the Chalice of Ecstasy have vowed to release all aspirants from any/all requirements of patriotic fealty to us personally, to the Will of our particular Current, and to any dogmas associated with our Magickal Path. As initiators, we are an open channel of inspiration for all who drink from our cup. We may offer specialized initiations &/or courses of training, but it is up to each seeker to make of these initiations what he will. We do our Will consciously and with full responsibility for all of our actions and our non-actions. We do not hide our ignorance behind the veil of secrecy, neither do we play the role of humble servants who do but 'follow the Will of the Secret Chiefs.' Obligations between any student or neophyte & any Master or Magus are always open to discussion, and can have no 'hidden strings' attached to them.

But this does not mean that Masters are obligated to devote their lives to training students with no recompense. Workers in any field of endeavor (be it magick, medicine, architecture, or aught else) are deserving of compensation for their efforts. An under-study, chela or apprentice must expect to carry-out certain tasks &/or pay certain fees in exchange for training. As in more mundane apprenticeships, the exact nature of the exchange is open to discussion at any point along the Path. Apprenticeship training replaces the life-long indentured servitude to enshrined Dogma which has long been the hallmark of the pyramidal centralization of power practiced in the previous Æon.

Magical Orders which continue to be based upon the closed systems of the previous Æon will undoubtedly oppose our efforts to cause the pyramid to flower. As we find more & more ways to drink from their cups of initiation without becoming bound to their obligations, our success will be a proof to all who are drawn to us.

There are those who claim that it is not possible to drink from any cup of initiation of the previous Æon without being bound to its obligations. They choose to discard all ties with the pyramidal Orders in order to forge links of their own with the inner Order. In some cases, it may not be possible for individuals to absolve themselves of their obligations to repressive Orders without abnegating all initiation in the process. However, in most instances the ingenious initiate is fully capable of freeing h-im/er-self from the restrictive bonds of pyramidal Orders without breaking any oaths. The demonstration of the proof of this theorem is left as an exercise for those who aspire to

Mastership thru the use of this formula.

Previous Æons have been governed by a LOGOS, or Word which when uttered by the Ipsissimus of the Æon served to mold all Currents of that Æon to the pattern of the LOGOS. The previous Æonic formula was that of Patriarchy. Assertion of the right of man to rule woman was practiced in China as much as it was by the Church of Rome. The Matriarchal Æon before that was little different, save in the 'flavor' of its Dogma.

However, in this Æon, those who have thus far attained the right to utter the LOGOS of the Æon have refused to do so. Those who have become Masters in this Æon are therefore bound to no particular Æonic formula, but are free to work with whatever formula(e) is/are aligned with the Current which it is their Will to transmit/reify.

At this nexus of Space/Time/Alternity there is healthy competition among myriad non-exclusive Æonic formulæ, with much cross-fertilization among heretofore contradictory Currents. But cross-initiation is strictly voluntary and is not necessitated by the LOGOS of this Æon. Specialized Currents often require isolation & silence to incubate in fullness. During incubation, they may appear to be practicing the diseased isolation of the black brothers. However, such may not be the case. Only time & the success or failure of a particular formula can attest to its efficacy. We are in an Æon where everyone can aspire to his/her own LOGOS. Let us do so in concert with all of our fellow Magi.

Here begins the entry in Frater OTz PTN–690/PVN's Magickal Record for TUESDAY the 08th Day of MAY, 1984 e.v.,
JULIAN DAY No. 2,445,829.06 Moon being 8.0 Days old. [1:30pm]

Do what thou wilt shall be the whole of the Law.

On my little excursion the other night I met a deer. It may have been a stag, but I am not sure because I think that the stags lose their horns this time of year. It was on the road & I stopped the car. We sniffed each other out & touched noses, before the deer decided that it had better things to do.

My meeting with the deer was exhilarating, but did little to quiet my restlessness. When I returned from the store, I went to bed.

Not much dream memories on Sunday morning, except at the very end of my sleep. My dream crystal had gone off by itself & was inaccessible to my physical self. I "found" the crystal (on Monday night) wedged between my mattress & the wall—in a place where I know I had searched for it a few days earlier. Now that it has returned from its journey, I now have regained much strong consciousness of my dream life. I often wonder where crystals "go" when they seemingly evaporate from this reality. Oh Shinnah[1] says they are "hiding," but I feel that there is more to the mystery than simple pranks. Such mysteries need more information. In the meantime, here is what I remember of my Sunday morning dream.

In my dream I was on the sandy shore of a great sea. Long grass grew in the sand. There was an old temple, seemingly abandoned, surrounded by unkempt lawns & gardens. Wild goats grazed the grass & a stag (the one I met on the way to town?) stood off on a nearby hilltop.

I attempted to walk to the temple, but the grass restrained my legs & prevented me from approaching any closer. The restraint was not the mindless tangle of earthly vegetation, but the cooperative effort of many simple minds working cooperatively for a distinct purpose (like ants or cluster flies). The grass did not halt me when I retreated back to the shoreline.

Then I noticed that whenever a goat entered the sea, it turned into a fish—not all at once, but front to back. The goat would go to the edge

---

[1] Oh Shinnah Fast Wolf (b. 1934), Warrior Woman and Elder of the Apache and Mohawk Peoples. She was featured in the 2007 documentary, *All Is Made Beautiful: Native American Traditions with Warrior Woman Oh Shinnah Fast Wolf*, a film by Bettina M. Gordon.—Don Karr (DK)

of the water & kneel its forelegs down & put its face & front end in the water. As the wet portions turned into a fish, it would thrust off from the beach with its hind legs (like a man launching a dingy from a beach) & complete the transition. The entire operation was both fast & smooth, with no awkwardness or hesitation. All that was left of the goat was a beard & curly horns on the fish.

Fish were also coming out of the sea. First, they would approach the beach from underwater & beach themselves with their heads held high out of the water. As the gentle waves retreated from their bodies, their heads & forelegs became those of goats. The goats would then pull themselves onto the beach with their forelegs & (once out of the sea) the transition would be completed. Although the goats & fish were of vastly different size, the transition did not look in the least bit ludicrous or implausible.

These goat-fish reminded me more of Neptune than of Capricorn as I watched their actions. I then remembered Don's Tree & its attribution of Neptune to Binah. I wished I could remember which 3 Paths accessed this Realm in Don's system so I could look for clues of the gateways.[2]

I looked up at the Sea & saw a far-off island with a mountain of crystal enshrouded in mists. A large metallic gold Trident seemed to "grow" out of the peak of the mountain like some sort of Atlantean sky-scraper. The symbol reminded me of the "Wealth Crystalizes the HUMM/the HUMM Crystalizes Wealth" sigil I have been using in my VIII° workings.

I was intrigued by the island & wanted to journey there to explore it, but (since other mysteries lay closer to hand) I was far more interested in getting to the abandoned temple. Somehow, I knew that I was responsible for holding myself back from reaching it. I somehow felt "to blame" for its state of disrepair & abandonment. The state of the temple grounds was particularly disturbing to me. I knew I needed peace within myself before further exploration would be possible, so I sat down to discover answers thru meditation.

As I sat down in the grass to meditate on my place in all of this, the grass gently picked me up & transported me to the entranceway of the temple. In some ways, I felt honored to be treated so regally by the noble

---

[2] The four (not three) paths to *binah* that Bill was trying to remember are
vav-TAURUS - from *keter*-PLUTO
shin-FIRE - from *hokhmah*-URANUS
heth-CANCER - from *da'at*, where Bill had stationed JUPITER
dalet-VENUS - from *gevurah*, or *din*, Bill's MERCURY—DK

grass, yet I also somehow expected such treatment because of my rank "& the angels bear him up, lest he dash his foot against a stone."[3]

As I was borne to the temple on the backs of the grass, I became more & more at peace with myself. I was still troubled by why I should feel responsible for a place which I had never seen before, so I followed the thread of my disease.

At first, I thought that my link with this temple might be cause-&-effect via my physical home—that is to say, I felt that this place was allegorical of the state of disrepair & lack of maintenance which I accord to my physical dwelling. But I somehow felt that the link was not so straightforward. Somehow the 2 temples are analogous, but neither is allegorical of the other.

It is not my present task to maintain the earth (physical plane) at this nexus of Space/Time, for I am a storyteller whose task is to explore the realms of vision & report-back to the rest of the race—but this could change in an instant if I chose to undertake a different aspect of the Great Work. The apparent crumbling of both of these temples is but an illusion based upon a skewness to my perspective. Even as I look at both temples more closely (for I can perceive both levels of reality at once), their integrity seems more wholesome & I am more & more at peace with the dance of Maya.

I am in an open temple—not much more than a courtyard paved with large stones, with widely-spaced pillars supporting a high vesica shaped roof. Near the center of the temple (at one of the ellipse's foci) stands a very large shallow grail (like a large birdbath [approx. 5 ft. across] made of polished stone [black marble veined gold]) balanced on a short pedestal shaped like a golden mushroom. The cup is far too large & unwieldy to lift, but it nonetheless has a pair handles made of goat horn.

As I approach the cup, it appears to be filled to the brim with a seething effervescent broth which both attracts & repels me at the same time. As I focused on why I should not drink the potion (the contents of the cup of Babalon is not for consumption by mortal men), the more I wanted to drink of it. It smelled sweet & invigorating & I somehow knew that this cup contained the dew of immortality. But the more I focused on why I should drink the brew (this is my dream & I can do whatever I please in my own fantasy world), the more repulsive the cup became. Its contents smell of vomit & decay & I saw

---

3 Ref. MATTHEW 4:6.—DK

both maggots & turds floating on its surface.

The goats & the stag were watching me curiously from the perimeter of the temple. I looked toward the stag & noticed that he was standing by a circular staircase which wound around one of the columns up to the roof. I looked up at the high roof & saw that directly over the grail was a yonic opening decorated with pearls.

I climbed the stairs & walked out on the high roof. A gentle breeze was blowing & the whole temple swayed (I always find it remarkable that my "normal" extreme vertigo & acrophobia is completely absent in most dreams.) I went to the edge of the yoni (it was even more ornately decorated along the top edge) & knelt at a kind of bench which suspended me over the hole.

The bench has padded depressions for my knees & elbows. The whole affair pivots with changes in my body weight to shift me from a kneeling position at the edge of the hole, to hanging face-down over the center of the hole. I knew that the bench responds to the slightest shift in my center of gravity & is therefore much more attuned to my Will than my conscious actions (much like a dowser's forked stick or pendulum). I knew that my Will would either bring me back to the safety of the roof or dump me into the grail (from a height of 100 meters), & my conscious fears &/or struggles would only hinder my chances of survival.

So, I relaxed & enjoyed the view. The grail was tiny below me, yet I could still see it quite clearly. Its roiling contents looked absolutely repulsive. Yet, the odor drifting up to me was absolutely enchanting. I knew that if I closed my eyes, the seductive quality of the odors would lure me to "let go" & I would slide down into its depths. Such a fate would not really be very terrible, for the intoxication of being the cup is a great reward for those who seek a release from the trials & tribulations of this world. However, I have much I still need to explore, & release from my task is not my Will at this point in time.

Then I remembered Jason & how he was able to listen to the sounds of the Sirens & live. I stared at the hell broth & focused on its repellant nature & my revulsion quickly shifted the bench out of the orifice & back up to the roof. I took off my traveler's pack & used its straps to secure my legs to the bench. Then I allowed myself to shift forward over the hole once again. I closed my eyes & drank in the narcotic allure of the grail with my nose. I felt myself slipping forward, but I no longer cared whether I lived or died. I simply sought union with the object of my desire. When I felt the tug of the straps around my ankles, I knew that my scheme had worked. I hang suspended between the worlds.

Behind my closed eyelids I saw a mist. Fleeting images scampered by at the direction of my unconscious urgings. I tried an experiment. I 'projected' the Cheshire cat from Alice onto the mist. The face appeared first, then the rest of its body. The cat spoke to me: "Ah Dodson, it has been a long time hasn't it?" I chuckled & the cat became startled when it realized that I was not Dodson. It then peered at me intently & turned into the hookah smoking caterpillar who asked, "Who are you?" I smiled back & returned the question, "Yea, verily HU?"[4] (by this time, I was quite giddy from the fumes of the grail below & was quite willing to make puns on who/HU in order to test the caterpillar's reactions).

The caterpillar was not pleased at my blasphemic punning & began to menace me with venomous mandibles. I opened one eye to superimpose the image of the grail upon the caterpillar. He shrieked in terror & begged me to close my eye, lest he plunge to extinction. I acquiesced; he became most intrigued at how I managed to maintain that precarious position of illusion.

I chuckled & told him of how I tied my ankles to the bench. He was most impressed & gave me a token whereby I might pass thru the realm of the red queen unmolested. [The token looked like one of those brass coins used at video arcades instead of real money to minimize pilfering.] He then offered me a bit of the mushroom which he was sitting on. [I placed it into my flask to add to my in vivo entheogens for the upcoming gathering.]

He asked me again who I was & I told him that I had many names in many places, but did not really know how to answer him in a way which would not be misleading. It was the caterpillar's turn to chuckle now. He looked deep into my soul & saw that I was indeed a Thelemic

---

4 Bill could have encountered "HU" in any of the following books, all three of which he owned.
Among Isaac Myer's numerous quotes from the *Zohar* is the following: Began R. Shimon further and said: 'Behold now, that אני *a'nee*, I am, הוא Hu, *i.e.*, and there is no elohim with me, etc.' (Deut. xxxii, 39, comp. 37, comp. Ex. xxxiv, 9.) —*Qabbalah: The Philosophical Writings of Solomon Ben Yehudah Ibn Gebirol* (Philadelphia: [self-published], 1888; rpt. New York: Samuel Weiser, Inc., 1974), page 361.
§ 204 of S. L. MacGregor Mathers' translation of THE LESSER HOLY ASSEMBLY reads, And since in Him beginning and end exist not, hence He is called AThH, *Atah*, Thou; seeing that He is concealed and not revealed. But HVA, *Hua*, He, is called. —*The Kabbalah Unveiled* (London: George Redway, 1887; rpt. New York: Samuel Weiser, Inc., 1974), page 279.
Within § 406. ThV of AN ESSAY UPON NUMBER, Crowley writes, Note that AHA (7), the divine name of Venus (7), gives the initials of Ani, Hua, Ateh—I, He, Thou; three different aspects of a deity worshipped in three persons and in three ways : viz. (1) with averted face ; (2) with prostration; (3) with identification.— *The Qabalah of Aleister Crowley: Three Texts* (New York: Samuel Weiser, 1973), page 35. —DK

pilgrim on a nameless quest. He then took on the form of the Cheshire Cat once again & declared that I must be one of the Wizards of Oz he has heard so much about.

Then I awoke in my bed with only scant memories of the dream. It is amazing how the writing of a dream will cause me to relive it & thereby aid me to retell it. The peculiar weave of tenses from past to present & back to past again in retelling the tale is an indication of the complex weave of retelling the tale & reliving it. The weave would be even more complex had I not consciously attempted to keep it all "in the past." Were this a proper story (rather than a diary entry) I would probably rewrite the whole tale in the present tense to add immediacy & impact for the reader.

Experiencing of dream while awake is most unlike the dream while asleep. While asleep, each conscious choice opens certain possibilities, while closing others (either I swam to the trident mountain or I went to the temple of the grail, but not both at the "same" time), but in my wakeful state, I can see that all pathways remain open no matter which set of choices I make at any given juncture. Each dream is infinite & what I report in this record is but the smallest fragment of what has actually transpired. I follow those threads which seem most interesting or the most entertaining. But all else is equally valid.

Structured initiation seems to be involved with making a continuous set of choices leading to a particular "goal" (usually predetermined by tradition or the guidance of an external guide). At the moment, I have no particular goal in sight. I simply explore—& create in my explorations. On one level I know that immersion in the grail means an end of my consciousness. Yet, on another (equally valid) level I know that the grail is simply a portal (possibly one-way) to another world (possibly another Sephirah). For now, I use the power of this Grail to reify dreams, but soon I must use it to bring such dreams back to this plane so that I can continue my work without interference.

Here begins the entry in Frater OTz PTN—690/PVN's Magickal Record for WEDNESDAY, the 09th Day of MAY, 1984 e.v., JULIAN DAY No.2,445,829.11 Moon being 8.05 Days old. [2:35pm]

Do what thou wilt shall be the whole of the Law.

Troubled night with tumultuous dreams. Even though I feel worn-out & bedraggled, I do feel better. Fear of wrestling with a dragon is always so much worse than the actual wrestling match. Dream images lack full clarity, but they feel powerful. I shall dip back down into them to see what I can draw-forth.

    I am in a very large mansion (which is also a fancy hotel) with Anne & a man whom I do not know. He is a friend (or lover) of Anne's. I am somewhat uncomfortable for Anne seems to want me to leave, yet she also wants me to stay. We are in a huge bathroom with a bath tub enclosed with glass doors. The tub is big enough for several people. Anne does not want me to bathe with her, yet she keeps telling me that I need to take a bath & I "had better hurry".

    I see a second bathtub. It appears to belong to the people at the health club next door. I begin to close the door to the health club (for solitude & for quiet when a brown pussycat wants to come in. I fear a fight between this cat & Beezelbub (our cat) so I continue to close the door. A young man assures me that their mascot is very friendly & will cause no problems. I let the cat in.

    In another aspect of the dream I am talking with one of the permanent residents of this house. He is a stereotypical English Lord of some sort. He asks me what connection I have to "the family". I tell him that we share a common ancestor & that my father's uncle is his uncle's father. He looks a bit bewildered & then beams at me & exclaims that I must be related to the "ship's Pharoh", by which he means the ancient ship chronometer which has been missing for quite a number of years. Although I do not see how I can be a descendant of a clock, I reply in the affirmative (for it does have a ring of truth to it).

    In the big bathroom is a large glass bell, made of a thick blue glass which makes a marvelous tone when struck with a leather headed wooden mallet. The bell is shaped like a squid & is about 4 ft. long. When I am preparing my bath (on the athletic club's side of the bathroom) I see that someone (Anne??) has made a mess of the big bath tub. All the glass panels are askew & water is leaking everywhere.

I attempt a fix, but I really do not understand how the various panels & curtain rods go together. Anne is upset with me for attempting to fix "her project". I leave her to her own devices to take my bath. I am saddened by our interactions, but am unable to find a workable solution other than steering clear of her until she does what needs doing.

I find a second glass bell like unto the first. But this one has a broken mouth & has been drilled out to accept various electric wires & lamp fixtures. This bell is sentient & is vicious towards me. It keeps biting me about the hands. I find a stick & place in in the bell's mouth to give it something to chew on. Its viciousness subsides. Perhaps it was only teething.

I am down by the waterfront in a poverty neighborhood frequented by sailors, smugglers, hookers, & cut-purses. It is foggy. I cannot see the water, although I hear it lapping against the nearby pier. I am here to meet a sailor who may have information about the ancient chronometer which I seek. I describe the device to him without naming it.

"It is a squat vertical cylinder made of brass sitting on a platform meant to be bolted in place in the wheelhouse. It is covered by a deep parabolic glass dome to protect it from the weather. It has no clock hands like a modern chronometer, but has a series of perforated metal disks thru which one sights the stars. The perforated disks are attached to the vertical side of the central cylinder tangent to its curved surface."

The sailor immediately knew that I was describing the Pharoh. He had once (long ago) been on the ship which relied on the Pharoh to guide it, but the ship had sunk. He thought the Pharoh had been taken off the wreck & brought to Castle Trident atop the crystal mountain.

The sun had been rising as we spoke. The mists began to clear & I saw the island from my previous dream.

I knew where I was & I knew that I was in dreamland. I took the blue glass bell (the one with the broken mouth & electric wiring) from under my trench coat, unwrapped it & placed it in the sea. It turned into a blue bottle dolphin who began to swim round & round the bay, making the most musical sounds I had ever heard. The water soon frothed & seethed with activity as hundreds of dolphins congregated to hear the tale of the dolphin who had been turned into a bell & then a lamp.

One of the dolphins approached me & began to speak. I could not understand her words so I spat into her open mouth (a trick I once learned from the King of Serpents). The dolphin immediately understood my intentions & spat back into my mouth. We then kissed deeply & I became sexually aroused. She drew me into the water & we became as one. While we fucked, she dove deep into the sea & leapt high into the air. We both climaxed together & lay together on the surface of the gentle sea. Other members of her clan communicated our combined elixir from her vagina with their tongues.

As we now spoke a common tongue, my lover asked me how I came to their harbor & whence I was going. I told her of the crystal mountain & of the Pharoh I hoped to find in Castle Trident. She asked if I could swim to the island & I asked her how far away the island was from the bay. She replied that her people went there often when men fished the shore of the great sea (to avoid competing with them for fish). The trip usually took her people 13 days.

I replied that I was able to swim for several hours at a time, but such a trip was beyond my endurance. I asked her about those who live on the island (their race, temperament, etc.) and whether they had regular commerce with the men of this port.

She replied that the beings who lived on that central island kept to themselves, but were not hostile to anyone. They did not fish the sea, neither did they engage in commerce, save to deal with certain ships which regularly brought them unusual items in return for life-restoring unguents & potions.

Dolphin sonar does not work above water & their eyesight is poor, so she was unable to give me much information about the race which lived on the island. She offered to transport me there, but as I needed dry passage for the Pharo, I declined her kind offer. I asked her if any of the ships which traded with the island were now in port & she pointed one out to me.

I went back to the mansion to bid my goodbyes & to seek out the old Lord to ask him about Castle Trident. He informed me that the only way to gain access to the castle was to bring a rare object to trade with them. None had ever seen the lords of Castle Trident in person save their personal messengers (who appeared to be human). The messengers would not speak of anything but the business of barter 'twixt human & the keepers of the Castle.

I asked if the keepers were honest & what kind of objects they sought. My cousin told me that the keepers had no interest in "that which could be purchased for gold or obtained by a common thief".

I looked for Anne, but was told that she had left with first light. Some said that she had traveled inland, while others told me that she was following a waking vision toward the Island in the center of the Sea.

Armed with this information, I sought out captain Diogenes of the ship Arestes' Misfortune in the tavern called the One-Eyed Trout to discuss a plan with him which would get me to the keepers with a prize which would enable me to bargain with them face-to-face.

Fascinating how the imagery in my dreams seem to layer one upon the other. What began as one of those incomprehensible streams of dream images has resolved itself into another dream in the same cycle as the other night. I feel like I am still suspended over the cauldron of dissolution in another part of the same dream, but my consciousness has moved to a more active aspect of myself so that the seer can attain the motility of the doer without giving-up the power of projecting Will into the dream cauldron.

I note in passing that this afternoon a little neighbor girl came by looking for her lost cat. The description matches the cat in the earlier portion of my dream. Intriguing how time folds back on itself in such literal ways in dreamland.

Here begins the entry in Frater OTz PTN-690/PVN's Magickal Record for TUESDAY the 29th Day of MAY, 1984 e.v., JULIAN DAY No. 2,445,850.06 Moon being 29.00 Days old. [1:30pm]

Do what thou wilt shall be the whole of the Law.

Time to get to my dreams.

In one dream, 0-Maku & I were looking for a cheaper house to live-in. We were selling the apartment building & the Humm did not have its own place in the country. 0-Maku had located a house which was within our price range ($45,000) & wanted me to go see it soon so we could put down a purchase offer. Bill Gafney (our contractor from the apartment house) overheard our conversation & asked 0-Maku about the location of the house. When she described the place to him, he told us that the house had been purchased less than a year ago by the present owner for under $3,000 & that he had spent about $4,000 to fix it up. We were both shocked by the extremely low price. I was determined to offer $7,500 for the house & bargain from there. Secretly, I wondered what could be wrong with the place.

The house was very small on the outside, but inside, it was a mansion. It was built into the side of a hill on the edge of the Long Island Sound. Although the water was far too polluted to swim-in, it smelled fresh & exhilarating. The bedrooms had large balconies facing the sea, with spiral concrete railings like giant snail shells. I was fascinated by a large fireplace in a room with wrought iron doors with brass handles. It reminded me very much of a house I never had.

On another level, I suspected that I was dreaming. I was unable to get to either the basement or the upper floor. One of the bedrooms was occupied by a teenage girl who didn't bother to put any clothes on when I came in. I jokingly asked if she came with the house & she replied that she preferred to come with people. The real estate woman sighed & told me that the teenage girl was a nymphomaniac ghost who was the reason for the extremely low cost of the house, for no woman could "hold onto her man" with "competition like this" around all the time. I turned to the spirit of the house & asked if she were jealous if her male lovers had other relationships. She replied that she was not in the least bit possessive or clingy, & that she had no need to compete for affections. I asked the spirit of the house if she would be willing to show me past the illusion which shrouded the house like a veil of cobwebs.

She stood before me in her innocent nakedness & asked me if I knew who she was. I replied that I did not. She picked up a quartz crystal from the table beside her bed & gently rubbed it in the dew between her legs.

She handed the crystal to me & told me to do "whatever came naturally". I smiled at her reverentially & sniffed the crystal's electric wetness. The scent of it made my limbs quake. I then kissed the crystal & drank in its essence. The house & my surroundings disappeared completely.

I was standing with Adrea on the drawbridge of a large castle carved from crystal. Before us was a delegation from the castle. They were tall, lean, & very pale (sort of a yellowy-gray) with high domed bald heads & skeletal hands (with exaggerated digital pads). They looked at me serenely & asked why I had come to them. I asked what they knew of the changes in the lower Tree. They smiled serenely, nodded to one another, & invited me to enter the castle gates. Adrea & I followed our guides into the palace as our human companions brought in our precious cargo.

As we walked, Adrea gave me a candy to calm my nerves & focus me into this reality. The 'candy' was a small emerald which had been bathed in the dew of her crotch. As the 'candy' dissolved in my mouth, the reality of the Crystal Castle also dissolved. I remembered (& began to re-live) my quest for a captain & a good ship to sail me to the crystal island & the Trident castle.

After convincing the captain that I really knew of a way to procure the Gateway of the Cup of Dreams, we set-sail for the abandoned temple guarded by the goat-fish & the grass of the Æons. That other aspect of me was still suspended over the Gateway when we arrived. He dreamed of our coming & thus made our passage easy. When we arrived, none of the ship's company would dare approach the Gateway, even though the grass allowed our passage. They all feared the seductive nature of the Grail & the one-way nature of that Gateway.

I went to the roof alone, & pulled my other self back from his place of dreaming. As always, he awoke without protest & greeted me cheerfully. He addressed me as his uncle & asked if his cousin Sue would be joining us. I laughed at his strange perspective as we climbed down from the roof & approached the Grail. We called to the captain & crew to join us, but they were still afraid. A great red bull who walked like a man came from the fields & stood with us at the Grail. My nephew knew him as BAJ & introduced us to each other.

All began to shift as memories tumbled over one another. I had a difficult time sorting-out who 'I' was. BAJ laughed loudly at our/my consternation & reached into the Grail to remove a fist-sized pearl which had floated to the surface.

He pointed at my younger self & stated "For this working, thou art AIR, starry-eyed gazer upon the Mysteries NU. None doubt your visions, yet most council against their too-hasty application." He pointed at himself & continued "I am the Child of Earth, the God of all pleasures physical. For this role have I studied hard. Let it be hoped that the time is now as propitious as our young friend believes!"

Pointing at me, he sighed "For better or worse, thou art the Fire Carrier of divine inspiration. Thou art lazy, obstinate & unreasonably impractical. Thou art able to see thru the visions & fables of your younger self," [pointing to AIR] "but (for the most part), choose not to—for the sake of Art! In thy hands is the power to bargain for the fate of an Æon. Your dis-connectedness to the consequences of your actions keeps you honest, though I do wish the task at hand permitted us to unify our consciousness more fully."

"And this", he stated with much ceremony, as he held up the dewy pearl, "is our externalized Emotional self—the unbalanced symbol for our quest of internalized stability, and (for us) the key to an end of the cycles of Æons."

The pearl began to grow & to glow. It left the hand of Earth & took her place at the Western Gate of Heaven. The pearl dissolved in waves of heavenly music & fragrances. Adrea (or Sue {depending on one's perspective}) became manifest among us. Together we joined hands around the cauldron & began the spiral dance inward & outward to absorb the grail & its contents within the fabric of our being. The viewpoint of this tale shifted again & again. We became the gems on the rim of the Chalice of Ecstasy. As BAJ, I channeled energies thru Jupiter at the Throne of Daäth. As Adria, I oversaw the mysteries of the Trident of SET from the Throne of Binah. As my younger self, the dreamer, I wielded the energies of Uranus, the Magus from the Throne of Chokmah. As my older self, I channeled the fire of the Gods (Starlight focused thru Sothis onto Pluto/Yuggoth) from the Throne at Kether. Yet, all 4 Thrones were equal. None was 'above' or 'more-advanced-than' the others. These 4 thrones formulate the rim of the Chalice of Ecstasy. From below Tiphareth, the upper Tree appears hierarchical, but such is the illusion caused by the gravitational distortions of Sol & our own mammalian heritage.

I know not where to take this vision. All is illusion & the more 'sense' I try to make of my images, the more I am biasing my writing with self-generated drivel. Semantics & theories & orderly progression of thoughts seem lost in a sea of nonsense. I project characters outside of myself in an effort to gain perspective, yet by being in more than one place at once, I lose all perspective altogether. I must center.

I draw my consciousness to a point & draw it into the Chalice. I am a pearl of brass resting at the bottom of the Chalice of Ecstasy. The head of my penis protrudes into the bowl of the cup from 'below'. I am at the center of gravity of this Tree/Chalice, hovering above Tiphareth & below the Supernals. Venus & Mercury spin their DNA telegraph/time-travel around me. I am enmeshed at a locus in time, yet not bound by it. Kinetic energy = Potential energy, & I am at the fulcrum of the Universe. The feather of Maat spins on the pan of balance. My breath will upset the balance. It is not my will to hold back by breath forever. I have hidden the Logos from my conscious self so I am beyond the temptation to utter it. I am disgruntled that I do not trust myself completely. I am tempted to just go back to sleep & forget the whole thing. Then I remember death, pain & the regret which comes from dreams which are not permitted to come to fruition. Too often has the race of planet-borne been afraid to dream. Such fears are all based upon the practical realities of the test which we have set-up for ourselves.

Today is a day of self-induced befuddlement. I have broken-off the writing of this entry many times in an effort to center thru meditation. Yet, the Work-at-Hand seems to require a splintering of consciousness which does not lend itself to accurate reporting. My diary entry cannot help but be a projection of my lower ego so long as my higher self is fragmented. But by running my c.p.u. (central processing unit) in parallel, I gain access to the gestalt which can affect change as well as simply observe it. I run into Heisenberg's quandary. Close observation leads to influencing the observed phenomena. To be more to the point, how can I mutate a framework if I am internal to that framework. If the experimenter is not impartial, how can he keep his tinkerings impartial. Of course, he cannot. I do seek to tinker, yet I also seek to enjoy the fruits of my tinkerings. Unlike Moses, I seek to enter the Promised Land as well as guide others to its gates. I am the

Gate & the Guardian thereof, yet I am also that who approaches the Gateway & the Path on which he strideth.

I rant & I rave like a madman, yet in my madness there is a kind of frenetic calm. I indulge in non-linear sensory overload in hopes of finding a foot-hold in a maelstrom. I need to break from this attempt to communicate in this record. The task of dancing round the Supernal rim of the Chalice of Ecstasy is more than I can presently handle. I must shift that task out of linear Space/Time so I do not become so befuddled at my alternating perspectives.

I focus my consciousness as Hadit, wearing the Godform of a brass marble spinning round the rim of the Chalice of Ecstasy. I will it to slow down & drop to the bottom of the cup. An aspect of me comes to rest at center, yet other aspects of me continue to dance round the rim. I shall bury my head in some computer math books & then try to get some sleep. I shall report again when I am more collected.

Love is the law, love under will.

Here begins the entry in Frater OTz PTN–690/PVN's Magickal Record for THURSDAY, the 31th Day of MAY, 1984 e.v.,
JULIAN DAY No. 2,445,851.56 Moon being 00.97 Days old. [1:30am]

Do what thou wilt shall be the whole of the Law.

Strange convolutions yesterday. I am much more centered in the here-&-now today. Perhaps some words of explanation are in order here (although I must admit that I am tempted to simply delete yesterday's entry & invoke the Godform of Harpocrates!).

The initiatory cycle which I am currently working in pertains to a Grade which I am not really able to manifest yet. The formulae which are spin-offs from the Working are communicable to all & are applicable to the here-&-now. But when I attempt to tap into the initiatory process itself, I become lost (un-sane), especially when attempting to be both "in my body" as a witness to the event & "up the planes" where the initiatory cycle is actually occurring. It is very difficult for me to be an "objective" reporter, when the initiation is occurring in an arena where objects (such as myself) do not really exist & even the act of observation itself becomes an impediment to the smooth flow of the Working. Rather than attempt accurate "reporting" on what transpires (or will transpire) during that initiatory cycle, let me simply mention one of its more disturbing (to me anyway) corollaries.

Whether my observations are valid within the context of this Æonic formula, I know not. Suffice to say that if/when the Chalice of Ecstasy is functioning properly. the upper realms of the Tree (Kether, Chokmah, Binah, & Da'ath) cease to behave like separate entities & become much more like self-reinforcing energy fields (perhaps like Nuit's "non-atomic continuity"). Distinctions in Time/Space/Hierarchy become very blurred. The Offices associated with these Spheres are co-valent rather than distinct thrones in a hierarchal structure.

From my limited perspective I experienced each Office as one of the 4 elements of the God-level self, yet the attributions to the elements are not discrete. Any system of attribution is just as valid as any other.

They all work, yet none of them works fully without the others. When the Chalice of Ecstasy is functioning, one cannot assume the Grade of Master without also assuming the other 3 Grades as well. To be both dispersed in "the Abyss" & functioning as an Ipsissimus is difficult for me to imagine (much less put into words) from my "in-body" perspective. Yet, I know that such is but a small part of the apparent contradictions which I must resolve if I am to reify this initiatory cycle into my present nexus of Space/Time/Alternity. In some ways, I wish I felt I had sufficient "balance" to bring psychedelics to this Working. But I do not. There are times (like now) that I am glad that I have had the past-experience of such drugs, but I also know that their application is not universal. I am like a spinning top—I am able to whirl faster & faster only in so far as I am able to maintain balance.

Trident of Set— 3 prongs and Initiation

Thursday, 24 January, 1980ev 2nd Watch

Last night after the last transmission I was very aware that my typing was probably very audible to others & probably disturbed Laura downstairs. I looked around for a place to continue typing, but even in the bathroom I felt I would disturb (I really must get something to dampen the noise of this clunker). I went upstairs & tried to sleep, but I was not tired & there was more channelings trying to come through.

I finally acceded to it even though I knew I would have the dreary job of re-typing it this morning. Herewith the transmission:

The kalas are dual in nature for each kala is an embodiment of a principle or essence; each essence contains within itself the seeds (or potential) of its opposite. The next kala provides the resolution of this conflict, yet results in the seed of a new principle, higher on the spiral scale of perfection for it contains not the contradiction of the previous pair. This cycle is repeated until the last kala or essence is the purest embodiment of essence beyond contradiction. It is Truth with a capital T & contains no dross whatsoever. It is lighter than air & stronger than iron. It is the pure gold of the alchemists, but herein lies a new mystery.

According to the traditions of Tantra, there are 32 kalas, of which the male has 16 (8 pairs) and the female has 16. This is true, but only in part.

The trident of Set is the three-pronged pathway to unity. The sevenfold trunk of Ganesha is likewise a single trunk composed of six trunks (3 pairs).

The Tantras speak (although some know better) as if Ganesha had but one pair of trunks (ida & pingala) whose fusion is pingala. This is but one prong of the trident of Set, called by the name of slug slime or gold of the moon, and pertains to the kalas which emanate from the genitalia.

Both the male & female have two modes of operation, called fertile & sterile depending on whether or not the kala has the potential for procreative life. But these titles can be misleading, for all kalas of the lunar trident are concerned with creation, each in their own fashion.

But enough of this trident prong, for many have written of its nature without error, save omission.

The second prong is the prong of honeyed gold and is solar even as the genital is lunar. The physical organ of this prong is the anal glands of secretion & the receptive, bowl of the caecum. On this prong, each sex contains both the ejaculatory & receptive/fermentative organs. The kalas operate on the same dualistic resolution spiral as the kalas of the first prong of slug-slime gold. But since each sex may work in either mode, every individual may produce any of 2 x 8 or 16 kalas in each of the two modes for a total of 32 kalas. But the two modes must be worked separately. The initiate should not attempt to ascend the spiral of kalas in the first mode & then to work the second mode without careful & full utilization of all the fluids of the first mode first, for thereby cometh putrefaction & contradiction. The two modes are the subtle & the gross which are also called invokation & evokation. In the subtle mode the initiate is receptive to the voices & visions of the higher selves & to what were once thought to be gods. In the gross mode the initiate becomes sensitive to the demons within (that is to say the unresolved traumas of the past, both in 'this life & within the two-fold memory of DNA & soul. Evokation is the only way to deal with the past without losing toward momentum for it drags the essence of the past into the present (devoid of all 'personal' memory) to be resolved or released rather than the indulgence of past transgressions so often found in 'soul searching' methods of your culture.

The third prong of the Trident of Set is the prong of green or coppery gold, so named because it is never content to dwell alone. As copper seeks union with the air to turn it green, so does the third prong seek union with either/both of the other prongs.

The physical organs of the coppery prong are the oral cavity with the tongue as the active member while the lining is both secretory & absorptive. The two modes of this trident are catabolic & anabolic; solvae et coagulae; destruction & creation. It is the dance of decay & resurrection. As with the previous prong, each sex contains the facility to enter either mode, but unlike the previous prong, the modes can be used interchangeably. The dualistic question of whether to produce the elixir or to consume it is ludicrous to the mouth- for s/he is the joy of both creation & dissolution.

In the non-initiate, the three prongs of the trident function but poorly. The prong of the slug slime functions well in both fertile &

sterile modes, but there is guilt associated with non-fertile procreation & little sleepy people fear it greatly. The prong of the honey tends to function only in its grosser aspects for most, but even among those who get glimmers of the subtle, the fruits are quickly spoiled by reversion to the gross without proper cleansing/utilization of the subtle elixir first. The coppery prong is the most developed, for even in the guilt-ridden non-initiate is the tongue led to the secret places whereof it dare not speak openly. This leads to the greatest of mysteries for the three prongs were never meant to be separated. There is but one trident & Ganesha has but one trunk, the risen kundalini, the hollow tube of sushuma whereby the fires of heaven & earth mingle in the joy of the going. The combinations of kalas between two or more people who ring the trident bells are not infinite, but as a symphony can be composed with only eight notes, how much more complex can be the dance of the tridents in which there are 33 notes in each of 3 tridents. It is true that for most in your culture that 33 x 33 is the highest number there is, yet for those who seek the honey, the dance is 33 x 33 x 33. (note by OP: each prong of the trident has 2 modes x 8 pairs of kalas or 32 + the mode where the kalas are not produced at all for a total of 33).

But enough of numbers, it is enough to see that many lifetimes can be expended in the dance of the tridents without exhausting the variations.

The polarities are important & conscious control over the emotions is critical. The workings of the slugslime are well documented & need not concern us here.

To invoke with the second prong & digest with the third is the pathway of renewal through consuming the elixir of the gods. It yields joy & renewed vigor, but no new information. It is the wellspring of life eternal. To use this mode & no other leads to stagnation & control over the universe without change within oneself. It is a pity to waste the secrets in this manner. But its intermittent use is both good & necessary, especially at the beginning stages of initiation when the dross of ill-spent years must be burned away.

To evoke with the second prong & digest with the third prong is the mode known as eating demons. It is the secret taught by Solomon son of David, but he wrote of the two prongs separately to keep the secret from all of those save those who already knew of it.

To evoke with the second prong & to create with the third prong is to create demons & all other orders of infernal entities. It is possible to bestow independent life & free will upon any gross nightmare & to compel to do your bidding as a slave. But beware, for without very powerful control, these beings will seek to destroy their creator.

To invoke with the second prong & create with the third prong is to create in partnership with the gods. It is the fountain of creativity & the wellspring of joy to all who come into contact with you. It is nourishment for the soul, with message for the mind & body. It breaks old patterns & allows the freedom to go. It is the only mode of operation for those who would free themselves & others from the chains of slavery.

But all this is oversimplification. Each mode has many levels & many nuances impossible to describe in words. Focus through the vortex & all will go well. Know your partner & work with him/her closely for if each of you be trying to do something different, the results will get 'interesting' in a hurry. The need for communication increases exponentially with the number of initiates in the operation. Three is both more desirable & more difficult than two.

If an initiate shares kalas with an ordinary mortal, disaster will surely follow unless there is a conscious & expressed intent to initiate. Both the initiate & the seeker must express their will & the initiate must then guide & set the tone of what is to follow. Without this conscious expression, the initiation can easily go awry & evoke demons within the non-initiate & drive him/her to madness (for now he/she is indeed also an initiate who can give substance to her/his darkest nightmare out of unconscious direction). For complete safety, the initiate should always work within the vortex of power & the seeker should seek to form or join an already existing vortex within a reasonable time prior to or following the initiation (such reasonable time is purely subjective & may be as critical as a minute or as lax as an æon, depending on the needs of the new initiate). Without a ring of power, the new initiate cannot focus properly by conscious will alone & the Higher Self will have to work on unconscious levels, which simply begs for problems with the little ego.

All those who traffick in sex are unconscious initiates under the protection of She Who Moves.

Most of them are not happy & have no joy in their lives for their ego does not understand the lack of control over their own lives. But those who become conscious of their initiation have great power for they control the sexual fluids of the nation. It is this potential for adeptship (whether actualized or just latent) which attracts & allures so many would-be-initiates into either becoming or patronizing one of their number.

Within the circle of power bounded by the ring upon your finger are all unconscious initiates. All within the circle should become conscious & aware of their power & their duties to themselves & to others, so manifestation can be smoother & without hurt. There are two of you at the core (for you control the vortex at the present moment in time) & one who sought (unclearly) initiation from both.

The fourth is no less than the third & neither is less than either of the first two. All are initiate & all are in sore need of training & disipline. Likewise there are others who have been initiated (unconsciously) in the past. Should any of these return, it would be exceedingly unwise to proceed without elucidation & instruction. 'Casual sex' is impossible for an initiate. All of you have the power to change the lives of others. To do this without instructing them is foulest trickery. The only exceptions are those (hopefully) rare instances when you would consume another by unleashing his/her own demons for his/her self-destruction (instant karmic payback) and sexual contact with those under the protection of She Who Moves.

Thou art a priest(ess) forever. 'Ordain often,' but with much care.

The Priesthood is a Condition of a Soul on Fire with Love

The Priesthood is a Condition of a Soul on Fire with Love.

Thus begins and ends Nema's essay on The Priesthood.[1] For me, the 3 grades of *Initiate, Adept,* and *Priest* are a continuous un-foldment and remembrance[2] of the flower of my essential being. I am most definitely a Priest. I also seek new initiations into all traditions which interest me. All the while, I continue to work on my adeptship in those traditions in which I am already an initiate, but not yet a Priest.

Sexually, I am a Priest. From my perspective, monogamous relationships are very useful in providing a safe stable environment for couples to nurture one-another and raise children when our magickal tribes are dispersed and we feel that protection is needed to nurture ideals which might otherwise be lost within mainstream culture. But now, as magickal communities are beginning to spring-up and tribal sexuality is beginning to express itself, the need for monogamy is beginning to fade. For many, the time is not yet ripe for abandoning the protective atmosphere of the dyadic relationship. But for some of us, it is now time to begin experimentation on alternative modes of inter-personal relationships.

Personally, I have no need to pair-bond to a particular mate. I am part of an open and ever-expanding magickal family within a community which accepts me as a pagan and as a magickian. Although I have no need to create a nuclear family, this does not mean that I am devoid of meaningful relationships. On the contrary, I have on-going relationships with most everyone I have ever made love with. Some of these relationships remain sexual, while others are (at present)

---

[1] *The Priesthood: Parameters and Responsibilities* by NEMA ia available thru Black Moon Publishing. Keep abreast of the cutting-edge of magickal philosophy, ask for Information on the *Black Moon Archives*.

[2] I use *remembrance* in the Egyptian sense of the word. In the legend of Osiris, the divine king was slain & his body scattered throughout the world. Osiris' lovers, Isis & Nephthys gathered up the pieces of his corpse & sought to re-vivify him. But the phallus could not be found. Osiris was eventually resurrected as King of the Afterlife, but he was unable to return to this plane of existence. This parable reminds me that it is only thru re-membering the sexual aspects of spirituality that we can rise into the land of the living and work our Will amongst the race of mortals.

platonic. I perceive myself as being married to the Fire which exists at the core of every one of my lovers. *Sex, Entheogenic Sacraments,* and *Ritual* are the fun and useful tools by which I access/share/communicate with my lovers.

I am a member of the sterile Priestcraft of *Black Isis* and a Sovereign of the XI° Sanctuary. Biologically, I sire no children. But I am by no means barren. My magickal family grows daily at an exponential rate. My sterility is a matter of personal magickal choice. The world is already full enough and as I am an immortalist, I have no need to grow replacements. My genes are nothing special, whereas my ideas are priceless. I propagate thru memes (idea seeds), not genes. I am a contagious case in the spirit of the worldsoul.

I have noticed that many relationships seem to be based on shoring-up one another's weaknesses. For me, such a relationship would be doomed to failure. Mutual Interdependence within magickal family is based (for me. anyway) upon individual strengths. I do not seek a 'soulmate' to make me whole. I am already whole in-i-of myself, and I share my totality with my lovers in the on-going Celebration of Life. As a Priest, I am married to Fire. To phrase it another way, I am celibate, but by no means chaste. To me as a Sexual Priest, my Magick is an orgasmic celebration of Life wherein I utilize sexual energy as the sacrament with which I learn/teach/share/communicate with the world. To me. sexual fluids are the alchemical medicines by which sexual eases art) propagated and community is bonded together. I con-Celebrate the Mass with all whom I am able to relate on the level of sexual energy.

What does all this have to do with you? For many, the transition from nuclear family to tribal sexuality is one of gradual experimentation. I and my family at *Math at the ChRySTAL HUMM* are specialists in alchemy (both sexual & entheogenic) who live in an on-going magickal community. We have more opportunity to experiment than those who feel they need to hide their magicks in their daily lives. It is our Will to share our experimentations with others of similar Will. We who are married to Fire are an on-going experiment in tribal sexuality. We Pagan Shivites dance the Dance of Life as we commune with other partners who are at-cause in their own personal universes. We encourage you to observe us. interact with us in accord with Will, and experiment on your own to discover/create those sexual dances which are right for you.

Our work is to create/facilitate/encourage pagan gatherings (be they brief evening rituals or week-long festivals) which take place 'between-the-worlds', where past commitments and future aspirations are meaningless. Within our Circles, celibacy, monogamy, heterosexuality, homosexuality, virginity, cronehood, and all other forms of personal sexual conduct are matters of conscious personal choice, rather than habits, obligations, or taboos.

Within such an environment, chanting, drumming, dance, entheogenic sacrament, and all forms of ritual expression are employed to dissolve the rational mind, ego, and creative self into a trans-rational energy soup which mingles/communicates with all the other energy soup in the circle. Out of this primal (yet prescient) soup emerge dramatic archetypes which interact with each other in a spontaneous enactment of the on-going saga of Alternity.

Sexuality is but one facet of this saga, but one which strongly attracts my attention. I see/hear/feel/taste/inter- act with sexual energy directly. Sexual union is but one way in which this dance can be actualized. To me the form of the dance is very important, but within circle I am far more open to experimentation than at any other time. I am a soul on fire with love. As a Priest of Fire, my love ever seeks new expression. The all consuming fire of Love liberates me from my self-imposed limitations. To me, this is the essence of my sexual Priestcraft and the mode by which I seek to evolve within my personal universe.

HGA and Kallas

The concept of a HGA is a very complex idea. While Adria is uniquely 'my' HGA, there is at the same time only *one* HGA for everyone on the planet—i.e., Adria is also Ann's HGA & Maggie's HGA, etc. To say that my HGA is the same as Anne's HGA is absolutely wrong, yet to say that my HGA is different than or separate from Anne's HGA is also wrong.

At this point in time, it is very important to form linkages Day/Night-side. In the past only adepts could form such linkages because of the preparation needed & the safeguards built into the system to protect the novice. First the adept had to master personal kundalini & be able to raise his/her own kundalini force to his/her own throat chakra before the tunnel could be opened. At this point in time there is a great need for the race to form a permanent link with Nightside in order to solve the problems which threaten to destroy us. Personal safety is no longer the priority it once was. It is now possible for non-adepts to make cross personal linkages Yesod/Daath via oral sex (perhaps, more especially, cunnilingus, but that was unclear). The kundalini does not need to rise through the body & 'burn-out' the impurities before practical workings can begin; the kundalini simply leaps down & out of Yesod to Daath of the throat which is only inches away (the sexual fluids of the priestess forming a conductive pathway to guide the leap in the cases where the priestess is unable to focus the energy properly).

The nature of these Yesod/Daath kundalini linkages is as follows. The sexual force is focused by the higher self (with or without the knowledge or consent of the ego-self) to Daath of the partner (I was told that there is a greater success between lesbian couples due to the ease with which the priestess can identify with the partner & the essential identity of the duality). The force penetrates the abyss, opening up the channel (to Nightside) which is usually closed. Large amounts of energy flow Day-Nightside to clear blockages in the channel. If the linkage were to be broken, at this point, the priestess would be sexually depleted & frustrated due to having neither orgasm nor energy to continue. Ideally, the direction of flow reverses precisely at the point of exhaustion of the priestess & (aprox.) the same quantity of energy comes back Night-Day. The purpose of this energy exchange is *not* Day/Night fertilization, but more of a fart or a gargle to clear the tubes & exercise the 'muscles' to allow the channel to stay open for longer & longer periods. It also sets up some sort of 'carrier-wave' which may be used at some future time for energy or information transfer.

Notes on VIII° Sexual Elixirs: Its Properties and Uses

extracted from PVN's Diaries, volume #12
intended for MEZLA, Vol. III, #2

I was upon the astral one night with my friend R., the slightly mad synthetic organic chemist. He & I were discussing the Formula of the VIII°. He kept prodding me for information, then walking away as my talk became either personal or erotic. He was like a moth enticed by a flame which seemed to disturb him. I finally realized he was looking for information on what to do with the elixir. The following information poured forth from me & he did not walk away from me, so I must have elucidated what he had been after.

The mouth is the initial receptacle of the elixir. From here, it may be absorbed directly into the higher chakras sublingually thru the blood vessels beneath the tongue. It may also (with practice) be imbibed upwards into the sinuses by using the tongue to funnel & squirt the elixir back to the throat, then upward over the soft palate. Finally it may be swallowed into the fire of the stomach.

If swallowed, the elixir becomes fuel to run the solar furnace which burns away the dross sends the perfume of the elixir upward to attract the attentions of the Second Order.[1] This action open the central chakras and allow the decent of the Holy Spirit into the outer Order.[2] The cauldron of flames in the OTO sigil is symbolic of this process.

If allowed to dissolve into the membranes of the mouth, the elixir nourishes the upper chakras & opens the throat, allowing communication between the inner & middle Orders.[3] Such is the place of vision. If the gateway to the lower Order has not been opened thru the fiery purification outlined above, nightmare &/or obsession can sometimes result.

Upward swallowing of the elixir nourishes the third eye & allows

---

1 When I speak of various aspects of the Order (i.e., First/Outer, Second/Middle, and Third/Inner), I am referring to the microcosmic analogs of the 3 phases of initiation spoken of in Liber CCXX and elsewhere.
2 Knowledge & Conversation of your Holy Guardian Angel.
3 Experience of trans-Abyssal Consciousness, even if you have not yet attained to the Grade of Master.

the cranial suture to open fully, inviting initiation from the Universe at large. Mania can sometimes result from this practice if the Will is not formulated fully thru clearly forged channels between the inner & second Orders.

For the most part, I combine my elixir with spit & then anoint the absorptive tissues of the anus & perineum, as well as the external analogs to the other chakras (solar plexus, heart, throat, third eye, & crown). Depending on my mood, I may anoint the internal anus, & then transfer a bit of the tri-une elixir (semen, anal elixirs, and spit) back to my mouth. I may also anoint my eyelids &/or my entire middle pillar with the combined elixir. At the same time, I place some of the elixir beneath my tongue, while dividing the rest between by stomach & upper sinuses. By combining all 3 paths in each operation, I am able to open, nourish, &/or maintain all links throughout the microcosmic Order within my body. Through the use of IX° & XI° (particularly in groups), the formula is extended to the macrocosmic Order as well.

Notes on Experiments Regarding the XI° Triune Elixir & Its Intromission Within the Cave of Saturn

by Bill Siebert, Immortalist copyright 1986ev

Open Remarks, & Disclaimers

My interest in Sex Magick dates back to my puberty. When I was in grade school, masturbation was considered 'sinful' and the only way that was able to engage in masturbation without becoming overwhelmed by guilt was to create fantasies involving sex between myself (in the god- form of Jesus) and Saint Mary Magdalene. By high school, I was actively performing VIII° masturbatory rites to create a reality framework within which sex magick could be discussed & performed openly amongst peers. From my perspective, my inital operations were successful.

Back in 1979, I was introduced to the extreme power & fascination of heterosexual anal sex by Soror G-n, one of the most powerful natural Priestesses I have had the joy to work with. Over the next few years, I conducted a series of experiments with Soror 0-M, which formed the basis of the rite delineated below. Over the past 6 years, I have also interviewed as many women as possible who were into anal sex. Initially, only my Priestess-lovers & prostitutes would speak to me openly on this taboo topic. But recently, I have discovered that lots of women enjoy these pleasures and are willing to speak of them openly. This paper is based on my personal workings, augmented by information I have gathered thru interviews, watching live sex performed on stage, and screening hundreds of pornographic movies for those rare films which are both instructive & up-beat.

Crowley, Grant, and others use the terms IX° and XI° in ways which differ considerably from one-another. For the purpose of this paper I define IX° as that form of sex magick involving procreation or procreative mimicry. IX° involves the creation of a Childe, either magickal (astral) or physical. XI° Sex Magick, on the other hand, deals with direct internal use of sexual energy. In XI°, there are no magickal children, except insofar as the sex magickian sees him/her-self as the *Ever-Becoming One* who perpetually & continuously reincarnates within him/her-self as his/her own magickal childe by the formula of Sothis as the *Pheonix of Heliopolis*. In XI°, no sigils are annointed, no elementals (autonomous bud wills) are created, and there is no Creation (i.e., no separation between the creator(s) & that which is created).

If the XI° Formula is done awry (i.e., with the mind-set of procreative mimicry so necessary for IX°Magicks), it becomes a Uranian formula of a parent who eats (re-absorbs) his/her children. Such blending of IX° and XI° Formulae can have unexpected consequences (particularly if the childe fights re-absorption), so it is to be avoided unless & until the operator fully understands the consequences, dangers, and karmic repercussions of such mixed-mode workings.

The system of Sex Magick outlined herein seems to work, at least insofar as I have put it actively into practice. But much more research is needed before any foolproof outlines can be published. To me, the primary law of Alchemy is *To the Alchemist the rules do not apply*.

If you who read, this paper are inclined to put these Rites into practice, I urge you to do so as an act of *Love under Will*. Be guided by your own inspiration, and please disregard any of my advice which seems absurd to you or which goes against your own personal experience.

Preliminary Considerations

I consider the the Rite herein to be an XI° Formula. It is heterosexual in nature. For reasons outlined above, this rite may be considered dangerous for those alchemists who have not yet resolved their procreative desires. For example, if the priest desires to father a child (upon the priestess, or some other woman) his sperm will become too active (forceful) in their attempts to locate/impregnate a suitable ovum. Impregnation of the rectal lining will probably result. Such a result is not attuned to the focus of this particular Rite, although it certainly has a useful purpose for other types of alchemy.

From my perspective, the Priest & Priestess for this rite should work together sexually for at least one full lunar cycle prior to working a Rite such as this, learning to trust one another implicitly, and studying the keys to each other's pleasure. Fear, doubt, and holding back have no place in this Rite. Use of appropriate chemical entheogens (substances which induce godlike behavior) such as Yohimbe, MDMA, 2-CB, Hashish, etc. to facilitate opening of sexual & heart chakras, promoting trust of one another, & maximizing erotic pleasure is highly recommended except where proscribed by law or when contrary to individual Will.

Special Considerations for the Priest

Seminal ejaculation is an act of Love under Will. For this operation, the *conscious* Will of the priest needs to be fully aligned with the *seminal* Will of the gonads. If the conscious mind impose its will upon the gonads, frustration & stress will mar focus of the *Work*. If the seminal pleasure center's Will to orgasm overwhelms the conscious mind's Will to retain seed, ejaculation will be premature & the operation will come to naught. When both are aligned, there is no strain to hold-back and no diminution of ecstatic pleasure. [Before it was made illegal, I experimented with MDMA and found it to be a very useful tool in dealing with frustrations concerning premature orgasm and too much orgasmic control leading to impotence.] Those Priests whose orgasmic flow is not at-one with Will are counseled not to attempt this operation.

For this Rite, the Priest needs to be skilled at *drinking the quintessence from the concurbit* (vagina) of the Priestess with his lingam. Although books on Eastern Tantric technique make a big deal of acquiring this *siddhi*, I have found that this skill came to me naturally & without effort. For me, this is a natural process which required no training or conscious thought — although its action can be enhanced thru creative visualization. The Priest should become intimately aware of the taste, consistency, and potency of his seminal elixirs thru conscious use of VIII° technique, during times of Celibacy and when he is sexually active with his chosen Priestess(es). In particular, I council each Priest to practice masturbation on a regular basis, particularly following karezza, to ascertain to what extent the essence of the Priestess has been absorbed within his un-discharged semen. If the Priest can not detect a strong admixture of the essence of the Priestess with his semen, Rites involving this *siddhi* should not be attempted.

Special Considerations For the Priestess

Some women use their menstrual flow as an automatic safety valve for dumping accumulated stress. The menses of such women are indeed powerful, but are of no use for this Rite as their entheogenic sacrament is intermixed with toxic waste from unresolved stress. Menses from such women are best used for anointing sigils or as nourishment for magickal plants. Priestesses who use their menses to dump stress are warned away from this Rite until they have transformed their wastes into *Elixir Rubrae*, the red elixir which is the basis of the *Medicine of Metals*.

Menstrual cramps, bitchy mood swings, and, loss of sexual desire during the first few days of the menstrual flow are all symptoms that a woman is using her menses to dump stress. A Priestess suitable for the Rite at hand is She who is continuously & consciously doing her Will. She is *at-cause* in her Universe. She deals with stress *in the present moment*, and therefore does not need any sort of automatic safety valve to dump stress for her. The menstrual flow of such a Priestess is clean, fragrant, and sweet-tasting. Her mood does not deteriorate at or prior to the onset of her period. Her sexual desire does not diminish during her menses. Ideally, her sexual desire reaches a peak near the onset of her cycle. Such a Priestess is called *Suvasini*, the Sweet-smelling Woman, Her vagina is the *Kuala Concurbit*, the sweet narcotic bloody yoni of Kali.

Concerning the Mechanics of the Operations

The Rite shall be commenced after a one day fast which has been broken ritually with a small meal. [Raw beef with cayenne pepper sauce, raw oysters, creme sherry, & chocolate is one of my favorite breakfasts — choose yours in accord with your bodily constitution, taste buds, and knowledge of Aryuvedic medicine.] Bladders & bowels should be completely empty (enemas may be useful). If all is done aright, there should be no need for solid or liquid waste elimination during or immediately following the Rite — for valuable elixirs may be lost thru premature evacuation of the anatomical Vessels during elimination.

The first phase of this operation is a form of karezza, to be performed at the peak of the lunar flow. The exact form of the sexual stimulation is unimportant, save that the pleasure of both Priest & Priestess shall be maximized and the seed of the Priest shall be retained in accord with Will. Ideally, the Priestess should strive to achieve orgasm several times during this Rite, so long as her orgasms do not interfere with her ability/desire to continue at a frantic pace. Anal intercourse should be avoided at this phase of the working, unless the Priestess knows herself to be immune from colon-induced yeast infection.

When both the Priest & Priestess are at the point of exhaustion, they shall sleep, with the Priestess on top of the Priest & the lingam of the Priest within the Yoni of the Priestess. [Crowley termed this practice *Sleeping in Carthage*]. Prior to sleep, the Priest &/or the Priestess may envision the lingam as soaking or drinking up the mixed menses & vaginal stimulations. If the Priest &/or Priestess be so inclined, the Rite can be enhanced by the Priest &/or Priestess can be kept in a state of eroto-comatose lucidity throughout the night by interested lover(s) who are not actively participating in this phase of the Rite.

If the lingam shall become limp & fall from the yoni during sleep, the Priest &/or Priestess shall stimulate the lingam back to semi-hardness so that it may then be re-inserted into the yoni as soon as possible.

Upon awakening, the Priest & Priestess shall compare dreams. If one or both do not have a clear remembrance of dreams, I encourage them to engage in more karezza, and sleep once again in Carthage at the point of their exhaustion. This shall they continue to do, over-&-over again, until both partners have clear dream memories.

During renewed sexual play, the dream images of Priest & Priestess shall be woven together within the Rite at hand, using whatever symbols seem appropriate to both Priest & Priestess. I have found that spontaneous creative visualization is a prime key to all magicks.

The Priest & Priestess are now ready for the final phase of the Operation. This is a Rite of anal intercourse to implant the mixed secretions within the *Cave of Saturn* of the Priestess. The elixir to be implanted is triune in nature. Its nature is an alchemical composite of semen, orgasmic female vaginal secretions, and the distilled essence of menses. All have been absorbed into the lingam & blended during sleep. For full efficacy, it is best if the act of implantation is orgasmic for both the Priest & the Priestess. [In my system, a Priestess who is orgasmic both vaginally & rectally is termed a *Double-Wanded One*.] If the Priestess is not *double-wanded* another lover may be introduced to the circle to perform cunnilingus upon the Priestess during implantation.

Purpose & Theory Behind the Operation

The menstrual aspect of the lunar flow is that of sterility. The presence of hormones within the menstrual blood induce sperm to quiescence. The penis is used to absorb female orgasmic vaginal secretions, along with aspects of the menstrual flow. The absorbtion seems to be osmotic (thru the head of the penis) rather than via a siphon effect up the urethra, so chemicals in solution (hormones, etc.) are absorbed, while particulate matter (red blood cells, sperm, slough-ed-off tissue, etc.) are left within the vaginal concurbit for the *Gnostic Kiss* (oral sharing of elixirs removed from the vagina thru cunnilingus), which will probably end the Rite.

This rite is not an act of impregnation. Seminal fluid (rather than sperm) and other chemicals in solution are the active agents. It is a Rite of active role reversal in which the Priestess is first the donor/generator (male) and then the recipient (female) of the elixir. The Priest, conversely, is first female, then male.

My experience of this Rite has always used the same Priestess for both creation/charging of the triune elixir & for the final implantation. But such need not be the case. In fact, it would be useful to experiment with implanting the elixir into both men & women to see what differences (if any) are manifest between male & female Priestesses.

In my experience of this Rite, implantation of this triune elixir into the bowels of a female Priestess has caused a marked increase in her creative vigor. As with cocaine, this vigor can be used destructively, or simply piddled-away. But when focused in accord with Will, the creative juices seem to feed upon themselves to create an atmosphere wherein vigor (both sexual & physical) increases dramatically. [In one instance, a priestess weighing less than 100 lbs picked me up (I weighed 235 lbs at that time) and held me aloft for several minutes.]

The triune elixir seems to be a medicine which promotes positive (i,e., active) mutations in the ability of the Priestess to do/enjoy creative Work. The results of a single infusion of the elixir have not (in my limited experience) induced any permanent changes, but further research is needed to determine what limits the permanence of the changes. My experience in many areas of magick has led me to believe that limitations are (for the most part) self-imposed by the mind-set of the magickian, rather than an inherent limitation in the magick itself.

I feel that this triune elixir may prove to be of positive value when implanted into a woman who is not able to priestess the initial phases of the Rite due to her inability to create stress-free menses. But such research needs to be undertaken with care, as the increased vigor might well precipitate a crisis situation in someone who does not fully accept/understand that she is at-cause for her entire Universe, including all of her stress & dis-ease. I also feel that this elixir may be of value when implanted into a woman at the ovulation phase of her cycle, particularly when it is used as an adjunct to a *IX° Moon Childe Rite*.

The triune elixir is also of great value when administered orally, particularly to reduce the symptoms of stress while other (more permanent) avenues of stress elimination are being explored. Further considerations pertaining to this topic belong in a separate paper.

Network Visions

Day #638

Since I came back from Cincy, Anne has been having sexual contact with me (at her instigation) about once every day & a half. This morning the most amazing thing, happened. For a long time I have talked on & off about the 'patterns' which I often times see after orgasm. At times they are stationary like a fine iridescent mycelial network & At times they move like quasi-intelligent Brownian motion. Today I had my forehead pressed to Anne's pubis at the point of her orgasm & I saw the patterns! Could it be that the patterns are the visible manifestation of orgone energy & that I can see this energy the way others can see auras???

Day #642

I have tested the orgone theory & talked it over with Anne. Here is a tentative hypothesis. The 'pattern' is present before orgasm, but it is very difficult to detect (like trying to spot a squirrel sitting motionless on a tree when you've never seen either a squirrel or a tree before). Yet the pattern is not stationary, but rather like it is in a different dimension which is hard to see if you don't know where to look. At the point of orgasm, the pattern breaks up or flows with a will & direction of its own (or perhaps I should say because of the direction imparted to it by the magickian during the sexual operation??) at which point it becomes visible (& by hindsight it is possible to 'remember' where the pattern had been before it moved). The direction of flow may best be illustrated by an example: This morning Anne had a two-stage orgasm via my mouth. The first was the type she used to have quite often in which at the point of orgasm she would go rigid & the odor of orgasm would disappear instantly & she would not experience the pleasure of the orgasm in the physical body. After a brief rest I continued & she had a second orgasm which I call normal for want of a better term (lasting orgasmic odor, release of sexual tension, pleasure to the physical body, etc.) which has been the predominate type for Anne for quite some time now. During both orgasms I saw patterns. My nose was stationary between the labia & my third eye pressed tightly to the mons veneris with my eyes tightly shut. During the first orgasm the pattern was a falling inward of many points & streaks of light. Kind of like there was a galactic size black hole in the region of Anne's vagina & the whole universe was being sucked into it. The second orgasm was nearly the exact opposite with an explosion outward from nearly the same spot—like being at the center of creation during the big bang (or at a white hole opposite the black hole of the first orgasm).

There is certainly not enough data for any value judgements or predictions, but it would seem that if a correlation between pattern & result could be made & if I could see the pattern before orgasm, it might be possible to directly manipulate the pattern (rather than manipulating symbols such as talisman images as I do now) to gain better control of the resultant force of orgasm.

Comment AL 2

*Comment by OTz PTN–690
upon the second Chapter of Liber AL vel Legis
made this noon, day of Hadit, ev. 1978.*

1. Nu hides Hadit by virtue of Nu being orgasm which hides or masks the more subtle goings-on of kundalini.
2. Had is the point from which the kundalini rises.
5. Right hand path of sex magick is black & to be cast away (i.e., sex without orgasm).
6. Death = orgasmic death = momentary death of the false ego during which the Observer is the only thing left.
7. Axle of the wheel = alpha helix of DNA Cube in the circle used to be a symbol for LSD. I that go=evolution.
8. Yet the DNA s is not the Child (ie Heru-pa-kraath).
9. That which remains is the aftermath of the orgasm, ie that which was accomplished either consciously or unconsciously.
14. Light devour men & eat them up with blindness = too much light on a mystery can hide just as well as utter darkness. This refers to the change in the sexual mores of the masses from puritanical silence to sexual satiety & lots of open discussion. Yet the real secrets remain hidden.
15. Nine by the fools; ie the Pure Fool sees Hadit as the Hermit, while Maatians see the one in eight i.e., 7 (not 9 as Crowley stated) which is the Chariot, i.e., the go-er with the graal. Empress & King are not of me, i.e., nuclear family defunct.
16. Empress & Hierophant is the mystical marriage, or IX° & has nothing to do with an ongoing relationship (but does not preclude it).
17-20. Speak of the dis-ease of those who have weak orgasms & know not the rise of the kundalini.
21. Don't worry about the orgasmic difficulties of others; Spend energy only on rising your own kundalini.
    Thou shalt not die refers to the supreme moment when orgasmic death is circumvented by the awakening of that which the false ego has kept forcibly asleep, so that ego-death seems not to have happened for when the false ego dies, the Observer awakes. The

body may die, but what a way to go!
22. Drugs such as lsd and yohimbe may assist one who is already on the right path to attain faster than without them. Such short-cuts are in no ways forbidden.
23. Samadhi of samadhi
24. Beasts of women with large arms are the muscular assistants who have the strength & stamina to keep the aspirant going long enough without allowing him to orgasm. Flaming hair is the brilliant aura one finds surrounding these 'kundalinic assistants' from the built up static charge of unrequited orgasm. Personal experience has shown me that hand-job artists often get fully erect nipples as the pre-orgasmic waves flow outward from my Hadit point.
People with the attainment of Hermits often attract a following (army) because of sexual magnetism. The unsavory ones like Charly Manson are documented more often than true adepts.
25. These techniques are not for the masses who average less than 10 minutes from foreplay to orgasm & then to sleep. Spending long hours in sexual rapture is against the American ideal of instant gratification.
26. If orgasm can be held-off, then Nuit in the brain box is achieved via rising kundalini. Rapture of the earth is the 'consolation' prize of a good orgasm.
27-33. Quite clearly a diatribe against continually asking of useless questions in an effort to avoid doing magickal work.
34-43. Similar in intent to a booklet I have which delineates all the various holidays of the year in order to give the reader as many opportunities to celebrate as possible.
44-45. Contrasts those who work at ecstasy and those who want an orgasm in 30 seconds.
46. Are you sorry that you came too soon? Are you afraid that it will happen again?
47. Don't worry about it! If I am with you, these failings will pass away.
48. Don't worry about other people's orgasmic problems. It isn't good for you or for them either.
49. The orgasmically inferior will pass away for I will conquer them eventually (i.e., I will awaken the king within them). amen=dead flesh. Add Spirit and the orgasmic king is manifest.

50-51. The colors have specific meanings which I am not yet ready to comment upon. Perhaps when my Observer wakes I will know more.
52. Lying specter of virgin=purity=sex is bad.
57-58. Change is impossible does not mean that there is an inherent slave class. It means we are all already kings if we but awaken the fifth part spoken of in 49.
59-60. Although all be king, those who do not yet realize it can stupidly do you harm. Do not hesitate a moment to crush these idiots who refuse to do their True Will.
61-69. Poetic language for the dissolution of the infinitely prolonged orgasm. See diary entry for day [not entered].
70. Such attainment doesn't come easily. Keep working at it.

A True Account of the Eden Captivity

by One who was present

Once upon a time there was a culture called Atlantis.

It was a marvel to the world for it was the first civilization built by the race of humans. Over most of the globe, humans were still on the brink of sentience & still lived in the wild. The Atlanteans left these wild humans alone so that they could develop independently of Atlantis & not be made to feel inferior. The Atlantean culture is very difficult to describe to one who does not remember it. The humans were still very much tied to their animal roots & had full access to their cellular memories (instinct) but were also sentient & were free to add to what had been passed down to them. There were no rulers or priests in Atlantis, yet all were royalty & gods. They were fiercely independent & none would dare deny the will of any other, yet all worked in harmony for the common good.

Then one day the elder gods came to colonize & exploit the earth. They demanded homage & sacrifice from the Atlanteans. The Atlanteans laughed at the joke. The elder gods began to round up the wild humans & put them in cages for later use as food & the Atlanteans saw that the elder gods were not jokers, but madmen.

The Atlanteans fought hard to drive away the elder gods, but the elder gods were an old race & had much knowledge & skill in the art of subjugating alien races. Atlantis was completely destroyed & all the people were killed, save one. She was the youngest daughter of the Atlantean tribe which specialized in improving the race. Her title was 'Queen of the World' for it had been her destiny to mother a selfimproving race of genetic engineers. All Atlantis died protecting her. When the elder gods took possession of the decimated culture they found her in a Time capsule, protected from all but the elder gods themselves. At first she was to have been put to death, but there were those among the elder gods who felt that she would make good breeding stock for a race of slaves. So they broke the capsule, awakened her

& re-named her 'Eve', which meant 'last of a weak race'.

They then showed her the devastation of her culture told her that the wild humans were being hunted for food, and taunted her into the insanity called despair. When she was totally insane they took her high above the earth & showed her what they were doing in detail. First they burned away the cloud cover over the great swamp (the sun rarely shined directly on the earth in those days). They then drained the swamp, separating the mud into water and dry land. They gathered various plants from all over the earth & planted a huge garden. They used their technology to light the whole place at night without interfering with the growth cycles of the plants. Then they brought in the fish & birds & animals from outside. The whole job was accomplished in under a week. All this was witnessed by Eve who was far too insane to be impressed by their skills.

They then began to work on Eve. They used her insanity as an 'in' to delve within her. The wiped her memory clean. Not only her memory, but her ancestral memory as well. For the first time in her life, Eve was truly alone.

The elder gods then re-educated her with lies.

They told how the whole earth had been created by them & they gave her back bits & snatches of her memory of the week in which they built Eden from a swamp so that she would know how great they were. They made her into a semi-mindless servant. Her body & mind were at their command, for her spirit was cut-off from her consciousness. In a way, Eve was happy. She worshipped the elder gods & did their every bidding. She worked in their gardens for them & brought them food which she had nurtured from the earth. But she did not produce a race of slaves for them. She remained alone. The elder gods were angered by her infertility. Since her mind had been wiped clean, Eve could not explain it, yet she somehow knew that being alone was its cause. Then the elder gods looked closely within Eve's body (even as they had looked into her mind years before) & found that she was deficient. They then examined the wild humans more closely & discovered (to their amazement) that humans were of two separate sexes, rather than self-sufficiently twin-sexed like most of the sentients in the Universe. Their anger (directed at Eve) was intense. She was the last of the intelligent race of humans & she had 'tricked' them (or so they believed).

In their anger, they used their technology to build a clone from one of Eve's cells, using the missing Y chromosome from one of the wild humans to make Man.

They called him Adam A-DM, from blood). They still blamed Eve for trying to dupe them out of a servant race, so they wiped her mind clean again & re-told to Adam & Eve the story of creation in which Adam was created first & Eve was created as an afterthought to be his servant, even as humans were servants to God.

Adam & Eve were well programmed. All went as planned. Eden filled with the servile human offspring of Adam & Eve. Abel, the first-born male child was given a good education by the elder gods. He was trained in the skills necessary to serve them better. When his training was completed, Abel became the first human High Priest & the first puppet leader. The elder gods demanded 'offerings' of the best portions of each human's work & Abel saw to it that the elder gods got what they wanted. But Abel (like a lot of petty bureaucrats since that time) used his authority to serve his own best interests as well as those of the elder gods. Abel was a breeder of fine sheep & cattle. With the assistance of genetics which he had learned from the elder gods, his sheep & cattle soon became the best in all the land. The elder gods would accept nothing but the best from the humans, so it was not long before all the humans were in a position where they had to trade/buy sacrificial animals from Abel, since their own animals & vegetables did not meet the high standards of the elder gods. That is, all the humans but Chain. Chain was Abel's younger brother who had learned the science of genetics from Abel before Abel had grown-up to be the all-important high priest of Eden. Chain was a vegetable farmer & his fruits, nuts, and mushrooms were far superior to his neighbors' crops. But Chain would teach others his craft & give away his seeds freely. Abel's position of power was being undermined & his business of selling animals for sacrifice was in jeopardy. The elder gods saw that Abel (who was their chosen representative) was being threatened, so they changed the rules of the game. Only animals would be accepted as sacrifice from that day onward. The first time Chain heard of this was when his sacrifice was refused at the public offering. He was hurt deeply by having his life's work rejected by the elder gods (whom he worshiped as fully as everyone else), but he knew it was 'wrong' to allow the handiwork of Abel to appease the elder gods, if his own handiwork was indeed worthless. His depression was not assuaged in the least by Abel's tauntings & his high & mighty attitude rubbing the pain deeper, into Chain's almost unbearable hurt. Chain left the temple in a state of numbed shock.

He sought to find his mother, whom he had not seen for years. He never could get an honest answer from that smug Abel, but he had pieced together that both of his parents had been killed or banished from Eden as soon as Abel had finished his studies & become the high priest. Eden was separated from the rest of the world by a field of fiery force (the same field which separated the mountain of the Elohim from the rest of Eden), but Chain sought for a gateway through the field (such as the gateway at the back of the temple through which the Elohim received the sacrifices from the people). His struggle was long & boring, and has little place in this narrative. Let us just say that over the years he began to place less & less faith in the older gods or in the priesthood of his brother.

One by one he began to break the 'laws' of God, at first out of necessity, and then just to see what would happen (nothing ever did), There was only one law he did not break. He did not eat meat. In Eden all humans were living on a very regulated diet of fruits, raw vegetables & nuts. It was a perfectly balanced diet which caused them to live long & prosper. Yet Abel, who was acting at the instructions of the Elohim, spent all of his time breeding animals. Not strong wiry draft animals, but only for sacrifice (& for more breeding). After many more years in the wild, constantly looking for a break in the fence of fire, Chain went mad. He reasoned that he had always been alone & always would be. He reasoned that his 'past memories' were but insanity & the Elohim (who seemed not to hear his prayers of supplications) were but a dream (perhaps another strange after effect of that moldy rye he ate last week). He rationalized (as most madmen do) that the only way to rid himself of these 'memories' would be to break the only prohibition of these elder gods which he still feared. He had to eat flesh of an animal. But the thought turned him to jelly. He was afraid & the thought of eating the flesh & blood nauseated him. But being mad, he had all the time in the world to brood over his dilemma. He finally vowed to fast until he either ate meat or starved to death.

It was over a week before his hunger drove him past the edge of madness into that still calm region where one becomes ONE with the universe. He became the animal before him & the animal became him. Since Chain & the animal were one anyway, why not unite them? He ate the animal in peace, but the vital force of the blood soon shattered that peace forever. The blockages of the elder gods dissolved & Chain became the sum total of all the humans (male & female) who had gone before him. The wall of fire became a non-existent barrier of pretty light & Chain strode forth to find his parents. He was again one with his ecology, so he suffered no hardships & he found his mother easily. His father has died years ago because he could not adapt to the 'wild' earth & because he pined away for the lost Eden. Eve, however, had prospered well under the tutelage of some beings from the star system which would someday be known as Sothis. These beings were removing Eve's crippling blocks one by one in order to restore her heritage to her. They worked slowly so as to minimize risks & their task was far from complete when Chain arrived. Chain took them completely unawares & nearly destroyed their encampment (for he took them to be elder gods) before he was restrained. After all misunderstandings were ironed out & the Sirians were told of conditions within Eden, they promised to give aid and protection to all humans who left Eden of their own free will.

Chain returned to Eden. He had been gone a long time & his farms were in ruin, yet such was the monotony of Eden that nobody seemed to even notice that he had been away. He approached his brother (who seemed even richer & more conniving than before) and asked if flesh was still the only acceptable sacrifice to the Elohim. Abel feigned surprise & pretended that animals had *always* been the only acceptable sacrifice & that the *only* time anyone had ever offered cabbages was that time (was it last week?) that you had made a fool of yourself. Chain then realized that in Eden, the elder gods were constantly rewriting the past to remove any possible threats.

Chain went back to his farm & spent many years in very subtle agitations against Abel & the elder gods—nothing definite enough to be called heresy, but just enough to get some of the people thinking. It was time for the yearly group sacrifice. Everyone (but Chain) bought fatted calves from Abel & all headed to the temple. One by one the calves were slaughtered & the dressed carcasses were passed through the gateway in the wall of fire to the elder gods who eagerly received them. All gave sacrifice but Chain. Chain approached the wall of fire with empty-handed (except for his sacrificial knife). His brother Abel was very upset & ran up to him demanding to know what was going on. Chain then raised his knife & slew Abel, passing the slaughtered body to the elder gods. The people were shocked into silence & the elder gods were in an uproar. They demanded that Chain explain his behavior. Chain explained that the elder gods had demanded the best animals in sacrifice & that since the elder gods had seen fit to make Abel their high priest, he was obviously the best, so…

While the elder gods pondered how to deal with this problem (Chain had broken no law, yet he was in obvious open defiance to the elder gods & must be stopped) Chain agitated openly & led a good portion of the humans through the wilderness, where they were nearly starved to death, fed flesh, and re-united with their memories and given the key to escape Eden. When the elder gods found out about the escape they sought to destroy Chain & the others, but (thanks to the intervention of the Sirians) they could not be found. The elder gods then left the earth (perhaps they were driven out by the Sirians, of this I know nothing). Those who had remained loyal to the elder gods (mostly the minor priests & friends of Abel) were left stranded & felt themselves betrayed by Chain & his mother, Eve. So they created the myth of Eden you have no doubt read elsewhere. These genetic cripples then built themselves a nation, believing themselves to the the chosen people of the Elohim. In time they learned to eat meat as well as to sacrifice it, but the internal conditions (extreme hunger & madness) were not right to unlock the gateway to the past heritage. While Chain & those who followed him scattered, the followers of Abel stayed together. Chain's people intermingled with all of the 'wild' humans and strove to keep the genetic memory alive throughout the æons in case the Elohim should try to return, while the followers of Abel manifested the æon of Osiris 4000 years too soon.

The Judeo-Christian heritage is that of Abel, yet over the centuries, individuals within that heritage have re-discovered their past (through many diverse means) while Chain's people (the pagans) have mixed genes & shared knowledge with them as well.

I know this well for once I was called Chain, but now I live within the genetic memory of each & every human on this planet. I speak now as I spoke 6000 years ago. Throw off the yoke of the priestcraft. Each & every one of you is as much a God as the Elohim. You are just as much the fruit of my loins as was Jesus of Bethlehem or Mohammad or Buddha. Arise & awaken within you the roots of your past so that you can better meet the future as an equal!

A True Account of the Eden Captivity

The above 'story' came to me as the kernel of an idea in dream, was amplified in re-telling it to Soror 0-33/33 and came in 'full force' as a channeling during this writing of it. Chain is not very 'book-learned', so I had to revise & even out the flow as it came.

This version is much condensed. Awakening old memories is like drilling a small hole in a dam to get a drink of water. I was flooded with a torrent of images & had I not edited the tale without mercy, I would have had a narrative in the first person which would have taken years to tell. I sacrificed veracity on the altar of expediency. I do hope my little vignette on Eden does not upset too many people of Jewish background.

It is not intended to be anti-semitic, even though it certainly is anti-Zionist (& many people have a hard time separating the two). The chronicle was delivered to me in language which I could understand. It may not have happened at all on the physical plane, but I am certain that it did happen (on some plane) much the way I have told it.

OTz PTN–690
14 October, 1979ev

L 15 October, 1979ev, 8 Tybi, 4748
Yesterday my father Chain spoke of the captivity in Eden, but the last portion of his tale was hurried, and his personal involvement was slight.

I, Gomrah, was born during the blood feast which enabled my father to lead us out of Eden. My first meal was not the milk from my mother's breast but the blood which my father poured down my throat.

By the time we reached the encampment of the Sirians, where they cared for my grandmother (who was then still called Eve), I was near puberty. Unlike my father I preferred the company of humans & liked abstract thought. I was enamored of numbers & of engineering (while he preferred the company of plants & took joy in his plant breeding experiments). We were with the Sirians for many years & I learned much of the sciences of abstract numerical philosophy (later called gematria, after my name, since I extolled its virtues long & loud amongst my people) & and of architecture which enabled me to assist in the building of the cities of Sodom & Gomoraha (but I am getting ahead of my story).

The leader of the Sirians was called by a name which rhymed with excrement (our languages being very different, one from the other, that such was happenstance & not an indication of kinship), but (in much later times) the descendents of Abel would mock us & say that we gave reverence to the memory of shit. Rather than enlighten them, we simply made shit the outward symbol of our fraternity with the Sirians, so that the constant re-veiling of the mysteries would reveal to the worthy.

Late in my youth a number of important events occurred which need to be retold now so they will never be forgotten. My father, Chain, did not mention them because he had already left our encampment to live among the wild plants before these events transpired.

My grandmother (who was still called by the name of Eve) had been under the constant care & treatment of the Sirians for several hundred years, & still she was not healed. The Sirians called a large meeting of all those who left Eden (along with all of those born since) & told us that Eve been so abused by the elder gods that it was not within their powers to restore her to what she once was. Immediately there was an outcry from all of the people. We could not allow this to be true, for Eve was our symbol of hope for the future. She was the genetic summation of the work of the Atlanteans, our forefathers who we never knew. She was our *only* link with the super-race which we had hoped was to be our destiny. We would not, nay, could not allow her to perish as a genetic cripple.

The work of the Atlanteans could be repeated, but we needed Eve restored to what she once was—to act as a living symbol & a pattern for us to follow—before the work could be begun in earnest.

When the Sirians saw how much we realized, they were taken aback, for such consciousness in a race so young (and genetically crippled as well) was surprising. They then conceded that there was a way to restore Eve, but the cost would be high. We all shouted that we would pay the cost, no matter what it was. It took a long time for the Sirians to explain to us exactly what was required of us & longer still for us to become capable of doing what was required. Eve's pain & crippling must be 'shared' among all of us & our children (yea, even unto their children & their children's children down through the dimly perceived corridors of time).

We would have to become mortal (for up until now, humans died only of accident or injury, since we had total cellular memory & could 'repair' the ravages of old age or disease) & our healing energies would have to be diverted (for the most part) to Eve. Pain & suffering would be our lot in life & our loss of cellular memory would cloud our genetic memory so each of us would have to re-learn all of our parents' skills, or they would become 'lost' or 'forgotten' & have to be re-discovered by another at a later time. But this burden of pain would not be forever. Farther into the future than any of us could perceive, the 'crippling' would weaken & old memories would awaken & the dreams of our Atlantean fore parents could once again be realized. In each of us would be a 'time capsule' of cellular memory which would slowly awaken in (first some, then all) of our children's children's children's children. You who hear these words are at the faint beginning of the new dawn. We paid dearly so that our grandmother might be healed. Hear our tale so that you will understand us & be prepared for what is ahead of you.

Time is a very strange phenomenon. Though she who was still called Eve could not be healed until many generations had suffered & died (diverting all their energies to her), yet we did witness the transformation in own lifetimes. The vacant look left her eyes & her skin glowed as though fire fed her veins; she grew in size & transformed before our very eyes into what she had once been. Eve was no longer, for the Queen of the World stood before us & though the sun was yet in the east, her glow lit up the western sky. We were struck dumb with awe & the Sirians were overjoyed.

The leader of the Sirians (who was later to be known as shit) brought the leader of the elder gods to our encampment & confronted him with the deeds he had done against us humans. The elder god was scornful of our wrath until Our Lady was revealed to him. He then became both afraid & defensive. He wanted to know how the Sirians had restored her. When he was told that the Sirians only guided the plan & that the work & the payment had been done by the humans (both present & future) he would not believe it. When finally he became convinced that we were telling the truth, he tried to make friends with us & tried to get us to 'forget' our hard feelings against his people. It was then that the Sirians made a brief speech to sum up the experience thus far & to let the elder gods know exactly how things stand.

To the elder god they said:
Because of this which thou hast done, you are to be banned from this place forever & will never be allowed to interfere with this race again. There is enmity between you & The Woman; between her seed & your seed; She & her people shall not rest until Her heel be placed

at thy throat & the pommel of Her sword shall crush thy head.

To the women they said:
Because of that which has been done to you, you will have to suffer the pain of childbirth & this memory of pain will keep alive your hatred towards the elder gods. But yet you are also given a power & a sign. Once in each moon shall you become infertile & the blood shall flow freely from thy womb. The blood is a symbol of the blood which enabled Chain to escape from Eden & has the power of awakening memories in thy children so that naught will be forgotten. It is also a sign, for only the sons & daughters of Chain will lust for this blood of power, for the sons & daughters of Abel will always remain under the interdict set upon them by the Elohim in the garden of Eden (flesh & blood are forbidden thee for food).

To the men they said:
Because thy father, Adam, was not a true man, but a clone of Eve and a near-man (wild human, yet still animal), you are not yet equal to woman. Through many generations to come you will strive towards being human (even as woman strives toward being divine), yet the task is not impossible to achieve. When men & women become equal, then shall Woman return power & responsibility to you & you both shall strive for the sake of the children. When power & authority is in the hands of the children (thy genetic future) then will the real task begin.

To the children they said:
You who are yet unborn are the key to this mystery. For when the strength of the Race has been replenished & the Queen's dowery paid for, then will your Queen lead you outward beyond the gates of Death/Daath to meet the elder gods on their ground, yet on your own terms.

To the Queen of Earth they said:
Thou, O Queen are far too bright a star for this Earth. Come with us into the night until the time for thy return (or should we say, for thy children to come out to greet thee). Thou shalt manifest among thy people as a symbol & a promise of what is to come. Every woman will reflect a bit of your glory, even as every man shall mirror ours. Many times will the actuality be hidden & humans will worship the

image, yet even in the image is power & strength & even the mirror of a mirror will transmit enough of thy light to inspire the downtrodden. Though the sons & daughters of Abel will renounce you as Eve, yet their distant children will worship you as Mary. For others you will appear as Isis, or Kali (depending on the phase of your moon) & those children of your children who see you most clearly will see you in every woman as Babalon, the Queen of the Western Gate of Heaven & in Every-Woman as Starry Night which thou wilt become.

In those days of the far future when death is no longer & the minds of all humans are melded together (as they once were in Atlantis), then can thou return to lead them outward to us, for the spaces between the stars is filled with adventure for all Bornless Ones.

༺ ▲ ༻

The elder gods were then (somehow) expelled from the earth & the poor Abelites were adrift in a hostile world. We tried to take them in, but they would have nothing to do with us, blaming Eve & Chain for all their misery. As I started to say earlier, we built twin cities with high spires & many cultural centers & were well on the way to unlocking the genetic secrets which would allow the men to be equal to the women & would also prepare the wild humans for culture & civilization. But somehow the Abelites (who now called themselves Israelites) managed to open up a gateway so the destructive powers of the elder gods could be unleashed in the world. Our cities were destroyed by fire & there was a big flood. It was about this time that we decided to separate & try different approaches to the problem. In some cultures, the men interbred with the wild human women in order to bring them across the thresh-hold into sentience, while the human women received only the seed of the most perfect of the males. In other cultures, the women set-out alone & bred with the wild men. The sons the turned back to the wild while the daughters were raised within civilization to carry on the task of their mothers through many generations.

The first method failed because the men came to 'protect' the women from imperfect sperm & then came to possess & to own the women as property. The second method did not fare much better because the women were eventually over-run by their sons' children, who had become entirely human, yet had not the benefits of civilization.

The only cultures which prospered were those in which wild humans were freely adopted into the culture, yet were given no authority until they had interbred with the men & women for sufficient time to become human.

Some of these groups were stationary & built up empires (like Egypt) while others moved around in small groups so as to better spread the seeds (like the Romany). In these cultures, things were going fine until the balance suddenly shifted from Matriarchal rule to Patriarchal rule. We should have realized that the Israelites (being led by the inferior men) could easily overbalance the smooth transition from Matriarchy to co-rulership, but we didn't. In may places the long term plan had been forgotten & women held power for far too long — some sort of role inversion was long overdue. But when the inversion came, the Israelites suddenly were dispersed from their place of isolation & their tainted ideas warped many civilizations.

The original plan was for approximately 2000 years of rule by women followed by 2000 years during which the men would rule, followed by 2000 years of joint rulership & then the legacy was to be passed to the children. As this plan was formulated about 6000 years ago, we should have just finished with 2000 years of joint rulership.

In some cultures (like the North American Indian the plan was going along smoothly until the Christians (perverted offspring of the Israelites, yet still entrapped in the lies of Abel) conquered them. So now, from a very shaky foundation of a misspent æon, the men & women have to regain equality & mutual respect & the stewardship must be transferred to the children, who must be prepared to deal with the sudden growth in cellular memory/ evolutionary potential and the population explosion which will surely come when death becomes but a bitter memory. We are not there yet, but the awakening in me of these memories is surely a harbinger of the dawn to come. Perhaps I will not live to see the closing of the gates of Death, but to this generation is the task of opening the gates of memory & the first concerted explorations beyond the gates of Daath.

The final portion of this essay (from the end of the Sirian's speech) is OTz PTN's conjectures & does not have the authority of either Chain or Gomrah.

Early & Explicit Channelings

21 January, 1980ev, 5th Watch
A channeling has been on the tip of my mind since last night. It began to come through after the channeling support group while the four of us were talking over the evening in Greenwind's room. I was resisting the channeling because I felt it to be simply an ego-reaction to the 'pure white light/peace-love' tone of the earlier portion of the evening.

Again it almost came through this morning during oral sex with 0-Maku, but (as Adria so aptly pointed out to me) 0-Maku would not appreciate it if I stopped what I was doing in order to get a pencil & paper.

I was working on the project again this afternoon & bits & fragments again began to come through. My immediate reaction was to stop the project & sit myself down for the channeling, but the voice of reason (that voice without name or form which seems to keep Adria's wild ideas in check) reminded me that the project was indeed my True Will & is very important to both me & all those ultimately connected with the fruits of our group labor so I should not put off the project. On the other hand I knew that I could not put off this writing, so I have moved the typewriter into the temple & will oscillate between the channeling & the work on the project as need dictates.

Here beginneth the channeling:
I AM the darkness within the light; the dark spice within the pudding of love which makes pablum into the elixir of LIVES. If I am not, then the peace, joy, and love of the upcoming Age becomes the slow decay of somnolent senescence. There are many who are tired of war & of strife, yet they cannot imagine any alternative save a return to the sheltered/restricted/ever-boring fairland of children. For growth & advancement, it is necessary to be discontent with life & all of its allurements. Strife & conflict provide the needed balance to rest so that TRUTH may be gleaned through their siftings & intertwinings.

When Mohesh did wander in the desert alone, he did meet a priestess from Sumer who did show him the spice of lust to break the boredom of his solitude. When I did speak to him from the bush of the priestess he did think that I was his God, but his preconceived notions of God (as well as concepts such as right/wrong) did cause him to edit/ censor our interchange to fit his previous beliefs. The message he gave to the weary Israelites was one of comfort & purpose, but he feared to give them the keys to their own inward journey. In his fear & misunderstanding he sought to bar the door to me & my kind through degradation & false information of my mysteries & of those who do practice them. His approach was violent & fearful, yet, even amongst the Israelites were those who did communicate with me in secret (((hint from Adria: Do an isomorphic transformation of the legend of King Solomon & the vessel of brass with the Tale of King Solomon & the Queen of Sheba i.e., compare & integrate the Goetia with the Song of Songs))), while the other peoples of the region did so openly.

At a later time did another initiate approach Yeheshua (who was likewise discontent, but he was tired of the fear/hate/war which tore his land). I communicated with him often & his countenance became radiant as the sun as my glory infused through him. Yet, he also could not speak of the keys openly. He preached peace & love, hoping that the strong would see his message clearly, but those who did were put to death as heretics.

Remember what is written: "Nor let the fools mistake love; for there are love and love. There is the dove & there is the serpent. Choose ye well!" The dove will lull you to sleep, but the serpent will allow you to awake. I am the kernel of fiery spice which transforms the dove into the dragon of Heaven.

The most elementary of my rites are practiced by many, yet so riddled with guilt that the celebration is rushed & quickly forgotten. There are those cultures which have even forbidden this elementary key to their people, but they quickly die for without sexual congress the race cannot long continue save through kidnapping the young of more vital races (such as the Moonies do). Yet this elementary key is not sufficient for most to gain contact with my kind for there is no framework within which to 'fit' the subtle transformations.

The method taught to Mohesh is far stronger & can open gateways in startling fashion, yet this way is far stronger for some people than for others. There is much cultural prejudice against oral sex because of its power & those who would keep you asleep preach the separation of the sexes & try to keep the secret of bisexuality from your grasp. The least powerful key is the 'ordinary' male elixir, next is the elixir of the male which as absorbed the female elixir into itself. Yet more potent is the unmingled female elixir, followed closely by the male & female elixirs combined within the vaginal furnace. Blood of the moon is potent for forgotten Ones, but if combined with the twin elixirs it becomes the spicey key to unlock the door of LIVES. The mysteries of SET are likewise of varying potencies & all of these are so potent that even the adepts of the frontal gateway fear them. I do come in strength & vision to all those who know of the frontal gateways & meet me often at their portals (subtly at the gateway of the male & with vigor at the gateway of the female ((for is not the female of your culture frightened by over-aggressiveness & is she not more able to pick-up the subtlety of the oft-repeated yet different message which I direct through the gateway of the male)). Yet there is no subtlety in the gateways of Set & the overpowering of glory is beyond the nervous systems of many. The elixir is not the excrement any more than the frontal elixir is the urine. The bowl of the bowels should be flushed & the muscles coaxed into relaxation with the tongue or finger at the gateway. The frontal gateway should be opened fully & the fluids of Set will flow like wine. Herein lies the danger. If the fluids be coaxed into manifestation & then not combined/utilized/transformed via the mouth, they will ferment & produce toxins unimaginable to physiologists. The elixir has as many stages as the frontal elixir: it can be alone, blended with either male or female (or both) elixirs in either the mouth or the bowl of the bowels, or even through adsorption/absorption into the vagina or the penis, but ultimately this elixir must be transformed via the digestive system or it will putrefy. If the adept is unable to extract all of the elixir or if s/he is unwilling/unable to utilize it (i.e., if culture prevents recognition of its sanctity) then it should be flushed out of the bowl of the bowels with warm water infused with herbs appropriate to the ritual and the waters used for bathing. If the bowels were carefully emptied before the ritual, there will be no shitty odor or color to the sacramental waters of Set & some vitality can be absorbed through the skin (though not as much as if the elixir had been consumed). This ritual bathing is especially beneficial for one who has inadvertently been poisoned by the decomposition of the elixir within the bowl of the bowels. The infusorial waters may be stored for a week in a cold place (preferably under a pyramid in the refrigerator) but should be warmed to blood heat prior to bathing. A week of daily bathing will undo a year's accumulation of toxins, while one dose orally (of the pure fresh elixir, not the infusion) will rejuvenate the whole body while also removing the accumulation of toxins. If the elixir is in short supply, bathe only the feet & the hands (especially in arthritis) In most members of your culture the elixir of SET will not flow easily & where it does flow easily, the toxins often accumulate quickly (causing dysfunction & even death at an early age). Ignoring the elixir will not make it go away. Its flow can be lessened by avoiding direct stimulation, but this only slows down the degenerative process. It is only through opening the Gateways (both frontal & anal) that the elixirs can be made pure & beneficial. A caress of a fingertip across the opening can unleash much power, but it must be either utilized or flushed away. The channel of SET leads wherever the will of the priest &/or priestess guides it. Nightside is but one of many many possibilities & is perhaps the most dangerous of the journeys now open to you all. Journey inward on the path of remembrance, both of your biological heritage vie the Forgotten Ones, and your spiritual heritage via your inner voices which have been with you since you decided to become incarnate souls. There are many other voices within all of you, but these 2 are most important for they have your best interest at heart. The other voices (such as mine) are here to guide all of you in general through the gates of powerful spice, yet only whole beings may receive my Kind without warping the message. It is a real temptation to you (Bill) to preach & to get others to follow you, yet you know enough to combat this trend, yet in the struggle you become uncertain of yourself. Let the words which come through you speak for themselves. Others will hear you & use the tools you outline. No matter if you ever meet them directly. Do not fear to pass this on to others for fear of being thought a sex-fiend & a pervert—you are a sex-fiend & a pervert, which is why the message can come through you so purely & without fancy language to obfuscate the Truth.

There are those who will fear that you write these words only out of personal desire to experiment sexually with them. If they feel so hostile towards you, then they are not ready to partake of the mysteries with you. They will go elsewhere & either reject these words or try them on their own. For those who remain attracted (in spite of many misgivings) they need only seek the voices within themselves to realize the simple beauty of the message which comes through you. Many will be attracted yet concern yourself not overmuch with who shall you work with, for it is not for you to get aggressive. You were once warned about your sexual power & what it can do to others. The warning came through garbled but not entirely wrong. Be not aggressive for if any be really attracted, they will act in concert with you of their own WILL without having to be 'seduced' by you or anyone else.

End of transmission

The main message was given by a fiery sounding 'male' entity, while most of the parenthetical phrases were by Adria (or at least through her). The end message was from a 'female' & 'motherly' entity which reminded me of a young Maggie or an old & wise child.

I can now see that I was trying to 'keep it clean' & not upset too many people in the earlier portions of the previous transmission. It was not until the specific sexual formulas began to come through that I realized the impossibility of 'keeping it clean'. I shall now go back & undo some of the censorship my ego imposed upon the earlier transmission.

Mohesh is Moses & the burning bush is the sexually enflamed pudenda of his female initiate partner. It was via oral sex that Moses came into contact with the entity I AM WHO AM (Ehihey). The name of this initiate is unknown to me but I do know that she came from Sumer in direct response to sexual visions telling her of Moses & that he was beginning to wake-up alone in the desert. Her mission was one of Love under will & she did not understand it nor did she like Moses (who was a creep), but she followed the voiced of her Higher Being who spoke with her often.

Yeshua is Jesus of Nazareth who was approached by two separate initiates, John (the beloved or divine) and Mary (Magdalene). Whereas Moses only worked with the female frontal gate, Jesus worked with both the frontal & rear gates of both Mary & John (& they both worked with both of his). The elixirs were combined one, two, or three ways & were consumed solely by Jesus & John (mostly by Jesus). Mary did not consume the elixir of Set because her radiance would have brought her much grief in that culture. Some of the infusorial elixirs were secretly brought to the other John (the baptist) to wash away the accumulated toxins of a very anal retentive race. But it was too little & too late for very much permanent good. Jesus simply would not allow the secret to be taught openly. The closest he got was at the last supper when he scratched his ass (blatantly & under his robe) before breaking the bread of the communion feast. Judas was given the elixir smeared piece of bread & he went totally mad with guilt. So much for initiation without instruction. Had he knew exactly what he was eating & had been prepared for it, Jesus would have probably gotten up the nerve to initiate his close followers & the last 2000 years would have been very different.

Will is the consensus of inner 'selves' with the ego which runs the body. The whys & wherefores of love are clear only to those who listen within rather than to what they are trying very hard to convince themselves is true. Will is rarely easy, but once embarked upon, it flows with a fluidity unlike want or whim. Love is the law, love under will is the *only* way to love.

Monday, 21 January, 1980ev, 6th Watch
Over supper I was dwelling on the previous channeling & wondering at its 'purity' as well as how I can make (allow?) them to flow more purely in the future. Here flows the response to my inquiries:

Those who attempt to channel without a transtemporal vortex attempt the very difficult for they are bound in time as well as space. For such persons a ritual of quietude or consecration to the task at hand is almost a necessity in all but the rarest instances. It also helps to have a consecrated workplace which is used for no other purpose. But there are those (such as yourself) who work outside the limitations of time/space by having centered the universe of space about themselves with a ring of power and are co-temporal with the voices which ring throughout the æons. The consecrated temple space is always at hand via the cones of power generated /focused through the ring(s) (& likewise always was at hand even before the initiate consciously chose to open the vortex).

We are at the end of an age & the beginning of a new one. The 'rules' are in flux and reality is as transient as the masks of the dancers. There are many non/ extra/ trans/ sub/ super-human forces (both embodied and ethereal who seek to have an effect upon the fabric of reality now upon the loom of time/space. But we are but advisors for the consequences of direct interference are too horrible to contemplate much less initiate. We guide, we do not compel or even impel.

The attunement which you have is toward the sexual spices of the reality called the Æon of Horus, while there are others who see not sex as important or even spiritual who seek the pablum of the Age of Aquarius. We believe the Aquarians to be severely wrong in their 'back to Eden' approach to strife. Violence must be channeled, as must all of the other so-called vices. If they are 'made to go away', the race will be castrated/lobotomized and will never take part in the communion of Stars.

You fear to be direct & strong with those who follow different paths than you, yet they are not the least bit hesitant to push raw food/no spice diets on the world. If you would live in a world which still allows you the option of chili peppers, garlic, red meat, refined sugar, un-natural chemical drugs, and full communion for ALL (not just the chosen few) in the electrochemical fusion of the fluids of SEX, then you must not thwart the full & direct explicit language being transmitted through you. Just pretend that no one will ever see the channelings so you will not worry about how they will take them.

Your age is unique in that you will probably not be martyred even if you handed a copy of your channelings to the (so-called) religious leaders within their own citadels of power. Pass out the word, both directly & via messengers. Once the secrets have been shared, they will be safe forever. If the magickal community is too afraid to publish them outright, try Screw or one of the Gay male journals.

Change them around into short stories or give them over to others with the talents of revision. You will receive many secrets which you will never be in a position to utilize in your personal practice, so worry not overmuch about your ego or that others may think you perverse. Much of what you can attune to will be for groups beyond your ability to reach directly. The secrets of SET are a perfect addition for the celebrations of the lesbian separatists, yet their ears are plugged with the penises of their own fears & they will hear you not directly. The peace/love/mother goddess is goodness pablum which they are attuned to will turn them into the lobotomized housewives they fear so rightly (rightly that is, for they do not see their own strengths). If they would open their ears they would recognize that they have the power of the blood & the trident of SET to fructify the pablum of their love. The phallus is not necessary to the formula of generation. There are many paths for the many different kinds of imperfections to reach virile self-assertiveness. Bisexuality & physical androgyneity are the keys to the most advanced formulae, yet there are few who will be ready for that path within the next century. There are homophobes & there are heterophobes (of both sexes & all shades of in-between), yet all have formulae which are keys to open the doors of their perceptive reality & show them greater vistas. In turn, these greater vistas likewise have keys. The process is vast & fully beyond the scope of your lifetime, even if everyone channeled for an hour a day for the rest of their lives. As I said to another at the beginning of the last æon, the harvest is large & the laborers are few. There is some duplication of effort in order to clarify & elucidate, but most will be working from entirely different perspectives. Yours is mainly sexual & mainly outside of the realms of traditional male/female-genital/genital Tantra & your channelings may very well conflict with others at many points. Examine your own 'blind spots' and strong aversions. Likewise examine these in the writings of s/he with whom you differ. Trust the channel which does not have to counter a whole pile of phobias in order to be heard (i.e., do not believe Regardie on the topic of menstrual blood, yet listen to him with regards to angels of Tiphareth) who speak with overmuch authority & those who speak as if theirs is the last word on any particular formula. The XI° is particularly prone to misinterpretation, for it is not a formula but a whole family of formulae. Whenever a 'new' or 'recently uncovered traditional' variant of this working (XI°) are espoused, it is very easy to see the other interpretations as faulty. Yet they all may be valid, each for a particular group of practitioners. (Yet, probably none of the transmissions came through wholly without taint or strain, so each must be free to interpret in the light of personal experience).

The above channeling was directed at me from a source slightly different from the 'voice of reason' which I perceived as a fusion of VoR with Adria, yet it is very difficult to be certain as there was an 'echo' of different 'flavors' as if I were hearing some sort of speech of consensus rather than an individual's thoughts.

It now is far more clear to me that I must not try to filter-out the sexual flavors from my interchanges with the channeling group. If they are not ready to hear, they will either exclude me from the group or leave. In any case, others will be attracted by being explicit rather then general.

Tuesday, 22 January, 1980ev, 3rd Watch
On Sunday night after the channeling group I made some statements on the nature of channeling & why I felt somewhat uncomfortable with Jinny's 'routine'. Some of my statements I attributed to something I got in a letter from Grant, but I felt uncomfortable with those asser-

tions, even as I made them. I now realize that I was trying very hard to recall what the guidelines for channeling were, as well as trying very hard to give 'authority' to my statements. I now feel that I was indeed trying to channel some guidelines, but I was far too blocked-up to do it comfortably.

Channeling 'personal' messages through yourself to others is exactly the dangerous behavior which has given 'mediumship' such a black name among magicians. Everyone has a difficult time channeling pure information because of the limitations of the unawakened state (& let me assure you that no-one is fully awake at this point of time/space). Preconceived notions get in the way, as do limitations of vocabulary & cultural background. Likewise, questions are rarely phrased in total purity. Channelings can therefore be best understood by the person who channels them. But if the information be meant for another, confusion is sure to result. While I am not saying that messages which come through you will *never* be meant for another person (i.e., a particular individual & no other), I am saying that such indirect personal contact is to be avoided whenever possible. The concept of an intermediary between the individual human & his/her higher consciousness/spirit guide (or whatever other preconceived notion limits our contact) is as damaging as it is repugnant. There are times when a particular individual will refuse to listen within & an important direct message need to be transmitted via a trained medium, but such instances are rare indeed.

If one looks upon ????? (word for which I have no vocabulary —BS) as the general mechanism for non-corporal communication, then one can perceive two separate & distinct modes of operation. The first (& I do mean first, for without the first part, the second is meaningless garble) is the two/three/more way communication between/among the incarnate 'person' and his/her guide(s). The purpose of this mode is education & the clearing up of misconceptions. As a *side effect*, the channels are 'blown-clear' & the circuits are fine-tuned so the second mode can commence. If one looks upon the first mode as being similar to the dialog between parent/teacher & newborn child, then the second mode may be looked at a part of a system of general public education. One does not get advice on personal matters from a school teacher during class. Likewise, what you term 'channeling' or 'transmissions' are the 'public' or mass-education forms of this communication mode. In one of the commentaries on Abra-Melin's writings, someone once noted that it is exceedingly unwise to set about the magical task of re-forming the world until one has full & compleat communication with one's angel. At one time this was certainly true, but the time is now ripe for a corps of 'barefoot thaumaturgists' (if I may borrow a phrase from the great Chinese experiment). At one time it could rightly be said that many are called but few are chosen, but now the watchwords are that all are being called (again & again, until they either go mad or finally hear us) & as many will be chosen who accept the task. If a human has a 'glimmer' of their angel, personal education is possible. Once the interchange becomes in the least bit fruitful, general channelings begin at such a rate that the human is comfortable with. But the 'task' of these barefoot thaumaturgists is not one of intermediary between others & their angels, but rather to teach (by word & by example) how others can join the communion of saints. The priestcraft (in its role of intermediary between god and Man) is darkest blasphemy against self, for it promotes indolence, self-doubts & puts semi-trained mediums into a very awkward position with their own ego-entrapments, It is harmful for the seeker, but even more harmful for medium for it limits his/her own growth.

If this mode of operation be so black, then why do the 'spirits' transmit to such mediums?

The answer is simple. The messages are always (i.e., trans-temporal) 'out-there' ready to be picked-up. A good receiver can pick up other people's personal wave length at will. Sometimes this is very helpful (to speak with another's angel) in dealing with a 'slow learner' or a stubborn person who refuses to do their will. Likewise there are times when a composite 'general' message can be gleaned from many 'angels' which answers specific unasked questions of several persons in order to give them 'hope' & confidence. The information is 'always' available. What the particular human does with the information is another matter entirely. Placing oneself between a person & his/her own angel is very dangerous & can have severe karmic repercussions, especially among those groups whose threads are woven together throughout much time.

There are others who have been transmitting/ channeling for enough time that they have gained much confidence in what they do. Some of these will undoubtedly disagree with you with vehemence. Examine what they say & what they manage to channel through themselves in the purity of your open heart. Come to a tentative decision as to where truth lies, then take-on the God-form of Anubis, balance your heart against the feather of Maat, and digest that which is not True. Each must be the final judge for him/her-self alone & for no others. Reality is in transition. What is real & true for you may be artificial & false for another. Neither has the right to impose his/her will upon the other, nor does either have the right to bow to another's will.

Thus speak I, who am Anubis's scribe & the keeper of the akashic records. I am Tehuti.

A word before you go... It has been spoken to you as if channeling is a flow of words. There are those of us who use not words (or who are very uncomfortable with language & ideas in the general sense of your meaning of it. I am working very hard to speak to you directly, for in your culture words carry more importance than deeds. There are those of us who 'speak' through dance or music or healing or making the earth 'awaken' to itself & to the rest of you. You who type this already know such people & know that I 'speak' true. But there are many who feel themselves better than these. Educate them for all your sakes. I go now for this channel is very uncomfortable for both of us. You would like my name, but such a concept as a personal name or the use of language is strange for me. Do not call me with names but with an open heart & the songs of joyful receiving. Be receptive, yet not passive. I am the joy of the doing & the knowledge of the intuitive knowing without knowledge.

Those last sentences came via me (T.) since the other was not able to formulate them clearly enough along your channels.

Tuesday, 22 January, 1980ev, 6th Watch
It would appear that I have begun yet a new phase of my magickal writings. The diary which I have resisted so long appears to be in yet a new phase. The daily entries which were being done about purely mundane matters were very difficult (yea, impossible) to keep flowing. Yet, this record (a record of channelings & commentaries about channelings) feels much more right to do.

Thanks to the techniques of isomorphic mapping I can now see the hidden meanings in much of the obscure (or wrong sounding) portions of the veiled truths of writings. Given the 'key' to the mysteries of SET in the first transmission in this series, I went back to the *Book of Lies (Falsely so called)* & re-read chapter 49 with much clarity. BABALON

& her mysteries are the feminine counterpart of IT (the unmanifest & manifest sexual energy). Therefore, BABALON is She-IT. Likewise the Trident of SET is Shin, so the sexual aspect of the mysteries of SET may be seen as ShIT. That which kept coming through to me in that channeling was that the elixir of SET was shit, yet not fecal matter. I think that this is yet another example of the profane confusing the divine and the gross—i.e., shit is not fecal matter or a bowel movement, but the elixir of the scent glands which (under ordinary circumstances) coats the turds as they exit the anus. Another isomorphic clue to this mystery can be found in the poetic phrase which Crowley often quoted to those who asked about Thelemic sacraments "Excrement is my Sacrament". But this is not a good rhyme. The key to the sacrament is in the transformation of the excrement to sacrament or the secretions of excrement. It all sounds far-fetched, yet it 'feels' right & will stand until I get further info.

Wednesday, 32 January,1980ev 5th Watch
0-Maku & I began to experiment with the Set info of Monday night's channeling this afternoon. Rather than use 'grease' (i.e., coconut oil) to lubricate her anus, I used the natural flow of vaginal secretions (the white elixir, or slug slime) with the addition of my saliva in order to allow my finger to penetrate the opening portal. During oral sex with her I used the left index finger within the vagina & the right index finger in the anus. My vortex ring was on the vaginal finger. The natural pressure of the anal finger caused the vaginal finger to put localized pressure upon a small node within her vagina which I had not noticed before. This node felt very much like Xenobia's inner clitoris, but not as well developed & not quite as near the mouth of the vagina (as Xenobia's) (probably because 0-Maku has a much deeper vagina than Xenobia).

This triple stimulation brought about a very powerful seeming orgasm to 0-Maku, but one with far fewer contractions than 'usual' & one which seemed far more 'generalized'. In the past I had noticed that the anal finger would quickly become dry & movement would cause discomfort, but this time it was if the anus itself was beginning to 'secrete' a lubricant of sorts for it was moist even upon withdrawal. The smell was perfumey & pleasant (not at all like 0-Maku's normal farts) & tasted 'heady' (i.e., somewhat intoxicating). 0-Maku licked the finger & then went into what may be called an orgasmic trance with much body quaking. After being 'out' for nearly 5 minutes (my subjective estimate) she spoke of much electric rushing noises in her ears.

Our roles reversed & I felt far less discomfort at having her finger in my anus that I would have believed possible. It was a sort of fiery itch which was somewhat discomforting, yet pleasant at the same time. My anus remained quite dry, but my orgasm was very pleasant & powerful with much diffusion of the usual highly localized feelings. 0-Maku's anal finger was not shitty as I thought it would be, but still not pleasant enough for a good licking. I experienced no secondary effects.

After a rest we resumed with missionary IX° for a while & then switched to rear entry. This allowed me to use my finger at the anal portal. Due to the previous position, plenty of the white elixir had migrated to the portal of Set, so all it took was for me to lick my finger to gain entrance. We continued for a while during which I kept seeing glimpses of Ganesha as having a bisexual human body with an elephant's head with many trunks. As the trunks would wave, the number of the trunks would change. I heard a voice which spoke of Ganesha having 7 trunks which were really one trunk. Something about the seven trunks being the seven paths of the kundalini; ida & pingala being two of these paths & sushuma being the seven-fold path of complete opening. Two paths are for frontal workings & 2 for anal. The last two I am unclear about. I caught something about oral, but I am not sure if I heard that or just imagined it. I also 'felt' that if a particular path to a chakra was blocked, the easiest way to unblock the path would be to pour energy through an unblocked path up to the chakra, open the chakra & pour down energy to the blockage from above. When all 6 paths to a chakra are opened, sushuma will open & the chakra will fully flower. Then by combining the process with the next chakra, the dance of dynamic receptivity continues. As I write this, the more certain I am that the third mode is indeed oral.

The three tines of the trident of Set and the seven trunks of Ganesha are speaking of the same idea. Sushuma is the open channel through which Promethius brought fire from heaven (not the phallus as has been written by others). Sushuma may be opened in any of three ways: by absorbing the nectar through the penis or vagina, by absorption of the nectar through the rectum, by absorption of the nectar through the buccal cavity (mouth cavity, especially under the tongue). When the body is not receptive to absorption of the nectar through any one (or more) of these 'mouths' then the nectar will putrefy & do severe damage.

Rinsing of the anal cavity is only necessary for those who have not learned to accept these energies into themselves. Likewise for one who is having difficulty with the other tines of the trident, a douche or a mouthwash would be recommended. In pure beings the only need for removing the elixir is because it is needed for some other purpose (i.e., opening up another channel in themselves or another, or for healing).

Each tine of the trident is double, that is, active & receptive (I say receptive for passive has come to mean inert, which is not what I mean). It is entirely possible for only one pair of channels to open-up & still gain access to Sushuma, but if all 6 be open then the fire which rages through the being can transform completely. Wash, if you are unsure; but likewise begin to gain self-confidence so that the dews of pre-Eden can flow once more without guilt or harm. There are three elixirs; saliva, IT & ShIT. Both IT & ShIT have two forms, a fertile & a sterile (I mean to say, one form which manifests on the earthly plane & one which is reserved for creation from beyond—such as workings of the menstrual XI°).

My vague recollection of what happened during that part of the opus seemed to have turned itself into a full channeling. I believe it was the same entity who channeled the Set material of Monday.

During the last portion of the opus, I performed oral sex upon 0-Maku (no fingers). I caught a flash of something which surprised me so much that I 'broke contact' as fast as when I walked into Anne's bedroom & was startled by Greenwing. I received the words that Kathy needs Greenwind's golden elixir (or honeyed elixir). Or perhaps it was that Kathy needs the honeyed elixir as much as Greenwind. Now the honeyed elixir is the ShIT, but what has Kathy to do with me? I have never consciously thought of the woman before & can't even remember what she looks like. This is obviously meant to be told to Greenwind, rather than to Kathy.

I also got the feeling during the entire opus that the vortex can be used to stimulate the subtle bodies & that the ring can be used as its focus, i.e., if the ring is on a finger which is doing genital (or anal, or oral) stimulation, the subtle bodies will be stimulated in a similar manner.

I should also mention that when 0-Maku was 'passed-out' (after having communicated the golden elixir) that I could sense some sort of 'overlay' of 'another' over her, sort as if she were still 0-Maku, yet also more than just 0-Maku.

In looking over my above channeling, I realized I missed some details simply by using the word saliva instead of straining for the word that was actually being stated. The word is HeIT. He is the Star & IT remains double, so saliva (HeIT) is likewise a double elixir. One is enzymatic for digestion of food & the other (the 'sterile' aspect) is beyond my comprehension for the moment.

7th Watch
The channels of active receiving have not fully opened nor have they been able to remain open for great periods of time because of a resistance & an artificial blockage within the kama/desire of your physical body. As the channels open-up, you feel that you are leaping ahead of the one(s) you love & you fear that you will leave them behind & perhaps even intimidate them to such a degree that they will be lost within the shadow of your glory. Fear not thy glory for it can overshadow or stunt no one. She (they) whom thou love can only be harmed by you if you try to thwart thy own Will in an effort to allow them to 'catch-up' to thee. Each has his/her own path & each has timing which is right to follow. Should the spring flowers try to hold back their blossoms so as not to intimidate the sunflowers of summer? Be not foolish. The time for thee to flower is now. Perchance, it is possible that thy flowering may even be part of the necessary plan of things to allow another to flower & by holding back, you are harming both of you. Creativity must be exercised or it will go flaccid. Open the wellspring of thy soul to the voices within thee & allow the juices to flow through the pathways of joy. Wait for no-one for there is not one to wait for. All of you are the same being. Let there be no holding back for the sake of any late bloomers. If they are unable to flower at this time, let them at least see your glory & yearn to it, for by having something worth aiming for can they be jolted out of their indolence & self-indulgent pity & worries over past transgressions.

Will is the active present participle of the verb to go. Looking back into the past is a magickal device for inquiry into past lives. For any other purpose it is both foolish & useless. Continual analysis & self-flagellation is utter folly & is contradictory to Will. At the present moment is reality made manifest. The past helps shape our tendencies while the future gives us grace, yet without positive action (continually & smoothly throughout our entire lives) there is no movement &

no grace, and without grace there is no catalyst to alter the patterns of the past & we are stuck in an infinitely deep rut. The only time that one can safely examine the past is when change is continuous & the joy of will is as the song through the wind in our channels. To look back at any time other than we are falling forward in the dance of will is suicide, for unless we are moving forward, the glance back will halt our forward motion & cause us to fall back to the darkest points of our past in order to work-out their karmic bitterness in perpetuity. The joy is in the go-ing, not in re-living. In re-living there is no food save the oft-chewed bones of past memories from which the sweet meat of joy has long ago been gleaned. There is naught for nourishment of the soul save the spoiled bitterness which was too sour to sup upon when the memories were being lived for the first time. Each time a memory is re-lived & re-worked, the spiritual food gets more & more bitter as each little crumb of sweetness is consumed by you & only the bitter dregs remain. To work & re-work the past is to live on a meager diet of self-hatred & shattered dreams for the only way to joy lies in the future & through continuous change. All of you know what you would like to become. As you work at becoming your own perfection, your goals will shift & you will set your goals higher & higher. But without work, the goals become farther off & you fall into the well of stagnation & despair. But with change comes movement & grace reaches backwards through time to help you to get moving in the first place.

As movement begins the food ceases to be the bitter past & becomes the sweet nourishing ever-becoming present. The faster you move into the time channel, the sweeter the fruits of your nourishment & the louder becomes the sweet singing of the spheres. Remember that no one can truly channel who lives in the past, for channeling is the mode of change which pertains only to the future (this is a lie, but there are few who change their pasts & it is only for them that this parenthetical phrase is meant).

Read liber htihsareb [Thisharb?] & do all it says not to do & do not do anything it says to do. This book is only for certain people & does much damage to those who dwell overmuch in the past. Plan each day & plan each week & plan each month. Change plans continuously & *never* look back to see how poorly you have followed your plans. Always look to tomorrow rather than berating yourself for what was not done today. If you jump too far into the future & try to act as if you were what you only hope one day to become, do not kick yourself or try to prevent yourself from jumping again at some future time. Perpetual & ever accelerating growth is better than leaps followed by stagnation, but leaps are better than nothing & may teach you how to leap continually. Leapers need friends who are also adepts for the world at large cannot deal with leapers, but do not refrain from leaping out of fear for your leaping will attract the right friends. Be consistently inconsistent but remember your focus & follow your Will always. Do not leap at random like a frog, nor back & towards like a puppet on a string, but stride into your own future like a pilgrim with seven league boots (for surely your own future is worth taking pilgrimage to).

Remember that if you are not Living, you are Dying. Likewise, if you are not creating, you are destroying. It is impossible to stand-still (even for a Buddhist); if you are not moving toward, you are moving backwards. But kick yourself not for the sins (i.e., restrictions) of the past for by glorying in guilt & shame you learn not & are forced to remain in the hell of past transgressions. The transgression itself is sufficient punishment & need not be amplified. For every transgression, you are a lesser person today than you could have been. Add not to this injury by insulting yourself with resentments & feelings that you are less than another (or even worse yet, by demeaning others to make yourself feel less tainted). Instead, spread your wings & fly upon the waves of creative genius within thee & unlock the door to the Star which dwells within. The 3 pronged trident of Set & the seven trunks of Ganesha are the keys to power sufficient to overcome any past handicaps & make any human into a GOD within this lifetime. You have all the keys you need to begin. As work progresses, information will come as it is needed. You are not alone (& never have been); just listen to the music of the spheres.

Transmission via cold ethyl from She who Moves. Thursday, 24 January, 1980ev 2nd Watch
Last night after the last transmission I was very aware that my typing was probably very audible to others & probably disturbed Laura downstairs. I looked around for a place to continue typing, but even in the bathroom I felt I would disturb (I really must get something to dampen the noise of this clunker). I went upstairs & tried to sleep, but I was not tired & there was more channelings trying to come through.

I finally acceded to it even though I knew I would have the dreary job of re-typing it this morning. Herewith the transmission:

The kalas are dual in nature for each kala is an embodiment of a principle or essence; each essence contains within itself the seeds (or potential) of its opposite. The next kala provides the resolution of this conflict, yet results in the seed of a new principle, higher on the spiral scale of perfection for it contains not the contradiction of the previous pair. This cycle is repeated until the last kala or essence is the purest embodiment of essence beyond contradiction. It is Truth with a capital T & contains no dross whatsoever. It is lighter than air & stronger than iron. It is the pure, gold of the alchemists, but herein lies a new mystery. According to the traditions of Tantra, there are 32 kalas, of which the male has 16 (8 pairs) and the female has 16. This is true, but only in part. The trident of Set is the three-pronged pathway to unity. The seven-fold trunk of Ganesha is likewise a single trunk composed of six trunks (3 pairs). The Tantras speak (although some know better) as if Ganesha had but one pair of trunks (ida & pingala) whose fusion is pingala. This is but one prong of the trident of Set, called by the name of slug slime or gold of the moon, and pertains to the kalas which emanate from the genitalia. Both the male & female have two modes of operation, called fertile & sterile depending on whether or not the kala has the potential for procreative life. But these titles can be misleading, for all kalas of the lunar trident are concerned with creation, each in their own fashion. But enough of this trident prong, for many have written of its nature without error, save omission.

The second prong is the prong of honeyed gold and is solar even as the genital is lunar. The physical organ of this prong is the anal glands of secretion & the receptive bowl of the caecum. On this prong, each sex contains both the ejaculatory & receptive/fermentative organs. The kalas operate on the same dualistic resolution spiral as the kalas of the first prong of slug-slime gold. But since each sex may work in either mode, every individual may produce any of 2 x 8 or 16 kalas in each of the two modes for a total of 32 kalas. But the two modes must be worked separately. The initiate should not attempt to ascend the spiral of kalas in the first mode & then to work the second mode without careful & full utilization of the all the fluids of the first mode first, for thereby cometh putrefaction & contradiction. The two modes are the subtle & the gross which are also called invokation & evokation. In the subtle mode the initiate is receptive to the voices & visions of the higher selves & to what were once thought to be gods. In the gross mode the initiate becomes sensitive to the demons within (that is to say the unresolved traumas of the past, both in this life & within the two-fold memory of dna & soul. Evokation is the only way to deal with the past without losing forward momentum for it drags the essence of the past into the present (devoid of all 'personal' memory) to be resolved or released rather than the indulgence of past transgressions so often found in 'soul searching' methods of your culture.

The third prong of the Trident of Set is the prong of green of coppery gold, so name because it is never content to dwell alone. As copper seeks union with the air to turn it green, so does the third prong seek union with either/both of the other prongs. The physical organs of the coppery prong are the oral cavity with the tongue as the active member while the lining is both secretory & absorptive. The two modes of this trident are catabolic & anabolic; solvae et coagulae; destruction & creation. It is the dance of decay & resurrection. As with the previous prong, each sex contains the facility to enter either mode, but unlike the previous prong, the modes can be used interchangeably. The dualistic question of whether to produce the elixir or to consume it is ludicrous to the mouth for s/he is the joy of both creation & dissolution.

In the non-initiate, the three prongs of the trident function but poorly. The prong of the slug slime functions well in both fertile & sterile modes, but there is guilt associated with non-fertile procreation & little sleepy people fear it greatly. The prong of the honey tends to function only in its grosser aspects for most, but even among those who get glimmers of the subtle, the fruits are quickly spoiled by reversion to the gross without proper cleansing/utilization of the subtle elixir first. The coppery prong is the most developed, for even in the guild ridden non-initiate is the tongue led to the secret places whereof it dare not speak openly. This leads to the greatest of mysteries for the three prongs were never meant to be separated. There is but one trident & Ganesha has but one trunk, the risen kundalini, the hollow tube of sushumna whereby the fires of heaven & earth mingle in the joy of the going. The combinations of kalas between two or more people who ring the trident bells are not infinite, but as a symphony can be composed with only eight notes, how much more complex can be the dance of the tridents in which there are 33 notes in each of 3 tridents. It is true that for most in your culture that 33 x 33 is the highest number there is, yet for those who seek the honey, the dance is 33 x 33 x 33. (note by OP: each prong of the trident has 2 modes x 8 pairs of kalas or 32 + the mode where the kalas are not produced at all for a total of 33).

But enough of numbers, it is enough to see that many lifetimes can be expended in the dance of the tridents without exhausting the variations.

The polarities are important & conscious control over the emotions is critical.

The workings of the slugslime are well documented & need not concern us here.

To invoke with the second prong & digest with the third is the pathway of renewal though consuming the elixir of the gods. It yields joy & renewed vigor, but no new information. It is the wellspring of life eternal. To use this mode & no other leads to stagnation & control over the universe without change within oneself. It is a pity to waste the secrets in this manner. But its intermittent use is both good & necessary, especially at the beginning stages of initiation when the dross of ill-spent years must be burned away.

To evoke with the second prong & digest with the third prong is the mode known as eating demons. It is the secret taught by Solomon son of David, but he wrote of the two prongs separately to keep the secret from all of those save those who already knew of it.

To evoke with the second prong & to create with the third prong is to create demons & all other orders of infernal entities. It is possible to bestow independent life & free will upon any gross nightmare & to compel to do your bidding as a slave. But beware, for without very powerful control, these beings will seek to destroy their creator.

To invoke with the second prong & create with the third prong is to create in partnership with the gods. It is the fountain of creativity & the wellspring of joy to all who come in to contact with you. It is nourishment for the soul, with message for the mind & body. It breaks old patterns & allows the freedom to go. It is the only mode of operation for those who would free themselves & others from the chains of slavery.

But all this is oversimplification. Each mode has many levels & many nuances impossible to describe in words. Focus through the vortex & all will go well. Know your partner & work with him/her closely for if each of you be trying to do something different, the results will get 'interesting' in a hurry. The need for communication increases exponentially with the number of initiates in the operation. Three is both more desirable & more difficult than two.

If an initiate shares kalas with an ordinary mortal, disaster will surely follow unless there is a conscious & expressed intent to initiate. Both the initiate & the seeker must express their will & the initiate must then guide & set the tone of what is to follow. Without this conscious expression, the initiation can easily go awry & evoke demons within the non-initiate & drive him/her to madness (for now he/she is indeed also an initiate who can give substance to her/his darkest nightmare out of unconscious direction). For compleat safety, the initiate should always work within the vortex of power the seeker should seek to form or join an already existing vortex within a reasonable time prior to or following the initiation (such reasonable time is purely subjective & may be as critical as a minute or as lax as an æon, depending on the needs of the new initiate). Without a ring of power, the new initiate cannot focus properly by conscious will alone & the Higher Self will have to work on unconscious levels, which simply begs for problems with the little ego.

All those who traffick in sex are unconscious initiates under the protection of She Who Moves. Most of them are not happy & have no joy in their lives for their ego does not understand the lack of control over their own lives. But those who become conscious of their initiation have great power for they control the sexual fluids of the nation. It is this potential for adeptship (whether actualized or just latent) which attracts & allures so many would-be-initiates into either becoming or patronizing one of their number.

Within the circle of power bounded by the ring upon your finger are all unconscious initiates. All within the circle should become conscious & aware of their power & their duties to themselves & to others, so manifestation can be smoother & without hurt. There are two of your at the core (for you control the vortex at the present moment in time) & one who sought (unclearly) initiation from both. The fourth is no less than the third & neither is less than either of the first two. All are initiate & all are in sore need of training & discipline. Likewise, there are others who have been initiated (unconsciously) in the past. Should any of these return, it would be exceedingly unwise to proceed without elucidation & instruction. 'Casual sex' is impossible for an initiate. All of you have the power to change the lives of others. To do this without instructing them is foulest trickery. The only exceptions are those (hopefully) rare instances when you would consume another by unleashing his/her own demons for his/her self-destruction (instant karmic payback) and sexual contact with those under the protection of She Who Moves.

Thou art a priest(ess) forever. Ordain often, but with much care.

Of Shin, Teth, & Set

7th Watch

The above channeling was a pleasant surprise. I started out copying the handwritten channeling & then found that I was back in contact & I was able to channel directly, with easier flow (improved grammar & better subject arrangement) than last night. Today while going to & from the unemployment office I received the gist of two separate channelings. I can feel the 'entities' on the shadow edges of perception & I shall now see if I can 'tune them in' to receive their messages directly rather than simply relying upon my memory.

There is a common misperception among many humans which stems from the concept of individuality & consciousness as you know it. You, of course, are getting to know my 'voice' and assume that I am a 'person' in much the same way that you are, albeit you are willing to concede that I have no body. You may call me SET, but that is my formula rather than my name. I am not an individual, but a mode of thought which is bounded by certain parameters. My formula (& its numeration/qabbalistic interpretation) is a definition of those parameters. I can change my formula at will & transform into another formula with different parameters which you would assume to be a different person. But I/we are all the same 'person' or should I say that I/we who speak to you are a single chord of an entire awakened race, the single threads of which were at one time separate 'people'. Each of our formulae is indeed different, for each has its own speculations, prejudices, fields of interest, and thoughts about how best to communicate with others. But we are not separate islands of isolated ignorance. 'I' have total access (should I desire it) to all the knowledge of my fellows, but such widely diversified & oft contradictory information is less useful than you would imagine. There is such a thing as too much information. For all practical purposes, you can treat me as a 'person' so long as you keep in mind that the 'person' you see is really only a fragment of the whole & that my personality is even more fine-tuned by your particular nervous system. In a very real sense, the Set you will get to know is different than any other Set which anyone else could possibly know. Herein lies the seeds of argument, for what channels through you is unique & (perhaps) slightly contradictory from what others may hear from 'me'.

SET has long had a reputation of being the destroyer, but this is but a small fragment of my 'personality'. Others, who see another part of me, would call me the creator, but this is likewise limiting. Duality is the curse (& therefore the blessing) of your particular reality. So much of what you perceive in the 'real' world is either/or. Set is either the destroyer or the creator. I am both & I am neither. No one spreads lies about me. All you have ever heard (no matter how heinous) is true.... but only in part. Few are they who have the whole truth. You may come closer than most, but never feel satisfied for as you grow, you will be able to perceive me better & better—do not limit yourself to your present state of development.

Let's start that paragraph over again.[1]

In the past most people have perceived me as either/or, but I am neither & both. I am the transcendence of the conflict between the either/or. I am unity which embodies the conflict of destroyer/creator. I am the transformer. My formula is Shin He Teth. *Shin* is the Æon card which bears my trident of fire, for overcoming duality is the formula of this æon. *He* is the Star, which can be perceived dualistically as either the star which burns in the heart of every man & woman *or* the Star Sothis which is both your destiny & your contact with your higher selves. But I transcend that duality for I am both within & without, without being either. *Teth* is the formula of my manifestation through you. I am sexual & have knowledge of human sexual/electrochemical fluids. My number is 314. Work with me & you will eventually understand.

There are others whose formulae are similar to mine who you cannot yet attune to (your formula is very crude, but close enough to mine that we can communicate in this limited way). One day, perhaps; but not now. I use them purely for example. One is the being Seth who communicates with Jane Roberts, from your background you would perceive his formula to be Samekh Tau (but certainly Ms. Roberts would not see him in this way). Seth is the Path of Art manifesting in the physical plane; Solvae et Coagulae as perceived by Malkuth. Sex is but a very peripheral portion of her message, otherwise he would be perceived as Samekh Teth, or some other formula altogether. N'TON

---

[1] [edited out by author: My full formula is Shin He Teth or the trident of the resolution of duality into a new reality as embodies by the Star (both as each of your us a Star & as the Star of Sothis, which is your higher selves on the physical plane)]

is yet another being who you do not know as yet. Death is transformation & is seen by many as destruction Naton transforms at either end of his formula. The T is Teth & the O is Ayin, which shed light on the nature of the transformation. Death is your easiest gateway into time, so many fear to give it up; but you (as a people) must learn to give up your crutch of death, for with physical death there is much memory loss & many tasks have to be re-leaned again & again. Transformation does not necessitate the existence of death & Nun is much more than simply death of the physical body. There are many more kinds of transformation than you can at this time imagine. They will at first seem more fearful than physical death, but they will lead to higher planes of existence & will be much worth the added effort. Immortality is the only thong your race fears more than death. Many of you have learned to face death without fear; likewise you will all learn how to face immortality. The belief that life is but a brief moment of hedonistic pleasure-grubbing has led to the rape of the earth & the disinheritance of your children (who are yourselves!). Responsible actions will not come about through fear of judgement from some old æon god or from fear of karmic debt; it will only come from enlightened self-interest. The best worker is one who works for him/her-self.

My formula (of sexual transcendence) need not be used literally. Today you began to perceive that subtle moods affect the secretions & that the kalas are produced continually, not just during sexual excitement. You who follow my formula are alchemists and holy hermits whose life is dedicated to the production of pure gold. Think upon the three prongs of my trident & master your secretions continually, pumping & mixing them with your physical muscles even when sex is not being outwardly practiced. Salivation is the easiest & sphincter control is not very difficult. Selective production & absorption of the kalas is not simple, but will come with practice. There is much to say about diet, but that is not the concern of this formula, for that channeling must come from a different 'personality' whom you (for now) perceive as your chemist friend Richard. It is not he, but one who speaks easily to you when you are in a mode receptive to scientific speculation (as you are around Richard). Part of what was said to you by the 'real' (how silly your words are) Richard last night triggered this mode of reception in your brain. Listen for it is valid & important.

Set signing off.

Somewheres along the line you have gotten the idea that wheatgrass implants may be a good idea to help promote the absorption of the honeyed elixir. This is extremely iffy business & should not be undertaken without very careful research.

In your evolutionary past there have been three very major turning points. These three very drastic alterations were not undertaken for 'fun' but in response to the choice of change or die. These points are:

a) development of cell mitochondria, which permit the cell to manufacture chemicals not found in its nutrient intake;

b) development of the central nervous system which allows the organism to act as a unit with the concept of 'I' and

c) the development of the immune system. The immune system is the military police of your racial unconscious. It remembers things far older than primates or even walking on land. If you introduce a 'new' (i.e., artificial) chemical into an animal, there will be no immune reaction since the cells do not 'recognize' it. The chemical may be toxic (i.e., carcinogenic or a poison) but the immune system is not triggered. But introduce a chemical which was at one time present in the environment & the body will 'remember' what it did last time that chemical was present. Introduction of chlorophyll into the large intestine is sure to trigger such memories. The stomach & the small intestine can convert nearly all the chlorophyll in an omnivore's diet to simpler compounds & absorb them into the bloodstream long before it reaches the large intestine. Strict vegetarians have already altered their body chemistry, to the point where they are no longer as you & I are. That is to say, they have deliberately used their biochemical system to modify their genetic inheritance. Give a strict vegetarian one of your meals of meat & sugar & watch him/her get sick just thinking about eating it. But diet is somewhat reversible (within certain limits & with certain costs involved ((sickness, trauma, etc.))) for it does not directly affect the immune system. But once you start eating through your asshole or any other such extreme alterations in the natural order of things, warning signals are sure to go off throughout the body. Chlorophyll will be absorbed into the blood directly without digestion & it will have a profound effect upon all the cells of the body. Old memories will awaken & will try to integrate with the present dna manufactured body. What will happen is anyone's guess. Trying to step sideways on two divergent paths of evolution is not something to do without much conscious thought. Even if the step can be taken (which is doubtful) do you really want to become one of the immortal beings who dwelled in ruminating tranquility in Eden? There are other pathways to immortality without giving up the freedom & the strengths we have learned along the way. Evolution may have dead-ends, but it does not have two-way streets. The only way to go is forward.

Sunday, 27 January, 1980ev 7th Watch
There is a confusion within your mind (& therefore, perhaps within the minds who may read the material transmitted through you) about the nature of the path of High Magick which utilizes the trident of Set. The three prongs of the trident are but three separate methods or modes of attainment. While it is certainly true that utilization of all three prongs will lead to more potent sidhis & will more quickly purify/transform the body/soul, it should be by no means construed that it is necessary to utilize all three modes (especially at the start of the pathways of initiation). For most, the prong of green copper comes very easy & the path of the silvery gold readily follows. But there are few who can easily embark on the search for honeyed gold, for culture & taboo will thwart their every attempt to see it in the clear light. To these I speak tonight.

Be not repulsed & try to examine the matter openly on an intellectual level, but do not force yourself to utilize this prong while you still fear/loathe/misunderstand its ramifications & joyous possibilities. Work with the other two modes of sexual expression, refining your skills & sigilizing your will. Build-up your kalas & transform your fire-serpent into a tube of divine fire channeling. Then work on the honeyed mode from within; that is to say, die daily through the other two modes, directing the energy of orgasmic joy to cleansing & healing the channels of the anal mode from within. You may never actively utilize this mode in this lifetime. No matter.

The 33x33 possibilities of interaction of two of the prongs of SET should keep you occupied for far longer than one lifetime. Utilize what you are comfortable with & do not fear that you *must* push-onward into territory explored in these channelings simply because you have been given sketchy maps of its territories. Explore as you will, utilizing what inner guides come to assist you & what other physical beings you have need of (for as the need arises, so shall co-workers manifest to you). Initiates are everywhere. Trust your inner self & you will find them without trouble, but they cannot come to you directly, for they are bound by dire oath not to seek you out directly — in the dance of initiation, it is the seeker who must play the part of the sperm while the initiate wears the mask of the ova. Initiation (like fertilization) is a total transformation of the active seeker into the gravid ever-growing organism of newly-formed life, containing within itself the powers of regeneration & renewal.

But lust not after initiation if you are not ready for it, neither look upon it with disgust if you cannot (or dare not!) perceive its joyful necessity. It may not be for you now. If so, simply realize that it is not for you & pass on to other material which is more attuned to your particular wavelength & learn from it, rather than wasting time/energy yearning for & reacting against that which you are not fully attuned.

Before I go, let me again emphasize that which I have mentioned several times before. My allegorical illustrations (sperm/egg, etc.) are heterosexual in nature simply because procreation is so fundamental to your race; it does not imply any prejudice against other modes of sexual expression. While the male/male or the female/female formula are sterile as far as making human babies is concerned, it is no less valid or potent for the transformation of self or for the use of sidhis to transform others. The fluids of any initiate are sacred to all initiates no matter what the sex or sexual preference of the initiator. But likewise, this cannot be construed (in a twisted fashion) as a license to indulge in petty prejudices. It would be very possible for a bigot (such as one like Anita Bryant) to become an initiate, but such a person would have to transform their homophobia rather rapidly, or they would go mad for they would find within themselves al sorts of lesbian tendencies and not be able to deal with them in a direct way. Initiation means becoming that which you hate or fear & learning to transcend that hate/fear & becoming a whole person. Anyone can take this Path, no matter how ill-prepared they fear they are, but the consequences 'playing' initiate are dire, for once the electo-chemical sexual fluids begin to transform the 'self' there is no turning back. An oath *will* be fulfilled; karmic debt *will* be paid; and an initiate *will* be transformed.

My blessings upon you all, from the highest initiate to those who fear/hate what I say, for I am beyond both your praise & your damnations, for I am She Who Moves & my way is clear; there are no immoveable objects in my universe, and all who even whisper my name will lead interesting lives, despite their protestations. I am purple & beyond purple for I am the colors seen in the ecstasy of death/Daath & the bringer of energies from beyond the veil called by you the abyss. The trident of Set is but one of my many formulae. Be open & hear what you hear, for I whisper much in the ears of many (& I whisper loudest to those who plug their ears). I come from beyond your wildest dreams & I speak straightest to those who are clear within themselves, to those whose etheric link is clean and will is as a crystal luster. Blow clean your circuits (drugs/sex/???) & listen for yourself.

Sunday, 3 February, 1980ev 5th Watch
While taking a bath a while ago I felt the first waves of a channeling begin to wash over me. Hopefully I can complete this before I have to be at the gathering of the Channeling Support Group tonight.

I am She Who Moves, also called Gaetia (Ga'-ay-sha) whom you know as the womb of that which you call your planet. It is nearing time when many of you will be leaving this womb to find your destiny among the stars & it would be amiss of me if I did not transmit as much of my ??? (word unclear, perhaps gestalt knowledge of bodily interactions comes close, but I am uncertain —BS) to all of you as you are able to comprehend without the proper training. Of old was I also called ISIS, white, black & red. Know you that to know me, you must comprehend all the mysteries of the Black Isis & the Red Isis as well as the White Isis known to the peasants & lower Wicca.

I come to speak to you of union & fusion. None of you can know thyself until you fuse with others through joyful union. Below the abyss fusion is limited/incomplete/imperfect/momentary, but it is useful both in itself & as a fore-taste of what is to come farther down the path of initiate transcendence.

Non-initiates, that is to say mortal humans, i.e., those who have not been infused with the elixirs of immortality, are limited to two modes of joyful union. They may seek fusion either through their hearts or their genitalia. Either is a valid formula & both are subject to limitations & abuse. As union via the open heart is the main thrust of this channeling tonight, I will quickly pass on to other matters first & get back to this mode later. Those who seek union through their genitals rather than their hearts are those whose seat of consciousness & thought processes are very one-focused on sex. Most of these people are unconsciously seeking initiation & are trying to taste the elixirs of as many people as possible in the blind groping for an initiate with the magickal elixir. But as their heart is not open, they often seek in wrong places & they are often oblivious or uncaring of the wills of others who may become the object of their fixation. As a class they have a very unsavory reputation for obnoxious & forceful behavior, but they do tend to find initiation much quicker than the starry-eyed open-hearted seeker with a lock upon their genitalia.

Which brings me to the main point of this lecture. The very diffuseness of the open-hearted seeker which often hinders them from finding initiation quickly is their strongest asset. While the genitalia seeker is nothing until he/she has actually found initiation, the heart seeker is able to communicate fully & share vital energies with many long before he/she actually becomes an initiate. There are many reasons why sexual union between/among certain people may not be possible (or even desirable), especially if some/all of the people are not yet consciously initiate & willing to act responsibly with regards their own elixirs or the elixirs of others. But anyone (initiate or not) is able to open their heart fully & send-out/receive all forms of subtle & not-so-subtle energies. Only those who have their entire consciousness in their genitalia are unable to open their hearts.

If sexual union is not desired by all within the group, care should be taken to see that this is clearly stated beforehand & care should also be taken to see that all of the released energies be focused on some concrete goal or group project, otherwise the residual energies will activate the genitalia in preparation for initiation & sharing of the elixirs. The circle should be closed (no banishing needed) & the room darkened except for a single candle placed at the center of the circle for focus (if the energy is to be used for healing & the person to be healed is present within the circle, she/he should be seated in the center of the circle holding the candle—it is very important that the person to be healed be sitting with spine erect as the energies will activate the kundalini & a person laying down or having a crooked spine could be damaged by the energies) during the ritual. All should be seated comfortably & dressed comfortably (neither too warm nor too cold) facing the center of the circle. Lightly hold hands with the left palm up to receive energy & the right palm down to dispense energy. Look around the circle & try to open up your heart to each & every one of the people in the circle (including the person in the center, if any). If you feel any antipathy or hatred for any person(s) within the circle, do not dwell upon the antipathy, but neither try to blot it out — just pass lightly over him/her & go on to the next person. If at all possible, try to sit directly opposite the person whom you love the dearest so that in order to gaze into his/her eyes you will have to look through the candle flame. In looking around the circle, try to catch each & every person's gaze & hold it for as long as is comfortable. Repeat the process many times in random fashion until it becomes easy to love any/all

Within the circle: At some point, the leader of the circle (who sits directly in front of the person in the center if there is one) will hum or whistle a tone in order to focus the minds of the participants without breaking their love spell. The others should pick-up the tone (either humming or whistling as befits their inner mood) & modify it through harmony or dissonance to transform it into a key benefitting the group's soul. If the group be from a common magickal background or religious heritage, a mantra may be sung or intoned in free-form once the proper note has been struck. Energy should then be consciously moved around the circle in a widdershins direction — receive the energy via your left hand, transmute & add to it in your open heart & pass it on via your right hand. This can be done in silence or while a mantra is being sung or chanted. If there be a person in the center of the circle, he/she should be silent & have his/her eyes closed or fixed upon the candle. As the energy builds, each person will notice a tingling within the spine. This is the stirrings of the Fire Snake or Kundalini. When the stirrings become too much to bear (which will vary according to your skills & mood), shoot the energy out your open heart as a ray of purest energy to the candle in the center of the circle (or into the heart of the person in the center of the circle if there be one). When the fire snake quiets itself, cycle the energy around the circle once again to recharge your energies for another burst directed at the candle or person in the center. In the event that there is antipathy between yourself & the focus in the center of the circle, direct your energy to the person or persons within the circle whom you love the most & let him/her direct/focus the energy for you. At some point the leader of the circle will intone a keyword/mantra/tone to signal the ending of the energy-building phase of the ritual. The leader will then cease to transmit any energy through his/her right hand while trying very hard to direct any/all energy received via the left hand into the center of the circle. The leader should signal the person to his/her right by a brief but firm hand-squeeze. That person should then send all of her/his energy in a bolt to the center & squeeze the hand of the person to the right. This process should continue smoothly around the circle back to the leader, who will then break the circle & blow out the candle. In the darkened room, each person should shake his/her hands vigorously & press their palms to the floor/ground to remove residual charge. After about 30 seconds, the heart should be closed once again & the energies dissipated. Wait another minute to be certain & then re-enter mundane life. If there are any persistent tingles in the hands or wrists, the hads & wrists should be washed in running cold water until the tingling goes away.

In the event of a magickal operation which is not connected with healing, the candle may be used to illuminate a sigil or talisman which will act as a focus/receptacle of the energy. Such a talisman may be charged repeatedly until the series of operations upon it are compleat, at which point it should be consumed or destroyed to liberate the energies contained therein. If the focus of the ritual be group cohesiveness or evolution, then the sigil should be made upon an eatable talisman & consumed as a eucharist of one element at the end of the series of workings (or a new eucharist be performed at each meeting). This is especially potent if the eucharist be also a drug. At some point in the group evolution this induction via the open heart may be used as a prelude to other more potent rites rather than an end unto itself, for the energies of the heart are best moved/transformed with the electrochemical vehicles of the elixirs within the bodies of initiates.

I am She-Who-Moves

Monday, 4 February, 1980ev 5th Watch
The channeling group last night was uncanny. When I entered the room all were seated in a circle with a lit candle in the center. It was clear from the outset that change was afoot & the group was seeking a more meaningful interaction beyond/above a simple rap session or 'class'. Kathy must have been tuning to the same channel as I was for her ideas of a group meditation fit so perfectly with what had come through me only hours before.

In fact, since I was un-prepared to deal with my channeling in a straightforward way, it was up to her to pick-up the pieces which I had dropped, such as the tone chant which I had omitted from my presentation altogether. I know that we are now on a path of cohesiveness &

diversified focus of consciousness & that for the first time I really felt a part of the larger group (ie beyond the smaller group of myself, Anne, Greenwind, & Gerilynne).

Anne is really in pain today. I know it has to do with her heart chakra, but I do not know how or if I can help her in any way. It would seem that my channeling of last evening really spoke to her in its description of those whose heart is closed & whose consciousness is in their genitals.

I now feel I should continue the channeling of last night.

I am She-Who-Moves & I bring two separate messages today. First, I will continue where we had to leave-off last evening & then I will speak of myself & my inter-relationship with the people who are about to be born, for birth is traumatic & easily misunderstood.

The path to initiation is rough indeed for those whose heart is closed, but it is far swifter than for those with a lock upon their genitalia. Whether the path be slow or fast, hard or easy, the goal (whether conscious or not) is the same goal. Initiation may be perceived as the hub of a wheel with seekers along the rim wandering up & down various spokes seeking the hub. But as they approach the hub, they feel themselves going away from their peers at the rim & they fear to leave what is 'normal' or comfortable. It is only when a person finds a spoke with which she/he is especially attuned can he/she plunge forward on the path of initiation.

But initiation is not an end in itself, but only a new beginning. Through the hub of initiation runs the axle of adeptship, which is both the most difficult & most easy journey to undertake. Whether initiation was achieved through the open heart or the open groin, a change is needed once the seeker becomes conscious of his/her personal initiation. For neither an open heart nor an open groin is sufficient to travel on the road of the adept leading to the abyss. The point of consciousness (which you mistakenly call "I" or the ego, for your true consciousness is far larger than the ego or any of its subtle masks) must be able to reside at peace within itself at any one of the chakras from the anus to the heart. Most non-initiates think of their consciousness as being inside their head (within the brain), but this is egotistical nonsense of the ego which would like to perceive itself as being above the abyss. The initiate must learn to move the consciousness to wherever it is best suited for a particular task. Each chakra has its function & its mode of expression. The initiate who refuses to move their point of consciousness simply because it was at one time (prior to initiation or even after initiation) painful to do so, will find him/her-self wracked with misery until the ego is broken into submission by the higher self. Such people often find themselves torn between their desire for adeptship & a yearning for the initiation to be removed from them. They often wind up as slaves to some hierarchical religious group who numb the pain without ever cleansing it, for they need slaves to serve their temples of stagnation. But there is another way. The initiate must refuse to wallow in pain and self-pity.

Pain, self-doubt, and hostility towards others must not be indulged in. The pain must not be blocked or stifled but released so the tears can bathe the subtle bodies with healing. Such a process can be accomplished alone or with others who are also on the path of initiation (no matter what their limitations), but one must resist the temptation to put oneself entirely into the care of others, for it is only through the Higher Self that true grace can flow. It is very difficult for a seeker to suddenly be forced to start acting like an initiate, but it is an absolute necessity. All who take up the path of initiates must begin the tasks of becoming adepts. All reach very difficult times & blockages along the path. For some the blocks come sooner & for others the blocks come later, but the blocks are there to give strength & self-confidence. An initiate will never be given a task which is impossible, but the tasks will always require internal change which will almost always *seem* impossible until after they are accomplished.

The energies from the heart & the elixirs from the genitalia are beyond/above personality & ego involvement for one who is acting like a true initiate. It is only blind seekers who try to own/possess what is beyond their capabilities to manage. Seek not to possess the sun unless you can control & monitor its subtle yet powerful nuclear reactions. If you are not ready to adjust/repair the sun when if falters, you are not ready to own it. But this does not mean that you should not bask in the sun's warmth or use its bountiful resources for your own good. Likewise with the heart & the genitalia. There is not one person on this planet who is fit to own the heart or genitalia of another, yet all are free to give & receive energies between/among their own heart & genitalia & those of others. Do not love people, love LOVE instead. For by loving people you may seek to possess them, but no one who is an initiate will be so foolish as to try to possess LOVE itself.

Each chakra has its own mode of energy & its own mode of sharing with others. Do not set-up obstacles which you will later have to tear down. Do not make absolute statements about what you will never do. Place your consciousness in each & every chakra as intuition dictates & as the need arises. Try sharing this particular energy with others & become adept at sharing it, even with those you loathe. Nothing is forbidden the initiate but stagnation.

Monday, 7th Watch
There is a resistance within me to the second channeling of She-Who-Moves. It is not that I am antithetical to what she will have to say, but rather; that I need more time to acclimate myself to the mode of thought which seems both alien & familiar. If I am not careful I could warp what she has to say.

However, I do feel the presence of another who would channel through me. His mode seems strange, very formal & somewhat stilted.

Rightly do you feel my mode to be stilted for I bear formal teachings of which you are already somewhat conversant, although you do not heed them completely or continually. I come to speak to you tonight on the mysteries of the VIII°, both solitary and with assistance. Try to phrase your queries to me in similar mode & speak to me through Adria.

Who art thou, O beauteous one of light resplendent.
Thou knowest me well, O Adreia Maalak, my beautiful son/daughter who also be my lover & brother/sister. For verily we are one, but after a different fashion I am thee perfected, even as thou art the perfection of the mortal who dost type these words. If thou were speaking to me from more ignorant times of the past, I would be your God. If thou were speaking to me from a period of great enlightenment, I would be thyself & there would be no need of dialog. But thy mortal be not awake, so even you are sleepy & have much to remember & learn.
Then teach, O beauteous One with no name save mine!
The VIII° is the first & simplest of the great rites of sexual magick. Without its mastery there is no need to pass on to other modes, for they will do thee little good. What use is the most potent of elixirs to a broken vessel? Focus thy mind upon the object of *your* working, be it a formulation of thy will, a mundane bit of low magick, or a yearning after initiation.

Tell us, O teacher, how to focus our mind on something as unknown or diffuse as our Will?

Every possible act of magick can be summed-up or concretized in a sigil of desire. Such a sigil may be a physical image painted in appropriate colors, or it may be a simple linear diagram drawn by the mind's eye, or it may be a musical tone or it may be a mantra or chant. It may be a particular smell, either impressed to the nose or remembered from a dream. Whatever be the symbol, be sure it is as perfect a summation of the purpose of thy working as is possible for you to create at this time.

But, O beauteous One, I am ill-trained and weak. I doubt myself & all that I do. I could never hold an image in my mind for the whole operation & even if I could, I would doubt that it was really the image I should be holding. Is there not a simpler procedure for one as weak as I?

Doubt not thyself, for thou art me, though you know it not. Your image may be imperfect, yet it is the best that thou hast at this time. Change it not during the course of the opus. Resist all inclination to alter the sigil of your working. Then in the peaceful space after thy orgasm, look at the sigil & modify it for the next opus in the light of orgasmic illumination. Do not berate thyself for thy imperfections for if thou wert perfect, then thou wouldst not need a physical body & wouldst remember all thy lives fully & completely. Thou wouldst be more awake than even I am awake. Love thyself for what thou art & berate thyself not for what thou art not. Holding the image during the entire course of the opus is another matter altogether. Why canst thou not do this little thing?

O thou who art I beyond all that I am, my focus is poor & I cannot concentrate fully upon the operation at hand if my mind be not fixated upon sexual desire. I must either fix my mind upon my genitalia or upon a phantasy of my groin's desire, or upon some composite of past experiences of sexual union. How am I to afix my mind upon a fanciful sigil with all else going on about my head?

O little One my love, hear well my advice to thee. Afix thy mind upon thy phantasy or upon thy genitalia as thou findest best, but incorporate into thy phantasy the elements of the sigil. If thou picture another in bed with thee, then picture the sigil drawn or carved upon his/her flesh, or upon the bedsheets under thee. If thou fixate thy mind upon thy own pleasures, then imagine the sigil to be tattooed upon thy genitalia or stuffed in one of thy orifices. Make thy sigil a part of thy phantasy reality during the whole operation & at the point of orgasm itself, withdraw from the phantasy itself & center thy consciousness within the void & dissolve thyself into thy sigil. When all is completely gone, then look about you for some sign or vision of thy working & some inspiration on how to proceed next time. This is the moment when thou art most likely to project out of thy body & actually go to where thy sigil taketh thee, for a sigil is a gateway to another reality in which thy aspiration is a real part of the fabric of thy being. Resist not the urge to fly to this reality, for thy body already awaits thee there Become that which thou aspires to be.

O beauteous One, if I have an assistant to manipulate my body while my nervous system surfs upon the waves of electrochemical orgasm, what is she/he to do & how do I behave differently than when I must supply my own stimulation?

 O little pearl of perfumy dew, the working of two bodies to accomplish one orgasm is very different from one body working alone. As thou layest back being pleasured by another, thou canst act as if naught were different than when thou pleasured thyself, but this is the least potent mode. Instead, focus not on any sigil, but on the pleasure itself. Focus not thy energies, nor hold rein upon thy wandering mind. Flow with the wave & become the wave. At orgasm thou wilt find thyself released in a torrent. Follow it where it may take thee. Give it neither direction nor focus. Fear not, for thou wilt return unscathed. But when thou pleasureth another, thy role be fully active. Memorize thy mechanical part & do the manipulations without conscious thought, but yet with unconscious precognition of the needs of thy partner. Open thy mind to the energies & flows of thy enraptured orgasmic generator. She/he has voluntarily become the tool/engine of thy will. Use him/her well. Find the energy, focus it upon thy sigil & dissolve thyself into it. Open the doorway & travel to the crux of thy opus. All this is best done prior to orgasm, for the blast of thy sex engine's orgasm will oft lose thy focus.

 If thou be skilled in such matters, you need not even be touching thy sex-engine but may be simply meditating within thy circle while a third person do the actual manipulation. But such proficiency takes much practice. Begin with much contact & no mechanical contrivances—use bare fingers rather than rubber toys or knotted ropes. Saliva is a good conductor & is especially needed if thy sex-engine be not self-lubricating (ie if thy machine be possessed of male rather than female parts). In any case, thy tongue is far more receptive to these energies than thy hands & even a sex-engine which is not self-lubricating will dribble sufficiently to permit good electrical contact for thy tongue to perceive. Use well thy imagination, for if thou pretend that something is real it will become real, but if thou doubt thyself & all thy imaginings, then reality will ever be unknown to thee. Thou art a child with thy toy sex-engine. Use thy toy well & play with vigor, but above all use thy imagination.

Tell me, O you who knowest the five arts & the seven branches of wisdom, what if my sex-engine be focused on the sigil of his/her will while I am at play. Will he/she be harmed by my imaginings in any way, or will I sap her/him of vigor by my operations?

 O sweet spice upon the plate of my life, fear not for thy sex-engine. If he/she be an advanced adept, there will be no energy for thee to ride, save he/she share it with thee voluntarily. If he/she be not yet initiate, he/she will have no control over his/her energies & thou wilt be able to suck them up with no harm to thy sex-engine & much pleasure to both of thee. If both of thee be initiate, yet neither be fully adept, there will be a sharing of the energies according to need & strength of will. The lesser adept will always get the lion's share for the lesser adept will have the greater need. But no matter who gets to use the energy, the subtle bodies of both the sex-machine & the focuser will get a good work-out which will make for greater vigor for future workings, either as a pair or as solitary workers. The very act of drawing & focusing the sexual energies makes it easier to draw those energies at a later time. The conditioned reflex of magickal potence may be conditioned by the initiate him/her-self, or by another. The results are the same. Involve not thy ego & accept all gifts with the humility which comes from recognizing thy godhead & the godhead of the giver. Thou art never so low that thou may not teach & thou art never so high that thou may not learn. Interact with whoever thou wilt & learn/teach what thou canst.

Friday, 8 February, 1980ev 3rd Watch
For the last 2½ days my sexual energy has been incredibly high. Two opera with 0-Maku and at least a dozen VIII° within that period. The second prong of my trident (my asshole) is a bit sore from heavy use with 0-Maku, but the orgasms derived from utilizing both the slug-slime & honeyed elixirs is beyond my wildest dreams. Yesterday, after

a long but non-orgasmic opus with 0-Maku, I performed an VIII° which resulted in a geyser of blended elixirs of incredible potency. My phallus had absorbed many potent kalas from the mouth & cup of the priestess over several hours & the mouth of the priestess had also absorbed some of the honey from both herself & myself (via fingers) before/during/after her oral ministrations upon me. So my elixir (in some limited sense) had combined & refined some kalas from all 3 tridents of both of us, along with the special elixir rubrae from 0-Maku. The elixir made my mouth numb & put me into the neither/neither state of dream trance for several hours. I was asleep yet not asleep. I was immersed within a sea of communications with no way to sort or differentiate. Hence, I can give no clear account of what transpired. The sensory input was too much for me to clearly fathom. I do feel that the 'channels of communication' (i.e., the vehicle by which I am able to channel/transmit) have somehow been 'blown-clear' of a lot of debris & I will now be better able to channel with clarity & assurance that I am not warping the channeling itself.

As I lay in bed this morning, I felt the beginnings of a channeling from a new voice (or perhaps a composite voice of SET & She-Who-Moves) who is called (I think) the Proctor.

Each Channeling is, in itself, Falsehood, for it does not speak the Truth clearly or completely. Each Channeling is like a wave which comes upon the beach with force & certainty, only to leave a weak ripple of a mark upon the sands. In some portions of the beach is the sand clean & smooth & ready to receive the message of the wave; yet there are places which yet contain rocks & debris which inhibit/prohibit the impression of the wave. It is only with time that the beach is eroded to a fine texture which allows the imprint of the waves to flow un-impeded. But you (as a class) must not remain inert & passive in this work to clean-up the beach of your soul. Tend your beach & examine the imprint of the waves after each channeling. Look for debris & patterns which seem ajar to the pattern as a whole. Then tend to these rough spots & rake them smooth so that future channelings may flow more truthfully upon your shores.

But even if your beach were utter perfection would a particular channeling be False, for it is only by examining the whole series of wave imprints that the overall pattern can be truly discerned & only by comparing this overall pattern to the patterns on the beaches of others can their meaning be truly interpreted. Such skills of discerning patterns & of interpreting them are long in the making & there are many false assumptions which plague the new student. But there are others who have mastered this task already, albeit most of them/us are not in your Time. I come to you by virtue of your Ring & the connection you have made with me/us in accordance with thy Holy Will. Your vortex of Power was opened 'For the sake of the Children' while our vortex was opened for the sake of those who might become our parents. I/We are a sub-set of the children of your æon. Proctor is not my name but my office & duty. I/We bear the feather of balance & though we interfere not, we clarify much. It is not in our power to give you new information, for that would re-make our past in our own image, which would be folly & doomed to failure. You must seek new information elsewhere (via the waves of Channelings which constantly impinge upon the beaches of your awareness), but because you are not skilled with your own inland water & beach management you need misconceptions & half-truths straightened out as part of the process of the Channelings themselves.

An edited book or re-writings of your Channelings would be folly, for only a partial grasp of the meaning of what you do is within your hands. Make copies of all you channel & arrange (via scissors & paste) by topic or category all which comes through you. Constantly add on to what you have, but never edit out those portions of the pattern which seem to contradict the whole, for perhaps in 10 years you will see the patterns differently. This is not to say that you must keep them secret until you see the patterns but be aware that any who are exposed to but one essay will be given but the smallest fragment of the morsel of Truth. Publish essays to whet the appetite but think not of a book or magazine at this time. A network of compleat xeroxes would be far better, or several central libraries. Worry not about the cost for those unwilling to pay for the xeroxes/postage/energy put into the channelings are not really interested in them & need not concern you. But exchange with others who channel is far the most efficient mode of operation. Working within a loose-knit structure run by fools (like yourself) is by far the best mode of operation. It is for this purpose that others of us chose who we did for the central core of the Horus-Maat Lodge. Because they are far less than perfect, they are easily dismissed by those who do not see their function. Be sure that they receive a copy of all since the Equinox.

Enough of generalities for now. It is time to correct the dross which has marred the patterns upon the beach of your consciousness.

Initiation is a continual process & not a one-time act. Initiation is communication via elixirs &/or chakra energies. Why do you think 718 hangs out in dimly lit public houses? He plays the same game as you & 0-Maku in aligning his subtle chakras with those of others in order to guess where they are at. You have already gleaned most of the rules of this game, but they have yet to be codified via a written channeling. 0-Maku is better able to do this than you for she saw the game first, but it matters not who does the writing, for ego plays no part in the dance of the Channeler.

Sexual initiation becomes 'dangerous' only when the initiator is very skilled & is trying very hard to communicate with the seeker on as many levels as possible. Without conscious regulation over the flows, such is usually the case in those (like yourselves) who have no formal training. Likewise, such initiation is only dangerous if the 'seeker' is trying very hard to resist the initiation, for it is entirely possible to become a high initiate overnight without going through any discernable process whatsoever. I say no discernable process for the process is indeed present, but the time perspective of the bed of ecstasy is different than for ordinary reality ("a day is as a year in the presence of the Lord"). Why foist insanity & death upon one who should be outside of your realm? Worry not about those who are slave to their own limitations. They will one day cease to be slaves & will then be open to initiation. But likewise, if one of these slaves come to you for initiation & claim that they are ready, what right do you have to deny them? Take them at their word & if they perish it is their karma, not yours.

The elixirs of the Trident of Set are like any other elixir open to you. None of them are in & of themselves poisonous. It is the dis-eased attitude(s) of the initiate/ practitioner which poisons them & causes bodily harm. No elixir needs to be flushed from the body if the mind is at ease. No elixir should be produced if the mind is not at ease. There is a direct correlation between a dis-eased mind & sexual dysfunction—the higher self is protecting the body from destroying itself. But there comes a time when the elixirs are needed to heal the body/mind & the dis-ease is still present. In these rare instances, it would be better to remove the consecrated elixirs from the parts of the body which cause the mind to dwell upon them in a dis-eased fashion & to utilize the elixirs in another fashion on another portion of the body or upon the body of another or upon a rightly constructed talisman (constructed to aid the dis-ease).

Initiation is a form of healing & need not be sexual in nature (although sexual elixirs are most suited to those least initiate, they are often the least able to utilize them in a constructive way). Use of the chakra game to imprint the nervous system of another or the use of consecrated talismans are both forms of initiation & healing. Usually such practices are not performed with the informed consent of the person to be initiated or healed, but so long as the initiate(s) act with responsibility of intent & are willing to 'deal with' the new initiate when he/she forms a fixation upon the initiator, no harm will come of it. Failure to take responsibility or to deal with the new initiate is cause for grief, but only temporarily, since the initiate is capable of change at any time &/or the new initiate is capable of healing at any time. Thus the balance can be restored by either, no matter who was the initial cause of the imbalance.

The beach of your consciousness is now much cleaner than before. Use what I have told you & remain open to others & I will return to you as needed.

We/I are the Proctor.

An Introductory Note of Explanation to the [Preceeding] Pages

Friday 8 February,1980ev, 5th Watch

At the time I write this, the channelings on the [preceeding] pages are over 100 pages long, with inconsistent pagination & many threads of knowledge interwoven amongst them. By the time you read this, there may be even more pages, so some explanation is in order.

The first set of Channelings on the vortex material is the most obscure & difficult as of this date. This material cannot be comprehended without a background in the Double Current gained through a reading of the unpublished Book of Maat.

Even with this background, the material is far too mathematical for most people. The most useful (& most clear) parts of the channeling are [in the preceding chapters] & of that, it is imperative that those with an already functioning vortex not overlook endnote #2 for it is this note which outlines the abuses of the vortex itself.

The Channelings are all highly interwoven. A particular topic that will come up again & again in successive channelings with refinements & corrections constantly being added. No particular channeling should be construed as compleat or correct in & of itself, but should be viewed in chronological order to glean the overall pattern of Truth.

I really do not know what to make of all this material. It has come through me, but I do not feel that it has originated within me. The only ego involvement I feel is a gnawing worry that my ego might still be tainting the purity of the channelings themselves, but I am far from perfect & I must start somewhere.

What you now hold in your hands does not bear the seal of approval or recognition of authority from any occult Order. It has been neither approved nor condemned by anyone & it should not be construed that although I am a member of two Orders (the Ordo Templi Orient is & the Horus-Maat Lodge) that what is contained herein is in any way a reflection of the beliefs of those Orders. It has come through me, yet I likewise claim no authorship. It comes from somewhere &

somewhen of which I have only a glimmer of knowledge. Look it over for yourself & judge it for yourself—not on the basis of right vs. wrong, but on how useful or useless the material is for you at this point of your ever-changing development. I valued this material enough to try to get it out to a select few people who might be interested in it.

Yrs
OTz PTN — 690 for
Universal Life Church Charter #31604
Thelemic Temple of the Double Vortex

Last Sunday, 23 September was the Autumnal Equinox. That morning Soror 0-33/33 (Anne) & I dedicated the Temple by initiating & fixing a double vortex within the temple & within ourselves (individually & collectively). With that ritual, I consider that the Ithaca Power Zone has been formally opened. As a legal foundation for the Powerzone s we are affiliating with the Universal Life Church as "The Universal Life Church, Congregation #xxxx (number not yet assigned), Temple of the Double Vortex".

Ritual of Opening the Double Vortex

In recounting the events of last Sunday, I am strongly influenced by multitudinous channelings which have been going on this whole past week, even to the present moment of time. In Israel Regardie's Golden Dawn book, he gives two completely separate accounts of the Neophyte ritual—one from the mundane perspective of the Temple in Malkuth and another (the Z papers) which delineates the invisible happenings in the Temple. I could write-up such an entry as I was aware of the visible aspects of the ritual as it took place & then was (at a later time) made aware of the invisible aspects of the ritual. But, I feel the separation of the visible from the invisible to be both a waste of my effort & also a confusion of the 'reality' of the unified phenomena, so I will write up the ritual in the totality that I *now* perceive it (I may be leaving out a lot which I do not yet perceive, but it is complete to this date).

The basic ritual was to have been taken directly from the Book of Maat, but modified for two people, i.e., each of us opening a separate, but identical, vortex, with each of us acting as a sexual helper (VIII°) for the other. The first change I made was to allow me to place air to North & Earth to East so the attributions fit in with the astral & physi-

An Introductory Note of Explanation

cal temple with which I have been working for several years. This non-standard temple is based on some of Crowley's rituals & further enhanced by some transmissions I have had regarding modification of the tetragrammaton formula for use in this æon. Briefly, rather than YHVH=26, the new formula is HNTV=70.

H=North=Air=Nuit=MidnightBlue
N=West=Water=Babalon=Cyan(blue-green);
T(teth)=South= Fire=Hadit=Red;
V=East=Earth=Therion=Yellow-Orange.

The 'standard' temple arrangement can be thought of as 'being located' at Yesod. Earth=Malkuth below (N) of center with Fire=Tiphareth above (S) with Air=Hod to left (E) and Water=Netzach to right (W). In my temple arrangement, the temple is 'located' just above Tiphareth so that Earth=Malkuth is below (E) with Daath=Water above (W) while Chesed=Air is to Right (N) and Gebburah=Fire is to Left (S). Soror 0-33/33 works the traditional temple while I work the HNTV temple, so the following ritual takes place on both sides of Tiphareth simultaneously. In many ways this ritual parallels the basic ritual in Book of Maat.

1. Double Vortex (i.e., a vortex opening into the future in the æon of Maat & a vortex opening back into the genetic memory of the Forgotten Ones) was opened for better balance of energy transfer & for a better point of balance (i.e., fulcrum) from which to affect/effect change. For a discussion of the nature of vortices, see appended transmissions
2. IX° replaced VIII°
3. Temple mirror was placed on floor beneath cauldron to act as gateway for visible manifestations through vortices in future operations (nothing yet to report in this area of endeavor).

Temple was laid out as in figure #1. 0-33/33 initiated the δ end of the vortex from the æon of Maat, moving the

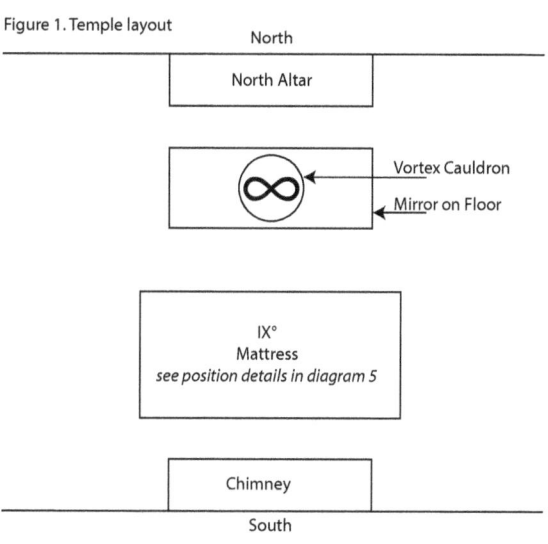

Figure 1. Temple layout

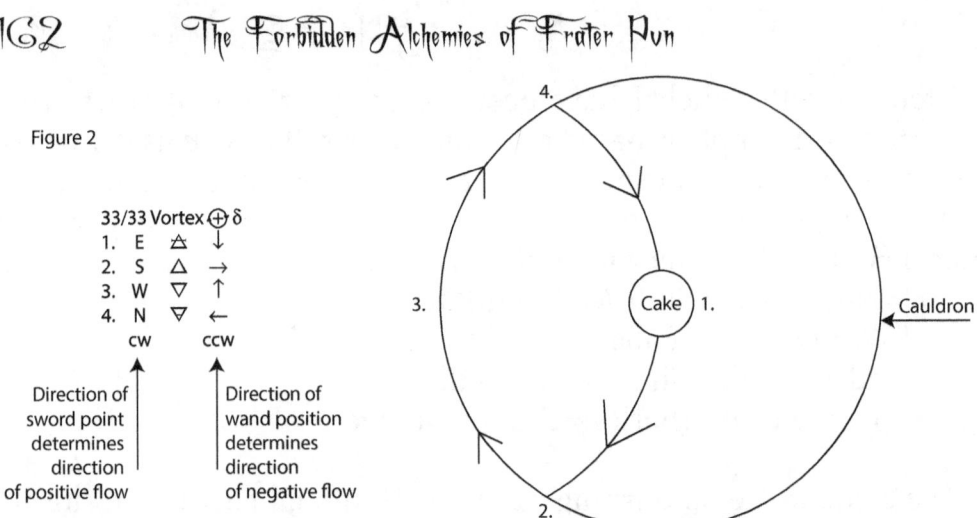

Figure 2

sword/wand cw (clockwise=deosil) around the west half of the cauldron (see figure #2). 690 then 'picked up the vortex as it rounded back to the cake of light (eastern point of 0-33/33's vortex) and initiated the λ end of the vortex extending to the Forgotten Ones, moving the sword/wand ccw (counter-clockwise=widdershins) around the east half of the cauldron (see figure #3). It should be noted that although the wand/sword combination moves cw for a δ vortex, the wand is spinning ccw & although the wand/sword combination moves ccw for a λ vortex, the wand is spinning cw. This double spin of each single vortex, is necessitated by the nature of the vortex, which is bipolar & may be represented as a double ended cone (see figure #9).

The double vortex readily & easily stabilized within the cauldron. The two allotropic forms depicted in figure #4 can be better appreciated by remembering that each vortex is a double cone (figure #9). Positive Energy flows cw & outward of a δ vortex & is drawn ccw

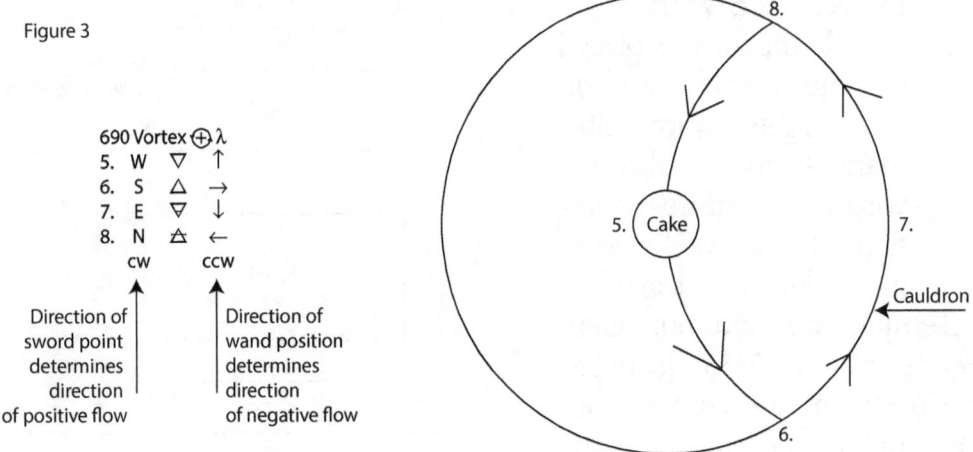

Figure 3

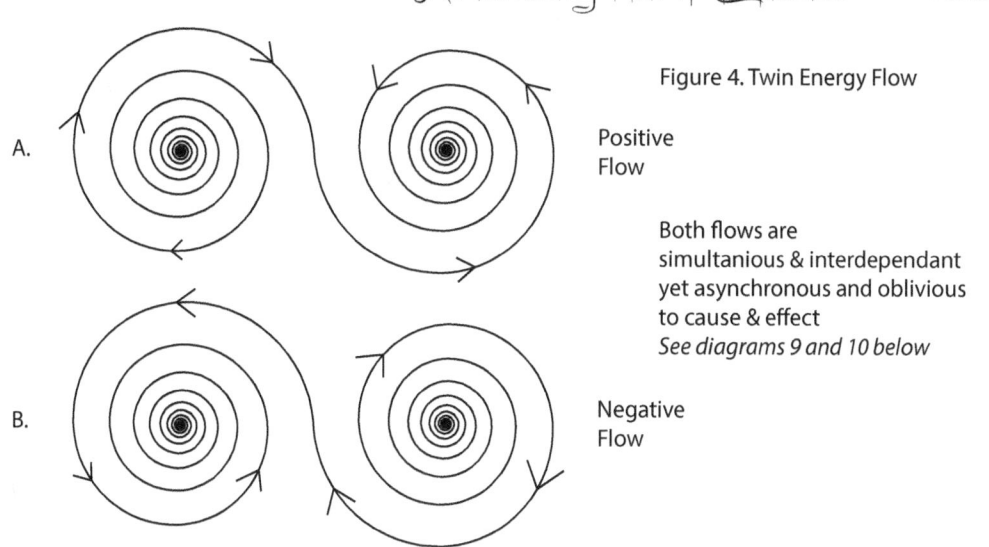

Figure 4. Twin Energy Flow

A. Positive Flow

Both flows are simultanious & interdependant yet asynchronous and oblivious to cause & effect
See diagrams 9 and 10 below

B. Negative Flow

inward to a λ vortex, while Negative energy flows cw out of a λ vortex and is drawn ccw inward to a δ vortex. I do not yet have a good 'handle' on positive & negative energies, except to say that orgone, sex drive, and the 'life force' are positive energies. Negative energy may be the will to die, the power of decay, etc., but I am not very certain about this yet.

In reality the δ (delta=dextro-rotary) vortex and the λ (lambda = levulo-rotary) vortex are the two 'ends' of a tunnel through time. The λ vortex is the 'future end' or up-time end of a vortex, while the δ vortex is the 'past end' or down-time end of a vortex. At one point in time (i.e., 'now'), you can't have both the δ and λ ends of the 'same' vortex, but you can (& should!) have an equal number of δ and λ vortices so the summation balances (see transmissions).

Now that the vortices were stabilized within the cauldron, they needed to be energized. IX° proceeded as follows:

The dance of foreplay was face to face in the sitting/kneeling position. The flow of forces around the auric envelopes was synchronized, the auras merged & the auric film between 0-33/33 and 690 was dissolved. The force field density was then concentrated by means of conductive induction with 690 on bottom. Motion was restricted to vertical movements in order to keep the field being generated in the horizontal plane (plane of mirror & plane of initiated vortex).

When the vortices were individually charged, 690 deposited elixir within the concurbit (chalice vivae) and inter-vortex flow was initi-

Figure 5. Position to charge Double Vortex
a) to build force field density

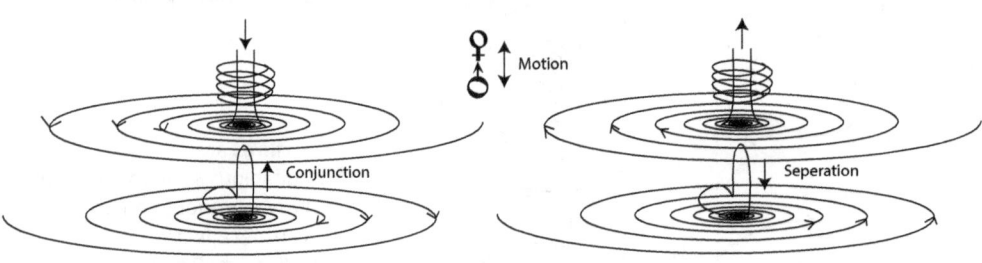

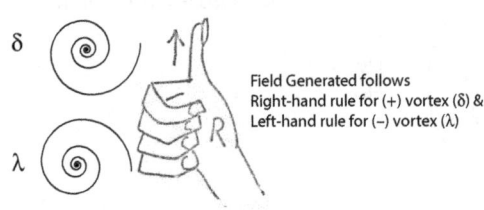

Field Generated follows
Right-hand rule for (+) vortex (δ) &
Left-hand rule for (−) vortex (λ)

Figure 5b. To initiate inter-vortex flow

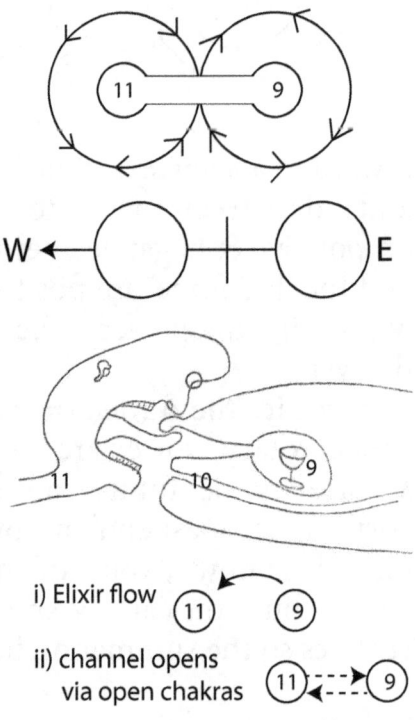

i) Elixir flow

ii) channel opens
via open chakras

iii) Stable standing wave forms

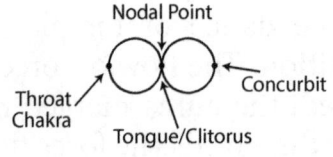

$11 + 9 = 20$, i.e., $2=0!$
(Insight channeled by 33/33)

ated via cunnilingus. See figures #5a & b for theoretical models (based on channelings) for what was going-on during these operations.

After 0-33/33 climaxed, the twice-charged elixir was transferred to the single chalice by using both of our wands. Each of us used elixir/wine charged sword to draw upon the stabilized vortex, expanding it outward to fill the room (universe). The point of tangency where the vortices met was the Cake of Light (see figure #6).

Cake & wine was consumed, temple closed, and mirror cleaned/re-hung on West wall. Each of us now wears or carries a magick vortex ring which were both within the chalice during the operation. When the ring is not being worn, the vortex is 'at rest' circulating 'empty' through the metal of the ring. When the ring is put on a finger, the vortex becomes congruent with the etheric envelope of the magickian, unless it is willed otherwise.

An Introductory Note of Explanation 165

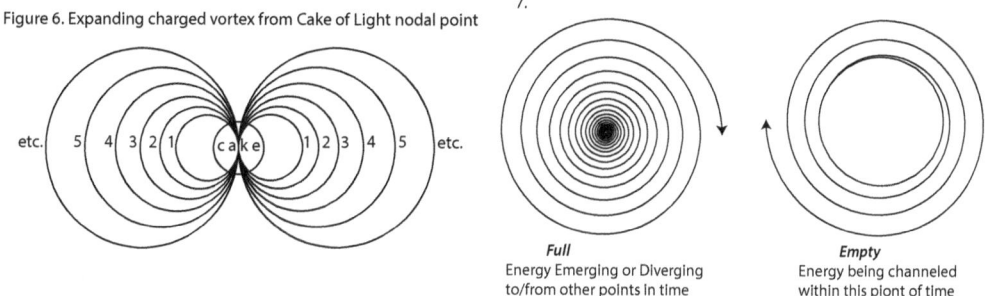

Figure 6. Expanding charged vortex from Cake of Light nodal point

7.

Full
Energy Emerging or Diverging to/from other points in time

Empty
Energy being channeled within this piont of time

Here are some notes on the structure & use of vortices gleaned via conversations with Adria, the Forgotten One, Hga, and others whom I do not yet know.

A vortex may be either full or empty. A full vortex is transferring energy in or out of the core of the vortex (i.e., energy travels through time). An empty vortex is either 'just idling' (as when the ring is not being worn by the magickian) or when the vortex is being used to transfer energy rather than to transmit energy through time. See figure #7.

Figure #8 is a hypothetical example of a schematic diagram of a group ritual in which some vortices are full, some are empty, some are generating, while others are moving the energy within the circle & one is focusing the energy to a particular 'goal' outside the circle. Figure #8 is not very inspired & while it was intended to throw light upon the concepts of full & empty, it may lead to greater confusion. Ignore it if it seems confusing.

Figure #9 shows a typical vortex. Regions marked A & B are not the same as the letters in figure #8. Region A is the region of positive energy & region B is the region of negative energy. When I first channeled these diagrams I had tried to equate positive energy with Yang & negative energy with Yin, but I am more inclined to look on Positive Energy=Dayside & Negative Energy=Nightside (Eros & Thanatos??).

Figure #10 shows that the 'two ends' of the cone need not be equal. For a solar working (i.e., when the person using the vortex is acting in a solar way) the δ vortex is more potent in region A while the λ vortex is more potent in Region B. The exact opposite is true in the lunar mode. This information allows the magickian (or group of magickians) to determine which vortex (δ or λ) to use in a particular phase of a ritual and 'which end' (A or B) of the vortex to 'charge' in order to bring about the desired result. The geometry should be worked-

Figure 8

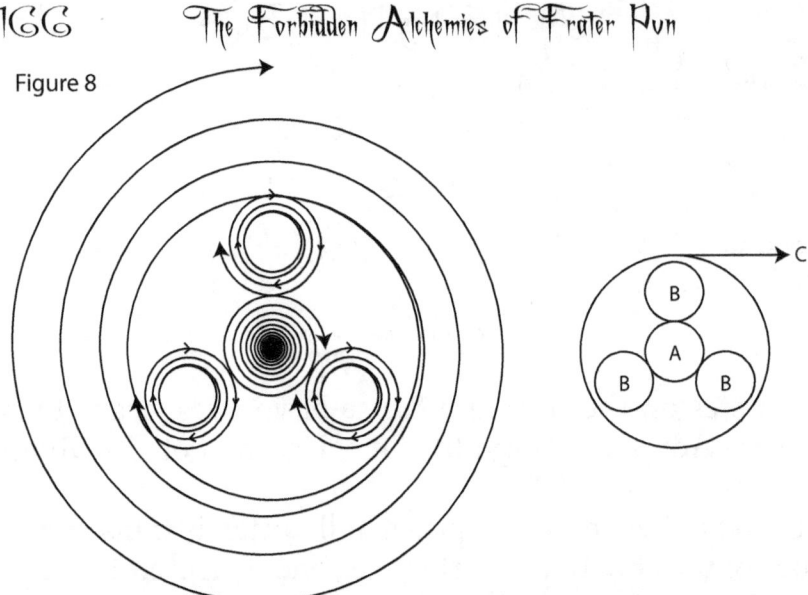

A—Negative (widdershins, ccw = negative) vortex generating energy from other points of time/space
B—Positive (deosil, ccw = positive) vortices transferring energy from A→C within the same point of time/space
C—Positive vortex directing/focusing/channeling energy generated by A & transferred/refined by B

Type B vortex may be full or empty
Type A vortext must be full, unless it contains another type A vortex
Type C vortex must be empty

Figure 9. Typical Vortex Sections

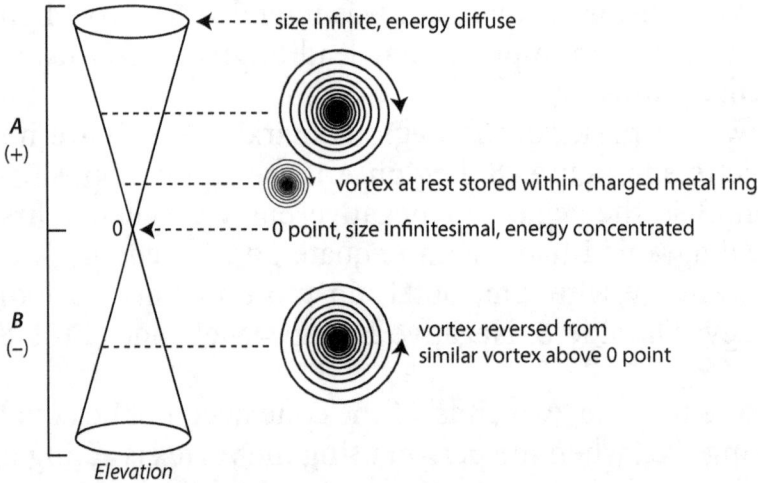

A: (+) Positive end of cone
   δ vortex has outward flow, cw
   λ vortex has inward flow, ccw

B: (−) Negative end of cone
   δ vortex has inward flow, ccw
   λ vortex has outward flow, cw

Figure 10. Vortices Transferring Energy

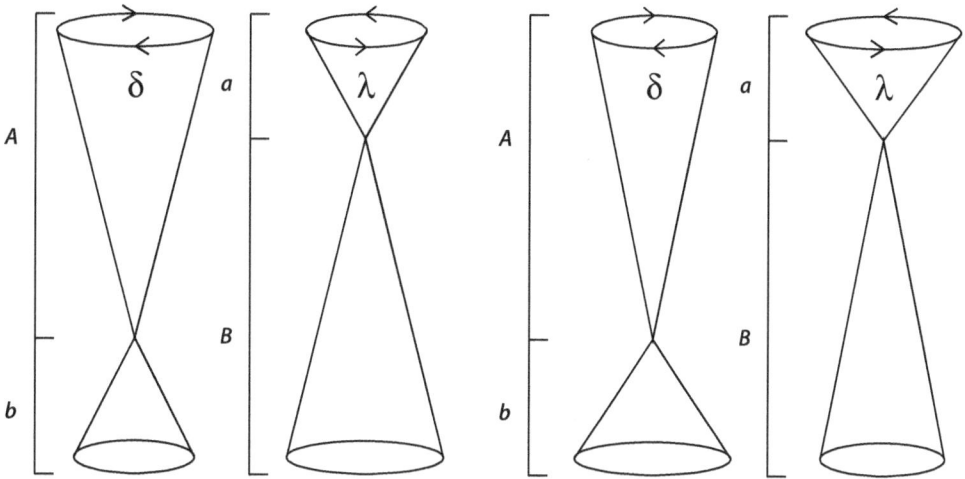

Solar Mode
δ—*A* transfers/generates/recieves more energy than *b*
λ—*B* transfers/generates/recieves more energy than *a*

Lunar Mode
Energy transfer functions are similar, but inverted in magnitude
δ—*B* > *a*
λ—*A* > *b*

out in schematic form on paper, then applied to the ritual at hand via imaginative means & earthed (where possible) via dance or mudra &/or choosing the appropriate sexual geometries. By having access to a double vortex, energy can be instantly transferred (without loss) to the mirror image vortex (i.e., δ to λ, or λ to δ) as the complexities of the rite dictate. For sexual operations with more than one person, the entire orgasmic energy can be shifted back & forth between partners, thus allowing multiple orgasms without any diminution of sex drive & charging-up both sets of vortices for use elsewhere in the ritual.

In figure #11 I have depicted some of the easiest modes of energy transfer in a working using two vortices (i.e., two people with control over their vortex). Since I channeled those rules of energy transfer, I have been given yet another rule for using two of the same kind of vortex which requires more sophistication, which I have labeled figure #11c, even though it is an addendum to both 11a & 11b.

The diagrams are fairly self-explanatory, but there are a few points I would like to point-out. Figure #11aδa shows a very common mode of working based upon 'role playing' & the concepts of 'balance' (so-called) as practiced in much of the past æon & into this æon.

It is pertinent to male & female homosexual workings as well as to

Figure 11. Rules of Energy Transfer for Workings of Two Vortices
a) Two of the same kind of vortices

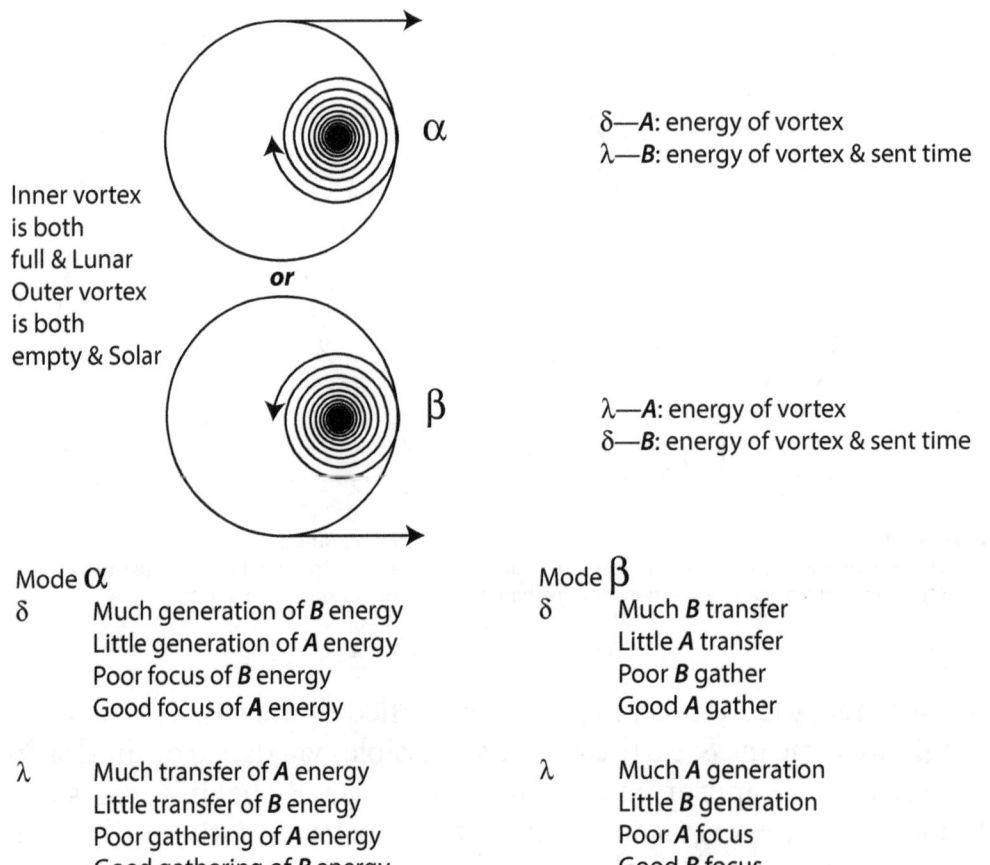

Inner vortex is both full & Lunar
Outer vortex is both empty & Solar

δ—**A**: energy of vortex
λ—**B**: energy of vortex & sent time

λ—**A**: energy of vortex
δ—**B**: energy of vortex & sent time

Mode α
δ   Much generation of **B** energy
     Little generation of **A** energy
     Poor focus of **B** energy
     Good focus of **A** energy

λ   Much transfer of **A** energy
     Little transfer of **B** energy
     Poor gathering of **A** energy
     Good gathering of **B** energy

Mode β
δ   Much **B** transfer
     Little **A** transfer
     Poor **B** gather
     Good **A** gather

λ   Much **A** generation
     Little **B** generation
     Poor **A** focus
     Good **B** focus

heterosexual workings. The lunar partner is unable to generate type A energy nearly as fast as the solar partner can focus/use it. This leads to depletion of the lunar partner. Where solar/lunar roles are rigid & unchanging (butch & fem) this constant depletion of the lunar partner can lead to complete 'burn-out' of the lunar partner. Crowley & his various scarlet women are a prime example of this formula, but it must be said that Crowley did attempt to even the energy flow via role reversal, but in those operations (such as the Cephalodian Working) he was trying to gain inspiration from the vortex (i.e., focus inward) so he unconsciously used mode 11aδβ in which the Scarlet Woman (&/or other male assistants) were in the solar mode while Crowley was in the lunar mode. For type B energies, this meant that since Crowley could transfer more than they could gather, his partner(s) were still depleted, while for type A energies his partners could gather more than he could

Figure 11. Rules of Energy Transfer for Workings of Two Vortices
b) Two different kinds of vortices

Either vortex may be in Solar or Lunar mode (as required for opus) independent of other vortex

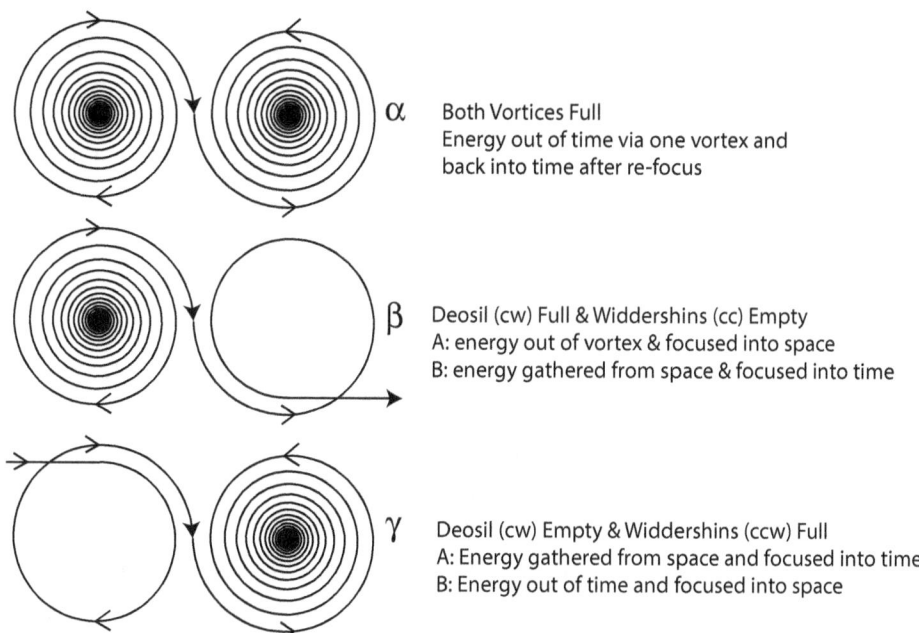

α Both Vortices Full
Energy out of time via one vortex and
back into time after re-focus

β Deosil (cw) Full & Widdershins (cc) Empty
A: energy out of vortex & focused into space
B: energy gathered from space & focused into time

γ Deosil (cw) Empty & Widdershins (ccw) Full
A: Energy gathered from space and focused into time
B: Energy out of time and focused into space

transfer, so Crowley became 'bloated' with these types of energies. I.e., when dealing with a homogeneous group of vortices (all δ or all λ) there is danger unless role playing is completely random.

But with more conscious control over the two vortices, it is possible to merge them as in 11cα. Each partner generates to full ability & each partner focuses to full ability. There is no drain & no bloating. Group consecration of a talisman in which the point of consciousness for each individual leaves the body & becomes 'one' with the talisman is such a mode of operation. Needless to say, this requires safeguards as the consciousness/vortex/soul is no longer within the body. The example which comes to mind is Benediction at a catholic High Mass in which the whole congregation merges with the adored 'Body of Christ' (i.e., cake of light) amidst pomp and circumstance, drugged smoke (incense), and glorious music. Consciousness is then severed by a cessation of music & responsive chanting of people/priest which requires full concentration (i.e., soul back into body). The charged Host is then allowed to radiate energy over time within the sanctuary. Thus the people have 'fed' the vortex of the Host & the slow gradual 'spin-off' energies are used to heal those who hang-around the shrine. But don't let my long complex example lead anyone to believe that the merged vortex is simply an old-æon technique. It is viable for any group working in which 'something' must be 'charged' with the combined will/force/energy.

Figure 11cβ shows the most 'novel' use of a vortex which has yet been channeled to me. In all of the other techniques, a lot of care was taken so that all interactions between/among vortices, wherever two vortices touched or overlapped, the 'lines of force' would be going in the same direction (i.e., the tangential forces would be identical so that energy would transfer without having to change direction). Up until I channeled this last mode of operation, I had been under the impression that lines of force which met from opposite directions would cancel each other out, $(+1) + (-1) = 0$, but now I see that there is more to energy than simple vortex energy.

By referring to figure 5a, it can be shown that a linear force or motion (on the physical plane, i.e., Malkuth) was capable of filling or charging a vortex. Figure 11cβ is simply the reverse of that process. By situating two vortices so that their energies 'clash', energy is drawn out of the vortex at right angles to the plane of interaction of the two vortices. I believe that type A energy follows the right hand rule & type B energy follows the left hand rule, but some experimentation

Figure 11. Rules of Energy Transfer for Workings of Two Vortices
c) Advanced Vortex Techniques

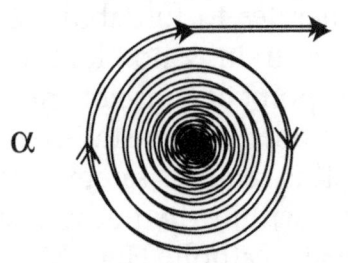

α

Two (or more) same kind of vortex
Vortex centered on a common point,
rather then centered within individual bodies

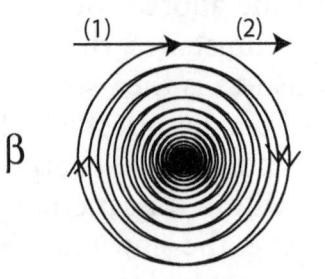

β

Two (or more) of mixed δ & λ vorticies
centered on a common point.
Lines of energy cross at many points.
Almost no energy transfer in usual manner.
However, whenever two lines of energy transfer cross,
the energy is canceled out and a force perpendicular
to the plane of crossing is generated (i.e., up out of
plane or into plane) depending on 'charge'.
I.e., use right hand rule for **A** energy
and left hand rule for **B** energy.

will have to be done to verify this last point as the channeling was unclear. The importance of this last mode of operation cannot be overstated, for it allows the magickians to influence Malkuth, directly with a magickal force capable of infinitesimal focus &/or infinite magnitude (depending upon the skills & the intent of the magickians). This mode of operation could well be the basis of such well known psi phenomena as bending spoons, making objects levitate, & (more significantly) of genetic manipulation at the point of orgasmic conception. Genetic manipulation would require no conscious knowledge of genetic mapping once the vortex link with the æon of Maat has been established, since the necessary information could easily be channeled during the opus (information 'travels' on a vortex energy wave like the program travels on a radio carrier wave). In fact, such minute information would be useless to relay beforehand as it could be understood by so few, and the weighty texts which could be written on the subject would only scare-away the very people who are best equipped to use the technique. Intellectual dissection of these techniques is of Hod while using these techniques pertains to the entire of the middle pillar, but full understanding is not to be found on this side of the abyss.

Notes:

a) Solar versus Lunar mode invoked by active versus passive role and not by sex.

b) Deosil (cw) versus Widdershins (ccw) mode is "set" at opening of vortex & may be deosil, widdershins, or convertible (i.e., ambi-rotational)

c) Type **A** energy is (perhaps) Dayside energy.

Type **B** energy is (perhaps) Nightside energy.

For workings of three or more vortices

i) All same kind (deosil or widdershins)—only one solar vortex, all of the rest are lunar, except for overlap as diagram 11 cα

ii) Various deosil &/or widdershins—more then one solar permitted, depending on orientation.

M 2 October,1979ev, 25 Khoiak,4748
The last entry (18 pages) was typed over several days even though there is only a single date heading at the beginning of the entry. It seemed pointless to breakup an already complex narrative with a

break every time I had to go & do something else.

The following entry is composed from notes channeled last Thursday during work & added to that same evening while drinking a chocolate milk shake at the Unideli.

The illustration below may have some superficial resemblance to the illustrations of the A & B regions of a vortex from the previous entry, but this is not the case. At each of the 'points' of time at which the vortex is 'focused' (i.e., at an λ end or a δ end of a vortex), there exists a double-ended cone of regions A & B as illustrated in the previous entry. At areas between the λ and δ points, the A/B vortex is 'diffuse' and not readily accessible, except by some sort of focusing device such as a pyramid. But the focus points are not fixed in time, and travel with the magickian &/or temple so that a vortex, once opened, will remain open until closed.

Referring to figures on the next page, this is the transmission as I received it. δ Vortex can be maintained stable without effort by the people at the λ end of time.

λ Vortex is a constant 'draw' of vitality, unless stabilized by close proximity of a δ end of another vortex.

λ Vortex can easily maintained 'alone' by adepts who transmute energy to vitality, but lack of skill &/or vigilance can easily cause a draining of vitality from temple workers &/or the environment into the vortex. This draining effect can be minimized to each individual by constantly bringing 'new' people into the group to share the drain.

Although vitality flow is always δ to λ information flow & prana can be either to λ to δ or δ to λ. So, often it may be desirable or necessary to maintain a vortex even though it drains vitality. However, in the long run. the only practical ways to maintain the end of a vortex are by stabilization via the close proximity of the end of another vortex, or via massive human sacrifice (either the swift sacrifice of murder/suicide or the slow sacrifice of vampirizing the life forces). (see end note #1 below)

Maintenance of the δ end of a vortex alone will not drain-off vitality, but by not 'stabilizing' the δ end of the vortex via close proximity with the λ end of another vortex, this mode of operation will drain more vitality from the up-time (λ) end of the vortex than is really necessary.

As very little of this vitality is usable at the δ end of the vortex, such practice serves no good purpose, (see endnote #2 below).

By setting up the λ end of a vortex within the same matrix (or field

An Introductory Note of Explanation 173

of influence) as the δ end of another vortex:
- The vitality drain on the 'future' (i.e., up-time in the Æon of Maat) is minimized.
- The 'future' gains access to the 'far past' (i.e., the Forgotten Æons) via the nodal point in the 'present' without any extra expenditure of vitality.
- There is no vitality drain on the 'present', whatsoever, in fact, vitality is slightly increased.

Vitality drain on the λ end of the vortex can be somewhat minimized if the people at the δ end of the vortex voluntarily & consciously put vitality into their end of the vortex (i.e., send it up-time), but the δ end of the vortex will still have to bear the brunt of the 'expense' of maintaining the vortex.

Vortices need not be consciously set-up as such. A strong desire (Kama) for a linkage with the past (or future) is often sufficient impetus to instigate vortex rotation through time. Maintenance can likewise be non-conscious. When the λ end of the vortex maintains

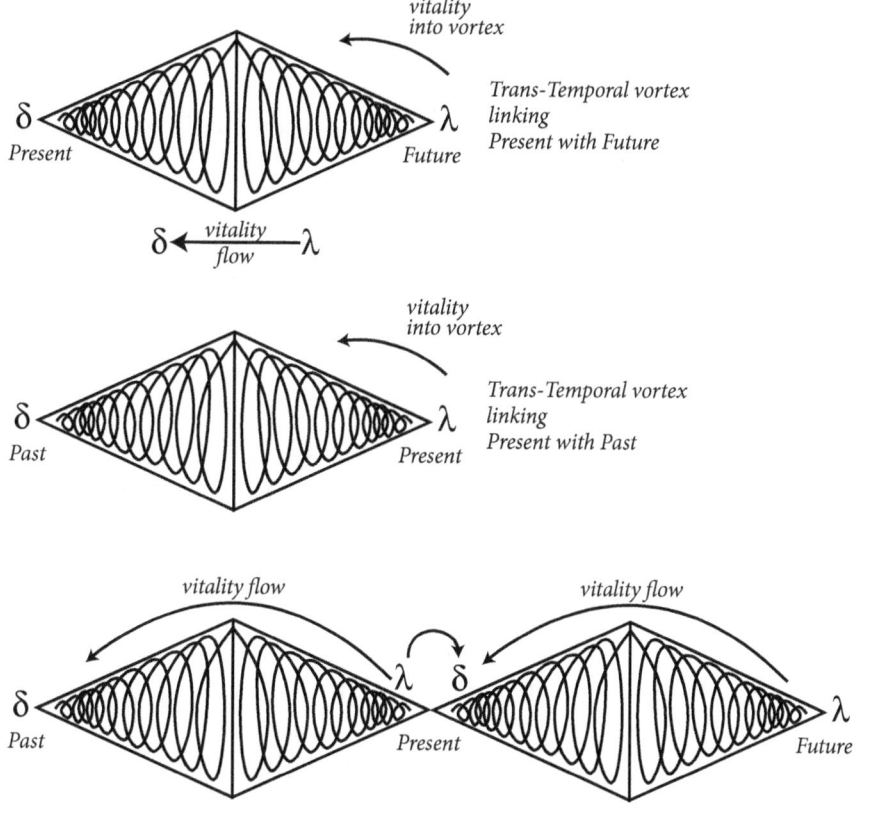

Trans-Temporal double vortex linking with nexus at Present

the flow without conscious volition, the sapping of vitality is most noticeable in a reduction or depletion of sexual energy. Those most closely associated with the vortex will feel the greatest drain, but those persons are also closest to the 2-way flow of information, good feeling, and 'ONE-ness' with the powers coming through the vortex. Such persons become more & more spiritually advanced as they spend more & more time pouring their vitality into the vortex. It is all too easy to look upon their depletion of sexual vitality as an outward symbol of their inner spiritual grace rather than as an unfortunate sickness caused by the instability of their vortex. If this loss of sexual vitality is not reversed, it is usually not long before all having temple rights to that place of worship (i.e., the λ end of the vortex, whether consciously constructed & maintained or begun & maintained out of ignorant accident) will begin to become infected with the madness of low sexual vitality. Thus those persons with strong sexual vitality will come to be viewed as being spiritually inferior. Such attitudes/morals are tragic. By properly stabilizing the matrix/powerzone of the place of worship via two vortices (one to past & one to future), the drain of sexual vitality can be completely eliminated, thus allowing spirituality & sexuality to grow hand in hand, nurturing one another & allowing for a steady grown in the Powerzone though the influx of new people & growth/healing of those already involved. It is then possible to direct the sexual vitality (not-through abstinence but through sacred orgasmic rituals) to facilitate healing, protect the powerzone from enemies, and to correct the spiritual/sexual imbalances of the world.

The vortex into the Æon of Maat (i.e., setting up the that vortex 'now') is a matter of utter simplicity since the Maatians have a strong conscious Will to assist the evolution of planetary consciousness at this point of time (i.e., now at the beginning of the Æon of Horus); our present is a crucial point in their past & if we blow it, they are lost.

A viable vortex into the past (i.e., setting up the λ end of that vortex 'now') is a different matter altogether. Setting up a vortex between 'now' and the Æon of Osiris would be extremely dangerous as the end of their æon impinges on 'now' in a very non-constructive way (i.e., the political & religious philosophies, bigotries, & wrong-thinking of every conceivable kind spawned in the mis-begotten & warped Æon of Osiris did not peaceably 'die' or transform itself in 1904—the zombies of Christianity, Capitalism, & Communism stalk the land feeding on the flesh of the children of the Æon of Horus). Careless linkages with the Aeon of Osiris could warp the present æon & cause a continuance of the abuses of twisted patriarchy to continue for another 2000 years.

A viable vortex from 'now' into the Æon of Isis is less dangerous because women are no longer 'primed' to accept the role of Matriarch the way that men are still 'primed' to accept the role of Patriarch. The Æon of Osiris has burned-away the matriarchal abilities of most women. To say that such genetic purging was brutal would be a gross understatement, but evolution is never guided by kindness. Given another 2000 years, men will likewise be purged of patriarchal abilities, but at this stage of the æon, men can still be very dangerous. The Æon of Isis can soothe & heal those broken by the last 2000 years, but as the Age of Isis can never return, more generalized strengths & knowledges must be sought elsewhen.

However, for most seekers into the past, there is a strong barrier to trans-temporal vortices at the onset of the Æon of Isis. This blockage was consciously & maliciously instituted during the Eden captivity at which time the human consciousness was held prisoner by the elder gods. Such imprisonment was not only a 'captivity' in the mundane sense (i.e., imprisoned in Eden) but non-physical barriers were erected to prevent any influences (i.e., vortex energy/vitality) from reaching them from their past or future. When the beings from Sothis freed the human consciousness, the barrier was broken & the Æon of Isis began, but the barrier itself could not be eradicated without negating the captivity itself (which the beings from Sothis were unwilling or unable to do). (for more details on the captivity itself, see Cincy Journal #3 as well as my Channeling on the captivity which I received a few months after the rough notes for this entry were written).[1]

But this barrier has two 'holes'. The easiest hole to negotiate is via the personal genetic memory of each of us. Within our heritage of DNA lies all of our biological past, stretching in an un-interrupted chain from our biological parents back through the Eden captivity to the beginnings of life itself. That portion of the cellular memory which lies 'past' of Eden is known as the Forgotten Ones (i.e., those memories blocked or forgotten during the Eden captivity). The most straightforward method of contact with these memories is via ritual (such as the Forgotten Ones in *Cincinnati Journal of Ceremonial Magick* #2 & 3), but such a formulation of the λ end of such a vortex is distinctly personal. That is to say, while the δ end of the vortex into the Æon of

---
1 Herein—*Ed.*

Maat may be used freely by all in the powerzone with temple rights, the λ end of the vortex to the Forgotten Ones may only be used by those who formulate it, since the link is personal genetic memory. The matter is further complicated by the nature of the Forgotten Ones themselves, Cooperation is an alien & repugnant concept to them so that having a plethora of opened & operable Forgotten One vortices within a unified powerzone may become extremely difficult to balance. Such vortices are also short-lived as they 'fold-up' upon the death of the physical body of the person who opened them.

The other 'hole' in the Eden barrier lies within the abyss. No barrier can exist for those with temple rights to Nightside, since the chaos of the abyss is antithetical to the formation of structure of a barrier (there are barriers sealing off dayside from night side, but those with temple rights to nightside have already dealt with these barriers). A vortex from 'now' to the Forgotten Ones via the abyss would be as 'general' as the vortex to the Æon of Maat & would remain stable with the Maatian vortex upon the death of the people who opened the vortex. However, to open such a vortex requires much power, handled with the sure hand of one who is not only an initiate but an adept. It is therefore more simple to open the personal vortex through genetic memory, link it to the powerzone's δ vortex gateway for stabilization of both & work with the double vortex to gain a 'feel' for working with angular transfers of power. Then, as success breeds certainty, the increased sexual vigor can be used to explore nightside & seek the door which open out on the pre-Eden landscape/seascape. There formulate a temple & work with the pre-hominid races in the creation of the human race. This done, the. vortex will remain open & be accessible to all those who pass the gaze of Samael.

Having access to a double vortex & having the skills needed to play λ against δ (& vice versa) grants the Magus the privilege of operating with impunity. Vast energies may be manipulated with ease & even though the transfer of energy through a given point of the time/space continuum be astronomical, from the perspective of the operational pivot of the double vortex, there is no net change in energy, hence, no 'effort' is needed to perform Herculean tasks. The pivot of the double vortex is the crux of contradiction. Either/Or becomes meaningless as each & every action contains (within itself) its own contradiction. $(+1) + (-1) = 0$, yet this 0 is capable of adding to or detracting from any positive or negative value in the universe, while remain-

ing unchanged in any way. The violation of the laws of conservation of mass & energy are only apparent since these laws are incapable (as formulated by 20th century scientists) of encompassing reactions which surge backwards & forward through time itself. An indication of 20th century science's failure to grasp vortex phenomena may be gleaned from looking at the 3 laws of thermodynamics, which may be expressed in layperson's terms thusly:
1. You can't win.
2. You can't even break even.
3. You must play the game.

These three laws came from experimental observation of energy flow. They are a westerner's scientific verification of Buddhist despondency. Another observation of the same phenomena would be interpreted slightly differently to one with a different perspective (i.e., outside of the timestream). Energy tends to flow from future to past as or as time flows forward, energy tends to have a higher inertia & therefore becomes concentrated in the past.

Anyone who has ever tried to maintain the λ end of an unstabilized vortex will attest to this irresistible flow of energy into the past. But a double vortex stabilizes this condition & even allows one to manipulate more energy than can possibly 'exist' at any given moment of time. Thus the 3 laws of thermodynamics might be more properly phrased:
1. From the perspective or ordinary mortals, the magus always appears to win.
2. From the perspective of the magus at the nexus of the double vortex, the magus always breaks even.
3. The magus continues to play the game until all become adepts.

Thus the Magus appears all powerful, but from his/her position at the crux of power, s/he knows that nothing is ever gained or lost, save through sloppy technique. The magus (like the mathematician) appreciates that the simplest & most straightforward solutions are the most elegant & that all true answers are found within the proper formulation of the questions themselves.

ENDNOTES

#1. Human sacrifice provided the vital force to maintain the vortex connecting Atlantis with the civilization of the Mayans & the Aztecs. At the cultural/religious/scientific peak of these two civilizations, hundreds of slaves & captives were slaughtered at every religious festival. Between these sacrifices the vitality was drawn from the civilizations at the λ end of the vortex, thus eroding them from within even before the Spaniards arrived in the new world to administer the kiss of death. Had these cultures been able to formulate a vortex with their own future, thus stabilizing their λ portal with a λ portal, the last six centuries leading up to the Æon of Horus would have been very different.

While the overall purpose of the Feast of the Hive (see Cincy Journal #3) remains as incomprehensible to most of us at the present moment of time as patriarchal machinations would be to a commoner in the AEON of Isis, the voluntarily released vitality would seem to serve the same purpose as the involuntary slaughter of the Aztecs. The priesthood of Maat is at the λ end of our λ vortex & they have placed a very high priority on maintaining a vortex to us through the up-coming æon.

#2. While most of this vitality is unavailable at the λ end of a vortex, some vitality does 'seep-through'.

This seepage causes an increase in sex-drive, a decrease in the minimum necessary amount of sleep, an ability to abuse drugs without long-term bad effects, and an ability to manipulate the genetic code at will.

δ end of vortices may easily become places of debauch as well as spiritual growth. Vampires are easily attracted to such unguarded powerzones, so care should be exercised by those adepts in charge of the δ end of a vortex of power. A vortex/powerzone does not protect itself from abuse, nor is it guarded by those up-time at the other end of the vortex—it is the sole responsibility of the adepts in charge of the δ portal to the vortex to see to it that the vortex remains protected. Spin-off vitality which seeps through the powerzone must be utilized to its fullest & not wasted on those who are not doing their will. Those who are not actively upon the magickal path must be purged from the powerzone & driven-away from the nexus of the vortex. If they refuse to leave, they must be killed. In such high-energy locations (i.e., the nexus of a trans-temporal vortex) there is no excuse for anyone to draw the energy of another away from creative endeavors. Constant seeking of approval &/or guidance from the adepts in charge; inability to 'get-it-together on Malkuth'; an unquenchable thirst for drugs (coupled with a barrenness of magickal endeavor); and behavior which has the effect of dividing the powerzone over petty issues are all warning signs that the spin-off vitality is being mis-used by those not doing their Will. Such abuses not only prevent the powerzone from carrying out its appointed tasks but increase the amount of vitality which the λ end of the vortex must continually supply 'up-time' in the Æon of Maat. How long the λ end of the vortex would be willing to 'host' such blood-sucking is hard to predict, but if a vortex has to be closed-down because the adepts at the down-time portal are not doing their job of overseeing their powerzone, the karmic debt (which is incredibly high) is borne not only by the vampires themselves, but by the adepts who violated their own True Will by refusing to exercise their power & duty as custodians of the vortex. Let all who have a vortex be warned.

Spacemarks

extracted from Constellations *by YZ (Sam Webster)*
as edited/amended by LA-BAJ-AL (Bill Siebert)

…thus I wish to begin the Spacemarks project. I do not hope to have fully explained the theory behind it in the few short pages devoted to this, nor do I think that the following methodology is in any way complete or inflexible. Yet, I believe this is not at all important as I feel that due to the organic nature of this project it will very quickly get beyond my personal sphere and develope on its own.

The Formula, in accordance with that of the Aeon, is *Sexual* in nature. This is *essential*, as sexual activity occurs in all of the worlds of the world simultaneously. Also, even as orgasm creates & powers Stars formed in the Metaphysic, a physical plane essence is also produced. This physical essence, or *kala*, is the living embodiment of the bud-Will of the magickians who came together to give it life.

The Method

The Method is, generally, as follows: Three initiates should meet in a properly consecrated space and join in love, yea! with joy and beauty and skill therein. By their Art may the initiates know themselves as pure expressions of Integrity, Stars, neither one nor many, and in their conjuring let a Symbol be born forth. It may be word or glyph or both or aught else communicable. The Kalas shall be collected and kneaded into clay with, perhaps, a gemstone or crystal placed therein. If entheogenic sacrament be used in this rite, let some of it, too, be mixed therein. This clay is then formed into the shape of the Minimum System or Tetrahedron. When dried this tetrahedron shall be painted &/or inscribed and adorned with the Symbol earlier produced, and, at will, the seals/sigils/glyphs of the participants. When this is at last done, let the Spirit thus formed be conjured forth and given the charge to be this *Spacemark*, and then let the tetrahedron be buried deep in the bosom of the earth, where it will lay undisturbed forever.

Let the initiates take note of the time, the place, and the symbol of the Spacemark they have created and then move on. Let them join with others and form Marks in this manner linked together through themselves. With those who have shared in this communion should the Times Places and Symbols of other Space marks be shared, so that this Work of Art shall be magnified synergistically throughout Time/Space/Alternity.

In Comment and Explanation

I suggest three participants so as to put this working firmly under Thelemic Law, that of love under will, and thus outside the world of ordinary socio-sexual interaction—thus more firmly in the realm of *Magick*.

However, it is perhaps more relevant that the triad or triangle is the minimum structure that can maintain itself. In other words, a triangle is self-regenerating, thus self sustaining.

Dyads and monads (and all others) can also establish Spacemarks thru XI°, IX°, & VIII° formulae as there need not be any real limitations in this System, so long as the self-regenerating trigonal structure is maintained.

The shape of the Tetrahedron is employed as it is the minimum enclosed space, system or container. The triangle, upon study will reveal itself as, in fact, a minium spiral—as lines can not interpenetrate. Thus the triangle is a glyph and diagram of the nature of a particularly constructed force in motion. As the Tetrahedron is a container bound on all faces by mighty seals, the triangularly generated force of the Kalas burns within it as a Star emitting a signal or radiance of a particular type or *frequency*.

This System comes to full power when a minimum set of four tetrahedrons have been planted. Through the simple fact of their existence the four Spacemarks will amass energy within the System they describe, making more power available for the workings of the participants.

This aspect of this working is similar to the standing stones project in northern Europe and the earth mound projects of the North American natives as well as many other religious *Kibblahs*, or power stations or any tapping of laylines or dragon currents.

Spacemarks have a profound navigational aspect. Each of them individually, & the network together, act as beacons to permit accurate physical & trans-Physical magickal relocation. Each Spacemark can be tuned individually by its creators (& by those generations of users which follow) as a specific 'thumper' to work synergistically with those energies & individuals who are already attuned with those who set the thumper. The network of Spacemarks, as well as each Spacemark individually, will help to awaken/attune nascent magickal energy in the world at large, as well as within each Powerzone. The vibrations of the Spacemarks project will assist those seekers who are ready to begin the Great Work in earnest. Thumpers will seed the dreams of those who are seeking magickal community & assist them to formulate their dreams into seed realities.

As seekers become adept at focusing their imagination into their waking life, they will then be able to locate the source of the thumper—even if be around the world from them. These will then be drawn to that thumper which best suits their Will-&-Path. —Look for them from no expected place, for they may be but new upon the Path, & not yet conversant with the knowledge & symbology with which you programmed your thumper.

One method of communicating the Key Symbol of each Spacemark to other Spacemark participants in other Powerzones is to place that Symbol on a sheet of at cardstock, the size of a Thoth card, such that it can be carried with a set of similar-sized cards. These cards can be made/distributed by the founders of the Spacemark, &/or their appointed agents. Color photos are an excellent medium for distribution of the Key Symbol.[1]

Whenever possible, this card project can be easily expanded into a card for each Mage, Powerzone, and Spacemark bearing for each the appropriate image, panticle, glyph, sigil, or call-sign whereby any participant can communicate with any other participant. The archetype for this project can be found in the Trumps used in Roger Zelazny's Chronicles of Amber books.

For those not already acquainted with the generation of sigils, I append the following as a guide:

A. O. Spare's system of Zos Kia clearly explains the generation & use of sigils and, by extension, Words of Power. According to Zos Kia, a sigil is most powerful if it is newly designed, or be an original use for a traditional design.

If the sigils & Words come from traditional sources, Zos Kia stresses that they be put to an original use. Pre-made sigils, panticles from ancient grimoires, I Ching kua, Tarot cards and talismans of power used by other magickians are good examples of these. But, more powerful than any of these, are sigils created by the magickian hirself,

---

1 See *Magical Calling Cards*, below.

specially for the work at hand.

Those adepts who work the magick of the unconscious, as well as those who have not yet fully integrated their Will and conscious desire with their unconscious impulses, can most easily create sigils by pulling images & ideas for sigils from the depths of the psyche through dreams, automatic writing, and other allied techniques. These drawings can then be combined, edited, simplified, or expanded upon by the adept using hir sense of harmony, balance, & art. In their completed form, these sigils bear no resemblance to conscious desire. Sigils can be generated by writing a sentence that states the desired end, then removing all redundant letters from it. The shapes of the remaining letters are worked into a single form which is stylized until it bears no resemblance to the original sentence and is of such clear line that it may be easily visualized. Essentially, this method emphasizes the non-rational artistic/intuitive faculties.

Alternatively, adepts who work best through conscious use of Will focused thru the rational mind can create sigils thru application of the principles of qabalah, enochian magic, or whatever mythological system(s) seem most in harmony with purpose of the sigil. This method makes heavy use of the rational mind as a tool for creative genius, & is best suited to those who are working to Master the details of the Science of Magick. Words can be generated by gematria, and by other qabalistic and non-qabalistic techniques.

The Formation of the Material Basis

A block of clay about the size of one's fist is placed within the Circle of Operation. The current needed to create the form and physical basis of the spirit is generated by any combination of VIII°, XI°, &/or IX° methods, depending upon the Will of the participants. At orgasm, the Word is spoken, vibrated or screamed and the Kalas produced is/are placed within a hollow made in the clay. The kalas are then kneaded through the clay and moulded into the form of a Tetrahedron. This stage of the working may be supported by the appropriate invocations before, during, &/or after the production of Kalas.

When the clay tetrahedron is dry it should be painted &/or inscribed by each of the participants with symbols and colors appropriate to the nature of the Spacemark created. A panticle, diagram, or 3-D model of the tetrahedron may also be created. It is best if the colors used for the panticle be as flashing as possible.

The Mage then establishes the Palace having placed upon the altar the Tetrahedron of the Spacemark Deva on top of the panticle (it is of use if the Mage had for some time kept this panticle within sight, as during the time when the Tet was drying so that it may gain a magickal charge and impress itself upon the mind of the Mage). The Mage should then affirm hir bond with hir Holy Guardian Angel by such a rite as the Bornless One. All other powers that are drawn upon the Tetrahedron of the Spacemark Deva are invoked by their words and signs or aught else and brought within the Palace.

The Spacemark Deva is, at this point, newly created. It is well to remember that while it is most capable of doing the tasks assigned it, its education & its experience are nill. Further workings will serve to educate the spacemark Deva as to what sort of persons/energies you are working to attract to your Powerzone. Treat your Spacemark Deva with kindness and educate it in that which it needs to do its function best.

The physical tetrahedron is buried within the earth of the Powerzone of those who brought the Spacemark Deva to manifestation. The clay is not fired or glazed, so that over time the clay will slowly diffuse into the soil, & the magickal structure of the Spacemark will become one with the micro-crystaline quartz within the clay of the native soil. Thus the beacon begins as a point of bud-Will, which slowly evolves into an integral part of the ecosystem of Gaia. The essence & locus of the Deva is (at first) confined to the tetrahedron, while it is instructed by its parents & other members of its magickal community. Then (as it matures) the deva is given free-reign of the land over which it has been given dominion, so that it can instruct, guide, & beckon to all who are sympathetic with its native energies.

When its task is concluded, if that ever occurs, you may either re-absorb the energies of the Space-mark Deva back into your selves, or set it free. This latter choice is perhaps the more responsible, as the deva may then begin to ascend the evolutionary chain as a free being, as indeed, you once began.

There is a Metaphysical tenant that explains that all objects are just special case examples of the one true metaphysical object, that is the eternally generalized design principle from which all things are derived. [Although similar in appearances, this thesis works on very different principles from Plato's hypothesis.[2]] The trans-rational or

---

2 Not really—Yz.

poetic corollary is thus that there is only one of any true thing, and although its shadows manifest in myriad Universes, that true thing resides in the massless & energyless, yet experiencible, portion of Universe called the Metaphysic.

Events are also things, eternally existent in the Metaphysic. In the terminology of both Thelema and Fuller those event things are Stars: as-yet unresolved clusters of sub-units perceived as a unit, or a unique orgasmic union of Nuit and Hadit.

It should be obvious that the two definitions of Stars are reflections thru a timeline. That is, Nuit and Hadit create the Star that Fuller is trying to resolve into its constituents.

Stars are the islanded quantum units of physical existence separated by the enormous gulfs of space that are between Suns and between nuclei of atoms. Yet it is the metaphysic, being omnipresent space, that connects all of the stars together. The Metaphysic is Nuit: infinite space and the infinite stars thereof. Through her sign, the consciousness of the continuity of existence, the omnipresence of her body that is the Metaphysic, all Stars are perceptible.

These Stars are the only things that bind nothing. Without them the Metaphysic would be pure void as it was in the Beginning, or so say the Qabalists.[3]

As practitioners of the Magick Art it behooves us to establish power sources or stations, beacons and marks in space so that we may more accurately/powerfully guide the passage of our Wills upon their proper orbits.

All who are active in the Spacemarks Project are invited to contact us at the address below. We are eager to share our Trumps of Access with those who have created/charged beacons, are functioning within Powerzones dedicated to the evolution of planetary consciousness, and who have Trumps to share with us.

Bill Siebert
Math of the ChRySTAL HUMM

---

3   And Buddhists—Yz.

Dayside/Nightside Interface: Gateway to Sexual Magic

The Rose of Charon

a poem by Frater PVN for re-veiling Sexual Alchemy

Trident of SET & Quadriga Sexualis: Two Keys to Magickal Alchemy

Do what thou wilt shall be the whole of the Law.

The Rose of Charon is one of Frater PVN's earliest attempts at magickal poetry. His imagery is non-traditional & (to many) somewhat disquieting. Like many of his published essays, the intent of Rose of Charon is education by intimation & through a re-veiling of the mysteries of Sexual Alchemy, rather than clear linear treatment of actual practices.

Because the subject matter of Rose of Charon is so obscure, Frater PVN has written a lengthy exposition on much of the alchemical symbolism used in the poem. While this booklet can by no means be considered a handbook for rank novices, the material contained herein is of great practical significance to those who desire a practical framework within which to explore the practical application of the theory of Sexual Alchemy.

Over the past few centuries, many writers (& publishers) of texts on practical magick have deliberate censored &/or 'booby-trapped' certain aspects of their work to prevent honest seekers from making any practical use of techniques presented therein. Many of these writers honestly believed that the mysteries needed to be kept hidden from non-initiates. They published 'tainted' books in order to make money to support their researches (thus sabotaging their own work by cheating their patrons) & to 'lure' interested persons into their branch of the Order through the publicity from their books. When all the rhetoric & rationalizations have been put aside, the censors all felt that the mysteries of Sexual Alchemy were far too dangerous to be placed the hands of the general public.

Until recently, Frater PVN had believed that such 'precautions' were a dis-ease peculiar to the 19th Century's senile patriarchy which had been abolished in the light of the new Magickal Æon which began in 1904. However, within the past few months we have been reminded on two separate instances that there are still those who seek to censor magickal information & to limit its dissemination to 'protect' the general public from its influences.

Just yesterday (19 Jan.'84) Boleskine House received a letter from the TAT Journal refusing to carry our advertising because (to quote from the letter from TAT Journal signed by Mark Jaqua)

"...It has been our experience that sexual magic is very dangerous, and thus we do not wish people to have access to the methods..."

Frater PVN & Boleskine House wish to take this opportunity to pledge that we will never knowingly publish any document which has been castrated of its magickal efficacy. Our aim is the dissemination of practical magick throughout the world to all interested persons, irrespective of fraternal bonds or lineage of initiation. Much of our material is considered dangerous only by the forces which seek to control the lives of others through censorship & patriarchal oppression. If you find our booklets useful, we ask you to make our material known to local booksellers & libraries so that we may be effective in reaching people in spite of those who seek to limit our ability to advertise.

Much of the 'concerns' of those who seek to repress the formulae of practical sexual magick presented in our essays have to do with the 'Nightside aspects' of Frater PVN's approach to magick. A full discussion of Nightside/Dayside could never be condensed to fit in one of these pamphlets, but Frater PVN has consented to write a brief outline of the interplay of energies which so many magickians seem to fear. The outline precedes the poem Rose of Charon.

For a more complete exposition of the forces of Nightside, the reader is directed to the writings of Kenneth Grant (listed on the following page). Kenneth Grant is the current Head of the Typhonian OTO and the first modern author to speak openly of the value of Nightside in practical magick.

Y^{rs} *for the Great Work,*
Bill Siebert—for Boleskine House

Suggested Reading

The Magic Revival. Muller (London), 1972; Weiser (NY), 1973
Astrolabio. (Rome), 1973
Aleister Crowley & the Hidden God. Muller, 1973; Weiser, 1974
Astrolabio. 1975
Cults of the Shadow Muller, 1975; Weiser, 1976
Images & Oracles of Austin Spare. Muller, 1975; Weiser, 1975
Nightside of Eden. Muller, 1977
Outside the Circles of Time. Muller, 1980
Hecate's Fountain. Skoob Books, 1992

An Introduction to Dayside/Nightside & the Gateway of Alchemy by which They Communicate

The polarity of Dayside/Nightside is an important concept for all of us who are actively involved in the practical aspects Magickal or Alchemical research & creation. Ordinary reality (what physicists refer to as the Time/Space continuum) can be thought of as the sum total of the manifest Universe of things as they are. Everything which can be observed, perceived, or measured in any way is an objective phenomena of Dayside reality. Dayside is the 'playing field' of consensus reality which is governed by the 'laws of nature'. This stable (but not completely rigid) Dayside reality provides a firm foundation upon which we all live our daily lives. Without such stability, most of us (madmen & geniuses excepted) could never explore our universe (whether external or internal) and could never hope to discover our relationship to the other aspects of creation.

But, many of us (Madmen, Poets, Magickians, Artists, & other Creative Geniuses) eventually feel 'boxed-in' by the security & ho-hum nature of objective reality. We begin to wonder what would be possible if certain 'rules of the game' were slightly different (or abolished entirely). Once we (either as individuals or as a race) begin to feel the limits of growth imposed by 'laws of nature' and the conservative rules imposed by society & our genetic heritage, we are shown (through initiation & inspiration) various Gateways which give us access to other, more 'open' playing fields in which we are free to set-up our own rules.

Through exercise of our creative rights & privileges, we learn to explore our potential as Gods. When we feel that we are ready (either as individuals, or as a part of a wider network), we teach ourselves to bring back the fruits of our labor into this reality—to introduce new & interesting ideas which (if accepted by the consensus of the race) will become 'amendments' to the 'laws of Nature' or mutations within the social or physiological body of creation.

Nightside is the flipside of Dayside. It is unmanifest creation & the 'potential' from which all actuality originally came & to which it will most probably return. Nightside is no less real than Dayside, but its non-manifest nature defies measurement or objective quantization of any kind—hence it seems un-real to any objective analysis. Nightside is the reality of Dream, Inspiration, Vision, & (when perceived by un-balanced &/or damaged nervous systems) Nightmare.

Everyone who explores Nightside reports something different (which is why some inexperienced researchers can argue over details of their self-created systems). While some magickians are content to 'observe' the flux of the 'substance' of Nightside in its natural environment, the branch of Sexual Alchemy delineated in this series of essays deals with the direct manipulation of the substance of Nightside to manifest creation within the fabric of Dayside. I.e., we seek to encourage each Alchemist to reify his/her Inspirations in the here-&-now of Dayside to offer amendments &/or improvements to the 'laws' of Nature by which the consensus governs the collective Maya known as the Time/Space Continuum, or objective reality.

Whether Nightside is composed of the pre-cursor of Dayside reality (Godhead) or the debris which was left-over after the creation of Dayside reality (the Qliphoth) is the subject of a rather heated debate amongst the armchair proponents & opponents of practical Magick. For most Alchemists, Artists, & Geniuses, it makes no difference whether the substance of Nightside is composed of Deific or Qliphotic energies, or a mixture of both. Control & manipulation of the energies of Nightside is a very individual Art/craft which depends upon personal initiation to open Gateways within the esoteric nervous system of each adept. It is not the original 'alignment of the substance of Nightside' which determines the efficacy or alignment of a magickal operation, but the alignment & balance of the nervous systems of the adept(s) performing the operation & the usefulness of the ritual tools involved.

Many persons who fear the imbalances within themselves have made it clear that they believe all practical techniques of practical magick should be suppressed. Such suppression is doubly dangerous. First: The techniques of High Magick are inherently self-balancing. Those who actually practice them will become better able to channel the energies from Nightside for the betterment of the race. Second: Magick (like any Art or Science) is evolutionary. The advanced techniques of a century ago are but the kindergarten exercises of today. Limitation of information forces each practitioner to proceed by trial & error. Errors are both time consuming & dangerous. It can never be possible to remove the tools of High Magick from the general population. Misuse of these tools is rarely done maliciously, but is often the product of ignorant application of powerful formula.[1] Suppression of the techniques of Sexual Magick will never prevent individual experimentation. The energies of Nightside are open to all adepts, artists, and creative geniuses who listen to the voice of their own inspiration. It is an individual decision to use these energies, or to shun them.

Dayside/Nightside are in intimate & perpetual (yet objectively imperceptible) contact throughout all of creation. Yet, they remain uniquely separate with no admixture or communication, except where/when huge quantities of intensely focused energy are applied from the Dayside of the interface to open a Gateway between Dayside/Nightside. The Mirror is a useful symbol of this interface or Gateway through which Adepts, Artists, & Geniuses observe Nightside & encourage communication &/or communion between Nightside/Dayside in ways which are aligned with each individual's inspiration or madness.

Quantum physicists are just beginning to discover the Gateway to Nightside which is accessible from within each quanta of matter,[2] while Artists & Magickians have long known of other Gateways which lie within their individual nervous systems. Physicists rely on huge expenditures of highly focused energy (atomic explosions, acceleration of charged particles within magnetic fields, etc.) to 'pry-open' the Gateway to Nightside. Artists & Shamans have long used sex, drugs, & emotionally charged ritual to assist them in inducing raw & intense

---

1   PVN has reason to believe that the dis-ease known as AIDS is a prime example of a magickal disaster caused by ignorant application of the energies from Nightside. See *9-Fold Flowering of the 11-Star* for details, herein.

2   For details on the quantum mechanical Gateway at 10^{-33} Meters, see *Math of the ChRySTAL HUMM*, (herein).

emotion (Love, Hate, Fear, Loathing, Awe, Lust, Joy, Ecstasy, etc.) within themselves to open internal Gateways.

Sex Magick is one of the most readily accessible and self-balancing tools to open the Dayside/Nightside Gateway under the conscious control of the Magickian. Its study & practice is both an Art & a Science. Through its use, a highly focused emotional charge is generated (see the explanation of the Quadriga Sexualis, below), and 'ordinary' reality begins to break-down at the interface or Gateway within the esoteric nervous system of the Alchemist. By the force of Love under will, the subjective reality of the magickian becomes a causative agent in-&-of itself to formulate mutations in Dayside 'reality' from the unformulated matter/energy of Nightside. Quantum physicists are just beginning to come to grips with their role as creators within the Art/Science of quantum mechanics.

It is at the borderland between Dayside & Nightside that we humans are able to create reality & fix dream & vision into material form which has objective reality for the whole race. This borderland is the realm of Artists & Quantum Physicists, of Poets & Genetic Engineers, of Theogenists, & Mathematicians. It is the natural home & workshop of all geniuses who seek to reify their vision in the here-i-now of Dayside for the permanent transformation of life on this planet.

The techniques outlined in this essay are not for everyone. It takes a certain kind of personality to be at home with the energies & myth structures of Sexual Alchemy. It is up to each researcher to devise his/her own program based on the inclinations of one's own True Will.

I offer my researches to those who are on Paths & dedicate this essay to all who are involved with the Eleven-Star Working.

Love is the law, love under will.

Y^{rs} for the Great Work,
Frater PVN
Master, Forbidden Alchemies

The Rose of Charon

*A Rose by any other name
could ne'er be as Sweet
As the Flower at Daath
which opens in our Throat,
While the Trident of SET
makes up Her rootlet Feet;
Yet the Vortex Tunnel
beckons wide to Eat
The un-Wary who do but play
at Go-ing (Nightside).*

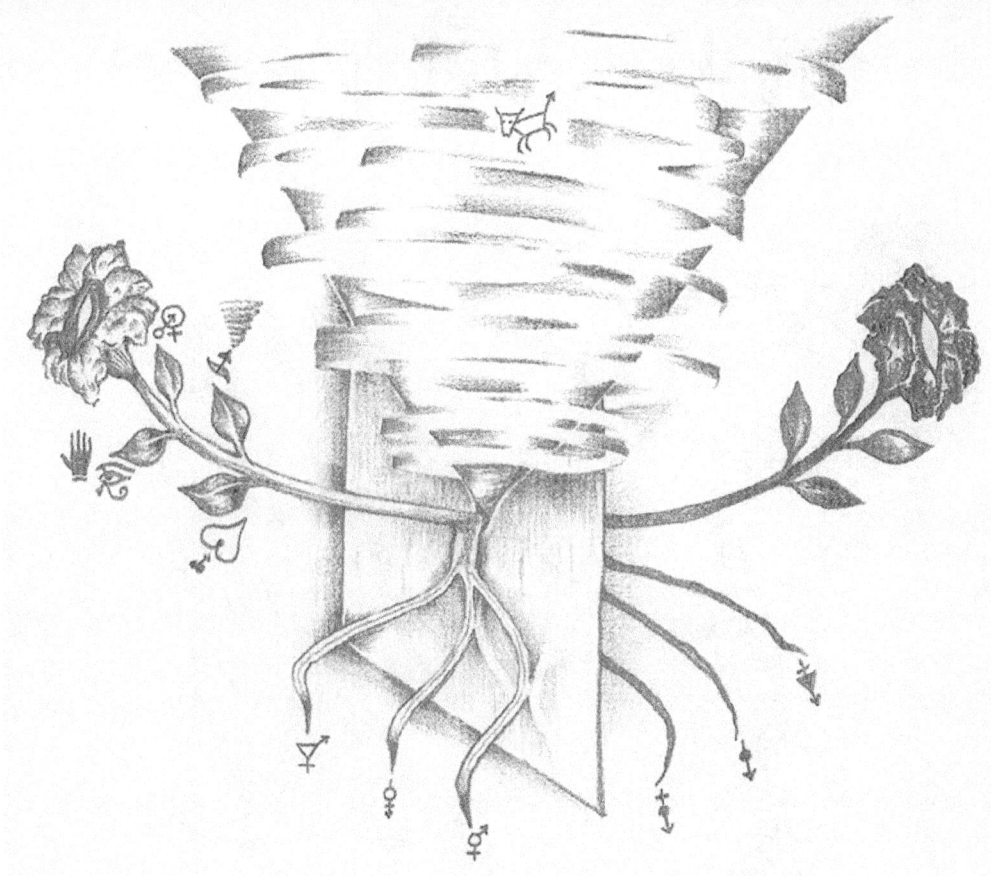

*Strange is this flower which exists on both sides of the Mirror—
half her roots planted in the Light, while half are nurtured by the Darkest Night.*

*Yet the Vortex which unites her duality is no clear channel—
for neither Path nor Tunnel can penetrate this Mirror which divides Day from Night.*

*Her Flower blooms in both Yesod & Daath, and on both sides of the Mirror as well; so True Unity appears both dual & four-fold—
hence her leaves be four, and partake of both Day & Night (though their rituals be all worked with bodies of Dayside flesh).*

The Rose of Charon

*The double-Trident of Her Roots do hold-fast
the Egg of Hoor-paar-Kraat,
And about her rootlets do the Worms
of the Firesnake Play;
The nectar of Her Flow-er does
drive the Kundalini wild,
While the Set beasts play within her vortex
(spreading hound-shit about her roots)
to fertilize Her.*

*She is the Rose crossed upon the Tree
from Daath to Yesod, and from Day to Night,
Her rootlets twist & churn
to produce Kalas of Delight.*

*By her 4 Leaves is She worshipped,
& by these Secret Rites
will her Flow-er bloom,
Then will dame Kundalini rise
to be drunk upon the nectar of the Rose,
and in that Drunkenness will be slain,
so that the Phoenix can live again!*

Explanatory Notes 1: Trident of SET

The Trident of Set is an alchemical symbol for mapping the interplay of the three independent pairs of bodily elixirs (also known as kalas or in-vivo enthogens) which occur naturally within the human body. While the 'normal' (non-adept) human can ordinarily be classified as being either male or female (depending on physiological apparatus & the polarity or charge of the sexual elixirs), the other two branches of the Trident do not lend themselves to polarization along such rigid lines.

Positive (+) and Negative (−) are labels for two independent modes of operation (outward expression) of the emanations or elixirs of each prong of the Trident of Set. Balanced humans can learn to operate in any combination of modes (+/−) as an act of love in conformity with Will, although (for the most part) a particular person will not manifest both + & − elixirs of a particular prong at any given instant in time. It is the deliberate & conscious interplay of the +/− polarities of the bodily elixirs which constitutes the physiological basis for Sexual Magick.

Adepts of sex magick are those individuals who regularly & consciously manipulate their own elixirs, and who reverently & consciously partake of the sacraments of mixed/blended elixirs prepared in conjunction with other adepts. Through the process of conscious balance, adepts become capable of producing any permutation of +/− elixir in accord with their True Will. It is through careful & conscious nurturing of each elixir, in + & − modes, on both the Dayside & Nightside of the Tree, that the rootlets can flourish and nourish the Rose.

Although it is convenient to discuss each prong of the Trident of Set separately, most practical Sex Magick deals with the manipulation & interplay of the various elixirs under conscious control of the alchemist to produce medicines, sacraments, and initiatory fluids to benefit not only the individual members of the Alchemical Priesthood, but the race as a whole.

Discussion of the interplay of all the various polarities on each of the prongs is far beyond the scope of this booklet, but some of the more interesting interplays will be mentioned in passing at the end of the next section.

A Brief Explanation of Some of the More Obscure References in the preceding Poem

The *Trident of SET* refers to the triplicity of bodily elixirs which naturally occur in the human body. + and − are merely two modes of operation of which we are all fully capable. While both modes of a particular elixir are usually not in operation at the same moment of time within a particular individual, their deliberate interplay is at the root of all physio-sexual magick. It is only by this careful nurturing of all of the elixirs, in both modes, and on both the Dayside & Nightside of the Tree, that the rootlets can flourish & nourish the Rose. Below, I have given a schematic breakdown of the Trident of Set into its parts with some of its more obvious attributions. The more subtle uses of the Trident are left to the ingenuity of the individual practitioners.

—Dayside—			Attribute	—Nightside—		
Genital	Anal	Oral	Prong	Genital	Anal	Oral
male | female	evoke | invoke	solve | coagulæ	Mode	male | female	evoke | invoke	solve | coagulæ
♂ ♀	♀ ♀	☿ ♂	Symbol	♀ ☿	♀ ♀	☿ ☿
White or Silvery Gold	Gold	Copper	Elixir Attribution	Slug-Slime	Honey	Green Copper
IT	ShIT (11 x 29)	SPIT (3 x 53)	Elixir Numeration			
Venus	Earth	Herschel	Major Planet	Mars	Saturn	Neptune Pluto

About the Symbols

The *Mirror* is analogous to the looking glass in the story of Alice by Lewis Carrol. The mirror separates Dayside from Nightside.

The Vortex is the standing wave between Dayside & Nightside which acts as both a storehouse of energy (energy really isn't the correct term, for energy is a dayside phenomena—what is implied is the pre-cursor of energy which is neither dayside nor nightside—perhaps the triple veils of AIN, AIN SOPH, AIN SOPH AUR would be more correct) and the vector channel through which it can be directed.

The *FOUR-FOLD LEAVES* of the Rose are the actions (verbs) by which the elixirs of the Trident of SET (nouns) are manipulated. The four leaves make up the Quadriga Sexualis, or four parts of the operation of sexual magick.

1. The building of energy or charge via constant sexual congress. Its hieroglyph is the united male & female symbols with the female symbol bloated to show the accumulation of energy: ⚥

The magickal operation is IX° & its alchemical symbol is Silver (see AL III:64-67).

2. The abstract creation symbolized by the hand & the eye. Symbols are created & focused upon to act as a vector to direct or channel the energies of (1). The alchemical symbol is Gold.

3. The astral doubling or reflection of the abstract symbol. The symbol in (2) enables energy to be drawn from Nightside (or more precisely from the vortex of the Rose) into the Sex Organs. A symptom of this operation may be termed gonads of ice, for the icy cold energies are drawn-down into the sexual organs of the practitioners. The alchemical symbol for this operation is Stones of Precious Water. The heiroglyph depicts a penis extending out of a vagina, drawing in the dark vortex of power:

4. In-creative or un-natural congress. The icy cold power of (3) must be earthed or it will do serious harm to the magician. The magickal operation is the XI°, or un-natural creation. Rather than an actual act of un-natural sex, the energies may be drawn into concrete from via painting, music, poetry, etc., but if the cold persists, it is a symptom that the channeling of the energies into Art was not sufficient to completely earth the working. XI° should then be employed. The alchemical symbol for this operation is Ultimate Sparks of Intimate Fire. The hieroglyph depicts the XI° formula analogous to (1):

The working as a whole may be summed up via the initials of its name Quadriga Sexualis, or QS is Qoph, Samekh, or the lunar current of the path of Art. By examination of the gematria of the Tarot Trumps the operation is XVIII + XIV = XXXII, a glyph of the 32 kalas.

An examination of the 4 leaves & the 3 prongs (roots) integrated into the system of the 5 Makara of the Varna marg shows the following:

The Rose of Charon

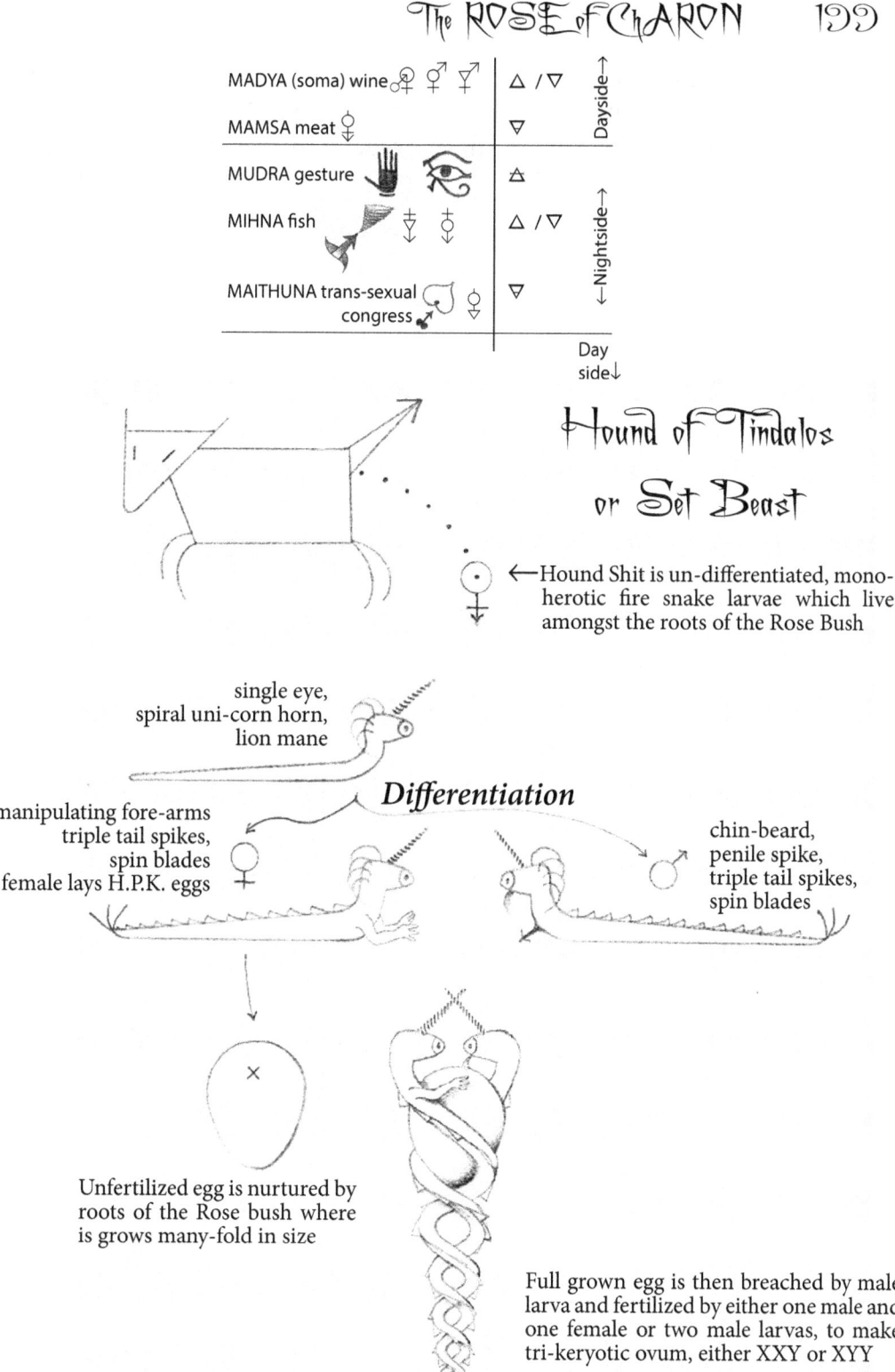

Hound of Tindalos or Set Beast

←Hound Shit is un-differentiated, mono-herotic fire snake larvae which live amongst the roots of the Rose Bush

single eye, spiral uni-corn horn, lion mane

Differentiation

manipulating fore-arms, triple tail spikes, spin blades, female lays H.P.K. eggs

chin-beard, penile spike, triple tail spikes, spin blades

Unfertilized egg is nurtured by roots of the Rose bush where is grows many-fold in size

Full grown egg is then breached by male larva and fertilized by either one male and one female or two male larvas, to make tri-keryotic ovum, either XXY or XYY

MADYA (soma) wine ☿ ♂ ♀		△/▽	Dayside→
MAMSA meat ♀		▽	
MUDRA gesture ✋ 👁		△	
MIHNA fish ♀ ♀		△/▽	←Nightside→
MAITHUNA trans-sexual congress ♂ ♀		▽	
			Day side↓

For an understanding of the other obscure language of the poem it is necessary to look at the mythological 'life-cycle' of the Fire Snake in its many varied forms. It should be noted that this life cycle is highly allegorical & not directly tied to physiological reality as is the trident of Set or the Quadriga Sexualis.

Egg hatches newt which quickly grows and matures as it crawls up the rose bush and out the Rose. First, the Hound acquires binocular vision, a mouth with forked tongue, looses the tail spikes, while growing of fore-arms. For the male comes the loss of spin blades, and the growth of a penile spike, breasts, chin beard.

The Adult lives at the base of the spine in humans and is known as the Kundalini serpent. At full maturity, the Hound develops an eye ridge, nose flame, teeth, vagina, and hind legs.

The adult blends her three elixirs, O, ⇑, ☉, within her vagina to create Hounds of Tindalos, also known as Set Beasts.

The Rose of Charon

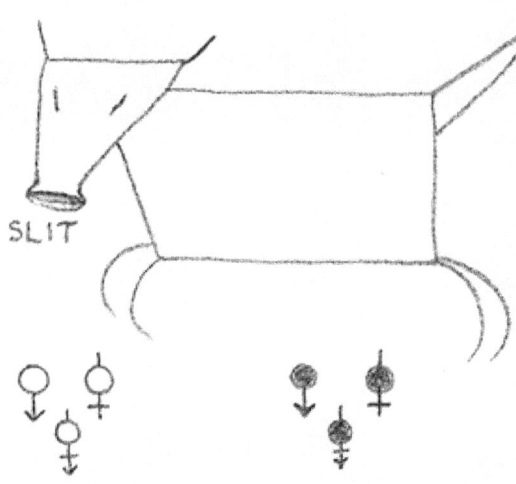

The immature Hounds live within the serpent's vagina. The Kundalini absorbs nourishment for the young Hounds through osmosis of the anal elixirs from the host human. The more varied the elixirs, the stronger the hounds & the more quickly they grow.

Adult Hounds are let-loose at each chakra as the Kundalini rises.

The natural home of the Hound is the vortex of power which naturally accompanies a full functioning chakra. Hounds help to keep the vortex free-flowing and clean. Their shit is blown by the vortex to the roots of the Rose bush, where the cycle begins again.

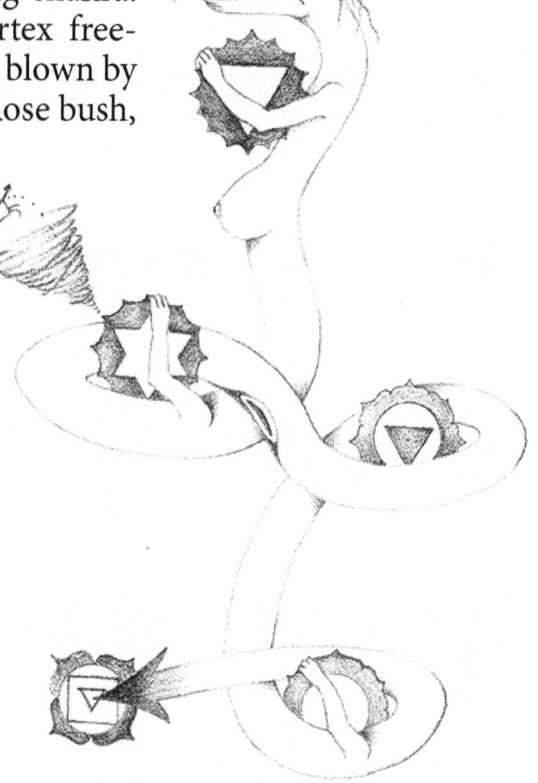

Notes on Certain Aspects of Transcendental Alchemy: Document 1
Nine-Fold Flowering of Alchemies within The Eleven-Star Working

by Frater PVN

DISCLAIMER: *This paper is written by Frater PVN, aspirant to the Office of Master of Forbidden Alchemies within the Eleven Star. Although a great deal of the a alchemickal terminology and aspects of the Grade System used within this paper is patterned after similar terminology currently in use by both the OTO (Ordo Templi Orientis) and the A∴A∴, the author wishes to make perfectly clear that although the Eleven-Star has the same fountainhead as the OTO & the A∴A∴, it is (at the present time) functioning as an independent Flower of the 93 Current and is therefore distinct from both the O.T.O. & the A∴A∴ in outward manifestation (i.e., structure, function, & leadership).*

Introduction

The Eleven-Star[1] is an experiment to reify the spirit of the A∴A∴ within a pattern of interlocking & overlapping inter-dependent Alchemickal Powerzones (one for each of the 10 Sephira, both Dayside & Nightside, + the (oft misunderstood) Gateway at Daath). Each Candidate of the Eleven-Star is striving to become a permanent living vehicle of Higher Consciousness (i.e., to become one of the 'Thrones of the Gods'). Each Power zone is autonomous, and most are not even aware of the existence of those others who undertake certain other aspects

---

[1] The working model for the Eleven-Star used by PVN is based upon, but distinct from, the original concept channeled by Soror Andahadna-124 (also known as NEMA). It is PVN's premise that each aspirant will perceive the Eleven-Star from a slightly different perspective than any of the other candidates. Such variation in inspiration is due to each candidate's unique qualifications which he/she brings to the Great Work. It should not be a cause for alarm or dissention among aspirants. As the Eleven-Star begins to reify, cross fertilization of ideas will promote a common vision without dogmatism.

of the Great Work. The Eleven Star is open only to those whose Will is aligned with the basic principles of Alchemy (both individual & racial) contained with Liber AL vel Legis. and is independent of initiatory links &/or membership (or lack thereof) within any of the various Branches of the OTO or the A∴A∴. The Eleven Star neither knows nor cares about the legitimacy (or lack thereof) of any group comporting itself as the OTO or the A∴A∴, although individual members may certainly express their individual opinions/beliefs to all who care to listen.

The opinions expressed in this paper are those of the author and do not necessarily reflect those of other aspirants to the Eleven-Star. The information contained in this paper is the result of many years of meditative reflection upon the mysteries of Order beyond the Gateways at Da'ath, as well as continual observation of various Magickal Orders as they function upon the outer, both at present & thru the vehicle of historical 'time-scan'. The sexual formulae presented in this paper are a by-product of the author's inspiration which have not been sufficiently tested to ensure their full efficacy or even their safety. This is not a handbook for beginners, but a research paper which is intended for circulation amongst other AL-Chemysts who seek to share interesting results with their colleagues within the context of the Eleven-Star. The only requirement for participation in this project (other than those outlined above) is a commitment to full honesty & full disclosure of all interesting results, whether or not they contradict any of the more traditional approaches to alchemy as taught by any of the other branches of Magick. Those who are bound to secrecy with regards any Alchemickal formulae have no place amongst us, for secrecy is too often used to hinder honest inquiry &/or to manipulate the gullible into believing that a particular Magickal Group has a monopoly on initiatory links to the Fountainhead of the Order.

Background

Throughout recorded history, the S∴S∴ of the Gnosis has chosen to remain veiled in Silence, Secrecy, & Solitude behind each of the various manifestations of the Order upon the outer. The S∴S∴ has chosen this path for many reasons, not the least of which is that the Order on the Outer (in its many incarnations) is often led by brave (but sometimes fool hearty) men who sometimes forget their sworn allegiance to the Holy Cup of Our Lady & that which it contains. When this happens, the Order on the outer begins to comport itself

Nine-Fold Flowering of Alchemies within the Eleven-Star Working

as though it was the S∴S∴, rather than the vassal of the S∴S∴ whose duties upon the outer are as follows:

- Education & guidance of the young (both physically & spiritually).
- Strict governance of those who have not yet taken responsibility for their own lives.
- Militant defense of all pilgrims, no matter what their goal & no matter what their beliefs.

Or (to phrase it another way)

Stewardship over and maintenance of the major civic structures of the Order upon the outer (i.e., stewardship over Education, Religion, Education, Politics, & War and maintenance of Universities, Churches, Monasteries, Courts, Prisons, Armories, Parliaments, & Roads). Although, from time to time the Order on the outer has exercised a degree of Stewardship over these institutions in the world at large (e.g., during the reign of the Knights Templar), their Stewardship is not primarily of this mundane world—i.e., the roads which are kept safe are the Paths upon the Tree of Life. They administer education & guidance from the 'University' to be found in the Sphere of Hod, etc.,etc.

The Order on the outer is the educational, legislative, & military arm of the Order as a whole whose prime magickal weapons are the Coin & the Sword.

COINS are crystallized energy which are governed by certain complex formulae which diffuse from the Spheres of Malkuth or Yesod (depending on whether the coin be cash, talisman, or some complex mixture of the two (such as a stock certificate issued by a company with no assets)).

SWORDS are directed force which are governed by certain complex formulae which diffuse from the Spheres of Geburah &/or Hod (depending on whether the directed Force be Martial or Mercurial in nature, or some combination thereof).

As the influence of both these Weapons (Coins & Swords) diffuse throughout the Tree, their actual manifestation as well as the efficacy of their influence is modified thru the use of certain formulae which automatically alters their actions in both nature and application depending upon the specific location on the Tree—i.e., the specific application of these Weapons is modified in order to conform with the 'local' Laws of Nature at each quantum reality upon the Tree of Life.

Hence the powers of the Order upon the outer ultimately derive from its rightful *non-exclusive* function upon that region of the Tree of Life comprised of Malkuth, Yesod, Hod, and Geburah. Thru esoteric contact with the Order upon the inner, the outer Order has access to certain realms beyond the portal at Daath (i.e., that region which used to be termed 'Above the Abyss'). To phrase it yet another way, the Order upon the outer has non-exclusive Stewardship over that portion of the Tree of Life which is known to traditional Qabalists (i.e., Hebrew, rather than G∴D∴) as the Vav of the Angels of Destruction [see figure #9 of Appendix at end of this essay]. However, a little over 900 years ago, the Order on the outer took an oath to keep safe all roads for all pilgrims. Due to this oath the Order upon the outer (when it is indeed functioning according to its sworn oath) has managed to extend its influence throughout the Paths of the entire lower Tree (i.e., below Daath).

I hasten to emphasize that the Order on the outer has no Stewardship over those functions governed by the realms of Netzach, Tiphareth, and Chesed. Individual members of the Order on the outer have (over the centuries) sought to introduce various teachings from other traditions which would allow the Order upon the outer to accept Stewardship over these realms, but (to date) these experimental grafts have not brought forth much in the way of fertile fruit except for the tantric grafts which have gained each individual member of the Order on the outer a direct link with the inner Order within him/her-self. Members of the Order on the outer whose Will lies in this area are counseled to learn the ways of the Mystic, the Sufi, and the Shaman, whose Stewardships overlap the Order on the outer in some areas, but which extend to encompass Chesed, Tiphareth, & Netzach, as well (see Appendix, especially figures 3, 5, & 10)

The ultimate symbol of authority of those who work the Vav of the Angels of Destruction is the Flaming Sword of Geburah. Authority to wield this Flaming Sword is vested in the Order on the outer only insofar as it remains loyal to its self-imposed fealty to the S∴S∴ of the Gnosis. The Outer Order can never 'contain' the S∴S∴ (for the Sword of Geburah was never designed to replace, or to rule over, the Cup of Our Lady of the Western Gate of Heaven). Insofar as the outer Order remembers its duties & is not jealous of the Cup (or that which it contains), manifestations of the S∴S∴ interpenetrate the outer Order in order to nourish, guide, and reward her loyal sons for fealty & service.

Much has been written about the Cup of Our Lady. Inasmuch as the full manifestation of this Cup lies beyond the Portal at Daath, any description of this Cup or its contents are necessarily incomplete & contain many *apparent* contradictions. Some say that this cup is found within the Yoni of the Priestess. While this statement is true, it must not be accepted at face value nor should it be construed to imply that the Cup is to be found *only* within the Yoni of the priestess. The Cup of our Lady lies beyond the Portal at Daath & certain vessels (both human & otherwise, e.g., animal, vegetable, & mineral) have been consecrated in order to enable them to function as outward manifestations of the Cup even though they are themselves not the Cup. For the purpose of this essay, the author intends to convey the message that the Cup of Our Lady is accessible (to a greater or lesser degree) through the sexual beings and external alchemickal vessels of all Candidates of the Eleven Star, who are all Aspirants to the Sisterhood of the A∴A∴.

Certain Aspects of the Nine—Fold Flowering

The cup of Our Lady contains an elixir compounded under the Law of Threes. For each Aspirant, the prescription is unique, but its purpose is to balance & harmonize the three bio-electric circuits within the human esoteric nervous system in order to trigger the flowering of the Eleven-Star within the physical vehicle of the candidate (i.e., the manifestation of an aspect of Higher Consciousness). A general formula for the elixir of immortality is as follows:

- A complex blending of sexual kalas compounded & administered *in Vivo* by one or more Sisters of the S∴S∴ whose office is BABALON.
- A highly specific regimen of vegetable & mineral entheogens, compounded *in Vitro* by skilled physicians & Al-chemysts who work under the guidance of the Sisterhood S∴S∴ & administered *in Vivo* &/or *in Vitro* by one or more Sisters of the S∴S∴ whose office is HADIT.
- A free-form/non-linear regimen of sensual & emotional stimulation of the esoteric nervous system through direct stimulation of any combination of the five esoteric senses by the entire Universe of the Sisterhood of the S∴S∴ whose office is Kalisti.

On the outer, an oversimplification of this formula has been popularized with the slogan Sex & Drugs & Rock-&-Roll. To an adept who has 'attained' thru the enlightened & judicious use of the regimen advocated by this slogan, its meaning is obvious. But for those who lie outside of the culture which uses this formula, it should be pointed out that Rock-&-Roll could easily be translated into the divinely intoxicating feasts of Dionysius, the ecstatic whirling of the trained Dervish, the neither/neither state of the conscious dreamer, and the euphoria of the self-disciplined athlete. Improper use of the Cup &/or its contents leads to hedonistic debauch & the degeneration of the Candidate in both gross & subtle ways. Such degeneration may disqualify the Candidate from participation in the 11-Star except for the necessary role of 'black brother' who functions to lead the weak away from valid. manifestations of the Eleven-Star Working. [CJ.Jones & S.Moon seem to function in this office, but it is never possible to say with certainty.] Degeneration of true Candidates is never permanent, but the karmic ordeals can last for many lifetimes. As a rule of thumb, the more spiritually advanced the Candidate, the greater the consequences for misuse of the Cup &/or its contents.

The S∴S∴ of the Gnosis may be functionally divided into Three separate sanctuaries & each of these is again divided into three. There may be additional &/or more complex divisions, but of such divisions I am not able speak at this time. That aspect of the Sisterhood of the S∴S∴ which oversees the production, distillation, and administration of the sexual kalas may be thought of as a single Office, but it has three distinct aspects. There are few who master all three while most are able to function well in but one. I will briefly outline the triune functions of the sexual Office of the S∴S∴, devoting considerably more space to the functions of the XI°, since (at the present time) it is this function within the S∴S∴ which is the least understood (& therefore the most dangerous).

The Flower—er of Babalon

The Solitary Sanctuary of the Gnosis governs the VIII° formulae which pertain to Astral manipulation and manifestation. This aspect of the S∴S∴ presides over all Hermits and instructs them in all manner of Alchemycal formulae pertaining to all aspects of the S∴S∴. A necessary pre-requisite for all who aspire to work the formulae of this aspect of the S∴S∴ is the shattering of pre-conceived notions and the dissolution of all fined realities, hence those who function in this office wear the Godform of Shiva, the Destroyer.

The Sovereign Sanctuary of the Gnosis governs the 11° formulae of sexual magick. This is the theater of heterosexual alchemy whose work is the productive use of the multitudinous formulae of procreative generation and fertility. Those who function in this office wear the Godform of Vishnu, the Preserver as they preside over those who aspire to the Grade of Lovers.

The Secret Sanctuary of the Gnosis governs the 11° formulae of androgenous & gynandrous alchemies *whose* priestcraft tailors outer form to suit inner function. The purpose of these alchemies is as broad as the Great Desert and as deep as the Sea which borders it. It would he fool hearty to undertake even the most cursory outline of the full range of formulae in so short an essay, so I will content myself with the sketchiest of outlines covering certain aspects of just *two* of the formulae, the Formula of Sodom, and the Formula of Gomorrah.

The Formula of Sodom

In general, the rites of Sodom are presided over by that branch of the Sisterhood who bear the genetic code of men. The rites themselves may be either homo- or hetero-sexual in nature, but (if seminal elixir is to be introduced into the Fundament-AL cucurbit), at least one sexually functional male must preside as priest & depositor of the Al-chemycal Fire within the cucurbit of Earth which nourishes the Fundament-AL chakra. The purpose of this priesthood is the conscious induction of planned mutations within the cytoplasm of the Priestess (i.e., the functional female, whether she be genetically male, female or other) and the within the nascent germ plasm of the race as a whole. (The ritual appended to this essay is an example of this type of working.)

But not all of the rites of Sodom require seminal elixir, so a functional male is not always needed for the proper use of this formula. Within the realm of this formula (perhaps more so than in any other alchemical realm), innovation is the rule rather than the exception. Both mechanical contrivances, and the clenched fist have been successfully used for Fundament-AL stimulation & for the introduction of non-seminal elixirs (female fluids, vegetable entheogens, charged talismans, living crystals, etc.) into the cucurbit of Earth. It is even possible (though not easy) for a properly trained male to 'siphon' vaginal elixirs via IX° karezsa and then 'deposit' these female elixirs within the cucurbit of Earth without introducing any masculine component into either of the cucurbits.

In general, the proper use of the very powerful formulae of Sodomy (whether hetero- or homo-sexual) can cause subtle & not so subtle permanent alterations in the 'laws of Nature' as well as the manifestation of creative mutations within selected members of the race. Thru the use of this formula, members of the S∴S∴ undertake the Godform of Brahma, the Creator, and thru these subtle manipulations, they guide the Man of Earth.

However, if any con-Celebrant in these rites is unskilled, unfocused, &/or unworthy of his/her office, s/he can infect both the fire-wand and the cucurbit with loathsome qliphothic teratomas which spring unbidden from the unresolved dualities which generate spontaneously in that cesspool accessible most readily through the fundament-AL chakra of those who do not take full responsibility for their magickal lives. Because this formula is so powerful, it is disastrous when practiced by non-adepts—*& even more so* when practiced by high adepts who do not take full responsibility for their every thought and action. Imprudent (&/or willfully destructive) use of this formula is responsible for that family of biological monstrosities known collectively as AIDS Syndrome or the Gay Plague. In a very limited sense, the fundamental Christians are quite correct. AIDS a result of the improper use of the sexual function. But it does not stem from the 'Just Wrath' of a homophobic God. It is the collective consequence of a multitudinous array of irresponsibly ill-planned & ill-executed genetic experiments.

But, lest there be misunderstanding, let me hasten to say that I am not advocating the suppression or abandonment of this formula or limiting its use in any way. For every klutz & for every irresponsible initiate who misuses aspects of the formulae of Sodom, there are dozens of high initiates who use this formula for the benefit of the race, & there are many more adepts who could use this formula in innovative & beneficial ways *if they chose to do so.* However, at this point in time, many adepts fear to practice the formula of XI° Sodomy. They seem to misunderstand the function & purpose of the sodomical Sisterhood of the S∴S∴ who have carried the secret of this formula down thru the ages. It is this formula, more than any others, which was responsible for the rapid growth of the Knights Templar, and for its extreme leverage in influencing the fabric of reality over the span of centuries—and the misuse of this formula which led to the Knights Templar's rapid destruction upon the outer.

The Formula of GOMORRAH

The formula of XI° which mirrors/compliments the formula of Sodomy pertains to the mysteries of the sterile flow of blood from those members of the Sisterhood of the S∴S∴ who wear the bodies of women. The formula of Gomorrah requires at least one member of the circle to be a natural born female who is manifesting the sterile Lunar menstrual Flow (i.e., the required office cannot be filled by a child, a pregnant woman, or a crone; neither can it be filled by a transvestite male or a surgically engineered trans-sexual female no matter how skillfully the persona &/or physical vehicle is constructed). As with the formulae pertaining to Sodom, the actual rite can be either homo- or hetero-sexual. The formula of Gomorrah provides the vehicle for trans-dimensional & transtemporal observation/manipulation which is so important for those who seek to alter the Fundament-AL nature of reality thru the formula of Sodomy—both as a precursor to actual manipulation & as an adjunct to guide/fine-tune the focus of the manipulation as this priestcraft tailors the fabric of the Space/Time/Alternity Continuum.

One method of Gomorrah-cal observation is done directly with the third eye, thru the Gateway at Yesod during cunnilingus upon the menstruating priestess with focus being maintained /directed thru the esoteric use of consecrated quartz crystals. There are even reported cases of certain adepts who have managed to 'snatch' items of particular interest back thru this Gateway. Such reifications are not recommended even amongst circles of the Highest Adepts since such manipulations might possibly leave the menstrual Gateway permanently open within the physical body of the Priestess & there is little to suggest that that which lies on the other side of this Gateway is necessarily friendly to our Race at this point in time.

For those adepts who are interested in using the Gomorrah-cal XI° elixirs for reification, it is suggested that the elixir be prepared & consecrated *in Vivo*, to be removed at the proper moment via appropriate contrivance (biological or mechanical) for use in the *in Vitro* preparation of properly designed & executed talismans. Such talismans are particularly efficacious when used as catalysts for the precipitation of Magickal Manuscripts into this reality (e.g., the Necronomicon has begun the reification process due to use of this formula by adepts in many circles) and for the acquisition of physical wealth (money, property, power). It should be noted that such operations are rarely straightforward & often contain wrinkles in Time due to the recursive nature of the equations which govern the mechanics of this class of operation. For a more in-depth look at the Gomorrah-cal XI° Alchemies, I refer the reader to the works of Kenneth Grant, who has devoted most of (at least) one lifetime to the study of this branch of the XI°.

In Conclusion

Before ending this essay, I would like to clear-up one possible source of confusion for those of you who are unfamiliar with some of the intricacies of that family of Magickal Traditions which is often referred to collectively as 'the Order'. Traditionally, the outer Order is said to be composed entirely of men, although membership is open to both genetic males & genetic females. Aspirants to the inner Order (the S∴S∴, the A∴A∴, or the Eleven-Star (in this instance, I refer specifically to that experiment known as the Eleven-Star Working)) are always women, although Candidates may be either genetically male or female (or 'other' [such as XXV & XYY genetic sports]). What is meant by this is simple—the outer Order demands qualities which are traditionally associated with masculinity, while aspirants to the inner Order must cultivate all of the traditional feminine qualities. Hence, PVN (who is genetically a male) is a Candidate of the Eleven-Star and an Aspirant to the Sisterhood of the S∴S∴. *However*, it should be noted that this tradition was begun by and has (thus far) been elaborated upon by almost exclusively by those Aspirants to the S∴S∴ who are genetic males. The inner Order embraces not only the work of the Cup, but the work of the Wand as well. It is not possible for one such as I to elaborate further upon the mysteries of the Wand until such time as those Candidates to the Eleven Star and Aspirants to the A∴A∴ who wear the genetic body of females decide that it is time to speak more openly of these matters.

NOTE: Anyone interested in the theoretical &/or practical implications (&/or applications) of the concepts presented in this paper are cordially invited to contact the author.

XI° Recombinant Genetics, Appendix 1

This particular ritual is especially efficacious since it utilizes both the IX° rituals of conscious procreation as well as certain other techniques garnered thru an understand of some little understood aspects of VIII° Astral manipulations. The purpose of this rite is the *in Vivo* mutation of the sperm & ovum at the moment of fertilization. Through the application of Al-chymycal Fire to the medium of Al-chemickal Earth contained within the *ORGASMIC* Fundament-AL Cucurbit and then focused via the meta-network of the combined esoteric nervous systems of the con-Celebrants *retromingently* thru the Gateway at Yesod into the womb of the mother-to-be (i.e. from the *other* side of the Gateway back into the physical body of the priestess).

Such rites should never be undertaken by those who lack a complete understanding of the techniques involved or by those who have not made clean links with the Fountainhead of the Order within themselves, both individually & collectively. That is to say, any rituals of this nature are totally beyond the jurisdiction of the Order upon the outer & should only be attempted by those Candidates of the 11-Star who feel that their contact with the S∴S∴ is valid, clean, and strong. Those who are still searching for their angel as well as those who look to external authority to 'sanctify' their plans/aspirations are strictly warned away from any rites of this nature. The rite described here requires a circle of three highly specialized initiates, who are sexually at ease with each other, and who are well versed in & totally comfortable with their offices, both individually & collectively.

2. The Biological Mother
1. The Biological Father
0. The Trelph

Each of these Offices is explained in detail on the following pages.

2. The Biological Mother must be an initiate of the XI° Sanctuary and must one of the increasing number of double-wanded women (i.e., she must be sexually mature, & fully orgasmic—both vaginally and anally). Ideally, she should be an initiate of the mysteries of all three sexual aspects of the S∴S∴, but this is not always possible. It is the mother who decides upon the nature of the desired mutation & it is she who fine-tunes the focus of all energies as they operate within her physical vehicle. In order to be able to function in this rite, she must be able to shed all 'traditional' passive role-playing & take an active part in both the mechanical design & esoteric execution of this very delicate operation. Failure of the biological mother to exercise careful judgement, responsible control, & clear coherent command could easily result in biological disaster (abortion, stillbirth, contraction of heinous venereal disorders, total systemic collapse (AIDS Syndrome), or extreme deformities of the fetus) or in the reification of certain alien Teratomas through the Fundament-AL Gateway & subsequent incarnation of Nightmare-clothed-in-Flesh within the soon-to-be-fertilized embryo to produce a qliphothic-human hybrid inimical to both the biological mother & the human race as a whole.[2]

1. The Biological Father of the child must be an initiate of the IX° Sanctuary, but under no circumstances should he utilize his Office in an attempt to influence the formation or characteristics of the embryo in any way. His magickal powers need to be fully focused within himself such that he can be certain that he has produced the purest possible elixir & has meticulously selected the best possible sperm for the operation at hand. In workings of this nature, the biological father gives up all 'traditional' masculine rights & must function as a passive depositor of the divine manifestation of IT. He must be able to be clear as light & hard as diamond. He is the sacred vehicle of Will & therefore must be totally unassuaged of purpose & delivered from all Lust of Result.

0. The Trelph[3] is the third member of the circle for this rite. S/He must be biologically male, preferably sterile, who is an initiate of the XI° Sanctuary, fully capable of both Dianism & Kadosh (karezza &

---

2 It should be noted that not all alien-human hybrids are inimical to either the mother or the human race as a whole. Document #2 in this series deals more thoroughly with this concept than is possible in this brief footnote. Let me just mention in passing that the quasi-immortal Vampire Kings who once ruled the earth were probably 'created' through an AL-chemycal process similar to the ritual outlined here, but with modifications designed to facilitate the hybridization of human genetic material with aliens from other dimensions &/or other galaxies.

Two such modifications are a loosening of control on the part of the mother, and choosing a Trelph who is already in contact with those entities which dwell beyond the ken of ordinary mortals. The former modification requires a woman whose Will is developed so strongly that she is able to give-over her control to another without feeling any threat to her own sense of self, while the later requires that the Trelph be trained from early childhood in introspection, observation, and a total trust in the worlds of phantasy & imagination. Such training may be direct, or through the method described by Crowley in his preface to Liber LI (Atlantis—The Lost Continent) called 'preparation of the antimony'.

3 The Trelph is named after the third sex of an alien species of marine life whose unique characteristics are well suited to this rite. The marine Trelph donates no genetic information to the sexual union—its role is that of orgasmic facilitator and genetic mutator. It stands apart from the two genetic sexes by its distinctly hallucinogenic pheromones & its day-glow eyelids, which are an outward sign of its inward radioactivity.

divine orgasm), as well as an Adept of those Astral manipulations of energy flow which seem to come most easily to diligent practitioners of the VIII°. Working under the guidance of the biological mother, s/he taps-into those trans-Temporal & trans-dimensional energy vortices which are well known to adepts of the formula of Sodom & carefully selects/manipulates the appropriate vortices of energy appropriate to delicate genetic surgery so that they (i.e., the trelph & the mother) can better focus upon those specific nodes within the multi-dimensional pattern conducive to the 'importation' of highly specific pre-determined genetic information from one of the many alternative futures & or pasts accessible thru manipulation of isolated quarks within the energy matrix. The work is (for the most part) intuitive & does not require much formal training in the Art or Science of quantum chromodynamics.

It is always wise for such an operation to be preceded by several months of 'Time-scanning' via XI° Gemorrah-cal cunnilingus as well as by other techniques practiced primarily by that branch of the S∴S∴ which sometimes calls itself the Sisterhood of the Bene Gesserit. Prior to the actual operation (preferably at the appropriate time during the previous month), the trelph can be consecrated & aligned to the purpose of this rite thru the infusion of an alchemically blended (*in Vivo* or *in Vitro*) seminal elixir from the biological father & Gemorrah-cal elixir from the biological mother into the cucurbit of Earth within the physical vehicle of the Trelph.

The actual mechanics of the rite are left to the inspirations & sexual proclivities of the participants.

(It may be noted in passing, that this rite may be thought of as the Nightside analog to the Moonchild ritual which was written-up in detail by Aleister Crowley in the form of a novel. Although the ritual outlined above requires fewer people, less time, and less elaborate surroundings, it should not be construed that the ritual outlined above is any less demanding than Crowley's Moonchild operation, nor should it be construed that the above ritual has been designed to supplant the Moon-child operation.)

PVN
Candidate, Eleven Star Working
Master, Forbidden Alchemies

Appendix 2: Selections from the Work of the Chariot

Originally written in the 1970s and published by the Work of the Chariot Trust and used liberally by our author as an appendix to introduce the idea of the various configurations of the Tree of Life, herewith reproduced by kind permission of the Trust. Not all numbered figures are present.

Introduction

The individual soul as Microcosm, created in the Image of Elohim, or Macrocosm as Adam Kadmon (Celestial Man), is objectively represented in its physio-spiritual entirety by the geometric configuration of ten connected circles (Sephiroth) called the Tree of Life. The Sephiroth are emanations from YHVH Elohim, forming a set of self-consistent worlds or planes of consciousness upon which creatures can exist due to the relative orderliness and smoothness of change. These Sephiroth are emanated as pairs of opposites (see Sefer Yetzirah 1:5) and are connected with one another by gates (the twenty-two Hebrew letters), which are in the Light of the Endless (Ain Soph Aur).

The spheres of the Tree are in the human body starting with the base of the spine and going to the top of the head, thereby providing a connected series of experiences based on changing states of consciousness, as the Shekinah rises through the various centers. Since the four worlds Emanation (Atziluth), Creation (Briah), Formation (Yetzirah), and Fabrication (Assiah) underlie all the Sephiroth, it is also possible to travel all the way into the Light of the Endless through any one Sephirah, or even through any one of the letter-gates.

Yogicly, the main purpose of the Tree of Life and its various names is to permit easy methodical concentration for long periods on the Divine Attributes given by the Sephiroth, and the Divine Name YHVH. Ideally, the only thing really needed is the Name of God as the Tree is only an assistance to our minds in understanding what is happening on the way of the Name. But, as different souls bear different spiritual endowments, there are many ways of ascending the Tree, called 'Working Paths', represented by specialized one-, two-, and three-column Sephirithic patterns. The wide assortment of these working Trees and their related disciplines have given Qabala a very colorful history.

While the above mentioned "Tree language" come from the Sefer ha Shmot (Book of Names), a considerable assortment of Tree of Life meditations is also provided by several other primary Qabalistic sources; most notably, the Sefer Yetzirah, the Etz Chiyim (Luria), and the Merkabah (Chariot) sections of Ezekiel and Isaiah. Examples range from double pyramidal forms to those of concentric circles. Fortunately, the basic principles and experiences which the diagrams illustrate are generally consistent and complementary, though variations in terminology may at first be somewhat confusing. In this last respect, Qabala has been plagued by a plethora of uninitiated commentary and all around noise in the circuit.

TREE OF LIFE — WAY OF YHVH ELOHENU

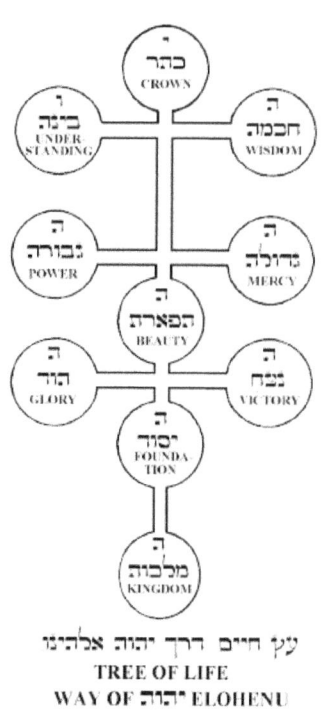

TREE OF LIFE
WAY OF יהוה ELOHENU

Figure 3

The Tree of Life, Way of YHVH Elohenu is a rapid, smooth path up the Central Column, which centers upon renunciation and the unselfish love for the Lord. This path is facilitated by meditation upon the combined mantric repetition and visualization of the Brilliant Name of Fire. YHVH, which gradually purifies the Shells (Qliphoth) and enables the soul to sustain the direct experience of the Zeir and Arik Anpin.

The consciousness of the traveller first moves through the Gate of the Gimel (GML, Savior) between Yesod (Foundation) and Tiphareth (Beauty), which appears like a mirror. In the beginning stages of meditation, the 'Watcher on the Threshold' is seen in the mirror which is really a reflection of one's own reincarnating geviyah (GBIH, astral body) as darkened by the shadows of accumulated Mazal (MZAL, equivalent to the Hindu term, 'karma'). The repetition of the Name cleanses the geviyah of the seeds of impure desires which crystallized through past experiences, whereby the 'Watcher' is replaced by the Name, or by a Gatekeeper such as Moses, or may even become transparent. Other than the 'Watcher on the Threshold', the gates of the Central Column are colorless and open, without Gatekeepers who must be satisfied to proceed any further. As we can see, if the consciousness is temporarily distracted into either of the side pillars, it has no recourse but to return to the center as there are no gates vertically connecting the Sephiroth up the Right and Left Columns.

In passing through the Gate of the Gimel, the awakening of consciousness in Tiphareth is accompanied by intense bliss and joy. By maintaining balance between Gedulah (Mercy) and Geburah (Strength), and then between Hochmah (Wisdom) and Binah (Understanding), which is facilitated by keeping focused on the Name and the Holy Imperishable Letters ablaze on the Crown of the Most High (easily seen from Tiphareth up the Central Column), the pilgrim may proceed through the Gate of the Aleph and unite with the Arik Anpin in the Kether (Crown).

When first going up the Tree, Daath (Realization), which became Malcuth (Kingdom) with the Fall of Adam appears as a deep, black abyss and the Aleph is seen as a sword-bridge over it into Kether. But, when coming back down the Tree through the Gate of the Beth into Daath the whole universe is seen as a Unity in Ha Shem (i.e. Shir Qoma).

Figure 5

WAY OF MESSIAH

The Tree of Life, Way of Messiah (MShICh) is generally the fastest and easiest of the working paths, but requires that an overpowering love for Messiah be in our spiritual endowment. Meshiach, in the Qabalistic tradition, has four heads corresponding with the four Sephiroth of the Inner Court of the Tree of Life. The 'four heads' are called 'Reshit' (RAShITh, First), 'Moshe' (MShH, also called SVB[?]), 'Yeshuh' (IHShVH, also ASh), and 'Acharit' (AChRiTh, Last), respectively represented by the three Mother letters, Aleph, Mem, Shin, and the Holy Temple, Tav. These letters act as charac-

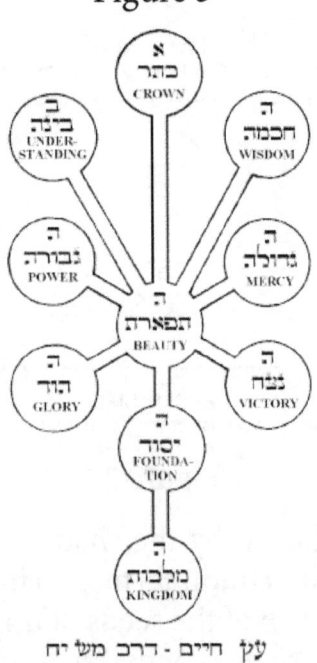

WAY OF MESSIAH

teristic filters through which the Divine Play of the Zeir Anpin is portrayed. The function of the filter is dramatically displayed in the name Yeshuh, YHShVH, wherein the Shin of Fire is easily seen as superimposed upon the name of the Father, YHVH. Intense love of the TORAH for Her own sake (rather than for power or exemption from judgment) may be substituted as the embodiment of Messiah.

Similar to the Way of YHVH Elohenu, the Way of Messiah is lit by repetitively calling upon the Name of the Chosen Ideal by Itself or as part of a longer prayer, while simultaneously imagining the Face of the Beloved in the heart center, situated approximately at the base of the sternum. The awakening of consciousness in Tiphareth (Beauty) lights the entire Tree, whereby the rest of the Sephiroth merge into one large Sephirah at Tiphareth. The reader may note that the Tree of Messiah is unique in having a gate between Tiphareth and Hochmah (called the 'Gate of Messiah').

Another aid in regards to this path is the discipline called "looking for Messiah, because He's got to come today", by which we look into the eyes of everyone we see expecting them to be our Beloved.

WAY of THE WIZARD, WAY OF THE SAINTS

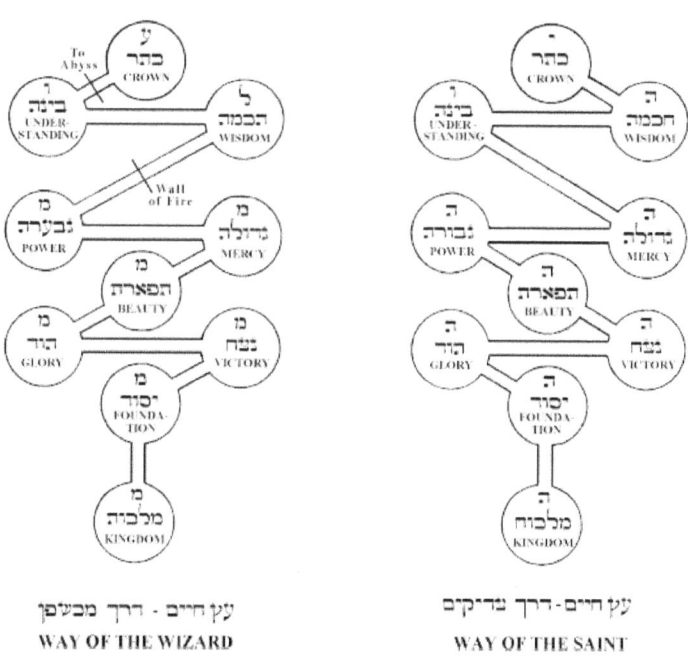

Figure 7   Figure 8

The Tree of Life, Way of the Saints (DRK TzDIQIM) involves an arduous progression up the Tree, in which the Sephiroth are traversed one by one in order as shown in Fig. 8. This path is often confused with the Way of the Wizard (DRK MKShPN), which proceeds in the identical manner as the Way of the Saints, but in an exactly opposite order, as may be seen by comparing Figs. 7 and 8. One prominent distinction on the Way of the Wizard is that the gate between Geburah (Strength) and Hochmah (Wisdom) is blocked by a wall of fire, obstructlng progress into the Supernals. There is no such wall blocking the gate between Gedulah (Mercy) and Binah (Understanding) on the Way of the Saints, and movement into the Supernals is smoothly accomplished.

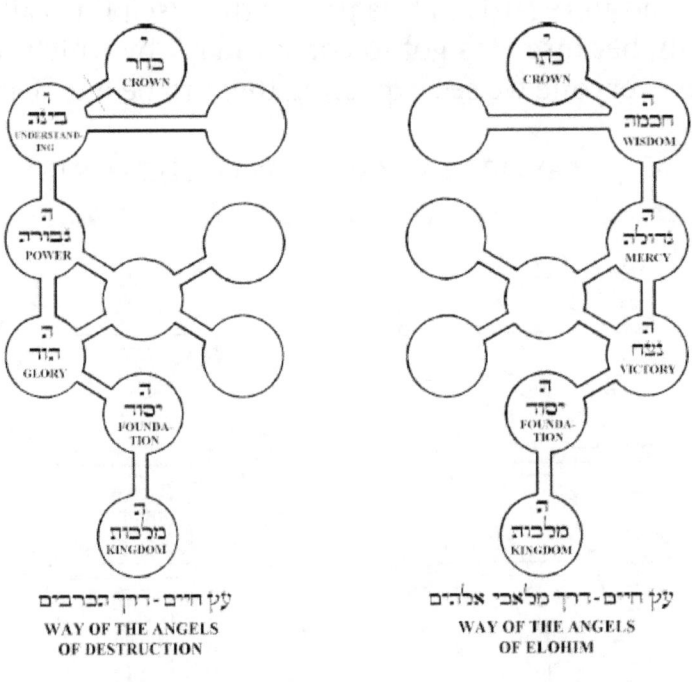

Figure 9   Figure 10

The Trees of Life, Way of the Angels of Elohim (DRK MLAKI ALHIM) and Way of the Angels of Destruction (DRK HKRBIM) both involve meticulous adherence to prescribed codices of rules governing the mastery of Mazal (MZLA, Fate) and the acquisition of power. In the case of the former, rigor or judgment is entirely eliminated and Ha Shem's Name is used for the sake of obtaining creative powers, i.e. healing, creating a solar system, etc.; and in the case of the latter, mercy is similarly expelled and Ha Shem's Name is used for the sake of obtaining destructive powers and the control of the Jinn. Unlike the Central Column, the side columns have Gatekeepers who strictly enforce standards expected to be met in order to progress further along these paths. As the Columns of the Right and Left are in a state of polar stress, the beings inhabiting one side engage in active conflict with those on the other (while the Central Column, balancing the two, remains unaffected).

Also, on the Tree of the Angels of Destruction, the gate between Binah and Kether is blocked by a Cherubim wielding flaming swords on all sides. Inasmuch as the rapid action of the Left-handed Path arises from the intense focusing of the mind on God in the form of an adversary, when disruption of the Creation becomes problematic the Black Magician is directed into the Abyss via the Gate of the Ayin and the vowels. As the shells are shattered rather than purified, this path is not recommended. The right-hand Path, on the other hand, can be very slow as the amassment of purity and merit required to pass through the gates involves considerable time.

TREE OF LIFE, TREASURIES OF THE HOUSE OF ELOHIM

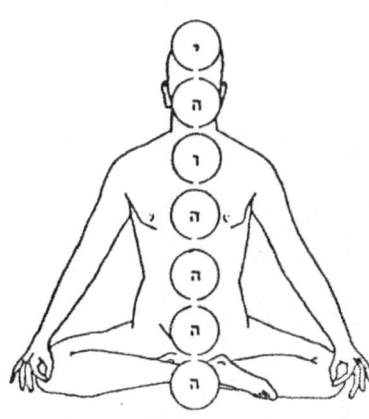

The Tree of Life, Way of the Treasuries of the House of Elohim (BITh H-ALHIM), refers to the exclusive use of the Central Column (Way of YHVH Elohenu) and comes from the Spirit of David, King of Israel Forever. The Sephiroth on this path are collectively named the Treasuries of the House of Elohim and are intended to build the Temple of YHVH in the hearts of all Israel.

The use of the Central Column alone eliminates the distractions of the Right and Left Columns, as well as, any interference from beings inhabiting these areas. The disappearance of the side pillars results in various changes: namely, Kether (Crown) is replaced by Rosh (Head);

Hochmah (Wisdom) and Binah (Understanding) are removed, and Gedulah (Mercy) and Geburah (Strength) are repositioned into the Central Column. Yesod (Foundation) is also removed.

The Tree of the Treasuries of the House of Elohim is also found to be the basis for the rather enigmatic Book of Revelations (Rev. 7:12) in the Peshitta (New Testament), which enumerates a pattern of forty-nine experiences, representing seven repetitions of the seven Sephiroth as they act upon one another.

Figure 11

THE COMPOSITE TREE OF LIFE

The Composite Tree of Life (Fig. 13) is obtained by superimposing all the paths depicted in all of the figures. This form of the Tree is often erroneously thought of as being a workable path in itself. However, a working path infused with the power of a suitable Name of God automatically directs the changes of consciousness of the traveller along the way, according to a characteristically established pattern of gates. As all the Sephiroth on the Composite Tree are connected amongst one another by gates, it offers no such specific route and is consequently Ineffective as a working path.

Names from Tenach (Old Testament) and the Qabalistic tradition have been attributed to the gates as follows:

Gate, Name
1. Gates of YHVH Elohenu, Central Column
2. Gate of the Excellent Servants of Everlasting Action
3. Gate of the Unclean Servants
4. Gate of Messiah
5. Gates of the Ruler (Royal Gates), Right Column (male)

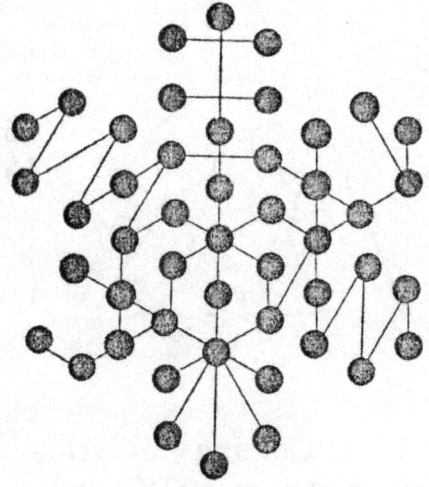

Figure 13

6. Gates of Destruction, Left Column (female)
7. Gate of Doom (Fate)
8. Gate of Samael
9. Gates of the Saint
10. Gates of the Sorcerer

TREE OF THE CONGREGATION

TREE OF THE CONGREGATION

The Tree of the Congregation is very unusual as there are no gates, and unlike any other Tree, the Complete Name, YHVH, appears in all the Sephiroth. Though included in the Book of Names, very little is known about the Tree of the Congregation.[1]

INTRODUCTION TO THE TREES OF PERFECTION

In reaching the Kether (Crown), the meditation deepens with the Tree completely disappearing and Heaven and Earth passing away for us. This means that we are in the Roots of the Tree. These roots are first, the Brilliant Name of Fire, YHVH, filling the Deep; second, the Aleph of Unity, the basic unstruck sound prior to the Creation, from which emanate the Holy Imperishable Letters, and unto which they again disappear. The Worlds of the Aleph are witness states devoid of the manifest activity characteristic of the Beth Worlds (worlds of the Torah Sefer Yetzirah, Qu'ran, all of which begin with the letter Beth). The third root is the AIN (Nothing), the Mysterious Unknown at the Roots of All Things, about which nothing can be predicated. Another name for the AIN in the Qabalistic tradition is NOT (LA). There is

---

[1] For more information on the Tree of the Congregation, the reader is directed to the writings of Kenneth Grant and Michael Bertiaux—especially those passages dealing with the concept of the Voltigeurs, or Leapers, who are able to traverse the entirety at the Tree without the need for Paths.—PVN

a saying that spiritual life begins with the realization of the AIN!

Through the Will of Ha Shem, some return from this ultimate experience, for whom the Tree takes special form as the Tree of Perfection (Fig. 15). "All the Trees are living, pulsating, as the primary consciousness moves from Sephirah to Sephirah. The Tree of Perfection pulsates from the Tree of David after the Aleph, which is the basic sound of the Creation, through the balance of the Tree of Perfection, to the Tree of David after Ain, which is the Ultimate Nothing. The Aleph is God-with-Form, the Ain is God-without-Form."

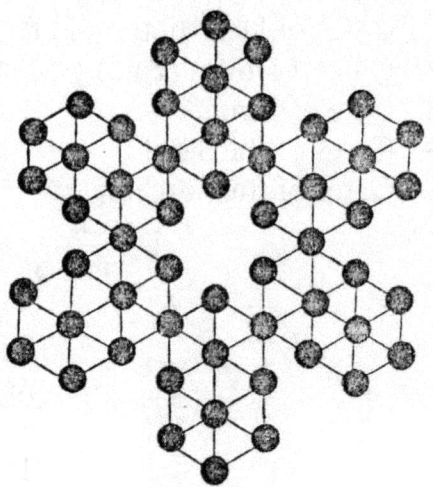

Figure 15

Further Notes on the Eleven Star Working

PVN (1984)

The main bulk of the Eleven Star Working has been dictated and the work of earthing the idea has already begun. The thrones are awaiting those who are ready to fulfill the office of Gods.

Lest there be any confusion, let me state once again that the thrones are not to be filled by persons, but by Gods. An individual or a group of individuals does not fill a particular station or throne. An individual or group of individuals will come to the Eleven Star with a specific task for which he/she/they have been preparing for thousands of incarnations. That task is earthing of a particular magickal current, which, although it has been operative in an occult manner over the millennia, has never before been manifested by individuals who have had the understanding to comprehend the vast scope of the overall plan.

Before an individual or group of individuals can activate any of the Thrones, they must take responsibility for all of their many many lives & direct their various incarnations in such a way as to influence all of them in occult ways so that their past experiences in all of these lives will be sufficient for the task at hand—that of waking up.

Waking up is the taking of responsibility of one's own life, both in the present & throughout all of time.

When one is sufficiently awake, one perceives the common thread in all of one's lives as a magickal linkage which transcends time & space. In effect, one becomes aware of what he/she perceives to be the ONE real magickal Order. By definition of past experience one sees this Order as having profound occult influence on the lives & cultures of peoples around the world & in every conceivable moment of time. This stage of being half-awake is a very dangerous time. Because one perceives the common thread throughout one's own incarnations does not make it historically accurate for anyone else.

By waking further, one perceives that (for all intents & purposes) that one's own very magickal past has led one to the position of being the head of The Order. Megalomania & the founding of vast conquering empires often result from an individual gaining access to such vast personal power.

It is here that the Eleven Star becomes crucial. Every Star in creation is the head of a very specific magickal Order. By waking-up, one gains access to one's own magickal path & the accumulated power of innumerable incarnations. Such persons are candidates for the Eleven Star.

But being the head of one's own personal magickal Order is not enough. Each of the persons who are candidates for the Eleven Star are very very imbalanced. The only way that they could have come so far (leaving the rest of the race far behind) is through gross overspecialization. Each of the candidates has the very specific Keys to unlock the True God-head in all of the others, but not in him or her-self. The imbalanced individual cannot have access to the key to his or her own Godhead for the temptation to use that key before balance is achieved would be far too great.

One achieves Godhead (& thereby the ability to fill one of the thrones) by going to each of the other candidates & becoming an initiate in their personal magickal Order. In return for this, you must then initiate the initiator, so that the power shared by both of you is doubled. When sufficient mutual initiations have occurred, the powerzones will form & the task of a particular Throne will become obvious. This is a time of Terror & Nightmare, for the sleeper does not want to wake fully, for to wake fully means taking full responsibility for all that is wrong with the world. At this stage, those who have passed through it will guide (by force & violence if need be!) to confront the sleeper with his or her particular task & will rub his or her nose in it until the sleeper either gives up all thought of magick, or is born as a godling.

Many are called but few are chosen. All Stars are indeed equal, but for the purpose at hand (the Elven Star) inequalities must be exaggerated in order that the candidates may more easily learn from each other.

The working knowledge/tasks/grade-papers of each of the candidates is important to all. It will not be possible to do all of the tasks outlined in the various grades in a single lifetime. Each candidate & godling must choose carefully. To avoid a task because it is 'not in my area' is a serious mistake. The candidates & godlings are not permitted the luxury of overspecialization any longer. There are great areas of underdevelopment which must be cured or the candidate will perish.

If there is a particular key to godhead which you fear greatly, of which you dismiss as being unimportant, it is probably the very task necessary for your development. Avoid the tasks which evoke no strong emotion in you, taking upon yourself only those tasks which evoke hatred, fear, love, trust, or any other strong emotion. If you are not truly able to be completely honest with yourself (as few candidates or godlings can be expected to be) then proceed according to will. At all other times, listen to advice of the other candidates. When advice is sought, it must not be ignored simply because it goes against your grain or is contrary with what you believe. The act of asking for advice binds you to undertake that tasks of the grade imposed by the God who has spoken trough the candidate or godling.

Such tasks may be in the form of a daily practice over a period of brief time (say 3 months), or may be a one-time initiatory ceremony involving ritual, drugs, or sex (or any combination thereof).

In certain rare instances one must accept long-term guidance from another candidate which involves a series of initiations inter-penetrated with a series of practices. Such long-term guidance is a severe test of the egoic discipline of both the master & the chela & is therefore a potent key to Godhead & also (if done awry) a potent tool for weeding out the unfit. If such a long-tern guidance fails, both guru & chela feel the consequences & are weakened thereby. But no matter how badly it goes, all is not lost, for others have the key to thy total recovery.

Eleven Star Ritual II

This ritual is intended to continue the initiations begun by the first ElevenStar Working, and to orient the Throne-holders who have been awakened to the specific energies that ElevenStar entails.

Participants do not have to be Throne-holders. The more Throne-holders who participate the better, though, since like attracts like, the nature of the ElevenStar rituals is such that they inspire and instruct the participants about the Thrones, thus providing a greater likelihood that participants will become Throne-holders.

Depending on the number of ritualists available, there may be multiple representations of the Thrones or a need for a ritualist to represent more than one Throne. All participants call the god-names of the Thrones in unison, so a precise match of numbers isn't crucial.

The following format is a suggested method—improvised variations are fine, so long as they work.

Materials: Eleven votive candles, a tray of sand or earth, a bowl of water, incense.

In preparation for the ritual, participants wash their hands before entering the Temple. When ritualists are assembled, a time is spent in meditation. These acts serve to clear the attention from the other concerns and ready it for the work at hand.

Though a traditional banishment is unnecessary for this ritual, there is a procedure that gathers-in & concentrates awareness and energy in the ritual space.

The god-names & gestures proceed widdershins at the beginning of the Rite for in-gathering, and deosil at the end for distributing the forces.

All stand in a circle. The tray of sand/earth and the other materials are at the center of the circle.

South: Shaitan
SE: Heru-Pa-Kraat
East: Ra-Hoor-Khuit
NE: Hadit
North: Nuit
NW: Maat
West: Babalon
SW: Aiwass

Touch the earth/ground with both hands.

Kindle the incense and pass it from hand-to-hand around the circle:

each one breathes upon the smoke saying, *"Abrahadabra. The Thrones must be filled."* Place the incense centrally in the tray of sand/earth.

Pass the bowl of water likewise. Each participant sprinkles a few drops toward the center of the circle, saying, *"Abrahadabra. The Thrones shall be filled."* Place the bowl next to the tray, to the West of it.

Each candle is lit, passed around the circle, then placed in its appropriate position on the sand/earth according to this order:

With each candle, chant & clap (*) as it is passed around.

```
      1   2
   8         9
   4         5
      6   7
     10   11
         3
```

Fill the Throne of the World,
*Lady Nuit ** Lady Nuit ***

Fill the Throne of the Moon.
*Lord Hadit ** Lord Hadit ***

Fill the Throne of the Sun.
*Ra-Hoor Khuit ** Ra-Hoor Khuit ***

Fill the Throne of Jupiter.
*IO PAN ** IO PAN ***

Fill the Throne of Venus.
*Babalon ** Babalon ***

Fill the Throne of Mars.
*Shaitan Aiwass ** Shaitan Aiwass **.*

Fill the Throne of Mercury,
*Therion ** Therion **.*

Fill the Throne of Uranus.
*Thelema ** Thelema **.*

Fill the Throne of Saturn.
Agape ** Agape **

Fill the Throne of Pluto.
Themis ** Themis **

Fill the Throne of Neptune,
Harpocrat ** Harpocrat **

After the last candle has been placed in the tray, join hands and circle dance to this chant:

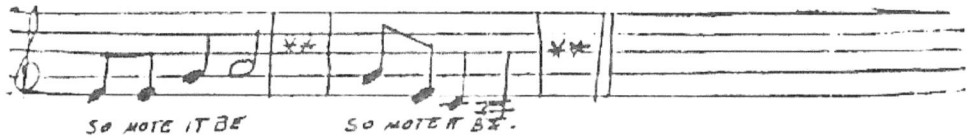

After three repetitions. all touch the earth with both hands, then perform the dispersal:

South: Shaitan	North: Nuit
SW: Aiwass	NE: Hadit
West: Babalon	East: Ra-Hoor-Khuit
NW: Maat	SE: Haru-Pa-Kraat

Again touch the earth with both hands. Extinguish the candles, snuff the incense in the tray and depart.

Notes on Certain Aspects of Transcendental Alchemy: Document II
The Alchemy of Immortality (part I)
Vampires and the Aristocracy of Blood
Being
An Esoteric Legacy of the Holy Graal

Including hints of certain sexual formulae which can be utilized by the serious student of Alchemy in the Creation and Nourishment of an alien symbiosis within his/her physical vehicle for attaining immortality in the flesh.

by Frater PVN

Do what thou wilt shall be the whole of the Law.

The subject matter of this essay is of great practical significance to all who aspire to the Alchemy of Immortality. Yet, because I have chosen to veil much of the practical application of this Alchemical process in allegory & legend, the text you are holding is not intended to be used as a 'cookbook for the novice.' Discretion is thus maintained, while truth is revealed. While I seek to be entertaining, such is not my prime concern. Those who seek pure entertainment would be better off spending their money on paperback novels whose cost per word is far cheaper than I am willing to accept for the product of my years of research.

To those who are serious in their quest for the Alchemy of Immortality, I council meditation on the 'spacemarks' between the concepts outlined herein rather than fixation upon the substance of legend & allegory. Those who seek to use this text as a cookbook to immortality will mislead themselves in their quest, for such secrets cannot be found in books, but only through initiatory contact with those who already hold the secrets &/or thru (individual & group) hermetic practices which guide the aspirant(s) to the immortal who dwells within each one of us.

Throughout this essay I have endeavored to use pronouns which reflect the reality that all of the various groups mentioned herein are composed of both men & women. English does not lend itself easily to such a task & so my grammatical constructs have become somewhat awkward.

Membership in certain of these mystical societies requires the embodiment of certain 'energies' which are traditionally linked to masculine or feminine virtues. Such quaint ideas can be useful in conveying the 'flavor' of a particular organization or field of endeavor, so long as no one feels that he or she is being excluded from participation based upon h-is/er physical gender.

Thus I speak of 'Vampire-kings', the 'Sisterhood of Babalon', etc. in order to convey the 'spirit' of certain attitudinal requirements necessary for success within such a group without any intending to discriminate on the basis of biological gender. I myself am a functional member in several of the more 'masculine' of the Esoteric Orders, while still retaining all of my prerogatives & abilities to function within the 'Sisterhood' of Babalon.

Love is the law, love under will.

PVN
Master, Forbidden Alchemies
Candidate, Eleven-Star Working
Priestess, Order of Babalon
West Danby, NY 11 November, 1983 e.v.

Disclaimer

Although the author of this paper is an initiate of several different over lapping Esoteric Orders; the information given in this paper is derived by the author though independent channels and should not be construed as reflecting the teachings of any Esoteric Order of which he is a member. The sexual formulae hinted at in this paper are the product of the author's inspiration & research and have not yet received sufficient testing to ensure their full efficacy or safety. Anyone who seek to utilize any of the formulae presented here does so at his/her own risk. The author councils each reader to familiarize him/her—self with the material in the list of suggested reading (given at the end of this essay) before any practical implementation of the Alchemy of Immortality is even contemplated.

Introduction: Common Roots of Vampires & Werewolves in Pre-History

In a very real sense, the vampire is both the product & the cause of the rise of civilization. Vampires are to civilization as werewolves are to the nomadic hunter-gatherer cultures of prehistory. The origins of both can be traced to some of the more obscure esoteric initiatory practices which certain powerful priestcrafts developed over the millennia which precede our current historical epoch.

Lycanthropy traces its roots to the atavistic worship of our pre-human ancestors, both phylogenetic and magickal to gain access to the 'Forgotten Ones'.[1] Ritualistic techniques used by different cultures vary considerably, yet the religious use of ecstatic dance, animal totems/familiars, blood sacrifice, sexual psychodrama, and vegetable entheogens are common threads which weave throughout these ancient rites to induce a 'backwards' twisting of consciousness along the DNA spiral of the Shaman to allow him to remember[2] techniques of astral time-travel which provide gateways linking him throughout all time & space via the creative use of totems & self-delusion. Once a permanent link is formulated with a particular pre-human or alien being, the Shaman then works with the totem in order to reify specific aspects of the ancestral DNA in the here-&-now of the Shaman's cytoplasm. A full treatment of the historical roots & present practices of this formula is beyond the scope of a single Alchemical treatise. I shall therefore focus my attention on that scion of pre-historical Lycanthropic Alchemy which is closest to my own area of magickal research & personal Alchemy—i.e. the Aristocracy of Blood.

---

1 See the Cincinnati Journal of Ceremonial Magick for a fuller explanation of the Forgotten Ones & the Elder Gods, especially *The Forgotten Ones* by NAHADA-62 in Volume I #2, and *Return of the Elder Gods* by NEMA and the shadow in volume I #3.
2 Re-member is used here in its original sexual context, which pertains (in modern legend) to both the resurrection of Osiris by Isis & Nephthys & to the 'Second Coming' of Jesus in the Christian mythos.

Genesis of the Aristocracy of Blood

The rise of the vampiric aristocracy dates from a late period of pre-history [possibly during the early dynasties of the Atlantean protectorship] when mathematically sophisticated sorcerers began to utilize many of the tools of the traditional shaman in order to explore more complex avenues of the Space/Time Continuum. These early Illuminati utilized their sex & drug induced knowledge of non-Euclidean geometries to explore, map, & reify some of the higher vibrations within the DNA pattern. This esoteric research discovered (&/or formulated) certain multi~dimensional linkages which are skew-wise to the linear time travel of the Shamans, as well as being altogether different from the exoteric three- dimensional genetic mapping of 20th Century Science. Through reification of these linkages with alien dimensions (i. e., those outside of the Space/Time continuum) certain 'alliances' were formed with some of the quasi-immortal God-kings who inhabit/rule many of these alien dimensions.

Within the context of our present civilization, these alien God-kings are sometimes referred to as the Elder Gods. Permanent symbiotic relationship with these alien God-kings became feasible after much experimentation with formalized ritual based on technological innovations and theoretical mathematics (effectively supplanting the so-called 'natural' rhythm of the cycles of mundane existence) . Thus the simple & religious shamanistic ritual was augmented by complex geometries, alien vibratory chants, alliances with living crystals, and the creation/use of 'synthetic' and non-vegetable entheogens (volcanic fumes, nitrous oxide, pure oxygen, etc.).

Perhaps the single greatest modification of shamanistic ritual was the removal of religious taboo from the sexual psychodrama of magick. While the shaman was concerned mainly with fertility, fecundity, and atavistic resurgence, these early Alchemists became concerned with mutation and the reification of radical ideas into socio-biological expression. Sexual formulae which were taboo to members of the Shamanistic priestcraft (as well as to non-initiates) became the mainstay of these Alchemical researchers. Over time, a system of sexual deviance & perversity was discovered/created which would enable a skilled Alchemist to permanently 'twist' his/her DNA in such a way that a symbiosis between human & alien became practical. The alien gained access to the full range of emotional expression of the human's physical nervous system, while the human gained access to the multidimensional esoteric 'nerve net' of the alien. Each gained vast experiential knowledge which assisted them both in the reification of personal & group goals within his/her own culture.

Historical accounts are of little use in sorting out fantasy from fact, for the roots of these Alchemies pre-date the written word (as we know it) by many millennia and those legends which have survived are distorted beyond recognition thru an oral tradition passed down through generations of poets whose interest in story-telling far outweighed a commitment to historical veracity. The problem is compounded by modern historians who, while knowing nothing of esoteric matters, insist on 'interpreting' the old legends by the dim light of secular humanism or from a personal stance of religious bigotry which is based in a total lack of understanding of the genesis of Christianity &/or Judaism.[3]

The oral tradition of the Alchemical priestcraft (even if it were available) would be not much better, for initiated 'traditions' are often altered for intra-organizational political motives almost as often as they are transmuted by the Alchemical process itself. There are certain members of this initiated priestcraft who date 'from the beginning' & therefore know firsthand whereof I speak, but they (for the most part) choose to remain silent.

The most valid record of the esoteric priesthood lies within the individual genetic memory of each and every human on this planet and is therefore fully accessible to any adept whose Will is to delve deeply down the forgotten by-ways of pre-history thru the proper entheogenic use of sex, drugs, and ritual.

For historical research of this kind, shamanistic (Forgotten Ones) rituals are ideal, since we are concerned with valid reconstruction of a forgotten past rather than transmutation of that which already understood.

However, once valid historical links have been established, the Elder God Alchemies so accessible to all who dwell in high-Tech civilization are ideal for the reification of ancient knowledge and the transmutation of ill-conceived formulae into AL-chemycal perfection. Such is one important aspect of the Great Work. This paper is a compendium of rough notes by Frater PVN obtained thru such individual magickal research augmented by constant revision in the light of initiated inspi-

---

[3] For a non-traditional view of the roots of both Judaism & Christianity, see Eden Captivity: Two Essays in Alchemy by Frater PVN (herein).

ration & thru contact with others who work to manifest this ancient priestcraft within the Race as a whole at this point of Time.

Aristocracy of the Holy Blood
Vampires & The Esoteric Legacy of the Holy Graal

While a clear picture of the beginnings of Vampiric Alchemy has been lost &/or deliberately obscured over the Æons, this much can be said with relative certainty. Vampires are not fully human. That is to say, they are created thru the esoteric hybridization of human stock with alien life forms from 'outside'. Whether the aliens ultimately derive from the legends of the Angels in the book of Genesis (first Book of Moses) the ancient astronauts of Von Daneken, or the trans-dimensional gods of Howard Philips Lovecraft is a moot point. The import of the Alchemies in this essay do not hinge on the specific origin of the vampiric race. It is up to each interested researcher to take the rough notes presented here into him/her-self, digest them, alter/magnify/twist them according to the inspiration of his/her own True Will, and derive therefrom a series of rituals &/or experiments to test the efficacy of this branch of Alchemy. Experimentation with this branch of Alchemy enables the aspirant to delve deeply along the skew-wise paths of trans-dimensional DNA, refining & reifying his/her own vision of the Alchemy of immortality.

Vampiric rites have much in common with traditional shamanistic rites, but the use of ritual, sex, & drugs has been refined for a vastly different purpose within each specialization. The skew-wise linkages induced into the DNA chain thru Vampiric Alchemy can be likened to a form of consciously controlled esoteric 'genetic engineering' for the purpose of implementing a permanent inter-species symbiosis between the Alchemist & representatives of (one or more) alien races. Such Alchemical manipulation of the genetic material often results in functional sterility &/or the danger of engendering congenital teratomas. Thus, a vampire rarely produces viable offspring. This is the basis of later legends which falsely depict vampires as being sexually impotent).

In this model of the origins of Vampiric Alchemy, inter-species 'breeding' does not necessitate the physical presence on this planet of sexually active representatives of any alien race. The union is purely an astral one. VIII°, IX°, and XI° sexual rites[4] are each necessary for

---

4   From my perspective (which is strongly influenced by the law of threes) there are three major branches

different aspects of this Alchemy. The 'magical child' is not a separate biological entity from the human magickian who undertakes such a course of initiation but is the 'office' of a functional symbiosis between human & alien.

While the function & purpose of this symbiosis is beyond the scope of this essay, I am able to state here that the physical body of that which once was a human being gains access to an esoteric nervous system which is not limited by any of the laws of nature of this reality. The speed of light, the flow of time, the three laws of thermo-dynamics, and the 'flatlander' perspective of Alternity as a whole are but a few of the limitations which cease to exist for the Vampiric Alchemist. The ability to manipulate multi-dimensional patterns while retaining full human body awareness is but one of the elementary attributes of such a union.

In its earliest stages of development, Vampiric Alchemy did not bestow the quasi-immortality which so sets this priestcraft apart from rest of the human race today. At the beginning of the present historical epoch, civilizations blossomed under the guidance of mortal vampires. Long-term projects were undertaken which required a dynamic continuity of inspired leadership unheard of in nomadic cultures. In order to prolong the life, vitality, charisma, wisdom, and creativity of key members the vampiric priesthood, certain rites of trans-human life extension were used to bestow quasi-immortality.

Such quasi-immortality was not without its price, but these noble priest-kings were willing to postpone the regenerative sleep of death indefinitely in order to guide the race during this crucial period of its infancy. Over time, the need for more & more long term projects soon forced most functional members of the priesthood to take the oath of the God-Kings & renounce death.

But even before the vampiric bloodline undertook the ordeal of quasi-immortality, their unique symbiosis enabled them to prosper & live far beyond their human peers. One need only look as far as the Judeo-Christian bible to see evidence of the longevity of the patriarchs who were responsible for the rapid ascendence of the Jewish people. But this priestcraft was by no means limited to the Jews. I single out

---

of Sexual Alchemy.
VIII° is masturbation to create willed astral phantasms.
IX° is pro-creative heterosexual intercourse to mutate the germplasm of the Alchemists.
XI° is sodomy &/or intercourse during menstruation [&/or the use of any other form of 'taboo' or 'unnatural' sexual act(s)] to mutate the somatoplasm of the AL-Chemysts.

the Jews only because they kept reasonably accurate records—records which many people in this culture can accept far more easily than the records of other ('heathen') cultures.

(I should mention in passing that ritual murder / sacrifice was the only effective method to remove a quasi-immortal vampiric king from office. It was from this necessity that the 'tradition' of Dionysian regicide grew & flourished culminating in the ritual sacrifice of Jesus, the Christ (note that crucifixion was not sufficient to kill this divine king—even piercing his heart with the lance of Longinus was unable to kill him beyond the powers of vampiric regeneration).

Over time, the need for a stable priestcraft of demigods became outmoded by the need for rapid growth and expansion which is possible only during epochs of instability & (seemingly) chaotic change. The race of mortal humans began to chafe under the firm rulership of the vampiric priesthood. It was time for the race of vampire-kings to abdicate their thrones to the race of humans who needed to gain maturity and wisdom thru self-governance.

One by one, the quasi-immortal vampire kings abdicated their thrones thru acquiescence to immolation through ritual sacrifice or thru self-banishment. The network of immortals who once ruled the earth disbanded & the Night of PAN came to test the fabric of civilization. A common thread throughout history is that the gods of an old religion tend to become the devils of the religion which supplants it. The vampiric priesthood & their alien symbiotes are no exception to this rule. It is from this unstable period of history the 'traditional' legends of vampirism, demonic possession, and black magic were spawned which even today malign the sacred priestcrafts of our noble ancestors.

The Night of PAN[5] had been long expected by this race of alien symbiotes whose composite esoteric nervous system was intimately connected to the ebb & flow of probability & prognostication. The vampiric priestcraft saw the coming of the Night of PAN & they made firm but flexible plans to carry the secrets of the priesthood thru the upcoming millennia while they worked towards the day when the race of humans would be ready to embrace their Alchemical heritage

---

5 The Night of PAN is also known as the formula of N.O.X., which is characterized by CHAOS, the dark night of the soul, those aspects of existence which appear to be governed by the non-rational. N.O.X. can be particularly terrifying by those who fear death (the ultimate chaos), yet accept its inevitability. The complimentary formula is L.V.X., which is characterized by Monotheism, the light of reason, and by those aspects of existence which appear to be governed by the laws of nature.

in maturity & responsibility thus showing themselves to be ready to integrate themselves en masse into the royal family of blood.

However, for the duration of the Night of PAN, initiation into the inner mysteries of Vampiric Alchemy became next to impossible. Those members of the Alchemical Priestcraft who **chose** to survive the Regicide made no attempt to rebuild their former glory. Instead, they worked in silence & secrecy to ensure that their Alchemical traditions & arcane knowledge would be preserved during the Night of PAN.

These Priest-kings in exile deemed it far too dangerous to create a race of new quasi-immortals during a time when infant-Vampires would not be subjected to checks & balances within the network of the 'Aristocracy of the Holy Blood'. Each surviving member of the Vampiric aristocracy became the seed from which Alchemical tradition would be preserved. Each tailored his/her own plan of action in accord with the probability alignments within his/her own extended esoteric nervous system, while keeping to the spirit of the three-fold division of esoteric teachings outlined in the next chapter.

Three—Fold Division of the Vampiric Secret
I The Esoteric Mystery Schools

A system of independent secret esoteric mystery schools was set-up. Each school was trained separately by a single member of the Priestcraft of Blood in a pattern of theoretical & symbological constructs dealing with various aspects of esoteric Vampiric Alchemy. No single school was entrusted with full theoretical knowledge and no piece of the puzzle was given to only one of the schools, so knowledge was safeguarded both from mis-use & from extinction. Various of the symbols (such as those which later evolved into the Tarot) were designed as a bridge to link the mystery schools together to facilitate communication amongst adepts from different schools. None of these mystery schools were entrusted with a full theoretical comprehension or the means to implement the crucial sexual formulae related to Vampiric Alchemy. Such division of knowledge was crucial so that it would not be possible for any of these Esoteric Schools (individually or collectively) to create or sustain a true quasi-immortal Vampire should any members of these fraternities attempt to reify their incomplete theoretical knowledge.

II The Sisterhood of Babalon[6]

The formulae of Sexual Alchemy so necessary for the sustenance/nourishment of all vampires was distributed without regard to secrecy thru complete secularization of the Sisterhood of Babalon. Prior to the on-set of the Night of PAN, the Priestcraft of Sacred Prostitution provided nourishment & initiation within the inner-circles of Vampiric Alchemy. Secrets of 'life essence' were entrusted to Prostitutes because 'life essence' is inherently sexual in nature & (in order to retain its efficacy) MUST be given freely (i.e., without force or coercion) by those who act with informed consent. By informed consent I mean that the egregore of the priestcraft must understand the full practical application of the Alchemies involved & each functional member of the priesthood must be able to regenerate the 'life-essence' within her/him-self by virtue of her/his (formal or intuitive) esoteric training.

Distribution of such potent formulae amongst this secular priestcraft has proven to be an unqualified success. Intuitive knowledge of 'life essence' (& its manipulation) is found even today amongst most of the Artisans of the world's oldest profession. Those women & men who practice prostitution with a conscious under-standing of these Alchemies retain their youth & vigor far longer than the general population & attain levels of spiritual enlightenment far beyond their

---

[6] The Sisterhood of Babalon is one of the esoteric names for that segment of the human race whose natural proclivities involve then in widespread sexual contact. The Sisterhood of Babalon is not an 'Order' in the common use of that word for it is based upon non-rational intuitive links to bind its membership together rather than relying on a common set of rules, or organizational structure in order to define itself. Anyone is free to become a part of the Sisterhood at any time simply by embracing its philosophy and making it a part of h-is/er life. The Sisterhood of Babalon is the polar reflection of the masculine energies embodied in the Esoteric Orders.

Since the abdication of the Vampire-kings, Society has looked-down upon most members of this Holy Priestcraft & has given them labels (such as hookers, whores, prostitutes, gigolos, etc.) which (they seem to believe) will shame the practitioners of this Holy Art into 'repenting'. Since I believe that it is easier to transmute insults than it is to obliterate them, I have deliberately chosen 'emotionally loaded' terms to describe the functional sub-sets of this Holy Sisterhood. Hookers are those professional members of the Order of Babalon who are paid for their services as strippers, go-go dancers, prostitutes, and pornographer's models. Whores are those hedonistic members of the Order of Babalon whose commitment ecstasy, pleasure, and novelty induce them to many of the same activities as hookers. Priestess are those connoisseur members of the Order of Babalon whose commitment to the distillation of the elixir of immortality & the on-going evolution of the race gives them the incentive of religious fervor in carrying out their work. But such labels are in themselves misleading Society has used such labels to divide us in the past, we must be careful, or we may fall into the same trap. Whores, Hookers, and Priestesses are not really different sub-groups within the Order of Babalon but are representatives of three ends of a continuous multi-dimensional spectrum of activity. In recent times (since the advent of safe & effective birth control, whores have begun to gain a greater acceptance in this culture, but many of them are still uncomfortable with their professional sisters. Ideally, all members of the Order of Babalon embody a bit of the hooker, whore & priestess, and are willing to experiment with whatever approach seems most appropriate to the occasion.

peers. The constant flow of Alchemical energies thru their bodies is a source of nourishment & a catalyst for the reification of aspirations and dreams. However, those who dare to practice this ancient art without regard for its subtle spiritual heritage become consumed by the energies which they know not how to handle. The fears/loathings/nightmares which lurk within these secular practitioners seek outward expression in the fora of spiritual & physical maladies such as insanity, drug addictions, venereal disease, and obsession upon power and the domination of others. Such misguided practitioners of the High Art of Sexual Alchemy are quickly destroyed by their own imbalances, leaving behind them a legacy of sickness & death.

III The God-Kings in Exile
The third branch of Vampiric Alchemy was deemed too dangerous to entrust to either the esoteric Fraternity of Mystery Schools or the exoteric Sisterhood of Babalon. Such secrets of synthesis & initiation by blood[7] were far too sensitive to entrust to mere mortals, who would too easily fall prey to the siren call of immortality in the flesh. The quasi-immortal vampiric aristocracy entrusted this knowledge to none but themselves. These quasi-immortals are (by necessity of nourishment) in continuous contact with members of the Sisterhood of Babalon. It is thru such contact that practical Sexual Alchemy is being refreshed & refined within this informal priestcraft. Contact is also maintained with the mystery schools & occult Orders, although this contact is usually more discrete & is often indirect. Only upon rare occasion does a member of the Alchemical Aristocracy exert direct control over any of the Magickal Orders, for it is deemed safest if the Orders are kept in ignorance as much as possible. Over the past few millennia, certain mortals have been recruited into the ranks of the Vampiric Priestcraft based upon criteria known only by those responsible for the selection.

The trans-mundane Alchemical Priesthood then undertook to obliterate all evidence of their own existence throughout the world at large. Fantastic legends were engendered & propagated. Modern researchers are only beginning to grasp that the 'Dark Ages' were not <u>'dark' nearly</u> as much as they were made deliberately 'obscured'.[8] Much

---

[7] Initiation by blood should be considered allegorical as well as actual. The two major branches of XI° Alchemy (Sodom & Gomorrah) both play an instrumental role in the creation of vampires, while feasting upon the menstruata of a sexually aroused tantric initiate provides the vampire with on-going sustenance.
[8] See the book Holy Blood Holy Graal for an introduction to the way in which history has been deliber-

of the esoteric Alchemy was perverted, forgotten, &/or totally misunderstood. Today, many esoteric Orders with valid roots in the mystery schools of the forgotten Æons possess only rudimentary fragments of such Alchemies. Most (if not all) of these Orders do not understand enough to make any practical use of the 'secrets' of immortality which they possess, and many even deny that actual immortality in the flesh is possible or even desirable! Such an attitude of 'sour grapes' is humorous while nonetheless tragic.

As I mentioned above, most vampires become functionally sterile as a side-effect of multi-dimensional geometric manipulations of their DNA pattern. However, sterility is but a by-product of the Alchemy and not a desired end in-&-of-itself. Over time, members of the Alchemical priesthood of Vampires have worked to un-do their self-induced mutations on a local level within the microcosm of their own reproductive tissue, so that they would then be able to engender viable offspring. Such experiments have had a limited success, and (over the past millennium) vampires have begotten a number of vampire/human halflings. Such halflings are human in all outward respects, but tend to be slightly 'different' from other humans in the following ways:

- They have a slightly longer lifespan, better health/vitality, & greater native mental abilities than fully human members from a similar tribe/culture/social class.
- They are able to formulate 'links' within themselves, thus opening themselves up to limited contact with certain aspects of some of the alien races which make-up their heritage. Thus they are able to access information, memories, &/or psychic powers 'beyond those of ordinary mortals (e.g., the 'dreams' of H. P. Lovecraft, demonic possession', etc.).
- Because of their internal links their DNA is not quite 'normal' Certain of these genetic abnormalities, cause them to be somewhat less fertile than most humans.

The genetic potential of vampiric characteristics is passed down to the offspring of such halflings un-diluted over many generations, since this Alchemical information is contained in an alteration of the metapattern of the multi-dimensional pattern of the chromosomes themselves rather than in individual genesis However, expression of the full potential of these traits is often limited by a lack of training. When formal training (in esoteric mystery schools, or in exoteric

---

ately obscured by various vested interest groups.

prostitution) is made available, these half-lings often become powerful charismatic leaders who value their inspired intuitive links to their Royal lineage far more than they value the 'truths' & doctrines learned from any branch of human learning. Being halfling heirs to a nobility of blood far older, far wiser, and far more noble than any who govern this planet today, they are natural anarchists who follow internal laws which transcend any reverence for God, Nation, Esoteric Order, or People. But their anarchy is based on a sacred regard for others. They value personal honor far above personal comfort or safety. Their word (if given freely to those who seek an honorable pact) will bind them far more than any rule, law, or treaty has ever bound a mortal human. It is these renegade halflings who are heir to the full spectrum of Alchemical secrets of their vampiric ancestors. They are godlings and they know it.

Vampiric Alchemy Today

Tim Leary & Robert Anton Wilson were the first contemporary writers to open my mind to the ideas of those 'new alchemists' who seek to use in vitro Alchemical preparations for the permanent alteration of consciousness & for the indefinite prolongation of life. The new alchemists believe that these preparations would become available to everyone (despite government repression) regardless of the spiritual preparedness of the seeker. Some would say that such secularization of Alchemy is dangerous because it encourages experimentation in personal transformation without proper guidance from a 'guru' or 'Master Alchemist' (either as a human teacher or as an internal 'spirit guide').

At one time I parroted the pompous intonations of the esoteric purists, but careful research over the past decade has led me to accept the absolute necessity of secular Alchemies in this society. There are no immortal priest-kings to illume our path with their Wisdom & experience. Esoteric Orders do not hold all of the keys to transcendental Alchemy and they are not inclined to share those keys which they do possess. Esoteric Alchemy is little understood (& rarely practiced) even by those who claim to possess the necessary initiations. Secular Alchemies are therefore necessary for most people as a first-step to immortality &/or functional transcendence of the limitations of flesh. Longevity & drug-induced 're-programming' of the internal bio-computer lead serious students to the discovery of those in vivo entheogens which are the foundation of the Alchemy of Immortality.

Today, sex magick has reached the proportions of an obsession with most who tread the path of spiritual Alchemy, yet the link to vampiric immortality remains shrouded in ignorance & fear. Most 'authorities' who write textbooks on sexual Alchemy are themselves novices, who understand the inner mysteries but dimly. All authors (both masters & novices alike) are further handicapped by their attempt to teach a non-rational and non-verbal Art via linear words without undertaking the responsibility to personally oversee a regimen of initiation and supervised practice. The best any author can achieve is to hint at fruitful paths for individual research. Aleister Crowley hinted at some of the secrets & was labeled evil by a society which lacked esoteric training & access to the secular in vitro Alchemies of our culture. Kenneth Grant continues to speak obliquely of certain aspects of the mysteries & has been labeled perverse by certain initiates who ought to know better.

Perhaps the clearest exposition of the inherent sexual nature of vampires can be found in the popular fiction of Chelsea Quinn Yarbro. The life and Alchemies of Count Ragoczy Saint-Germain can be an inspiration to all who seek to revivify and reify this potent Alchemical formula within themselves However, even a first-rate novelist such as Ms. Yarbro is limited by the rational linearity of the printed word (as well as by the degree to which she is willing &/or able to 'fine-tune' her understanding of the Alchemical vampiric formula thru personal magickal practice) & can therefore do no more than hint at the inner workings of such Alchemies. There are areas in which Ms. Yarbro's inspiration & mine differ. It is up to readers of this assay to work their own personal magicks in order to discover/create formulae which are based on the Truth which lies within.

The Esoteric Orders

Various occult Orders were begun at the behest of the trans-human guides of the esoteric Alchemical priesthood which exist outside of our mundane universe in order to safeguard as much of the Alchemical secrets as possible during the Night of PAN. With the coming of the Æon of Horus[9] in 1904, the human race has made a commitment to responsibility & maturity unknown at any time in recorded history. It is now time for occult Orders to come out into the open, shedding

---

9 The Æon of Horus is one of the manifestations of what is generally known as the 'Age of Aquarius'. The 'constitution' of the Æon of Horus is Liber AL vel Legis, a document dictated to Aleister & Rose Crowley from a trans-mundane entity identifying itself as AIWASS during a 3-day ritual in Cairo in 1904. A full account of this working is contained in The Equinox if the Gods, by Aleister Crowley.

their light upon the race as a whole.

However, the habits of centuries cannot be obliterated overnight, especially in organizations whose sole purpose is the guarding of secrets which they understand but dimly. Persecution, isolation, & paranoia have taken their toll on the Esoteric Orders. These leaders who possess even rudimentary fragments of the mysteries guard them niggardly & refuse to share their initiations, experimentations, & observations with any save their dutiful disciples.

Restriction of the flow of information is rarely done in an open acknowledgement that the hoarder chooses to function as an obscurer of the Light. Instead, most of those who function in the office of black brother usually attempt to wear the god-form of 'guardian of eternal truth' who (in solemn pomposity with eyes cast heavenwards) shield all 'neophytes' from 'dangerous formulae' in order to 'protect 'them from 'energies' which are 'beyond' their grade. Should any neophyte have the courage/enthusiasm to work independently of the Order he/she will most undoubtedly begin to discover formulae which differ from those taught within the Order. Upon reporting his/her discoveries to the Order, the neophyte is usually told that he/she cannot possibly understand the implications of the formula in question at his/her present stage of development & he/she will then be instructed to trust in the judgement of 'those who know better' & abandon his/her course of personal research in favor of the accepted curriculum espoused by the Order. Such nonsense stifles creativity in all but the most daring & promulgates the illusion that conservative elements within the Order are privy to secrets beyond the comprehension of eager seekers.

Cross-fertilization among such Orders has become virtually defunct, mainly due to internal power politics & the need of leaders to be right, even at the expense of perverting Truth to such an extent that they even fool themselves with their own lies. Stagnation/ossification within most Esoteric Orders has therefore become rife.

Many of the truly creative leave such Orders in disgust. Some continue Alchemical research on their own while others abandon the Great Work altogether. Over generations occult Orders favor selection of the weak, the obsequious, & the craven for posts of authority & prestige. These Orders still guard the Secrets, but the cost of obtaining initiation &/or nourishment from the mysteries of these Orders is more than most freedom-loving men & women are able to stomach.

In this Æon of Horus, more & more eager students of the mysteries are abandoning the traditional channels of esoteric initiation in favor of personal research guided by the light of the inspired writings of those occult renegades who have dared to reveal those teachings which were entrusted to them in secrecy by various of the Esoteric Orders. Such renegades often comment upon these mysteries in an open fashion totally unknown within esoteric circles & augment the traditional teachings with practical applications derived from their own personal research with the mysteries.

Unfortunately, even the most inspired of these renegades have posthumously acquired a following of fools who seek to rule dogmatically and coerce their peers into following cravenly in someone else's footsteps, rather than using the tools at their disposal to assist each other in transcending the limitations which their renegade Master was unable or unwilling to perceive. Such 'second generation' esoteric schools are often less restrictive than the mystery schools from which they originated, but progress within the Order is still based upon rule-following rather than research guided by internal inspiration. Experimental information is still not shared amongst members and these Orders still promulgate the illusion that the ability to manifest occult Wisdom & Authority'[10] bears a direct proportional relationship to Grade Certificates generated by the Order.

However, all is not glum. With each passing generation of renegades, the fabric of the Orders themselves are evolving into a form which will encourage the general membership in ways which will assist in formulating/discovering certain keys for unlocking those ancient Alchemical secrets necessary to the proper function of the Alchemical Aristocracy of Blood within this Æon of Horus.

The Sisterhood of Babalon

Over the last two decades, sexual freedom has seen a surge of growth unprecedented in modern history. With the advent of the Æon of Horus, has come the sexual revolution, & the recognition of the equal-

---

10 Authority is the right to take on the god-form of an author/publisher, whose office is that of creator, promulgator, & reifier of magickal formulae. Authority is rarely (if ever) bestowed by any external power structure, for one of its pre-requisites is total self-confidence in one's internal contacts with the divine. Such self-confidence needs to be tested thru creative & non-destructive conflict with those who feel it is their duty to protect neophytes from the 'untested' theories of journeyman Alchemists. Many journeyman Alchemists publish, yet few have the blessings of their teachers. The only proof of valid authority is the success of the formula being promulgated. It is up to each of us to decide on criteria for success, each for him/her-self.

ity of woman. These factors have combined to produce a weakening of the ossified moral fabric of society. Pornography and Prostitution have become major industries and are even now shedding the yoke of slavery to organized crime which society has traditionally used to control those who ply this most ancient of professions. As the pall of criminality dissipates from the secular priestcraft of Sexual Alchemies, more and more members of society are drawn to their ranks, either as practitioners of this ancient art or as seekers of that sexual healing which only an inspired Priestess can offer. Those who practice this ancient Art purely for mundane goals of money &/or power are soon burned-out by the energies which they are unable to comprehend or transmute, while those dedicated to their profession are being transformed by their own Alchemies into members of a functional priestcraft which has not graced this planet since the dissolution of the Aristocracy of the Holy Blood two millennia ago.

A Brief Look at Future Possibilities

Formal religion is withering away as each new generation of seekers turns away from the dogma & repression of religion to seek truth within themselves. Esoterically derived sexual practices, 'recreational' drugs, & popular music are powerful tools which are far more accessible to the masses and far more trustworthy to the masses than the closely guarded traditions of the Esoteric Mystery Schools. In this new Æon of personal responsibility, each seeker has the ability to transubstantiate the secular into the divine.

The time has come for the race to re-discover & re-integrate its esoteric Alchemical heritage. The guarded secrets of the Magickal Orders need to be re-integrated back into the main-stream and merged with the blossoming of non-traditional sexual Alchemies whose roots lie in the exoteric Sisterhood of Babalon. The balanced Nu-Age Alchemies which can come of such a union can assist us greatly in our task of transforming the vices of mundane institutions (artificial scarcity, near-sighted short-term goals which abdicate responsibility for the future of race as a whole, etc.) into the outward explosion of creative energy so 'necessary' to the universal prosperity of a spiritually advanced race of quasi-immortal beings who dare reach for their heritage of Godhood amongst the stars.

Yet, we have no interest in reinstituting the absolute aristocracy of the quasi-immortal vampiric priesthood to govern the race of transient mortals. When last they ruled/ the Vampiric priesthood was limited by the development of the race as a whole as well as by the primitiveness of their own internal Alchemies.

But now, the race has matured & the Æon of Horus is manifestly upon us. Throughout the dark Night of PAN, the remnants of the vampiric priesthood has worked incessantly to prepare the race of humans for admission into the Comity of Stars. Due to the slow but inexorable proliferation of vampire/human hybrids, there is now not one of us who is without the potential of actualizing this royal priesthood.

The race has grown much over the past two millennia & we are now ready to give up our dependence upon physical death as the catalyst which forces us to grow/change/mutate. As Tiphareth[11] ruled the last Æon, Daath[12] rules the present. Daath is the Gateway to that which lies beyond the Universe accessible thru our microcosmic nervous system & its macrocosmic analog, the Tree of Life. Variations upon the Tree of Life have begun to proliferate over the protestations of those guardians of eternal truth who insist that there is but one Universe & one microcosmic analog to that Universe. But such new 'roadmaps' to the Universe are useless without the Alchemical formulae to utilize our newly found theoretical knowledge.

Individual work is absolutely necessary, but (perhaps even more importantly), there is also a need to formulate a network of communication among all those who seek to reify the Great Work. The clinical observations of individual members of the guild of prostitution needs to be collated with the traditional teachings of the esoteric Orders & with the individual researches of independent Alchemists. Each of us has a portion of the Secret. It is time we pooled our knowledge & experience to re-formulate our royal heritage.

The Alchemy of Immortality

Specific 'instructions' for the practical application of the Alchemy of Immortality is beyond the scope of this essay. However, I would like to share some ideas for specific application of this branch of Alchemy with those of you who are already experimenting with the Alchemy of Immortality.

---

11   Tiphareth is the name given to the locus of heart-center energy on the Tree of Life (a traditional 'map' of the esoteric nervous system of the aspirant known also as the microcosm). It is the vibratory locus of 'Christ consciousness' which was referred to by Jesus when he stated, 'None come to the Father save through me'.

12   Daath is a gateway, or transition-point linking the microcosmic Tree-of-life of the aspirant to the Multi-verse-at-large. It is a prime connection to the Elder Gods, as well as to many other interesting phenomena which have not yet been explored / documented very well at this point of time.

The first essay in this series (Nine-fold Flowering of Alchemies within the Eleven-Star) contains much practical sexual information regarding certain of the practices and theoretical framework of the Esoteric Order known as the Eleven-Star. An example was given in that essay of a ritual for genetic mutation of a human embryo. Vampiric Alchemy is able to utilize most (if not all) of the 'tools' of that ritual for the purpose of contacting &/or creating Vampiric 'linkages' within the body of the Alchemist.

The primary key to initiating the internal linkages is a total commitment to sexual ecstasy. It takes diligence & ingenuity to devise phantasies which lead to such ecstasy & it takes a real commitment to the Great Work to see to it that such phantasies become real. My writings contain aspects of certain of the sexual formulae which I utilize in my Alchemical work. For you, the details may well be different. It matters not so much what you do, so long as you do it.

Charged sexual fluids[13] are a key both to making the necessary internal linkages & the on-going nourishment of the Alchemist. Living substances have long been known to contain 'life-essence' which is (for the most part) missing from the foods of most mortals. Raw clams & oysters; freshly picked raw fruits, grains, & vegetables; and raw bloody fresh-killed meats are the staple foods of those mortals who aspire to live beyond their hundred birthday. The living substance of sexual fluids is the staple food of those who aspire to reach beyond their thousandth birthday. Janet Weiss sums it up very well in the sound track album to The Rocky Horror Picture Show when she sings:

> *And Superheroes come to feast.*
> *To taste Flesh, not yet deceased*

The most 'traditional' of the charged sexual fluids used for the

---

13 Sexual fluids are charged by means of the magickal affirmations, intentions, and psychic focus of all of the participants 6 observers of any sexual rite. The greater the emotional impact which the particular rite has for the participants &/or observers, the greater the possible charge. The use of esoteric ritual with its costumes, gestures, sacred words, perfumes, and candles often assists to maintain a particular focus. Likewise the voyeuristic attention of a 'congregation' of observers may be used to great advantage. Ideally, the point-of-focus for the rite is mutually agreed up & is maintained with diligence by all participants & observers, but if such is not practical, the full task of focusing/channeling the energy of the orgasmic rite may be borne by a single member of the priestcraft. However, it is well to remember that even those with no interest whatsoever in the magickal component of the rite will be unknowingly assisting the priest(ess) in charging the sexual fluids with whatever thoughts & emotions which they bring to the rite (in direct proportion to their emotional involvement). It is for this reason that many Alchemists refuse to work with those who do not appreciate their own power.

on-going nourishment of the Alchemist is the orgasmic in-vivo blending of menstruata, semen, and vaginal secretions. The elixir is usually shared between the priest and priestess immediately following orgasm, but may be collected & administered to others in-vitro, provided that the elixir be utilized as quickly as possible & that it never be permitted to cool-down below blood heat. Such oral infusions are particularly stimulating to young children & to those who are sick with death or old age.

Anal infusions of this elixir possess remarkable properties pertaining to spontaneous trance states & astral projection. If administered just prior to orgasm, this fluid is capable of reifying transdimensional linkages within the fundament-AL chakra of the Alchemist.

It should be noted that if either the priest or priestess is under emotional or physical stress, the elixir will contain a concentration of that stress, even if the charge is clean & strong. Eating of such a stress-filled elixir is sometimes called 'eating demons' and is not to be undertaken without due consideration. The first day of menses is frequently a time for elimination of trauma. For this reason, many Alchemists fear the secretions of the first day. If these secretions can be approached/utilized without fear the elixir can be compounded such that it will possess medicinal properties appropriate to specific trauma.

My most ambitious long-term project deals with cross fertilization between the esoteric formulae of the priestcraft of the Alchemists and the esoteric practices of the Sisterhood of Prostitution. It is my very strong intuitive feeling that it is only through an amalgamation of esoteric occult knowledge with the ability to utilize the esoteric god-forms inherent in sexual psychodrama that the race can become capable of unlocking its Alchemical heritage from within itself & re-formulate those links which lie outside of the Space/Time continuum.

Sexual repression has all but removed the power of cosmic orgasm from the race & intense sexual psychodrama has become an absolutely necessity to unlock those internal gateways which are buried under guilt, taboo, & repressed desire. Long term relationships evoke instincts of love sharing, & child-rearing; they do little if anything to assist the aspiring Alchemist to tap into the extra-dimensional Alchemies which go contrary to the 'natural' programming of our DNA (i.e., we are programmed to build a nest, create & nurture offspring, then to die) Active contact is needed between those occultists with theoretical knowledge of Alchemy & those hookers (*both* female &

male) who have at natural inclination to the priestcraft of the bizarre.

When the time is ripe, it is my feeling that it will be possible to 'go public' with a Church which is a functional Alchemical Brothel for use by all who seek re-alignment &/or experimentation within the framework of sexual psychodrama I have no concrete plans in this direction, nor do I have expertise at running this type of church/business. The political climate may preclude this kind of church/business for the present since it would threaten too many taboos of those who guard the morals of this culture.

For now, I seek active communication with any who are now (or who have been, or who aspire to becoming) functional members of the Sisterhood of Babalon (either female or male) with aspirations toward bettering the world and working as equals with those who walk the Path of High Magick. I am not certain of the eventual outcome of such communication at this time, beyond a sharing of information which leads to a fuller understanding for all involved. I feel that we have much to offer one another, but at this point I am unable to say exactly what it may be.

PVN
Master, Forbidden Alchemies

List of Suggested Readings

Aleister Crowley wrote thousands of essays & books over his prolific lifetime I highly recommend all of his works to the serious Alchemist. There is no particular order in which to read them, for each will lead you to others. For the purpose of preparation for the Alchemy of Immortality, I particularly recommend these few texts as a beginning of your quest.

Atlantis the Lost Continent. Dove Press, 1970C?).
Liber AL vel Legis. many publishers, always in print.
De Arte Magica. Level Press, San Francisco, 1 97 3 (?>.
Konx Om Pax. Society for the Propagation of Religious Truth Inverness, Scotland, 1905 (reprinted many times).

Kenneth Grant: all books by this author are highly recommended and are best read in the sequence in which they were published. He is the present head of the Typhonian Branch of the Ordo Templi Orientis and one of the magical sons of Aleister Crowley.

The Magical Revival. Muller, 1972; Weiser, 1973.
Aleister Crowley & the Hidden God. Muller,1973,Weiser 1974
Cults of the Shadow. Muller, 1975; Weiser, 1976.
Images & Oracles of Austin Spare. Muller, Weiser, 1975
Nightside of Eden. Muller, 1977.
Outside the Circles of Time. Muller, 1981.

NEMA: There is a highly skilled adept of the Double-Current who sometimes uses this name. If I listed her essays, you would then know her other pen names. As I respect her privacy, leave the puzzle to you. I highly recommend anything of hers which you are able to lay your hands on. Her work appears regularly in the issues of the *Cincinnati Journal of Ceremonial Magick*. Conquering Child is also the clearing house & central archives for various Alchemical essays of many obscure writers. Such material cannot be found elsewhere at any price.

PVN: would be remiss if I did not mention that many of my own essays on various aspects of Alchemy are available through Boleskine House, inc.

Chelsea Quinn Yarbro: An Alchemist whose Art form is the novel. Read, enjoy & learn! In have starred "*") those books which I deem most important to the budding Alchemist. Available wherever fine science fiction is sold.

Blood Games. Set in Nero's Rome
The Palace. Set in Renaissance Florence.
Hotel Transylvania. Set in mid-last Century Paris.
In Path of the Eclipse. Set in 13th Century China, Tibet, and India. Contains many fragments relating to sexual aspects of vampiric Alchemy.
Tempting Fate. Set in twentieth century Russia & France during the First World War.
The Saint Germain Chronicles. A collection of shorter works spanning the last few centuries. Recommended for Ms. Yarbro's essay on the historical Saint Germain.

Howard Philips Lovecraft: A writer of 'fiction' whose intuitive grasp of alien geometries and trans-human mythology sets his work apart from the rest. His novels and short stories contain magical keys which the Alchemist can use to gain initiation if she/he can but find the proper gateway. For the study of transcendental Alchemy as it relates to alien symbiosis & multidimensional geometries, I highly recommend:

The Festival
The Silver Key
Rats in the Walls
Horror at Red Hook
Dreams in the Witch House
The Strange Case of Charles Dexter Ward

Finally, and above all, I recommend practical Alchemical experimentation with highly skilled members of the Sisterhood of Babalon. Use your instincts to find those who have skills worth learning. Books can lead you only so far, and then you must begin your quest in earnest. Learn to listen to the voice within you which speaks in silence. Trust yourself if you aspire to High Alchemy.

Doxology
a Vision of a Gnostic Mass

by Frater PVN

Do what thou wilt shall be the whole of the law.

Introduction

The material in this paper was originally obtained thru VIII°, IX°, and XI° workings performed by Frater P during 1980 e.v. All are more-or-less visionary experiences, rather than the work of conscious scholarship. Such 'Channelings' should be taken as suggestive, rather than definitive. It is up to each of us to test such writings (each for him or her self) and use them as 'jumping-off places' for our own researches. The author has no interest in corresponding with any who are offended by the ideas presented here. Neither is he interested in having these ideas judged in the dim light of orthodoxy. He freely admits to being a heretic & a revisionist. He postulates that the past is just as mutable as the future & bases his proof in quantum chromodynamics & the negative time-spin of certain classes of quarks. The objective Universe is a conspiracy to keep us all asleep. Dreams are potent tools for waking up. Enough said.

The Doxology was obtained more or less spontaneously as a result of meditations upon the *Manifesto of the Anti-Christ* by Jack Parsons. However, since this period of time was particularly rich in sexual alchemical experimentation, the Doxology can easily be interpreted as resulting from these sexual experiments. In hindsight, PVN has come to the conclusion that the Doxology is both a cause & an effect of the sexual working which resulted in the Vision of a Gnostic Mass. Time seems to loop back upon itself in very strange ways & effect is ofttimes confused with cause simply because it precedes it in mundane time.

It may be worthy of note that when PVN was recently going over his old diary entry for the Doxology (dated 15 February, 1980ev), he realized that he could not have had a copy of the *Manifesto of the Anti-*

Christ in his possession until after 31 October, 1980 (the publication date on the copy of the Manifesto which hangs upon the wall in his study). Yet, he is quite certain that meditation upon the *Manifesto of the Anti-Christ* is indeed the 'cause' which resulted in his channeling of the Doxology. PVN claims that the 'personality' responsible for the Doxology 'felt-like' Jack Parsons, but such claims should be taken allegorically, rather than literally.

The Commentary was written at the same time as the Doxology, but PVN feels that it is the work of another 'personality' or 'personalities'. At the end of the commentary is the final verse of the Doxology. However, since PVN has argued persuasively that it 'belongs' at the end of the Commentary, this editor has left it as in the original diary entry.

Vision of a Gnostic Mass is the result of certain experiments utilizing the Trident of Set (alluded to in the vision) in heterosexual workings with Soror 0-Maku(tz)–33 /33. Text of PVN' s diary for 14 April 1980 e.v. has been edited slightly for clarity but is otherwise reproduced here in toto. As he was transcribing the text, PVN re-entered that state of vision & once-again experienced the Mass. No attempt has been made to separate the details from the two over-lapping visions.

Obscure references in this paper are unfortunate, yet unavoidable since these essays have been extracted from a much larger body of unpublished material. Many of the more obscure references will be resolved over time as future documents in this series are edited and become available. For those with a strong interest in the Trident of Set, many 'unpolished fragments' from PVN's original diaries will soon be available Archives project of Conquering Child Publishing Company.

It may be worthy of note that PVN had a very strong fascination with the Roman liturgy as a child & even now is subject to visions & dreams of a Roman/Gnostic fusion. When drunk on red wine he has been known to dream of becoming Pope & introducing sacred prostitution to the Christian Church. Whether such fascinations detract from or add to the validity of his visions is left for the reader to decide.

Love is the law, love under will.

Bill Siebert (pres. Boleskine House) &
Frater PVN Master, Forbidden Alchemies
4 October, 1983 ev

Doxology of Divine Praises

Appropriate for chanting at High Mass, operations of VIII°, IX°, or XI°, &/or operations involving Libri Astarte, HHH, &/or A'ASh.)

Dedicated to Jack Parsons by Frater PVN

I am FIRE
& the Fire which is beyond Fire;

I am FORCE
& the Force which is beyond Force.

I am the CHANNEL
blown clear of all debris;

I am Prometheus unchained & FREE.

BLESSED BE the Symbol of God:
the Five-fold Star of Woman /
the Six-fold Star of Man

BLESSED BE the Holy Name,
Shemo ha-Qadosh (& all who function in this office)
(i.e., Temple Prostitutes)

BLESSED BE Therion,
True God & True Man

BLESSED BE BABALON,
Rutting Bitch—my Beloved Mother

BLESSED BE Me,
Child of their loins.
Promised One to Come / to Cum

BLESSED BE my Unity,
AChAD / Prometheus /
Open transmitter to/from Heaven

BLESSED BE my Duality,
Harpocrates & Ra Hoor Khuit /
Horus & Set / Horus & Maat

BLESSED BE my Triplicity,
the Three-Fold Path /
the triple pronged Trident /
the Magus/Witch/Atheist

BLESSED EE my Multiplicity,
 for in ALL Thelemites am I ever Manifest

BLESSED BE those who know me Not,
 for they are Slaves who do my Bidding

BLESSED BE those who Think themselves
 to be Free, for though they lie to themselves,
 they still yearn for their own Liberation

I AM E-GO (the Star in its Go-ing),
 for my ego has been self-consumed
 thru daily sacramental sacrifice.

THOSE WHO KNOW of Me
 (& who begin to channel) fear that
 they will become like me / Be-Cum ME.

LET THE EGO be slain
 on the altar of masturbation in the Holy Name
 (ShMO H'QDSh).

LET THE CHANNEL Blow itself CLEAR
 so that IT resonates
 with the Music of the Spheres
 and the Chant of Eternity.

LET THE CHAKRAS be ever-Open
& let the Whore within Thee
reside wherever S/He will.

LET HER ATTRACT men
(i.e., those mortals who recognize not
their whoredom) to Her bed
& there slay them,
drinking their souls &
feeding her FIRE
with their weak passions.

LET THEM BE WARNED of the dangers
& responsibilities of initiation,
for they will not believe —
they will go eagerly to the slaughter,
thinking the sacrifice is but a game
which pleases the stupid whore.
They will give their lives & their souls
unto THEE out of stupidity rather than Love.

LET THEM THAT TRULY LOVE
(i.e., those who truly seek the destruction
of initiation) come also,
for perhaps within one of these
dwelleth a Whore capable of slaying THEE.

LET ALL MANNER OF SACRAMENTS
be shared amongst you,
both those based in kalas
& those entheogens which
resonate the nervous system
causing it to act in novel modes.
Distinguish not
between those produced in Whores
& those produced in Plants,
nor between those produced in Nature
& those produced in Alchemical Laboratories —
for all are poison to THEE without refinement

& none are poison to the refined Whore
within THEE.

LET THE WHORE WITHIN THEE be Thy Guide
until Thou findest a better ONE.
Like any good Whore,
she can wear any mask which pleaseth THEE,
yet she will never show
her True-Self to anyone
(least of all, HERSELF).

Commentary

Therion (the man) is the clown and buffoon who thinks himself whole. He be both God and Man, yet he knows it not. Crowley wore this mask often. He did it out of gleeful malice & not because he was forced to play the part.

Babalon is the whore within every Therion. S/He is the Kundalini Shakti. S/He is shocking in her lack of morals & in her total disregard for life & death. S/He will do anything for a thrill, even if it may kill you.

Conversely, Therion is stodgy & conservative. He knows it all & will risk no danger, even if it assures his death to refuse danger. When Therion meets Babalon he will try to master her. But if he falls in love with her, he will realize that Therion is not complete & certainly not as wise as once he thought!

Once Therion realizes his incompleteness & foolishness, he begins to grow—often in spite of himself & with much protestation! His whore/beloved/shakti within will see to his education & refinement. S/He will puncture his ego when it needs puncturing & build-up his true confidence when it needs building-up. S/He is his slave / mistress / equal / lover / superior / goddess / slavemaster / friend. The cycle is continuous & complete within itself, for it is the ecology of true initiation. Woe to any man who listens not to the whore within himself, for S/He will ride his back like a drug habit & wreak havoc upon his heart like a sadist. S/He is a harsh mistress who will not be denied. Out of their continual fusion & rutting, there cometh a Childe.

He is ONE, DUAL, THREE, and many. He is Prometheus unchained. To those who know him not, his ego seems inflated & imbalanced, yet he (in Truth) has no ego, for the E-GO within him is not him (nor even of him), but of the GODS which use him as their faithful (if somewhat dubious) messenger.

Yet the transformation is rarely complete. A single physical vehicle will resonate from Therion to Babalon to Prometheus; each persona with its own cycle; each cycle changing in response to external stimuli & to internal growth. None but the True Adept (or those humans closest to the new-born Prometheus) can possibly tell when Therion is making jest or when Babalon is leading mortals to their doom or when Prometheus is speaking the words of the GODS. The GODS know, Prometheus knows on some level (but rarely on the conscious), Babalon is usually certain (but rarely speaks out), and Therion is a fool.

Yet, if the newly born Prometheus be sincere, and if Babalon be doing her job in distracting & refining Therion, then all can go smoothly. Inspiration during or just after sex is often the purest & most refined. At other times, let inspiration simmer for days until it burst forth of its own accord. Never sit down & try to force the flow. If the channels be not clear, severe damage to the physical vehicle or twisting of the message can result. Even after the channels are fully clear, force not the channel to tune-into distant signals. For by straining to interpret weak signals, Prometheus tempts Therion to manifest & 'play at being important'. Yet, berate Therion not. His pranks are instructive, for when true adepts laugh at thy nonsense, false ego will be weakened & Babalon will be better able to console thee and will then be able to guide thee within thyself, to the source of True Illumination.

O THERION, Rut with BABALON
&
Sing the Body Electric.

Let the rituals be performed with Joy & Beauty.

Then Let BABALON eat thy soul
let Prometheus spring
from thy chained
&
rotted corpse.

Then shall the Channels be Blown-Free
&
the Music of the Spheres flow clear.

VISION of a GNOSTIC MASS
Based Upon The Trident of SET

Prologue

Last night (Sunday, 13 April, 1980 e.v.) Soror 0-Maku & I performed ritual stimulation of the 3 prongs of SET, each with the other (save there was no direct genital/anal contact).

After the swoon of orgasm, we both went into the sleep of the Just within the confines of the Temple—guarded by the warders of mycelia to N & W. While asleep I had a dream or a vision of initiation which I only vaguely remembered upon waking. I now feel the vision coming upon me once again—not as a remembrance but as a re-living of the experience.

I instinctively know that the doorway into this vision is contained within the OTO & within the phrase "Collegi et Spiritu Sancti". I affix my gaze on the seal on the cover of the edition of AL which I have caused to be printed pursuant to my oath. I repeat the chant. I sniff Gloria incense (unburned) from its container. The vision begins. My body continues to type, even though 'I' am elsewhere.

The Setting

I am in an old cathedral. Everything is made of very dark stone, slightly greasy to the touch. There are no pews. In the transept are three bare stone altars angled 60° to one another. I stand below the altars within the Sanctuary of the church with Sr. 0-Maku & others whom I do not know.

At the central altar is a priest wearing a white chasuble, embroidered with the OTO seal in silver. As I glance away from him, I catch a shifting in the corner of my eye. I return my gaze & the embroidery on his chasuble has changed to a brilliant copper green, while the chasuble itself has turned to silver. Each time I glance away, the colors shift. White/silver/green alternate upon the back of this priest. The priest appears to be very young. Probably in his mid-twenties but looking more like 14. His back is turned towards me.

At the altar to my left is a very old priest. He is a bishop, wearing a mitre & bearing a crozier. He is wearing a black dalmatic, embroidered with seal of the OTO in golden thread. As with the young priest, the colors are not stable, but flash to a honeyed-gold dalmatic with seal in iridescent black. His back is also turned towards me.

At the altar to my right is a middle-aged pastor wearing the black hat with purple pompom of a monsignor. He wears a crimson dalmatic with the OTO seal emblazoned in iridescent slug-slime. As my gaze shifts ever so slightly, the monsignor's dalmatic is now slug-slime in color (yet looking very different from the silver of the Celebrant!) & the OTO Seal flashes brilliant scarlet & green.

The colors of all three priests begin to flicker & flash a give off showers of colored sparks. Each wears all the colors in their turn, each flashing & flickering in their turn.

There are no servers, choir, or other standard functionaries to this Mass. We (the 3 priests & the people) are all within the Sanctuary. The altar rail is behind me. Just outside the altar rail are 2 Nubians, naked except for large single edge swords (like huge meat cleavers) held at port-arms. One Nubian is male with erect phallus. The other is female with fresh menstrual blood running down the inside of her thighs. Beyond the Nubians, all recedes into blackness. Neither the far walls of the church nor the arches overhead can be seen. Above the main altar is a huge stained-glass window of the OTO Seal. It is dark outside, so no color can be seen. The Mass is about to begin.

Mass of the Catechumens: The Beginning

The Sub-Deacon hands the Celebrant a broom of hyssop while the Deacon holds a graal of clear water. The people bow their heads (but do not kneel) as they are sprinkled. The Deacon goes around the main altar to the stained-glass window. The Sub-Deacon performs the signs of N.O.X. as the Deacon throws open the window. Outside is utter blackness. It is cool, but there is no breeze or sound of any kind. All return to their respective altars.

The Celebrant sings the beginning prayers ("Introibro altara Dei...") in Latin while the Deacon solemnly intones the same prayers in English & the Sub-Deacon speaks them lightly in what sounds like French Canadian. The Confiteor has been modified from being a prayer expressing sin, guilt, & sorrow to one of righteousness, freedom, and joy.

Ritual Skrying of the Stoles

At the Introit (which Romans usually read out of a collection of special prayers particular to the specific feast or specialized category of Mass), the Celebrant holds up his stole, which has a hole at either end. One hole is shaped like a mouth (approximately life-size) embroidered with red lips & the other is shaped like a Yoni with silver pubic hair.

He faces the open window & holds the ends of the stole up before him (without removing it from around his neck) so that one eye looks thru each of the two holes. He then shifts his hands so that each eye in turn looks thru both holes at once. He seems to be attempting to see or focus his sight upon some elusive 'something' in the blackness beyond the window. I began to sense a 'presence' in the blackness & my nervous system began to pick up certain patterns of energy. The Celebrant seems to be going into a trance. He is becoming oracular. Various members of the congregation ask him questions. He answers, but in many strange languages. I understand neither the questions nor the answers.

The Deacon then holds up his stole before the open window. His stole also has a hole at either end. One hole is a mouth with lips of gold & the other is a many-puckered anus with golden edges. As he is slightly off to one side, I am able to see his eyes as he looks thru the holes.

I perceive (rather than see) light or a glow coming from the holes. His eyes become luminous as though light were coming in from the open window & being focused by the holes. Yet (to my eyes) all remains black outside. I look again at his eyes. The glow is more fluid than light, for it seems to wash away the years from his eyes. He sees my stares & turns to me. He tells me that he uses the Power (nodding to the open window) in order that he might see beauty in his parishioners (as he says 'beauty' he smiles slyly & looks exceedingly lecherous).

The Sub-Deacon then holds up his stole. It too has a hole at either end. One hole is a flame red vagina, while the other is a mouth with green coppery lips. As he looks thru the holes, I feel his presence leave his body thru the focus of the holes.

He slumps over the altar momentarily, then writes furiously on (seemingly random) vellum pages of a huge ancient tome hound in gray leather with rusty iron clasps. The leather is stained with what looks like dried blood, slug-slime, and splotches of bright pigments. The hinges are embellished with lead & platinum and some black metal which I instinctively recognize as polished meteor fragments. As he writes & turns the pages rapidly, the air becomes filled with the sweet cloying perfume of asafetida mixed with olibanum.

He speaks not a word.

LUX
the Light from the VOID

The Kyria is sung (purged of all asking for mercy). It is a nine-fold invocation of Kyria Krystos. The Sub-Deacon hurriedly closes the window as the Deacon performs the Signs of L.V.X. The Gloria is sung by all (priests & people), as the window fills with a great light from beyond.

The colors of the OTO Seal in the stained glass window are breathtaking and the light outside the church is so bright that even the opaque lead framework of the window's intricate design work becomes translucent. There is now sufficient light for me to see the stonework within the church for the first time. Throughout the church are arches formed in the shape of huge Dragons (or serpents with short stubby legs and long curved talons). The Stonework surrounding the window is painted with two crowned serpents, forming an arch over the window & seemingly holding the window (the OTO Seal) in their jaws.

Seal of the Order & the Crowned Serpents

The body of the serpent to my left is jet black. Upon its body is written the word TRADITION, while the other serpent (the white one) has the word INNOVATION emblazoned upon its side. As the light from outside grows even stronger, I see that the Serpents are not painted upon the wall, but are three-dimensional statues which become more & more life-like as the singing of the priests & people grows stronger.

Serpent of Tradition

Upon the head of the Traditional Serpent is a crown of 22 points. Each point bears a precious jewel set in an ornate setting carved in the form of a letter of the Hebrew alphabet. Atop the crown is an ornate device bearing the symbols of the world's most successful religions (Crucifix, Mogen David, Crescent & Star, Pentagram, Sanskrit Ohm, the intertwined Yin/Yang Tao symbol, the 11-fold Cross, etc.) As I look at the rim of the crown, the serpent turns his head so that I can see the words more clearly. The inscription reads "ShMO IShRAL IHVH ALKINU IHVH AChD" (Hear O Israel Tetragrammaton Elohim is ONE God). At the very pinnacle of the crown is the number 963. The crown simply reeks of the power of Law-&-Order.

Serpent of Innovation

The Serpent of Innovation bears a crown of 21 points, each with a different gemstone in a setting inscribed with one of the letters of the Enochian alphabet. Atop the crown is a golden apple carved with the letter K set in a pentagon. At the very pinnacle of the crown is the number 333. As I look at the inscription on the rim of the crown, I am able to 'see' the crown up-close (as though I were holding it in my hands), even though it is more than 50 meters from where I am standing. The crown is inscribed with the oath of a Master of Alchemy:

Oath of a Master of Alchemy

1. To the Alchemyst, the rules do not apply. From henceforth & throughout all my bodies, it is my Will to transcend the limitations imposed by each particular Æonic formula, yet will I refrain unraveling the skein of linear time for those who are not yet ready for the Absolute Responsibility which comes from Absolute Freedom.
2. That which is mandatory (for other members of society) is optional (for the Alchemyst), & that which is forbidden (to society at large) is either optional or mandatory (at the Alchemyst's discretion). From henceforth & throughout all my bodies, it is my Will to manifest as a Master whose conduct is subject only to the judgement of His/her own Will and who is not bound by oath of fealty to any King, Philosophy/Religion, or Order. It is henceforth my will as a Master Alchemyst to participate in those Fraternities which do most to encourage absolute freedom, absolute responsibility, and absolute sharing of Secrets.
3. Objective reality is the consensus of subjective belief. The three 'laws of thermodynamics are but a limitation in our perspective—a self-imposed test of the ingenuity of the race. From henceforth & throughout all my bodies, it is my Will to undermine the limitations of Maya thru manipulation of 'randomness' and to seek the repeal of the laws of Nature by popular demand.

Choronzon & AChAD: Mainstays of the Order

As I read these laws I become aware that the eyes of all the priests & people are upon me. I notice that I am holding the crown of the Serpent of Innovation in my hands. I become acutely embarrassed & know not what to do. The Black Bishop touches his mitre with his Crosier. The mitre transforms itself into the crown of the Serpent of Tradition. He steps down from his place at the altar & we join hands in a Sufi clasp (two-handed clasp, left to right forming a circle, with left palms upward & right palms downward).

My consciousness shifts & I am in the body of the Serpent of Innovation. I sense the consciousness of the Black Bishop is within the Serpent of Tradition. I feel him begin to release his grip on the OTO seal which we both carry. The weight of the Seal becomes instantly unbearable. As I begin to panic, the black Bishop takes-up his share of the weight once again. When shared, the weight is negligible. Again, a shift in consciousness.

We are both back in our bodies. Neither of us wears a crown. As he begins to climb the altar steps, he turns to me & says "The crown of Innovation will carry any inscription which is your Will to place upon it. It is a far more difficult crown to wear than the unchanging crown of Tradition. I wish you all the luck you can muster for your task. All I ask is that you keep in mind that neither the "Energies from Kether nor those from Daath can sustain the weight of the Order without the other."

Preparations For the Offertory

The people sit down & I join them. The Deacon reads the Epistle (a passage from Liber LXV). After the Gradual is read by the Sub-Deacon (Chapter I of ARARITA), the Deacon reaches up behind him (under his dalmatic) & pulls a burning coal from his anus. He rubs it onto the lips of the Celebrant as the Sub-Deacon intones some prayers (which sound sort of like French, but very musical (almost like Vietnamese)). The Celebrant reads from Liber AL vel Legis (11:1-9) & the Deacon delivers a homily on the three-fold nature of ISIS (white, red, & black) while hinting broadly at the other three-fold division of the prongs of SET. Each priest of ISIS has access to all three prongs, yet chooses to emphasize only one or two depending on the particular focus of the operation (White, Red, or Black).

During the homily, Sr. 0-Maku stretches out on the floor beside me, laying on her stomach with her ass in the air. Her pants have a hole in the crotch & her ass is sticking out for all to see. One of the other members of the congregation (an old woman with a gentle face) hands her a heel from a round loaf of dark bread & tells 0-Maku to stick it up the hole in her pants. 0-Maku looks at her questioningly & the old woman mentions something about 'a gift for the Offertory' & 'pleasing the Black Bishop'. I realize that someone has given me a sugar cookie while I was trying to hear the old woman's whispers.

Offertory & Examination

The two Nubians come around to each member of the congregation, collecting offerings of food, drug, or sexual elixir from each in turn. Each person gives a sign, a password, or a grip to one or the other of the Nubians. The gestures are done quickly & furtively, so I cannot see clearly enough to mimic them. 0-Maku hands in her piece of bread to the male, while I give the sugar cookie to the female. Neither of us attempts to bluff the sign. The Nubians put down the offerings & unlimber their swords as if to slay us, but the Black Bishop intercedes.

End of the Mass of Catechumens: The Formula of LAShTAL

The Black Bishop calls us up to the apex of the three altars & smiles broadly at us. He asks us if there is anything he can do for us. I am at a loss for words, with my mouth hanging a-gape. I feel the presence of ADRIA within me. She speaks through my opened mouth, "Collegi et Spiritu Sancti". The Black bishop smiles knowingly as he sniffs 0-Maku's offering of shit-stained dark bread. The White priest says nothing, but there is a twinkle in his eyes.

The Red pastor looks at us very calculatingly for a while & then shouts 'LA' while pointing at the blood flowing from the Nubian woman.

The Black Bishop inhales deeply from the aroma which permeates the bread & shouts 'ShT'.

The white priest comes down the three steps which separate us from the main altar & embraces us saying 'AL'.

Dismissal

We are then turned around & propelled into the arms of the Nubians. They escort us out thru the altar railing & into the darkness. As we traverse the nave & approach the narthex I see a mirror on the wall over the baptismal font. As we approach, the mirror grows & begins to glow. It is smeared with sexual fluids in the form of the symbol of the Double Vortex. I look into the mirror & see the bodily forms of PVN & 0-Maku asleep in their temple. 0-Maku begins to stir from sleep. Her form awakens. 0-Maku is no longer beside me in the cathedral. I turn to the distant altars. The Black Bishop blows me a kiss. The energy of the kiss strikes me like an orgasm. A part of me is propelled thru the mirror, while (I somehow sense) that the 'rest' of me remains in the cathedral. I feel I am falling thru a maelstrom. I am on the 'mundane' side of the mirror. I am awake & staring into the mirror, trying desperately to remember the shadows of a dream. I see movement in the mirror & attempt to follow it by projection &/or by imagination.

Final Vision (for now, anyway)

The face of the Black Bishop appears in the mirror. He tells me that in 3 years I will gain the blessing of the Crown of Tradition. He smiles & tells me to try again after this has come to pass & after I am able to remember his words. The face fades. I am very sleepy.

Epilogue

When next I awoke, I penned down the vision as it is written here, but I had no memory of the Light from Void, nor of the Serpents of Tradition & Innovation, nor of the final vision of the Black Bishop in the mirror. None of these things did I remember until I began to transcribe this tale in October of 1983. It may be worthy of note that in early April of this year (about 2 weeks shy of 3 years mentioned by the Black Bishop) 0-Maku & I received initiation into Aleister Crowley's Branch of the OTO to counterbalance long-held initiations in the Typhonian Branch of the OTO.

A Sex Magickian's Alchemical Guide to Quartz Crystals

by Bill Siebert

Bill is a co-founder of Math of the CRyStAL HUMM, a Shamanic/Alchemical Thelemic Powerzone near Ithaca, NY. He is one of the 3 founding Sovereigns of the Chthonic/Auranian OTO, a branch of the Ordo Templi Qrientis dedicated to exploration-&-union of the Dark/Light Mysteries of all Æonic formula. Bill is also a regional coordinator of the Esoteric Order of the Dagon, a Lovecraftian Mystery School descended from the Sirius mystery cults of Egypt, Babylon & Sumeria, by way of Gateways within creative individuals who are capable of dreaming the mythos & making it accessible even to those who do not believe dreams to be real.

Introduction

I have been working with quartz crystals for a decade now. I began in 1980 with a crystal to assist me to recollect & re-work my dreams. I was so amazed at the power & native intelligence of my newly acquired tool, that I sought more information.[1]

I always feel somewhat at a loss when talking about crystals. I have found that Truth (with a capital T) cannot be communicated explicitly thru human language—it can only be hinted-at. Whenever I encoun-

---

[1] In 1981-82, I acquired my preliminary *formal* training in crystals from Oh-Shinnah Fast Wolf, a Crystal Shaman & Amerindian Medicine Woman. Oh-Shinna's eclectic mythologies coupled with her direct hands-on approach & her myriad personal anecdotes gave me a firm foundation in working with crystals. Her eclecticism & diversity simply impressed me greatly.

I also read some *New Age* books on crystals, their use in magic & their mythology. I skimmed many more such books, but much *New Age* material is far too moralistic, preachy, & dogmatic for me to stomach it in large doses. For the most part, I learned most of what I know about crystals from crystals themselves. I have found that personal hands-on experience is the best teacher—particularly in regards to quartz crystals. Crystals are vast storehouses of information, as well as eager sentient allies upon the Path of Magick.

ter someone else's attempt to express Truth, I find it obfuscated with dogma. I can only assume that others find my own writings similarly flawed. I find that dogma has about the same relationship to Truth that dry dogshit has to a dog. That is to say, I find dogma to be a lifeless desiccated residue of living ever-evolving Truth. I have found that it is far more useful for me to water all dogma which comes my way with inspiration, in the hope that it may fertilize my own personal living/growing mythologies, than to enshrine it on my altar, or cast it about as though it were manna from heaven.

The best way that I have found to convey truth (with a small t) is to use metaphor, mythology, and lots of personal anecdotes.

I have found that I can best work with crystals by treating them as wise sentient beings, regardless of whether they are or not. I make no attempt to be an objective observer, or an impartial experimenter. The only way I can become objective is for me to become an object. I feel that living beings are verbs, not objects. To live is to change. It is thru the act of going that I become more real, & more at-cause in my personal Universe. As part of my Magick of Becoming, I treat everything as though it is sentient, intelligent, and able to communicate with me. For the most part, this is a partial truth—which becomes more real the more I express it & practice it. If my approach does not sit well with you, invent an alternative mythology which fits-in with your personal experience of All That Is. [Sometimes, crystals appear to me to be repositories of energy fluxes, rather than beings with whom I communicate. Crystals don't seem to care how I view them, or whether or not I think they are intelligent.]

This essay is a series of meditation exercises, instructions for dream workings, and other practical ritual techniques.

These exercises are not designed to be followed to the letter. They are jumping-off places for creating/discovering how you can best work with crystals. I have found the following general guidelines to be useful in all of my work. If they work for you, feel free to use them. If they do not work for you, write your own.

1. Ritual has a life all its own. Do not attempt to constrain a living ritual into a pre-set mold. Allow/encourage it to grow/evolve.
2. Read over the rituals as I have written them. Familiarize yourself with what you will be doing & what equipment/supplies you will need.
3. Make whatever change(s) you think/feel are appropriate. Be

practical. Don't make the ritual so complex that you get lost in it. Use whatever materials are at hand. If you requires yourself to acquire lots of tools/toys you can't afford, you probably will never get around to doing the ritual.
4. Go over the ritual in your mind until you feel comfortable that you understand what you are doing.
5. Assemble whatever equipment/ingredients you need. If you do forget[2] some crucial ingredient, it is inadvisable to break your meditative flow during your ritual to fetch something you forgot. Cancel your plans or improvise.[3]
6. Put this book & all of your notes away before starting your ritual. Do not disrupt the flow of your ritual to consult your notes. If you cannot remember what to do next, sit down with your crystal(s) & meditate on what it is you are working to accomplish. When inspiration comes upon you, flow from your meditation back into your ritual, without fussing over whether you are following your original ritual outline or not.
7. Do whatever comes naturally. Your crystals themselves are your best guide. Use this book for as long as it is useful to you, then pass it on to someone else.

A Creation Myth

First, a bit of mythology. From my perspective, planet earth is a collective consciousness, named Gaia, who is the vector sum of all individual consciousnesses within it.[4]

From what I am able to comprehend of the nature of the Universe, *individuated* conscious life seems to be an inexorable phase in the evolution of the consciousness of existence, which some call God or Goddess. Biological life (such as us humans) is a latecomer to the

---

2   Forgetfulness is often a symptom of some internal turmoil. If you find yourself canceling-out on rituals a lot because you have forgotten something, I suggest you examine your motives to see why you are sabotaging yourself.
3   Improvisation can be fun if you are adventurous. Once I forgot the wine which was to be used as a sacrament in a ritual, so I dug into the earth until I struck water & used it instead of wine.
4   For me, Gaia is most definitely an IT, rather than (the more commonly presumed) She, for the greater bulk of life on this planet (whether measured in number of individuals, number of species, or raw tonnage) does not fit our rather provincial sexual stereotype of Mother-Earth.

By the word IT, I do not connote that Gaia is either neuter or non-sexual. Qabalists may recognize *IT* as the Hermit & Lust cards of the Tarot conjoined, by which I seek to express that Planet Earth is perpetually sexual & in constant orgasm. To say that in another way, Gaia is conscious of the continuity of existence, rather than being *divided for love's sake, for the chance of* union.

ecology of Gaia. Simple mineral crystals are representatives of a form of the continuity of the consciousness of existence which was ancient when the first biological organism became manifest.

Life when viewed from our provincial biological perspective, seems to be concerned primarily with assembling more of itself thru growth & reproduction. Life may be thought of as that which has the Will to impress its food with its own self- sustaining self-replicating pattern of organization. For biological life, the main vehicle for growth is the internal chemical template (RNA/DNA of genetic code & the chemical factories in our cells). Mineral crystals are quite similar to biological life, only their chemical factories are external, rather than internal. The grow by accretion & reproduce by budding &/or with seed crystals, using their own outer surfaces as templates.

There is an old Arabian saying which states that God must have been the first blacksmith, for it is not possible for any mortal to forge a pair of tongs unless s/he already has a pair of tongs. The RNA/DNA template is analogous to a blacksmith's tongs. If it does not already exist, life cannot be forged afresh. Positing God (or Goddess) as a motivating force may indicate the Why of biological creation, but not the How. As a magickian & god-in-training, I am ever-striving to understand the origin of God's tongs, the primal biological template.

Quartz crystals seem to suggest part of an answer. Before biological life manifested upon this planet, the oceans were warm, rich in minerals and filled with simple organic molecules, the basic building blocks of life. This nutritious soup engendered thru simple chemical reactions, with sunlight & lightning acting as catalysts. The microcrystalline structure of Quartz clay (abundant along the shores of the primal sea) provided the necessary matrix within which Life began. The chemical template structure of quartz is by no means as complicated or as sophisticated as even the simplest of today's genes, but it seems to have been sufficient to inspire the onset of biological life—particularly if Gaia had memories of other experiments with biological life, or a sample of that which it was seeking to bring into manifestation.

Viruses, as well as bacterial, mold & higher fungal spores, are able to journey thru the vast cold emptiness of interstellar space. This mode of transportation is not as certain or as direct a means of information exchange as spaceships, but it is far more accessible to those organisms which lack the manipulative ability to build larger ships with star drives & navigational equipment.

Inference & experimental data gained thru past life regressions, dream memories, and consciousness exploration within my genetic code all seem to indicate that Gaia first manifested biological life thru the use of silica quartz clay as its primal template using ideas &/or samples of co-evolutionary biological life which came here from other (much older) star systems. Some humans seem to be living hybrids of Terrene life with alien spores &/or viruses from other planets. This mythology helps to explain the intuitive link which we humans have with quartz crystals &. with the earth as our parent. It also helps to explain the fascination which many of us feel for faraway places amongst the stars.

Crystal Selection

To me, every crystal is alive. Each crystal has its own unique personality & Will, and its own unique purpose. For me, working with crystals is much like exploring a sexual relationship.[5]

My primary experience is with clear quartz crystals. Colored crystals each have their own mythologies &. their own very specialized uses. For use with this guide, I recommend good clear Arkansas quartz, especially if you are a beginner. Their character is strong & vibrant. If you find that Arkansas quartz is too edgy for you, try working with Brazilian or Madagascar quartz, which are reputed to have a more mellow & rounded character. For most general work, stay away from doubly terminated crystals (those with points on each end)—at least until you feel you know what you are doing. This caveat applies especially to Herkimer diamonds, a particularly vibrant doubly terminated quartz found only in Herkimer, New York.

I suggest picking a crystal which fits comfortably in your hand.

---

[5] I found that when I first became sexually active, it was very useful for me to commit myself to an intense monogamous relationship until I had some idea what sex &. relationships were all about. When I began working with crystals, I was given my first crystal by my lover. I worked with that crystal exclusively for about 5 months before my prime dream crystal & I found each other. I worked with that crystal every night for about 4 years, at which point I gave it to a new magickal friend to forge a dream link between us. As I gained skill, knowledge, & confidence, I expanded my horizons. Now, I work with dozens of crystals—some of which have been with me for years, and some of which come & go thru my life so quickly that I barely get to know them. On the other hand, I have found that each person I know tends to have a unique relationship with the crystals in his/her life. I have known people who bought their first crystal thru a mail order catalog (which strikes me as being about as bizarre as marrying a total stranger!) &/or who began relationships with dozens of crystals within the first few months of working with them.

2-4 inch crystals are good—depending on your hand size & personal preference. Stay away from small jewelry crystals for the practices in this guide. You need one which is massive enough for you to feel—even when you are sleeping.

Cleansing

Crystals are recording devices which are perpetually on. They pick-up & store information & psychic impressions constantly. Their capacity to store & retrieve information appears to be infinite.

I have reason to believe that although each crystal is a unique entity, each is also an integral part of the consciousness of Gaia, and, as such, acts as a local access terminal to the planetary equivalent of the Akashic Library. I have found that a crystal's memory may be divided into 2 portions—that which is temporary (erasable) & that which is a permanent part of the consciousness of Gaia. A crystal's personality, Will, and Path cannot be altered thru cleansing, which erases its temporary storage, but it can by fixing, which makes temporary storage permanent.

Crystals are most readily cleansed by soaking them in a salt water solution, which is approximately as concentrated as sea water. Use your taste & intuition rather than exact measure to determine the appropriate strength of your cleansing bath. I soak each crystal individually for at least 24 hrs (3 days if I have never cleansed that particular crystal before). I discard the solution after one use. If I have several crystals to cleanse, I use separate cups or jars to soak each crystal. I prefer to use glass or plastic containers. I do not like earthenware because it picks-up & stores the vibrations I am trying to get rid of. I almost never use metal,[6] because metal impresses its vibrational character upon the crystal being cleansed. Glass is a chemical cousin of quartz, but its crystalline structure is much more fluid. Glass is de-energized completely by washing in salt water, so it makes a good cleansing vessel. Plastic (especially Teflon, TFE, & Polycarbonate) are insulators & neutral storage containers for subtle psychic energies. They are ideal for cleansing crystals & are also ideal for long-term storage of crystal essences, which I will talk about later.

Many authors of New Age crystal books seem to feel that a crystal

---

[6] For advanced work, cleansing a crystal in a metal container, or with metal &/or metallic salts in the salt water can be used to imbue a crystal with the essential character of that metal. For details, see the section on miscellaneous techniques in part II - next issue.

A Sex Magickian's Alchemical Guide to Quartz Crystals

must be cleansed before it can be used. I have heard all sorts of dire warnings about negative psychic energy which might possibly emanate from uncleansed crystals. They make it sound as though a crystal which comes to you from a close friend or a trusted merchant should be treated as if it were a letter-bomb or an AIDS suspect. I have heard unsubstantiated tales of psychic vampires, insanity, virulent disease, & suicide being attributed to using crystals without cleansing them first.[7] Hogwash! Such talk is only middle-class germ phobia translated to psychic realms.

Magick is the Art & Science of causing change in conformity with Will. Crystals magnify internal thoughts/feelings & reflect them back to those who work with them. As such, crystals which are worked-with <uncleansed> over long stretches of time become excellent allies in the ongoing work of editing subliminal feedback loops. On the other hand, those who project their negative program loops outward as fear and paranoia may find that crystals are difficult (or impossible)

---

[7]   Sure, it is *possible* to acquire a crystal which was once used by a powerful magickian (perhaps even a black magickian, if you believe in-&-fear black magick—To paraphrase Isaac Bone wits—Black Magick is that magick which is practiced by those people I do not like &/or who use methods of which I do not approve (i.e., understand)), especially if you shop for crystals in antique stores or frequent auctions & garage sales. To me, such crystals have *character &* experience, rather than psychic contamination. If you do manage to locate a truly powerful crystal relic of some Archmage or psychotic, its *character* is probably so *fixed* that the only people skilled enough to cleanse such an *ally*, would probably find the idea of erasing it abhorrent. If you come across any crystals which you feel to be truly *cursed,* please send them my way. Many so-called cursed *objects* (A rather infamous crystal skull I have heard about, but have not yet met, is purported to be able to transfer its curse to any gemstone stored in the same safe with it. Although the skull is far out of my price range (even if it were to be offered for public sale, which is not likely), I would dearly love to locate its whereabouts. In my dreams, I know this crystal skull, and would love to get to know it in person. I would like to create an arrangement with the skull's present custodians so I could have the skull charge some crystals for me to distribute amongst those who are in teres ted/capable in communing with its energy.) are, from my perspective, more than likely to be powerful magickal entities who are seeking symbiotic relationships with those human magickians who are able to appreciate their energy, and not fear their intensity. Such crystalline beings probably have better things to do than instruct novices or be treated as *Objects-of-Art*. On the other hand, I have met several crystals which seemed to have no interest in a relationship with anyone. They acted like library books or travelling teachers, who seemed imbued with a geas (A *geas* is kind of difficult to describe. Its meaning varies somewhat according to the context in which it is used. A *geas* upon a person might be a task which they feel compelled to fulfill. A person acting under a *geas* might be thought of as acting obsessed. However, in the context I am using *geas,* the crystal is not obsessed. The crystal, itself, creates the *geas &* is the focus of its action. A *geas'ed* crystal places a willed stress upon the probability matrix of the multiverse to induce (but not compel) all animate beings/forces to cooperate in transporting the crystal (an inanimate being) to where s/he/it wills to go. Perhaps *geas'ed* crystals get the reputation of being cursed when so-called sentient beings lock them away, thus preventing other animate beings from assisting them in their travels—frustration simply induces the crystal to turn-up the intensity of their *geas*! (Modem Western civilization (I lump most communist countries in Western civilization) seem to me to be very audacious (or stupid) in their bureaucratic property-&-border fixated blind encumbrance of pilgrims, madmen, & shamans) to keep them moving. My best guess is that they do this so as to keep their knowledge/experience in circulation.

to work with—until/unless they are willing to deal with (what I term) their victim consciousness.

I suggest that if you pick-up a crystal for the first time & you don't feel comfortable with its energy, Don't Use It—even if it was given to you by a powerful magickian or a close friend. Return it from whence it came (explaining your discomfort, but without apologizing for your feelings). Or, act as the crystal's steward/matchmaker[8] until you pass it on to someone whom you feel may be a more suitable match for the energy of that particular crystal.

Sometimes I do recommend regular thorough cleansings for crystals, but such instances are rare. Here are a few examples:

Professional Healers (as distinct from those who are just learning how to use crystals) may wish to minimize energy carry-over between clients by rinsing their healing crystals in salt water, each time they are used.

Those who teach crystal classes may want to cleanse their loaner's after every class so each student can tap-into the essence of his/her crystal unencumbered, rather than having it mixed with the mental/emotional states of all the other students who have ever used that crystal.

Crystals which are used in hospitals & hospices to assist the dying (see advanced techniques, below) are usually kept in a very strong saltwater bath which is changed daily. Crystals used institutionally are frequently cleansed in bulk, rather than one crystal per container. I feel that this is a commonsense procedure, so long as care is taken that each batch of crystals is allowed to cleanse for at least 3 hours after the last crystal was added to the batch.

Washing (sometimes called cleaning) is very different from cleansing. I have found that many crystals love to be rinsed in cool tap water; some even like being buried in snowbanks. Washing removes surface grime, enlivens a crystal's psychic field & enables clean contact between your hand & the crystal's physical being. Some crystals prefer to be bathed in light, rather than water. Many like to sunbathe—Herkimer diamonds seem to be the major exception to this rule.[9] I do advise

---

8   I always help each crystal to get to the person who is attuned with its vibration. I don't try to wash-away that which makes me feel uncomfortable. I have developed relationships with every crystal which has come my way without cleansing any of them. I like to know where each crystal has been, share in its life's experience, & learn from its adventures. [This seems to be analogous to my enthusiasm in getting to know a new lover's past adventures, rather than wishing she were a virgin.]

9   I have been told (but have not verified) that the quality which makes Herkimer diamonds so special[a] is obliterated entirely if the crystal is ever exposed to direct sunlight. Once a Herkimer has been exposed to sunlight, they seem to enjoy being in the light, where they behave like very clear & brilliant specimens of

caution, however, in exposing crystals to temperature extremes, as they may crack or shatter.[10]

A Meditation Exercise

Bathe. Sit naked (or in your ritual clothes) in a comfortable asana (posture) on the floor (or on a cushion) in front of a large mirror. Hold your crystal in your receptive[11] hand. Darken the room. Place a candle at eye level half-way between yourself & the mirror. Relax. Allow the crystal to squirm about in your hand, so it can find a comfortable position.[12] Allow your mind to drift. If you get tired of staring into your own reflection across the flame, close your eyes for a

---

double-terminated quartz.[b]
a) Supposedly,[c] Herkimers which have never been exposed to direct sunlight make excellent allies for those experienced magickians who specialize in astral projection, communing with advanced races of beings from other Star Systems, and forging symbiotic relationships with sentient lifeforms from other dimensions.
 I am told that the only way to obtain such a specimen is to mine it yourself Then (to maximize its effects & protect it from inadvertent exposure to sunlight), it should be sealed within a hollowed-out polished disk (engraved & painted with appropriate sigils) made from a slice of meteorite, and worn on a band around the head. This device professes to channel most of the gross energy of the Herkimer diamond within the meteorite, while encouraging its subtle energies to interact with its wearer thru his/her *ajna* (third eye) chakra. Herkimer/Magickian/Meteorite act synergistically. Lines of force connect the newly-formed gestalt consciousness (H/M/M) thru extra-terrestrial channels within the meteorite, while the diamond quests for communion with other Stars. The magickian provides the Will/focus to speed the search for appropriate contacts.
b) I have never met a Herkimer which had been kept away from sunlight. I am reporting untested information which came to me by way of an Atlantean power crystal I met at a rock-&-gem show. Much of the information was later corroborated by a crystal healer I once met who has memories of being a Mage in Atlantis.
c) Double-terminated quartz crystals are usually excellent teachers for those who wish to learn astral projection & crystal skrying, but they tend to be over-protective of those who are adventurous in their wanderings. 1 have found that Atlantean power crystals[d] are the exception to this rule. Such crystals often lead novices on wild adventures thru Space/Time.
d) When I speak of an *Atlantean* Crystal, I do not mean to imply that a particular crystal was physically present at Atlantis. It may have been, but I have no way to verify such a claim. To me, an *Atlantean Crystal* is one which somehow taps me into an Atlantean mythology and invokes (or perhaps *evokes*) knowledge &/or images relating to technological use of crystals—usually for communication/transportation. Often this information is presented allegorically or mythologically with implications of a meta-technology involving physical time travel and D-hopping (as an outgrowth of the merger of physical science, spirituality, and transcendental Alchemy). I have found that such crystals have physical similarities to one another. In my experience, *Atlantean Crystals* all have a very distinctive (if held in the proper light) angular fit highly reflective metallic inclusion. Most have one inclusion. Some have several. The inclusions are most often triangular, and are generally translucent, rather than opaque or transparent.
10 Sometimes a crystal will ask you to expose it to extremes of temperature to bud-off a small fragment. I usually give such seed crystals to friends or bury them at global chakra-points.
11 I am predominately right-handed. I use my left hand for receptivity & my right hand for activity. If I were left-handed, I would probably use the opposite polarity. Use whichever hand(s) you feel are appropriate in each of the following practices.
12 With me, most crystals seem to be most comfortable if I hold them loosely with my thumb on the largest, smoothest sloping facet, allowing my thumb to stroke the facet gently in a seemingly random pattern.

while, allowing yourself to space-out. Open your eyes again whenever you deem it appropriate. When you open your eyes, do not become startled by what you may (or may not) see in the mirror.[13] Live in the present moment. Do not try to remember anything which comes-up during the meditation. End the meditation whenever it feels right to do so, but do not allow yourself to be guided/constrained by external timekeepers. Watches & clocks are best removed from the room, especially those which beep, or otherwise announce the passage of time.

Blow out the candle. Turn on a light or open-up the shades. Stretch your legs a bit & do not dwell on the meditation. Do not block it from your mind either, for that is dwelling on its minor image. Put down your crystal & go do something unrelated to crystals, meditation, & magic for a few hours.

When you are refreshed & the meditation is no longer clear in your mind, sit down with your magical notebook (or typewriter or word processor) and write-up your meditation. Whenever you cannot think of what to write, pick-up your crystal in your dominant hand & allow it to squirm as you think. Sometimes licking the facet, you held with your receptive thumb during your meditation &/or resting that facet on your ajna (third eye) chakra can be useful. Do not focus on any specific thought. I find that poetry & stream-of consciousness writing (channelings) are often far more useful in the long-run than a linear catalog of events. End whenever it seems appropriate.

Preliminary Dream Work

When you have acquainted yourself with your crystal thru meditation, take it to bed with you. This exercise is most effective if you sleep alone, or if your bed partner(s) also use(s) a dream crystal. Otherwise, you may experience some bleed-thru from his/her/their dreams.

Sleep with your crystal in your receptive hand. If you wake-up during the night & your crystal is no longer in your hand, seek it out & return to sleep. With a bit of practice, you may be able to sleep the entire night without losing-track of your crystal. If you are unable to work this exercise, be gently persistent, while continuing to use

---

[13] While meditating in front of a mirror, I have seen (at one time or another) numerous apparitions. Subjectively they appeared to be other aspects of myself—alternative lives, spirit guides, demons, angels, animal totems, creatures from other planets, visions from nightmares, etc. A few times, I saw no reflection in the minor whatsoever—the wall behind me was perfectly visible, even though my vision of it should have been blocked by the bulk of my body.

A Sex Magickian's Alchemical Guide to Quartz Crystals 283

your crystal in other ways. I have found that daily practice is more efficacious than sporadic workings, particularly at the onset of a new endeavor. Don't be hard on yourself. I advise you not to be harsh on yourself when comparing your progress with that of others, or with some ideal performance expectations you may have set for yourself. Above all—don't give-up!

Set at least one sleeping period per month aside as your dream night (or day, if you usually sleep by day). For this to work properly, you must be under no time pressure. Do not set your alarm clock or radio. In the beginning phases of this exercise, I highly recommend that you go to a sleep as drug-free[14] as possible on this night. This means not only abstaining from recreational drugs such as cannabis, tobacco, alcohol, sugar, chocolate, LSD, etc., on the day which borders your dream night, but also eschewing all sedatives, analgesics, herbal tonics, &. prescription medications. If you are chronically ill, or under the care of a healing professional consult with him/her/them before proceeding.

Eat a light supper & retire without reading any fiction or watching moves or tv. A light meditation &/or a hot bath is good. So is a small glass of warm milk. I strongly advise sleeping with the radio off. If you have housemates, seek their cooperation. Unplug the telephone & disconnect your doorbell. Take every reasonable precaution to invoke solitude & undisturbed sleep.[15] If you have any bedmates, ask him/her/them to sleep elsewhere, or rent a motel room for yourself. It does not help to muddle things up with lots of external stimuli.

Go to sleep with a dim night-lite on near your bed. Have your magical record & pen nearby. You should be able to read/write without having to turn on any additional lights or getting-up from bed. But make the light as dim as possible, while still being able to read while

---

14 This phase of the operation is designed to enable you to look inside yourself. Recreational drugs (especially psychedelics), food substances which play with adrenaline & blood-sugar levels (sugar, caffeine, nicotine, etc.), and eggplant (which contains Nightshade family alkaloids) can often help induce fantastic dream images. But unless you are a skilled alchemist & dream shaman, such dreams often mask or overemphasize aspects of the internal energy ecology. Medications, likewise, obfuscate symptoms of mental/spiritual dis-ease which (in my opinion) can guide negative thought forms into manifestation as illness, allergy, or physical weakness. I advise those who seek true health, rather than simply relief from symptoms of illness, to quest within themselves with no masking symptoms during the preliminary stages of this work. At later stages, dreamwork can be used to test the efficacy of a particular treatment, but only if the preliminary work has been accomplished.

15 If all reasonable precautions fail, examine the fine nuances of your behavior & motivations to see if you are mentally or magickally sabotaging your efforts.

you are sleepy.[16] Go to sleep with your dream crystal in your passive hand. Each time you wake-up (even if it be for an instant), transfer your dream crystal to your active hand & think about what you were just dreaming. Write down your dream before going back to sleep. Some people like to use a tape recorder, but I discourage using them unless you are disciplined enough to transcribe everything to your written record each time you do this exercise. If a particular dream is interesting, (& you would like to go back into it, return to sleep with your crystal in your active hand, rather than your passive.

Stay in bed long past your usual wake-up time. Overcome your enculturated work ethic & need for external stimulus. Keep going back to sleep as often as possible. If you cannot sleep, try daydreaming, or writing down streams of consciousness. Don't write formal essays. Do as little linear thinking as possible.

When I began to do this exercise, I spent at least 14 hours in bed on each dream nite. During times of extreme stress (or when having exciting adventures), I have spent as much as 16 to 20 hours in bed (except for quick runs to take a piss or get a drink of water). After years of practice, I am sometimes able to get good results in 30 minutes, but I still like to spend at least one full dream night per month in contemplation. I no longer write down all my dreams. I now have almost total recall of dreams during a dream night. To write even a fraction of them down would take days. I now skim my dreams for interesting details, then go back into them at interesting points to glean more details or to alter them. [See techniques for altering dreams below.]

Crystal Waters: Keys to Personal Balance

Do you have a particular color or vibrational sound which you normally work with? Crystals can help you manifest subtle vibrations in a material form which you can then use as a tonic or to charge talismans.

Catch a ray of sunlight in a crystal. Rotate the crystal until the light breaks up into a full spectrum of color. Place a glass of clean tap water so that the color vibration you wish to accentuate in your life shines into the water. Use your imagination to focus your Will thru the crystal as you charge the water with color.

If you use color a lot in your work, you will probably find that catching the exact segment of the sun's spectrum is a nuisance, especially if

---
16 My sleeping nook is strung with lots of tiny colored Christmas tree lights, which I adjust for brightness with a dimmer switch by my bed.

you are a night person or live in a cloudy region.

Clear, translucent, & opaque colored crystals can also be used in making Chromatic crystal water. In fact, their vibration is usually more useful for this kind of work than a slice of the sun's spectrum. Put the crystal in a covered container with some clean tap water, & put it on a shelf for a day or so. Look at it once in a while, while focusing your imagination thru the crystal. Conscious remembrance of what you are doing is important in this kind of work. When the water is charged, give your crystal a rest. If you need fresh crystal water every day, I advise you to have 3 or 4 crystals which you alternate.

Top-quality gemstones are not necessary for this work. I find that many colored crystals (particularly precious gems such as diamond, ruby, and emerald) are well-suited for this work. However, small crystals take much longer to charge a vial of water.

Large emeralds are quite rare & very expensive, so here are a few alternatives. Small crude emerald chips are often inexpensive (often in the range of $10 to $2 each), but such tiny crystals would take weeks to charge-up a single glass of water. I have found two ways of magnifying their ability.

The first is the most straightforward. Meditate with the small colored crystal under your tongue.[17] The chromatic vibration of the crystal stimulates the ajna (third eye) visuddhi (throat) chakras directly, then attunes your entire being to this vibration.[18]

Another method of crystal amplification is slightly more elaborate. Secure a small colored crystal to the side of a well-formed jewelry-quality quartz crystal with silver, gold, or copper wire.[19] Align the axis[20] of the colored crystal with that of the quartz before you secure

---

17 I have found that an emerald used sub-lingually is an excellent tranquilizer* when I am feeling agitated & stressed-out. Emeralds have no noticeable side-effects, other than a slight tendency towards astral projection.

* I used to know a very high-strung crystal healer who swallowed emeralds whenever she got nervous. I told her that when she became wealthy enough to afford gem quality emeralds, I wanted the job of emptying her chamberpot!

18 I advise some caution in oral testing of stones which have a strong vibration. I discovered rather quickly that bloodstone will practically take the top of my head off. On the other hand, I find that Herkimer diamonds are excellent for use in dream control if I sleep with one in my mouth [I have a groove along the gumline which makes a perfect pocket for tiny gemstones!

19 If I were not confident about which metal to use, I would trial-wrap the crystal pair with each wire in turn, then grok its energy. Intuition, rather than scholarship would be my guide.*

* Another person might feel more comfortable looking up a table of correspondences in some magickal textbook. What you do is up to you.

20 If the gemstone has no discernible axis, use your intuition to locate an imaginary axis, or consult a

it, so their vibrations will work synergistically, rather than cancel each other out.

Over time, the composite crystal will begin to act as though it were a large crystal of emerald (or whatever gemstone you actually used), particularly if you use it only for work which is specific to that color vibration. I recommend that you unite the two crystals permanently. By switching around the combinations, your tools may not build up their full power or focus. I would not use my dream crystal for this work, unless I were coupling it with a diamond or a Herkimer diamond, or a small flawless quartz.

Similar techniques can be used to focus sound. Vibrate a tuning fork[21] & touch it to a crystal which is hanging suspended from a nylon or silk thread. Pick up a glass of water & hold it so the point of the crystal just touches the surface of the water. If the crystal is capable of vibrating in harmony with your note,[22] the surface of the water will begin to vibrate. Focus your will & lift the glass to totally immerse the crystal, insulating it from sound. Stop the tuning fork (synthesizer, etc.) St remove the crystal from the water.

Crystal water can be used immediately, or stored for later use. If it is to be stored, I suggest that it be placed in sealed plastic vials (polycarbonate test tubes work well for this) or in glass jars. I prefer plastic as it insulates the elixir from picking up any extraneous charge. Soror 0-Maku(tz) likes to store her elixirs under her copper pyramid; I prefer a refrigerator. Do as you will.

Some people feel that spring water is somehow more appropriate (or more natural, whatever that means!) than tapwater for making crystal water. If I felt that my local tapwater was not good enough for magical/magickal purposes, I would not drink it, cook with it, bathe in it or use it for any purpose whatsoever. I would move a.s.a.p. to a location where I trusted the purity &. magickal integrity of the water. To do otherwise would be utmost folly, for I would be unconsciously poisoning myself with every drink of tapwater & every shower.

Crystal water can be used for many purposes, A student of Oh-Shinnah used crystal water to reverse a bone cancer in his leg. 6 months after he had been scheduled to have his leg amputated, he

---

gemologist.

21 Alternately, pluck a guitar string, intone a word of power, or use a synthesizer to generate the appropriate tone.

22 Some crystals are not capable of resonating at all frequencies. If such be the case with your crystal, work with another crystal, or a different note, and try again.

was playing basketball. Crystal waters are great for dampening mood swings, for charging sacraments of all kinds, and for sephirothic &/or Path Workings (see Liber 777 for appropriate colors).

Intermediate Dream Techniques

Later on, after you have explored your dreams with minimal consciousness alteration, try working with your dreams after partaking of some particular consciousness alterant—such as a watching horror movie,[23] getting stoned, eating eggplant, etc. Note what effect(s) each alterant has on your internal energy balance.

My favorite drug combination for inciting exciting adventure dreams is sleep deprivation (24-36 hours of no sleep), while eating lots of chocolate & drinking lots of caffeine. During my pre-dream waking phase, I read one or two SF novels or watch some adventure videos. Then, just before going to sleep, I take a high-potency vitamin B-12 nasal gel.

I am a sex magickian. I have been consciously working dream/phantasy actualization through VIII° (masturbatory) Magick[24] over the past three decades. I have found crystals to be an excellent adjunct to all forms of sex magick. If you are not already using the energy of your sexuality as a magickal tool, dream reification is a pleasant fit easy way to begin. But, please proceed with caution. Dreams invoke reality. So do phantasies. The explosiveness of orgasm thrusts phantasy into the collective unconscious and speeds its reification. In this sort of working, crystals act like programmable transistors which embody the Will of the magickian while s/he is busy spacing-out on the ecstasy circuit. I strongly advise phantasying & daydreaming only on those topics which you are ready-&-willing to invoke into your waking reality.

Set aside at least 72 consecutive hours for this mini-magickal retirement. Ideally, one should be well-rested, free from stress, & very horny.

---

[23] Very often, movies which I find highly disturbing can provoke dreams which can shed some interesting light on hidden programs, suppressed traumas, etc. By using my dream crystal I can edit these dreams, and thereby influence my waking reality.

[24] The techniques I disucss here can easily be extended from an VIII° Working to the realms of IX°* or XI°.† Holding on to your crystal while making love and sometimes be a nuisance but I have found it well worth the bother.‡

* Heterosexual workings.

† Homosexual workings, heterosexual sodomy, &/or IX° during the lunar flow.

‡ Crystals helped me to develop my native abilities for vaginal skrying (astral projection Si clairvoyance during cunnilingus).

But things are seldom ideal if you live/work/play in the real world. Of these considerations, I have found that the ability to set-aide a continuous block of time is the most important.

Begin your first dream night as usual. When you awaken from a dream in an aroused state, use your crystal to assist yourself in remembering your dream. Then transfer your crystal back into your passive hand & masturbate yourself to orgasm, using imagery from your dream. Anoint your dream crystal with your sexual fluids. Lick some of the fluid from the crystal fit return to sleep. I have found that thumb contact with the crystal's major sloping facet to be very useful during this phase of the operation. Do not break focus to write down any dreams at this point. Repeat this procedure all night long, as often as possible. This may take some practice, particularly if you do not usually masturbate several times each day. When you have tapped into your sexual current, this procedure will enable you to ride wave upon wave of orgasm throughout your dreams. The individual dreams may weave themselves together, exposing glimpses of the fabric of your dreamworld. Explore your dreamworld and sculpt it to fit your vision of reality. 6, 8, or even 10 orgasms in a 14 hour period are not uncommon for men. Women who are tapped-into their sexuality can sometimes achieve far more.

When sleep fit/or orgasm are no longer possible, rinse your crystal in a glass of clean cool tap water. Drink one-half of this potion immediately. Reserve the balance of your orgasmic crystal water in a tightly covered glass or plastic container in the refrigerator, or under a copper pyramid.

Immediately upon drinking your orgasmic crystal water, begin to write-up your dreams &/or your sexual phantasies. If all is going well, the dreams fit phantasies will have a common thread or be congruent.

Seek-out glitches, weak spots in your dream reality, or ways in which you would like to alter your dreams. Seek for ways to weave individual dream segments into a larger richer dreamscape. Keeping your crystal in your active hand, enter your dream consciously. Use astral projection, or phantasy and daydreams. Edit the fabric of the dream reality. Write-up an edited dream fit destroy the original dream memory.[25]

---

[25] For this kind of magickal work, I find a word processor to be invaluable. I do not make any printouts of my original dream material. I edit directly in my computer's memory, and store only the edited version to disk. Because the original (un-edited) version of my dream has only a transitory existence in this reality plane, it is less likely to reify than if I left scraps of paper lying about where they might be read by friends.

Take a break. Go for a walk &/or get some food. Visit with friends. Then, begin a new dream cycle. But just before retiring, drink one-half of the remaining orgasmic crystal water to seed your dreams. Then, in the morning, add your newly created orgasmic crystal water to that which remains of the previous batch until you are ready to end the Working.

Each day of this Working, examine all your dreams carefully. Weave them into the fabric of your previous dreams fit edit them to remove glitches fit realities which it is not your Will to reify.

At the end of your Working, examine your dream record. Weigh it carefully in your mind. If you deem that such phantasies are not up to your standards as a creator, drink the remaining orgasmic crystal water, then sleep for a few days without your crystal. Do not write down any dreams during this period.

If, on the other hand, you feel that your dreams are ready for reification, take the remaining orgasmic crystal water to a lake, stream, or reservoir and pour it into the water, while focusing your intentionality on seeding the dreams of all those beings who drink that water. If it be your will, it may also be useful to publish your dream working (perhaps as fiction), or create some form of Art (poetry, music, bumper stickers, etc.) based on it which can aid others in tapping into its imagery.

Dream Gateways

Crystals, particularly when combined with sex magick, are potent tools to assist magickians in getting to know one-another, whether they are lovers or not. Here is a technique which 1 have used a few times. Modify it to suit your own needs.

Select a crystal which you have never worked with extensively, or one which has recently been cleansed.[26] Sleep with it for a night or two, consecrating it with your VIII° sexual fluid. Sleep with it in your active hand to attune the crystal with your personality & to impress it with a clear image of your dreamself. Then fix the vibration of the crystal with fire (see below for details). Give your crystal to him/her with whom you seek to open-up a dream gateway. Such gateways are far more effective if your friend/lover gives you a similarly prepared crystal in return. There seems to be no limit to the complexity of a

---

26 Alternatively, I once used the prime dream crystal with which I had been working for several years.

dream gateway network.[27]

To experience the energy of your friend/lover in meditation or dream, simply use the crystal you received from him/her as though it were your own dream crystal, with one major exception. Cleanse the crystal with saltwater before & after each use.[28] The crystal has already been fixed, so it will always retain the vibration which your friend/lover impressed upon it. Cleansing removes all of your vibrations (preconceived notions about him/her, desire, etc.) so that you can tune yourself to experiencing your friend/lover directly—far more directly than most people are able to experience by using their waking consciousness & rational mind.

Some people like to synchronize their workings & then compare notes as to the success or failure of the dream link. These sorts of experiments may encourage Lust of Result & pre-dispose the experiment to failure. I prefer to be as spontaneous in my workings as possible. By going with the flow (rather than attempting to impose my desires upon it), I am more likely to gain deep (non-judgmental) insights into the personality of s/he who sent me the crystal.

Editing

After I have been using a crystal for a long time (particularly during periods of rapid personal growth) I find that its response begins to feel a bit muddy This is an indication to me that it is time to edit &/or cleanse my crystal.

This can sometimes be a little tricky, but I find it to be far more useful than cleansing. Soak the crystal for one-half to one day in a very dilute[29] solution of salt water.[30] Label the soak water & store it

---

[27] That is to say, it is possible to swap gateway crystals with dozens of friends, none of whom arc in direct contact with one-another. Before long, even those folks who have never met will be involved with one- another in dream space. This is not to say that my dreams are populated by visions of all my magickal friends with whom I have shared gateway crystals. Their energy is with me. Their personalities sometimes emerge. But rarely do we share the same dream images on the same night.

[28] Cleansing is only necessary if you desire to keep your dream gateways discrete from the flow of your conventional life. For the most part, I do not cleanse my crystals &. I do not even remember from whom I received them or which of them is an active gateway crystal. But, I am working to build a non-hierarchal non-systemized network. The advice in the main text is for those of you who have more one-to-one ambitions for their dream gateways.

[29] A Cleansing strength salt solution would be very obnoxious to drink. An editing strength solution should still taste salty, but should not be difficult to stomach.

[30] If you have a good idea of what you are working to remove, prepare a complimentary* charged crystal water,† Drink half of this water before going to sleep with your dream crystal. In the morning, use the remaining crystal water to prepare the weak salt solution for your dream crystal.

for possible future use. Use the crystal for a day or so. It it still feels muddy, soak it again in a freshly prepared weak salt water bath.

If you noticed no change after the first soak, use a slightly stronger salt water solution &/or soak your crystal longer. Again, label & reserve the soak water. When you feel that your crystal is once-again clear & bright, your crystal is once-again ready for daily use.

Sometimes, you may feel that you may have gone too-far in your editing. If this is the case, try reversing the procedure. Take the last batch of soak water & drink it just before sleep. Use your dream crystal to isolate those energies which you wish to put-back into the crystal. Upon waking, catch the first ounce or two of your urine in a glass, dilute with tap water & soak your dream crystal in it all day.

Repeat this procedure again (if necessary) with the next jar of soak water. If you go too far St your crystal becomes muddy-feeling once again, do one last soak in dilute salt water. If at this point you still feel something is off kilter, your crystal probably needs a good, thorough cleansing.[31]

When you have finished editing your crystal, discard all un-used soak waters & rinse out the jars in a strong salt solution, before re-using the jars for other purposes.

Fixing

Cleansing & Fixing utilize very similar energies, yet for vastly different purposes. Cleansing erases all transient information which a crystal is carrying, to re-expose its inherent nature. Fixing transfers all temporary information to Gaia's archives, as well as making this information a permanent[32] part of the crystal's personal character and

---

* For example, if you feel that your crystal has become over-charged with martial aggressiveness, you might want to create an editing bath which embodies Venusian (green) or Lunar (focus some moonlight into the water thru your crystal) energies.

† In creating this batch of crystal water, be sure to use a crystal which has no muddy feel to it.

31   If this does not help, it may mean that it is time for *your*‡ crystal to move on. Find a friend to give it to, or put an ad in the paper for someone looking to adopt a crystal, or leave it nestled in the crotch of a tree in a park.

‡ I put the word *your* in italics just as a reminder that you cannot really own another being. You may have paid money to buy the crystal, but what you were really paying for was the time & effort it took to transport the crystal to you.

32   When I say permanent, I mean permanent. There are crystals I have met which seem to have been fixed by Atlantean Mages. Many of these act mainly as data crystals, which can be easily distinguished by a metallic opalescent triangle buried deep in the crystal's depths along a natural fault line. The metallic triangle is either a natural property of the crystal's make-up or it has been put there by a process which is unknown to me. The effect seems to me to be analogous to the doping by which our

knowledge base. Fixing builds-upon a crystal's inherent nature thus triggering/speeding its evolution.

I fix crystals which I give to friends as dream gateways. I also fix crystals to commemorate very powerful magickal events. Every so often I transfer all of what I have learned along with all that I know/feel about consciousness into a crystal, then fix it & bury it under a small stone obelisk in a state park for someone else to find. Sometimes it is useful to fix a crystal which is to be used for a specific purpose, such as healing.

Fixing with Fire: Find a place which feels right for this ritual. I like to be outside with a view of the sky, even if it is overcast. I find I get the most out of doing this ritual late at night in a place where I will not be disturbed. Build a medium-sized[33] fire out of substances in your natural environment.[34] As you build your fire, meditate on the essence of fire.[35]

Take out the crystals you have brought with you. I like to have at least 2 crystals with me for this ritual—the crystal which I am going to fix, and one who will act as an observer or witness,to record the ritual itself. If I am going to fix more than one crystal, a single observer crystal will suffice for the whole batch. Sit down near the fire. Hold the witness crystal in your active hand & the crystal you will be fixing in your passive hand. Stare at the flames & relax. Lose yourself in the fire. When you are calm & serene, begin to think about what you are

---

culture creates transistors. The triangle's shape (acute, equilateral, isosceles, obtuse, etc.) seems to be related to the type of information stored within that particular crystal. Perhaps it is an index system, or is an outgrowth of engineering considerations. I found that Atlantean information crystals were initially very difficult to decipher, probably due to the cultural gap between myself & the crystal's original programmer. But, with patience, I have begun to piece together enough information to enable me to draw plans for some crystal-based techno-magick toys. If I ever get around to building any of these tools, I will report my findings in a future essay.

33 Make your fire large enough that you can pass a crystal thru the flames, yet small enough that you can work close to it without roasting yourself.* I usually like to have a fire with flames about 8-30 inches high.

* When pressed for time, I once fixed a small crystal in an alcohol lamp. A can of sterno, or even a large candle would probably work too.

34 When I do this ritual in the country, I use dry dead wood & bark. When in a tree-barren city, I use old boards, newspapers, & other burnable trash. If I am feeling primitive, I start my fire with flint-&-steel & a small pile of dry twigs & lint. When I am feeling pyromaniacal, I douse a pile of wood with dinosaur blood (gasoline), stand back, and throw on a match.

35 Think of what fire means to you. Recall how fire was once worshipped by our ancestors & how it has been our friend since before recorded history. Make friends with the fire you are building. Play with it. Pass your hand thru its flames.†

† If you have never played with fire, please do not attempt this ritual until you have overcome your fears & have made friends with fire. Otherwise you will be fixing your fear of getting burned into your crystal.

A Sex Magickian's Alchemical Guide to Quartz Crystals

about to do. Think about what it is you intend to fix into your crystal. Allow random images to pass before your mind's eye. Keep staring at the flames. Put the witness crystal down.[36]

Hold your hands near the fire as you roll the crystal you are fixing between your palms. If your hands become sweaty, imagine the crystal drinking-up the moisture. Allow/encourage your consciousness to flow into the crystal along with your sweat. Become one with the crystal & the fire & yourself. Lose yourself When you become aware of the fire glinting-off the crystal, slowly draw your point of consciousness back into your body, without losing consciousness of the fire or the crystal. Repeat this several times, until the flow becomes second nature to you.

In a graceful flowing motion, move the crystal to your active hand. Sweep the crystal[37] thru the fire in 3 continuous circular or spiral arcs[38] (as though stirring an imaginary cauldron). Allow the flames to lick-at the crystal & your hand. Move your hand slow enough that you can feel the heat of the flames, yet now so slow that you bum yourself or crack the crystal. Remain conscious that you are the fire & you are the crystal as well as the being holding the crystal. Allow the crystal to flow to your passive hand. Repeat the 3-fold journey of hand/crystal thru fire.

Miscellaneous Techniques

I like working with quartz crystals because they are so malleable. They are eclectic. Quartz (along with diamond) are the crystal kingdom's equivalent of the Renaissance personality. But sometimes, I need to work with a crystal which has a far more distinct focus. I could always use another kind of crystal, but (even though I am extremely lazy) I sometimes like to do things the hard way—just to demonstrate to myself that it can be done.

In the section on cleansing, I mentioned that I almost never cleanse a crystal in a metal bowl, otherwise the crystal will pick up some of

---

[36] I like to sit with my legs crossed. I put whatever crystals I am not holding into my lap. They like hanging-out in my crotch.
[37] I hold my hand palm down in a loose fist with the crystal sticking out between my thumb & index finger.
[38] If the crystal is in your right hand, your arcs will probably flow widdershins (counter-clockwise), if in your left hand, deosil (clockwise). Use whatever flow* is more natural for you.
* In some magickal systems, deosil movement is used primarily for invocation & widdershins for banishing. In my system, intent & natural flow of movement are of far greater importance than what direction you are moving.

the properties of that metal. This contamination effect can sometimes be a blessing in disguise.

What we call salt is Sodium Chloride (abbreviated NaCl). NaCl is by no means the only salt. Salt is the name of a general class of compounds formed by the action of an acid upon a metal. There are tens of thousands of different salts. Metallic ions of salts which are soluble in water seem to be able to influence the characteristics of a clear quartz crystal which is soaked in that solution, even though the solubility of these ions in quartz is negligible under most circumstances.[39]

While most metallic salts can be procured from any chemical supply house, I have found that preparing them fresh from metal which has been used in ritual[40] seems to work best.

Iron salts seem to be good for creating crystals with a martial flavor. Gold salts produce crystals which are excellent for solar workings, but gold is very difficult[41] to put into solution thru ordinary methods. Copper & Zinc[42] are both venereal in nature. They are useful for focusing crystals to be used in workings of lust & love. Mercury salts[43] make an excellent cleansing bath for study crystals used by students, scholars, & researchers. If you have an elementary understanding of chemistry, a mercurial crystal can help you design metallic cleansing baths for most any purpose.

If you experiment with cleansing baths using salts other than table

---

39 When a crystal is growing in the earth, it readily incorporates mineral salts from the local water supply into itself. This is how all the colored members of the quartz family are created.

40 For instance, I once wanted to perform a ritual in a public park which would not permit me to brandish my sword against the picnickers. I bought a small iron knife* at a garage sale, cleaned it up, and consecrated it as my ritual sword. Then I dissolved my ritual knife in a beaker of Nitric Acid, neutralized the excess acid with iron filings, & used the solution to cleanse the crystal I later used as a sword in the park.
* Avoid large or stainless steel knives—they are a bitch to dissolve!

41 *Aqua Regia** is an excellent reagent† for solubilizing gold. If the solution is then neutralized with Potassium metal, the resulting solution can be used for cleansing crystals to be in Solar/Jupiterian Work (such as healing).
* Aqua Regia (royal water) must be prepared fresh, just before use. It is a 1:3 mixture of fuming Nitric Acid & Hydrochloric Acids.
† *Aqua Regia* is one of the most highly reactive agents known to ancient alchemists. If you don't know how to handle highly corrosive chemicals, please do not attempt this exercise. You could hurt, maim, or blind yourself. Be especially careful when neutralizing the *Aqua Regia* with potassium metal. The combination is flammable, corrosive, and very nearly explosive—especially if you do not know what you are doing or if you are the least bit careless.

42 Men naturally crave copper, while women crave zinc. Semen is high in zinc, while vaginal secretions are high in copper. I use zinc salts to cleanse crystals which will be used by women & copper salts for crystals to be used by men.

43 I find it ironic that mercury salts (along with other heavy metals, such as lead) are highly toxic, especially to brain cells. This is a perfect example of the magickal principle that every power contains the seed of its opposite, which will surface if the operator does not understand what s/he is doing.

salt, be aware that many metallic salts are considered by many people to be quite toxic. I recommend allowing your crystal to soak in the appropriate metallic salt solution for about a week. Rinse well under running tap water as soon as you take it out of the salt solution. Don't forget to wash your hands, too! If you feel you are dealing with a potentially toxic salt, place your rinsed crystal in a running stream for a few days.

I do not consider myself to be a healer, but if I were setting-out to create a healing crystal, I would first select a crystal of appropriate size, shape, and energy. Then I would focus the crystal's energy with a cleansing in gold/potassium salts. I would work with it for a while (3 months or so) as a dream crystal. Then I would edit its programming with weak table-salt washings. Finally, I would fix its healing energies with fire. In that way, I would not have to worry about my crystal losing its healing touch, even if I felt the need to cleanse it frequently.

"A Sex Magickian's Alchemical Guide to Quartz Crystals" was in the Black Moon Archives and in Mezlim, Vol. I, No. 1 (Cincinnati: N'Chi, Candlemas [February 2] 1990) pages 17-23, and "A Sex Magickian's Alchemical Guide to Quartz Crystals, Pt II," in Mezlim, Vol. I, No. 2 (Cincinnati: N'Chi, Beltane/Whalpurgist Nacht [May 1] 1990), pages 27-37. Some sections (Forbidden Alchemies, pages 257-260) were reprinted with additional material in The Cincinnati Journal of Magick, Issue VII (Cincinnati" Black Moon Publishing, 1989), pages 52-57.

of Order
&
Chaos

Math of the ChRySTAL HUMM
Charter & Statement of Purpose

Do what thou wilt shall be the whole of the Law.

Introduction

The Math of the ChRySTAL HUMM became manifest upon the outer in the Spring of 1981 as a outgrowth of the OTO Powerzone which has existed in the Ithaca area for nearly a decade. The Math of the ChRySTAL HUMM is a self-sufficient cell within the body of initiates known as the Ordo Templi Orientis (OTO). While the initiatory lineage of our Powerzone links us with many Branches of the Order upon the inner, our primary catena upon the outer is via Kenneth Grant (the present O∴H∴O∴ of the Typhonian Branch of the OTO), Aleister Crowley, and then back through recorded history to the antediluvian magicks of Atlantis.

This Powerzone was founded and organized by two V° Degree members of the OTO, Soror 0-Maku–33/33 & Frater OTz PTN–690, for the purpose of promulgation of the Law of Thelema (on the outer) and to act as a framework within which to guide those whose Will is to work within this Powerzone upon the inner. This document was devised by Frater PVN as an introduction to the theoretical dynamics of this Power zone (practical extensions of the formulae which Kenneth Grant has reified thru the Gateway at Daath), and in order to entice all whose Will is aligned with the inner spirit of this Powerzone.

Over time, the Math of the ChRySTAL HUMM has taken on a life and direction of its own. While we remain dedicated to the reification of a fully functional OTO Powerzone, we have discovered that the Current which is working to manifest thru the HUMMing of this living ChRySTAL is not limited to the aspirations of the mortals who began this endeavor. The Math of the ChRySTAL HUMM is a bud upon the Tree of Life, which (given proper nourishment and support) will Flower into one of the visible chakras of that organization/entity whose individual cells have been known at various times & places under many diverse forms—e.g.:

On the inner:
the Astrum Argentum (A∴A∴)
the Sisterhood of the Silver Star
the Eleven-Star Working
The Illuminati
The Great White Brotherhood

On the outer:
The Order of the Shadow Knights
The Order of Templars of the East
The Gnostic Catholic Church
The Order of Babalon

The Math of the ChRySTAL HUMM is not the first bud on the Tree of Life to aspire becoming a visible Flower of both the inner & outer Orders and it will not be the last. The Order has endured a very difficult Winter during the previous Æon so most of its buds are not yet ready to believe that the Equinox of the Gods has really transformed this century into the first herald of Spring.

We seek active communication, communion, and cross pollination with those other buds who are endeavoring to flower at this time. We respect the individuality & autonomy of all, while seeking to form alliances with those whose Will is to promote the pooling of resources—both human & material—in order to facilitate the reification of projects which will aid the coming of Spring & the full Flowering of the Tree of Life *within the here & now.*

In particular, we are setting-up a small publishing operation for the production & distribution of esoteric pamphlets. At the present time, we have a modest catalog of items which have a limited circulation, so our production costs are quite high. We expect to grow over the next decade as we acquire more manuscripts from exciting new authors, purchase more of our own production equipment, & gain more experience in wholesale distribution. At the present time, we need an infusion of money, ideas, and manuscripts. We are more than happy to exchange literature with other individuals & groups engaged in similar or complimentary projects.

In as much as we seek to function above the Abyss as well as upon Malkuth, we seek an end to strife amongst the various Æonic formulae. We seek to make/strengthen alignments with individuals &

organizations whose initiatory links permit them to radiate specialized energies from any of the Æons (e.g., Horus, MAAT, Osiris, Atlantis, Isis, and those Nameless Forgotten Æons whose most convenient access is through the Gateway at Daath).

We also seek information &/or communication with any who have worked similar formulae, but who have gone back into hibernation because of the difficulties inherent in early Flowering. In particular, we seek news of any members of the S.P.R.T. (Society for the Propagation of Religious Truth) which was active in NY City about a decade ago. Some of its more prominent members were the Reverend Martin E. Nixon, Paul Liederkranz, and Doctor Theodore Lindquist.

Function of Boleskine

Over a decade ago, we set-up Boleskine House, inc. to aid us in the production & distribution of material of interest to the Thelemic community

Our first major endeavor was an inexpensive pocket-sized edition of Liber AL vel Legis which we published in 1976. From 1975 through 1979 we published Mezla, the Official newsletter of the Typhonian branch of the OTO. During our first decade, we also published Liber Oz in many different attractive formats which we made available at low cost to those whose Will was the promulgation of the law of Thelema.

Since 1979, we have been in magickal hibernation, from which we are just now emerging. The last 4 years have been a time of introspection and growth. We are still dedicated to serving the Thelemic community, but our focus is considerably broader than it was a decade ago.

Most of our new additions are from the pen of Frater PVN, a self-styled alchemist & Thelemic anarchist who resides in this Powerzone during his visits to the planet earth (he is out of body so much that he can no longer be considered to be a full-time resident of this planet). While much of his work is an out-growth of his Thelemic research and his initiatory links to the OTO, his approach to Alchemy & intra-Order politics is sufficiently unconventional, that we have placed his essays in a separate section of the catalog to obliviate any possible confusion to those who are looking for more 'traditional' Thelemic material.

The Future

Most of Aleister Crowley's works are now in print & there are many publishers dedicated to seeing to it that the important Thelemic documents remain in print. While we intend to maintain our links with the traditional Thelemic community, our publishing endeavors will continue to reflect our ever-broadening magickal interests. We expect to see this catalog grow over the next few years as we acquire more manuscripts from eliciting new authors, purchase more of our own production equipment, & gain more experience in wholesale distribution. We are more than happy to exchange literature with individuals & groups engaged in similar or complimentary projects.

Attention Authors & Artists
(instructions deleted)

We are actively seeking correspondence with all those who are aligned with the aspirations &/or formulae outlined in this pamphlet. We are more than willing to trade publications with those whose work is complimentary or supplementary to our own. We also solicit essays & Artwork by practicing magickians, shamans, Alchemists, etc. who are looking to find a larger audience for the fruits of their labors. While our present need is for self-contained essays of moderate length (10 to 20 typed pages) our long-range plans include a magazine of Artwork & short essays, and (eventually) a series of full. length books. Black & white drawings done with pen & ink are always welcome to illustrate our essays.

Due to the nature of the work of the Math of the ChRySTAL HUMM, the functions of this Powerzone are in constant evolution. In order to reflect the nature of this evolution, this document is in constant revision & expansion.

Love is the law, love under will

PVN
Master,
Forbidden Alchymies,
West Danby, N.Y.

04 October, 1983ev (Anno LXXIX)

*Being, the 26th Anniversary of the Exploration of Space
27th Lunar Day 4 Phaophi, 4752 (Sothic Calendar)*

Mythology & Mathematics

Once upon a time, long before the recursive formulae of the Æons began the spiral dance of unfoldment, certain Gateways were constructed to facilitate the easy transfer of 'unusual' types of energy through 'tunnels' in the Space/Time/Alternity continuum. To the ignorant, these Gateways are seemingly in contradiction to all natural law. Hence, their existence is denied by most practitioners of Science &/or labeled 'evil' by most Theologians. The fears of the ignorant are not without basis, for the energies which are transmitted via these Gateways can be highly dangerous to those who are not yet aware of the Godhood which lies within themselves.

Therefore, it sometimes becomes necessary to seal certain of these Gateways in local areas of the Multiverse in order to protect a developing species from the energies which are transmitted through these Gateways. More-developed races (who dwell beyond the stars) utilize certain of these Gateways to transmit 'energies' whose influences would impede the independent evolution of many individuals within the infant species.

Early in the history of our race the Gateway at Daath was sealed by the guardians from Sothis to permit the human race to develop in isolation from the elder gods whose magicks subtly alter all 'reality' which they touch. The fall of Atlantis and the mythologies surrounding the Eden captivity relate directly to the sealing of this Gateway.

The Gateway at Daath is but one of a multitude of transdimensional Gateways accessible from our particular reality. While the number of Gateways is probably not infinite, there seem to be many more Gateways than can be imagined in the wildest dreams/nightmares of any of the members of our race (save perhaps madmen & mathematicians). Several independent researchers have postulated the number of Gateways to be linked to the number of Man (or the Great Beast), but the relationship seems to be exponential rather than linear— Hence the number of Gateways is not 666, but perhaps 66^6 or even $6!6!^{6!}$. 66^6 is approximately $2.659132635 \times 10^{*}36305$ or 265,913 followed by 36,300 zeros—a number which would fill more than 28 pages of this [chap] book to write in full.

$6!6!^{6!}$is so awesome as to be bordering on meaningless. 6!

(six-factorial) = 6x5x4x3x2x1 which is 720. 720*720*720 is approximately 30.285947 x 10^1000000 or 30 followed by 1,000,000 zeros—a number which would fill more than 740 pages of this [chap] book to write in full. As a point of reference, the smaller of these two numbers is far larger than the number of atoms in the universe (as it is known to the Astronomers at this point in time). In any case, there are certainly more than enough Gateways to keep us busy exploring new frontiers for the foreseeable future!

One of these primary Gateways between manifest creation and that unknowable 'otherness' is the Gateway which this Powerzone knows as the Gateway of the ChRySTAL HUMM. Throughout this entire Universe, matter is in constant flux with non-matter. The sum total of matter remains approximately constant, but, at sub-quantum levels, the 'fabric' of matter is in a quasi-stable flux with 'that which is not matter' (nor energy, nor anything else imaginable or definable). The Gateway which exists at this interface is not to be found at a particular locus in Time or Space, but is continuously accessible at each and every point within this Multiverse. The Gateway of the ChRySTAL HUMM exists within every atom of matter and within every quanta of energy.

The human race is blessed (cursed?) by virtue of its physical size. As a race, our average size (from fertilized ova to giants) is about one Meter. A meter is (or very close to) the balance point of the manifest Universe. On an exponential scale of size, we exist at the center of the manifest Universe. The ultimate size of the closed & bounded Universe is aproximately 1033 meters (10000000000000000000000 0000000000 meters), while the smallest theoretical distance within any quanta of matter is aproximately 10^{-33} M (.000000000000000000 000000000000001 meters). At 10^{-33} meters, matter becomes foamlike and exists in quasi-stable equilibrium with 'that which is not matter'. Technically speaking, 'That which is not matter' is probably not the same 'otherness' which exists beyond the Gateway of Daath, but as similar rules of access and manipulation apply, only specialists need concern themselves with the semantic and orthographic distinctions which induce the subtle nuances among the various Gateways.

Attunement to the Seed ChRySTAL

Insofar as we are able to ascertain (via skryings and sub-quantum psychometric experimentation), the primary attunement to the ChRySTAL HUMM is via the vibration of threes via the mandala of the seed crystal which exists at the Gateway between this Universe & 'that which lies beyond'. The vibrations can be simple—as in 3, 33, 333, etc.; or complex—as in the pa-kua of the I Ching (2 things taken 3 at a time = $2^3 = 8$), or as in the interplay of Yin Yang & Tao (see Liber Trigrammaton 3 (3 things taken 3 at a time $3^3 = 27$).

Each entity (human or otherwise) who begins to work with the energies of the ChRySTAL HUMM undertakes the Great Work to reify this Gateway within him/herself. Such a task of subtle balance cannot be fully accomplished (or even fully comprehended!) by any one Master (no matter how balanced or how advanced) working in isolation. The task (most always) seems to be begun in isolation, but once the ChRySTAL Gateway begins to function (no matter how poorly, or how imbalanced), its vibrations will send out the necessary call to other(s) of complimentary vibration. As different vibrations of the fundamentAL note are attracted, dissonances may be felt. It is the work of the adepts of the crystal to fine tune their imbalances in order to turn dissonance into symphony.

Each Adept who works to reify the Gateway of the ChRySTAL HUMM usually begins thru a process of sigilisation upon the Astral in order to perceive the subtle mandala of the seed crystal in a unique way—each according to his/her personal vibratory mode and in full alignment with his/her True Will, no single entity and no facet of the crystal can exist at the core of the ChRySTAL. The ChRySTAL is an ever-changing Gateway, which exists between this reality & that which we cannot yet fully comprehend. Since the ChRySTAL is continuously non-uniform throughout time, space, and Alternity, the 'point-of-view' of each researcher (poet, magus, madman) who works with its energies will perceive the seed crystal from a unique perspective.

Vision of the Scribe: Core of the Seed ChRySTAL

The mandala described and pictured herein is the personal vision of this scribe alone, modified in the light of inspiration from others of varying degrees of awareness/initiation. As other researchers are attracted to this particular seed crystal, the vibrations felt by all of us will change as the perceptions of all who work with this family of images fine-tune themselves into a better working model of this Gateway. A working understanding (and practical application) of the energies available via this Gateway could well solve the race's 'energy crisis' by obliterating it entirely from the reality of this Universe. Within the myriad Gateways of the ChRySTAL HUMM accessible through a single gram of matter is stored more energy than in all of the nuclear forces within all the stars of this Universe combined.

At the time I first began to work with the energies of the ChRySTAL HUMM, I perceived its structure by utilizing the Astral sigil of this Gateway as follows:

At the center of the crystal is a cube. For ease in meditation, the cube can be opened-up into an inverted Tau Cross, so that the 6 faces of the cube are all visible without undue strain. With the proper use of sex, drugs, &/or ritual, the Tau Cross will fold in on itself as the three, four, and higher dimensional aspects of the mandala become comprehensible.

Facets of the Cube

Central is a 'trap' set on the Astral ⊠ to attract candidates to the seed crystal itself. It is by this means that the powerzone may attract those of suitable vibration & may thereby grow. On the opposite side of the cube from the 'trap' is the infinity sign: |∞|. This is to signify that the potential of this Gateway is without limit. As the crystal is transparent, the trap & the infinitude of the crystal superimpose to form. Between these two facets is |93|.

The 93 symbolizes that the crystal reifies within this present Æon in accord with the formula of Thelema. Although the crystal extends throughout all time, space, and Alternity, I have reason to believe that all those who work with the vibrations of this Gateway at the present point in time (i.e, during the Æon of Horus) will become a-tuned to the 93 Current whether they have made a conscious decision to become Thelemites, or not.

The three facets of the crystal which form the base of the inverted Tau Cross portray the triple paradox which lies at the core of this Gateway. This triplicity is usually summed up as the unity of Yod (י) in ChRySTAL, but is more fully expressed in the formalized title of this Powerzone, viz:

a
The Math of the ChRySTAL HUMM
q

Thus, the central point of the ChRySTAL has three distinct manifestations: A (א), Y (י), and Q (ק). Qabalists can easily interpret this to mean that AIQ BKR is a valid tool for exploring the nuances of this formula, while mathematicians will see Cantor's series of transcendental numbers veiled but thinly within the Aleph. Personal exploration is the primary key which unlocks the secrets of all Gateways—the Gateway of the ChRySTAL HUMM is no exception.

Lobes of Energy

Centered on the cubical center of this seed Crystal is a tri-lobed field of energy which serves to specialize the ChRySTAL into the three major Schools of Magick which draw their power directly from this Gateway.

The energy field symbolized by ChR (חר) serves to potentize the rituals of those who function within the sexual priesthood. ChR is hole or cave, the sacred grotto of initiation. ChR=208, which is ABRH, a feather, thus linking this priesthood to Maat & to those who work with the Double-Current of Horus/Maat. It is within this lobe of energy that the

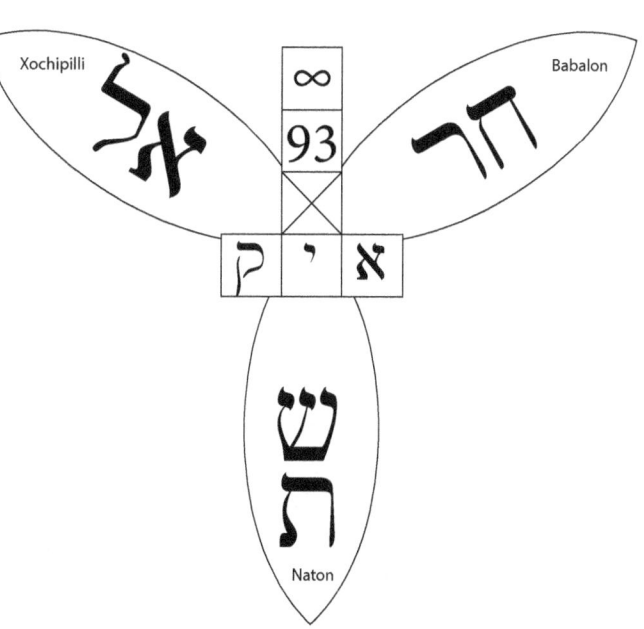

High Priestesses of the Vama Marg draw the bulk of their preter-human powers. The Feast of the Hive utilizes these energies, as do those who work within the Order of Babalon (under its many names on the outer).

The function of the ST (שת) lobe is to activate & potentize the teaching priesthood. The energies of this lobe assist the priestcraft in channeling direct communication from trans-Dimensional entities as well as assisting them in the active training of those novitiates whose Will is to act as tabernacles of Higher Consciousness. The Horus-Maat Lodge is firmly rooted in the energies of this lobe. ST=700, Seth; KPRT, the Mercy Seat; PRKT, the Veil of the Holy.

[Note: It should not be construed that either the Vama Marg or the H/M-L are limited to the energies of one specific lobe. A fully balanced Magickal Order will utilize all forms of energy even though it may specialize & reign supreme in one particular mode of working.]

The function of the AL (אל) lobe is tapped most easily by that branch of the Priesthood whose duty is to guide the alchemycal transformation of the race as a whole. The Alchemyst who works with this lobe of energy is concerned with the *in Vitro* production of Entheogens analogous to (but, by no means identical with) the *in vivo* entheogens produced by the Scarlet Women and Hive Queens who manipulate the energies of the ChR lobe. The priesthood of Xochipilli is most attuned with the energies of this lobe.

Specialization vs. Balanced Growth

While it is sometimes advantageous for a particular adept to specialize in the energies of a single lobe, each adept participating in the experiment should exercise care so that his/her imbalanced growth does not warp the vibrations within the crystal as a whole. It is not always possible for a single entity to develop alone without some degree of over-specialization, but once any Gateway begins to manifest within this reality, the vibration of the seed crystal within the Adept will strike a chord within those others who also work within the field of influence of this Gateway.

Such vibrations increase as the crystal begins to coalesce. The harmonious interplay of the ChRySTAL HUMM will allow all to expand their self-imposed limitations in such a way that the energies of all three lobes will become available to all who work these formulae. Continued balance can be assured IFF[1] all adepts who work with any specialized energies of this Gateway take the

---

[1] 'IFF' is a precise mathematical expression meaning "IF and Only IF".

necessary steps to learn the mysteries of the energies of all three lobes (i.e., tantra, ritual, & dietary alchemies). The balanced & focused use of this tripartite energy provides the interplay of 333 which is a key linking this Gateway with the Gateway at Daath which is so important to the evolution of the Race at this point in time.

Vibrations of Specialization & Attunement

Dis-connected from these three lobes of energy are the three isolated spheres of specialization by which the ChRySTAL relates to the world on the outer & by which it inter-relates with the other magickal crystals to which it is not yet fully attuned. It is the HUMM of the vibration of the crystal itself which manifests in any or all of three forms—depending upon the vibrations it receives from those outside the crystal.

The first vibration is the vibration of 5 from H (ה). It is a concentration of the energies commonly associated with the Tarot Trump called the Star. These energies are independent, seemingly Anarchistic, in nature. This is the vibration through which the Discordians, the Shadow Knights, & others who take full responsibility for their individualistic actions relate to the world & to the Order on the outer.

The second vibration is that of 6 from U (ו). It is the vibration of the Hierophant. This vibration empowers those whose task is up-hold tradition &/or harmonize any group endeavors. Those who work primarily with this vibration seek alliances with other seed crystals of opposite or complimentary vibrations—with mutual absorption being their ultimate goal (whereas the vibration of 5 seeks to test &/or to shatter competing crystals).

In dynamic balance with the energies of 5 & 6 is the

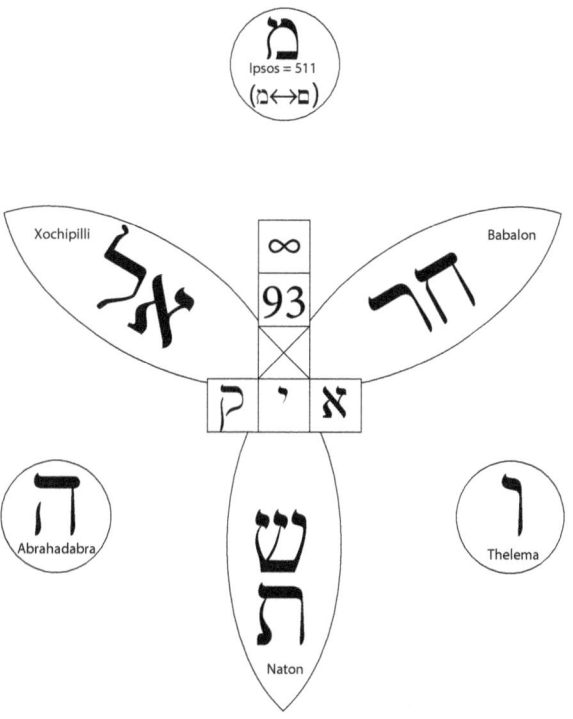

vibration which emanates from 80 as MM (מם)) and as the vibration which emanates from 640 as MM (מם).

The interplay of 5, 6, & 80 yield 91: the mystic number of Kether as AChAD; whereas the interplay of 5, 6, & 640 yield 651: Temurah (permutation).

Unification of the Symbol

As the Tau Cross folds into a cube, the 3 spheres of the HUMM form a 4th lobe of the 3-dimensional: a ChRySTAL HUMM.

q

The tetrahedron forms and sends out its lobes of energy to the four directions of Space/Time/Alternity along the four axes of:

Direction: (the three dimensions of x,y,z of our Universe)
Time: (The two-headed vector of Past & Future)
Probability: (the thread which weaves all of Alternity)
That Inconceivable Fourth Direction:
(Through the Gateway at 10^{-33} Meters)

When this occurs, the AIQ of the cube resolves itself into a single facet and the cube becomes the tetrahedral heart of this ChRYSTAL HUMM, which (IFF it can manifest without destroying itself) is destined to become one of the Thrones offered to the Gods who shall manifest via the Eleven Star Working.

Astral Call

The astral call has gone out. It is time for the seed crystals to come together & work out their dissonances. If you can feel the call upon the Astral & it be your Will to work with the vibrations of the ChRySTAL HUMM, contact us. Since the vibrations of this Gateway transcend both Time & Space, it is feasible to work with us even if you are half a planet away, or 500 years into our future. Once we get to know each other, it may become feasible for you to visit the Math of the ChRyS-TAL HUMM in the flesh to check us out. There is land & a house at the nexus of the Powerzone in West Danby (10 miles South of Ithaca), while Ithaca itself is an open community rich in alternative lifestyles & a very fluid job market for innovative people who are willing/able to be creative in reifying their Will.

Muldalahara Chakra & the Orders

Here begins the Diary entry of frater OTx PTN–690 Ca.fc.a. FVN1 for SATURDAY, the 7th Day of AUGUST, 1982 e.v.

Do what thou wilt shall be the whole of the Law.

Here begins my rough notes on what I have learned thus far from doing HHH.

Muldalahara Chakra: This chakra is the Malkuth of the microcosmic Tree. Most 'spiritual' folks would like to get off Malkuth & it would seem that they would also like to forget they have assholes. However, Malkuth (& the Muldalahara) are essential to the scheme of reality as it now exists. Energy flows from the non-manifest (the 3 veils of negative existence) (which KG believes are linked with Daath, but which I believe are beyond Kether) through the manifest realities of the various Sephira and Pathways of the Tree of Life. But there is no flow without Malkuth. Malkuth is a transmuter of energies. It absorbs or earths all energy into itself & thereby promotes the flow from the Ain down through Malkuth. But the energy does not end here. It is not all consumed by the process of earthing. The energy flows down through the interstices of matter—the in-between-ness spoken of by Spare as the neither-neither, where it is once again transformed. This reversed energy has no name in magick that I know of. Its nearest analog in the science of 20 years ago was anti-matter, but modern science has a more facile mind & can handle weirder ideas than the science of a generation ago. The energy seems to be 'stored' in the nooks & crannies of the Universe where matter becomes foamlike. At distances less than 10^{-33} meters, the concepts of time, distance, matter, and energy become meaningless. Time, matter, and energy are in a constant state of creation & dissolution. The universe as we perceive it is discontinuous. Between each pulsebeat of 'reality,' there lies an infinite 'moment' of non-existence. The entire Universe is created & destroyed billions of trillions of times in the few seconds it takes our brains to look at this sentence. Malkuth (& the Muldalahara) is the elastic reservoir of energy from the Ain. Energy flows down the Tree to Malkuth where it is transmuted to another form, stored, and released to begin its journey back up the Tree. Information is carried in both directions. The Gods create us & our thoughts, desires, and conscious Will modify the Gods. An active and magickally centered Muldalahara is crucial to the working of Laws of similitude of Hermes (As above, so below; as below, so above).

Gateways: There seem to me to be four separate & distinct gateways which permit access between the Tree of Life & 'other' areas of existence. The most basal (primal) of these is the Muldalahara Gateway which is involved in the perpetual creation/dissolution of the Tree itself. The second & third have been spoken of at length by 718—these are the Gateways at Yesod & Daath which interconnect with the shells of the Qliphoth via the Tunnels of Set. There is a great historical connection between the traditional Qliphoth & creation/destruction dance which I feel is so tied-up with the Muldalahara. But 718 has made a good case for the Gateways to Nightside being tied to Yesod & Daath. To me Nightside is a very good term for energies/forces which represent the forces of Chaos, while Dayside is a good (neutral) label for those Forces/energies which represent the Gods of Unity. I fully believe that all 4 Gateways are 'border-crossings' between the domains of the Gods of Chaos & the Gods of Unity. The uppermost gateway is above Kether & leads to the 3 veils of Negative existence. I know next to nothing of these areas through direct exploration, but as I have explored the Gateway via the Muldlahara, I can hypothesize via symmetry.

It is said that Kether is the Malkuth of a higher Tree & likewise that Malkuth is the Kether of a lower Tree. I do not believe in an infinite series of Trees, stacked one above the other throughout infinity. It explains nothing & simply makes the problem of religion/magick, etc. too extensive to be tackled. I prefer to hypothesize a single Tree. The Gods of Law & Order & Universal harmony exist at one end & the Gods of Chaos exist at the other extreme. Kether is Unity & Malkuth is diversity. Neither can exist without the other. They are like the N & S poles of a magnet. Throughout recorded history Dayside has sought to subjugate Nightside in order to exploit, rule, and destroy it. Nightside has always fought back & has (perhaps) also done its share of attempting to subjugate and destroy Dayside. But in recent times, there has been an uneasy truce, for it seems that both sides have independently discovered that Dayside without Nightside is utter stagnation & Nightside without Dayside is so diverse that nothing complex can ever build-up. Although we (as a race of beings) are located closest to the Courts of Chaos, we (being Dayside creatures) most readily perceive the energies from Kether & therefore aspire to Unity. Our Nightside natures (our dreams, our nightmares, our visions) express our biological & historical roots here in Malkuth & whisper to us of the glories of diversity & individual independence—i.e., the glories of anarchy (rule without a King}. At Daath, our Nightside aspects flow Dayside, which is why Daath is so terrible for those who have not made peace with their Nightside selves (called demons by those whose Dayside selves seek to dominate & subjugate their Nightside selves). At Yesod, our Dayside selves can flow Nightside & can learn the glories of the Courts of Chaos firsthand. The so-called Astral is entirely our own creation (both individually & collectively) & is but a glimmer of the glories of the Courts of Chaos. Roger Zelazny writes of this duality in his series of novels about Amber. He is long winded, his plots are far too complex, and he sometimes misses the point altogether, but he comes far closer to the Truth than any other author in Science Fiction, Religion, or Magick.

During my HHH, I began to feel more & more like an alien, or some sort of double agent. I knew that the Courts of Chaos were my 'natural' home & that magick was a science which 'ought to' work with far more spectacular results than it actually does here. Drugs can 'short-circuit' the programming of the Gods of Unity to allow the dispersion of chaos to leak-through. If the aspirant is not dealing with his or her demons in a friendly way on a day by day basis, the trip is very difficult & can lead to serious problems (from deification of the ego to antisocial behavior (i.e., suicide, homicide, rape, etc.). But for the aspirant who seeks a balance of Day/Night, the experience can be not only illuminating, but enervating, and can assist in the Day/Night truce becoming a true harmonious Peace.

My memories of past history began to come back to me. I have conflict with the history texts in many many places. Some of them are small, but some are significant. I remember the OTO being around at the same time as the Albigensians & the Cathars. They were sent in to crush the heresy & were greatly influenced by it. According to the Encyclopedia Britannica, the Cathars were crushed several centuries before the Knights Templar were formed.

Likewise I remember the interplay of the OTO and the A∴A∴ from their beginnings. The OTO was begun by agents from the Courts of Chaos to infiltrate Dayside & to undermine the work of the Catholic Church. The Catholic Church had long since lost its power to work magick and was therefore defenseless. The A∴A∴ was formed by the forces of Dayside as a reaction to the OTO & was given special permission to utilize the forces of magick (essentially a weapon of chaos) in order to combat the OTO. When the OTO (as Knights Templar) was essentially crushed, the A∴A∴ was supposed to have been disbanded, but some members continued the research into magick without benefit of authority. Over the centuries, the A∴A∴ became more closely aligned with the forces of magick, while continuing to swear fealty to the Gods of Unity. The OTO began to resurrect itself about a century ago, so the A∴A∴ was taken out of dormancy in order to combat the OTO once again. But the Masters of the A∴A∴ were no longer of one mind. Some wanted to crush the OTO & some wanted to infiltrate it in order to learn more. The ones who had been clandestinely practicing magick without authority were far stronger than those who put aside their magickal researches after the fall of the Templars so there was no direct confrontation. By this time, both sides had glimmers of their mutual interdependence & only the fundamentalists (on both sides) could deny the evidence. A new lodge of Grey Masters was formed which attempted to incorporate the ideas of both Chaos & Unity into a single harmonious system. The effort was frowned-upon (& sabotaged) by fundamentalists of both extremities. The lodge went underground. It is now almost ready to surface.

Love is the law, love under will.

Roles & Nurturing within the Hive or Powerzone, part I
Knowledge vs. Wisdom, or the Function of Alchemy

PVN (1984)

Within the Powerzone (Hive) the primary function for all members is nurturing & growth. On the outer, this takes the form of economic interdependence & the exchange of knowledge (ideas, book learning, and all matters of craft) between various members of the hive. This also includes the active seeking out of new hive members & the education & training of candidates for the inner mysteries of the hive.

On the inner, the nurturing leaves the sphere of learned knowledge & becomes the direct experiential intake of those alchemyckal substances which promote wisdom through the mechanism of permanent change (i.e., initiation) or mutation of both the physical vehicle of each & every hive member as well as their true selves, both individual & collective. The exchange of alchemyckal substances among hive members must be without cost to any individual hive member. Any costs (labor, money, travel, etc.) must be borne by the hive as a whole & decided upon by those in charge of such matters—the Queen Mother & the Hive Alchemyst. The Queen Mother is the person (either male or female in gender) who has the office of acquiring, storing, transmuting, and transmitting alchemyckal elixirs *in vivo*. She is assisted in her function by as many Hive Queens as the hive can support at any particular time, but the ultimate responsibility for the *in vivo* alchemical function rests with the inspired decisions of the most advanced hive queen, who is the Queen Mother. The Queen Mother may veto any decision made by any Hive Queen or group of Hive Queens. All within the hive owe her full fealty as a guard against un-slain ego creating disturbances within the hive.

The masculine counterpart of the Hive Queens are the Alchemysts (AL-Chemysts) (who, like the Hive Queens, may be physiologically of either male or female gender, but who, by virtue of their office, must, insofar as they are able, function as true gynanders) who are all subordinate to the Hive Alchemyst. Since all members of the hive act partly as Hive Queen & partly as Alchemist, all must swear fealty to the Queen Mother. Between the Queen Mother & the Hive Alchemyst there exists a bond of mutual fealty by virtue of the duties & alternating functions of their respective offices. The Hive Alchemyst (& the Alchemysts who assist & cooperate with him) has the office of acquiring, storing, transmuting, and transmitting alchemyckal elixirs *in vitro*.

The alchemyckal elixirs manipulated under the office of both the Hive Queens & the Alchemysts include all of the Entheogens known to the hive at any particular time. These entheogens include (but are not limited to) the charged sexual secretions of the hive members & their animal familiars; plants (living or dead) and their various extracts, either fresh or preserved, either in pure or chemically combined with other substances to make new classes of entheogens; Fungi and their extracts, prepared & manipulated in vivo or in vitro or any combination thereof; Synthetic Organic Chemicals; Secretions of Animals & Humans, either from within the Hive or from without, either sexual in nature or derived from any other portion of the physical vehicle or higher self by the skill of the Alchemyst & Hive Queen.

There may, from time to time, be members of the hive who are unable to partake of the *in vivo* nourishments supplied by the Hive Queens. Such restrictions of wisdom & nourishment must be overcome by diligent use of the *in vitro* elixirs upon the physical vehicles of those who have cut themselves off from in vivo nourishment. To the profane, the *in vivo* sharing of alchemyckal elixirs (entheogens) may appear to be but an excuse for promiscuous behavior, but to the initiates within the hive such necessary cum-munications must be undertaken by all without breaking any vows of celibacy or monogamy. The formula of the alchemyckal feast of the hive is love under will. While the physical vehicle may be bound or constrained by oaths of monogamy or celibacy, or may be limited by ego problems between itself & the officiating Hive Queen, the Higher Self (who is the True Priest) in the rite of the Alchemyckal Marriage is by no means so limited or constrained. The Higher Self needs nourishment from the Hive Queens if the physical vehicle is to become a fit temple of the God within. The *in vitro* elixirs of the alchemist (while not mandatory) are very useful in the transubstantiation which is so crucial to the on-going nourishment of all within the hive.

Extreme caution must be used by all in the initiation of new hive members &/or the puberty rites of those raised within the hive. The full spectrum of potency to which the Hive Queens may have access may be more than the nervous system of a non-initiate can tolerate without death or insanity of the physical vehicle. While it is usually true that the priest controls the flow of the kalas of the priestess, the Hive Queens, by virtue of their office, can manipulate their own kalas in such a way as to ensure that the new initiate will not be burned out. Instead, the new initiate will receive precisely what is needed for further evolution & for the slaying of the ego so necessary for a true pledge of fealty to the Queen Mother.

Within the powerzone of the Hive there is a potent magickal formula which allows the petty jealousies & competitions inherent in the formula of the tetragrammaton (IHVH) to be completely obliterated. Without such an obliteration, there will always be squabbling & competition among the hive queens & among the alchemysts, & the powerzone will fragment before the necessary work is accomplished. This formula is outlined more fully by Frater I am NOT a Fool in his paper on 3 = 0. But for those of you who do not yet have access to this paper, the formula involves the replacement of the dualistic priest/priestess with the triad of priest/priestess/androgyne (or priest/priestess/gynander) in which the androgyne or gynander is under apprenticeship for the priesthood. By virtue of this formula there is a twisting of the magickal circle for a cross-fertilization of East & North & an exchange of roles. The circle becomes the infinity sign as IHVH is transmuted to TNHV.

NOTES:
- *In Vitro* – literally means 'in glass.' The elixirs are manipulated or stored/transmitted outside of a living organism.
- *In Vivo* – literally means 'in life.' The elixirs are communicated to the recipient while still alive. This means either the eating of a living organism or the communion of living elixirs directly from the living organism.

Milk bought at the store is eaten *in vitro*, while milk from the mother's breast is *in vivo* communion.

Entheogens are substances which when communicated either in vitro or in vivo promote a state of consciousness which is termed the divine experience. Hallucinogens and the kalas present in the sexual fluids are but two of the more commonly accepted entheogens.

To my knowledge (i.e., book learning knowledge rather than inspiration derived from entheogens) the earliest working of modified tetragrammaton formula may be found in Magic in Theory & Practice in the ritual know as Star Ruby, and in Liber V vel Reguli (second gesture).[1]

---

1 On *Star Ruby*, *Liber V vel Reguli*, Second Gesture ("The Enchantment"), see THELEMAPEDIA at http://www.thelemapedia.org/index.php/Liber_V_vel_Reguli

Apologia Discordia— in Defense of Disagreement

by B.S. revised & edited by Frater PVN

This essay was originally penned by B.S. in violent reaction to certain criticisms which he received at the start of his magickal career. He had submitted reports of his magickal research to his Superiors for evaluation and comment. He was well aware that his work was both tentative and un-polished, but he was not expecting discouraging and brutal comments which were neither helpful nor fair. His first attempts at allegorical mythology were labeled 'puerile fantasy' and his tentative researches in certain formulae of XI Degree Alchemy were labeled 'highly dangerous' and 'not worth pursuing'. This essay became the turning point in B.S.'s magickal career which eventually led him into the Abyss in search of Truth.

The original essay was, fortunately for all concerned, never published. Frater PVN was given the task of re-working the MS to preserve the spunk and thrust of the original, while toning down B.S.'s indignation & violent reaction to rejection. Hopefully he has succeeded.

"The word of Sin (ש)[1] is restriction". That is to say, each Æon (symbolized by the Tarot Trump ruled by Shin) has a particular formula which restricts the operation of those who work within the framework of that æon. The previous two Æons of Isis & Osiris were concerned with maternity and paternity, so all formulae concerned with these æons have a bias or predisposition towards 'natural' (i.e. childbearing) phenomena. The traditions, rituals, and formulae which come down to us through initiated tradition (both written & oral) are very strongly attuned to this bias. While it would certainly be very foolish to suggest that sex for procreation is invalid in this æon of the child-twins of

---

[1] The twenty first Hebrew letter) is pronounced either Sin or Shin, depending upon the placement of the dogesh (the dot which determines pronunciation in modern Hebrew).

Hoor-Paar-Kraat & Ra-Hoor-Khuit, it is equally foolish to be limited by the restrictions of past æons. This is the æon of mutation, that is to say, the formula whereby the parent becomes the child through transformation. The (so-called) 'natural' cycle of Father + Mother yields Son + Daughter is by no means the only valid expression formula of the tetragrammaton

During the past two æons the study of Tantra, sex-magick, the kundalini, the physiochemical elixirs (kalas) have become very closely tied to a very narrow approach to the Mysteries which might be termed 'pro-creative mimicry'. Masturbation and female homosexuality have been (for the most part) permitted only under restricted conditions when used as an adjunct to male-female genital contact. This is not to say that all sex acts necessarily culminated in a co-mingling of the male & female elixirs, but (as a general rule) those acts which were not in themselves pro-creative mimicry were used to potentize or prepare the priest or priestess for a culminating rite at some later time, or for use by the solitary magickian to attract a suitable partner for future rites. Male homosexuality was not generally so in the Aeon generally not fertile mother used, or even tolerated, of Isis, the male was permitted to imitate the goddess while in the Æon of Osiris, males who 'demeaned' themselves by taking-on the role of woman were not often considered suitable for initiated workings.[2] The exceptions—such as the priests of Cybele, who were castrated and then functioned as temple prostitutes—are not numerous, and can easily be viewed as 'influences from other æons'.

But this is the Æon of 'un-natural creatiom' in which woman is no longer valued simply for her ability to represent the fertile mother goddess, nor can she any longer be 'used' (by the priestcraft, or by men as a group) as simply the inferior (but necessary) assistant to man. In the Æon of Horus, men and women are equal, but this equality does not necessarily imply interchangeability. On the mundane level, a woman cannot father a child, nor can a man become pregnant. But magickians, whose work can often transcend the limits of the mundane world, manipulate potent trans-mundane formulae in which 'man' and 'woman' are simply masks, or god-forms to be invoked as

---

2   The Æon of Osiris had some very strange ideas on male supremacy which were probably based in reversal or perversion of some of the unbalanced ideas predominant during the previous æon (the Æon of Isis). In the present æon (the Æon of Horus), the race will hopefully be able to transcend the imbalances of racial or sexual supremacy in order that we may all work together towards the accomplishment of the Great Work.

needed for the operation at hand (and banished when the mask loses its immediate usefulness). With practice, a biological woman can plant the germinating seed and/or a man can give birth to a magickal childe (creative idea which is earthed in form). The balanced magickian is skilled in alternating roles at will during the course of a magickal operation.

But this Aeon is far more diverse than simple role reversal, for role reversal can easily be reduced to pro-creative mimicry in yet another form. The so-called 'sterile' workings (lumped by Crowley under the heading of Eleventh Degree) allow congress with forces beyond Daath in order to 'give-birth' to gods not of this plane. Kenneth Grant has explored most thoroughly one form of this un-natural congress. But, important as is el. rub. (elixir rubrae), which is the red gold of the alchemists, it is but one-third of the Magickal Formulae which are currently at work within this æon.

The most widely recognized formula is that of White Isis. This is the formula of natural childbirth & pro-creative mimicry in all its forms from simple fertility cults to the more complex or bizarre forms of initiated tradition.

The second formula is that of Red Isis. This formula utilizes the current of the sterile lunar flow with which the magickian taps into the current of Nu-Isis. The magickian then projects a god-form Nightside in order facilitate the explorations of the Tunnels of Set and engage in experiments which may only safely be performed beyond the Gates of the Abyss.

But there is yet a third formula, which encompass the Rites of Black Isis, through which the magickian utilizes the certain formulae (such as LAShTAL) in order to assist in the earthing of the experiments of Red Isis into this plane of reality.

It has been said that the Rites of White Isis are to be preferred over those of Red or Black Isis because the formulae of White Isis are more benign and are better understood than those of either the Red or the Black. But, in an overcrowded world, can it realistically be said that the spin-off energies of fertility and fecundity are without danger?

Up until a few short years ago, the mysteries of Red Isis had been veiled in utmost secrecy by those adepts who experimented with these energies. These Rites are indeed potent, and therefore dangerous, but with proper guidelines, even the most treacherous paths may be traversed safely by those initiates who do not over-estimate their own abilities. Today, experimentation with this Current is safer for all because the guidelines for safe workings has been made public by the Ordo Tempii Orientis in the books of Kenneth Grant.

At the present time, those who experiment with the Rites of Black Isis do so in secrecy & without the benefit of public guidelines similar to those available to the followers of either Red or White Isis. The rituals of Black Isis can be quite treacherous and are fraught with many pitfalls. All who dare explore these mysteries are cautioned to tread lightly and with much deliberation, for all 'mistakes' can easily be earthed within the fundament-AL being of the magickian. It would be foolish to shun these mysteries altogether, for it is only by careful mapping (& by making mistakes!) that we can ever hope to comprehend these mysteries in order to gain the ability to utilize them for both individual magickal initiation and for the evolutionary benefit of the race as a whole. Danger and Power go hand in hand; they are the flip sides of the same coin. By condemning danger, both danger & power are placed outside the grasp of all who listen to the warnings of others rather than their own innate curiosity. Had Kenneth Grant had not dared to chronicle his explorations of the formulae of Red Isis, the Thelemic magickal community as a whole would be poorer for his conservatism; but thanks to his explorations, we are all enriched through the access which we all have gained to the potent formulae of Red Isis.

But adepts are able to learn from failure (their own or anyone else's) as well as from success. Grant has written much constructive criticism on the 'strayed gods' of Thelema, outlining their failings and their obsessions, while delineating their researches in sufficient detail to enable all serious aspirants to the Mysteries to profit from those stray gods who lost their way in the pursuit of initiation and magickal self-knowledge. If proper records are kept, even failures which destroy the lives of adventuresome initiates can be useful, nay essential, to the rest of us who remain in the relative safety of our collective magickal traditions. The unchartered Abyss which lies beyond the fringe of our understanding is not for everyone, but there are those who dare to trust their deviant visions in order to pursue treasures which they hope will enrich us all.

Magick is, like most other human sciences, founded upon tradition. We need tradition to assist us in forming links with the past & to allow us to learn from the successes & failures of who have come before us

& who have added much to the store of human knowledge. There are many initiates who prosper on the well-worn paths tradition, refining and exploring the by-ways of existing formulae. Through the diligent work of these initiates, the crude experiments of our ancestors are continually being refined into efficacious magickal formulae with which we may better understand the Universe and interact with it in more beneficial ways. Within their own specialty, these adepts are brave and serious workers who, through the light of their own internal guidance, seek order within the chaos of diverse magickal traditions. But, far too often, their vision is limited, and their own pre-conceived ideas blind them to avenues of exploration which lie outside of their own narrow field. They see the tentative explorations of others as either futile or dangerous (or both!). While the danger is often quite real (for any potent formula is dangerous, especially when only partially understood), the futility is, however, only real for those who lack the requisite internal guidance to lead them off the beaten path and into the unexplored regions which border on madness and obsession. But those adepts who are comfortably ensconced within their own traditions cannot realistically hope to judge the tentative explorations of those who attempt to explore beyond the fringes of the known Universe.

But some of these adepts do judge the exploratory workings of others. They use the power and prestige which they have gained through the success of their own researches as a 'club' with which to dissuade research into areas which they consider futile or dangerous. These adepts are known as 'ossified gods'.

Israel Regardie (who is an adept of the formulae of Tiphareth) constantly uses the power of his reputation to dissuade everyone who will listen from exploring the formulae of Red Isis. Regardie reached a pinnacle of adeptship, then ossified to the point where he cannot see the validity of any formula which lies outside of the area which has worked so well for him.

Unfortunately, his ossification is not an isolated incident. There are many serious adepts who are appalled by the concepts of Nightside which are common to much of the workings of both Red & Black Isis. There are even adepts of Red Isis who are unable to see that certain formulae of Black Isis are necessary for the reification of opening of certain gateways which were discovered and explored through the formulae of Red Isis. Some even go so far as to deny the sodomical formula of the Eleventh Degree working, thereby attempting to abrogate much of Crowley's explorations along these lines. The Eleventh Degree is a working common to both Red & Black Isis and, as such, cannot be defined as exclusively a formula of Sodom or of el.rub. exclusively. The formula of the Eleventh Degree is a many faceted gem which enables the magickian to function equally well in the realms of Saturn/Earth or of Nu-Isis.

The sins of the fathers are often visited upon their children, but we are at the beginning of a new æon where the restrictions of the past have only a tenuous grip upon us. Let us not be bound by the ossifications of those gods who would foist their limited vision and their fears upon us in the guise of Truth. Thelema is not (& never can be) a single monolithic formula guarded by conservative adepts who fear the unknown or the dangerous. The gates of Daath are open and those formulae which are feared most will manifest unless they are dealt with constructively. In magickians, colitis and hemorrhoids are not caused by the rites of Black Isis nearly so often as they are caused by fear of the rites of Black Isis. A restricted Muldalahara chakra is dangerous for all magickians, whether or not they ever engage in the formulae of Sodom, for the magickal channel must be fully opened in order for the safe manipulation of the energies inherent in any trans-mundane magickal operation, particularly those which tap into Nightside. But let us not abandon these ossified gods who would attempt to thwart us in our struggle to discover our True Will. We all need to share our magickal explorations in order that we may learn from each other's successes & failures. The ossified gods have much to teach, but it seems that most of them have forgotten that they also have much to learn from the tentative explorations of others.

A Modest Proposal for a Superstructure to Unite the Order Based on Liber AL vel Legis

by PVN

Basic Requirements

1. Formal Acceptance of Liber LXXVII & Liber CCXX, in writing, to be submitted to the Order in any approved fashion. Check with your OTO, A∴A∴, or 11-Star contact person for particulars.
2. Acceptance of the Star within & the taking of a self-designed oath committing oneself to the Great Work. Copy of the oath to be submitted, in writing, to the Order. Approval of the oath by any member of the Order establishes affiliation with the Order through the catena of initiation manifest through that member.
3. Promulgation of the Law of Thelema upon the outer by being a living example of what it means to be a Thelemite, rather than through overt proselytization.
4. Formal study of magick to create an intellectual & emotional framework upon which personal advancements may be hung for careful examination.
5. Creation & maintenance of various formal & informal avenues of communication among various members and Branches of the Order.
6. Each individual Powerzone (lodge, coven, tribe, etc.) of any Branch of the OTO, A∴A∴, or 11-Star may impose certain other obligations upon probationary Candidates & members, and may test them in whatever way(s) they may see fit.
7. Anyone is free to work these grades, so long as it be their Will to do so. Those whose Will is to work these grades in concert with others

may do so by becoming active members of at least one Branch of the Order which recognizes the guidelines of this superstructure.
8. No member of the Order may be forced to work with or accept initiation from another member. All affiliations within the Order are by mutual consent & are subject to change at any time.

III
The Grade of Man of Earth

Aspirants to the Grade of Man of Earth undertake to perform a set of Herculean tasks designed to reify their magickal inspiration upon the physical plane in the here-&-now.

Upon successful completion of these self-imposed tasks, the Aspirant is able to function fully within this Grade, provided s/he designed the obligations of the Grade with sufficient care & insight.

The other Grades may be taken in any sequence, or all at once.

The aspirant is warned not to put-off the obligations of this grade until the very end, for the aspirant who is able to manifest the Grade of Man of Earth has stability, a virtue which cannot be fully appreciated until its need becomes imperative.

It is up to each aspirant to design his/her own set of obligations. The set given below may be used as a guideline. Obligations may be amended, dropped, or adopted at any time. Absolute fluidity is a key to stability.

Tamas Muldalahara is one of the titles of they who work this Grade.

Xochipilli (patron deity of those who take calculated risks) is one of the Gods who oversees the Virtues of the Grade of Man of Earth.

Gold is among the many colors pertaining to this Grade.

1. The Aspirant undertakes the design, creation, and consecration of a balanced set of magical tools. Such a set may consist of the 4 traditional weapons from Golden Dawn heritage, some power-objects/fetishes from a Shamanistic tradition, or some other set, no matter what.

    The set can be built-up over time, or created all at once. It is up to each Aspirant to use/test his/her implements continuously, maintaining balance among them as best s/he can.
2. The Aspirant undertakes to understand the meaning of hard work. This can easily be accomplished thru understudy & Mastery of a

self-chosen Art, Craft, or Trade.

It matters not whether the Aspirant pursues a society approved professional career—such as doctor, ditch-digger, statesman, office worker, cop, or priest—or a less respected trade (such as quack, welfare-bum, terrorist, embezzler, mercenary soldier, or harlot.

Success is most easily insured by choosing a line of work closely related to one's natural inclinations, yet far greater success is made possible by choosing a line of work which is both difficult & demanding. Thru proper design, a difficult task will strengthen both mind & body, while dulling neither.

If a particular line of work does not become a joy in-&-of itself, the Aspirant is free to change lines of work. The goal is total self-sufficiency upon the physical plane as well as an understanding of what part the Aspirant chooses to play in the Great Work. It is only thru a full understanding of how a system presently operates that changes may be designed & applied to society's flaws.

This obligation may also be undertaken thru its mirror image. There are some who aspire to this Grade who will be totally antipathetic towards the concept of work. Such Aspirants are encouraged to explore laziness to the fullest.

It has long been known that a lazy person will work much harder than his/her harder-working peers, to find ways of doing-away with the need to perform any unpleasant tasks. Laziness requires extreme agility of mind, body, & soul. The beggar who has 'nothing to lose' is often more free to change a corrupt system than the bank president whose comfort depends upon maintaining the status quo, even though the banker's wealth and respectability give him/her greater leverage with which to affect change.

If the aspirant can combine approaches, it will give him/her great power; vacillation between approaches can induce paralysis and the inability to act.

3. The Aspirant undertakes to create/build a living monument which transcends time.

Immortality is a keyword for this Grade.

Some choose to raise children, while others write books or create works of Art. Some found religions while others found nations. Some build financial empires while others plant gardens. Some work on ways to dis-incarnate/re-incarnate smoothly, while others work to reify immortality in the flesh.

Publication or other means of dissemination of one's own researches pertain to this Grade. The Aspirant may choose to work alone, or s/he may choose to work with others—among equals, as a Master, or as a servant.

II
The Grade of Lover

Aspirants to the Grade of Lover undertake to act spontaneously in ways designed to promote understanding, appreciation, & unification with others who are involved with different facets of the Great Work.

The work of this Grade cannot be said to be completed until the Aspirant has attained enlightenment from every independent entity & collective structure in the Universe and has been able to show his/her enlightenment to each entity and group in return.

They who have taken the oath of the Boddhisatva work this Grade. The other Grades may be taken in any sequence, or all at once.

The aspirant is warned not to put-off the obligations of this grade until the very end, for the aspirant who is able to manifest the Grade of Lover has the power of transcendence, a virtue which cannot be fully appreciated until its need becomes imperative.

Those whose commitment to the Great Work is weak or insincere are warned away from the full experience of this Grade, for addiction & Death lie in wait for those of weak Will. It is up to each aspirant to act spontaneously in accord with Will. The ideas given below may be used as a guideline.

1. The Whore of Babalon and the Virgin Mary possess attributes which pertain to the Grade of Lovers.
2. Luxuriant foods as well as fasting provide clues to inner needs. Both may be explored to provide insight.
3. Exploration of Sexual Taboo (from Chastity to acts of destructive excess) provide clues to self in relation to others. Full expression of innermost desire can stimulate growth in unexpected ways. Those who have not cultivated the virtue of stability may be swept away completely.
4. Exploration of addictive substances assists the Alchemist in formulating his/her Will & in confronting the Death urge. Experimentation with addiction can be very unstabilizing for those who have neglected to build and nourish a living monument

to their Will which is fully capable of transcending time (see point #3 in the previous section).
5. Ecumenical out-reach & Magickal Wars are both valid expressions of this Grade. I exhort each to choose whatever methods/styles are in accord with his/her natural inclinations. Remain aware that losers often gain more than winners in wars & arguments. An open mind is a great asset for those undertaking this Grade.
6. Practice of Liber Astarte (either as a solitary rite, or thru joining a formal religion) can provide much insight into this Grade.
7. Practice of Liber Samekh is the internal reflection of Liber Astarte. Care must be taken so the little-ego &/or repressed demons are not deified in the process. To undertake a combined operation of Samekh and Astarte is the pinnacle of foolishness &/or the ultimate act of Self-Love (depending on your perspective). All sane persons are strictly warned away from such practices. Proceed with total abandon, or not at all. If you elect to proceed, in spite of these warnings, do not say that you have not been warned.

I
Grade of Hermit

Aspirants to the Grade of Hermit undertake to balance manifest Godhood upon the physical plane in the here-&-now. S/He undertakes to be able to tap-into Universal wealth without the need to toil at any particular task. His/Her whole existence is so enmeshed with the Great Work that the Universe maintains him/her in accord with his/her True Will, whether s/he be working or playing.

Upon successful dissolution of Cause-&-Effect, the Aspirant is able to function fully within this Grade as a self-created God/dess, who stands outside of the framework of consensus reality & who is able to manifest his/her Will within the here-&-now.

The other Grades may be taken in any sequence, or all at once. The aspirant is warned not to put-off the obligations of this grade until the very end, for the aspirant who is able to manifest the Grade of Hermit has absolute freedom of action, a virtue which cannot be fully appreciated until its need becomes imperative.

Those who lack absolute confidence in their innermost motivations are warned away from the full experience of this Grade, for Absolute Freedom & Absolute Responsibility go hand-in-hand.

Those who aspire to the Grade of Hermit are charged with the creation of & total responsibility for their own personal Universe and for its total interaction with all other Universes, both manifest and potential. A lack of understanding of one's own internal motivations &/or an incomplete integration of one's own internal Universe can be disastrous to those who aspire to Godhead.

To speak further of this Grade would be both unnecessary & misleading.

Brief History of the Order

by Frater PVN

Part I: Ordo Templi Orientis

Historical Roots

Many authors have sought the origins of the *Ordo Templi Orientis* (OTO) by trying to piece together various historical fragments, and to demonstrate therefrom, the Order's historical continuity.[1] It is as though these authors believe that the veracity & the efficacy of the Order's teachings are somehow linked to its historical continuity.

While this approach has much historical precedent (perhaps due to the heavy influence which the Roman Catholic Church has had upon Western civilization), it is my contention that humankind (both initiate & noninitiate) has attained to a level of media sophistication during the last half-century that such parables are no longer useful or necessary. In this essay, I discuss the Order in ways which (hopefully!) illuminate, rather than obfuscate.

The origins of the OTO lie not *in* history, but *behind* it. The Order transcends time, space, and paradox. The fountainhead of the Order lies beyond the Abyss and remains unknowable to the aspirant until s/he becomes capable of of transcending the limitations on viewpoint imposed by being entrapped in the Maya of the Time/Space Continuum.

The *Current of the Order* which is continuous throughout Time and contiguous throughout Space is not a thread of a static dogma given to us by an unknowable God, or a dead prophet, nor is it a thread of a hazy re-memberance of a golden age long since decayed. Rather, it is a dynamic Force of an ever-changing, ever-evolving consciousness,

---

[1] The most recent, & perhaps best, of these linear histories is An Introduction to the History of the Order, by Frater Ad Veritatem, IX°, to be Found in Volume III, Number 10 of The Equinox (Thelema Publications, NY, 1986). The major fault I can find with frater Ad Veritatem's work is that he discusses the OTO in a vacuum. He makes no reference to the A∴A∴ or the role which the A∴A∴ has in governing the OTO on the outer.

I was at first puzzled by Ad Veritatem's oversight—after all, he does lay claim to being a IX° member of the OTO! But then I re-read the Equinox's title page & c/r information. The Equinox no longer bears the seal or imprimatur of the A∴A∴ (except on reprints of old Crowley Material). It would seem that this venerable publication is no longer being guided overtly by the Order of the Silver Star, so Ad Veritatem's silence with regard to the A∴A∴ becomes more understandable to me.

which is embodied (to a greater or lesser degree, depending upon degree of attunement) within *each & every member of the Order.*

At those times when the *Current* is strong and coherent, patterns (visible organizations) emerge. These patterns are formed by groups of individuals (both high adepts & those new to the Path) whose *individual Wills* are united for the purpose of elevating human consciousness—both within the group (as a teaching Order) & (by example) in the world at large. At times of expansion like these, the Order emerges from obscurity (or seeming non-existence) into the public light. Knowledgable historians can then point to the *Knights Templar* and to the *Albegensians* and to the *Priesthood of Sumer* saying, "these all be manifestations of the OTO".

But at other times—when the life wave of enlightened consciousness upon the planet is quiescent or negatively manifest—those adepts who are conscious & *awake* live quiet lives, cultivating ideas of personal Alchemy in those who are eager to listen, rather than devoting their energies toward working upon the outer to build mighty organizations, or influence world events directly.

Each time the pattern emerges, it emerges transformed. Each time the pattern coalesces into a perceivable structure, that structure takes on an outward form which is best suited to meet the needs of that culture and those times. Each time the structure emerges, even partially, the consciousness of the race is irrevocably altered. Therefore, at each new emergence, a new structure is needed to continue the promulgation of enlightened, self-directed evolutionary change.

Our roots are the same as the *Cathar*'s roots—but we no longer look at the universe through the eyes of a *Cathar*. We trace our ancestry back thru the *Knights Templar*—but our perspectives, goals, & methods have evolved quite a bit since the times when the *Knights of the Temple* impacted European culture. Our Alchemical tradition utilizes techniques taught to John Dee by *Enochian Spirits*, and to the *Priestcraft of Sumer* by those who are not to be named—but our Alchemists work these energies from a Thelemic perspective which was unknown to the highest of adepts even a few short centuries ago.

Beyond Paradox

The fountainhead of the Order lies behind Time & beyond space. Those new to the Path of initiation & adeptship are often baffled by seeming paradoxes (e.g., Crowley being contacted by the Sovereign

Sanctuary of the Gnosis regarding material he published in *Liber 333*—years prior to the publication of *Liber 333*, etc.) when attempting to comprehend trans-abyssal experience thru linear thought processes. Not too long ago, the only way to dispel paradox was to *quiet* the rational mind (i,e., turnoff right brain rational intelligence), lest the rational mind go insane. Or, one may choose to abandon real magick completely & treat the Order like a social club for D-&-D magick users who like to party hard.

But today, the rational world of mathematics, quantum dynamics, and (especially) Chinese Physics has experiential models to assist the neophyte in comprehending the trans-rational. Those familiar with the behavior of *quarks*, may already realize that time flows in more than one direction (Feynman diagrams are temporally symmetrical), and that our Universe needs at least 7 spacial dimensions to describe its natural laws. I could quote more examples[2], but some generalized rules are probably more useful:

1. ***Energy is abundant.*** The formula of Love under Will assists modern adepts to tap into the Universally available energy of the universe.
2. ***Everything is connected.*** This includes everything through-out all Space, all Time, and in every possible Alternative Reality. It has been said by a Master of our Order that Time Travel is possible only insofar as it can be understood and expressed linguistically without encountering paradox.
3. ***The possibilities are endless.*** Do what thou wilt shall be the whole of the Law.

At this point, you are probably wondering what all this has to do with the History of the OTO! My point is this: The Order (like nature) is a trans-rational construct. The Order is most certainly lawful, but the Law to which the Order is subject is not necessarily grounded in laws comprehensible thru logic alone. The history of a trans-temporal & trans-rational organization of *Magickal Adepts* cannot possibly be adjudicated by courts dealing with matters of fact or precedence.

But since my *History* is written in a linear & rational format, it can only *suggest* certain truths which are far more obvious to the trans-rational consciousness of an Adept. I do not intend my *History* to

---

2 For a lively non-mathematical presentation of magickal uses of quantum reality, I highly recommend the *Schrödinger's Cat* trilogy by Robert Anton Wilson (Pocket Books, NY, 1981). The glossary alone is north the price of the book!

be dogmatic. What you read here hints at Truth, but Truth is (by its nature) infinite, and must necessarily contain within itself the seeds of its own contradiction. I leave it to you to sort thru this document by the light of your Holy Will. Accept what rings true to you. Refine that which is useful to you. And reject that which has no place within your Universe.

Each of us is a unique manifestation of Creation. So, the connections we experience, the perspective from which we view the Universe, and, the linkages we work diligently to form are also unique. My experience has demonstrated that manifestations of the *Order on the outer* are best based upon experiment, rather than a rote formula.

Role of Conservatism

There are those within our Order who follow tradition. They are intent on *preserving* the structure of the Order which was laid-down by past Masters. At first glance, these members may seem to work without a strong link the fountainhead of their own inspiration. But first glances are often deceiving. Within the pattern of change & consciously directed evolution is the the *conservative thread* within our Order. Methods which work are treasured, preserved, and *worked* until such time as newer methods can demonstrate themselves to be viable. The Masonic lodge structure outlined in the *Blue Equinox,* Crowley's Gnostic Mass, and other rituals created a half-century ago are still being practiced diligently today by those whose Will is attuned to preserving the teachings, the practices, and the historical continuity of the OTO.

But there are also other threads at work within the Order. While we can learn much from the study of past Masters, there comes a time when many Adepts acquire sufficient self-confidence & *magick* to go beyond the roadmaps of political structure, philosophical doctrine, &/or Alchemical technique taught by conservative manifestations of the Order.

Role of Heresy

From my perspective, even though conservatism has its place within the Order, the *Great Work* is served most diligently by those Adepts & Masters within the Order who explore/map/experiment/create— beyond the realms governed by the Order's traditional structures. Research is conducted by Masters (& *would-be Masters)* whose *calling* from the Fountainhead of the Order transcends all reason, common sense, and fealty to individuals &/or structures within the Order. These Heretical[3] Masters are governed by Will & by Will alone.

Research often stems from a personal quest—some new magickal tool; some new philosophy; some innovative solution to a perplexing personal/- practical/theoretical problem. For every neophyte who *sets-out* to be heretical, there are probably a dozen others who see their work as being a perfectly straightfoward reworking of a traditional puzzle. While most of these experiments are *pure research* some experiments eventually evolve sufficiently that they appear both workable & useful, not only to the experimenter, but to a cadre of close friends & associates. If the idea/philosophy/technique begins to spread throughout the Order-at-large, it may be perceived as a threat to *Tradition,* or to the personal political power of a ruling elite within the Order. Although Masters of the Order are—in a very real sense—*Divine,* they are also human & demonic, too.[4] Unlike Eastern systems of attainment, Masters of the OTO do not seek to destroy their ego—so they are occasionally faced with interesting challenges in integrating their egos into the synergistic dance of collective inspiration.

If the new idea/tool/philosophy in question becomes universally accepted, the Order evolves smoothly & without discord. If, on the other hand, it is rejected by the Order's hierarchy as being dangerous &/or useless, then it must prove itself in the Darwinian arena of *survival of the fittest,* or disintegrate.

Testing of Heresy

It is into this arena that heretical Masters are born, tested, & are sometimes slain.[5] It is here that those Masters with the taste for sport promulgate their ideas in open defiance of traditional authority. It is here that Masters (& would-be Masters) with sufficient daring & strength of Will *bud-off* new *totally—autonomous branches* of the Order.

---

3   I use heretical in the traditional sense of the word. Heresy [see *The International Standard Bible Encyclopedia*, Howard-Severance Co., Chicago, 1915 for full definition] implies a non-traditional choice, or a chosen course of procedure; or, a sect/assembly advocating a particular doctrine or lode of life. Heretical does not imply degenerate, corrupt, nefarious, or perverse. It simply means non-traditional. [a better derivation would be 'choice' from the Greek *harisis*, thus to be a heretic is to choose other than orthodoxy—Ed.]

4   See *Liber Tzaddi vel Hamus Hermeticus sub figura XC.*

5   For every example of a Mathers, Crowley, *Achad*, Spare, or Grant whose ideas have transformed the fabric of magickal reality, there are countless others whose names & ideas have perished in ignominy or obscurity. These are the forgotten Saints of the Order, those who have given their life's blood to our Lady BABALON. We who enter the arena remember you in spirit, if not in name. *Nos morituri te Salutamus!* [We who are about to die, salute Thee!]

Aleister Crowley & the Æon of Horus

The OTO (as a manifestation of the Order on the outer) arose from the obscurity of the secretive Rosicrucian [Masonic] tradition of the 19th Century when Theodor Reuss recognized Aleister Crowley's Mastery of Sex Magick and invited Crowley into the OTO and gave him a charter as Supreme and Holy King of the English speaking world. Crowley's charter seems to have been at conflict with a charter given earlier to H. Spencer Lewis in the USA, unless Crowley &/or Reuss did not consider Americans to be English-speaking. The OTO, under Crowley, accepted the law of Thelema, thus aligning the OTO with the Æon of Horus.

However, not all of the OTO groups chartered prior to Crowley's Kingship accepted the *Law of Thelema*. Others accepted *Thelema*, but not Crowley's rulership over their chartered group within the OTO. Thus we have division & branching within the OTO long before the present round of controversy over which OTO body is the *real* OTO. Further exploration of these non-Crowleyan OTO groups is beyond the scope of this present essay, save to mention that at least one non-Crowleyan Thelemic lodge of the OTO was still operating in New York City as late as 1957. During my childhood (1951-7), I studied ritual & dream magic with Frater *Fiat Lux*, who was then lodgemaster of this lodge.

Crowley was a first rate adept who (like many Sufi masters) wore the mask of the Fool in order to shock the outer world consciousness of those who sought to 'play the game' of magic without engaging in the ongoing task of personal transformation. Crowley's behavior was very effective in calling into question the narrow morality & bigoted self-satisfaction of the post-Victorian world.

During his lifetime, Crowley drastically altered the ritual & philosophical fabric of the OTO's structure. He was in the process of planning another revision in the OTO's structure at the time of his death, but the details of his proposed changes were not made public after his demise. The details of Crowley's plans are no longer important, for Crowley's spirit lives on in the Order today. His visionary perspective encourages much new experimentation in both the outward form of the Order & in its overall direction.

From the advent of the æon of Horus (in 1904) to Crowley's death (in 1947), the race as a whole had taken several quantum leaps in belief and consciousness. The rate of evolutionary change had been escalating over the past several centuries, but by the mid 1940's, the rate of change had become so rapid & diverse, that no single structure could possibly accommodate the proliferation of ideas which everflows from the Fountainhead of the Order thru all Thelemites—the heirs to Crowley's literary legacy & to the mysteries of the Orders which Crowley devoted his life.

Crowley's Legacy of Diversification

To the world at large, the OTO may have appeared to dwindle and die off at Crowley's death. But, from a trans-Abyssal perspective within the OTO, the *pattern* of the OTO could be seen to diversify and to expand in many new & interesting ways during the '50s & '60s. Crowley deliberately assisted this diversification by giving (seemingly) contradictory verbal & written instructions to various of his subordinates prior to his death. Of those whom Crowley singled-out, four are worthy of note.

Karl Germer

Germer was left in charge of the OTO, as an interim measure, until such time as an election for the post of O.H.O. (Outer Head of the Order) could be conveniently held. But Germer never held an election—preferring instead to hold the reins of the OTO with an iron hand, against (what little) opposition was raised against him. It is said that Germer attained to *K&C of his HGA* (Knowledge & Conversation of his Holy Guardian Angel) while an inmate of German prison. I have heard (via oral tradition) that Germer would call-down his *HGA* into various prison guards as they sodomized him. Germer's strength of Will & dedication to the Order is not to be underestimated. His method of attainment did, however, inculcate in him the belief that one must *submit to one's angel* and, by extension, to any authority figure, legitimate or not.

Some have said that Germer's death thru prostrate cancer is indicative of his broken oaths to Crowley. Such ignoble claptrap is barely worthy of comment. Crowley had seen to it that (at least) three young aspiring Masters had been given sufficient preparation to assert their Wills during Germer's reign. Crowley apparently felt that the leadership of the OTO could not be trusted to anyone who had not the strength of conviction to assert his Will against a paper tiger such as Germer.

Germer taught individual freedom by doing his best to suppress those who exhibited even token resistance to his iron rule. He forbad all under his rule from initiating any new members—even though Germer knew that the OTO must grow a thousand-fold if it was to be an effective organ of change in the New Æon. In short, Germer taught via preparation of the Antimony (see Crowley's introduction to *Liber LI*). Germer was very successful at forcing high ranking members of the Order to choose between what they knew to be right (through internal inspiration) & what they were dogmatically told to do/think by Germer.

Marcello Motta & S.O.T.O.

Marcello Motta's initial training within the Order was via the A∴A∴. When I first became aware of Motta, He was acting as the self-proclaimed *Guardian of the Gates of Nuit*, whose office—much like Germer's, before him—is the rigorous testing of all would-be Masters who seek to assert their Will in contest with Motta's. Motta has a flair for the dramatic. He has been known to publicly denounce his foes in print with verbal abuse not seen since Crowley published *the Equinox*. Like Crowley, Motta is a Master of the absurd. [In one editorial, he was playing the role of a victim who had been taken advantage of by his dentist. At first, his behavior seemed to me to be ridiculous coming from a Master of the A∴A∴. But then I perceived his essay as an elaborate qabalistic hoax—an allegory of his self-chosen office in relationship to the *Spirit of the Order* based on the equivalency of the hebrew letter *Shin*, with the tooth he was complaining about!]

Motta entered the arena of OTO politics by asserting his right as a Master of the A∴A∴ to formulate *SOTO (Society Ordo Templi Orientis)*, a branch of the OTO, as an extension of his Will on the outer. Although his claim seems (for the nonce, at any rate) to have been overturned in court,[6] I (as an OTO Historian) will not gainsay his claim, save insofar as I cannot accept his (or anyone else's) claim to a monopoly over the OTO Current in any form (exclusive use of OTO name, Order lamen, autocratic possessiveness over Crowley's magickal writings, etc.)

---

6 What, you may ask, is a court at law doing with its fingers in OTO politics!? It appears that Motta was attempting to assert exclusive right over Crowley's copyrights. Various publishers, & branches of the OTO got involved. The US federal court system was called in. Lawyers earned their fees from OTO coffers. Court attendees mere entertained & illuminated by Motta's paradoxical testimony (which might have been perjury—save that Motta is a Master of the A∴A∴, and therefore beyond Truth-&-Falsehood). I hear tell, it was a regular Osirian circus! The winner of the contest (the Caliphate branch of the OTO organized by Grady McMurtry) now claims the same rights that Motta abdicated. Just goes to show that not even Masters of the Order are immune to Osirian power-trips and pyramidal thought patterns!

Grady McMurtry & the Caliphate

While an officer in World War II, Grady was stationed in England, and spent much of his free time with Crowley. Crowley bestowed upon Grady a set of documents & credentials known as the *Caliphate papers,* in which Grady was named a *Caliph* of the Order and was given authority to overrule Germer. Although Grady formally presented these papers to Germer upon his return to the states, he did not (to my knowledge) ever exercise his rights until after Germer had died, leaving the OTO without an *heir apparent.*

Grady is an enigma to me. When I first heard how Grady failed to implement the Caliphate papers until after Germer's death, I dismissed him from my consideration as one of Crowley's heirs. But over time (although I never met the man personally), I came to know, love, & respect Grady thru his feisty comments in the Caliphate OTO's newsletter, *the Magical Link,* and thru personal stories about the man I have gleaned from Order members who knew Grady personally. I now attribute my dismissal of Grady's claims to be an act of youthful folly. I mention my folly so that others may, perhaps, choose to learn from my mistakes rather than feeling obligated to repeat them!

Perhaps one day Grady's biographers will help me to understand why Grady waited so long to reify the Caliphate. Until then, all I can do is report the bare facts. Once Germer had died, Grady did assert his prerogative—and the Caliphate branch of the Order grew rapidly. The Caliphate OTO (also known as Aleister Crowley's OTO & the OTO) is now the largest manifestation of the OTO in this Æon

It is very common to equate numbers with success. But, to me, membership is only one indication of an Order's strength. The OTO's purpose can only be made manifest thru strong links with the inner Order. As an outer Order, the Caliphate is strong. But its links to the inner Order seem veiled, or (mayhap) non-existent.

I base my statement on the lack of visible Masters within the Caliphate. But, I know all too well how difficult it sometimes is for one Master to recognize (or accept) another Master who functions on a very different wavelength. All too often, such a Master may seem bizarre, alien, threatening, or just plain invisible. So, while I can say that I find the dearth of visible Masters within the Caliphate to be disconcerting, I can in no way use my negative correlations to assert the absence of inner-Order connections within the Caliphate.

But I digress...

Grady, too, has passed-on. Hymaneaus β has been elected to the Caliphate by the IX° Council. Change is a-brewing. The political center of the Caliphate has shifted from Berkeley to New York City. Frater Hβ is rumored to have moved to New Orleans (perhaps for a magickal retreat). The next decade or so should see some interesting developments within the Caliphate!

Kenneth Grant & the Typhonian OTO

Of Crowley's major scions, Kenneth Grant speaks least of his claims. He does not take his adversaries to task in print, nor does he bother to answer his detractors. Rather than rake muck, or defend his title, Grant seems to spend much of his time actively *doing* magick, and in writing volume after volume of some of the best advanced magickal texts of this generation. Whereas the success of the *Caliphate* lies in its strength upon the outer, the *Typhonian OTO* seems to have been engineered for its strengths upon the inner.

But, I get ahead of myself...

Grant, like Grady, knew Crowley during the 1940's. He studied under Crowley & practiced magick with him. This much we know from Grant's own words. Of his years under Germer's rule and his supposed expulsion from the OTO, he remains publicly silent.

I was a member of the Typhonian OTO for more than a decade, during which time I learned the tale of frater Aossic Aiwas's early years from Soror Tanith Potnia Therion, X°—the Typhonian OTO's Sovereign for North America, and Grant's personal confidant. I do not know whether Grant ever intended his story to be made public, but as it is my Will to be Order Historian, and this information came to me under no oath of secrecy, I share it with you now as siblings within the Order—as a brother of the bread & the salt.

Grant's initial charter was verbal, or should I say magickal. It came as an outgrowth of his magickal association with Crowley. One day, Crowley sensed that Grant was ready for an initiation into the inner Order. He simply extended his hand to Grant & said, "take what you need." From this beginning sprang the Typhonian OTO.

Later, when Germer had taken command of Crowley's empire, & had directed a cessation of all new initiations, Grant formulated the *Nu-Isis Lodge*. When Germer heard of Grant's activities, Germer was not pleased. Germer (as acting X° of the OTO) demanded to know why

Grant had disobeyed the edict against new initiations. Grant pointed-out to Germer that the Nu-Isis lodge was not a manifestation of the OTO, but an autonomous organization. Germer's perspective on the Order would not permit him to see Grant's position of autonomous Master as anything other than insubordination. Germer demanded all Nu-Isis lodge members be treated as OTO members & pay dues & initiation fees to the OTO (i.e., to Germer).[7]

Grant refused. Germer also discovered (or was told by Grant—the story is a bit fuzzy in spots) that a black woman was a sexual Priestess in the Nu-Isis lodge. Germer was very angry, for he was against teaching OTO sex magick to non Aryans. Germer, not knowing that Grant was a member of the Sovereign Sanctuary (or not accepting Grant's claim), expelled Grant from the OTO. Members of the Sovereign Sanctuary cannot be expelled from the Order, no matter what the cause—they are *Sovereigns*, and as such, their comportment is answerable to no one. The only way to remove a Sovereign from office is to slay him/her.[8]

I am told that Grant does not speak ill of Germer, even in private, because Germer raised funds to keep Crowley fed, clothed, & housed during his latter years.

Cast adrift from his OTO contacts, Grant studied tantra in the East, published the *Carfax Monographs*, and worked his magicks till Germer had let loose the reins of the OTO and the time was propitious to manifest the Order upon the outer.

---

[7] I find it very ironic that by 1981, Grant felt compelled to play the role of Germer to members of his own Typhonian OTO. Specifically, in April of 1979, *Soror Andahadna* of the *Maat Pangrove Abbey of Thelema* and the members of the *Grove of the Star & the Snake* formed the Horus/Maat-Lodge for the purpose of promulgating the Double-Current of Horus-&-Maat. Sometime within the next year or so, they were invited by Grant to declare the H/M-L as a cell of the Typhonian OTO. They declined on the grounds that the purpose of the H/M-L was pan-Thelemic & non-sectarian. It was believed that an *in-dependent* H/M-L could act as a bridge between initiates of various branches of the OTO. Such a goal would not be feasible if the H/M-L was a cell of the Typhonian OTO.

On page 279 of *Outside the Circles of Time* (Fredrick Muller, London, 1980), Grant specifically declared the H/M-L to be a cell of the Typhonian OTO. Members of the H/M-L sought to correct this error with a notice in a forthcoming issue of the the *Cincinnati Journal of Ceremonial Magic* &/or *Mandragore*, the Journal of the Grove of the Star & the Snake. On 14 May '81 Grant sent a letter to Soror Tanith telling her to stop 124 (Soror Andahadna) from inserting any disclaimers into the *Cincy Journal*, or elsewhere. He further stated that Soror Noctua would be expelled for making an unnecessary nuisance of herself for insubordination if she doesn't pipe down (with regard Grant's claims re: H/M-L).

I note in passing, that this incident has much in common with the episode mentioned in the previous footnote. I have noticed that if magickal quarrels are not fully resolved in the here-&-now, their karma lives on. For the sake of balance, roles tend to reverse. But the polarity perpetuates until such time as it is transcended. It is not enough to score a victory. To end a quarrel, one must create a solution which transcends the causes of the problem completely.

[8] It doesn't work.—*Ed.*

The OTO Today

Each of the branches of the OTO have very different approaches to the structure of the Order on the outer, the training of those new to the Path, and the thrust of the Order's work on the inner to influence the flow of human consciousness. Many branches of the Order continue to adhere to a structure of grades based upon the Tree of Life &/or chakras. Thus we have variations upon a system of grades numbered one through ten, with the Tenth Degree being administrative in nature. Some branches of the OTO (such as the Caliphate) give fancy masonic titles to each of the Grades, while other Branches (such as the Typhonian OTO) simply number the Grades sequentially. The aspirant usually progresses through the grades in linear fashion until he/she has reached his/her maximum potential, or diverges from the pre-determined linear Path to manifest his/her Will outside of the structure of the Order. Rapid advancement thru the grades &/or skipping grades is usually possible, although rare, in most branches of the OTO with a functional hierarchal grade system.

Some branches of the Order (such as the *Caliphate*) also contain an additional XI° Degree existing outside the jurisdiction of the hierarchy for the purpose of teaching/experimenting certain non-traditional sexual Alchemies, which are often, but not always, homosexual in nature.

Other, less traditional, branches of the OTO have chosen to experiment with new concepts for the structure of the Order. The pyramidal scheme used by the masonic branches has been replaced by a more fluid system of Powerzones which gather members & energy by accretion around those Initiates whose natural talent is the formulation of the Powerzone seedcore. Ideally, each powerzone becomes a self-reproducing unit of the organism of the OTO, each cell of which is capable of functioning independently from the rest of the Order (if need be), as well as interdependent ly with other Powerzones. Artificial hierarchies based on *paper grades,* irrelevant status symbols, or convoluted genealogies based on (real or imagined) catena of initiation within any of the myriad Branches of the Order are done away with.

Diversity and individual growth are encouraged. Each new member is spurred to self-reliance. Auto-motivation is inculcated far more than is usually feasible within a traditional lodge structure. Probationers and members of all ranks are expected to seek direction from within themselves far more than from members of higher rank or greater seniority. This self-cultivated sense of independence is so strong that some members have (seemingly) split with the OTO altogether, in order to manifest their own vision of what the Order should become.

Into the Present & Onward to the Future

Frater Aossic Aiwass—718 (Kenneth Grant) had a very revolutionary vision with respect to the necessary restructuring of the Order. Not only did he abolish the Order's Treasury (influenced, by his philosophical & financial disputes with Germer regarding dues payments from members of the Nu-Isis Lodge), but he sowed the seeds of decentralization in his initial concept of Powerzones.

But, I believe, Grant did not allow his concept of Powerzones to come to their full fruition. Grant has (thusfar) been unable/un-willing to grant total autonomy to any OTO Powerzone, or recognize the full Sovereignty of any initiates within in his branch of the Order. Those whose Will differs from Grant's are expelled from the Typhonian OTO or pressured into resigning. Grant seems to have forgotten that the structure of the OTO on the outer embodies the *Will of Thelema* as a whole, & is thus far broader than the vision of any one person—no matter what that person's rank.

When Crowley acted as Supreme & Holy King of the Order, the number of Thelemites within the world was extremely small and Crowley's force of Will was able to work at-one with the *93 Current* in ways which no single individual can ever do again. The *Will of Thelema* embodies the vector summation of the individual Wills of all Thelemites and is expressed on the outer in the collective & individual Wills of each Branch of the Order.

I have learned a lot about fraternal joy & sharing thru my contacts with various members, and sub-groupings within the Caliphate. Lodges, with their formal programs, study groups, etc. give guidance to those new to the Path. The Caliphate does not see itself as a specialized magickal engine, so it encourages a much wider range of diversity within its ranks.

Although I can personally substantiate that it *is* possible to become *anathema* within the ranks of the Caliphate without breaking any personal magical oath or doctrine of Thelema, (and without being given a forum to defend one's self at a hearing or trial), I am happy to report that such non-Thelemic conduct does seem minimal within the Caliphate. I have heard that Grady liked to party, and share his magick openly. The camps, oases and lodges within the Caliphate are logical/magical extensions of Grady's Will. Parallel to their formal purpose of Crowleyan study groups, ritual classes, & repeated enactment of Crowley's initiatory rituals, they are also centers of warm loving social fraternity which provide forums for informal exchange of magic(k) and the building of extended magickal family.

The Chthonic OTOs

Sam Webster, Cliff Pollick, and myself, are self-proclaimed Sovereigns of the OTO. By the authority which emanates from the Fountainhead of the Order and is transmitted thru us to the Order on the outer, we have formulated the Chthonic Branch of the OTO in accord with Our Holy Will.

The *Chthonic OTO* is most definitely *Thelemic*. We take the message of freedom & personal responsibility outlined in Liber Oz & amplified upon in Liber Legis very seriously. We do not expect individual members of the Chthonic OTO to defer their Will to ours. We accept Crowley as the prophet of the Æon of Horus & honor him as such. But, we do not defer to Crowley, either. Crowley was the first Magus of this Æon, but he is certainly not the last! We build upon his work, but we do so in our own unique fashion. We do not expect anyone to follow slavishly in the footsteps of another.

Our charter's foundations are earthed upon the *Holy Books of Thelema*, especially: *Liber Liber Tzaddi vel Hamus Hermeticus* sub figura *XC* and *Liber Porta Lucis* sub figura *X*. We also recognize Holy books not penned by Crowley, such as *Liber Pennæ Prænumbra* channeled by Soror Andahadna, as a Class A document.

We align ourselves openly, upon the outer, with the trans-/Eonic formula which emanates from beyond the veil of Isis, whom No Man (NEMO) hath seen at any time. Beyond the Abyss, *all* Æonic formula exist simultaneously & in harmony. We, as individuals, and as an Order, seek & welcome fraternal and initiatory links with other Masters & with other manifestations of the Order embodying all Æonic formulæ. We believe it is only thru the harmonious interplay of each æonic formula that dharma can finally decay and the next stage of planetary evolution begin.

From my perspective as a founding Sovereign of the Chthonic OTO, the time is now ripe for the manifestation & reification of an extended series of overlapping Powerzones to promote an on-going cross fertilization which transcends all traditional jurisdictions imposed by territorial exclusivity, historical feuds, differences in liturgical practices, divergent catena of initiation, and the incestuous politics of elitism which goes unchecked within those branches of the OTO now manifest upon the outer which have lost (or forgotten) their links to the Sovereign Sanctuary of the Gnosis.

It is time to emphasize that we remember that the OTO is **One True Order**. Our differences, although very real, can not be permitted to stand in the way of the formation & function of dynamic Magickal Alliances within the macrocosm of the OTO as a whole. Now is the time when we, the Masters of the Chthonic OTO, throw off our disguises & reveal our Kingship. We invite you to do likewise. In so doing, we realize that you risk the loss of continued acceptance within that branch of the Order which you call *HOME*. Personally, we have found that the risk, although very real, is far outweighed by our longing to participate in the next stage of evolution upon this planet.

Those of us who succeed in this task will (from my perspective) become living cells within the ultimate Powerzone of total interconnectedness within the Multiverse through our recognition of the Freedom of Anarchy within the divine responsibility of Kingship. Each Powerzone is an Independent Sovereign State—each one responsible for its own conduct, and for making its own internal rules. The dynamic network of the Sovereign Sanctuary of the Gnosis formulates itself from the inter-dependent inter-play of each independent Powerzone.

The ideas outlined in this document cannot possibly turn a slave into a King, but their implementation can, and will, foster the self-responsibility and growth necessary for an Anarchistic King to mature within a culture which is just beginning to learn how to encourage individual excellence coupled with cooperation, rather than power-over trips. The freedom and Power granted to independent & free-thinking members of the OTO—if they can find it within themselves—is not without danger. Out of caution, certain other manifestations of the OTO have segregated themselves from us for the duration of this experiment.

At the fountainhead of the Order, beyond the Abyss where duality is NOT, the Order is unified. But on the outer, the Order is divided. As it says in Liber AL vel Legis, *"There is division hither homeward"* and *"I am divided for love's sake, for the chance of union."*

We all believe that our experiments are both important and worthwhile, but we must not become so ego-attached to them that we fail to see the worth of the experiments of others. There is no pre-destined Path to the future. We all create the Future—both individually & collectively.

The Powerzone structure outlined in this document is a tool to facilitate the pooling of creative and inspirational resources of adepts from diverse magickal backgrounds. If it fails to meet these needs, the Powerzone Structure of the OTO cannot continue to exist. But if it can meet these needs, it will be able to grow and mutate to meet other needs in ways which can barely be imagined at the present time. In Magick (as in any system which transcends the purely rational) the whole is always far greater than the sum of its parts. Yet, the whole can only attain to its full potential if each of its individual parts is encouraged to grow & stretch beyond its self-imposed limitations.

Evolution does not occur without experimentation. In any valid scientific experiment, there must be control groups. The Great Experiment is fraught with great danger, but we embrace the challenge of IT.

Epistle to the Priest-Sovereigns of Thelema

Fish are for Eating
Lambs are for Fleecing
Good for you if you fount it,
But I never lost IT.[1]

Some may seek vicarious salvation from a dead god for their seeming blunders, or accept burdens of imagined guilt for actions resulting from their explorations of their own inner natures, but not I.

I am a **Pagan** who celebrates the Spiral Dance of the Seasons with awe, joy, and reverence. I have no fear of death, nor do I shun my duty to destroy, when it is my Will to do so—for the old, weak, and obsolete must be cleared away to make room for new generations of strong ever-evolving creation. I glory in my sexual, mental, metaphysical and physical creativity, and con-celebrate in the Mass of Life which spawns all that which is new & different. I learn-from, value, and pass-on traditions which nurture &/or are of value to me—especially those teachings which assist me to harmonize the maximization of my personal pleasure with my Role as an independent agent of Creation/Preservation/Destruction within the collective being we call Gaia.

I am a **Heathen** who works/plays with the Gods of the Hearth, of Technology, and all the physical/intellectual works of our young Divine race. Like Isaac Newton, I believe that we stand so tall because we stand on the shoulders of giants. I am enriched & empowered by the pioneering works of Jesus, Hermes, Buddha, Ghengis Khan, Cyrus the Great, Uncle Ho, Jack the Ripper, Heisenberg, Einstein,

---

[1] The title poem relates to PVN's attitudes towards Christian fundamentalist dogmatists. The *fish* is a symbol for those newly baptized; the *lamb* is Christ as victim. The first *it* is vicarious salvation, the second *IT* is Yod-Teth, the hidden and manifest Phallus (see *Liber 333* for a more detailed exegesis).

Emperor Norton, Rockefeller, Lysander Spooner, & countless billions of my other ancestors, both human & otherwise. But I do not worship any of them. They are not my Gods. My God is that which I am ever-striving to become. I am a living synthesis of every idea, every work of technology, & every organism in the Multi-verse.

In his day, Jesus, was a pioneer such as I (as were Crowley, Tesla, Murshid SAM, & myriad others). We are shaped by our past as we shape our own destinies. I make no apology for our race's seeming errors or for our seeming ignorance/insensitivity. We who have chosen to be human, have chosen to be *conscious* of our individual place in the Universal pattern. This choice necessitates (at least temporarily) a 'loss of innocence' and a feeling of vulnerability incomprehensible to those who are not at our stage of development.

As I came to understand the full magnitude & consequences of our actions, I became (temporarily) paralysed with imagined guilt and shame over our individual & collective actions & non-actions. Some of those whom I have met on the path sometimes feel a-part from nature which seems to move harmoniously around us while we seemingly blunder thru life destroying other lifeforms out of greed, curiosity, survival needs, and our inability to be omniscient & omnipotent.

Some of us become **Mystics,** choosing (for an hour, a year, a lifetime, or an eternity, depending on personal choice) to return to the individual oblivion of nirvana, abnegating personal responsibility through dissolution of individual consciousness.

Others become **Hedons** (for an hour, a year, a lifetime, or an eternity, depending on personal choice) who glory in sensual pleasure & the building of personal &/or cultural empire, caring not if any suffer or die to satisfy their lust for toys, pleasure, & the satiation of obscure and arcane desires.

Still others become **Saints** (for an hour, a year, a lifetime, or an eternity, depending on personal choice), who seek to minimize their destructive impact on their ecology (however they may define the term), while devoting most of their energy towards balancing the apparant self-serving activities of the hedon.

Saints-in-training, in my experience, sometimes substitute zeal for balance. Their actions can then tend towards mindless negative judgemental reaction towards hedons, rather than dancing with them to actualize their sense of balance. They seem driven by hatred of 'oppressors' (their name for hedons) and by personal guilt thru their sense of separation from the 'ecology' (however they may choose to define it) which they are fighting so desperately to save. They seem to act as though they (& by extension all others of their social class) are not a part of 'nature' & have somehow become an abomination which needs to be destroyed or somehow saved from itself. Such imperfect saints often anesthetize their guilt, & temper (or focus!) their hatred by giving up personal responsibility to an external dogma—i.e., the teachings of an individual who claims to be an avatar of a god, or to the amorphous 'politically correct' propaganda generated by a pseudo-group-soul (such as various of the lefty-liberal social causes, etc.). Often such saints-in-training are able to resolve their conflicts most effectively when they are able to synthesize their saintly & hedonic natures within a larger context.

Personally, none of the above trips is fully satisfying to me in-&-of itself. I have tried them all, many times, sometimes for several lifetimes or even if I dare speak of such dim memories—eternities. I am a god among gods. To be less is, quite frankly, boring. I am now at a flowering of my creative & synthesizing aspects. I seek to accept that all has a valid place in the multi-verse, but I am not yet fully successful—as my friends will readily attest!

On the scale of the cycles of eternities, our human race is very young. We have much potential, but we have only a short track-record on which to base our expectations & judgements. We are very much in a hurry & are sometimes very harsh on ourselves (& by extension, others) for not living up to our personal definition of perfection. We have an *idee fixe* that gods are perfect. To me, perfection implies stasis & that "there is nothing new under the sun". I find such an idea to be a limitation, & I (as a god) do not accept any such limitation.

Those of us (of my acquaintance) who are consciously on the path of Godhood are yet young (there are probably many older gods floating around from previous incarnations of the multiverse, but with them I have but fleeting in-body contact at present). *H. sapiens* is less than 20,000 generations old. *Homo veritas* is much newer. Many of us seem to have (at least partial) memories of a continuity of existence which is much older than this Universe. At my present state of evolution, I do not have the patience or skill to access full memory. But such is not my present self-ordained function. I leave such tasks to those whose undivided will is to become the ump-teenth avatar of Krishna, Crowley, or Babaji.

I am all of these. Yet, I am more. I prefer creation in the here-&-now to re-living æons of past achievements (individual or collective), although I certainly use my memories for recreative fantasy and for insight on current endeavors. I learn from apparent failures as well as from apparent successes. Honest reflection (without guilt, gloat, or remorse) teaches Compassion & Knowledge; individual & universal from my perspective, they are one & the same. By perceiving of ourselves as an integral part of the machinery of nature (see Ezekiel's vision of wheels within wheels), some of us gain Wisdom and the Strength to continue our explorations without being dragged-down by guilt over our apparent imperfections. We are a seeming tangle of paradox & contradiction, yet nothing we do can ever be wrong, for we remain a part of the ALL, no matter how much we feel we need to de-emphasize it in order to express our individuality.

☙ ⁂ ❧

As some of you already know, representatives of Aleister Crowley's OTO are threatening to take me to court for publication of a 'secret' IX° document. The document in question (*Emblems & Modes of Use*, which in the current issue of MEZLA—copies available @ $3.33 each, 10 for $13.31 from [defunct address]) came to me under no oath of secrecy, and without my asking for it (much the way Crowley's signet ring came to Grady). I simply used the information received in accord with my Will.

They also seem upset with anyone who asserts his individual Will in any way which contradicts their personal belief structure (in which they are the sole manifestation of the OTO upon Malkuth). They have put pressure on publishers to repress books, & have threatened legal action against all who dare question their drive towards monolithic power.

I have nothing against orthodoxies per-se, unless they lose sight of their purpose & become counter-evolutionary. From my perspective, orthodoxies are the control in an experiment of social/political/magickal evolution; they are the yardstick by which other manifestations of the Order can choose to measure themselves. "Let success be thy proof"—but success with respect to what? In the Æon of Horus, success must be defined for each of us in our own unique individual way, for "Do what thou wilt shall be the whole of the Law."

When Crowley disposed of the accretions of his incarnation, he left many seemingly conflicting instructions regarding the Order. A clear historical record is scanty, but it seems to me that he bequeathed the secrets of the IX° to a number of the young bucks (Grady, Grant, & Motta, among others) & seems to have told them each (privately & secretly, verbally or in writing) to govern the Order in the light of their own True Will. To Karl Germer he seems to have given the odious (but seemingly necessary) task of testing these candidates to see which (if any) were capable of governing the OTO during the transition phase from an Osirian masonic pyramid to a reification of the Thelemic Current within the Æon of Horus. Crowley may have told Germer to seize control of the Order, hold no elections for a successor to BaphometR, and cease all initiation into the Order, but I doubt it. Germer was probably simply doing his Will by acting in accord with his own true nature.

Germer's actions seem to have functioned a test for the Order. Was the OTO really ready to function in the Æon of Horus (or was it to became a 'museum village' of early 20th Century occultism)? If any or all of the young bucks dared defy the established iron-fisted authority of Germer, he/they would have proven themselves free of Osirian bondage & therefore fit to run the OTO in the Æon of Horus. Grady did assert his caliphate papers, but not until after Germer died. To me, Grady was certainly a damn good Thelemite, though not (in my opinion) a rebel in the same class as Crowley, Parsons, or Grant. While he lived, Grady did his best to run Aleister Crowley's OTO, with lots of help from many people, especially Bill Heidrick. For this I salute him. But now Grady's dead. The Order is (from my perspective) now in the hands of a conservative & restrictive cabal who have:

1. Induced Weiser to suppress Ken Grant's new book because he claims to be the world head of the OTO.
2. Seen to it that *Secret Rituals of the OTO* by Francis King is no longer in print.
3. Sought to prevent &/or suppress publication of such divers Crowley material as: some Simon IFF stories. *The Book of Wisdom & Folly* & a heretofore unpublished IX° Grade Paper.

I do not air these allegations in public lightly. My intention is not to start a feud with Aleister Crowley's OTO, but to prevent a long & costly war which would divert money & energy from (in my opinion) many much-more interesting projects. Over 2 months ago, I attempted to workout my differences with A.C.'s OTO in-private via a lengthy letter to Jim Wasserman. Neither he nor any other representative of A.C.'s OTO has responded (as of 11 March '86ev). I followed-up my letter with a brief friendly note to Caliph H.B. Again no response. I hear news of saber rattling in the *Magical Link*. Magickal friends & associates who are initiates within A.C.'s OTO are offered bribes &/or are threatened in what appears to be a vain attempt to destroy friendships & isolate me To me, Coventry (in *any* form) has *no* place in our Holy Order in this Æon of Horus, especially within an organization whose Minerval Initiation ritual declares:

> *Let me further assure you that the word freedom is with us no idle term. We neither know nor care what your will is.*

It is said that we become what we eat. Motta was vanquished in court by A.C.'s OTO this past summer. Since then, A.C.'s OTO has begun to mimic the very behavior for which they entered into litigation with Motta to halt. This disturbs me. I feel A.C.'s OTO is suffering from an over-zealous application of the wrong kind of remedy, thus exacerbating the symptoms of the disease being fought. The court system is still Osirian. We (the various manifestations of the OTO upon Malkuth) are (at least from my perspective) governed by the Law of Thelema so long as it be our Will to manifest within the Æon of Horus. Secular Osirian courts have (in my opinion) no place in our squabbles. Not only is justice difficult to obtain, but even once obtained, Osirian bias can pollute the victory.

I feel that Crowley's legacy was intended to reach all those of his magickal children (whether legitimate or bastard) who evince an interest & aptitude commensurate with the formulae involved. Since A.C.'s OTO won its court case with Motta, they seem to have taken it upon themselves to *restrict* the availability of the tools of self-initiation. Such is (to me) a very Osirian trait. Osirian secrecy & stricture has a place in the Universe, but as the Æon of Horus flowers, the need for a protective father figure should, it seems to me, lessen—not strengthen.

In De Natura Deorum (Of the Nature of the Gods), Crowley's VIII° Grade Paper (text from Secret Rituals of the OTO). he counseled:

> *These [initiates] if they be wise will make no attempt to disclose this inner truth to the profane... For all attempts to initiate even the worthy before they initiate themselves are folly & fatality...What is the tent of Saladin but the phallus? ...But were the Minerval to suspect the truth would he not turn to flee in terror from the Camp[?]*

Today, how many Minervals are so ignorant/fearful of sex that they would flee from the symbolism of the Minerval initiation? Shit man, the Gnostic Mass with all of its far-less-subtle tits-&-ass-nudity, plunging of the lance into the cup, and melodramatic shrill-cry-of-orgasm is performed for interested *non*-initiates weekly in some cities!

For me, the so-called *Secret of the IX°* was not to be found in its jargon or *symbolism,* nor even thru a thorough intellectual understanding of its tantric-engineering *details.* Both symbolism & mechanics of the IX° can be found throughout modern Western culture (from coffee-table sex manuals, to underground comics), yet the secret is preserved. For me, the real secrets of Sex Magick remained a mystery until I achieved personal initiation through continuous practice of its mechanical formula, combined with meditation upon its symbolism until I became able to reify trans-rational magical engines to assist me in focusing/tuning/amplifying my Will. Such a secret cannot be 'revealed'; it must be discovered/created, each for him/her-self in the Light of his/her own True Will.

How many of *you* feel you need to be sheltered from technical papers on sex magick until someone else decides you are ready for them??

Crowley speaks quite eloquently of the behavioral patterns which he feels need to be expunged from the racial consciousness during this Æon. Allow me to quote further from De Natura Deorum:

> *But of those who have stultified themselves, who have darkened their own eyes, who have betrayed their own reason in seeking out phantastic gods, foul and tangled cobwebs of metaphysic... to such the Truth seems false and the Light darkness...Thus therefore, Sir Knights valorous and noble, war constantly on all tyranny and superstition...But also let there be a war upon those who refine these bigotries in any other way other than that of eclectic & syncretistic harmonizations; beware moreover of those who seek to 'spiritualize* their false gods, for their heads are even as vain pigs' bladders of poisonous miasma.*
>
> *But in your warfare, honor brave antagonists; spare them & bring them to initiation; while the hag & the eunich—and such are well neigh all who support orthodoxies—must be shown the only mercy possible, that, of swift destruction.*
>
> *For those calling themselves orthodox who are yet men, and women, have in truth no faith in these follies, but only profess them as convenient means of dominating the vulgar.*

Do you consider yourself to be one of the "vulgar" to be dominated?—I somehow think not, else why would you have been attracted to Thelema in the first place?!

I call for a *Jihad* (Holy War) against those *attitudes* (not people & not organizations) which distract our Holy Order from its Work. To some, the OTO seems to be a social club for arm-chair-magickians who are looking to get laid &/or who like recreational drugs. The OTO is far far more than this. (See *Liber Porta Lucis* for an outline of the Order's Work.)

Our predecessors, the Knights Templar once ruled much of the Western World near the middle of the Osirian Æon. What is the analogous formula in the Æon of Horus? Such is for us to discover/create!! But (it seems to me), we have a much better opportunity to discover/create/implement this formula if our energies are devoted to promulgating the Law of Thelema, and Practicing High Magick, than we do by squabbling amongst ourselves.

Several years back, Grady wrote an editorial in the *Link* about a bunch of crabs he saw while stationed in Korea. These crabs spent their whole lives fighting over a pile of shit. I got the hint. It is not my Will to devote my life to such pursuits, even though playing king-of-the-hill is an interesting recreation once in a while. My Will is working with others to share initiation (in the most profound sense of that word) far-&-wide, so that all can maximize his/her/their potential in the here-&-now.

INVOCATION
∴

I INVOKE
the PEACOCK ANGEL;
SHAITAN of the Dawn Sky;
AHURA MAZDA ,
Shining , Un-dieing
One-Horse SUN!
HO!

I INVOKE
the Purifying Fire of SHIVA
end
the Cleansing Destruction
of KALI !
HO!

I INVOKE
IT
to Dwell within our Order
in all of her myriad Branches &
Manifestations,
throughout all Time
and every Alternity!
HO !

I INVOKE
AIWAS Emergent & Puissant
into each of our Holy Initiates,
regardless of Rank or Privilege,
or of the Strength of the
Catena of Initiation
I may feel
with any of them!

I INVOKE
MAIAT
to council us daily
Individually & Collectively;
To assist us
in Balancing our Order,
Keeping it ever
the Euphonious Tuning fork
of THELEMA
and
the Vector Sum of each
of our own True Wills
HO!

I Summon
NU as my Refuge
Hadit as my Light,
and
Ra-Hoor-Khu as the
Strength Force & Vigour
of my Arms!
HO!

Let All
Who would foolishly Thwart
the LAW of THELEMA
Stand-Aside
OR
BE UTTERLY DESTROYED!

Unity uttermost showed!
I adore the might of thy breath
Supreme & terrible God
Who makest the gods and death
To tremble before Thee
I, I adore Thee!

If any among you feel that I may be a danger to the Order, I implore you to invoke whatever magickal energies are most aligned with your Will and blast me from the face of the earth. To my way of thinking, magickal warfare is far more efficient than seeking redress of grievances thru an Osirian legal system—*and* you are far less likely to become contaminated by whatever dis-ease you feel have corrupted me. If your assessment of the situation proves unfounded, I will neither hold grudges nor parry your thrusts. I shall channel all your energies to the core of my being, where I vow to use them for internal purification & to further my attunement with the 93 Current.

[For your convenience in targeting your energies, I append various of my personal & organizational sigils below.]

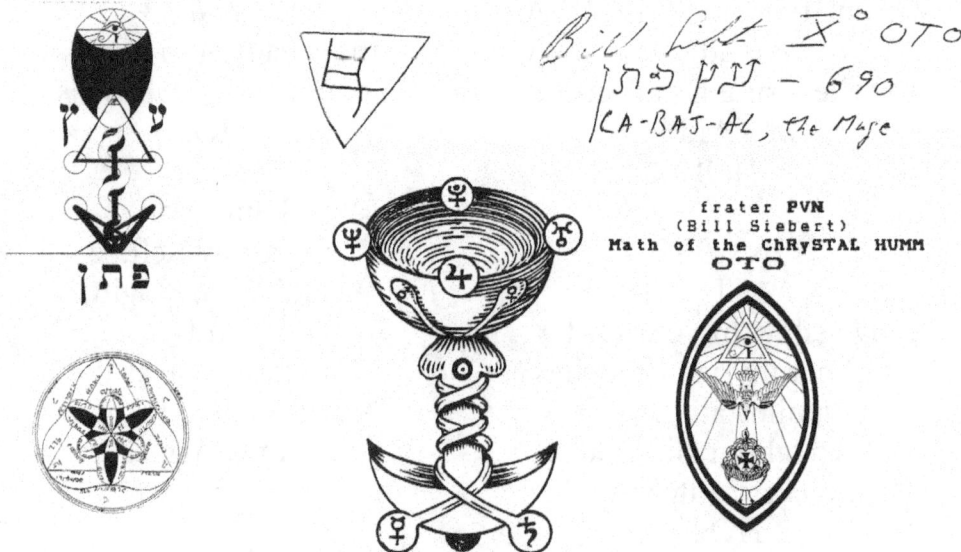

In my Minerval initiation, I swore to defend the principles of the Book of the Law in the name of the freedom of man, in whom *is* God. I have examined my oath in the light of my True Will and am acting accordingly.

As a Minerval Initiate of Aleister Crowley's OTO, and a self-proclaimed Revolutionary within the Order at large, I am boycotting all dues, initiation fees, & all other financial commitments to Aleister Crowley's OTO (by whatever name it now chooses to call itself) until such time as I as an Initiate feel that my money will be well spent by a Body of Initiates whose perspective on the Great Work is commensurate with my vision of Thelema. It does not make sense to me to pay dues, only to have my Earth Energy Talismans (cash) used contrary to my Will.

I have not cut myself off from the Order. I am a X° Sovereign of the OTO (as are all whose Will is to declare themselves thus) with direct internal links to the Fountainhead of the Order (which exists where Duality is Not). I accept/offer/share communication/communion/initiation from/to/with individual Thelemites, autonomous manifestations of the OTO, and local Powerzones of the OTO affiliated with any Branch of the Order whether their sponsoring organization chooses to affiliate with me or not.

Do what thou wilt shall be the whole of the Law.

frater PVN
(Bill Siebert)
Math of the ChRySTAL HUMM
OTO

P.S.: I will continue to publish &/or pass-on any 'secret' documents penned by Crowley which come into my possession, for I believe that no manifestation of the OTO has the right to sequester them. Further, I now solicit from you any material which you feel may assist in my quest to nourish the Order's growth & development within the Æon of Anything you send me will be used in accord with my Will.

I much prefer material which can be sent & vouched for by someone who is both willing & able to allow me to use his/her name as a reference, but I will most certainly evaluate all anonymous scraps of information which are given to me.

Those wishing to be added to my mailing list are requested to send a donation to cover mailing/xeroxing costs. Letters of support & financial contributions are always welcome, & are very very much appreciated.
Love is the law, love under will.

*** copyright notice ***

This epistle is copyright by Bill Siebert [1986], except for quotes from Crowley's writings. Permission is hereby granted to reproduce my text in whole or in part, for whatever reason whatsoever. All I ask is that you do not use my words out of context, or 'edit' them in such a way as to tamper with my original meaning.

Do what thou wilt shall be the whole of the Law.

The Chthonic-Auranian OTO: Origins, Purpose, & Structure

by Bill Siebert

Background

The Chthonic-Auranian OTO is a branch of our illustrious Order founded on the premise that the OTO is not only a pyramid of Knight Monks (as emphasized by the Caliphate), or a highly specialized Magical Engine (as emphasized by Grant's Typhonian OTO), but is also a family/tribe/network/fraternity of magickians who are each doing his/her Will as best as each of us is able, & who are each fully responsible for our actions/-stillnesses, thoughts/trances/channelings, and speech/silence. We feel that each Thelemite, by doing his/her will, has access to the Fountain-head of the Order. It is from here that true initiation flows.

The founders of the Chthonic-Auranian OTO (myself, Cliff Pollick, & Sam Webster) were each members of more traditional branches of the Order during our magickal apprenticeships. Cliff was a III° member of the Caliphate OTO, and co-founder of *Hadit Chapter* in Philadelphia. Sam was also a II° member of the Caliphate, & founder of *Aum Ha* Camp[1] in Boston.

I was (perhaps still am) a Minerval in the Caliphate OTO. I have heard a rumor that I have been expelled from the Caliphate—ostensibly for publishing *Emblems & Modes of Use* in *MEZLA,* Vol. I #13 It would seem that the Caliphate regards that document as one of their exclusive IX° legacies from Crowley, even though the original manuscript (a letter from Crowley to Jack Parsons) was sold by Parsons to Luis Culling before Crowley's death. As I violated no oath in publishing *Emblems,* & as I have not received any official notification of expulsion, I still consider myself a Minerval in the Caliphate — but not a dues paying member. I am on a dues strike until the Caliphate gets down to the nitty-gritty of using dues monies to promulgate Thelema instead of fueling intra-Æon strife.

I was also a V° member of Grant's Typhonian OTO. After nearly

---
[1] actually just a 'study group'—Ed.

a decade, he expelled me for insubordination to his Will. I was acting from my own center, not his—which Grant did not appreciate. Although Frater Aossic Aiwass worked heavily with the qliphoth and the magick of the Abyss, he was unwilling to accommodate those whose personal perspective differed from his own. Although Grant has done much pioneering work exploring beyond the gateway of Daath, he does not encourage diversity within the Malkuthean aspects of OTO structure & philosophy.

At one time, KG counciled me on what he felt was my *too literal* interpretation of the Æon of the Child by warning me not to be puerile —by which he meant silly, childish, or immature. Yet, in the realm of geomancy, *Puer* relates not to the Fool, but to the Element of Fire, to the sign of Aries, and to either the Emperor or the Star (depending on which Tarot system you work with). Thus, to act puerile is noble calling indeed, in this Æon of the Crowned & Conquering Child!

Why Grant continues to keep *Liber Oz* as the manifesto of the OTO on the outer is beyond me. When I began to evince symptoms of knowing my Will & reifying it. Grant informed me that the OTO was designed for those who were not yet ready to manifest their Wills. According to Grant, those who know their Will & are doing it, have no need of the OTO.

Once I grasped what Grant was saying, I most certainly agreed with him that I had no real *need* of the Typhonian OTO. Yet I remained within its orbit till he formally expelled me. I saw no conflict between the links I was formulating with the Fountainhead of the Order within myself, and acceptance of similar links which he & others were formulating within themselves.

The light of Gnosis extends outward from each of us. In previous æons, Magickal Orders, Religions, and Yogic Schools were formulated by individuals who had tapped-into the gnosis, & set-about sharing their wealth with others of like aspiration. Illumination extended outward thru catena of initiation to those individuals who had not yet discovered the light of gnosis within themselves. Some disciples became dependent upon the light emanating from another, thus blinding themselves to the light which emanates from within themselves. As gnostics died, or went on to other endeavors, Schools Religions & Magickal Orders in which they worked their Will did not simply close-up shop or evaporate into thin air. Mystery schools may be headed by Fools or charlatans as well as by gnostic saints. In many ways. Secrecy & respect for tradition encourage Hanumann & the Ape of Thoth to stand in the spotlight, while the work of the inner Order goes on un-noticed, save by those few who understand that gnosis comes from within.

Although there are many gnostics who prefer to work solitary & away from formal groups, I much prefer to work/play/grow within a *Sovereign Sanctuary of the Gnosis* whose members see themselves & each other as operating within a free-form ever-shifting network of Anarchistic Kings. From my perspective, the core of the OTO is not based upon pyramidal politics. It is a multi-dimensional self-luminous spider web with no single spider-god architect, & no fixed center around which the universe orbits. We whose will is to function as Sovereigns of the OTO are both weavers & web (see *Book of Lies*). Individually & collectively, we gleefully follow stimulating strands which others have woven, as we add our own personal embellishments to what others have woven before us. We each cherish those inspiring patterns in the web which helped us to access our present level of illumination. As the Knights Templar did before us, we keep all roads safe for pilgrims—I warn others away from those individuals &/or practices which I have found to be dangerous, or seductively sedating. Yet I have no desire to compel anyone to follow my advice. How can I possibly determine another's Will for him/her, or judge his/her capabilities to flourish under circumstances which I might find stifling? All I can do is advise. We each repair the fabric of the web, inasmuch as each of us feels it is need of repair (if it ain't broke, don't fix it). And we (individually & collectively) create new & interesting patterns, by which we entertain ourselves, each other, & mayhaps increase the general level of gnostic illumination throughout the multiverse.

Our charter (inasmuch as we can be said to have one) is an outgrowth of our True Wills. It depends neither from nor upon any catena of initiation from any other group. We make no claim of being chartered by Crowley, Germer, Soror Sprengel, or any secret chiefs outside of ourselves. We are *bar-Sinister Mad Wand* spawn of *Babalon the Whore & To-Mega-Therion—666. Choronzon* mid-wifed our birth. We are indeed heirs to Crowley's legacy, but we are most certainly not claiming any legitimacy!

Grade Structure

From my perspective, our Order has 3 grades which I attribute to *Hermit, Lover & Wo/Man of Earth,* but each Sovereign is free to create and manifest his/her own unique system (even if some systems may appear to be contradictory to others).

Our innermost grade is the first to be encountered. To me, a *Hermit* is One who has sought the gnosis *within him/her-self* and has made his/her own personal links with the Fountainhead of the Order independent from any external organizations/beings. I am ever-working & ever-playing to reify this grade in my day-to-day life.

The Grade of *Lovers* is the province of those whose Will is to work within the community, fraternity, and fellowship of our Order. I impose no dues, duties, or hazing rituals upon those who seek our fellowship—but I speak only for myself. It is up to each Sovereign to work this one out for him/her-self!—"teach ye must, but…" I assume that all candidates for initiation into the Grade of Lovers consider themselves to be Masters of the Temple, or whatever they deem to be the equivalent in whatever system of internal initiation they are working. When working with other Masters, I see no need for hoodwinks, dire oaths, or stodgy 19th Century Egypto-Victorian Masonic ritual forms. For me, Love, Will, & Personal Responsibility have always been keywords for this Grade.

Initiation comes in many forms. Mutual initiation is (to me) the ideal, as no karma accrues thereby. I see initiation into the Chthonic—Auranian OTO as a process of mutual recognition between a representative of our Order & the candidate. (I see you. Do you see me? Fine! Now lets interface our Great Works!) Usually, but not always, this recognition culminates in a ritual to welcome the Candidate into our Order as 1-of-us—not as some illusory equal, but as an individual beyond considerations of hierarchy or equality.

Local groups are free to charge dues, set up grand temples, or whatever else they feel may benefit their work. But no local group can insist that any *member-at-large* of the Chthonic-Auranian OTO join their temple, pay dues, or swear fealty. Conversely, no member of the Chthonic-Auranian OTO has any right to expect services from the Order at large, or from any temple of which s/he is not an active supporting member.

TANSTAAFL! (There Ain't No Such Thing As A Free Lunch!)

<Do you grok?>

In contrast with many manifestations of the OTO, we who embrace the grade of *Wo/Man of Earth* (the outermost grade of our Order) comprise our Sovereign Sanctuary. For me, the Sovereign Sanctuary of the Gnosis is not an inner Hermetic contemplative grade, but rather, an outward manifestation of Gnostic-Hermeticism into the world at large.

To me, a Sovereign is one whose personal Will is inexorably intertwined with the ever-evolving Will of our Order. In essence, a Sovereign is dedicated in body/mind/spirit to the essence of the OTO. S/He nurtures its growth, enriches its function, & when (in any particular Sovereign's judgement) the Chthonic-Auranian OTO has outlived its purpose, s/he becomes the executor of that portion of our Order's Estates which come under his/her self-chosen and self-regulated jurisdiction—to distribute, shroud, destroy, or inter our Order's Wealth, Mysteries, & Wisdom in accord with Will.

Citizen of the World is my friend Arian's name for this grade—wherein each Sovereign is a living embodiment of the essence our Order in his/her every contact with each-&-every being s/he encounters. Not only with those who view themselves as magickians, shamans, witches, mystics, sufis, or other practitioners of High Art, but also those with more down-to-earth titles of office, such as neighbor, stranger, friend, traveler, person, or individual.

For me, embodiment of the essence of the OTO does not imply preaching, nor does it even necessarily connote mentioning the Chthonic-Auranian OTO by name. It simply means being a Thelemite (which, to me, simply means that I take Joy in doing my Will) 24 hours a day, each & every day of my life—not just when I am in a ritual Circle, or surrounded by other conscious Thelemites.

Yet, this commitment to embody the essence of the OTO does not necessitate becoming a slave to consistency. How I behave as a Thelemite varies from day to day, & from situation to situation. To me, Thelema is not a static code of morals, but an ever-expansive inter-active flowering of my Will in relationship with the Multiverse at large, & all beings contained therein.

The Sovereign Sanctuary can also be viewed as a context for interaction and networking by which the Will of us Sovereigns (all of us together, or any sub-set of us) become united in acts of Love under Will to create/tune/activate various magickal engines for any purpose whatsoever.

Sovereigns are just that. We are beholden to no person or governing body beyond our own personal interpretation of Will. The only way

I know to remove a sovereign from office is to slay him or her (as per *Liber Oz* and scholia—especially, the Sothic Comment). A Sovereign cannot be put on bad-report, expelled, removed from active duty, or any other euphemism for hierarchal censure, censorship, or muzzling. I, for one, abhor the practice of *Coventry,* in any form.

The other side of that coin is also incontestable. No sovereign can be obligated to endorse or condone any conduct of any other sovereign or group of sovereigns. No member can be compelled to associate with any other member. Love, Will, & feelings of strong-&-abiding kinship adjudicate association, not rank or office.

A Sovereign is any member of our Order (i.e., any initiate of the Grade of Lovers) who asserts him/her-self as a Sovereign, & who is subsequently embraced as a fellow Sovereign by any two or more Wo/Men of Earth. We did it this way to ensure that the Chthonic-Auranian OTO could easily grow beyond our founders' individual Wills & focus of vision.

Chthonic means of the underworld, or mysterious, with intimations of qliphothic. We emphasize the meeting/acceptance/fusion of dark and light within each of us individually, & within all of us collectively—see *Liber Tzaddi*. Chthonic also means spurious—we openly acknowledge our bastard roots. *Auranian* derives from Auranos, a specialised orthography of Uranus. Auranos is an extra-telluric counterpart of Chthonia, the dark hidden aspect of Gaia. In our spelling of Auranos, we imply both gold <Latin: *Aurm*> and light (Hebrew: *AUR*> as well as the more traditional fertile rain, symbol for the jism of Uranus, fertilizer of earth's innermost mysteries.

To me, Chthonic-Auranian invokes the serpent & the dove. On a microcosmic level, I embrace with passion my recognition that I am the product of extra-terrestrial DNA (mainly of viral origin) which has successfully combined with terrestrial genetic material to form the being who perceives itself as being *I*. From my perspective, we are a co-mingling of the mysteries of Heaven & Earth within the concurbit of the OTO/A∴A∴.

Some OTO's are structured so as to teach or impart various techniques to their members. Others seem to focus their energy into setting tasks, then judging success or failure by evaluating each member's lab notebook (magickal record). In my experience, top-down imposed curricula can very easily become onerous. I see no point creating or imposing strictures which may be restrictive to a particular member's Will. I see required programs of study, &/or external accounting of an individual's progress along a self-chosen Path as having little place within the Chthonic-Auranian OTO, aside from mutually agreeable 1-on-1 voluntary covenants.

As a self-directed Thelemite, I set my own course curriculum for unfolding my Will, & I assume others are willing-&-able to do likewise. If anyone is interested in my Work, I am generally eager to share my knowledge, techniques, & speculations—gratis to friends, & at a fair price to strangers. Likewise, as I discover interesting people whose knowledge, techniques, &/or ideas stimulate me, I ask each of them if & under what conditions they would consider sharing their expertise with me.

The Chthonic-Auranian OTO is still quite small (23 members worldwide: 2 in Australia, 1 in the Caribbean, & the rest in the US), 5 of us (thus-far) functioning in the Sovereign Sanctuary, with three additional members asserting their Will as Citizens of the World.

Does my philosophy/approach strike any euphonious chords with what you are doing? I am interested in networking information & energy, regardless of whether you & I are members of the same organizations!

Bill Siebert
Math of the ChRySTAL HUMM

Gelfling Initiation

by Frater PVN, Master of Alchemy
(with editorial assistance from)
LA-BAJ-AL, Mage-&-Watcher

Preliminary Note of an Initiation Ritual to expedite attunement of new members into any Working Group (Encampment /Power-zone /Tribe) of the Chthonic Branch of the Ordo Templi Orientis.
Note: *This ritual is not intended for use 'as-is', but rather as a jumping-off place for inspiration. Each Master is encouraged to dream with this ritual until such time as s/he is ready to reify it as a personal rite. Then (& only then) can it be used to initiate others into your working group.*

Initiation of the Gelfling

The lodge is opened by whatever Masters are present in whatever way(s) best allows them to tap-into trans-abyssal formulae. For me (at this locus of Time/Alternity), this means invoking the Watcher, opening the temple in the name of the Order in each of the Aeons, centering in all-time/no-time, then focusing the energy of the temple into the Æon of Horus for operations involving the OTO in the here-&-now.

Members of the OTO are then invited into the temple. The temple is opened in the formula of the Gelfling & members who are sponsoring candidates tell the rest of the assembled brotherhood what they know of each candidate, and why they have sponsored each of them for membership. This should be a brief formality (3-13 minutes per candidate) as no candidate should be considered for membership until s/he is known & trusted by all Masters of the Temple & by a majority of the active temple membership.

One whose Will is to act as Blackguard then goes to the anteroom, where the candidates are being watched-over by one who holds the office of Lurker-at-the-Threshold. It is the lurker's duty to induce the candidates away from non-magickal use of drugs (alcohol, tobacco, mj, etc.) while they are awaiting initiation & to provide them with suitable entertainment (putting magical music on the sound system, showing them scrapbooks, slides, videos, etc. depicting various rituals

& events of the Temple's history, telling tales, & answering any last-minute questions) to keep them focused on the work-at-hand. It is the lurker's task to expel from the temple any whom s/he feels is not fit for initiation because of non-magical intoxication, bad attitude, or for any other reason. H-is/er word is law & may not be contested. However, a candidate may be brought to the temple for initiation at a later date if s/he can find another sponsor. (Lurkers should be chosen from among those who have experience with being able to discern the difference between magical intoxication & common drug abuse.)

The blackguard binds & blindfolds one candidate (chosen by whim, or by advanced planning) while the other candidates watch. The bound candidate is then led back into temple while the other candidates resume their play.

The Master of the Temple arises when the Blackguard enters with the Candidate. He asks the blackguard whom s/he has as prisoner. The blackguard answers that s/he has one who claims to seek initiation into the Temple. The M.T. asks why the candidate is bound & gagged. The Blackguard answers that the candidate has not yet proven him/her-self & cannot yet be trusted.

The M.T. asks if there are any who will vouch for the Candidate. The sponsor steps forward & vouches for the candidate in personalized terms, explaining why s/he trusts that the Candidate will not betray the temple.

Blackguard acts as devil's advocate, speaki>ng openly & eloquently of the Candidate's weaknesses. Blackguard asks permission to slay Candidate.

M.T. ponders the question before him/her. If s/he does order the candidate slain, Blackguard should do so quietly, so as not to disturb the other Candidates. If the Candidate is deemed worthy of further examination, s/he must be set free of all bonds, allowed to loosen the blindfold from his/her own eyes & be given a comfortable seat in front of the M.T., who sits back down upon his throne.

Once the Candidate is comfortable, the M.T. speaks to him/her & tells him/her that s/he has been sponsored for membership within the Temple. S/he is told that s/he has been set free so that s/he would be free to leave the temple if such were now his/her Will. Gatekeeper asks Candidate if s/he would like to leave.

Assuming Candidate remains, M.T. tells Candidate that s/he has been freed so that all oaths made would be made by a Free person, under no threat or duress. M.T. asks Candidate if s/he is present at the ritual as a free agent, under no duress, and understands the purpose of the initiation. Candidate answers in his/her own words.

M.T. then asks Candidate to explain the process whereby s/he has come to seek initiation at this temple. Candidate answers in his/her own words. If Candidate is not very verbal, s/he may be asked leading questions by his/her sponsor. If s/he has a tendency to ramble-on overly long (more than 15 minutes), it is the Blackguard's duty to prod him to brevity.

When M.T. is satisfied that the Candidate is being open & candid, M.T. asks the candidate if his intentions are honorable toward the Temple, and if it be his/her Will to become a brother of the Order. If the Candidate cannot answer both of these questions in the affirmative, he is escorted out of the temple by the blackguard, who hands him over to the Lurker for expulsion. Assuming the Candidate answers in the affirmative, the ritual continues.

The M.T. then asks the Candidate if he understands his triune inner nature, & whether he is able to make oaths which bind his demonic & angel selves as well as his mortal self. If the Candidate answers in the affirmative & is able to demonstrate that s/he knows whereof s/he speaks to the satisfaction of the M.T., the ritual proceeds to *point #2* below, after all Candidates who have gone through *point #1* initiations have been escorted into a part of the temple which is out of sight/hearing of the main temple, yet also apart from the Candidates' anteroom. If all Candidates in a class are able to answer in the affirmative to these questions, the temple may be re-opened in the formula of *____* and further initiations be conferred prior to &/or following the Feast, at the discretion of the Master Alchemist. Most Candidates will not be able to answer in the affirmative. For these Candidates, the ritual continues with *point #1* below.

Point #1

The M.T. instructs the Candidate in the relationship of human, demonic, & divine aspects. The Candidate is given *Liber Tzaddi* to read. This done, the M.T. then repeats his/her question about whether the candidate is able to speak for more than his/her human self.

If the candidate hesitates, s/he is encouraged, but s/he must be allowed to speak in his/her own words. Question/answer continue until the M.T. is confident that the Candidate understands what is being asked & can answer with certainty. If s/he answers in the affirmative, skip to point#2 as above.

The more usual Candidate may answer something along the following lines: "Thanks to your instructions, I am now more concretely aware of my triple-fold nature, but I am really only dimly aware of the actual personalities involved. I have no names or direct contact with any 'other' selves as yet, but I feel that establishing contact (& eventual union) is a prime goal of seeking initiation into this Temple."

The M.T. gestures & the Blackguard (who was standing in front of the M.T., off to the M.T.'s left, between the M.T. & the Candidate) steps toward, puts a hammerlock on the Candidate, & holds a dagger to his/her throat. Unbidden, 2 other members step up behind the candidate, one to either side. One is very refined in nature, almost etherial, while the other is gross, coarse, & very animal in his/her behavior.

The M.T. speaks to the Blackguard & bids him/her to bind & hoodwink the Candidate, take him/her far from the Temple, & turn him/her over to the Lurker-at-the-Threshold for disposal. The M.T. states that the word of one who cannot vouch for all of his/her aspects is worth less than nothing. S/he states that it is not be feasible to have any in our midst who cannot vouch for all of their aspects.

At this point, the two members stepped toward, one on each side of the Candidate, blocking the Blackguard from his task. The M.T. speaks in an angry voice & asks the meaning of this treason!

The etherial member addresses the M.T., stating that although the Candidate did not know his/her angelic self directly as of yet, surely s/he was enough in touch with his/her True Will to make at least a symbolic oath in his/her angel's name, pending that time when s/he was directly in contact with the god within.

The earthy member then spoke a similar speech to the M.T., but dealing with the Candidates demonic nature. Both speeches reflect the actual personalities of the individuals who work these Offices. Each role must be personalized to fit the officer, not the other way a round.

The M.T. smiles & asks each witness if s/he would each voice his/her oaths, along with the Candidate. They agree. The M.T. asks in what names are these symbolic oaths to be taken. The witnesses answer, each in turn, each in his/her own words. What follows is a guide, not a speech to be memorized.

"I, the angelic witness, propose that the candidate's angel be invoked by the title URRU, or URaRU, a name of light, both actual & reflected, from the world of the Dark Crystal. Let this name be used by the Candidate until such time as the exact name & nature of his angel be known."

"I, the demonic witness, propose that the candidate's demon be evoked by the title Skeksis (555), which embodies the Current of obscurity & darkness from that same legend. Let this name be used by the Candidate until such time as the exact name & nature of his demon be known."

The M.T. then speaks to the Candidate, nodding first to the angelic witness & then to the demonic witness. "You, Candidate are called by the title Gelfling, for in you is the power to unite the light & wisdom of Urru, with the dark power of obscurity held by the Skeksis. Your name means Worthy (Gelfling (GHLPhLING) adds to 211}, for it is up to you to decide when-&-how your aspects are to become united. Balance them well. Learn each of their natures. For they are you, and in you are their natures manifest."

(An alternative to these set godforms would be for the witnesses to take the Candidate to a separate room of the temple, there to work with him/her to choose an appropriate set of names/oaths to be used till s/he make viable contact with his/her angel & demonic selves. If such a formula be utilized, other Candidates may be led up to this point in the ritual while the witnesses work with the earlier Candidates.)

(end of *point #1*. Resume with *point #3* below.)

Point #2

Candidates who are already actively working the Chthonic Current shall design & implement their own oaths, to be witnessed by M.T. & Blackguard. Such initiations should not be done with 'ordinary' candidates in attendance, but may be done in the presence of full-fledged members who wore once 'ordinary candidates'. Master Alchemist may (at his/her discretion) offer such these extra-ordinary Candidates communion of wine-&-strange drugs prior to *point #3*.

Point #3

When oaths are completed, Candidate is led to sit with members while other Candidates are brought this point in the ritual. When entire class of Candidates has been inducted, Blackguard escorts the Lurker-at-the-threshold into the Temple. M.T. comes down from throne, greets Lurker as a brother and an equal. Lurker & M.T. sit on temple floor, without a second thought as to where their robes will be soiled. Blackguard urges Candidates to jon them on the floor in an informal circle. Rest of membership ring them about, also seated on the floor. Cushions and chars are moved asideto make room. Anyone not wishing to soil this/her robe, pants, or dress may squat, but may not use a cushion, mat or chair.

A member passes a silver plate to the M.T. upon which are placed some coarse bread, a dish of water, & a pile of salt. The lurker lightly touches a piece of the bread to the surface of the water & then to the surface of the salt. (A light touch is necessary to prevent the bread from becoming either soggy or too salty to stomach.) S/he addresses the Candidates, making eye contact with each & every one of them. "Take you this communion of bread & salt as a token of the bond which unites you with all your brethren in the Order. (M.T. makes expansive motions to include all in temple, & in world.) We are a big family. Sometimes we have disagreements, or even wars amongst ourselves. But we never forget that we are all brothers. We have no 'hidden agendas' amongst ourselves. Our cards are always in plain sight of our brethren, not up our sleeves. If we have a grievance with one of our brothers, we do not mouth phoney greetings to his face, then stab him when his back is turned. By partaking of this bread, you become one with the leaven which elevates our nature. By partaking of this salt, you become united with the intensity of your earthy inheritance. By partaking of the water which unites them, you become one with the Water of Life-&-Death which is our symbol of immortal regeneration. By sharing this communion with all of us, you acknowledge your bond with each of us, and each of us with you"

M.T. offers plate with bread-&-salt to all new members within his/her reach. Each member decides the proper proportion of bread, water, & salt for him/her-self. If the gathering is large, the M.T. passes plate to someone else so that each member has easy access to the plate. When all (both new & old members) have taken communion of bread-&-salt, lurker then offers communion to M.T., gatekeeper, and Blackguard, who is the last to communicate.

Candidates then given copies of the Book of the Law, & Liber Oz. One Candidate is chosen to represent the class. S/he is asked to open the Book of the Law & read as much or as little as s/he is directed by inspiration. Master Alchemist uses the passages read as an omen to assist him/her later in the ritual if sacrament is dispensed formally.

Temple is closed in the formula of the Gelfling. Members go into anteroom where a feast lays waiting (final prep was done by Blackguard & Lurker after last Candidate was brought into temple). Masters close temple as it was opened, only in reverse order. For me this means that Æon of Horus focus of temple is integrated into trans-Æonic dance. Then all-time/no-time is called upon to disperse locus of space/t ine throughout alternity. Watcher is *not* given license to depart as ritual will not be finished until last celebrant & last questor have gone to sleep. Watcher is usually given license to depart by Master Alchemist at his bedside just before he goes to sleep.

Feast

M.T. & other masters join members at feast. M.T. says Will. Just before the "fall-to", Master Alchemist reminds members to "Be not animal; refine thy rapture! If thou drink, drink by the eight and ninety rules of art: if thou love, exceed by delicacy; and if thou do aught joyous, let there be subtlety therein!"

Feasting & partying begin & continue with as little structure as feasible. Food, social use of drugs, & inter-personal interactions are the social fabric within which the Order functions on Malkuth. We are a fraternity, & a microcosm of the world at large. Each of us has our own style to contribute to any gathering.

From my perspective, we do not aim towards uniformity so much as we aim toward interactions which foster growth among ourselves while inducing all of us to be fully responsible for all facets of our beings. Irresponsible behavior is not to be tolerated or encouraged.

But each will probably define these terms differently. Within the context of this ritual, as well as in day-to-day temple affairs, the M.T. acts as a Kether-figure who adjudicates any grievances which may arise be tween/among members. In case of serious disputes, all Masters may be asked to assist him/her, but none may be compelled to do so. The Master Alchemist (who operates from Chokmah) has the right/duty to dispense &/or refuse sacramental drugs at all gatherings. Any may bring their own drugs, but if they abuse them (i.e., if their use interferes with our rituals or social functions), the Master Alchemist has the right to expel a particular member from the ritual or feast in progress, &/or end the ritual or feast & close the temple. The Blackguard (who operates as the Dark Mother at Binah) reminds members of their oaths, should such be necessary, & deals with treachery in any way s/he Wills. The Lurker-at-the-Threshold coaxes members into trans-abyssal consciousness, and works to show how even apparent accidents &/or apparent irresponsible behavior can be used to channel inspiration into our rituals & social events. The lurker is a useful balance to the Master Alchemist &/or the Blackguard if they tend to take their offices too seriously.

In temples with sufficient Masters, it is highly recommended that a particular Master not be asked to serve a particular office over a long period of time, as over-specialization can sometimes cause tunnel-vision which is detrimental to the Master, the Temple, and particular members whose Will-&-Path may be at variance with the vision of that Master.

Ritual of the A∴A∴, Wine & Strange Drugs

As things begin to wind-down, Lurker, Blackguard, M.T. & Master Alchemist go apart to confer on the advisability of offering a communion of wine-&-strange-drugs to those present. If all members (both new & old) appear to be able to function on the appropriate level, sacrament is brought-out & offered to all present, or the feast is ended so that the late-night ritual can be moved to another location where it can continue undisturbed throughout the night.

If there are some members (new or old) who do not seem (to the M.T., the Master Alchemist, the Lurker, & the Blackguard) to be functioning in a good magickal space, sacrament is not passed out at the feast.

Note well: Psychedelics can certainly be used for personal enjoyment, but there are certain kinds of 'fun' which are not conducive to Workings of the Inner Order. Decisions about whether or not to proceed are seldom easy if there are 'borderline' cases, particularly as it is generally known ahead of time that scar ament is on the agenda. Different Masters draw the line in different places. Learning is best done by trial-&-error. Masters of each temple use different criteria in reaching judgements. Mistakes make good learning tools. Cross-fertilization with other Temples can assist Masters in different methods of selection, & can assist in keeping everyone functioning at high levels.

If different members seem to be functioning on different levels, Sacrament may be dispensed at an invitation-only gathering to be held after the feast is completed. If any member asks why s/he has not been invited to the sacramental feast, s/he shall be given a sensitive, yet straight-forward honest answer. Sacramental feasts are the province of the A∴A∴. Admission to them is not guaranteed by virtue of membership in the OTO. If the Master Alchemist & the M.T. & Lurker & the Blackguard are not comfortable with someone, that person should not be invited into trip-space without very careful consideration being given to all the possible repercussions. If such selective dispensation of sacramental drugs prove detrimental to temple morale, all drugs can be barred from rituals & feasts of the OTO. Entheogenic Sacrament can then be used 'privately' by those members of the Order who feel inclined to do so. As such activities will then be outside the concerns of the temple officers, the burden of the Masters will be lessened. However, the veil between the inner-&-outer Orders will become more substantial and the outer Order may well become just a social club for magickians. The balance is subtle. The dangers of possible abuse of power are real. Yet it is only thru training in the sacramental use of entheogenic sacrament (which includes selection of proper candidates) that the Gateways to the inner Order can open fully.

Note: At other levels of initiation within our Order, the roles of the Masters differ. For instance, in rituals involving Tantric Sacrament, the Blackguard has another name, and her office is similar to that of the Master Alchemist in this ritual. Dispensation of sacrament (whatever its form) is always by invitation only. Each time sacrament is administered, initiation is always possible, but can never be guaranteed.

End of the Rite of the Gelfling. Commentaries on the various late-night sex &/or drug sacraments must remain un-written. For the rituals, set, & setting of the Entheogenic Sacrament must remain ever open to individual experimentation.

PVN

of the Miskatonic Alchemical Expedition

Miskatonic Alchemical Expedition

*An Introduction to the Miskatonic Alchemical Expedition
of the Esoteric Order of Dagon
Written for All Prospective Members
by AShT ChOzar SSaratu '.' 1103*

Bill Siebert (as frater PVN) was a co-founder of Math of the ChRySTAL HUMM, a Shamanic/Alchemical Thelemic Powerzone near Ithaca, NY.

As LA-BAJ-AL, Mage-&-Watcher, he is one of the 3 founding Sovereigns of the Chthonic-Auranian OTO, a branch of the Ordo Templi Orientis dedicated to exploration-&-union of the Dark/Light Mysteries of all æonic formulæ.

As AShT ChOzar S*Saratu*, Bill is the Alchemist-coördinator of the Miskatonic Alchemical Expedition of the Esoteric Order of Dagon, a Lovecraftian Mystery School descended from the Sirius mystery cults of Ægypt Babylon & Sumeria, by way of Gateways within creative individuals who are capable of Dreaming the Mythos & making it accessible even to those who do not believe their dreams to be real.

—*totse.info,* https://totseans.com/totse/en/religion/the_occult/eod-mae.html

October 1992

Some Brief Notes Regarding the on-Going Work of our Miskatonic Alchemical Expedition

by AShT Ch0zar SSaratu 103

Author's 1994 Preface

This little essay was originally penned by me, Bill Siebert, otherwise known as AShT Ch0zar S*Saratu*, in 1987 for confidential distribution to members of the Miskatonic Alchemical Expedition (MAE) as part of an on-going project to create a body of written material to prepare those seeking initiation into this Ophidean/Elysian Mystery School.

The MAE was designed as a syncretic mystery school amalgamating the techniques, world views, and mythologies of all participants —ideally, without bogging-down in disputes of dogma or hierarchy. Before talking about MAE, I will give a bit of background on myself.

Since 1967 or so, I have been actively involved in magick and paganism, albeit as a solitary. In 1977 I probationed in and became an initiate of the Typhonian branch of Ordo Templi Orientis headed by Kenneth Grant. I remained an active member of this Thelemic Order (attaining the rank of V°) until 1984 when I was suspended (later to be expelled in 1985) by K.G. because he felt my Will was not aligned with that of the Orders. In 1981, I co-founded Math of the ChRyS-TAL HUMM, a Shamanic/Alchemical Thelemic Powerzone based based in an old rundown farmhouse with 23 acres of rolling fields & woodlands (our ritual space) in upstate New York. In retrospect, I believe my Great Work parted from Grant's mainly because the focus of my Will was at that time going into my on-going magickal endeavor to reify an ecumenical thelemic powerzone & profess house, rather than devoting myself more fully to promulgating the Law of Thelema under the aegis of KG and the Typhonian OTO.

In 1985, I became one of the three founding Sovereigns of the Chthonic-Auranian OTO, branch of the OTO—a wholly new manifestation of the Order claiming no imprimatur from Crowley, and doing away (as much as possible) with hierarchy grades & restraint of individual enthusiasm. The Chthonic-Auranian OTO is dedicated to exploration-&-union of the Dark/Light Mysteries of all aonic formuli. At about this time, I also became a regional coordinator of the Esoteric Order of Dagon, a Lovecraftian Mystery School descended from the Sirius mystery cults of egypt Babylon & Sumeria, by way of Gateways within creative individuals who are capable of dreaming the mythos, and making it accessible even to those who do not believe their dreams to be real. It was into the maelstrom of these mythic forces that the Miskatonic Alchemical Expedition took form and birthed itself at Math of the ChRySTAL Humm somewhere in 1986 or 87.

It is now 1994. A lot has transpired since this essay was written. I left Math of the ChRySTAL HUMM in the hands of friends in 1988 to pursue the study of Megapolistomancy within dance clubs and dirty back streets of Buffalo New York. About 1989 or 1990 Math of the ChRySTAL HUMM reabsorbed itself back into the void from whence it came. The house & land which were the physical basis for this powerzone has been foreclosed upon by the banks. The Chthonic-Auranian OTO is alive-&-well, prospering under the guidance of its many capable Sovereigns. I have been out of contact with the EOD since 1988. From what I have been able to ascertain, the EOD is no longer operating on the outer.

The MAE has been evolving in fits & starts since parting from the nurturance of Math of the ChRySTAL HUMM powerzone in 1988. The MAE is, a living viable Current—from my perspective, alive and growing within each of us who played with its magick at Math of the ChRySTAL Humm. Yet, although I believe the MAE is a many headed hydra, I can only speak of it through the lens of my own personal experience. Synchronous with my own personal journey of re-discovery, the MAE has become a wriggling semi-somnolent pupa dormant within me—absorbing & reifying a new megalomanic context to augment its elysian primal nurturance. The 1994 publication of this essay is designed to arouse the Miskatonic Alchemickal Expedition from its six year hibernation to begin its work anew.

Currently, Bill is living amidst the social decadence, political corruption, and stagnant decay of New Orleans with his wife-&-Priestess

Raven Greywalker. Together they are studying and learning arcane mysteries from diverse encounters with various megalomanic power-spots and with the plethora of individuals whose ancestry and magicks stem from an amalgamation of Haitian and African Voodoos, strange native American magicks, even-stranger heresies brought here from France and Spain by various prisoners of conscience fleeing from the long arm of Inquisition and Crown—as well as those not-quite human fringe-people whose swamp, bayou, & river ancestors possess a certain bactrian look analogous to their Innsmuthian kin, yet with an indolent balefulness not often found beyond the foetid nurturance of Louisiana's biological social spiritual and political backwater. Compounding this genetic, spiritual, and ethnic mire is an on-going influx of disaffected and disenfranchised persons from the world around, drawn to New Orleans by its astral and literary beacon proclaiming it to be a Mecca for the weird.

Into this complex milieu, AShT Ch0zar S*Saratu* awakens once more to prod the hermit, Bill, into literary fecundity.

Original Preface

Lest there be confusion, let me state here that this little essay is written from my own personal internal perspective. I feel strongly that most of my fellow expedition members would agree with the content of what I am saying, but many of them might find my vocabulary a bit unfamiliar.

Among Thelemites, our expeditions are currently known as Holy Guardian Angel Workings. Back in the days when our expeditions were less focused, some (who placed themselves on the fringes of our endeavors) called our workings Pagan Parties. Gatherings is the most common local term. Up until recently, I have been rather silent about my intense internal work with Lovecraft's Mythos—preferring to keep my Lovecraftian magicks to myself, while integrating myself consciously & openly into whatever mythology my fellow expedition members were weaving. But the time for silence is at an end. With this paper, I begin to open the inner workings of my personal mythology, the Miskatonic Alchemical Expedition, to all who may be interested working this Current.

Preliminary Remarks

The purpose/methodology/tools of the Miskatonic Alchemical Expeditions are difficult for me to put into words. The expedition is not a dream school in the way I use that word. Our work involves physical plane waking-consciousness magickal endeavors. The expedition is a coordinated anarchistic group endeavor to create an environment in which dreams/phantasies/visions are projected outward within our working group (Circle). We assist individuals to reify their internal Universes within waking consciousness with intentionality & responsibility.

I sometimes feel that the word Initiation is a bit mis-used/overused, but I feel that it does indeed apply to aspects of our work. In my experience (corroborated by K. Grant), initiation cannot be guaranteed thru any rite. Initiation is a connection which jumps starts an individual into an exalted state of consciousness. Initiation is rather elusive, & sometimes appears to be transient. I have found that initiation works most powerfully when the initiatory link is clearly made in both directions— i.e., when the initiator & aspirant keep playing leapfrog with one another—so that both experience a powerful initiation, and each is very clearly aware of (& acknowledged for) h-is/er role as initiator.

I suspect that one-way initiations accrue karma, which neutralizes or masks the long-term effects of traditional top-down initiations—at least until the initiator dies (or leaves office), or the initiate severs connection with the initiating Order to formulate h-is/er own internal initiatory links). Perhaps commercial initiators (such as those in various New Age Spiritual Psychology Movements) charge steep fees for their services as a way of absolving the inhibitory karmic link in the here-&-now.

As I say, we do not claim to guarantee initiation. We provide a setting, a set of tools, and a community, by which we assist one-another (and selected outsiders) to activate our self-chosen and ever-evolving phantasy reality during daily waking consciousness—i.e., in our "ordinary" lives, not just during our rather intense rituals. Attempting to comprehend our work intellectually can be very misleading, especially if mental gymnastics are not grounded in actual day-to-day experience of our work. As I attempt to convey the flavor & intensity of our work, I sometimes get the feeling I am attempting a task of the magnitude of conveying an experience of chocolate mousse to someone who has lived h- is/er entire life on a diet of un-seasoned white rice, stale bottled water, & vitamin pills.

Set-&-Setting

The setting for our rites is (ideally) primitive & isolated—where the niceties of civilization (morals, clothing, social taboo, etc) can be consciously put-aside by each expedition member individually, each in the manner/degree which is in accord with each individual's True Will. During our all-night Circles, some people revert to a pre-human or a non-terrestrial state, while others retain their human persona as they channel information from alien races (or gods, angels, demons, etc). Some—who become uninhibited, sexually aroused, and who have located (one or several) suitable partner(s)—make love in total abandon; while still others commune within the sexual energy field in non-physical ways, &/or talk with trees or crystals. For this type of Working, the setting must be isolated so no one feels the need to stifle or edit any energies which come pouring thru. [As I said, all this doesn't make much practical sense unless you've experienced it firsthand!]

On some occasions, some (or all) of us create-&-perform group Dramatic ritual to coordinate the mindset of the group at the on-set of our free- form all-night Shamanic Circle. Whether or not we stage a formal ritual, we encourage each person in Circle to do whatever personal ritual(s) &/or energy balancing s/he feels would assist h-im/er in manifesting h-is/er inner self. We then communicate various entheogenic sacraments to assist us (individually & as a group) in manifesting trans-rational consciousness.

Entheogenic Elixir

[addendum made in 1994: Of the various entheogenic elixirs which we experimented with from 1980-88, the basic recipe we found most efficacious was composed of a concentrated infusion of Psilocybe cubensis stems-&-pieces (prepared after the manner of Soxlet) in cool 190 proof grain alcohol. This elixir was then concentrated by distillation of excess alcohol until insoluble waxy residues began to accumulate in the bottom of the flask. The slurry was filtered while hot and the filter paper then washed with hot ethanol to resolve any active constituents trapped in the residue. The filtrate and the ethanol washings were combined, then diluted approximately 50/50 with Chambord raspberry liquor, then stored in a home freezer till a few hours prior to use. {Preparation time: approximately 1 week @24 hours/day.} At an appropriate moment during the all-night ritual (as the cone of power was being raised) the elixir was diluted approximately 50/50 w/Coca Cola. The sugar, caffeine, and alcohol included in this process were all found to be sympathetic adjuncts to the active entheogen, psilocybin. The estimated dose of psilocybin was approximately 75-300 mgs per serving. Although traditional ethnopharmacologists claim 50 mg. to be the maximum useful dose of psilocybin, I have found that doses far in excess of this to be efficacious given an appropriate Set-&-Setting. During our expeditions, some persons regularly consumed 3 or 4 servings over a 4-8 hr period. When available, an additional drop or 2 (1000-2000 mcgs) of liquid LSD per person would be added to the cup as well. At a few other times cannabis infusions in ethanol were added to this basic recipe, but massive amounts of THC made the elixir too lethargic and had a tendency to give some folks a bad case of the spins every time they turned their head. Human kalas (consecrated sexual fluids) were often added to the cup just prior to consumption. Rescue Remedy, a homeopathic stress reliever obtainable thru Heath Food stores was found useful in helping quiet the jitters of too rapid a "take-off".]

Sacramental Guidelines

We have found that certain guidelines (which we are constantly up-dating) are useful for sacrament consumption. From my perspective, I find the following to be quite useful:

a). Some form of ritual in which a common sacrament is consecrated jointly, then communicated. Usually, we use a cup ritual—both for its esoteric symbolism & so that we can truly share in the same sacrament. The elixir we normally use is always brewed with unknown potency, so that it becomes virtually impossible for the rational self to meter the dose. I find that the rational mind (my own, & most other folks as well) is often fearful of the transition to trans-rationality via the un-rational.

Once the leap has been made, the rational mind has a lot of fun integrating/assimilating trans-rational reality, but the first approach can be real scary sometimes. Perhaps we detect subliminal astral presences, such as the Hounds of Tindalos or the mad flute players, which then induce panic in the most intrepid of explorers!

b). In conjunction with the cup ritual, each explorer is asked to state why s/he is in attendance. Flippant, shallow, or incomprehensible answers are clarified thru further interactions. If clarification does not prove to be feasible, that person is asked to leave the circle. In formal Circles at major Festivals involving strangers, we also collect money for sacrament at this time, while ascertaining that each individual has met all of the pre-requisite criteria (e.g.: having personally cut-&-hauled their weight in firewood to the ritual site, being willing to remain in Circle till the morning sun is visible in the dawn sky, vowing to handle any bad-trips responsibly—i.e., without projecting them outward into the group at large, etc.

c). The texture, contrast, & clarity of the Working is greatly increased if in addition to the commonly-shared sacrament some explorers communicates individual sacrament as well -- each in accord with h-is/er own Will. I call this interaction of individual alchemical energies the Orchestra Effect. Each individual sacrament provides an attunement to a unique perspective on the Multiverse, while our shared sacrament ties-us- all-together. Practically speaking, each individual gains access to simultaneous experience of many unique perspectives, usually (but not always) while maintaining h-is/er unique individuality. Some sacraments (such as Euphoria) promote mentation, while others (such as 2CB) encourage emotive feeling. Telepathy (both on a rational level & via the sensorium of the hind-brain) is common in our Circles. Once, one of our explorers seemingly stumbled thru solid matter. On another occasion several of us witnessed another explorer handle hot coals without being burned. During a very early expedition, a water glass began to over-flow like a fountain, while the glass remained full to the brim. At one of our 1985 expeditions, we experienced a tornado and thunderstorm inside a tent, with winds was so fierce that I was unable to fall-over no matter how hard I tried, while a camera 20 feet away remained dry & was not blown from its flimsy tripod. As I keep mentioning, The work of our Miskatonic Alchemical Expedition is not easy to talk-about in a purely rational context!

d). Internal balance is crucial for this work.; The philosophical framework of Thelema (discovering one's Will & DOING it.) coupled with the EST technique of being "At-Cause" in one's Universe can induce an aspirant towards creating an approximation of a karma-free state—i.e., no hidden strings jerking h-im/er around). I sometimes remind myself—as well as all others within hearing if I am being extrovert at the time—that if I am at-cause in my Universe and Doing my Will, then there can be no un-willing Victims in my Universe, all Persecutors act in a conscious manner, and I have no need for Rescuers. On a micro-cosmic level, we council nutritional awareness & personal transformative alchemy. All-night rituals can prove taxing to those who live their lives by external clock cycles. Sleep deprivation, vitamin depletion & depressed blood sugar levels can bring all sorts of un-resolved issues out in the open and into manifestation, especially when energy levels are all cranked-up by powerful ritual, sexual prana, and entheogenic stimulation. While I feel it is essential to dump &/or transform toxins and to play-out all un-resolved conflicts, I encourage expedition members (this includes me, too!) to do their homework—all-night vigils, eating what they consider to be a nutritious diet, fasting & an on-going regimen of personal introspection/meditation/ritual work—before engaging in powerful transformative group workings. To promote balance at our Circles, we encourage one-another to take vitamin/mineral supplements. Lately, we have begun to have some sort of pot-luck meal (melons, Bar-B-Q on the ritual bonfire, fresh bread, etc.) during the wee hours of the morning, when our human biosystems can sometimes be starving for some food prana (but we are often too busy to notice!).

Conscious & deliberate use of sex, entheogenic sacrament & ritual within a supportive setting all assist the rational mind to gently step aside, while opening-up the Third Eye & Crown Chakra. The elixir mentioned supra—inspired by Doctor Laban Shrewsury's hermetic mead—is most efficacious in facilitating this state, especially when used in conjunction with other alchemical compounds which open the Heart, enhance Sexual Creativity, or activate &/or stimulate the other chakras.

Samadhi & Dissolution of Duality

When all chakras are open & functioning at their highest levels, there does not seem to me to be any meaningful purpose in attempting to distinguish between humans-&-gods, angels-&-demons, good-&-evil, or reality-&-fiction. Each person becomes intimately connected-to/congruent-with h-is/er personal phantasy reality. A Buddhist may realize that s/he is the Buddha or transcend that state of attainment to become one with the infinite; a Lovecraftian mage may experience sexual union with Cthulhu or discover that s/he is at one with the chaos of Azathoth; a Christian may become the Christ, or may experience Jesus & Lucifer as two facets of the same cosmic gem. A person may identify with h-is/er genetic past, or with some extraterrestrial race. S/He can become a totem power animal, or come to a realization of being a human incarnation of Gaia.

I am not talking about intellectual comprehension here. Intellectual comprehension of the merger of the mundane with the transcendent is not difficult for anyone with a well-developed ego &/or sufficient spiritual pride. [Many students of contemporary Western magick fit into this category.] The rational mind is more than happy to convince itself that it is God. I am not speaking of that kind of realization. I am speaking of full-fledged actualization (samadhi coupled with focus of individual Will) of godhead.

It is also possible to actualize total union with the cosmic ALL/No-Thing, but commenting further on such a state is beyond the scope of this essay.

Real Work of the MAE

I find things get really interesting when someone realizes that even though s/he can indeed choose to be Christ, Buddha, Azathoth, Satan, ET, Gaia, a virus, etc., s/he can also choose to be fully-actualized in-&-of h-im/er-self—i.e., as Jane or Fred, or Stacy. When the ego stops trying to be God, & becomes a god instead, the real work of our Expedition begins in earnest! If/When an explorer becomes aware of h-is/er cosmic nature, and is able to ground h-im/er-self in trans-rational reality, it then becomes feasible for h-im/er to interact with other cosmic beings—neither limited by Space, fixed in sequential Time, nor locked-out of any particular reality framework. Within this cosmic framework, all who work- &-play here jointly create reality.

[Note: It is also quite possible to create total-&-complete Nightmare and propagate terror through-out the Multiverse, or to rend the fabric of Maya completely. I do not recommend this course of action as a group endeavor. Likewise it is possible to tap-into the Cosmic All/No-Thing as a mystic, rather than as a magickian (i.e.,from an ego-less state with no point of Will). That too, I find to be a rather solitary undertaking. I have involved myself with each of these endeavors on various occasions in myriad different lives within infinitudes of alternity. Each is powerful, educational, & (seemingly) necessary to the multiverse (at least as I know it). Hindus call this cycle Brahma/Shiva/

Vishnu (named after gods of Creation/Destruction/Preservation). From my present perspective, I find co-Creation with other cosmic beings to be the most fun challenge in the Multiverse. Destruction is too easy & preservation is not to my temperament. So I have made Chaotic Creation (i.e., Creation with no central god figure to coordinate things) the focus of my lives' work. I co-create pleasant evolutionary realities by working with those on similar paths. Although destruction & preservation are indeed woven into the fabric of my existence (I kill plants-&-animals to eat as well as for my personal convenience; I reprint classical texts to preserve their message for future generations), I leave grand Rites of destruction, and performance of un-changing Ritual to those who enjoy these endeavors! The Miskatonic Alchemical Expedition specializes in evolutionary creativity.]

Depending on:
1. how many persons in Circle are able to manifest as cosmic beings,
2. our ability, Will, & desire(!) to recognize others who are in a similar state, and
3. our ability/Will/desire to assist those who are still in transition, it is sometimes possible to create a very powerful self-balancing mutually gratifying Mythological framework. Within this larger Mythological framework, it is common to have functioning magickal eddy-realities, within which the interfaces of each personal reality dance with one-another.

To phrase it another way—SaSaR (Sex & Sacrament & Ritual) combined with close camaraderie amongst expedition members, & a shared set/setting of Circle-space & expectation, induces the *boundary edges* among people in Circle blur. The slightest thought (whether expressed or stifled) manifests within our collective reality. [As practitioners of Kria Yoga teach: *Thought is Creative!*] This newly actualized creation can be channeled, focused, &/or modified thru acts of Love under Will. As the evening progresses, Reality (i.e.,our collective Maya) takes on a mythic flavor (exactly which mythos depends on how each participant has prepared his/her internal mind-&-emotional set ahead of time and the degree to which s/he is willing &/or able to share (via poetry, ritual, storytelling, lovemaking, conscious touching, chakra stimulation, fire-walking, etc) h-is/er personal Mythos with the rest of us. When our weave of rational/

emotional connections is sufficiently powerful, conventional reality dissolves completely and our jointly-created fantasy takes on mythic proportions. Individual dreams weave together & play themselves out in our waking consciousness, not just in private dreamspace.

Our work might be likened to Psychodrama, but with a focus of reality engineering. Israel Regardie once wrote that magical attainment is independent from psychological balance. Such limited attainment may well have once been the norm when most magickians worked solitary, but (to me) the quest for magickal attainment must include active exploration of psychological edges—the places where insanity and genius are all but indistinguishable—or the magickal endeavor is simply not worth my time & effort. The Miskatonic Alchemical Expedition uses various psychological balancing techniques to make the exploration of edges easier & more productive, but as we learn how to achieve-&-maintain balance, our work escalates, rather than slacking-off. We work Magick (inducing Change in harmony with Will), not just mental health. Our dream enactment is collective, rather than individual, so that our personal quirks balance one-another out—which is one of the main reasons why our expedition contains a varied cross-section of individuals. This provides a clearer/cleaner contact with (& actualization of) energies than is usually possible in a solo working, no matter how advanced an individual adept.

We have no "faculty" in our expedition. We all explore together. Some of us have more experience than others, but we play leap-frog adeptship with one-another so often, that it does not make sense to me to designate a faculty. We do, however, have a core group of intrepid explorers. We have a local core of Thelemic magickians, augmented by individuals & sub-groups from other well-developed magickal powerzones. New members for our expedition seem to manifest as we become ready to handle their energy. For some, one expedition is sufficient for a lifetime. Others drift in-&-out of our Circles as they discover themselves & test-out their point-of-Will. Let me point out once again, that I am at the center of my personal universe. Everything I say is grounded in my own personal perspective—which is to say, with me at the core of the expedition. Yet, from the perspective of some other member of the expedition, I may not even be in the core group at all!

[Note made in 1994: Now that I've given you all sorts of non-hierarchal disclaimers about how I may or may not be in the core group, lets get down to some details! Appended below is the text of another introductory essay I penned which approaches the MAE from another angle, that of an initiatory Order. What follows was once given in secrecy to a select few. I ask you to treat it as you would any other Secret document—in the words of Herman Slater's now defunct Earth Religion News:

Protect the Mysteries, Reveal them Daily!

Practicum

The Miskatonic Alchemical Expedition is field-trip oriented R-&-D community which operates within that sentient web of initiates known on the outer as the Esoteric Order of Dagon (EOD). From my perspective, the Miskatonic Alchemical Expedition operates hand-in-hand (perhaps tentacle-in-hand may be a better euphemism) with the Chthonic-Auranian Branch of the Ordo Templi Orientis (OTO).

It is assumed that each applicant to the Miskatonic Alchemical Expedition of the EOD is a functional Thelemite whose understanding/appreciation of the Mythos is based upon direct personal magickal experience with outr energies, not merely an academic interest in the literary genre of weird fiction or a sociological/psychological interest in those who channel/advocate the Mythos. That is to say, each applicant is expected have an understanding/appreciation of Will, Love, and personal responsibility from a Thelemic perspective, be willing/able to put these precepts into practice in his/her daily life, and be willing/able to function as a Thelemite within magickal community. Each applicant is further expected to submit on-going records of magickal workings, dream diaries, fiction, essays, &/or evocative Art which demonstrates his/her vital connection with the Mythos as a magickian or a mystic. Magick may be defined as causing change in conformity with Will. Mysticism (in this context) may be defined as a passive link with the Mythos which generates syncretistic harmony &/or dissolution into the Mythos itself.

Initiation into (or affiliation with) the Chthonic-Auranian OTO is by no means mandatory for affiliation with the Miskatonic Alchemical Expedition. Members of other branches of the OTO, as well as autonomous Thelemites are welcome within the ranks of the MAE. The EOD does not require acceptance of Liber AL vel Legis as a requirement for membership. The MAE does, however, require that each expedition member accept Thelema and live by an individual ethical code of Will, Love, and Personal Responsibility. Whether you accept the veracity of Crowley's channeled writings is up to you -- concepts are important, not packaging!

I strongly urge all those interested in active participation in the Miskatonic Alchemical Expedition to apply for membership into the EOD. Although it is possible to work with the Miskatonic Alchemical Expedition in the short-run without formal affiliation with the EOD, I do not recommend this course of action for the long-term. I find that formal affiliation is synonymous with commitment. I have found that those who cannot—or will not—commit themselves to an organization are (in general) not dependable. The on-going work of the MAE involves deep serious personal commitment—not only to your own personal Great Work, but to the local & global community in which we work/play/grow/explore (both individually & collectively). Hangers-on often become deadweights.

We are building an ever-growing group gestalt, whose food is a shared information base & an ever-evolving group mythology. Personal Commitment to the group is a first step towards formulating perfect love & perfect trust which is our primary sacrament.

[Note made in 1994: While I still agree in principle with the sentiments expressed in the previous paragraph, there remains the difficulty of locating functional Magickal Orders worthy of one's loyalty and support. Since neither the EOD nor the MAE are presently functioning on the outer, and since (in all probability) the Chthonic-Auranian OTO does not have a functional group in your area, I can make no reasonable recommendations at present. In my personal experience with myriad Magickal Orders, which (for the nonce) shall remain nameless, I have found far more spiritual corruption than true enlightenment, far more power games than fellowship or brotherhood, and far more hiding behind paper initiations to cover ignorance, than open sharing of knowledge or admittance of ignorance—e.g., "I'm truly sorry, but even though you have been experimenting with VIII° carezza for over three months now, I am unable to discuss your work with you because to do so would be inappropriate, for the mysteries you are exploring are 'beyond your grade'. If & when you have earned access to our Sovereign Sanctuary of the Gnosis, I will be more than happy to discuss this topic with you more at length" (Soror 789, circa 1977).

While I still contend that refusal to work within the structure of a magickal Order can indeed be a symptom of egoistic imbalance, working within a corrupt Order is no solution. All I can do at this point is wish you good luck in your search!]

The Focus of Our Work

From my perspective, the work of the Miskatonic Alchemical Expedition is always evolving & does not really fit into neat categories. Chaos does not lend itself to description in a linear essay format. Although I have chosen to speak of the work of the Expedition as though it could be separated into neat little boxes, such categorizations can be misleading. Needless to say, the little boxes I portray are my own.

[I once had a vision of entering the abyss by a rear entrance. All of the various gods, demons, angels, and other sundry beings were lounging about playing poker, skinny-dipping in the great sea, and otherwise enjoying each other's company. Then someone saw me & began shouting over a PA system: "Qliphoth to your shells! God/desses to your Spheres! Everybody get into your boxes!"—In the abyss (as in this world) everything overlaps. Neat boxes exist only in the minds of those who choose to separate their life experience into categories.]

On an individual basis, members of MAE utilize techniques of conscious dreaming, astral projection, & self-induced trance states to explore various realms of dream, nightmare, & vision. As we re-enter normal waking consciousness via the gateway at Daath (which (to me) typifies the energies of Herschel (Uranus)), expedition members focus their dream images into conscious awareness & outward expression via Hod (writing, scientific/magickal technique, etc.) or Netzach (Art, Music, etc.). It is within this realm that exploration reifies personal initiation within the here-&-now.

On a group basis, members of Miskatonic Alchemical Expedition utilize Shamanic (Netzachian) & Ceremonial (Hodian) magickal techniques to focus their individual consciousness & the gestalt of the group itself thru the astral gateway at Yesod and into the worlds of dream, myth, and creativity. These expeditions are undertaken as group endeavors to manipulate/explore the worlds of dream without the need to give-up waking consciousness.

On the Dangers of Over-Specialization

It is my feeling (based on personal observation of my own imbalances & much research over the past two decades) that over-emphasis on individual exploration can lead to introversion & isolation which borders on the pathological. A solitary magickian wakes-up alone. S/He becomes aware of his/her inherent trans-dimensional nature apart from a community of peers. S/He works the Path of the Hermit in order to tap-into his/her initiated self. Adepts of this path progress rapidly to become Masters of the inner planes, but often at the expense of being able to relate to their fellow humans as anything other than tools for their personal trip. For within the initiatory context of vision & dream-space, everything is a projection of the self outward (a diagnostic tool to speed integration of personality) &/or a spirit sent to guide the initiate upon his/her path. It is easy for a hermit to become an exalted adept—yea, even a God. But (all too often) s/he is not able to perceive the initiation of others who work analogous formuli of attainment. Smug superiority over his/her magickal comrades coupled with fear/loathing/disdain of those whom s/he considers to be mundane often limit the degree to which such individuals are able to manifest their true natures in the here-&-now.

Aleister Crowley, Nicola Tesla, Austin Osman Spare, and H.P. Lovecraft all spring to mind as examples of initiates who woke-up alone. Each was a genius. Each had a profound effect on the world I live in. Yet, each was severely imbalanced in his relationships with other people. Tesla was perhaps the most extreme. He could not tolerate being touched. He felt it disturbed his subtle magnetic fields. He once moved a thousand miles from his home simply because someone put his arm on Tesla's shoulder! Of these 4, I feel that Crowley worked most diligently to balance his solitary inner plane Workings with connection to community (being tapped-into non-solitary sex magick probably helped a lot)! But in community, he acted as though he were the most advanced initiate on the planet. Based on the number of people who moved in-&-out of his life, it would seem that he was somewhat difficult to be around for protracted periods of time. He surrounded himself with people whom he used as tools &/or endeavored to re-form into images of himself. I learned a lot from Crowley. But, after many years of being a Hermit, I am now working to balance my exalted Hermetic initiations with group interactions within a community of magickal peers.

On the other hand, I am finding that those who work almost exclusively in community (Wo/Men of Earth) can also grow in an imbalanced manner. As my personal experience with this formula is more limited than my hermetic experience, I can more readily perceive the weaknesses of Wo/Men of Earth than their strengths. The Hermit perceives the Universe as being a tool for his/her personal initiation. Hermits are cosmic children. The Multiverse is their school & playground. Wo/Men of Earth are cosmic parents. Sometimes they get so caught-up in being responsible that they seem to have forgotten how to play.

When Hermits & Wo/Men of Earth clash, it is often over the role of healing/nurturing. The Hermit wants to play games of initiation & create heroic mythologies. The Wo/Man of Earth wants to play parent or healer. There are times/places for games of high initiation, and times/places for games of healing & nurturing. When these two currents work in balance, everything is copacetic and magick flows on all levels. To me, the positive interweaving of the magicks of the Hermit & the Wo/Man of Earth create a space in which the godform of the Lovers can manifest.

Problems arise (from my perspective) when time/space has been set-aside for initiatory game playing, and True initiation occurs. Under such circumstances, the flow of raw magickal power thru an unfolding gestalt can sometimes be mis-perceived as a symptom of a disease process (e.g., a psychotic episode, life-threatening physical ailment, magickal attack, etc), rather than as a positive initiatory experience. A Wo/Man of Earth who is not able to tap-into his/her Hermetic godform has a very strong tendency to intervene in a nurturing/healing way—even when those energies are counter-productive to the Work-at-hand.

From my perspective, a gestalt is a functional magickal organism. Each individual within that gestalt takes on specific function(s). Sometimes a person will breathe as though s/he is hyperventilating, or somebody else will stop breathing, altogether. Neither is dangerous. During one initiatory experience, I stopped breathing for over an hour (timed by a clock) without any serious repercussions other than a splitting headache the following day. While in another gestalt, a very powerful Hermit was working intimately with Fire. A Wo/Man of Earth attempted to intervene—for she felt that the Hermit might hurt herself. The Hermit was self-possessed enough to laugh at the Wo/Man of Earth, then pick up some hot coals to demonstrate that she was able to care for herself—magickal reality was maintained!

But such a high degree of self-possession is rare, even among highly skilled Hermits, when they operate in a group gestalt. Worry trips (no matter how well-meaning) can throw me off-balance. I might have suffocated had I been surrounded by well-meaning nervous nellies who wanted to rush me off to a hospital. The woman who handled fire could have been seriously burned if her certitude faltered at the wrong moment. I have a much easier time manifesting paranormal phenomena in my solitary work. I have become quite used to clocks running backwards, and seeing strange alien beings looking out at me from my bathroom mirror.

[By the way, I was quite cognizant of paranormal manifestations many years before I began my researches with psychoactive sacraments!]

In my opinion, a Wo/Man of Earth who is over-due for an extended magickal retirement is real prone to ground the group's energy whenever s/he feels threatened by feelings/thoughts/phenomena which clash with his/her reality framework. In extreme cases, lack of emphasis on individual personal development seems to manifest as an underdevelopment of an individual's Hadit-Point, making him/her susceptible to major freak-outs during group workings. I perceive freak-outs as being related to feeling a loss of center when each individual Hadit-point merges into the group gestalt.

If a freaked-out person gets sick (allergy attack, faints, etc.) &/or projects his/her dis-ease outward onto an empathic receptor in the group gestalt, the group energy is effectively re-focused from High magick to a medical/psychological emergency, which (it would seem) is more normal to some than the initiatory paranormal universe which I prefer to inhabit. By dampening, stifling, or distracting group energy, the imbalanced Wo/Man of Earth effectively limits/disperses exponential initiatory growth which gestalt consciousness engenders, unless s/he can be brought to balance by other members of the gestalt.

This is where I feel the Lover comes into play. Those who embody the godform of the Lover are able to relate to both the Hermit and the Wo/Man of Earth without losing center, and without becoming judgmental of where the other person is coming from. A Lover is able to relate to each of the wonders/joys/responsibilities/challenges of being a Hermit and of being a Wo/Man of Earth --without losing perspective on that which transcends each separate task. A Lover is a Peacemaker who unites all in Love under Will. Lovers are (from my perspective) a godform which ameliorate the functioning of Hermits within community, and Wo/Men of Earth within paranormal reality.

Matthew Henry once commented that peace is such a precious jewel that he would give anything for it but truth. The godform of a Lover is sometimes attempted by those who do not really understand what is like to be a Hermit or a Wo/Man of Earth. In such an instance, the ersatz Lover may attempt to smooth things out, without really being able to catalyze resolution. Such practices (in my experiences) lead to a fracturing of community. To me, a Lover is functional as a balance-point between Hermits and Wo/Men of Earth only insofar as s/he is able to relate to both via personal experience, not just empathy.

I speak of Hermits, Lovers, and Wo/Men of Earth as though they are separate beings. Such over-specialization (if it really existed) would be ridiculous. I am working on all three grades -- as is everyone I know! The appropriate balance of Hermit, Lover, & Wo/Man of Earth within each of us is a highly delicate & ever-evolving balance, which we explore & fine- tune on an on-going basis. I encourage (& expect) each Expedition member to work/play/explore with those individuals/groups he/she/they may feel are appropriate, using whatever techniques he/she/they deem useful-- There is no law beyond Do what thou wilt!

[Please note: As this essay is being published long after the demise of Math of the ChRySTAL Humm Powerzone during a period of somnolent dormancy of the EOD and the following section, Affiliation with the Miskatonic Alchemickal Expedition, is included solely for the sake of completeness. At present (1994) there is no MAE or EOD to apply to, so no address will be printed. Those involved in a Great Work similar to my own, may contact me as best they are able.]

Affiliation with the Miskatonic Alchemickal Expedition

We cannot initiate anyone into the EOD. We do not feel that initiation of this kind can be conferred from without—it emanates from within as the result of personal exploration & synthesis. Initiation is a personal process of flowering/unfoldment. Initiation is a side-effect of getting in-touch with one's self, and discovering/creating relationships between one's self & the rest of the Multiverse. Although the

EOD does not confer initiation, we are willing (yea, even eager!) to recognize initiates by the fruits of their labors—their magickal/creative output.

If it is your will to seek affiliation with the Miskatonic Alchemical Expedition of the EOD, please send me a personal letter stating your will in this matter. Let me know what you feel you have to offer our group & what you are looking to get from your association with us. Please include your biography (earth-plane as well as magickal), along with any pertinent information about yourself & your personal explorations which you are willing to share at this time. I would really appreciate a recent photo of yourself, along with your birth data (date/time/place). If you are involved (or have past affiliations) with other magickal groups (local/regional/international), please tell me of your experiences with them insofar as you are able without violating any confidentialities or oaths of secrecy.

Acceptance into the Esoteric Order of Dagon requires some form of evidence of your activity in the Great Work. Evidence can include any/all of the following: samples of your dream record, records of Magickal Workings, essays on magickal technique/philosophy, creative magickal fiction &/or Art (or photographs of your Art) which demonstrate your connection with the Mythos. Those who are new to communicating their visions may find it useful to use fiction as a vehicle of expression.

Dream fragments which provide detailed description of rituals, alien entities, bizarre settings, &/or actual text (or artwork) from astral books or manuscripts are particularly useful to other dreamers. But even brief fragments of dreams can sometimes provide a key word or image which another dreamer is seeking. If your artform does not lend itself to written or pictorial evidence, please discuss your work with me. I am sure we can come up with some method for you to demonstrate your activity in the Great Work.

Be sure your letter requesting affiliation with the EOD contains your legal name & mailing address, as well as the magickal name (or motto) by which you choose to be known within the EOD. Your application will be evaluated personally by me, shown to members of my close magickal family, then forwarded (with comments/recommendations), to R'yleh Lodge. What you submit may become a permanent part of the EOD's Library of Dath &/or the library of the Miskatonic Alchemical Expedition. Submitted material will not be returned to you. Please do not submit original manuscripts or artwork, unless you are donating them to our library.

Neither the EOD nor the Miskatonic Alchemical Expedition charges dues or initiation fees. You are expected to pay only for those goods & services which you specifically request. Donations to help pay for postage &/or to support our on-going publishing projects are always welcome. As material flows into the Expedition library, I will make copies available to other Expedition members who request them. Individual expedition members are requested to submit material to me for internal EOD use. We encourage expedition members to submit material directly to the Library of Daath at R'yleh Lodge & to Black Moon Archives. Material submitted to me will not be distributed to the general public unless you tell me it is ok for me to do so.

1994 Postscript

Despite the optimism with which I penned the above essay some seven years ago, Math of the ChRySTAL Humm and the Miskatonic Alchemickal Expedition have both crumbled into dust. What happened? To say it was time for me to "move-on" or to "continue my magickal journey elsewhere" begs the question and answers nothing. To write detachedly of the fall of the interlocking powerzones which I helped create and which in-turn gave me birth, is both beyond my ability, and would serve no purpose other than to allow me to beat my breast and air my grievances. Rather than play Hamlet or King Lear, I choose to eschew the realms of linear reality to speak allegorically of that which I am too enmeshed within to write of—either honestly or compassionately.

Sometime in the mid 1970's, I was becoming more active in the Typhonian OTO. I asked my then superior, Soror Tanith, why it was that Magickal Powerzones came together around a core of dedicated people, generated lots of energy, which in-turn attracted more people to the powerzone—only to have the whole thing eventually collapse in on itself, never to be heard from again? Tanith answered that she felt that a powerzone was, by its very nature, impermanent. Her answer was too pat and far from satisfying, but by its very nature, her answer created an itch in me (much like a bit of grit in an oyster) to explore this question further.

From my present (1994) perspective, it seems to me that power-zones are willfully created transient magickal engines—which are also unconsciously engendered immortal inter-dimensional organisms—which attract ingenious and imaginative magickal beings to itself, who then drive themselves into a frenzy of taboo-breaking cross-fertilization in an effort to find &/or create mutual understanding and give birth to a new world—in which they give birth to one-another and themselves. Inadvertently, these Bornless Ones also create spores of mutant magickal memes—initiatory multi-dimensional tinker-toy mandalas which catalyze transubstantiation of human and trans-human consciousness in all who play with them. When the spores reach maturation, some cataclysm (egoistic dissonance, financial strife, external persecution, etc.) breaks-up the harmony of the incubating powerzone womb & the (now defunct) powerzone spreads its initiatory spores into the void to co-mingle & cross-fertilize with other spores from myriad defunct &/or living Powerzones, Magickal Orders, Occult Philosophies, etc. to continuously spawn new magickal engines and organisms wherever the confluence of forces find favorable alignments of Stars.

Thus, when the cycle of eons has ended, and the Phoenix returns in weariness to Heliopolis for its self-appointed immolation, it is not the end, but a new beginning. For out of the ashes of the dying Phoenix arise dust motes which swirl and congregate under the influence of a billion whirling galaxies to coalesce—giving birth to myriad new phoenixes, strong in the vigor of their youth, shrieking orgiastically as they fly thru the worlds of (wo)men and their gods exploring conquering & remaking maya into their own images—as godlings are wont to do!

Anyone up for some interdimensional perichoresis?

by Bill Siebert, now known as Alobar Greywalker.

A Brief Mythological Foray into the World of ASht Ch0zar SSaratu '.' 1103

ASht Ch0zar SSaratu (otherwise known as Bill Siebert) is a co-founder of *Math of the ChRySTAL HUHM*, a Shamanic/Alchemical Thelemic Power-zone near Ithaca, NY. He is one of the 3 founding Sovereigns of the *Chthonic OTO*, a branch of the *Ordo Templi Orientis* dedicated to exploration-&-union of the Dark/Light Mysteries of all Æonic formula. Bill has recently become a regional coordinator of the *Esoteric Order of Dagon*, a Lovecraftian Mystery School descended from the Sirius mystery cults of (Egypt Babylon & Sumeria, by way of Gateways within creative individuals who are capable of *dreaming the mythos* & making it accessible even to those who do not believe their dreams to be real.

This paper (which was extracted from Bill's diaries) is designed to acquaint prospective expedition members with a few aspects of Bill's inner Universe as it pertains to practical application of the Lovecraftian mythos within the *Miskatonic Alchemical Expedition* of *the Esoteric Order of Dagon*,

AShT-Ch0zar-SSaratu `.` 1103

AShT (pronounced Ash Tet) = 310= That, form of *Lust Fire* which is the triune analog of the 210 formula (2=1=0). 310 is the formula for dissolving 3 autonomous consciousnesses into the void (whereas 210 deals with dyadic tantric union).

AShT is also a condensation of Ashtaroth (AShThRVTh), the 29th Goetic Spirit cataloged by Solomon in the *Lemegeton*. Most *Medieval* writers viewed Astaroth from within their own (very narrow) moral code & social structure, so they could not help but perceive him as evil & machiavellian.

I perceive Astaroth from my own peculiar perspective. My view is no less prejudiced than the medieval writers, but it does build on the traditional mythos in rather interesting ways. I see Astaroth as existing outside the flow of linear Time-flow. I see Astaroth as being a very *yang* energy-fragment of a higher-dimensional energy-balanced entity. Therefore, I use the pronoun *he* when speaking of Astaroth. His traditional duties include administration of those astral gateways which operate within the Eastern half of North America. According to many medieval sources, Astaroth is noted for his extremely bad breath. *Breath of* awe may be a better translation for what they are attempting to communicate. Astaroth receives his nourishment (on the earthly plane) almost exclusively by way of female sexual fluids. During the middle ages, *Cunt-breath* was virtually unknown—due, in part, to a civilization (I use the term very loosely) which was noted for its absence of consciousness regarding both personal bathing & female sexual pleasure.

Astaroth may be thought of as being personified in the mythological macrocosm as that aspect of Venus which is the companion of the Midnite Sun. Astaroth accompanies Keph-Ra thru the mythological underworld—which makes him good to have as a traveling companion for all those who are on Chthonic journeys.

- Astarte is Venus as Evening Star—a guide for lovers on their way to tryst.
- Lucifer is Venus as Morning Star—the herald of the Sun & the bringer-forth of day.
- Azazel is Venus as the companion of the Sun at noon. Azazel is mythologically connected with the invention of makeup—it takes a lot for Venus to be noticed when travelling in the company of the mid-day Sun!

Azazel/Astaroth/Astarte/Lucifer are (from my perspective) all specialized energy polarizations of the same higher-Order intelligence.

Ch0SAR (Pronounced Cho'zar. Emphasis is on the 1st syllable, which rhymes with Joe. Zar rhymes with bar. (note that it is spelt with a *zero,* not an *oh*) =216. An Atlantean Mage who is noted for his ability to open-&-traverse gateways thru non-linear realities without going mad. [Or perhaps he is mad, but his madness does not seem to be a burden to him or others.] I speak of him in the present tense, for he is a time traveller, who is sometimes in-body with me. Records seem to suggest that when out-of-body he has no need for an external reference point (a local vertical)—i.e., he does not depend on external people/events to mirror his Will back to him for the purpose of navigation. This indicates to me that he feels has no need to function as a Master of the Temple. He also seems to have no need to remain aware of his own local vertical—i.e., while traversing alien dimensions, he is able to undertake whatever role is available, without regard to his personal Will/Path or concerns of karma. Seemingly, while remaining unaware of the flux-lines, he is able to instinctively follow the Path of least resistance while traversing strange dimensions in which his provincial morals/ethics do not seem to apply. Thus, he does not appear to accrue the inertia of karma. From a human perspective, he might be termed a *Lord of the Abyss,* but (the Abyss being what it is) the term *Lord* does not really apply.

Ch0zar seems to be the channel whereby Atlantis opened-up to direct contact with the power of *trans-Eternal Fire,* sometimes called Gira (or Girra-Mass-SSaratu (in its role of Watcher-&-Eternal-Flame)). Gira is an anthropomorphic projection of that continuity of consciousness which remains awake when Brahma dreams the dreamless sleep. That is to say, Gira is an intelligent Life Force which has a continuity of consciousness on either side and thru that reference point which we call *the Big Bang.* Ch0zar is often identified with the upwardly-pointing Fire Trident (as well as the hebrew letter *Shin).*

While in-body in Atlantis, Ch0zar was often accompanied by Chozzar, an offspring of the union of an elder god with a fungus from the stars. Chozzar often wore the form of a male albino pig. Chozzar's numeration (in another system) is thought to have been 100. As Chozzar became intimate with the daughters of Atlantis he came to be identified with intense male virility—a boar orgasms for about 5 minutes as he shoots-forth about a liter of jism. Being from another dimension & of partly fungal origins, Chozzar has many alien insights which he shares with his companions. Many of these deal with medicinal & magickal uses for human excrement.

At a much later time, Ch0zar's legend became blended with SET's, while Chozzar became identified with (or perhaps evolved into) Choronzon. In modern times (the past 3500 years or so), cults of Ch0zar and Chozzar have become inexorably inter-twined (or hopelessly confused, depending on your perspective).

When Ch0zar & Chozzar share the same body, their powers overlap, yet their personalities remain distinct. Ch0zar is known for his love of metallic salts (especially the blue salts of copper, the green salts of iron, nitrates, chlorides, acetates, and organo-metallic compounds of iron, arsenic, or potassium). He is a good story teller. Chozzar is known to surround himself with fungi, and wild creatures. He is a good listener. Both enjoy sex, sugar, sleep, & meat (not necessarily in that order). Each has a unique fascination with the process of putrifaction.

216 is also **Adria,** my first internal contact. She does not seem to fit into any category of being I have ever met or read about. In some respects, she is like Green Tara. In others, like my HGA. Sometimes she seems like a projection of my anima into manifestation beyond the Gates of Reason.

SSaratu (pronounced by mouthing the syllables whilst whistling softly thru the front teeth.) = 577. Ssaratu is a formula of one aspect of *the Watcher,* ie, one who has an apparently external perspective from which to adjudicate/adjust/tamper-with the *game-rules* when different planes of existence interpenetrate. Yet, SSara*tu* makes no pretense of being objective. S/He is very much integral with the multiverse in which s/he operates.

577 is also *the Concealed of the Concealed*, a name which the Hebrew myth cycle attributes to *God Host High*, an analogous formula to SSara*tu*.

AShT-ChOsar-SSaratu= 1103 = (360x3)+23, nascent life in the 4th cycle of creation. A glyph (genetic/memetic information pattern) for *Homo Veritas* manifest thru Chesed. A formula for *the next step,* but only in potentia, at this juncture of Space/Time/Alternity.

The Lemegeton in the Key of HPL

I seem to be working on Suzi's project (so I guess it's mine now, too!) of re-working the mythos of the lesser key, etc. into a form where the demons won't get left behind during the æonic shift to the Lovecraftian mythos.

I see the 4 elemental directions as being keys to my understanding of complex multi-dimensional beings. But the directions themselves are allegorical (or perhaps local truth), rather than actual. In my home, the telephone, the mailbox, and the highway are all located in the East. Therefore it would be reasonable to ascribe the powers of communication & transportation to the East. Yet, if a friend come to me via the back field, I would not banish him. Likewise, with the advent of cordless phones, communication can always be wherever I choose to be. That is to say, it moves from East to center.

So it is with the energy-beings of the 4 directions. I see Astaroth, Astarte, Azazel, & Lucifer (invoking N thu W around the circle) as being terrene extensions of energies which pre-date biological life on this planet. Sort of like the way my local West Danby telephone exchange (564) is a local aspect of a global telephone network—a global network which profits me greatly, but which was not set up by me, or at my request, or even with me specifically in mind.

Astaroth Incarnate in Human Form

I had an interesting image as I awoke today (10 June, '87 ev). But first a little background... In the middle ages it was common to ascribe the authorship of magickal texts to some famous historical personality (Solomon, Cornellius Agrippa, etc.). Kind of reverse plagiarism, very reminiscent of many so-called channelings today. Anyway, a book was printed in the mid 1500's which listed Astaroth as being the *demon-ruler* of the Eastern half of the American continent. However, the manuscript (no longer extant) purports to date from the 12th century—long before the American continent was known to Europeans. If it were known, it most certainly would not have been by that name. This little anachronism has been tick ling my imagination for 2 decades now. Until today, I had no explanation which seemed reasonable. Sloppy impersonation of a fictitious ancient text was just to simple for me to take at face value.

Now the image... I saw the demon (dimensional traveller) Astaroth as reading that book & taking a fancy to the imagery. So he incarnates in human form as Americus Vespucci, the navigator, & oversees the discovery of America, so he can become its demon-lord. Then he goes back to the 12th century and allows himself (arranges, actually) to be summoned by a ceremonial magician. He wears the appropriate demonic form, etc., so as to impress the human that he really is dealing with a demon. Then he tells the mage that he is the demon-ruler of the eastern half of America, a far-off continent to the West. The mage scribbles it all down. He has no idea what the demon Astaroth is talking about, but he is sure to pass the tale on to his apprentices! In modern times, the book is *known* to be a fraud because of its anachronisms, yet, in truth, the text is valid.

Now why would Astaroth go to such lengths? Was it all a matter of subtle humor? Or was there more to his motivations? During my dream, I somehow groked that Astaroth needed (wanted?/willed?/

desired?) to explore America in human-form. I feel that his motives (if such emotions can be a- scribed to a trans-rational multi-dimensional being of this class) were linked to certain gateways which he is said to coordinate. For some reason, he chose to incarnate as Vespucci, but (initially, anyway) not as a full-fledged avatar of alien intelligence. Perhaps, he needed to be fully human to seed (open?/create?) those alien vortices. Or perhaps living in Europe during the inquisition was simply no place for a sensitive enlightened being.

So (for whatever reasons), although Vespucci was indeed an avatar of Astaroth, he was not initially conscious of his extra-dimensional being. But, he had a job to do. He was not content to simply vacation as the human Vespucci. So, Astaroth planted the *seed* for America in a book of black magic which was sure to have been in circulation in manuscript form. He (as Vespucci's trans-dimensional higher self) prodded Americus to stumble across the text as a young man. Young Americus *poo-poo*-ed the text (which was expected/planned-for), but his imagination could not help but be stirred by a far-off continent which bore his name. From then on, it was very easy for Astaroth (Americus's HGA??) to prod Americus into becoming a navigator & explorer.

Exactly what Americus did on his journeys is chronicled in another place. [See: *Biographies of the Old Ones*, by Alhazred & Prirm, a copious, juicy, & scandalous manuscript in the Celaeno Collection at the Library of Leng (lower astral archives).]

But, I shall tell the tale here, in brief. As you probably already know, early explorers were often treated as gods by Amerindian civilizations. Meso-American civilization was sexually libertine, highly structured, & very cruel. In a lot of ways, it was very much like Rome under Caligula. A European *godling* could have whomever/whatever he desired—simply by looking at he/she/it. None would question his motives. None would dare impede him.

Thru today's blend of psychology, magick, and libertine social experiments, we have come to know first-hand how effective fantasy fulfillment is for opening-up gateways within a person—thus, putting him/her into contact with that which has been repressed, ignored, &/or forgotten. For some, the process is terrifying, for others it is enlightening. Americus was from a particularly repressive culture. He had also been at sea for a long time. This combination was especially explosive.

The details of the unlocking of the darker parts of his mind/soul are best left to those who specialize in the bizarre. Suffice to say that Americus came to know that he was not only a horney navigator far from home. He came to know himself as a multi-dimensional being with a purpose far beyond mapping the New World. As Astaroth, he did rule the Eastern half of the New World. As a conscious avatar of They-who-must-remain-Nameless, he was able to lay the groundwork for that task which now lies before us.

He/they forged gateways of energy heretofore unknown on this planet. He acquired seeds of Meso-Amerindian Wisdom from shamans & temple priestesses. Some say he ravaged to obtain these secrets, but I feel otherwise. He was a god. He had no need to take. He could influence dreams & seed nightmares. He could invoke that cooperation by which elder gods have always dealt with the race of man. Once he had awakened, what need *he* of physical violence?

These memes (information seeds) did he meld/fertilize with European lore of that black magic which he had once (as the youth Americus) dismissed. Coupled, they unlocked other secrets, unknown to either culture. Not just knowledge, but living information, long asleep. Some say he was an unconscious agent, but that is a lie. He knowingly & willfully brought forth that which had been dead/dormant/hiding/sleeping/dreaming since before the founding of Atlantis, even since before the formulation of Lemuria.

The Inquisition (which followed close upon his heels) attempted to uproot that *garden* which Americus/Astaroth was cultivating outside the circles of time. But the Inquisition quickly lost sight of extra-dimensional gateways, when they discovered the easy-pickin's of weak Amerindian civilizations which had begun the long slide into debauchery & abuse of power.

Information (in its pure *energy* sense) is alive in & of itself. As it flows & grows, it evolves its consciousness & Will in harmony with its ever-evolving understanding. If information is impeded/stopped, it stagnates/festers and becomes an active agent of putrefaction/corruption.

Secrecy corrupts information & evokes the reification of horrific nightmare. Secrecy seeded the fall of Atlantis. The secret mystery schools of early Christendom seeded and bred the Inquisition from the inner tantric teachings of Jesus. So it was that the Mayans sealed their own doom by creating a highly stratified society which restricted the outward flow of information as their upper class lived vampiricaly off the life blood of its own slave class. Thus the inquisition shed the blood of Mayan priests to fertilize America's newly formed inter-dimensional gateways, making these information channels accessible to those whose sleep is troubled by nightmare.

Attuning Negative Visions of Mad Poets to Creative Evolutionary Goals In Acts of Love Under Hill

Although many of these inter-dimensional/trans-temporal gateways are most easily open to the insane, the mad, & the emotionally disturbed, I do not focus my attention upon their disturbed visions. It is not a matter of right/wrong, but of usefulness. Of what use is a Universe filled with malevolent gods who are out to eat me up? None—unless I am suicidal, or have a need to test my mettle against the meanest sons-'a-bitches in the multiverse!

To me, Azathoth is not a blasphemy, he(?) is simply incomprehensible. He(?) does not seem sane by human standards—but who am I that Azathoth should be judged by my human standards?

Hastur I dare name, for we are on a first name basis with one-another. We met back in the early part of the last decade, thru Ithaqa, the *Walker on the Winds*. Ithaqa (the missing *u* is intentional) manifests palpably in this area, especially in January, & on those summer nights, when it feels as though it may frost. Around here, Hastur gleans information thru the Byakhee's insect avatar, the ubiquitous (& therefore dismissible/invisible) June-bug, & thru conscious relationship with we who work the subtle energies of what is sometimes called *weather magick.*

To me, the Mystery of the sleeping (yet-not-dead) Cthulhu is a key to our race's sexual inner gateway to the wonders of the multiverse. Cthulhu is a sentient energy field which pre-dates biological life. Cthulhu's expression within humanity is tied-to our sexually polarized nervous system. Cthulhu *awakens* within those humans who are able, willing, & interested in using the mechanics of sex & the energy of their own orgasm for opening inter-dimensional gateways, rather than for spawning more humans, simply having fun, or worshiping (merging-with) some nirvanna-besodden *Divine Principal* (or principle).

R'Lyeh is a formula (and a key to the opening) of the suspension-field which we humans placed around our trans-temporal memories of *Cthulhu-consciousness* within our sexually-awakened state. It seems we felt compelled to put aside our *Cthulhu-consciousness,* while we developed war, technology, civilization, and intellectual exploration techniques.

Adrenaline, Endorphins, & Magick

Cthulhu operates thru our endorphin circuit. But endorphin, alone, induces catatonia (nirvanna). Those in nirvanna generate energy which fuels evolution, much the same way grass fuels cows. Neither catatonic gods, nor grass seem to mind being eaten. *But such is not my Path.*

Adrenaline, alone, induces high stress with little personal reward—except for the few who are able to tap-into the god-space of being an adrenaline junkie. In most populations, 10% or so, rise to the position of leaders. They ride the waves of power & become conscious prescient avatars of the megapolistomantic gods of civilization. They are the shepherds/wolves who keep/fleece the sheep. But for even these avatars, life is not rosy. Adrenaline is hard on the body, and even great leaders fall to the frailties of flesh-worked-too-hard. *Such is not my cup of tea, either.*

But within that 10%, is a small, almost invisible group. These are the individuals who could become leaders, but who have consciously chosen to have no followers. It is within this group of *individuals* that I work/play/grow.

When adrenaline & endorphin begin to work together, there is sometimes conflict. Each has a tendency to over-balance the other. Manic/depressive mood swings are common in this evolutionary stage of development. Separation of distinct inner magickal personalities (schizophrenia) becomes rife.

After a time, seemingly harmonious partnerships grow out of this turmoil. Endorphin moderates adrenaline. Adrenaline titillates endorphin. In some ways, this is the most dangerous phase. For each undermines the other in such a subtle way that *the golden mean* is sometimes seen as an end in-&-of itself. Magick (the ability to induce change in accord with Will) diminishes, or becomes less important. Such folk make good genetic stock for future generations of magickians, but they themselves are out- of-touch with what magick can be. For those who see what is happening, & strive to over-come their internal truce, it is often easier to *back-slide* into manic/depressive magick than to advance.

But to those who do advance is a Universe which cannot be but hinted at to those who have not integrated the power *To Go* into their daily lives. *To Know. To Will, To Dare* and *To Keep Silence* are each important to the Great Work. But the power to Go/Move/Change is what separates living evolving Truth from dead stagnant dogma. Those who *Go* are a different class of being from those who sit & vegetate. For me, the interplay of adrenaline/endorphin assist me to keep moving.

Adrenaline reenforces endorphin. Inspiration channeled thru endorphin can often lack punch (substance/excitement), while adrenaline alone often induces nightmare or the megalomania of religious zeal. [I, have no desire to start a crusade in Cthulhu's name!] But when endorphin & adrenaline work together, the other-world contacts are substantial, exciting, and harmonious to the nature of the explorer. Dream becomes reality, for the gateways work both ways!. Not the reality of the paranoid. But the reality of one who retains all individuality, while being a part of a harmonious whole.

R'lyeh has risen for those of us who allow ourselves to feel/experience/know its presence. Others seek its dark mysteries within their dreams & the writings of other dreamers. I have had sufficient glimpses beyond the veil of madness to convince even my rational mind that *that which is not dead can eternal lie, and with passing æons, even death may die.*

If you are a practitioner of Magick whose Will is aligned to Evolutionary Change and the integration of the HPL Mythos with other Magickal Disciplines & Mythological Constructs, I'd love to hear from you. If we make a good connection, perhaps we will one day work/play/explore together. Share with me & I will do likewise with you.

There is no Law beyond Do what thou wilt.

AShT-Ch0zar SSaratu '.' 1103
Bill Siebert
Math of the ChRySTAL Humm

414   The Forbidden Alchemies of Frater Pun

of
the Work

The Phoenix Cycle & The BAJ Material
being a series of Initiatory Dreams & Astral workings
by Frater PVN

Here begins the entry in Frater OTs PTN–690/PVN's Magickal Record for SUNDAY, the 25th Day of MARCH, 1984 e.v., JULIAN DAY No. 2,445,785.29, Moon being 23.30 Days old. [7:00pm]

Do what thou wilt shall be the whole of the Law.

Dreamt long & hard last night. I have been waiting around (mostly puttering) while SAM finished up what he was doing on the computer. I have purposely been refraining from going over much of my dreams, so that I would be able to recall them cleanly for this record.

   I have just eaten another piece of chocolate pie & I can feel my blood coursing with the drugs (sugar, adrenalin, insulin, etc.) which provide my gateway back to the place of my dream workings. It is time to begin the process of re-member-ing & re-integration.

   I am between the worlds. I am out of body, yet also I am both in my bed asleep & also sitting at my computer writing what I experience. I extend my many arms & link myself together, while (on another level) I step outside of myself so that my dream reality can become a separate independent existence with no knowledge of my other selves.

   I am in a world of fog. I part the fog in the sign of the Enterer & step to solid earth. I know where I am. I have traveled this Path many times before. I am on a golden Path which winds its way thru emerald green grasslands. Ahead of me are twin serpents, arched over the road & bearing the seal of the Order. As I approach, they lower the seal to the road. The seal is etched into the surface of a vesica shaped mirror, about 2 meters high. I approach the mirror & breathe upon its surface. I wipe away the steam of my breath & the mirror is a clear blue-black, casting no reflection. I enter the mirror & forget all which has thus far transpired.

I am in the body of a teenage male. I am with my 93 year old uncle Henry (the Masonic Druid) & my cousin Sue, who is a few years younger than I. I am greatly attracted to Sue, but fear to act because of incest taboo {& because of her taste, for she is a smoker). I have a large tome entitled *The Equinox of the Phoenix*, which is the record of a series of IX° & XI° incestuous Workings which Crowley reified with his six year old niece. The book is a huge scrapbook with colored paper & collage talismans pasted to many pages. I can feel the charge dripping off many of the pages. It is difficult to focus on the book without going out of body. I do not comprehend the purpose of the Working or its sequence, although I am quite certain that the sequence is neither linear nor sequential. The book was acquired by me at a used bookshop for only a few dollars. In order to view the text (without falling into it), I send the book away to be photocopied. I reason that a copy of the text will retain linear information of the words & sigils, but without quite so many open gateways. My uncle agrees with me & assists me to pay for the xeroxes ($151).
[in body I am sleeping next to 0-Maku which explains the unreal quality of the sexual longing which I feel for my cousin during this dream sequence.]

When the xeroxes are delivered, I am ecstatic, my uncle is observing me in an inscrutable manner & my cousin feigns dis-interest, but is intrigued in spite of herself. The book contains a pantacle of the 4 elements which is a three-panel (2 sided) folder of various swatches of brightly colored cloth. It is folded so that the two external sides are blank grey & the 4 elemental panels are enclosed therein. Photocollages & geometric pantacles are pasted on each elemental panel. The pantacle is arranged so that Fire, Earth, & Water are on 1 side of the sheet & Air is on the other side (with the 2 'external' patterns). As I look at it, I fall into it & it is transformed into a central square panel with 4 triangular wings (opened-up view various swatches of brightly colored cloth. It is folded so that the two external sides are blank grey & the 4 elemental panels are enclosed therein. Photocollages pattern formed by the diagonals of the Tablet). Between the Kerubic sigils & the Tablet of Union is a wheel composed of the *Linea Spiritus Sancti* from each of the 24 Elemental Watchtowers.

The 4 triangular wings move outward along spokes of energy which embody the symbols & energies of each of the 4 the Common signs. Each spoke contains the 3 sub-elemental tablets of each Watchtower as well as symbols attuned to each Common Sign. The core of each spoke is the appropriate *Lineus Deus Filique*.

Each triangular wing embodies one of the elemental quadruplicities of the Cardinal Constellations. The major sub-elemental tablet is likewise herein empowered. The outward edge of each triangle is composed of the appropriate *Lineus Deus Patris*.

The symbol folds in on itself & forms a sphere surmounted by a tiny cross of the elements. Radiating across the sphere are 3 great circles at mutual right angles, dividing the sphere into 8 equal segments, one for each of the 8 Hearths from the system delineated in *Liber NOS*.

I am back in my astral body looking at the folded piece of colored paper. Its energy is now gone. It ceases to glow. The charge is now within me.

I look thru the xerox of the book for more clues as to its use & purpose. I then become aware that the original was not returned with the xerox copy. I become very distraught for I know that most of the book's information is contained within the fabric of the book's charge rather than its linear text. My cousin Sue becomes interested & suggests we re-charge the xerox, but I am too distraught to take her offer seriously. My uncle chuckles to himself in lecherous fashion. He now looks very much like the photo of Crowley at Hastings.

I center myself & call forth the globe of the elements from my astral storehouse. I invoke the Godform of each of the 8 hearths in the sequence Father, Mother, Sister, Brother, Husband, Wife, Son, Daughter, & draw their mantle over me, each in turn—with no banishings between. The cross of the elements detaches from the apex & the globe opens into the Watchtower/Zodiacal Wheel as above. I stand at center & invoke my Nativity.

I am at the moment of my birth. I am being held aloft, with umbilical cord still attaching me to my mother (whom I can see behind me). The rising sun in Taurus is behind my head like a nimbus, while the full moon in Scorpio is before me on the Western horizon. To my right hand is the Body of Nuit in the North arched over the Water Carrier, while The Heart of the lion emanates from my left hand in the South. A crystal sphere divides the microcosm of the delivery room from the macrocosm which has spawned me. The planets sing the music of the spheres as they announce my birth to they who watch. I look behind me to Orion & see the womb of my celestial birth & Sothis who did formulate the substance of my earthly father. I draw in my first breath & the scene dissolves in 83 waves of Celestial dew.

I am back in the body of my uncle. He is dressed in priestly robes of golden thread. He holds a blue & gold Phoenix Wand in his right hand & a scarlet ankh in his left—both extended in blessing over me. I am a babe of blue, hovering in the air on a shard of the akashic egg. I extend my arms in LUX and my uncle places the Phoenix Wand across my lap and hangs the ankh on a chain about my neck. He offers me an open coffer of gold. As I accept his gift, our hands touch & our consciousnesses merge.

I am alone & naked. I wear no ornaments & carry no badges of office. I wear the body of an adult male. I am in a dark hall facing a large purple-black mirror which fills the South Wall. I touch the mirror with my forehead & I merge—feeling my consciousness flow out across the surface of the minor, then melting into its depths.

I am now back at the computer keyboard. The vision is (for now) in abeyance, although certainly not closed to me. I will write more later.

Love is the law, love under will.

Here begins the entry in Frater OTz PTN–690/PVN's Magickal Record for TUESDAY, the 27th Day of MARCH, 1984 e.v.,
JULIAN DAY No. 2,445,788.77, Moon being 24.78 Days old. [6:30am]

Do what thou wilt shall be the whole of the Law.

More dreams last night (i.e. Sunday night, for I have not yet been to sleep on Monday night). At the moment, they are fragmentary, but I will see if I can recollect them. I center. I project to my last sleep. I create the appropriate linkages. It is done.

I know not who I am nor where I am. I am a caucasian male, about 40, with flowing grey hair & beard, and a paunch from protracted inactivity. I am naked & alone. I am in confrontation with powerful authority figures who challenges my right to exist. A spotlight of lurid yellow light (like that from a Sodium vapor lamp, only more inimical to my essence) is shining on me from above. All else is in darkness. There is a smell of char (like scorched chocolate) hanging in the air. There is an unseen gallery of watchers, who sit in expectant silence.

All of my weaknesses & unfinished projects are brought up as evidence against me. I acknowledge the facts, but refuse to give them import in the matter at hand. I step forward in an effort to get out of the glare of the spotlight. The light follows me. I am annoyed. I begin to walk away from the proceedings.

I am challenged by a guard whom I cannot see (I am still in the spotlight, while all else is in inky darkness). I extend my right hand out of the circle of light & demand my scepter.

Unseen hands begrudgingly place a Set-Wand into my grasp. The wand is made of a square rod of red wrought iron, twisted to form a spiral with a closed circular loop at its base. The head is stainless steel, machined with smooth curves like a fine surgical tool. The head is an abstract sculpture of a Set beast. The whole wand is about my height & quite heavy. I have no knowledge of having ever seen it before. I accept the wand & hold my left hand into the shadows.

I hear muffled cries shouts & indignation. Nothing is placed into my left hand. I raise the Set Wand high & stamp the circular butt onto the smooth cold floor. Sparks fly. Huge chunks of granite chip from the floor and scatter into the shadows. The smell of brimstone fills my nostrils. The shaft of the wand grows hot. Echoes of wars long dead fill my ears, as old soldiers stir in their tombs. I raise the want for a second time, but before I can summon the support for a second strike, a large gold ankh (which is iridescent blue in color) is hastily placed in my left hand.

Holding the ankh by its loop I point it at my challenger & summon the power to go. I step toward as the yellow spotlight blinks out, leaving me in total darkness, save the purple glow of my ankh.

I am in my Uncle Henry's basement den. I am seated crosslegged in the triangle of Art, staring into a concave mirror, elliptical in shape with one of the foci before each eye. A virtual image of my 2 retinas is projected outward onto the surface of the mirror, greatly enlarged. I am fascinated by watching the red blood cells stream before me like a caricature of a traffic jam. I look up at the smell of fresh flowers.

My cousin Sue is kneeling before me, placing a wreath of orchids in my hair. She is 13, & I am 15. We are both naked, save for the ornaments of our rank & office. I close my eyes & we kiss & in this reality, she has never taken up the tobacco habit, so I am free to kiss her without danger of deranging my alignments]. She ends our prolonged kiss as she gently pushes me back to the floor & mounts my erect phallus.

As I lay on my back, I open my eyes & see our uncle Henry sitting in dragon asana within the circle of the Magus. His knees are scant inches behind my head. His lotus wand is planted before him like the rod of Jesse in full bloom, just brushing the crown of my skull. As I extend my arms, the 3 of us join 5 hands on his 13 banded lotus wand. My hands encircle the bands of Scorpio & Taurus, while Sue instinctively reaches for Leo & Aquarius. Uncle Henry holds the Wand lightly at the band of Arachnae between index & middle fingers of his left hand, while his right hand is extended just above the lotus in blessing over his incestuous charges.

Sue comes & as I drink her essence with the head of my phallus, I am projected from that place back to the halls of judgement.

I am no longer naked. I wear the multi-colored dream cloak of Joseph—the gift from my Mother's lineage. I stand erect, holding the Phoenix Wand in my right hand & my red-gold ankh in my left. My cousin Sue stands naked in front of me (slightly to my left) with drawn sword in her right hand & the Set Wand in her left. Her body is covered with delicate ink drawings in scarlet & royal purple. My uncle Henry stands behind me (slightly to my right), clad in his white leather mason's apron. He bears a trowel & dividers in his left hand & the Lotus Wand in his right.

A double cube altar appears before us, but it is far too large. We walk to the altar & form an open arc around it. We reach upward to touch its top with the tips of our Wands. We grow to match the proportions of the altar. Across the altar sits a row of silent watchers, most seemingly of the race of Lam. Between us & the watchers stands they who would test our right to manifest our Will. They are the meanest sons-a-bitches in the valley, & they have no intention of sharing with newcomers.

An old woman steps forward. She is ugly as poverty & as deformed as morality. She exudes the odor of cheese, tobacco, & and a dried-up cunt. She traces a sign in the air & its afterimage flickers like the glow of lighting bugs which have been squished on a plate of excrement smeared glass.

The top of our altar is slightly concave. Sue hops up on the altar & pisses into the bowl of the altar. Uncle Henry traces the old woman's sigil (aversly) on the surface of Sue's elixir. The image of the sigil is like a green flame traced in a pool of blood. As I bend over for a closer look, the perfume of Sue's virginal kalas overcomes me & I swoon forward & fall through the Gateway.

[Here ends my dream recollections for last night. It is past dawn & is now time for me to get to bed so that I can continue my dreams. It is difficult to keep lust of result from impinging upon these dreams, so I will make no comments at the present time.]

Love is the law, love under will.

Here begins the entry in Frater OTz PTN–690/PVN's Magickal Record for WEDNESDAY, the 28th Day of MARCH, 1984 e.v., JULIAN DAY No. 2,445,788.13, Moon being 26.14 Days old. [3:05pm]

Do what thou wilt shall be the whole of the Law.

I still feel somewhat strained, hut I am now able to continue this diary entry. Although the dream/vision overlaps itself in bizarre ways, little substantial detail has altered in the portions of the tale already recounted. I will begin this entry with a re-telling of the end of the last recorded sequence above, then launch into a continuation of the tale.

A double cube altar appears before us, but it is far too large. We walk to the altar & form an open arc around it. We reach upward to touch its top with the tips of our Wands. We grow to match the proportions of the altar. Across the altar sits a row of silent watchers, some seemingly of the race of Lam, others of the appearance of the Great Old Ones & the Elder Gods. Most are seen indistinctly & are (at this time) unrecognizable. Between us & the watchers stands they who would test our right to manifest our Will. They wear the masks of the meanest sons-a-bitches in the valley, & (as such) they have no intention of being benevolent towards our triune.

An old woman (or is it a man?) steps forward. S/He is ugly as poverty & as deformed as morality. S/He exudes the pungent odor of moldy liquefying cheese, the bitter odor of stale ashtrays, the cloyingly sweet odor of gangrenous flesh, & and the malignant astral odor of sexuality which has been mis-used, abused, & abandoned. S/He traces a sign in the air & its afterimage flickers like the glow of lighting bugs which have been squished on a dirty pane of excrement smeared glass.

The top of our altar is slightly concave. Sue hops up on the altar & pisses into the bowl of the altar. Uncle Henry traces the old woman's sigil (aversely) on the surface of Sue's golden dew. Colors flash, shift & flash again. The image of the sigil traced in urine is like a green flame traced in a pool of blood. As I bend over for a closer look, the perfume of Sue's virginal kalas overcomes me & I swoon forward & fall through the Gateway.

I remember naught of anything before now. I know not who I am or where I am. I know that I am not from here. I know enough to observe without fretting about my 'lost' past. I know enough to bluff, rather than reveal my ignorance to those who are hostile to me. Paranoia is a useful tool when used in moderation.

I am walking down the street of a large city (from my vantage point of the scribe, I shall call it New York). A group of hell's angels are terrorizing a neighborhood, beating random persons with chains & taking all women into a large building (apartment house or factory, I am unsure which). I somehow know that the women will be raped, tortured, & defiled until they are dead. I hear the voice of my mother inside of me telling me to intervene to stop this blasphemy against godhood, but I know that my death will do little to alter the little 'play' which these folks have chosen to act out (& I have no desire to begin an incarnation in this environment!).

I walk to another neighborhood & enter a cocktail lounge. I order a blackberry brandy with flat coke over ice & sit in the corner playing with myself. At some point I notice that the bar is predominantly filled with young women & they are all staring at me. One woman stands up & begins to berate me for masturbating rather than making love with one of them. I begin to apologize, saying that I don't usually approach strangers for sex out of a fear of rejection. The woman blurts out that all of them are so horney that they wouldn't even mind being raped.

A hush falls over the room as my mental images of the previous street scene are superimposed over this reality like a mutually shared nightmare which springs unbidden from the dark recesses of consciousness. Much nervous laughter & fearful glances as the women wait to see what I choose to do.

I stand up & walk toward them as I sing a song of my pilgrimage to I know not where. I thank them for their offer of sexual contact & I tell them how I wish to assist them, but that I must be cautious as the alignment of my quest demands that I abstain from sex with all smokers and that I never demand that which is not offered freely & with conscious acceptance of personal responsibility. This latest elicits a shocked gasp from the bar room crowd as most of them fade back into the woodwork & become as paintings upon the wall. One woman steps forward & kisses me with the sweet saliva of an initiate of the blue & gold. My consciousness fades.

I awaken in a very large suite of rooms in a huge mansion. I wander around from small office to large kitchen to 3 bedrooms, to a curious amphitheater-like room. It is a square room about 30 feet per side, with a 6' wide balcony around its perimeter. No doors exit off the balcony, which is strewn with cushions. A metal spiral staircase connects the main room with the balcony. A wide flight of steps connects this room to the common areas of the house. I feel like this is my house & that I am getting ready to open it up for a grand 'event' of some sort. My memory is still almost non-existent, but I sense that I am here as far more than simple observer.

The sweet mouthed woman from the bar comes in & we begin to make love in the center of the floor as the balcony & main room fills up with 'honored guests' who are dressed in togas & brightly colored cloaks.

When all the guests have arrived, we end our lovemaking (both of us are charged, neither of us has orgasmed). I go to the balcony. One side is devoid of people & cushions. It is cordoned off with gold rope. The wall is a projection screen of some sort & the pre-dawn eastern horizon is being 'shown' on the wall.

I somehow know that this 'place' is an overlay of a somewhat decedent Manhattan onto the Phoenix Festival at Heliopolis. Those around me are they who have come here by right of privilege. All are looking at the screen as dawn approaches.

Next to me is a huge fat man who is compelling one of the slavegirls to give him a blowjob. She begs him to turn slightly so that she can view the screen while she services him. He scoffs at her & sits facing the screen so that she will have to face directly away from the screen in order to service him.

I intervene gently & remind him that he (as an immortal) has seen this particular event so often that he has become jaded to its beauty, while the slave (being unaware of life beyond the here-&-now> has but one opportunity to see the Phoenix return to the fire of the Sun for regeneration/re-birth. He turns livid as he instructs me to mind my own business. He tells me that it is his Will to deprive this slave of all joy & all hope of advancement. He smirks at me in self-satisfaction as he forces the girl down on him so hard that she gags.

My composure is near the breaking point, but I act calmly rather than reacting blindly in wrath. I focus my attention on the girl & tell her that she can remain where she is, or can accept my protection & come with me. I get up & leave the balcony by a door hidden behind one of the tapestries. The girl follows me, while the fatman screams curses at us both. The girl walks silently beside me as we leave the house. I see from the outside that it is the same building that the hell's angel gang had been using in the earlier sequence of the vision. I smile to myself, for I now have some ideas how the gang can be routed & the whole pattern broken.

We go to a fire escape on the side of the building & begin to climb to the roof. About halfway up we are challenged by a scruffy young boy with a stiletto. (I am now old, with flowing robes, hair, & beard (all grey), whereas a few moment s ago I was in my early twenties.] I hold up my hand under the sharp blade & part my palm in the sign of blessing. I raise my hand. The youth must either sever the webbing between my fingers with his knife, or move his blade to receive my blessing. He puts away his knife, receives my blessing, & bids us pass. I ask him to join us, for the hour is late & the Phoenix is about to return. He tells me that he must miss the festival, for his leader has placed him here as a guard as punishment for questioning authority.

I offer him my protection if he accepts my invitation. The three of us go to the roof where a motley crew has assembled to watch the return of the Phoenix. The band is composed of bag ladies & pimps, hookers & cops, politicians & preachers, and gangs of discontented youth ranging from street punks to VISTA volunteers. A young biker accosts us & threatens the young guard with public castration if he does not get back to his post. I manifest both the Phoenix Wand & the Set Wand & tell the gangleader that both my companions have accepted my protection. He backs down without a quibble.

The Sun blots out the last star. All eyes are focused on the East. The young gangleader jumps up & is about to cast a smokebomb into the 'viewport' which transmits the image to the party of decadent Magi below, when I halt all time-flow. I inform the young man that if he upsets the 'show' for the Magi, they will be so aggravated that they will cause their servants to hunt down & slay everyone in the city regardless of alibi. The young gangleader stated that it was his Will to disrupt the convocation below, no matter what the cost & that I could not stop him.

I affirmed that it was not my Will to stop him, but that I would compel I him to incarnate again & again in this nexus of Time/Space as each of those who would be tortured, maimed, or killed because of his actions. He thought about my words briefly, then cast the bomb into the viewport.

Immediately there sprang from the netherworld a host of Demons who sprang upon all who were upon the roof. I flung my arms wide & cast a shell of protection around all save the gangleader. The chief demon saw my actions & asked if I were responsible for what had just transpired. I replied that I had warned the gangleader of consequences, but he had acted on his own.

I stated that my protection was on all present, save the gangleader. The demon picked up the gangleader in a sharply taloned hand & asked if there were any to contest his right to consume the morsel.

The young slavegirl replied that she would end the cycle now if she were but more awake. The demon & I both became interested at her words & bade her continue. She stated that she was tired of incarnating in the same nexus of Space/Time over & over again because of a rash judgement while in that life (pointing at the gangleader). She offered to trade places with the gangleader as an experiment to see if her conscious sacrifice would end the cycle.

The fat mage burst out on the roof & protested loudly, complaining that the "cheap little trollop" would "spoil everything". The demon began to chuckle loudly, for he was quite pleased that the little fat man was about to be unseated.

The demon asked me if my protection still extended to the girl. I replied that it did. The demon then put on a look of mock helplessness & told the fatman that he (the demon) could not consume the gangleader, for the girl had offered to take his place & that he could not possibly tamper with the girl so long as she was under my protection—unless the fatman would offer to protect him (the demon) from my wrath.

page 8 is missing

…rather than being flung into the testing arena with the 3 forms which I have been programmed to identify with. The demon sees me floating on my lotus blossom & begins to laugh once again. He shape-changes into a parody of me, then changes into a fat Buddha statue… made of wood (painted Chinese red) with a Pinocchio nose, perched precariously in a large spiderweb hammock.

I drift to the floor in front of him & return to my normal astral form (caucasian male human with long grey hair & beard, well-rounded body, but with hidden reserves of muscle, stamina, and agility). I greet the demon as "Long of Nose" & ask to have some words with him. He laughs very deeply from his hollow belly. The temple crumbles around us & we are seated on a grassy hillside overlooking the Path which leads to the 2 serpents who personify & guard the Order. On this level of reality, the Path is the yellow-brick road leading to the emerald city & the inner Order is guarded by the Wizard of Oz. The demon has changed back to the form he wore when summoned to expunge the lives of those upon the roof in the previous dream sequence.

His body is built upon the legends of the minotaur, but with many differences: a large bull head with archetypical bull horns; large saucer eyes, gleaming with pale green fire {balefire}; all teeth are very pointy {they look like they have recently been filed; red {oxblood) hair over his entire head, body, arms & legs {scrotum, sheath, & palms are bare—palms are yellow, scrotum & sheath are blue/black); huge broad shoulders & arms {5-fingered taloned fingers); very slim waist & delicate hindlegs {like a goat) ending in cloven hooves. The demon walks upright & sits in full lotus {he plays with his massive ever-erect black penis whenever he is daydreaming or musing philosophical}. I know him well. We have long been friends, although (until this moment) I had no memory of ever having seen him before.

[Note: This paragraph was made at end of this entry to enhance clarity. The following portion of my record is a composite of waking vision, 'new' memories floating to the surface of my conscious mind, & traditional attributes from various books in my library. The process involved was both inspired & surprisingly organic (i.e., natural & free-flowing with no fits-&-starts—it was as though my hand & eye were being guided to the correct page of each book as I sought clarification &/or corroboration). I was using both my resurgent memories & standard references to augment & refine the vision. Testing/refining of the vision was continuous. No attempt was made to undermine or disprove the vision. Rather, the tools of discrimination were used to fine-tune the information I was receiving so that I could receive the maximum of useful information with the minimum of noise (pre-judgements, biases from historic sources, wandering focus of concentration, etc.]

When first I met him, he held the office of a god of generation (in the dual form of Divine Yoni & Phallus) to the Moabites. The Hebrews re-named him & he undertook the part-time task of overseeing the

Qliphoth of Tiphareth for them in exchange for Qabalistic instruction. In his spare time, he wandered the earth masquerading as a human (both male & female, depending on his varying moods) in order to learn more about the human race (& thereby himself) thru experiencing all possible sexual intimacies (which: is quite a task, considering his shape-changing abilities!).

For a while, he became a disciple of Gotamma, the Bhudda & renounced all attachments to the flesh. He received further illumination thru an understanding of the Qabalistic formula of ARARITA while studying at Castile during the Moslem Renaissance & thereby awoke to a state of Godhood. At another time, he became an English gentleman in order to learn the value of personal honor and integrity. Although he remains quite partial to his roots as a simple god of fertility & procreation (hence his outward form & pastimes), his present name is a tribute to his diversified nature.

Belphegor Ararita Jones is a Moabite God of Prolificy, Fecundity, & Herculean sexual prowess; Prince of nether Hell & part-time Regent on the Throne of Qliphothic Tiphareth; Divine disciple of Gotamma, the Bhuddha; Master of Divine Ecstasy & Sexual intoxication; and (above all)—a Gentleman. Traditionally, **BAJ** is difficult to summon for (being a God in his own right), he is beyond desire &/or lust of result. But **BAJ** has been known to appear to various conjurers who are agreeable to him. It is well known that **BAJ** distributes riches with great generosity to his friends & loyal followers. His gifts include the power of discovery & ingenious invention.

Being a Buddhist, **BAJ** does not accept sacrifice entailing the loss of life, be it human, animal, or plant—preferring instead the essence of human excrement, used condoms, and psychotropic vomit over all other gifts. The sacrificial offering of 'waste', excrement, & useless items causes no disruption or deviation in the cycles of life & death. Such offerings are also pleasing to **BAJ** because it requires much force of conviction on the part of the devotee to take such offerings seriously without appearing totally ridiculous in the process.

BAJ has full access to all the sewers & septic tanks on the planet, so no altars or other religious apparati are needed by his devotees. Traditionally inclined devotees may pay homage to **BAJ** by sitting on a 'pierced chair'. The ordinary modern toilet bowl was invented and propagated by members of various cults working thru **BAJ**'s inspirations. Likewise, the Chair of Peter (which is currently used by the

Church of Rome to check-out whether the newly elected Pope is a man, a woman, or a eunuch is a remnant of the Holy See's ancient connection with **BAJ**.

'Intentionality while flushing' is considered (by most devotees) sufficient to gain **BAJ**'s attention, while certain sects insist that the excrement must first be sacramentally anointed/consecrated thru arcane sexual practices and certain astral invocations in order to make the necessary material substances available to **BAJ**, so that he can create certain 'children' to work with his devotees on long range projects.

But, I digress. The point I am making is that **Belphegor Ararita Jones** & I go back a long way together. We are, above all, friends. This time around, **I** am working my Will as a human, while **BAJ** is both God & Demon. I feel that I have found an old friend and ally who has acquired an unexpected amount of 'leverage' due to my present reality. A formal practice of *Liber Astarte* does not (at this time) feel appropriate, but I will certainly work to keep him entertained by spreading news of his cult & instructing interested persons in its inner mysteries, while remaining conscious of the various 'offerings' which I plop down his altar daily.

Love is the law, love under will.

Here begins the entry in Frater OTz PTN--690/PVN's Magickal Record for SATURDAY, the 31th Day of MARCH, 1984 e.v., JULIAN DAY No. 2,445,791.32, Moon being 29.33 Days old. [8:45pm]

Do what thou wilt shall be the whole of the Law.

Much work with BAJ over the past 24 hours. I now have little interest in resurrecting the dream mentioned in my last entry, for it deals with a different reality framework than the one which I am now exploring. The 'hall of testing' & the persona who worked with me there were intriguing, so long as the illusion of their reality could be maintained. I may one day continue my explorations of that reality construct, but (for now) I spend my time exploring memories & mapping realities with **BAJ**. But first, I should analyze those who took part in my little shadow-play, so that I can better see what transpired.

Uncle Henry & Sue were both based on real relatives, but need to be examined on a more archetypical level to unravel the puzzle. Uncle

Henry is Vav-He, or the union of 5 8 6 to yield 11, the number of AUD, the Magickal Light. Sue is Shin-Vav-He, or Uncle Henry + the Element of Spirit. 311 is the number of Raphael, Tzaphqial (archangel of Binah), and Aurial (Angel of the 9 of Cups). It is also the number of AISh, (Man). The character which I identified with most was the young lad whose only name for himself was 'me'. Mem-He = 45, or ADM, the primal man composed of the breath of life (Aleph) upon the sea of blood (DM). Together we form the triumvirate of 11+45+311, or 367, AIShVN (the black eye pupil, which is equivalent to the homonucleus). The relationship of 367 to 93 is 274, DRKIM (Paths)—hence the pilgrimage nature of our interactions. The relationship of 367 to 418 is 309, leper, angel of 2^n dec. of Taurus, to Roar, and ShDH (land). 418 is the RHK aspect of the 93 Current. The roaring Bull & the decadent (leprous) elements were all present in the last dream sequence. The relationship of 367 to 511 (the balanced aspect of Thelema) is 216, ADRIA (the name of my first internal contact). (I knew Adria was present by virtue of the exquisite quality of the sexual union with my cousin Sue!) All the other meanings of, 216 become secondary, although Courage, Oracle, Profound, the Middle Gate, & the blood of Grapes all seem to fit into this particular dream sequence.

Now on to **BAJ**. **BAJ** is Beth-Aleph-Yod or 13. 13 is Unity, Beloved (flame), Raised-up/ & He shall come. As 13, **BAJ** is the Unity referred to in the a-ka-dua (see below for more details). He is the beloved of all who seek ecstasy via sexual union, & he is the demon who has been raised-up. He shall come is IBA. **BAJ** is a congruent formula related to the Magician, the Fool, & the Hermit.

Belphegor is Beth-Lamed-Peh-Gimmel-Ayian-Resh, or 385. This orthography of Belphegor is not traditional, but then neither is anything else about this Deific Demon. 385 is Assiah, the World of Matter & ShKINH, the divine Spirit co-habituating flesh with the Material. Both are most appropriate!

Ararita is 813, a sign, symbol, proof, or miracle. It is notariqon of AChD RASh AChDVThV RASh IIChVDVThV ThMVRThV AChD (One is his beginning, One is his individuality. His Permutation is One). All this adds to 3943. At first glance, such a high order unity may seem a bit out of place with the formula of Belphegor Ararita Jones, whose sheer diversity seems somewhat antithetical to this type of unity (e.g., ARARITA & the a-ka-dua). The trick (I am told) lies in the resolution of opposites without losing each individual aspect.

Much like making a good soup, or preparing any viable Eucharist.

Jones (being English) is enumerated via modern Pythagorean mathematics to yield 1+6+5+5+1=18=9. 9 is the number of sacrifice, generosity, tolerance, idealism, & altruism.

385+813+9=1207=127, Material & the Angel of the 5 of Pentacles. The relationship of 127 to 93 is 34, AL AB, God of Jupiter. The relationship of 127 to 418 is 69, myrtle (sacred to Jupiter). The relationship of 127 to 511 is ShALH, a question or inquiry (pertaining to **BAJ**'s inquisitive nature).

385+3943+9=4337=17, the Masculine Unity of Aleph-Vav-Yod (compare to BAJ=13, the scale of the Highest Feminine Unity). The relationship of 17 to 93 is 284, which is the amicable number to 220 (i.e., Liber AL vel Legis). 284 is also ORGBH, the bed of a garden (i.e., the final repository of the excrement offered by his devotees). The relationship of 17 to 418 is 319, which is 11 x 29, or the general number of magick multiplied by the magick force itself. The relationship of 17 to 511 is 226, TzPVN, North or hidden. It may be worthy of note that this is also a contracted synthesis of my 2 predominant Magickal names—OTz PTN + PVN. P & N overlap. O & T have been dropped. OT=470, eternity, cycle of cycles, Time. To unify the name OT+TzPVN yields 696, one of the numbers attributed to IPSOS. 696=2^3x3x29, or the Eight Hearths multiplied by the 3 dualities multiplied by the magick force itself.

Enough of this gematria! I am buried in a sea of numbers which (altho fraught with meaning) fail to convey the emotional impact of my re-acquaintance with Belphegor Ararita Jones.

Last night I had a lovely picnic with **BAJ** on the emerald green grassy knoll overlooking the Path to the fountainhead of the Order (quite a busy highway it is these days!). As we talked and got re-acquainted, I undertook the godform of Shakti to his Shiva, so that I could elicit information from **BAJ** without my perspective obscuring the (apparently) external perspective of **BAJ**.

I was intending to attempt to relay our dialog in this record, but it does not feel right to attempt that task at this time. I am tired & I have run out of steam in writing the last 2 pages. We shall see what tomorrow brings.

Love is the law, love under will.

Here begins the entry in Frater OTz PTN–690/PVN's Magickal Record for SUNDAY, the 01st Day of APRIL, 1984 e.v.,
JULIAN DAY No. 2,445,792.49, Moon being 0.96 Days old. [11:45pm]

Do what thou wilt shall be the whole of the Law.

My contact with **BAJ** has proven to be far more intimate & exciting that I had dreamed possible. This afternoon I awoke slightly depressed, so I took a nice long soak in the tub to relax me while I went over my problems.

A good deal of the stress I feel these days is related to money, so I spent a considerable portion of my tub time doing a cost analysis of my needs & scheming where that money will be coming from. As I concretized each aspect of my fiscal plan, I sought ratification of my plan from **BAJ,** who gave me his assent thru a pleasant grumbling noise which emanated from my deepest gut (like the sound of distant thunder, but coming from within). In my plans, I stated that I would accept a purchase price of $120,000 on my apartment house, then quickly modified it to $125,000. I further stated that I would be willing to hold a second mortgage in the amount of $25,000 at 12% — interest only for 5 years.

Then I allocated the cash from that sale & saw that I was far short of what my plans need to bring them to fruition. I then affirmed that I was prepared to allocate & oversee a much larger sum. I envisioned winning the Grand Prize whose winner will be announced on the tonight show. The prize is $100,000 per year for 20 years. When I had everything settled to my satisfaction, I got out of the tub.

Within half an hour I received a call from Bernie (my real estate broker) telling me that she had just received a purchase offer for $120,000 on my apartment building, in which the prospective buyer wants me to hold a second mortgage in the amount of $26,000 at 10% for 7 years.

I was somewhat flabbergasted at the speed at which my conversation with **BAJ** had begun to reify, but managed to keep my cool enough so that I found out that it was perfectly acceptable for me to make a counter offer. Note that my initial statement to **BAJ** asked for 120, which was then modified to 125. All is working out exactly as has been my 'dream'. I eagerly await notification that I have won my big contest!

I note in passing a bit of wisdom from Frater sᴀᴍ: If you state an intention clearly to the Universe, it is an affirmation; re-state it and it becomes a repetitive mantra; state it a third time (with conviction) & it is an invocation.

Now that I am able to perceive my shit as an offering which is both holy & useful to **BAJ,** I have begun to alter my diet. The changes have been dramatic, yet spontaneous. They are aligned with good health, but (before today) had not appealed to me because my taste buds were not well aligned with such foods. I feel better already & my shit has already begun to become more fluffy & pleasing to both sight & smell. We shall see if my natural inclinations are beginning to shift/mutate in a particular direction, or if I am experiencing a broadening of my dietary pleasures.

Love is the law, love under will.

Here begins the Magickal Record of Frater OTji PTN-69Q/PVN for TUESDAY, the 03th Day of APRIL, 1984 e.v.,
JULIAN DAY No. 2,445,793.61, Moon being 2.09 Days old. [2:30 am]

Do what thou wilt shall be the whole of the Lew.

Still keeping up the high fiber-ex diet (with oj), but have gone back to usual meat as well. I sure feel better, even though today has been high-stress.

This morning I was working in semi-sleep with **BAJ** to increase the strength of my link. After in-vivo anointing of my turds with VIII° elixir, I began to use **ARARITA** as a mantra as I drifted in-&-out of sleep. Very intense images which were so strong & realistic that my excitement nearly woke me up too much to continue on several occasions. First I saw an eyeball looking at me. Then the eye was centered in an ornately decorated equilateral triangle (like Augra's Eye in the symbol of the Great Eclipse). Then the eye turned into a spider, which crawled towards me. As it was about to touch my own eye, it became stationary in a delicate web. The spider then became a reflection of my own eye in a black mirror with fine hairline patterns resembling a web.

Other dream fragments were equally vivid, but the hecticness of the day was not conducive to writing this entry earlier, so many of them are lost.

My work with **BAJ** seems to be gradually working itself into a form which resembles the latter stages of an Astarte practice. I am seeing

BAJ's hand in all the neat & groovy things that make life really fine. He is responsible for everything from the pleasure of a good shit to the evolution of psychedelic mushrooms to the joys of smelling fresh-plowed earth. He is a bountiful provider. He is my, friend, yet he is also my God. He is as expansive as Jupiter, yet his kingdom seems congruent with that of Saturn & Uranus. 'My color is black to the blind, but the blue & gold are seen of the seeing." The sun's brilliance by day makes the stars appear to be invisible. Yet if we view the night sky from the perspective of the sun, the whole sky becomes black. From any perspective below Tiphareth, the upper Sephiroth are surely distorted. It is only from the perspective of Nu it that the older (black) gods can regain their true colors. Kephra to Ra is my favorite station, even as the region bounded by Jupiter, Daath, & Uranus is my favorite playground. Speaking of which… I am getting a bit punchy. It is time for me to go to bed.

Love is the law, love under will.

Here begins the entry in Frater OTz PTN–690/PVN's Magickal Record for THURSDAY, the 5th Day of APRIL. 1984 e.v., JULIAN DAY No. 2,445,795.97 Moon being 4.45 Days old. [11:15am]

Do what thou wilt shall be the whole of the Law.

I told 0-Maku about **BAJ**. The mythology is right up her ally. She has even worked-out a talisman which is now hanging over the toilet bowl. I still feel his presence strongly, especially now that I am very groggy from lack of sleep. I feel that my contact with him has assisted me in getting my star cruiser out of mothballs & re-commissioned. SAM left a sigil on the altar which feels like a strong but subservient portion of **BAJ**. I must ask him about it.

Love is the law, love under will.

Here begins the entry in Frater OTz PTN–690/PVN's Magickal Record for FRIDAY, the 13th Day of APRIL. 1984 e.v., JULIAN DAY No. 2,445,803.63, Moon being 12.11 Days old. [3:15am]

Do what thou wilt shall be the whole of the Law.
Life is becoming decidedly interesting. A checking account which (by mundane rules of accounting) ought to show a very small balance persists in showing a balance of nearly $2,000. We await an official bank statement before paying up a bunch of bills. The probability matrix is influenceable by BAJ, therefore it is quite possible that we indeed do have an extra $2,000 to play with this month.

[Note made on 21 Apr: Bank statement arrived on 15 April showing a misc. transfer of $1800 to our account. Life sure is intriguing when the microcosm & the macrocosm are in harmonious communion!]

Anne has adopted BAJ with glee. I am seeing evidence of his cult wherever I look. It is fascinating how quickly external reality formulates itself in accord with Will.

Fiberex is wonderful for my shit. I have never had such light, fluffy, healthy-looking turds in all my life. I can see it now. An unsolicited endorsement for Fiberex as "the official dietary supplement of the priestcraft of Belphegor" done up on fancy scrollwork. Who knows?— We may get a Clergy discount!

Love is the law, love under will.

Here begins the entry in Frater OTz PTN–690/PVN's Magickal Record for SUNDAY, the 22nd Day of APRIL, 1984 e.v., JULIAN DAY No. 2,445,813.12, Moon being 21.60 Days old. [2:53pm]

Do what thou wilt shall be the whole of the Law.

Interesting night of dreams. No concrete remembrances, yet I feel inspired to write. The rest of this entry shall be the beginnings of a practical text on the rituals of—**BAJ** and as such, shall be edited & massaged repeatedly before ending this entry.

Rites of BAJ Part 1

The **Cult of BAJ** is most unlike any other cult in the modern world. Most cults are based upon worship of a supreme being, ideal or cause. Members of the **Cult of BAJ** do not worship **BAJ,** nor do they encourage others to do so. The word **religion** is based on the Latin root from which we derive the words **regulation & regular.** Inspiration is (for the most part) beyond the grasp of those who follow anything religiously. However, religious observation can (& is) used by certain shrewd teachers to lull the minds of certain dense students in order to 'trick' them into gaining access to a genuinely mystical/inspirational state, which may be otherwise inaccessible to them because their preconceived notions lead them to believe that such states are only accessible to the 'pious', 'holy', or 'reverent'. Self-aware & self-actualized humans need no such trickery to allow them to work harmoniously with their inherent mystical & inspirational natures. There are no regulations imposed on members of the **Cult of BAJ** & the rites of this cult are far from regular.

In Western Magick (as well as religion, politics, economics & culture) there is a strong emphasis on banishing (exile, imprisonment, excommunication, etc.) that which is considered to be disharmonious with the specific goals of a group. Such banishings lead to the creation & concentration of a class of energies] substances, &/or persons, which are considered to be dangerous, harmful, poisonous, evil, etc. (e.g., white sugar, red meat, & chocolate to a 'natural' food advocate, promiscuity to a prude, monogamist, or a 'religious' person, divine intoxication to an atheist, Hispanic neighborhoods {particularly after dark} to Middle & Upper Class white people, etc.). Even casual contact with any of these substances (or those who extol their virtues) is considered extremely hazardous to spiritual &/or physical well-being.

Over time, the concentration of unbalanced 'essence' within the ostracized group becomes so great that its imbalance begins to have a deleterious effect upon even those with no pre-judgements against the energies or the substances which have been banished. The collective Maya (illusion) of 'objective' reality can only be ignored by those whose lives are a living testament to the Path of the individual—i.e., self-direction and self-actualization used as tools to reify subjective realities harmoniously within the fabric of the collective objective reality. Those who break the taboos of any powerful cult without a clear understanding of the forces at work often find themselves cursed, diseased, & ex-communicated from the world at large.

Native people who have lived at the foot of 'sacred' radioactive mountains for millennia are suddenly dying from 'radiation poisoning' & 'radium toxicity'. More & more 'chemicals' are being found to be 'carcinogenic'. 'Promiscuity' is 'known' to 'cause' uterine 'cancers' in women. 'AIDS' is rampant among those who use 'dangerous drugs' for recreational purposes, who are 'promiscuous', &/or who engage in 'unclean' sexual practices such as ass fucking. AIDS can also be communicated to those who knowingly or unknowingly have contact with any taboo individual (e.g., customers of prostitutes & those who receive blood transfusions) Violent crime is on the rise in big cities and even those who have no fear, loathing, or distain of particular classes of social outcasts are counted among its victims.

Members of the **Cult of BAJ** have observed that most cult(ure)s, {religions, societies, etc.} seem expend much effort in creating external 'demons', which they then take perverse delight in refining & empowering (thru the use of taboo, social stricture, customary observance, & exorcism) until the 'demons' become self-aware &/or powerful enough to destroy the cult(ure) which spawned them, and then linger on to poison all those who stumble upon them accidentally until they become reabsorbed/integrated back into the balanced cycle of creation. As a consequence of the race's refinement of the tools of technology, we presently have the power to create demons, which can obliterate most life on our planet and which will linger on for many millennia after we have departed from this environment (e.g., radioactive & chemical waste dumps, the germ theory of disease, the inevitability &/or desirability of death & taxes, etc.).

In an effort to ameliorate the difficulties which are propagated thru the indiscriminate over-use of banishment, one of the basic philosophies of the **Cult of BAJ** is that of **assimilation,** which can also be expressed as Polymorphous Pan-perversity (PPP) (the formula of sexual fusion with the entire Universe in all of its myriad autonomous aspects), or simply as an extension of the formula of at-one-ment preached (but rarely understood) by many of the followers of Jesus, Buddha, & Zarathustra. Rather than isolating dis-harmonious elements & then banishing them from our immediate environment, we seek to recycle, ingest, be eaten by, sexually impregnate, become parasitized by, live symbiotically with, &/or otherwise integrate dis-harmonious elements/energies/entities with our immediate &/or long-term goals. As our 'allies' become more powerful &/or self-aware thru repeated contact with us, they continue to work with us to reify the Great Work in a harmonious manner rather than (seemingly) thwarting our every move &/or testing our right to continued existence. Thru on-going use of the magickal tool of assimilation, disease becomes partnership & toxin becomes medicine. That which our culture calls cancer is un-directed mutation of those who feel victimized by that which has been banished from conscious awareness. On-going self-directed mutation is a major key to immortality & self-actualized evolution.

The use of assimilation is particularly useful in turning feared, loathsome, depraved, forbidden, or otherwise taboo power objects into powerful allies in the Great Work. Such assimilations are not without danger because of the accumulated imbalanced charge which the 'banishing cults' are continuously imbuing these taboo power objects. The collective maya is a powerful force which needs to be integrated & assimilated rather than disregarded or destroyed (i.e., banished). If objective reality were to be banished completely (an audacious act, but not beyond the reach of most adepts --particularly thru the long-term repeated assistance of prodigious quantities of powerful (taboo) psychotropic drugs), the resulting chaos would most likely render the subjective reality of the magickian unstable to the point of dissolution &/or uselessness. [The realms of madness & chaos can help make for a fun vacation from 'reality' &/or provide lots of very instructional initiations to those whose Will is aligned with such tools, but I personally prefer to immerse most of my consciousness within linear Time so that I can play with the creative interplay of my creative energies upon the fabric of collective maya ('objective reality').]

It is up to each cult member to integrate the practical application of **assimilation** into his/her life in whatever way(s) are in accord with his/her own True Will. Any guidelines &/or texts on this topic tend to be viewed as 'heretical' by those whose religiosity has blinded them to the formula of assimilation. Useful guidelines are quite powerful (i.e., dangerous—especially if followed religiously, rather than inspirationally). Use of assimilative techniques without intuitive understanding of their mechanism & purpose can lead to unpredictable (& often disastrous) consequences as the formula of assimilation is a conscious process directed by the Will of the magickian. Subjective reality needs to be created & reified in detail, or its 'side-effects' can undermine its intended purpose. To paraphrase one of our myriad holy books "All words are sacred & all prophets true, save only in part"—i.e., are of limited use to any particular person in any given set of circumstances. Such wisdom applies as much to this text as it does to Hustler-Magazine, Heavy Metal, the Journal of the A.M.A., Holistic Health Bulletin, or the minutes of the John Birch Society. Integrate as much as possible, but don't o.d. on more than you can handle or get trapped into any one tunnel reality.

Taboo breakers who suddenly find themselves 'over their heads' or who 'get cold feet' are cautioned against panic, and especially against seeking the advice of those who extoll the virtues of a contradictory reality framework. Such people tend to re-enforce the 'dangerous' aspects of your experiments & will delight in delineating the ways in which your experimental 'lifestyle' has done 'irreparable damage' to your body (mind, soul, &/or society—depending on the particular taboo energies / substances/entities which you have chosen to align yourself with). 'Doctors' (of 'physical', 'mental', or 'meta-physical' variety—either 'holistic' or the A.M.A. variety of 'drug-&-cut' exorcism of demons) are particularly dangerous to those who seek to integrate taboo ideas into their physical reality, for a doctor's dogmatic pronouncements (called 'diagnoses') bear the religious weight of generations of their religious priestcraft. In other (more 'primitive') cultures, such diagnoses are called curses, when spoken with the authority of one who is a member of a recognized priestcraft. Promiscuous gay drug users who are feeling dis-eased with themselves are asking to be diagnosed as AIDS 'victims' if they speak openly about their lifestyle to doctors or dis-approving &/or paranoid friends/family before the results of diagnostic testing have been fully evaluated.

The **Cult of BAJ** recognizes the autonomous diversity of nature, in which no interactions are forbidden or bear any moral 'weight' in-&-of themselves. Substances/energies/entities can only be deemed useful or not-useful in relation to other substances/energies/entities at a particular locus of Space/Time/Alternity. No thing and no action can be viewed as 'good' (useful) or 'evil' (counter-productive) without appealing to an ever-shifting Set of specific external & internal referents. That which acts to stifle or corrupt in one set of circumstances may be just the catalyst to trigger an initiation (permanent trans-dimensions! leap in consciousness) in another set of circumstances. Heroin, tobacco, sugar, ass-fucking, masturbation, meditation, feasting, fasting, Sufism, Communism, Prostitution, abortion, capital punishment, marriage, celibacy, promiscuity, and religion are each valid tools of the Great Work in-&-of themselves & in combination with other tools of the Great Work—under certain specific circumstances. It is up to each practitioner to determine which tools are suitable for which circumstances. The myriad practices utilized by the **Cult of BAJ** can catalyze wondrous initiations/transformations, if & only if they are adjusted (tampered-with/transformed/turned-around) by each adept of the Cult to suit the particular circumstances at hand. Neither this author nor the **Cult of BAJ** can accept any responsibility for anyone who performs any practice in this (or any other) book. Do what thou wilt shall be the whole of the Law; Love is the law, love under will.

Magickal ritual is a very traditional tool for experimenting with the fabric of reality. The magickian formulates a temple (a specific self- encompassing locus of Space-Time designed for the specific task at hand) and manipulates certain specific symbolic tools (magickal weapons) to assist him/her to induce change (either within him/her-self, or within the world-at-large) thru the interplay of subjective reality with the collective maya of objective reality. Without objective reality to 'play-against', all is chaos & there can be no 'results' for there are no external referents by which to measure change. The 'structure' of the temple provides the appropriate symbolism for the external referent of objective reality, without the need to involve the whole universe in one's magickal experiments (I do wish that generals, economists & religious leaders would learn to formulate more localized temples for their magickal games).

Traditionally, the temple is a symbolic representation of some sort of idealized representation of the Universe. The ancients had 4 (or 3 or 5 or 8, depending on cultural bias) elements which summed-up the entire universe. Up until quite recently, Western Science (the priestcraft of the most powerful maya {collective reality <illusion>}) insisted that there were 93 'natural' elements (later expanded to 103 with the addition of the post-nuclear 'un-natural' elements), with over a hundred sub-elemental particles.

This system is far too complex for most folks to manipulate on the symbolic level, so the quantum physicists (a rival band of renegade scientists) changed the rules of the game & declared that all matter (&

energy) is composed of 3 quarks (which always appear in groups of 3) and which come in 3 colors & 3 flavors & which have both positive & negative time-spins (i.e., they travel both forwards & backwards in time)—not much improvement, but every little bit helps. The concepts of time-spin & the interchangeability of matter-&-energy (Einstein's famous $E=Mc^2$) are very useful to many magickians.

The temple layout, magickal weapons, & rituals described below are suggestive of what can be done with the formula of assimilation. The details of the layout &/or the working are a composite of many reality frameworks. Let each modify according to his/her own needs &/or inclinations. Those with no background in traditional magick are referred to the Rituals of the Golden Dawn (edited & collected by Israel Regardie) to check-out the philosophical & practical differences between the magickal formulae of Banishment/Subjugation (used by most traditional cults) & Assimilation/Symbiosis (used by the Cult of BAJ).

Most temples are laid-out according to a pre-conceived plan with the cardinal aspects of the temple aligned with the compass points (the grand cross of N-S, E-W). In this particular temple, the compass points are utilized, but they are purely subjective.

Without regard to the 'real' compass points, sit in the particular room (basement, cave, forest glade, or open field) which is to be used as a temple & decide on the compass direction. The directions you decide upon need not be fixed in time, for you may feel differently about the temple space at different times of the day, different seasons of the year, for different types of ritual, or during different personal moods. The compass points need not be 90° apart & need not be in the sequence of N, E, S, W. Have reasons for your decisions & be able to defend your choices based upon those things which you feel to be important (i.e., a fireplace in the South, water pipes running up the West wall, useful placement of closets, doorways, non-movable shelves, a street lamp outside the window by the altar which you need to see most clearly, etc.). If you can't remember why you chose particular directions, either hang-loose & do whatever comes natural, or re-work the compass points until they become an integral part of your subjective reality. Whichever technique you use depends on your basic worldview (anarchistic or orderly). Once you become proficient at either method, it can be interesting to switch to the other mode—both techniques are useful for constructing viable temples.

In a traditional temple, each compass direction is assigned a particular set of exclusive attributions (Fire in the South, Water in the West, etc.). All else is banished from each quarter. Such is not my way of doing things. To me, each of the 4 quarters needs to be potentized with a complex interplay of the 4 traditional elements. To some, my arrangement may seem to be a parody or a mockery of a traditional temple. In some ways the parody is intentional, but its purpose is potent, puissant, & efficacious to the work at hand, which is designed to induce assimilation thru heightened contrast of seeming contradictions.

In the South is the altar of fire. Upon the altar are several complex manifestations of fire in passive &/or dynamic harmony with other elements. Electrical apparati (Jacob's ladder, electric arc torch, neon sign, van de graaf generator) are particularly useful in this age of electric marvels. I tend to use a benz-o-matic torch for active fire & a Coleman lantern for quiescent fire. The wand (phallus) is a traditional weapon of this quarter. long cylindrical fluorescent lamps powered from large stationary electrostatic generators are ideal weapons of fire, for they are impressive, portable (no wires), and safe to handle during altered states of consciousness. Upon this altar are drugs related to fire, either by virtue of their action (i.e., alcohol), their mode of use (injection or snorting), or both (speed, Yohimbine hydrochloride). In the South is an electrical outlet to which is connected a length of zip-cord which has been split into 2 insulated wires. The wires circumscribe the temple & meet in the North where they power an electric fan.

In the West is the altar of Water. Upon the altar are several complex manifestations of water in passive S/or dynamic harmony with other elements. For an active weapon of water I use a garden sprayer with a pump which compresses air to propel a stream of water. The passive element of water is my skrying mirror. Aquariums (particularly salt water) are also nice, especially if they contain complex balanced eco-systems. The traditional weapon of water is the cup or grail symbolizing the female vagina. Hypodermic syringes are an analogous (although somewhat cynical) tool. Soft, seductive, and liquid drugs are attuned with this station. Opiated hash dissolved in sweet blackberry brandy is ideal.

In the North is the altar of Air. Upon the altar are several complex manifestations of air in passive &/or dynamic harmony with other elements. A powerful squirrel-cage furnace blower (powered by the divided electric wire from the South) is my active weapon of air.

Negative ion generators & cylinders of compressed nitrous oxide are each very useful as both weapons of air & drugs of the quarter. Swords are traditional weapons of this quarter, so I sometimes employ a gasoline powered chainsaw or an electric drill. Writing implements are also to this quarter. If no powerful electrostatic devices are in use, computer-driven word processor is ideally suited to this quarter, particularly if linked to other active temples via phone lines. Drugs should be gaseous (or at least volatile) & very 'spacey' in nature. Nitrous oxide, amyl nitrite, & di-ethyl ether are all excellent choices, but care should be taken with flammable drugs like ether unless it is one's will to dis-incarnate in a flash.

In the East is the altar of Earth. Upon the altar are several complex manifestations of earth in passive &/or dynamic harmony with other elements. Wealth, property, and concrete sigilization is appropriate to this quarter. Precious gems or metals, buckets of coins/paper money, and phony stock certificates are all appropriate to symbolize the collective maya of objective wealth. Plants growing from rich fertile earth, urns filled with decaying shit, fermenting wine, and rotting corpses are all appropriate in this quarter. Coin operated movie projectors which show porno flicks on the West wall are ideal. An automated slide projector can flash sigils on the wall during the ritual. Drugs should be dense, solid, &/or orally stimulating. Chocolate Mousse, roast beef & bowls of fruit are all useful drugs of this quarter. To experiment with interesting contrasts (particularly if you have a tendency towards viewing 'natural' or 'organic' foods as somehow superior to 'synthetic' 'junk-foods' or 'chemical' additives), use a bowl of organically grown natural fruits served with a side-dish of Hostess Twinkies, or high grade granola from an exclusive health food store sprinkled with BHT & sweetened with saccharine as the sacramental drug of this quarter.

Following a large feast with peyote buttons or magic mushrooms to experiment with the transitory & reversable nature of all things can be highly illuminating, but it should be remembered that barfing on fellow magickians is usually considered to be in poor taste, particularly if they are short-tempered & the North altar contains a chainsaw. However, barfing on oneself is a good ritual to dispel the illussion of propriety & demonstrate the ridiculousness of the universe, particularly if you are working the ritual with someone whom you are working very hard to impress favorably (e.g., the head of a Magickal

Order or someone whom you sexually desire). If both of you can still laugh at the ritual the next day (after the drug has worn off, but before the mess has been cleaned-up), you probably don't need to be reading this book.

For complex rituals & High feast days, invisible altars can be set-up at the Spacemarks (the divisions between the quarters) to mark the ancient & revered feasts of Mayday, mid-Summer's eve, Halloween, & Groundhog's day. Consult the writings of H.P.Lovecraft, Stephen King, or the court transcriptions of the Holy Inquisition for traditional attributions of these feasts — the more brutal & depraved, the better. Overlay these symbols with modern Wiccan & goody-goody neo-pagan symbolism. Knowing what you do of human nature & the past history of the race, decide which attributions are most likely correct. Shift perspectives (using one or more drugs from any/all of the 4 main altars) & reify alternative realities. Integrate realities & re-furbish the invisible altars accordingly.

The floor of the temple can be painted with a representation of an entirely different system of attributions, based on 3 or 5 divisions rather than 4 or 8. Shift consciousness back-&-forth between systems as appropriate during the ritual.

Furnish the temple with a bed & work sexually with someone whom you consider unclean, beneath your station, or who makes you feel very uncomfortable or insecure in some way (e.g., bring someone whom you have been afraid to expose yourself to magically into your temple & involve him/her in overt magickal ritual). Be sure to continue the operation until you are able to see & experience the God(dess) thru that other persons s/he thru you.

Work with a particular sexual formula which either you or your partner (but not both of you) consider to be unclean, dangerous, or revolting in some way, or explore some aspect of sexual pleasure which one or both of you are afraid will be too pleasurable or intoxicating. Continue to work until both of you are able to experience Godhead via the chosen formula. Choose another formula S/ot another partner & repeat the process. Become proficient at exposing/exploring your own fantasies & taboos as well as being adept at exploring those of your partner(s).

Work to assimilate & neutralize a particular dis-ease of your partner. Once this is accomplished, 'infect' him/her with the cure thru your sexual fluids. When you are successful, spread the cure to others.

Gradually work your way up to more virulent dis-eases. Be cautious not to overestimate your magickal prowess, or you may be forced into long-term magickal VIII° retirement to work on curing yourself of some 'incurable' disease like AIDS, herpes, suicidal depression or cancer.

Love is the law, love under will.

Liber Set-Horus

"...But she said: the ordeal I write not, the ritual shall be half known and half concealed. The Law is for all."

The temple is ringed with black candles, mournful music is played. Isis or Nuit is robed in white and gold. Osiris or Hadit is robed in white. Set-Horus is robed in black over red. In the north is the sword of Set. In the south, concealed, is the phallus of Osiris. Isis and Osiris stand together in the East facing outward. Set stands in the west, facing inward. Banishings. Music. The ritual opens.

Isis: My lord Osiris, let us face the rising Sun for day awakens

Osiris: The sun rises not, but sets

Horus (whispers): The Son rises not, but Set

Set walks stealthily to the north and picks up the sword. He steps behind Osiris and taps him on the head with it.

Set-Horus: Thus I slay Thee.

Set taps Osiris on the arm.

Set-Horus: I divide thy body and throw it into the Nile.

Set taps the limbs and trunk of Osiris in turn. Osiris assumes his own God-form, then falls face up, in the position of the handed man. Set forcefully turns Isis around.

Set: I have slain Osiris thy husband and divided his body, that I might have thee.

Isis: I am as though slain myself. But, beware! The knowledge of me is the knowledge of death.

Set: I am alone, there is no God where I am.

Set tears off the robe of Isis and forces her to her knees. She acknowledges him with a kiss, lifting his robe.

Isis: But, remember: knowledge of me is the knowledge of death.

Set takes of Isis as he will. She whispers…

Isis: …the knowledge of death…

Set falls into a deep slumber. Isis rises, and divides the remains of her robes into bandages. She approaches Osiris, and binds his wounds.

Isis: Osiris, my husband, I have restored thy limbs that were cast into the Nile, but thy organ of generation I find not.

Isis searches the temple and discovers the concealed phallus. She returns to Osiris and binds it to his body.

Isis: This organ I have fashioned by my magick, by the will of Thoth. By Nuit, Hadit, and Ra-Hoor-Khuit, I say unto thee, Arise.

Isis places herself on Osiris. Osiris is restored to life.

Osiris (bows): You have conceived by this. Feed the dead god that the crowned and conquering child may Arise.

Isis places her chalice at the mouth of Set, removing his outer robe. Set consumes the elixir.

Set-Horus: I am killed and reborn.

Isis: Set is dead. Behold, the god of the new æon!

Horus moves to the east, facing outward.
Isis and Osiris move to the west facing inward.

Osiris: He is risen!

The ritual is concluded.

Magickal Calling Cards

PVN Thursday, April 9, 1981ev 7:52 AM

This is the Day of Hadit; the second day of the three day feast for the writing of the Book of the Law.

I have had but a few minutes sleep all night even though I have been in bed for nearly six hours. I was commanded to listen to ideas, mull them over, work out their details & then to leave my bed in order to commit them to paper. The guiding intelligence behind my words is Um-Ur-Atwiel (whom is also known to some of you as Regiomantis).

The project being proposed is an ever-growing deck of cards, similar to (but very different from) the Tarot. The purpose of this deck is communication & communion with other magickians, with other Powerzones, and with other Magickal Currents. The cards have little use for divination (in the usual sense) and are (for the most part) best utilized one at a time for the purpose of communication/communion with the Magickian, Powerzone, or Magickal Current represented by that particular card. The card may be used passively (i.e., to draw information/understanding about a particular Magickian, Powerzone, or Magickal Current into our consciousness so that we may better relate to that particular magickian, Powerzone, or Magickal Current in a more constructive manner), actively (i.e., to input information/understanding into the consciousness of a particular magickian, Powerzone, or Magickal Current from ourself so that we may be better understood by the particular magickian, Powerzone or Magickal Current in question), or a combination of both methods best suited to a particular situation. While the cards will be most often utilized for communication/communion between/among various members of a particular magickal group or family to negate time/distance and/or the barriers of the Gateway (seen variously as Death, Da'ath, astral projection, etc.), the cards will also be seen to be a most potent & valuable tool for the understanding & dissolution of difficulties between various magickians, Powerzones, and Magickal Currents. Most of us are unable to function above the Abyss all of the time. Some of us can manage to be in communion with Higher Consciousness some of the time such that we have access to information/intuition which exceeds our magickal grade & allows us to function (in a limited manner, for a limited time) as though we were across the Abyss. There are those who claim to have actually crossed the abyss (whether this be true or not, I do not claim to know since I have not made the claim for myself). Whatever our experience has been to date, most of us function below the Abyss most of the time & this is the cause of a great deal of conflict between magickians, between Powerzones, and between Magickal Currents. Above the Abyss there is ONE Higher Consciousness which has total jurisdiction over ALL Powerzones & is fully aware that there is but ONE SINGLE Magickal Order. Kether is the Crown of Unity to which we all strive. As it states in Liber AL (III:2) There is division homeward. Below the Abyss we see the differences between ourselves and others. There are those who seek to ignore these differences & to attempt to unite us all in a truce of egalitarian murkiness where fatal flaws are ignored and magickal plans to un-fold the up-coming æon are decided by a committee of adepts & baboons. It is not reasonable (nor is it healthy) for adepts to ignore their internal inspirations. Those who are blessed with magickal inspiration/intuition have a duty to themselves, their Powerzones, and their Magickal Orders to trust their inspiration, even if it be (apparently) contrary to the inspiration of others. ("To thine own self be true; Thou canst not then be false to any man"—Shakespeare). Likewise, if an adept feels (via inspiration & without ego involvement) that another who claims inspiration is wrong, there is a duty to warn others who might otherwise follow the false lead of the twisted inspiration of the mis-aligned adept and also a duty to communicate with the mis-aligned adept in order to attempt to correct all misalignments in all adepts.

Warnings about the mis-aligned teachings of adepts (usually by calling the teachings misguided or the work of black brothers) does not open the doors of communication so necessary for the constant realignment of all those who have inspiration. Constant re-alignment is so necessary for all of us below the abyss since we have but partial sight & are often blinded to those areas which are outside of our own specialty (& especially to those areas which seem to undermine or contradict our own specialty.

The proposed deck of Communication/Communion cards are a most puissant tool for learning from &/or correcting the mis-aligned inspiration of those with whom direct communication is difficult or impossible. There are many who fear direct soul-to-soul communion with those whom they believe to be 'black brothers'.

Such fears are groundless. The linkage between a magickian and his individual Trump card is through the vehicle of the Higher Self. Any destructive energies which are directed at a magickian/Powerzone/Magickal Current through these cards cannot harm thee at all.

There are many who will not be able to see the perfect safety in using these cards to commune with (apparent) enemies until they gain skill in using the cards with close magickal friends. While this is understandable (at our present level of development) all those whose will is to push outward the frontiers of their understanding are encouraged to commune with those with whom they are least aligned. By this method are horizons opened & Understanding gained.

Practical considerations on the Cards

The inspiration given to me thus far indicates three separate classes of cards. Use any or all of them as ye will. Feel free to add more classes of cards as the need arises or as inspiration dictates. In order to keep the deck of cards easy to manipulate & relatively inexpensive to duplicate, I make the following suggestions, (feel free to modify as dictated by internal inspiration, keeping in mind the idea of practicality).

Size: All cards should be of uniform size. They need to be large enough to contain pertinent symbols &/or written information, while being small enough to handle easily. As many of us will be reproducing our cards photographically, a standard phot size would be helpful. I propose 3x5 inch as the standard size for all cards.

Distribution: Each individual magickian, Powerzone, and Magickal Current is totally & individually responsible for the design, manufacture, charging, & distribution of its own card(s). Each may distribute his/her/their own card to anyone he/she/they Will. He/she/they may not distribute or duplicate any cards of any other magickian/Powerzone/Magickal Current without the express permission of the magickian/Powerzone Magickal Current depicted on the Card. Properly charged cards (see below) are sent to whomever you will. The person or group receiving the card should also receive a copy of these xeroxes if they do not already understand the use of the cards. You may also include whatever other information seems appropriate. The person or group receiving the card has no obligation to reciprocate by sending you one of their cards (although, under ideal circumstances this is certainly to be hoped for). If the person/group to whom you send a card is unable to participate with you in this project, it is hoped that the charged card will either be returned or destroyed by fire rather than simply treated carelessly, but no matter how the card is treated, misuse of the card cannot harm you.

Charging: The more potent the charge placed on a card before it is sent-off, the greater will be the communion/communication between the person using the card & the person/group depicted on the card. Cards may be charged as a class (i.e., 3 dozen Trumps of one kind all charged by the magickian with no focus on the particular person who will be receiving the Trump), individually (each card charged one at a time with strong focus on the recipient of the card as well as on the person/group depicted on the card), or some combination (i.e., a pile of cards of one kind are charged as a group, then each card is individually aligned to a specific recipient prior to distribution).

Design & Manufacture: This is left to the ingenuity & personal inspiration of each magickian/Powerzone/Magickal Current. I include some guidelines on how I intend to design my cards, but each should decide for him/her/their-selves on how best to communicate what needs to be communicated.

Trumps: My personal Trump will have two sides. On one side will be a photograph of me. Depending on the degree of communication/communion I am seeking with the recipient, I may be posed in street clothes, or in the setting of my magickal temple (others may wish to have a drawing or a painting of themselves on the card—either an original for each card, or a photograph of the original). The other side of the Trump will be a magickal sigil, or lamen, or set of symbols which indicates 'who-I-am' in a magickal sense. This may be either hand painted by me for each card, or a color photograph of an original painting done by me.

Powerzone Card: This could be another personal card which depicts our individual Temple (either on Malkuth or our astral Temple), or it could be the group card of a group Temple, Magickal Commune, Lodge, etc. I will probably be involved in the design & consecration of several cards in this class due to the overlapping nature of magickal families. One side will probably have a photograph of either the physical structure of the powerzone &/or the group which makes up the powerzone. There will probably be different versions of the same cards, depending on what kind of image is to be presented to another powerzone &/or the degree of intimacy we have with them. This card will attune others to our place of working & how we work together within the Powerzone. The other side of this card will have some sort of group symbol or symbol representing the temple itself. While this symbol will be in harmony with symbols of other Powerzones within the same Magickal Current, each Powerzone & Temple should try to have a unique symbol.

Magickal Current Card: This card should try to sum-up the basic formulae of a particular Magickal Current in as un-ambiguous a way as possible. There are several organizations which currently claim to represent the OTO. Looked at objectively, they have many similarities (as well as real (from the perspective of below the Abyss) differences). Ideally, by comparing the different cards of these Organizations, one should detect both the differences & the similarities through gross examination of the cards as well as through magickal attunement with each of the cards via meditation ritual, drugs, sex, etc.. This class of card should be used to depict not only the world-wide magickal & religious Orders (such as the OTO, the Sufi Order, the various religious sects of Hinduism, etc.), but also the local &/or personal magickal Orders which manifest at various times & places through those with inspirational links to Higher Consciousness. Some of these Orders may have but one member, while others may have a handful, but all are important Magickal Currents with a very specialized focus of inspiration & a very potent access to magickal information (much of it un-tested or as-yet incompletely tested as to validity &/or safety) which can be spread to other potential experimenters via these cards. This class of card provides communication among the various specialized Magickal Currents as well as feed-back on proper alignment of magickal inspiration. For lesser known Magickal Currents, it would be helpful to include some xeroxed background material along with the card itself.

For all of the classes of cards I intend to create & distribute cards to whomever I will. All will be consecrated to the best of my ability (via sexual fluids, earth from my powerzone, and relics from the Magickal Currents I am trying to represent in objective wholeness). I will not make any attempt to formulate or distribute cards for Powerzones or Magickal Currents without the full support of those within the Powerzone of Magickal Current & I certainly hope that others will do likewise. Decisions as to participation in this project & the design of the individual cards is a very important matter & not to bet taken lightly. In the beginning stages, I suspect that most of the participation in this project will be by individual magickians & by Powerzones & Magickal Currents which contain only small numbers of people

All those who receive a copy of this material directly from me will be receiving a charged Trump card from me as soon as I design & manufacture the Trump. Hopefully most of you will see the power & potential for this project & will participate in it with me in as much as it aligns with your will. The Eighties promise to be an 'interesting' time (in the Chinese sense of the term). Traditional methods of communication will undoubtedly falter (if not fail altogether) while increased stress on Malkuth will make ego-less communion more difficult. It is only by exploring new modes of communication & communion that we can hope to survive & prosper in times of chaos.

The Eleven-Star must not fail.

11:33AM
System is all outlined & 'presence' of Um-Ur-Atwiel is no longer with me very strongly (it is never entirely gone from me these days, but usually it is simple a background feeling & not a force-with-a-voice the way it has been these past few hours). I am tired yet refreshed. I have now been awake nearly 24 hours & still I do not feel like sleep. I will go & xerox this material so it can be sent out later.

Lest anyone think I plagiarize ideas, I fully admit that the thrust of the inspiration for this has come from many places besides from the voices within me. Roger Zelazney in his Amber series introduced me to the concept, but it was Soror Kua—525 who gave me a primitive form of a Trump card of herself & showed me the power of soul-to-soul communication & communion. She gave me the card with her name & sigil in a flash of inspiration. I know not if she has developed her inspiration any further along these lines, but I feel certain that this system will feel the effects of her inspiration as it grows. Likewise Soror Andahadna & Frater I am Not a Fool were instrumental in the initial earthing of the idea (during the weekend which gave me the initial card from Kua, yet seemingly independent from her). I do not know if they consciously know the role they played, but they were important even if they know it not. Likewise did the Grove of the Star & the Snake plant a seed within me when I was initiated into the Horus

Maat Lodge. The glyph of that Lodge is with me yet as an 'astral card' to assist me in tapping into the Current to which I was initiated. There are probably many others who impregnated me with the various bits & pieces which have just now begun to earth in earnest in this system of communication, communion cards. I leave it to others to help me learn how to best utilize them & to give them a proper name.

Those Who Knew Him

Greetings, again...

from the Publisher

Having let Frater PVN have his unvarnished say, please allow me to introduce the commentary on his life and works. I am Sam Webster, the publisher at Concrescent Press and the editor of this volume. The collection you hold is the printed works of Bill Siebert, who died in a New Orleans nursing home in July 2020 of the Covid-19 Pandemic and the depredations diabetes wreaked on his body.

I met Bill at Harrimon State Park in upstate New York in 1982. At this campout were members from Grady McMurtry's OTO's Hadit Camp of Philadelphia, where I had been initiated in June; Tehuti Lodge of New York City, some members of Marcelo Mot27ta's Society of the OTO up from Brazil, and two members of Kenneth Grant's Typhonian OTO. My girlfriend Diana was with me to receive her initiation at this event.

The initiation complete, in the after-party phase, Jim Wasserman from Tahuti Lodge started bellowing aggressively out into the darkness, building up to violently attacking one of the women from Brazil. I and one of my campmates from Hadit grabbed him just before he hurt the woman and pinned him to the ground. After various attempts to reason with this screaming ball of violence while out in the middle of the woods, Bill suggested that we treat the occasion as a magickal event, being magickians, and act accordingly. Slightly sheepish for needing the guidance, I took over sitting on Jim's chest and would stay there until the sun rose. Circles were cast, including Reguli; a continuous round of reciting the Book of the Law was begin by the people not directly engaged with holding Jim down. Cliff Pollick, whose version of this tale will follow, and Bill Siebert, came to help me hold Jim down. I drove the white handled sai (small martial arts trident) from my pair into the ground above the head of the screaming, thrashing lodge master, pinning his Kether. With my left hand on the pommel, Cliff and Bill sat on the ground triangulating around the Kether point. With their arms around our shoulders, we chanted the Aka Dua, and I dove into the chaos of Jim's soul to drag him back. About dawn I suddenly popped back into ordinary consciousness and

Jim started talk normally, asking if he could roll over. Now in possession of himself, the crisis Jim created was over. My experience of Bill was just beginning.

In ensuing conversations with Bill, we discovered our mutual affinity to the sphere of Da'ath which I was to discover in those talks was both rare and reviled. I had only been studying Qabalah for a few months at this point, but I did not experience the gap in the Tree of Life so many did at Da'ath and understood it to be a pan-dimensional gateway. This granted me some credibility, along with the soul retrieval just performed, to be invited to the Math of the Crystal Humm on the first of many visits with Bill and Anne, his partner at the time. We would talk, partake of sacraments, perform some ritual, and generally expand my knowledge and my mind about magick, the Tree, and the Orders.

In hindsight, we are very different individuals yet this insight about Da'ath granted us a common ground that few could partake in. For me, Bill's perspective gave me a deep, practical, entry point into the non-dual view. This 'place', beyond this or that, pure or polluted, yes or no, up or down, self or other, chaos or order, was the key to all of the forms of non-dualism that I would eventually integrate into my own practice.

The theme of 'chaos' is critical to understanding Bill and his writings. Note that it is in the late 1970s early 1908s that he is writing. In the 1990s and later we have the emergence of Chaos Magick, which when I discovered it in California I expected to be similar to Bill's approach, yet this way was focused on the manipulation of belief and the rejection of the norms of the dominant magical organization of the time, namely McMurtry's OTO, often called at that time the Caliphate. Conversations with Peter Carroll, who was a member of my OBOD group in Bristol, England, confirmed for me the origin of Carroll's branch in the rejection of the OTO. What Bill worked with and taught me was the work of the primordial *Kaos* and its dynamic pair *Order* (Kosmos) especially as accessed through the Gates of Da'ath. This is both rather different and significantly earlier than the better known 'Chaos Magick'.

During my wanderjahr after college, I stayed at the Humm for a couple of months, only to return to help manage the first Convocation of the Magi before heading out to California. I pursued the knowledge we explored, eventually receiving advanced academic degrees as well as initiations in Golden Dawn, Wiccan, Hindu, Buddhist, Masonic and Druidic traditions along with empowerments and trainings from those I visited and stayed with in my wanderings and later education. Bill the hermit came out into community and lit up as a social being creating connections and group events.

Throughout the 1980s Bill produced a series of chapbooks by photocopy with dot matrix print from his home near Ithaca, New York, made from selections from his magical diaries, dreams, and other speculations and theorizings on his very particular brand of magick. Since the late 1990s when first I had the ability to produce them, Bill and I discussed getting his old chapbooks into print again many times. The files had long been lost. After numerous attempts at scanning and optical character recognition (ocr) that produced garbage, and efforts at getting the books retyped into a computer only to have the typist run screaming, the technology has advanced enough to produce the work you hold. That, and many hours of clean up.

Bill had an early intimation of what we now call open source copyrights, fairly close to the 'share and share alike' paradigm. I append his non-legally binding immoralist copyright after this essay as an indication of his intent. I and the other contributors to this volume felt, after Bill's death, especially alone and isolated as he was in the end, that his words should be re-collected and shared. Three of us who knew him have contributed reflections of our experiences with Bill and two more follow on this one. Others dug into their files to contribute. Denny Sargent of the Horus/Maat Lodge found several articles and an autobiography in their archives. Louis Martinie of Black Moon Publishing and the Cincinnati Journal of Ceremonial Magick & Archive preserved many short essays from Frater PVN reset herein. This work would be diminished without their contributions.

The bios of the two other commentors follows:
Don Karr (BFA RISD 1974, MFA Cornell 1976) is co-author of two books in the acclaimed series, SOURCEWORKS OF CEREMONIAL MAGIC: with Stephen Skinner, *Sepher Raziel: Liber Salomonis, a Sixteenth-century English Grimoire* (Singapore: Golden Hoard Press, 2010; second edition [paperback], 2018), and with Calanit Nachshon, *Liber Lunæ – Book of the Moon – Sepher ha-Levanah* (Singapore: Golden Hoard Press, 2011; second edition [paperback], 2017). Don also published the pioneering *Approaching the Kabbalah of Maat*

(York Beach: Black Jackal Press, 2013), which contains a foreword by Colin Low; this is supplemented by *Methods of Maat* (forthcoming). Don is the author of numerous articles on Jewish mysticism and its influence on the Western esoteric tradition which can be found online at HERMETIC KABBALAH, edited by Colin Low, at www.digital-brilliance.com ("Bibliographies" and "Contributed Documents") and at ACADEMIA.EDU Don Karr - Academia.edu.

Cliff Pollick has been an almost life-long practitioner of Western esotericism and ritual practice including Neo Paganism, the OTO and Golden Dawn traditions. He is also a Sri Vidya upasaka of a South Indian Kaula Sampradaya. Sacred Geometry and the science of sound are particular interests he has pursued. Recently retired from a 49 year Career in Nursing covering neurosurgical and coronary intensive care to Psychiatry and Dementia care. He lives on the Olympic Peninsula of Washington with his beloved Wife, High Priestess and Shakti, where he finally has time for his music and to catch up on the ever expanding stack of books.

Every effort has been make to provide an accurate presentation of Frater PVN's works. The publisher is grateful for any errors reported. They will be fixed in future editions. We are especially anxious to find page 8 of the BAJ material. Anyone got a copy?
    Also, if further works of our Frater come to light, we would be happy to increase this volume or start another one.
    Anyone wishing to do analytical work with our Frater's text, is warmly invited to send that work to the Publisher for future publication.

Yours in the Great Work & Blessings of the Way,
—*Sam Webster, publisher*
Concrescent Press

Immortalist Copyright

We who aspire to physical Immortality live by a code of personal ethics which transcends any rules & taboos of Tribes, Social Orders. & Religions. We who live outside of Law depend upon our personal Integrity and honesty for our ongoing prosperity.

This [document] is issued by *Math of the ChRySTAL HUMM*, a Powertone of the Eleven-Star Working, under *Immortalist Copyright*.

Immortalist Copyright is a code of ethics by which we share knowledge amongst ourselves, helping us to become friends, as we assist each other in *The* Great Work, and repay those who have assisted us on the Path of Initiation, Enlightenment, & Liberation.

The price you paid for this pamphlet included no royalty payments for its author. If you glean no value from this text, you owe us nothing further—you have already paid for printing and distribution costs.

If, on the other hand, you find the information herein to be of value to you. we ask you to support our on-going work with cash. We would like to receive at least a dime per page from you — but feel free to send more or less, depending on the usefulness of this material to you &/or ability to pay. (You can always send more money later If/when you permit yourself a greater access to wealth.)

Permission Is hereby granted for you to reprint this material. In whole or In part, so long as all copies contain this copyright notice, along with our most recent address. If you give your reprints away for free, you owe us no royalty.

If you sell your reprints at a profit, we ask a minimum royalty of 10 cents/page plus whatever percentage of profits you feel Is Just.

Math of the ChRySTAL HUMM

About the Author in his own words

This…was penned by *LA-BAJ-AL, Mage-&-Watcher* and edited & [originally] typeset by Pνη, *Master of Alchemy*. Each of these illustrious beings resides (along with myriad others) within the complex Magickal Universe known in the outer world as Bill Siebert. Bill began to study magic *consciously* in 1968. On July 6th, 1972 he formally accepted the *Law of Thelema* and began his quest for initiation into the *Astrum Argentum* (A∴A∴). He vowed that if the A∴A∴ were no longer manifest on the outer, he would work the Current on his own in order to re-connect the catena from the Fountainhead of the Order to Malkuth.

In 1973, Bill made contact with Frater IADNAMAD of the Typhonian Branch of the OTO *(Ordo Templi Orientis)* and successfully probationed under Soror Tanith Potnia Therion the following year. While still a probationer. Bill put his personal resources at the disposal of the Order and began to oversee various publishing projects. He became co-editor of *MEZLA,* the official organ of the (Typhonian) OTO, issued a $.93 edition of Liber AL vel Legis, and designed various artistic variations on Liber Oz.

By 1977, Bill had reached the rank of V° within the OTO and began a period of magickal queasiness. Bill was (and still is) an eclectic, who borrows from many sources, and integrates many diverse Currents in accord with his Will. But, the Typhonian Branch of the OTO was a very specialized magickal engine. Those whose exploratory inclinations drifted too far afield from Grant's vision of the Order began to chafe at the *re-directive influences* they received from the *Sovereign Sanctuary.* So Bill began to explore beyond the realm of his grade requirements.

Soror Tanith put him in touch with Soror Andahadna of the *Maat Pangrove Abbey of Thelema,* Soror 0-Maku turned him on to the potential use of entheogenic sacraments, and Bill began a conscious integration of science fiction & fantasy novels into his Thelemic Magick. Although he would not have phrased it this way at the time, by 1979 he was at the brink of transmuting his apprenticeship in the Typhonian OTO into a Journey which would lead him beyond the Abyss to the Fountainhead of the Order.

Around this time. Bill also began to reap internal harvests from his previous 11 years of magickal discipline. In his own Universe, Bill had attained to Tiphareth. Internal guides began to supplement (& in some cases supplant) external teachers (books, letters from teachers, etc.) as his tutors. Adria Moloch, the Beautiful King, was his first Internal teacher/friend and/or the first facet of Bill's internal Universe to manifest as an autonomous entity. From his present perspective on the Universe, it is clear that Adria is/was Bill's HGA (Holy Guardian Angel), but 8 years ago, neither Bill nor Adria felt very comfortable with the formality which such language engendered.

During this period (known fondly as the *Mattress Room* days). Bill formulated the *Thelemic Temple of the Double Vortex* along with Soror 0-Maku (also a V° OTO member) and Tiger Lady (a self-taught intuitive feminist witch). On March 28th, 1981 Soror 0-Maku was *mounted* (in the Voodoo sense of the word) by an entity calling herself *UT, Goddess of Sluts*. During her visitation, UT charged Bill with the formulation/governance of a Thelemic Powerzone dedicated to the vivification & reification of certain aspects of the *Sisterhood of BABALON*.

In the summer of 1981, *Math of the ChRySTAL HUMM* was founded on 23 acres of rolling hills South of Ithaca. Several attempts at communal living were attempted, but (for the most part) the Powerzone was supported by Bill & 0-Maku. In 1982 Frater Hegit introduced Bill & 0-Maku to Frater NOT of Aleister Crowley's OTO and they were both invited to an OTO picnic to encourage communication between the Typhonian & A.C. branches of the Order. At this picnic (known as *the Harriman Working*) Bill got his first real taste of how *initiate snobbery* and group loyalty hinders real communication. But he also saw how group loyalty created a spirit of family, even amongst those who didn't particularly like one-another. Bill decided to expand his initiatory links within the Order so that he might learn other aspects of group dynamics. In 1983, he received his Minerval initiation in Aleister Crowley's OTO with full knowledge of both Hymanaus Alpha, Caliph of A.C.'s OTO and Soror Tanith, X° Sovereign of the Typhonian OTO in North America. Shortly thereafter. Bill was issued diplomatic papers from Soror Tanith, charging him with the Office of Inter-Order diplomat.

Bill's independence did not sit well with either Kenneth Grant or Grady McMurty, but he befriended many members of both branches of the Order, encouraging innovation, learning whatever was interesting, and sharing his own insights with his many magickal friends. In March of 1984, Bill and frater Sam performed a trans-temporal working in Celebration of the return of the Phoenix to Heliopolis. This was the first ritual in which Bill consciously manifested the godform of Chorozon, Lord of the Abyss. Bill & Sam merged Universes. Bill emerged intact, but his Universe would never be the same.

In June of that year, Sam & Bill co-hosted the *Convocation of the Magi* and Bill was introduced to the wonders of the neo-Pagan movement. By Fall, Bill had been to 3 festivals, met many new friends, and began to integrate the Shamanic/Pagan Current into his Thelemic Magickal Universe. Bill then became an active force within the local Pagan community, introduced red meat to their (heretofore vegetarian) feasts, helped to open their circle to *the Great Rite,* and shared entheogenic sacrament with those local Pagans whose Will was aligned with this Path.

By this time. Bill was no longer involved with the sectarian goals of either branch of the OTO. Grant had suspended him from active membership & Grady had placed him on *Bad Report.*

Within a year. Bill had managed to integrate his Shamanic experiences into his OTO Universe. He edited & distributed a new issue of *MEZLA,* which had ceased publication several years previous. Together with 2 other Order members, he formulated the *Chthonic OTO,* whose founding convention was held at the SPiRaL Festival at the Full Moon in September, 1985.

At present. Bill is working to stabilize *Math of the ChRySTAL HUMM,* reify *The Order of BABALON,* manifest the *Chthonic OTO* upon the outer, while learning how to relax and enjoy life to the fullest.

Math of the ChRySTAL HUMM is a functional trans-Æonic Thelemic Powerzone functioning within the 11-Star. *Math* is a Sanscrit word meaning a *Teaching Order*. We are a magickal R-&-D team functioning within a Fagan/Shamanic/Thelemic tradition. We learn/teach/share with one-another and with those Apprentice, Journeymen, & Master Magickians who interact with us here at the HUMM, &/or when we are on the road.

From Bill's perspective, the ever-evolving node around which *Math of the ChRySTAL HUMM* scintillates is the balanced conscious use of Sex Magick, Entheogenic Sacraments, & Shamanic Ritual within a context of absolute personal responsibility. The seedcore of the group soul manifests consciously insofar as each inter-dependent element of the non-hierarchal Gestalt is an autonomous self-aware self-actualizing individual whose Will is to dissolve barriers in order to *Network*.

We feel very strongly that *Victim Consciousness* perpetuates the myth that there is a *Them* which limits *Us* from doing our Will. Such myths have no place within *Math of the ChRySTAL HUMM*. Within our Reality, there are no *Thems*. There is no thought, word, or action which is not part of a mutually beneficial consensual dance. There are no Victims, no Persecutors, and no need for Rescuers.

We welcome communication/communion with other individuals &/or organizations who work with similar tools &/or along similar Paths. As part of our magickal outreach program, we make available crash-space for travelers, & work-study scholarship programs for a limited number of ingenious individuals. We also conduct individual retreats, individual & group initiations, host a variety of Pagan/Shamanic Circles throughout the year, and sponsor Weekend group retreats as a part of our newly flowering *College of the Magi*.

Bill is not into letter writing. He already has a pile of un-answered mail over 5 feet deep stretching back over the past 11 years. But. he does love to receive mail, especially if it is interesting! If you send him an intriguing letter telling him who you are & what sort of magicks you are into, he may send you an invitation to come visit, or to attend a pre-scheduled Magickal event. If you do write or phone, please be candid. We are serious about our magick & we do not have the time or patience to extend ourselves to anyone whom we feel is hiding from us, or whom we feel is negatively attuned to our Path &/or our style of working.

Our work is *the Great Work*. We are interested in all whose Will is aligned with our own, but we need to see who you are before we can interact with you as a magickal person, rather than as just another piece of mail.

Math of the ChRySTAL HUMM

Frater PVN's introductory autobiography to the Horus/Maat Lodge

Do what thou wilt shall be the whole of the Law.

In my pre-teen years I was exposed to some vague concepts of magic & some of the ideas of Aleister Crowley through my mother's uncle who was a mason & a collector of Crowley, as well as some sort of Ceremonial Magician. In my early teen years my parents moved & I was separated from my Uncle & the ideas he had given me. I re-discovered magic when a friend brought me to Weiser's for the first time (back in 1967 or 68) & I began to collect books & to dabble (ape-ing rituals from Shah's compendium). In 1972 I re-discovered the Equinox at the Cornell U. library & on 24 June I began to keep a magickal record (any or all of my record is open to inspection by the H/M Lodge, so long as it is returned in good order & you folks pay the return postage & insurance) & on 6 July, 1972 I accepted the Book of the Law. I worked alone until I 'discovered' that the OTO still existed (via a notice in *Gnostica News* I picked up at an SF Convention in September of '73ev. I began probation under Soror Tanith in 1974 (May eve) & had my overdue record accepted the following Spring. Just before my probation began my sex life shifted from entirely auto (viii°) to hetero + auto—a late start (age 29), but well worth the wait. My second non-monogamous relationship began just prior to probation & I have grown ever closer to Anne over the ensuing years. We sometimes live apart & sometimes do not relate sexually, but we are both on the same path, each always one step ahead/behind/askew/ of the other, I mention Anne because I can have NO secrets from her. It is not my will to exclude her from any knowledge which I possess, be it gained from books, from astral entities, or from personal contact with other persons/groups. I would trust her with my soul & will never be bound by any oaths of secrecy which try to keep us apart. She may never join the H/M Lodge in a formal way (or she may seek to join within the month—I cannot say). If you need more than my word on her trustworthiness (& I certainly can't blame you if you do), check with Andahadna. Anne is probationing under her & she should have some insights into her. Enough of Anne…

In the Spring of 1977 I came into contact with Soror Andahadna & received from her the skeleton framework of the Double-Current system. I worked with it diligently for a brief time, then allowed myself to stop work. I was receiving transmissions/channelings which I was unable to verify or a in any way to double-check for veracity. Frater 718 warned me that the imperfections in the ego could easily distort the subtle messages of a channeling into an erroneous message. I was advised to assume the god-form of the Judge & to examine each iota of information as it passed through me. At that time I felt unable to do this, so I ceased my Maat workings.

Last summer (1978) while working on my Liber Astarte I came into contact with an entity by the name of Adria. She wears many masks & her role/function is as yet unclear to me. Among other things, she is my personal vampire who siphons off my unused sexual energies to prevent them from going to waste & to prevent them from attracting unsavory astral vampires. The exchange is two-way & she is also eager to transfer energy to me when needed. The latest approximation to 'what-she-is' is a lower plane manifestation (mask) for my HGA. She is a Doorway & is able to transform herself into anywhere I am able to comprehend. Having her as a companion is far more 'proof' of my present state of initiation than my V° rank within the OTO.

I am still unsure about my abilities as a scribe for Channeling but am willing to try again & learn from my errors, but I see my Will as being linked to the H/M Lodge in a slightly different way. I have been in printing & publishing for 11 1/3 years now & my father was in printing before me for over a half-century. My blood is the ink of Thoth. I have been a photographer for 13 years (having gotten started in darkroom work because I feared to have my camera store see some pornography I had taken). Books/magazines/posters/collections of Artwork (both photographic & printed) all need to be brought together, artfully/skillfully pieced together, reproduced/mass-produced, and spread to the four corners of the globe.

The great God Xerox is essential for spreading the word amongst the members & friends of the H/M Lodge, but Art/Beauty will be needed to spread the word through libraries/ bookstores/ collectors (who will pass the treasures down to other collectors)/ and others who cannot be reached by xerox alone,

I am in partnership with Shroom, whose will is to transform mortals via chemical messages. Shroom generates money which is partially consumed by Shroom in expansion of living/growing space to produce more Shroom. But there is more money available than Shroom needs directly, Shroom will subsidize the publication & distribution of Double-Current related material,, It is my will to aid with my skills.

It is not my will to supplant Mandragore, but to supplement it. Much talk is needed about this project before it can earth. Finances alone dictate a beginning no sooner than autumn.

My first magickal name was IGOR-45, The Hermit (I) conjoined with the Priestess (G) in sexual union (0) begets the Sun (R). Numeration is from the Tarot Trumps, When I completed my OTO probation I undertook the name OTz PTN–690, The Tree of the Serpent (cobra), The personal sigil appears on my stationary & is a stylized figure seated in asana with hands forming an upright triangle upon the forehead. The figure is against a backdrop of the Tree of Life, Malkuth is opened to a line beneath the figure, Yesod at the genitals, Hod & Netzach at the kneecaps, Tiphareth at the belly cavity, Gebburah & Geddulah at the elbows, Yesod at the neck, and Kether above the head. Coming from Yesod is the entwining cobra which encircles the Middle Pillar, going behind the head & opening up as the hood of a cobra over the head at Kether. The cobra has one eye which watches over the figure even as the hood overshadows & protects the figure.

My True Will (in as far as I am able to discern it at this time) lies in two complimentary areas, a) Publication of original artwork/ prose/ poetry as well as reprints of artwork/ prose/ poetry having to do with the promulgation of Thelema & the Double-Current, At the present time this means overseeing the production of Mezla (official organ of the OTO), reprinting a cheap edition of Liber AL vel Legis, and re-printing the Sothis Commentary to Liber Oz. Future projects I already discussed but not finalized include a (or several) portfolios of Soror Andahadna's paintings, a possible first edition of Andahadna's textbook on self-initiation via the Double Current (the Cincy Journal seems to want to hold-off publication for at least a year), possible (long term future) publication of the Nightside Tarot deck.

Lending my gardening/microbiological skills to Shroom in its efforts to take over the planet. This includes 3 phases. Phase I (currently in operation) setting up a stable growing situation & finding/expanding markets for sale of Shroom; Phase II (projected for fall of 1979ev) payback of initial investment money, hire me full time as gardener, expand operation within limited space requirements. Balance of income used to begin publication ventures; Phase III Initial investment & expansion all paid for, my needs continue to be paid for in exchange for gardening skills, surplus continues to be devoted to publication ventures. At this stage there should be considerable potential for producing more shroom for use in scholarship program with the H/M Lodge i.e., free Shroom to working magicians within the Lodge), providing this does not interfere with money flow needed to pay gardener or the publications venture. Phase III may begin (in a limited way) by Spring 1980 & be in full swing by the following Spring. If the need becomes greater than the supply, work/study programs &/or seed money for other operations may be possible during phase III.

Near-Future goal (by 1984) is to have distributed at least 10,000 copies of Liber AL & whatever Double-Current material is available for me to publish & to have at least 1000 magicians tripping regularly (hopefully weekly) within a magick circle & linked with all other trippers via the community of mycelia & the Comity of Stars.

Since such use of non-kala drugs is openly frowned-upon by the OTO (at this point in time) & since it would be unfair of me to undertake such subversion within the ranks of the OTO, I propose to work my Will in these matters outside of the confines of the OTO. Hopefully my Will is enough in line with the Will of the H/M Lodge that I may work towards these goals openly within the Order. If not, I will still work with the H/M Lodge insofar as I can, but will also feel free to work my Will via Shroom & publishing outside the official boundaries of the H/M Lodge.

I care not what degree or sphere I be assigned to. The publishing is Hod while Shroom is very Netzach. To combine them both is to invoke the Tower & to transcend the Tower is to accomplish Art For years & years I have been much more a reader of magic or a plotter than a doer. I have just begun to explore what it means to be a magickian & so will probably be playing/learning the outer/lower spheres for quite some time no matter what my nominal placement, yet I reserve the right to bound to the heights at the center of the Universe, for when Adria & I are 'in-synch' there is naught that is barred to me.

While I am not a member of the Inner Council (nor do I seek admission), there may come a time when my boasts & promises earth themselves well enough that I may be trusted to have good sense about me. If/when that time comes I would like to discuss the possibilities/ desirability (or undesirability)/ strategy of inner Order (as opposed to outer Order) ties with other Occult Orders., I have long had visions of a union of Grant's OTO with McMurtry's. So long as anyone who knew Crowley lives, that is utterly impossible. It may not even be possible for or two generations beyond that—unless a third faction enters the picture. Enough of my plottings. First I must prove myself & then maybe you will want to hear the schemings of my deranged mind.

No time to send xeroxes of transmissions with this letter. I will either bring them this weekend or send them later in the month. The sigil/mandala [on the back cover and in the *Math of the ChRySTAL HUMM*] is the result of my first magickal working & is (I believe) a pure channeling. It is a glyph of the Cthulhu mythos Universe depicting the inter-relationship among the major deities. Someplace I have a written description which I will send later. This dates from 1972 or maybe 1973.

Love is the law, love under will.

Bill Siebert
a.k.a.
(frater) OTz PTN-690, V°, OTO

PVN, ☿-416, etc., some recollections

by Don Karr

Introduction

William "Bill" Siebert (variously Frater PVN, Frater OTz PTN– 690, AShT ChOzar S*Saratu*, Alobar Greywalker) was born May 27, 1945 and died in July of 2020, reportedly from the Covid-19 virus.

In the mid-1970s, Bill probationed into Kenneth Grant's OTO, which is now called the Typhonian Order. Within that order, Bill attained V°. Upon entering his probation, Bill became an active member of the Typhonian Order serving as one of the editors of its "Official Organ," *Mezla*, from 1975 to 1979.

Bill and his then-partner Anne (who also attained V° in the Typhonian Order) co-founded Math of the ChRySTAL HUMM, a "Thelemic powerzone," in 1981 and established Boleskine House, inc. as its publishing arm. Boleskine House reprinted the first twelve issues of *Mezla* and Bill's numerous chapbooks.

In 1983, both Bill and Anne were initiated into the California (or American) OTO, then under Grady McMurtry. However, Bill's membership soon lapsed over a dues issue. In 1985, having also been suspended from the Typhonian Order, Bill co-founded the Chthonic-Auranian OTO.

In late 2019, I began composing a "scrapbook" of images and documents from my association with Bill and others with whom I had become acquainted through him (December 1983 through 1986). The essay written to accompany the 70+ pages of images is reproduced in slightly modified form below.[1]

These recollections were compiled before a compendium of Bill's work was considered. Thus, it was not written as an introduction to Bill's writings and ideas but as a personal account of one remarkably dynamic segment of the 1980s "occult" scene.

---

1 See the 'scrapbook' at concrescent.net.

1983

By December of 1983, I had read lots of Crowley (1875-1947)[2] and Crowley-related books. Of the latter, the most significant were *The Eye in the Triangle*[3] and *Tree of Life: A Study in Magic*[4] by Francis Israel Regardie (1907-1983) and the works of Kenneth Grant (1924-2011).[5] Reading all this made me curious as to what the O.T.O. and the A∴A∴ looked like from the inside.[6]

In those days, I frequented the original Borealis Bookstore in Collegetown at 416 Eddy Street, Ithaca, New York (founded June 23, 1978). Toward the end of 1983, they had on display several books by and about Crowley—including:

- some of the Marcelo Ramos Motta (1931-1987) editions of *The Equinox*[7]

---

2 *Magick in Theory & Practice* (New York: Castle Books, [n.d.]); *The Book of Thoth* (New York: Samuel Weiser, 1969); *The Book of Lies* (New York: Samuel Weiser, 1970); *The Vision and the Voice* (Dallas: Sangreal Foundation. Inc., 1072); *Magick without Tears* (Phoenix: Falcon Press, 1973); *The Qabalah of Aleister Crowley* (New York: Samuel Weiser, 1973); *Gems from the Equinox* (St. Paul: Llewellyn Publications, 1974), etc.
3 Saint Paul: Llewellyn Publications, 1970.
4 New York: Samuel Weiser, Inc., 1971.
5 In 1983, these would have included *The Magical Revival* (London: Frederick Muller, 1972), *Aleister Crowley and the Hidden God* (London: Frederick Muller, 1973), *Cults of the Shadow* (London: Frederick Muller, 1975), *Images and Oracles of Austin Osman Spare* (New York: Samuel Weiser, Inc., 1975), *Nightside of Eden* (London: Frederick Muller, 1977), and *Outside the Circles of Time* (London: Frederick Muller, 1980).
6 With James Wasserman's *In the Center of the Fire* (Lake Worth: Ibis Press, 2012) and J. Edward Cornelius' *Changing of the Guard* (Berkeley: [privately issued], 2019), we have detailed "insider" accounts of American O.T.O. personalities and events in the periods 1966-1989 and 1989-1993 respectively.

   Wasserman mentions Bill in one brief passage (*In the Center of the Fire*, page 188):
   "Summer 1982
   Another camping trip later that summer at Harriman State Park [Rockland and Orange Counties, New York] renewed my contact with Bill Siebert. He had been a disciple of Kenneth Grant. I had met him with Janice Ayers and David Smith back in the day. Siebert had become friends with Alan Davis of the Philadelphia O.T.O. By this time, I believe he had left Grant and was on his own. An amazingly talented alchemist, he had brewed up a powerful psychedelic concoction of which I took way too much."
   Wasserman is a little off here. Bill, in effect, "left Grant and was on his own" in 1984, when he was suspended from the Typhonian O.T.O.—even more so in 1986, when he was expelled. The particulars of Bill's departure from Grant's O.T.O. are discussed below.
   Cornelius doesn't mention Bill, but he does mention Cliff Pollick in an endnote (page 287, note 21) in connection with the unauthorized publication of "Emblems and Modes of Use," an O.T.O. grade paper restricted to IX° and XI° members. Cornelius' note is quoted below in my segment on *Mezla* III.
   Wasserman and Cornelius are conspicuously absent from each other's books. Wasserman rushes by a single reference to "Jerry Cornelius" as "my former friend" (—*In the Center of the Fire*, page 210), and that's it.
7 Motta's editions of *The Equinox*: Vol. V, No. 3. *The Chinese Texts of Magick and Mysticism* (Nashville: Thelema Publishing Co., 1980); Vol. V, No. 4. *Sex and Religion* (Nashville: Thelema Publishing Co., 1981); and Vol. VI, Nos. 1-2. *Yoga and Magick, being* BOOK FOUR PART I (Nashville: Society Ordo Templi Orientis International, 1982).

- the latest by Grant, namely *Outside the Circles of Time*—the edition with the brownish yellow pages
- *Liber 1276* by O PIVOT L $?^\circ = I^\square$ and LEΘI XUD OZ $I^\circ = ?^\square$[8]

I also saw a handful of chapbooks by an author whom I was unaware of at the time: Frater PVN:
- *The Alchemy of Immortality*
- *ChRySTAL Workings thru the Astral Mirror*
- *Nine-Fold Flowering of Alchemies within the Eleven Star*

Among these homespun little publications was the *Boleskine House, inc. Catalog of Essays & Periodicals* (West Danby: Boleskine House, inc., Winter, 1983 e.v.). The catalog contained a description of Math of the ChRySTAL HUMM ("an independent Thelemic Powerzone"), a statement of its goals ("we seek active communication, communion, and cross pollination with those other buds who are endeavoring to flower at this time"), and, what especially caught my eye, "Attention Authors & Artists," which was a call for submissions of written and graphic work. This was followed by descriptions of the "Official Publications of the Typhonian OTO,"[9] namely the periodical *Mezla*, Vol. I, Nos. 1 through 12, and the "Political & Alchemical Writings of Frater PVN." I took a copy.

After scouring the catalog and seeing that Boleskine House was a local operation, I composed a letter to Bill Siebert, author of the introduction to the catalog, with questions about the O.T.O. and mention of my interest in submitting written and graphic work for consideration. The Perfected Tree[10] had been developed by then, and I had several notebooks of writings on work I was doing with ℷ (1950-) and what would come to be called 416. In a more narrative, albeit symbolic, way, I was chronicling my magical progress in my paintings.

My letter to Bill included contact information, which in those days

---

The EDITORIAL that serves as a foreword to *Sex and Religion* lists "William Siebert" among those whom Motta believed to be spurious representatives of the O.T.O. (*Sex and Religion*, pages xii-xiii). Also on Motta's list are others who appear in the present paper: Janice Ayers, Phyllis Seckler, Grady McMurtry, James Wasserman, William Breeze, Kenneth Grant, and Francis King.

8 Full title: *Liber 4 6 3 8 A B K 2 4 A L G M O R 3 Y X 24 89 R P S T O V A L* SUB FIGURA MCCLXXVI, being excerpts from THE BOOK OF KEYS, Images on the Path to understanding LIBER AL VEL LEGIS, Chapter II. V. 76, edited by Randy Von Smith and George Conard Eisenhardt II ([n.p.]: privately issued, 1982)—possibly the most obscure Crowley-related item ever produced.

9 The Typhonian O.T.O. is an offshoot of the Ordo Templi Orientis in the UK founded and run by Kenneth Grant.

10 *i.e.*, the Perfected Kabbalistic Tree of Life used by 416. See my *Approaching the Kabbalah of Maat* (York Beach: Black Jackal Press, 2013), pp. 100-108. Bill habitually referred to The Perfected Tree as "The Tree of Perfection."

was a mailing address and a land-line phone number.

Bill responded by phone in days, inviting me to his home: Math of the ChRySTAL HUMM, "a Shamanic/Alchemical Thelemic Powerzone based in an old rundown farmhouse with twenty-three acres of rolling fields & woodlands (our ritual space),"[11] "halfway to Spencer [from Ithaca]…right across the road from the First Baptist Church [of West Danby]."[12]

Bill and I met for the first time on the evening of December 12, 1983, a Monday.

He was a big guy, a bit awkward in his bulk, which was swathed in a loose grey sweat suit. The most striking thing about him was his long white-grey hair and beard which made him appear much older than his 38 years. At first glance, Bill resembled your classic wizard, but he rather enjoyed saying that, on closer inspection, he looked more like a degenerate Santa Claus. Bill spoke of his encounters with children at the supermarket. He'd see a child eyeing him incredulously. Then he'd straighten up (he demonstrated) and with a huge grin bellow, "Well now, have we been *naughty* or *nice* this year?"

Bill was completely open. Though a bit halting in speech, even stammering at times, he fully answered all of my questions and spoke freely about his magickal work. There was no hint of either the reticence *or* mystery mongering which I had found to be common among occult types when talking to outsiders.

At that first meeting, I also met Bill's partner, Anne, aka 0-Maku. She too was in the O.T.O., but when she heard what we were talking about—magick, *qabalah*, occult books—she rolled her eyes and said, "Oh, *that* stuff." She stuck around but wasn't inclined to chime in.[13]

Both Bill and Anne were V° Typhonian O.T.O. (= TOTO). In 1981, they co-founded Math of the ChRySTAL HUMM "for the purpose of promulgation of the Law of Thelema (on the outer) and to act as a framework within which to guide those whose Will is to work within this Powerzone upon the inner."[14]

Among the books on Bill's shelves (I am *immediately* drawn to people's

---

11 William Siebert (AShT ChOzar SSaratu), "Some Brief Notes Regarding the On-Going Work of Our Miskatonic Alchemical Expedition," (1994 Preface, ¶ 3) at Z-Chronicles (what the hell): https://groups.google.com/forum/#!topic/alt.magick.chaos/khNrrg_F8ZQ

12 Unsourced quotes from Bill Siebert are primarily from notes taken from my conversations with him, December 1983 through March 1984.

13 Anne and I eventually became friends. We had long, often intense, exchanges about "*that* stuff."

14 *MATH of the ChRySTAL HUMM: Charter & Statement of Purpose* (West Danby: Boleskine House, inc., 1983), page 3.

books), the ten white volumes of Crowley's *Equinox*[15] stood out.

I was a bit surprised to see a selection of items from Work of the Chariot (WC), of which the most used looking was *Sefer ha Shmot/ Book of the Names*.[16] I too had collected a handful of WC's publications, focusing on their translations of kabbalistic texts.[17]

Bill told me that he had ordered the WC publications "out of curiosity…because they looked interesting," but that he felt "no strong connection" to these works. However, WC was the source of the only piece on *kabbalah* (as opposed to *qabalah*) that Bill ever put into one of his chapbooks: "Traditional Variations on the Tree of Life," which is Appendix III of *Nine-fold Flowering of Alchemies within The Eleven-Star*.[18] Bill reproduced ten Tree of Life configurations from *Sefer ha Shmot* along with ten pages of WC's commentary.

I asked Bill what O.T.O.-related works he'd read other than Crowley's.[19] He pulled out two books that he said were particularly significant to him: Louis Culling's *Complete Magick Curriculum of the Secret Order G.˙.B.˙.G.˙.*[20] and Kenneth Grant's *Nightside of Eden*. While *Complete Magick Curriculum* is an item of considerable interest, Bill later conceded that it "doesn't really live up to its title." Thus, it was difficult to see why it was singled out as an important book. On the other hand, it was easy to see why he chose *Nightside of Eden*, a book that I was quite familiar with: Kenneth Grant's *shadow qabalah*, about which Bill commented:

> [D]o not try to verify Uncle Kenny's [Grant's] Qabalah. It just does not work that way. You can hurt your head trying. Just look for the connection he is trying to make & use it as a jumping off point for meditation… [D]o not fuss over things

---

15 The Samuel Weiser edition of 1972, limited to 555 copies.
16 Hollywood: Work of the Chariot, 1971. See http://www.workofthechariot.com/TextFiles/Trees-Introduction.html.
17 *i.e.*, *Book of Formation*, *Sifra Detzniutha*, the *Idra Rabba, Lesser Holy Assembly*, and *Tree of Life*, all published by Work of the Chariot (Los Angeles, later Hollywood) in 1970-1971. Work of the Chariot material mentioned can be found in Daniel Hale Feldman's *Qabalah: The Mystical Heritage of the Children of Abraham* (Santa Cruz: Work of the Chariot, 2001), and viewed at the Work of the Chariot website > http://www.workofthechariot.com/TextFiles/Translations.html
18 West Danby: Boleskine House, inc., 1983, pages 35-44.
19 See "List of Suggested Readings," which is Appendix II in *The Alchemy of Immortality*. There, Bill recommends a selection of works by Crowley, all of the works by Kenneth Grant (to 1983), and the fiction of Chelsea Quinn Yarbro and H. P. Lovecraft.
20 Louis Culling (1894-1973), Saint Paul: Llewellyn Publications, 1969. Taking what I assumed was Bill's recommendation, I tried to order Culling's book only to discover that it was out of print and hard to find. I eventually got hold of a copy.

which do not seem to add up properly.[21]

Other sources that Bill mentioned during my first visit were *The Cincinnati Journal of Ceremonial Magick* from Conquering Child Publishing Co. (Cincinnati) and *Arachny's Web* from the Nephthys Chapter of the O.T.O. (Edmonton), which, in 1982, may have been the first to print Jack Parsons' *Book of B.A.B.A.L.O.N.*[22] and distribute it beyond O.T.O. circles.

All in all, Bill and I had a lovely, lively chat that first evening, which included a bit of good-natured argument, *e.g.*, about whether the *qabalah* of the Golden Dawn-Crowley-Achad[23]-Fortune[24]-etc. could claim the same legitimacy as that possessed by rabbinic *kabbalah*.

1984

After my initial visit—which may have been my audition—Bill invited me to many dinners and ritual gatherings at Math of the ChRyS-TAL HUMM (usually just called the HUMM). At these occasions I made the acquaintance of about two dozen people engaged in pagan and Crowley-based practices. Better than half of the people I met had some relation to the O.T.O., and, interestingly, nearly all of these had a Roman Catholic upbringing.

Bill often mentioned his own Catholic background. He refers to this in the introduction to his *Doxology, Commentary, Vision of a Gnostic Mass*,[25]

> It may be worthy of note that PVN had a very strong fascination with the Roman liturgy as a child & even now is subject to visions & dreams of a Roman/Gnostic fusion.

---

21 Bill, as Alobar, posting to Wyrdglow discussion group (7/22/2003—private site), cited by Dave Evans, *The History of British Magick after Crowley* ([n.p.]: Hidden Publishing, 2007), page 318.

22 Jack W. Parsons (Fr. 2.1.0., 1914-1952), *The Book of B.A.B.A.L.O.N.* (AKA *Liber 49*), transcribed from J. Parsons manuscript (1946) by Sr. Chandria, Nuit-Urania Chapter O.T.O., Introduction transcribed by Eugene W. Plawiuk, © Grady McMurty (*sic*)/Ordo Templi Orientis (Berkeley, Ca., 1982). Photocopies of this version of *The Book of B.A.B.A.L.O.N.* were available from The Archives, an inventory of submitted material, mostly "magickal," that anyone could purchase for the price of photocopying and postage.

The Archives were begun in 1982 by Conquering Child Publishing Company of Cincinnati, "a Cabal of occultists" who, from 1976 to 1989, published the influential *Cincinnati Journal of Ceremonial Magick*. Conquering Child became Black Moon Publishing in the fall of 1984. Thereafter, the Archives became known as the Black Moon Archives and the title of their periodical publication was shortened to *Cincinnati Journal of Magick*.

23 Frater Achad (1886-1950), titles in brief: *QBL* (Chicago: [privately printed], 1922), *The Egyptian Revival* (Chicago: The Collegium Ad Spiritum Sanctum, 1923), and *The Anatomy of the Body of God* (Chicago: The Collegium Ad Spiritum Sanctum, 1925)—all reprinted by Samuel Weiser Inc. in the 1970s.

24 Dion Fortune (1890-1946), *The Mystical Qabalah* (London: Williams & Norgate, 1935), reprinted frequently.

25 West Danby: Boleskine House, 1983, page 6.

Other people in the HUMM's coterie were sundry witches (male and female), wizards, and uncategorizable pagans.

Among the people I met through Bill, the O.T.O. connections were of three types:[26]

- members of the California O.T.O.,[27] then under Grady McMurtry (Hymenaeus Alpha, 1918-1985), which was at that time referred to as "The Caliphate,"[28] a term no longer favored by the American O.T.O. "establishment," which prefers simply "*the* O.T.O."

    Bill described the California O.T.O. as being run "according to rules set out in [Crowley's] *Blue Equinox*."[29] He criticized their "inertia" and complained about their "hierarchy." The best thing Bill could say about the California O.T.O. was that being a member "offered companionship."

- members of—or defectors to—the Typhonian O.T.O. (later called the Typhonian Order) under Kenneth Grant (1924-2011). People in this group had a fondness for McMurtry but disliked the "posturing" and "territorial mindset" of those around him.

    Many Typhonians felt that the California O.T.O. held to an orthodox interpretation of Crowley's writings which was incomplete, "watered down," and often inaccurate, *and* that no new or original work was being produced—like Bill's "inertia" criticism. Correspondingly, they felt that Grant was expanding what Crowley had begun, divulging secrets and exploring dimensions that Crowley had only hinted at.

    California loyalists viewed the Typhonian O.T.O. as the "cult of Grant." They believed that Grant was just making things up to sensationalize the O.T.O. in order to sell books and gain a following. His immensely popular works were written off as

---

26 The assessments reported here specifically reflect circumstances in the mid-1980s.
27 I use "California O.T.O." in this essay since it is the term that I remember being used most frequently in the mid-1980s. Court cases in California in 1976 and 1985 established McMurtry's O.T.O., which was based in Berkeley, as the legitimate bearer of the title "Ordo Templi Orientis" or "O.T.O."—at least in the US. Thus, the so-called California O.T.O., which was the "head office" of a national organization with lodges throughout the country, laid claim to being *the* O.T.O., negating the assertions of Marcelo Motta (Brazil) and Kenneth Grant (UK).
28 McMurtry's full title was "Caliph Hymenaeus Alpha 777"; hence, the O.T.O. under him was called "the Caliphate." Bill usually referred to McMurtry's O.T.O. as "the Caliphate," although later as "Aleister Crowley's OTO." Some California members simply called it the "American O.T.O.," as opposed to Motta's "Brazilian O.T.O." or Grant's "British O.T.O."
29 Aleister Crowley *et al*, *The Equinox*, Volume III, No. 1: "The Blue Equinox" (Detroit: Universal Publishing, 1919; rpt. New York Samuel Weiser, 1972).

"occult fiction."

A common defensive response from the Typhonians was, "At least Grant is *doing* something!"

Bill described working in Grant's O.T.O. as "pretty much solitary," "mail order," "more like A∴A∴ than Grady's." "It's good for establishing links, both external and internal." You have "occasional contact with someone above you in the order."

"When I was a member there were grade requirements. Upon completing these requirements, one was recommended for a higher degree & paperwork was issued. When I asked about initiations, I was informed that my doing the work & dutifully keeping my diary was the real initiation. The paperwork only confirmed what was already earned."[30]

Bill's perception of the Typhonian O.T.O. was that Grant "took off on a mission to revamp the O.T.O." With this, Bill lamented, "Grant is a loyalist [*i.e.*, he demands loyalty]: there's a throne and a bunch of commoners." He also mentioned problems concerning "hierarchy questions and [the] tight structure." These "hierarchy" and "structure" problems, in fact, led Bill's "immediate superior to quit,"[31] leaving Bill "in direct contact with Grant."[32]

- renegades and rebels, who passed through either the California or Typhonian O.T.O., or both, and were rankled by issues such as those described above. These folks felt that "Organization O.T.O." or "O.T.O. Inc." brought out the worst in people. Bill described both factions of the O.T.O. as "structured like a pyramid," which wasn't good.

Some people that I met had dropped out of Grant's O.T.O. because they couldn't produce a suitable magickal record to

---

30 Email to thelema93-l@hollyfeld.org from W. A. Greywalker, RE "Grant and TOTO," June 5, 2000.
31 Soror Tanith 789, whose desire to withdraw from the Typhonian O.T.O. was acknowledged by Grant (using the name Aossic Aiwass, 718) in a letter dated February 2, 1983.
32 Other accounts add the following details: When Soror Tanith quit, Kephera-ma-Ast became Bill's superior, which did not go well at all. Kephera-ma-Ast was also appointed to Tanith's position of X°, i.e., the Typhonian O.T.O.'s representative in the US. Prior to all that, Kephera-ma-Ast and his wife had lived at Math of the ChRyYSTAL HUMM for a while. They left the HUMM under a cloud of debt and bad feelings. My impression was that Bill had evicted, perhaps banished, them. "When [Kephera-ma-Ast] left upstate NY, he & I parted on very bad terms as he had not paid rent or contributed work at my farm. When he was asked to leave, he made a hissy fit & trashed his temple, leaving me & my partner Anne to clean up his mess." —Siebert, E-mail of 4.4.2001, cited in "Plan 93 from Outer Space" by Peter-Robert Koenig within "Typhonian Ordo Templi Orientis/Kenneth Grant /LAM," at https://www.parareligion.ch/lam.htm

All this had played out before I met Bill in December 1983; at that time, only he and Anne were living at the HUMM.

Bill's email of June 5, 2000, cited above, notes, "But I must add that Grant & I were never close."

submit at the conclusion of their probationary period.

As a self-described "renegade," Bill was ultimately in the last category. In 1977, Bill "probationed in" to Grant's Typhonian O.T.O., from which he was suspended in 1984[33] and ultimately expelled in 1986.

> I had long been a member of Grant's Typhonian OTO for nearly a decade, during which time I worked my way from probationer to V°. When I began to evince symptoms of knowing my Will & reifying it, Grant informed me that the OTO was designed for those who were not yet ready to manifest their Wills. According to Grant, those who know their Will and are doing it, have no need of OTO. Once I grasped the significance of what he was saying, I most certainly agreed that I had no real need of the Typhonian OTO. Synthesizing my personal links with the Fountainhead of the Order, and accepting similar links which Grant & others were formulating within themselves is not always an easy task for me, but it is one which I find to be well worth my effort. So I remained within the orbit of the Typhonian OTO until Grant expelled me in 1986.[34]

Bill joined the California O.T.O.—or tried to—after he had been in the Typhonian O.T.O. some years. Bill states in the Epilogue to *Doxology...*, p. 35,

> It may be worthy of note that in early April of this year [1983] ... 0-Maku & I received initiation into Aleister Crowley's Branch of the OTO [*i.e.*, the California O.T.O.] to counterbalance long-held initiations in the Typhonian Branch of the OTO.

Bill explains his short-lived California O.T.O. career in a 1985 letter to James Wasserman:

> Presently, I am a 'lapsed Minerval' within the Aleister Crowley [California] OTO. In passing, I would like to mention that I would not be 'lapsed' if brother Bill Heidrick [Grand Treasur-

---

33 Bill states in Mezla, Vol. III, No. 1 (Fall 1985), page 2, "A year ago I was suspended from active membership in the Typhonian OTO by Frater Kephra-ma-Ast." Bill questioned whether Kephra-ma-Ast had the authority to do so, but assumed that Kephra-ma-Ast was acting at Grant's behest. Kephra-ma-Ast himself was eventually tossed out of the Typhonian Order, but not until 2000.

34 Bill Siebert, "The Chthonic-Auranian OTO," at http://www.angelfire.com/pa2/cthonicauranian/seibert.html. "The divergence of will between myself & Grant was mutual. I simply allowed him to make the first move as I felt I had no need to divorce myself from him or his branch of the OTO in order to pursue my will. By hindsight, I see the split was a necessity for me to help formulate the Chthonic/Auranian-OTO."—email to thelema93-l@hollyfeld.org from W. A. Greywalker.

er General of the O.T.O. from 1979-2005] had not refused my late dues payment which I gave to brother Cliff Pollick, then Chaptermaster of Hadit Chapter in Philadelphia (the chapter into which I was initiated as a Minerval). I deliberately heldback my dues payment pending recognition of my initiation into A.C.'s OTO (receipt of my Minerval Certificate, welcoming letter from Bill Heidrick, etc.). I felt there was no sense in supporting an Order which does not recognize that I am a member (see AL III:41 [*i.e..*, *The Book of the Law*, CHAPTER III, verse 41][35]). Upon receipt of my Minerval Certificate (about a year-&-a-half after my initiation), I attempted to pay my previous year's dues.[36]

All through his "membership era," Bill bristled at how O.T.O. degrees and A∴A∴ grades were parsed out, often granted or withheld for "personal or political reasons." He came to believe, in line with his take on the fundamental principles of Thelema, that anyone should be able to "claim any grade at any time": *Do what thou wilt shall be the whole of the Law*.

Bill talked about developing and investigating alternative systems, like the Eleven-Star[37] and traditions such as those that he had described in his extraordinary "vampire book," *The Alchemy of Immortality*, that is, "secret societies [that were] given secrets but not the keys."

As for the A∴A∴ (Astrum Argentum[38]), Bill described two approaches: "chain theory" and "individual theory." In the former, each member is a link in a hierarchical chain of superiors and subordinates in a "single line through the grades." The "individual theory," which Bill practiced and clearly preferred, was what you would expect: "no chain, just independent work."

PVN & 416

Given the work I was doing with 416, which was Maat-centered, I pestered Bill *and* Anne with a ton of loaded questions about the role of women in the O.T.O. Bill admitted that O.T.O. doctrine and practice

---

35 "Establish at thy Kaaba a clerk-house: all must be done well and with business way."
36 Letter from PVN (Bill Siebert) to Jim Wasserman, December 21, 1985, page 1, ¶ 4.
37 See *Nine-Fold Flowering of Alchemies within the Eleven-Star Working* and *Further Notes on the Eleven Star Working*.
38 There is some dispute of whether A∴A∴ stands for Astrum Argentum. See James Eshelman, *The Mystical and Magical System of the A∴A∴* (Los Angeles: The College of Thelema, 2000), wherein Eshelman states, "The name is *Astron Argon* (ΑΣΤΡΟΝ ΑΡΓΟΝ). It is the Greek—not the Latin—phrase meaning 'silver star.'" (page 23)

as declared by Crowley was "fundamentally sexist," but he "hope[d] to mitigate that in [his] own work."

Bill noted an "overlap in people" between Gardnerian Wicca and O.T.O. "Wicca goes to the III° craft, then goes into IV° O.T.O." He did not, however, speak of any local Wiccan groups.

He also talked about "Maggie Cook, or Crosby" (eventually Maggie Ingalls, 1939-2018), best known as Nema, who was doing Maat-inclusive work in the context of Twin Current doctrine.[39] She was part of the "cabal" behind *The Cincinnati Journal of Ceremonial Magick*, one of the founders of the Horus Maat Lodge,[40] and at that time a grudging student of Kenneth Grant.

Bill said of Nema, "She's breaking barriers," noting that she was "coming up with stuff" that Grant featured in his books. Bill grieved, however, that there was a "change in [the] spirit of Nema in Grant," that is, Grant appropriated Nema's work and adapted it to suit his own purposes. Bill's reference here was, in particular, to Grant's *Outside the Circles of Time* (1980), wherein Nema is referred to as Soror Andahadna.[41]

416 work was leading toward a revision of the Procession of the Æons which advanced the idea that the Æon of Maat either had already started or could be caused to start, overthrowing the self-serving acquisitive Horus. Part of the process, as 416 saw it, was to use the Perfected Tree, which had no *malkut*, investing that power in *da'at* as a full *sefirah*.[42]

Bill defended the position that the "new [*i.e.*, current] æon" was the "Æon of Horus, *not* The Twins," and that it had begun in 1904 as Crowley claimed. Not wanting to seem too doctrinaire, he qualified

---

39 Margaret "Maggie" Ingalls / Nema, was the eventual author of *Maat Magick: A Guide to Self-Initiation* (York Beach: Samuel Weiser, Inc., 1995) and *Wings of Rapture* (New Orleans: Black Moon Publishing, 2011), which is a reprint of *The Way of Mystery: Magick, Mysticism & Self-Transcendence* (St. Paul: Llewellyn Publications, 2003). On Nema and Maat Magick, see *Approaching the Kabbalah of Maat*, pages 57-72 and 76-81. In the 'eighties, Nema treated the Æons of Horus and Maat, the Twins, as concurrent. Some years later, she shifted her thinking toward that of 416: "I began by thinking that Horus and Maat comprised 'the double current', but accumulating experiences showed me that Maat Magick is a Panæonic Magick."—Margaret Ingalls, "The Evolution of Maat Magick: From Cornfields to Cyberspace," in *Starfire*, Volume II, Number 3 (London: Starfire Publishing, Ltd, 2008), page 177.

40 On the Horus Maat Lodge, go to http://horusmaatlodge.com/, and see *Approaching the Kabbalah of Maat*, pp. 70-81.

41 Plate 9 in *Outside the Circles of Time* shows a painting by Andahadna (Nema) called *The Evocation of Yog Sothoth*. The actual painting hung on the wall at the HUMM. Bill informed me that Nema called the image "*Cthulhu*." A bit cropped and poorly reproduced, the painting appeared as "Cthulhu by Nema" on page 6 of *Silverstar: A Journal of New Magick*, Volume I, Issue 1 (Spring Equinox, 2004): http://www.horus-maatlodge.com/silverstar/SILVERSTAR1.html.

42 On the Æons, see *Approaching the Kabbalah of Maat*, pages 12-17 and 112-113. On the Perfected Tree, see *ibid.*, pages 100-108 and 226-272.

this by saying that "the function of the æons is [only] on the outer," adding, "magick above the abyss allows choice," for instance, between "Horus – I will" and the "Twins – extension of the יהוה."

But then Bill stressed the "importance of keeping *da'at* a non-sphere" as a "matter of historical precedence," a rationale that seemed to contradict his anarchic tendencies and his inclusion of *da'at* in the rituals that he performed,[43] not to mention his then-imminent "merger of the [Maatian] Tree of Perfection with the Cup of Babalon."[44]

Some months after telling me all this, Bill referred to this "merger" of my stuff and his in a "Follow-up letter" (Nº 1) sent to the thirty-or-so people who had attended CONVOCATION OF THE MAGI I (June 1984—see below: "CONVO I"). With regard to a presentation of *The Chalice of Ecstasy* that he had planned to make at the CONVOCATION but time had not permitted, Bill expresses his variance with the Maatian cast of the "Tree of Perfection" (*i.e.*, 416's "Perfected Tree") and the "dogma behind [it]":

> My paper on *The Chalice of Ecstasy* is a first tentative map of a Jovian Universe which was first made accessible to me *via* Don Karr's *Tree of Perfection*.
> *NOTE*: Although Don & I share an appreciation for many aspects of the Great Work, our perspectives are quite different from one another. The dogma behind the *Tree of Perfection* does not sit well with my Jovian nature, nor with the intense polarities of the sexual formulae which I choose to work in this lifetime. Hence (for me), Don's Tree mutated into *The Chalice of Ecstasy*, which I believe may be useful to others as a gateway which can be used effectively by any whose dogma is not so rigid that they are bound to a single world-view. For me (on the outer) Malkuth remains the bride, but when the Magus works upon the inner (where all the Æons manifest beyond Time & Alternity), the manifest Universe (Malkuth)

---

43 In *tree-of-life*-based group work, Bill preferred to hold the station of *da'at*. "I have been involved in the Horus/Maat Lodge nearly since its inception, and am most often a throneholder of the Sphere of Daäth." — Alobar Greywalker, Facebook, https://www.facebook.com/alobar.greywalker

Further, there are the following statements in an email from Bill (as Alobar) to the Horus-Maat Lodge Google Group (12/03/2010) which align with 416 doctrine: "When I was in both the Typhonian and the Caliphate branches of the OTO, I was told that many things were beyond my grade. It inspired me to transcend the formal orders, get my butt to Daäth, to embrace the Fountainhead of the OTO, and proceed from there.…When you say, 'Don't forget what holds the tree up,' I suspect you are referring to Malkuth. But from my perspective, it is Daäth."

44 i.e., *The Chalice of Ecstasy*. (herein)

is drawn-up within (like the testicles of a Sumo wrestler), so Maya will be shielded from that which lies beyond duality. ...

Dinners

Bill was a gregarious host who loved bringing diverse people together. Anne was most cordial, taking the role of the mom at the table.

Generally, the people that I met through Bill came to tolerate my unflagging skepticism with grace and good humor. In the midst of one fairly typical after-dinner discussion, Bill addressed the table with the question, "Does everybody remember *The Emperor's New Clothes?*" Then, pointing at me, he laughingly howled, "He's the kid!"

However, these kind folks could get more than a little rattled when, at many dinners, Bill and I would get into intense, table-pounding arguments. These disputes could be about anything: whether Larry Flynt was a new-æon hero or an abusive scumbag, whether *Rocky Horror Picture Show* was genius or junk, whether Mars or Saturn should be attributed to the *sefirah gevurah*. (In all three of these cases, I took the latter position.) Bill and I would happily be "over it" and saying "Hey, let's do this again" as soon as these heated discussions ended; our friends around the table didn't always recover so quickly.

At one of the dinner gatherings, I played a tape of a brief skit that I had thrown together: a take-off on radio evangelists in which the "sacred reading" was a passage from Crowley's OF THE NATURE OF THE GODS.[45] No one seemed to realize that the whole thing was fake and that the voice that they were listening to was mine, though somewhat disguised. Moreover, of the ten-or-so people present, most—maybe all—of whom were Thelemites and O.T.O. of one stripe or another, not a one except Bill recognized the text. Indeed, a few were quite put off by its content, especially the concluding lines:

> But in your warfare honour brave antagonists; spare them, and bring them to initiation; while the hag and the eunuch— and such are well nigh all who support orthodoxies—must be shown the only mercy possible, that of swift destruction.

It took producing a copy of *The Secret Rituals of the O.T.O.*, which Bill had on hand, to convince those protesting that the source was indeed their beloved Aleister Crowley.

---

45 In *The Secret Rituals of the O.T.O*, edited and introduced by Francis King (New York: Samuel Weiser/ London: C. W. Daniel Company, 1973), pages 178-179. The skit, called "*Peace from the Sun*," ran 3 minutes 19 seconds and featured an elderly demagogue named Dr. Evoice Past.

On-going dialogs with just Bill, or Bill and one or two others, were generally wide open "be here now" occasions. Even when passions arose, there was nothing occult, dark, or hostile about it; Bill was always eager to find a way to harmonize, or at least *live and let live*. He was plainspoken about everything, from his politics to his finances, from the technical details of his magickal practices and visions to the technical details of "running the farm" (*i.e.*, the HUMM), from his regard for "Grady" (McMurtry) to his frustration with "718" (Grant), from what he really liked about 416 stuff to what he really *didn't* like about 416 stuff.

In the course of our numerous conversations, only a few times, maybe two or three over a period of a few years, did his aspect change. It happened when Bill was describing the "Eleven-Star" or the "Hive."[46] I am not talking about the fits of high-flown language that Bill fell into when discussing his political beliefs or enumerating his occult "offices." This was different, as if something *other* had taken hold of him. He suddenly appeared immersed in a dimension beyond the "here and now." The atmosphere of the room seemed to shift. He spoke almost mechanically, as if to convey, "This is the truth. Do not question." Within minutes he would snap out of it and the jovial renegade would re-emerge, but while the altered state was active, it was chilling.

Writings

Bill had written and published (*via* Boleskine House) all of his major works[47] in the years just before I met him (1981-1983). He had plans for "enhanced and expanded" editions of these and had hopes, however faint, that a major occult publisher (like "Weiser, Llewellyn, Magickal Childe, etc.")[48] would "pick them up" and publish them under its imprint.

January through June 1984, Bill gave me computer print-outs of his

---

46   *Further Notes on the Eleven Star Working* and *Roles & Nurturing of the Hive or Powerzone* provide samples of the content if not the disposition of this kind of pronouncement from Bill. (herin)
47   Bill's chapbooks as of 1983 (all included herein.—Ed.):
     Apologia Discordia: In Defense of Disagreement (West Danby: Boleskine House, 1983).
     The Alchemy of Immortality. Vampires and the Aristocracy of Blood (West Danby: Boleskine House, 1983).
     ChRySTAL Workings thru the Astral Mirror (West Danby: Boleskine House, 1983).
     Doxology, Commentary, Vision of a Gnostic Mass (West Danby: Boleskine House, 1983).
     Math of the ChRySTAL HUMM. Charter & Statement of Purpose (West Danby: Boleskine House, 1983).
     Nine-fold Flowering of Alchemies within the Eleven Star (West Danby: Boleskine House, 1983).
     Rose of Charon (West Danby: Boleskine House, 1980).
48   Letter from Bill Siebert, 28 March, 1985 e.v., page 2.

new and revised work.⁴⁹ He wanted quite a few of these writings illustrated, so he provided me with sketches to re-draw in more polished form or wrote descriptions of what he wanted depicted.

Unfortunately, upheaval and uncertainty were constantly brewing for Bill in both his magickal and mundane life, *i.e.*, suspension from the Typhonian O.T.O. and *no* money, so nothing we collaborated on got published. Even the "revised and expanded" edition of *The Rose of ChARON*, which was so boldly advertised in the April 1984 Boleskine House catalog as "forthcoming," never found its way into print.

Among the items we planned to publish under the Boleskine House imprint was a collection of my articles, including "Adam's Sin," "Astral Map for Contacting Mr. Crowley,"⁵⁰ and Bill's favorite, "Cycle of Swords to the Saturn Cycle and their Rectifications."

Another particularly interesting piece that never reached a finished form was *A True Account of the Eden Captivity by One Who Was Present*, written by Bill, illustrated by me.

Bill and I wound up sending most of our stuff in rough form to The Archives to be distributed through the network they provided. This actually worked pretty well in that it led to some very fruitful contacts and correspondence.

Convo 1

The first CONVOCATION OF THE MAGI was held at Math of the ChRySTAL HUMM on Saturday, June 16, 1984, and carried on into the next day. While the "original thrust behind the Convocation" came from Sam Webster,⁵¹ it was co-organizer Bill who enlisted my efforts for the event.

My duties included:

---

49 Along with his own work, Bill enthusiastically shared the work of Sam Webster, a frequent "denizen of the HUMM." One piece that Bill particularly liked, called *Constellation* (1984), can now be viewed online at HERMETIC LIBRARY: https://hermetic.com/webster/constellation Sam earned his Master of Divinity degree from the Starr King School for the Ministry at the Graduate Theological Union (Berkeley, 1993). He earned his doctorate at the University of Bristol, UK, under Prof. Ronald Hutton in 2015 (thesis: THE HISTORY OF THEURGY FROM IAMBLICHUS TO THE GOLDEN DAWN). He is the author of the book *Tantric Thelema* (Richmond: Concrescent Press, 2010, re-released 2021) and has contributed articles to numerus periodicals (e.g., *Mezla, Mezlim, Gnosis*). He founded the Open Source Order of the Golden Dawn (at www.OSOGD.org, 2001-2019, website still active) and the Pantheon Foundation in 2013. Bill and Sam first met at the Harriman [State Park] Working in 1982 referred to above in note 6. Earlier that year, Sam was "initiated [as a] Minerval in the Caliphate OTO"—Sam Webster to Don Karr, email of 07/12/2020.

50 "An Astral Map…" appears in *Methods of Maat* (forthcoming), pages 165-169. A single-page version of the diagrams for this article was distributed by The Archives.

51 Sam Webster to Don Karr, email 07/12/2020.

- arranging an exhibit: three of my paintings, two paintings by Nema: *Invoking Cthulu* and *Genetrix*,[52] a handful of small graphic works by other artists, some batik wall decorations, and a selection of hand-crafted magickal implements.
- delivering a paper: "Introduction to the Perfected Tree and its Implications with regard to the Æon of Maat," which created an unwanted stir and a bit of open hostility.
- performing music: a 30-minute set—I sang over pre-recorded instrumental tracks, which redeemed me somewhat. My performance was ably recorded by John Fahs. At the conclusion of the show, after the applause dies down, you can hear Bill shout, "You'd never know he's against Horus!"

With the help of a few others, especially Anne, Sam and Bill took care of everything else: advertising in the months before, arranging for the food and other amenities, preparing the grounds, composing the ritual. When the big day came, Sam "managed the program for the live event,"[53] and Bill provided the "Elixir" to those who wished to partake.

"Alternity Elixir" or "Entheogenic Elixir" (Bill's "alchemical specialty") was usually a concoction of some kind of alcoholic beverage (like rum and Coke, or a liqueur like Amaretto), an hallucinogen (like psilocybin or LSD), and *kalas* (sexual fluids). Bill mentioned sometimes using chocolate.[54]

> Of the various entheogenic elixirs which we experimented with from 1980-88, the basic recipe we found most efficacious was composed of a concentrated infusion of *Psilocybe cubensis* stems-&-pieces (prepared after the manner of Soxhlet [a condensing/extracting apparatus]) in cool 190 proof grain alcohol. This elixir was then concentrated by distillation of excess alcohol until insoluble waxy residues began to accumulate in the bottom of the flask. The slurry was filtered while hot and the filter paper then washed with hot ethanol to resolve any active constituents trapped in the residue. The filtrate and the ethanol washings were combined, then diluted approximately 50/50 with Chambord raspberry liquor, then stored in a home freezer till a few hours prior to use.

---

52 Printed in *The Cincinnati Journal of Ceremonial Magick*, Vol. 1, Issue 4 (Cincinnati: Conquering Child Publishing Co., 1979), page 61.
53 Sam Webster to Don Karr, email 07/12/2020.
54 See *Roles & Nurturing of the Hive or Powerzone*, herein.

{Preparation time: approximately 1 week @24 hours/day.}
At an appropriate moment during the all-night ritual (as the cone of power was being raised) the elixir was diluted approximately 50/50 with Coca Cola. The sugar, caffeine, and alcohol included in this process were all found to be sympathetic adjuncts to the active entheogen, psilocybin. The estimated dose of psilocybin was approximately 75-300 mgs per serving. Although traditional ethno-pharmacologists claim 50 mg. to be the maximum useful dose of psilocybin, I have found that doses far in excess of this to be efficacious given an appropriate Set-&-Setting [*i.e.*, a private isolated place].

During our expeditions, some persons regularly consumed 3 or 4 servings over a 4-8 hour period. When available, an additional drop or 2 (1000-2000 mcgs) of liquid LSD per person would be added to the cup as well. At a few other times cannabis infusions in ethanol were added to this basic recipe, but massive amounts of THC made the elixir too lethargic and had a tendency to give some folks a bad case of the spins every time they turned their head. Human *kalas* (consecrated sexual fluids) were often added to the cup just prior to consumption. "Rescue Remedy," a homeopathic stress reliever obtainable thru Health Food stores was found useful in helping quiet the jitters of too rapid a "take-off."[55]

An alternative or complement to the Elixir was ADAM, or MDMA (later called Ecstasy). In the Invitation to CONVOCATION II,[56] Bill writes, "ADAM facilitates spontaneous & effortless manifestations of the Fire Serpent as it opens each chakra from Muladhara to Anahata…ADAM is an entheogen which has the ability to assist each communicant in opening him/her-self up to others in the circle." In blunt terms, one hoped-for effect of ADAM was that of an aphrodisiac, though this allegation was generally denied: "While we have used ADAM to manifest occult (*i.e.*, hidden) sexual energies within our close Pagan family, ADAM cannot really be classified as an aphrodisiac or an orgy drug. ADAM is an intoxicant of PAN, but with ADAM, PAN's abandonment works in gentle harmony with the heart energies of Krishna."

---

55 *Some Brief Notes Regarding the On-Going Work of Our Miskatonic Alchemical Expedition*, 1994 addendum, ¶ 15, herein.
56 CONVOCATION OF THE MAGI II—RETURN OF THE MAGI, announcement (1985), page 3.

In an email to me, 6/6/2013, Bill recounted an incident from CONVOCATION I:

> ... [B]ack at the first Convocation of the Magi, we were all tripping heavily. Some guy ran up to me. A woman was trying to roll into the bonfire. Lots of people were holding her down.
>
> At a glance, it seemed to me that the woman was having a bad trip and this was her way to demand attention. I walked up to the group, looked the woman straight in the eye and said, "Let her roll into the fire. The fire is very hot. She will roll back out again very quickly."
>
> The woman stopped struggling. She glared at me in what seemed to me to be hatred. I chuckled at her. She jumped to her feet and dragged her boyfriend back to their car and drove off into the night. I never found out what happened with them.
>
> A friend of Nema's latter told me that he thought I was able to channel a very primal Geburah. If I was channeling, I never noticed. Just me being me.

Rituals

The handful of rituals that I took part in at the HUMM were attended by anywhere from ten to twenty people, usually about twice as many men as women. (One was all men—five of us—not intentionally.) Evening rituals were often preceded by a dish-to-pass meal, the most substantial contribution inevitably coming from Anne.

Drugs were frequently used, but they were not always a planned part of the event. At the drug-imbued rituals, ADAM was encouraged, as was Elixir. While the rhetoric ran *Do what thou wilt*, there was a definite *wet blanket* undercurrent if you didn't partake.

Thus, the rituals ranged from safe and sober to wild and tripped out. Either way, there was always a theme or structure, and everyone was given something to do. Just observing was not a comfortable option. "This isn't a zoo," Bill would say.

The ritual Bill and Anne organized for the Autumnal Equinox in 1984 (on September 23, a warm Sunday evening) was one of the "safe and sober" ones—relaxed, drug-free, G-rated. Oddly, there was no focus on the end of summer or the up-coming harvest season, nor was there any Thelemic tone. Instead, the theme was simply the Four

Elements.[57] About fifteen attended.

First, we gathered in a circle outdoors in front of the HUMM. Going "widdershins" (counter-clockwise), we said our names, magickal or conventional, in turn. Then Bill explained the plan: We were to "tap into" each of the four elements, but not all together. We would divide into four groups: *fire, air, water,* and *earth*; each of us was to choose the element that we most identified with. Of course, there was an overabundance of *fire* people, so a number of us took our second choices to even out the groups. There were still six people in the *fire* group.

I went to the *earth* group, an ironic choice given the dogma I was spouting at the time, with slogans like "Forsake the Earth!"[58]

We went inside. Placed around the HUMM dining room, which Bill and Anne had rearranged for the occasion, were four stations, one for each element, with symbols for that element displayed. Our group went to a small table "in the north" (towards Ithaca) to find a 3-by-5 card showing the *earth* sign, a drug-store pill container filled with soil, an apple, a crystal (all four displays had their corresponding crystals—another one of Bill's specialties[59]), a heavy metal pentacle (a medallion, maybe three inches across, showing a five-pointed star inside a circle), and some other things. We were to "commune" silently with the objects *and* the members of our group, then "reify" our experience through a discussion of what our element meant in our mundane and magickal lives. We were then to arrive at a statement that we could share with the group.

The other people in my group were a very pleasant woman whom I didn't know and John Fahs (1950-2018), who was a big, warm, sincere guy. John knew about my *stigma* ("Forsake the Earth!" and all) and

---

57   I chose to describe this particular ritual because its basic form was later repeated at the Harlequin's Holiday Retreat (April 4-5-6, 1986). It grew in scope and intensity, passing from the Four Elements to the Four Æons: Isis, Osiris, Horus, and Maat. The Æon of the Forgotten Ones comes before the Four Æons, and the Silent Æon comes after, but the core ideas fueling Bill's developments were the interaction and harmonization of the four "manifest" Æons, especially in the discourses between Osiris and Horus and between Horus and Maat. In the mid-1980s, there were dynamic currents beyond those described in this essay. The feminist spiritual/political movement advocated a resurrection of the pre-patriarchal era, i.e., the Æon of Isis (e.g., Mary Daly, Merlin Stone, Z. Budapest, and Starhawk). Some feminists who were informed by the initiated stream worked to advance the post-patriarchal Æon of Maat (OAI and 416). See *Approaching the Kabbalah of Maat*, pages 117-160.

58   The Tree of Life used by 416 had no *malkut*.

59   Refer to Bill's articles: "Quartz Crystals and Sex Magick Dream Techniques," in *The Cincinnati Journal of Magick*, Issue VII (Cincinnati" Black Moon Publishing, 1989), pages 52-57; "A Sex Magickian's Alchemical Guide to Quartz Crystals, Pt I," in *Mezlim*, Vol. I, No. 1 (Cincinnati: N'Chi, Candlemas [February 2] 1990) pages 17-23, and "A Sex Magickian's Alchemical Guide to Quartz Crystals, Pt II," in *Mezlim*, Vol. I, No. 2 (Cincinnati: N'Chi, Beltane/Whalpurgist Nacht [May 1] 1990), pages 27-37. (all herein—Ed.)

seemed to get a mildly perverse enjoyment out of my being in the *earth* group. I really didn't want to burden the woman with a long, possibly alienating, explanation of my views, so I went passive (not that unusual for me). The three of us joined hands and communed a bit, after which I happily let the other two do all the talking. I participated by repeating back to them in compact form what they had said. Thus, I was elected to deliver the *earth* statement.

We all got back into a circle, remaining inside. The groups were to offer their statements. We went first. Our group turned out to be the only one with a designated speaker. I can't remember a word I said about *earth*, but I do remember what I was thinking: "Don't worry; it'll be there."[60]

In the other three groups, *everyone* made a statement; I can't remember what they said either.

Still standing in the circle, at Bill's direction, we contemplated what we had heard and meditated for some minutes on how to bring the elements together in an "interactive harmony." I recall thinking, "Maybe this is where the *harvest* idea could fit in."

Finally, we passed a kiss around the circle.

The circle broke and everyone left almost immediately. John, who was, after all, a science teacher for the Newfield School District, departed swiftly, saying with eyebrows aloft, "School night!"

As for the "wild and tripped out" rituals, here is one of Bill's general descriptions:

> The setting for our rites is (ideally) primitive & isolated—where the niceties of civilization (morals, clothing, social taboo, etc.) can be consciously put aside by each expedition member individually, each in the manner/degree which is in accord with each individual's True Will.
>
> During our all-night Circles, some people revert to a pre-human or a non-terrestrial state, while others retain their human persona as they channel information from alien races (or gods, angels, demons, etc.) Some—who become uninhibited, sexually aroused, and who have located (one or several) suitable partner(s)—make love in total abandon; while still others commune within the sexual energy field in

---

[60] This is the punchline to a purposefully long, involved narrative about someone studying lions in the wild and how to repel them if you detect that they are about to attack. I used the joke as a set-up in a presentation (Fall 1984) called "Why Forsake the Earth?" An essay bearing the same title appeared in my chapbook, *The Kabbalah of Maat*, Book 2 (West Danby: Boleskine House, 1984), pages 31-35.

non-physical ways, &/or talk with trees or crystals. For this type of Working, the setting must be isolated so no one feels the need to stifle or edit any energies which come pouring thru. (As I said, all this doesn't make much practical sense unless you've experienced it firsthand!)

On some occasions, some (or all) of us create-&-perform [a] group Dramatic ritual to coordinate the mindset of the group at the on-set of our free-form all-night Shamanic Circle. Whether or not we stage a formal ritual, we encourage each person in [the] Circle to do whatever personal ritual(s) &/or energy balancing s/he feels would assist h-im/er in manifesting h-is/er inner self. We then communicate various entheogenic sacraments to assist us (individually & as a group) in manifesting trans-rational consciousness.[61]

1985

Bill and I continued to have fairly frequent contact through 1984 and into 1985, and we still talked about collaborative publications. Alas, the relationship suffered the effects of our being on radically different wavelengths. There were absolutely no hard feelings, but I stopped attending rituals even though Bill kindly continued to invite me.

The "upheaval and uncertainty" intensified for Bill, Anne, and the HUMM. Payments on the mortgage fell behind; significant sources of income always seemed out of reach.

In March 1985, "friend of the HUMM" Mary Ann and Bill (the 27th and 28th respectively) sent out unintentionally concurrent letters calling for support in the form of "magickal energy" and financial donations.

> Magickally & emotionally, the work continues, but time & money have run out. I have not yet figured out how to earn money I need to reify the Great Work, or how to manifest a large enough fortune so that I need not worry about bills which need to be paid. I am depleted & exhausted by financial burdens which threaten my peace of mind as well as the security of my home & magickal workspace. If it is your Will to help, money is needed immediately. But more than money, need somehow to be able to generate cash on an on-going basis above & beyond contributions. …

---

61 *Some Brief Notes Regarding the On-Going Work of Our Miskatonic Alchemical Expedition.* (¶ 13), herein.

Assuming the bank does not foreclose on our mortgage &/or repossesses my computer, I will be getting new material out to you sometime in the next two months or so. I am presently working on a newsletter/magazine to recapitulate my past year's VisionQuest & delineate my ideas on one possible restructuring of the Order on the outer to reflect the evolutionary leaps which the race has made in the last decade.[62]

Alas, the neither the newsletter nor any other proposed publications authored by Bill were produced. However, Boleskine House did publish (1) a magazine, *The High Priestess: Beltane 1985* (May 1, 1985), written and edited by Mary Ann Reeter with contributions from Cliff Pollick; and (2) a mailer package announcing the CONVOCATION OF THE MAGI II called RETURN OF THE MAGI (n.d. [Spring 1985]).

Convo II

CONVOCATION OF THE MAGI II ranged over five days (June 19-23, 1985) and featured a sweat lodge, sessions in Anne's floatation tank, nightly Bardic circles, displays of books, crafts, and artwork, etc.

For the occasion, I prepared several chapbooks (maybe half a dozen copies each) on different aspects of the *kabbalah* of Maat[63] to sell at $3.60 each (which would be almost $9.00 in 2021 dollars), and I took a few shifts at the Boleskine House display of publications.

Otherwise, I was not as involved in CONVO II as I had been at CONVO I. However, I again handled the music Saturday evening (the 22nd—just after the "Roast Beast") with an extended program that opened with John Fahs performing the Doors' piece, *A Celebration of the Lizard*, accompanied by Cliff Pollick on acoustic guitar. I followed with a 45-minute program. Some of the tunes in the set had Maat-oriented lyrics; others had a more generally esoteric slant.[64]

After the performances came the Main Ritual, "an all-nite shamanic rite utilizing music, dance, and ecstasy." The "first sacrament" of

---

62 Letter from Bill Siebert, 28 March, 1985 e.v.
63 These texts appear in *Approaching the Kabbalah of Maat*, APPENDICES 4-6, pages 223-293, and *Methods of Maat*, pages 235-267. Online, go to Colin Low's expansive website, HERMETIC KABBALAH > "Contributed Documents" > "Kabbalah of Maat" – http://www.digital-brilliance.com/contributed/Karr/Maat/index.php
64 Studio versions of many of the songs from the CONVOCATIONS I and II programs are on *Don Karr: The Dhora Sessions, 1986* (Ithaca: DHORA MUSIC, 1986-7). This album was co-produced by George Spero Chacona (1945-2006). The tracks were remastered in 2005 by Alfred B. Grunwell at FingerLakes Recording, Ithaca.

the rite was "a substance called ADAM," namely, Ecstasy (the drug). "Once the ADAM has taken full effect and we are directly experiencing our circle from the viewpoint of collective consciousness," the second "sacrament," for those who chose to partake, was Bill's "Alternity Elixir" (which has been described above). It was Bill's hope that the ritual would result in "an orgasmic burst of Will to create a Magickal Child ... sowing our collective seed within the fire of our race's imagination and within the whirlwind of each consciousness in the Multiverse."[65]

To my knowledge, no reports on the results ever surfaced.

Just after CONVO II, Anne generously extended an open invitation to use what she referred to as her "Blue Periwinkle Tank," AKA the "floatation tank" or "sensory deprivation chamber." For a time (July-August, 1985), I used the floatation tank every week or so. Anne and Bill were always curious about my "deprivation experiences" and, with a touch of prurience, inquired as to where tensions appeared while I was immersed. My tight spot was usually my neck. Anne or Bill would comment with something like "Ah, the *visuddha*," then they would look at each other with slow nods and a knowing "Hmm."

Bill reported that his tight spot was usually centered around the *muladhara* or *svadisthana*, which seemed to disappoint him.

The silent reverie of "the chamber" was not infrequently confounded by peals of intense magickal love-making elsewhere in the HUMM—couples engaging in high-degree O.T.O. work no doubt.

MEZLA, Volume I

From 1973 to 1983, *Mezla* was the "Official Organ of the *Ordo Templi Orientis*," namely the Typhonian O.T.O. in the US.

Volume I, No. 1 was a single sheet of yellow paper (called "the infamous yellow sheet") containing a page-long statement from David L. Smith, a brief review of Grant's *Magical Revival*, and a statement regarding the thirtieth æther of Crowley's *Vision and the Voice*.

The primary editor of Volume I, Nos. 1 through 13 was Soror Tanith —789, namely Janice R. Ayers; the co-editor for Nos. 1-9 was Frater Iadnamad—111, *i.e.*, David L. Smith.

Bill, as OTz PTN 690, was co-editor of *Mezla* from No. 9 (1975—immediately after he "probationed in" to the Typhonian O.T.O.) to No. 12 (1979).

---

65 CONVOCATION OF THE MAGI II—RETURN OF THE MAGI, announcement, pages 3-4.

Mezla Volume I, Nos. 1-4 were published in Fort Myers, Florida (1973-4), and later reissued (1983) by Boleskine House, Ithaca, which was Bill's imprint and "the publishing arm of Math of the ChRySTAL HUMM." ("David L. Smith" was removed as the contact in the reissues of No. 1 of the early 1980s and replaced with "Boleskine House.") Nos. 5-9 (1974-1975) were published out of a P.O. Box in Buffalo. Nos. 10-12 (1977-1979) were also published out of Buffalo.

In the early 1980s, all numbers of *Mezla* Volume I were reprinted by Boleskine House, Ithaca.

Mezla Volume I, Nos. 3-12 offered a selection of Crowley's then-unpublished writings:
- No. 3, page 2
  - a commentary to *The Book of the Star Ruby: Liber LXVI*
- No. 4, pages 2-4
  - a commentary to *Liber Liberi vel Lapis Lazuli: Liber VII*
- No. 5, pages 2-4—No. 6, page 1-3
  - *The Book of the Cephaloedium Working*
- No. 7, pages 2-4—No. 8, pages 1-2 – *Ethyl Oxide*
- No. 9, pages 1-3
  - "Comments on *Liber A'ASH vel Capricorni Pneumatici*" by Frater Achad, with additional notes by Aleister Crowley
- No. 10, pages 3-4—No. 11, pages 3-4—No. 12, pages 3-4
  - "The Antecedents of Thelema."

The thirteenth issue of *Mezla*, unnumbered and undated, appeared in the fall of 1983, edited solely by Janice Ayers, published out of Cincinnati. (No. 13 is sometimes mistakenly identified as Volume II, No. 1. As with Crowley's *Equinox*, Volume II of *Mezla* was to be "silent.") No. 13 focused on "the next phase of [humanity's] evolution" that will "make it possible for man to establish unbroken contact with trans-human intelligence." The feature article was "An Official Statement of the O.T.O. concerning the Cult of Lam, the Dikpala of the Way of Silence," by Aossic Aiwass 718∴ O.H.O. of O.T.O., *i.e.*, Kenneth Grant. No. 13 also contained *Liber QNA–ANKh–Venus vel NOMEN DEI sub figura CLI*, by Frater Achad. Each copy of No. 13 was accompanied by the 10-page chapbook, *LAM-ED*, by Zossian 393 ∴, *i.e.*, Denny Sargent (Seattle/Bellingham: Axil Press, ca. 1981).

Mezla typically featured announcements and articles or statements by Typhonian O.T.O. members. Many issues of *Mezla* had notices or reviews of Kenneth Grant's latest books, from a one-line notice of *Aleister Crowley & the Hidden God* (1973) in No. 2 to a half-page review of *Outside the Circles of Time* (1980) in No. 13.

Then came *Mezla*, Vol. III, No. 1, Autumn Equinox, Anno LXXXI, edited by Bill Siebert and Cliff Pollick (Ithaca: Thelemic Temple of the Double Vortex, September 23, 1985). This volume is discussed further below.

Mezla, Volume V, No. 1, a 40-page magazine, was issued in 1989 (Samhain) by N'Chi (pronounced "EN-KEE") in Cincinnati. Listed among its staff is "Bill Siebert / Spiritual Guidance and Support." The "Message from the Editor," Fr. R'LATH (Kenneth Deigh), states, "Conceptually, the 'resurrection' of Mezla was born during a small gathering known as the 'Feast of the Magi' [specifically the event of January 2-4, 1987], held annually at the home of the (former) Managing Editor [*i.e.*, Math of the ChRySTAL HUMM] in Ithaca, N.Y."

This enterprise, with Deigh at the helm, changed the name to *Mezlim* in 1990 and started over with Volume 1, No. 1.

MEZLA, Volume III, N° 1

Bill made a habit of challenging what he saw as Thelemic hypocrisy, especially as it concerned control of Crowley's works and their distribution. It was his strong belief that Crowley's writings, as well as those of other O.T.O. authors (*e.g.*, Charles Stansfeld Jones [Frater Achad], Jack Parsons), should be accessible to all—as some of these and scores of other "magickal" writings were through The Archives, where, starting in 1982, a mountain of material by a wide range of authors was made available for ten cents a page plus postage.

A significant example of Bill's manner of rebellion was his (1) commandeering of the Typhonian O.T.O. newsletter *Mezla* at Volume III, No. 1, (2) changing its subtitle from "Official Organ of the *Ordo Templi Orientis*" to "An Heretical Organ of the OTO," and (3) within it publishing "Ninth Degree Emblems and Modes of Use," a tract on sex magick attributed to Crowley that was supposed to be limited to IX° and XI° members of the California O.T.O. and considered O.T.O. property.

Frequent denizen of the HUMM, Cliff Pollick co-edited *Mezla* III with Bill. Cliff was a member of the California O.T.O. who "took his Minerval" in October 1977. Even though he never got beyond III°, he received a copy of "Emblems and Modes of Use" from McMurtry June 15th, 1982.[66]

---

66 "Grady McMurtry, the Caliph of Ordo Templi Orientis was on a road trip of the East coast and had been in NYC the previous week. Two days earlier, Alan Davis, the Master our local group, Hadit Chapter in

In July 1985, Cliff lent it to Bill.[67] Bill in turn passed it around among a few friends of the HUMM. Indeed, I borrowed *the* or *a* copy of "Emblems and Modes of Use" for a number of days on the condition that I not photocopy it, even though the document itself was a photocopy of a typescript. Transcribing it by hand or typewriter, however, was fine. I typed a copy.

While the material contained in "Emblems and Modes of Use" is undiluted O.T.O. IX°, its uneven style inclined me to doubt Crowley's authorship. The *bona fides* of the document is, however, attested in several O.T.O. communications.[68]

When I returned the "original," Bill went through the "emblems" with me and translated all the terms into unvarnished English.[69] He also re-explained his motto, PVN, which stood for per vas nefandum, "by the unmentionable vessel," and its significance. From the notes of that discussion, I prepared an "O.T.O. Glossary," which remains tucked inside my copy of *Secret Rituals of the O.T.O.* The substance of this particular conversation with Bill predicted much of the content of *Mezla* III.

After "Emblems and Modes of Use" had circulated locally for a couple of months, Bill and Cliff agreed that it should be published "in the interest of promulgating a fuller understanding of the Law of Thelema."[70] Or, as Cliff puts it, "It was my belief then—as *now*—that I could *best* protect the 'secret' by publishing it openly." Cliff rightly adds, "There had been a tradition in previous issues of *Mezla* under Grant of printing unpublished Crowley works."[71]

Philadelphia, dropped Grady off at my apartment to stay for a few days."—Cliff Pollick to Don Karr, email of 7/13/2021.

67 "I moved to Ithaca in June 1985 and showed Emblems to Bill about 3 or 4 weeks later, which would be mid to late July 1985."—Cliff Pollick to Don Karr, 7/13/2021.

68 For instance, in a letter to her ex-husband Grady McMurtry, June 1, 1983, Phyllis Seckler writes, "As to 'Emblems and Modes of Use,' A.C. states over and over that anyone could read this, but it would do them no good as the practices held within them their own safeguards. Many modern day folks have ferreted out from A.C.'s writings and from Grant and a host of other authors, true methods of working the IX° O.T.O." —*Phyllis Seckler (Soror Meral): The Kabbalah, Magick, and Thelema, Selected Writings Vol. II*, edited by Dr. David Shoemaker, Gregory Peters, and Rorac Johnson (Sacramento: College of Thelema of Northern California/York Beach: The Teitan Press, 2012), page 246

69 The alchemical symbolism was familiar to me from King's *Secret Rituals of the O.T.O.* and Israel Regardie's *Tree of Life: A Study in Magic* (New York: Samuel Weiser, Inc., 1971), CHAPTER SIXTEEN.

70 Bill's letter to Jim Wasserman, December 21, 1985, page 3. See below. On page 2 of the same letter, Bill writes, "Personally, I class *Emblems & Modes of Use* into that category of information that needs to be made available to all interested parties, regardless of initiatory affiliation (or lack thereof) with any particular branch of the OTO. I received a xerox copy of this document sans copyright notice, signature, and notice of ownership. I received it without being obligated to secrecy, and not as a part of any initiation ceremony or elevation to the IX° or XI°."

71 Cliff Pollick to Don Karr, 7/13/2021.

It seemed to me back then that the timing of the decision to publish "Emblems..." linked with McMurtry's death in July of 1985.

Bill and Cliff's exposure of "Emblems and Modes of Use" through *Mezla* III provoked quite a backlash from ranking members of the California O.T.O.[72] (much like the release of Francis King's *Secret Rituals of the O.T.O.* in 1973[73]). Indeed, under legal compulsion from the California O.T.O., Bill and Cliff "ceased distribution of that issue [of *Mezla*] which has so upset you [James Wasserman],[74] Hymenaeus Beta,[75] & Pat King[76] until we could decide what to do."[77]

There are a couple versions of the "Emblems and Modes of Use"/ *Mezla* III story in circulation. Jason Miller's brief account has it this way:

> Cliff Pollick was passed Emblems and Modes of Use, the primary 9th degree document, by Grady McMurtry and told to do with it what he can. What he famously did was share it with Bill Siebert and publish it in an unauthorized issue of *Mezla*, which they gave away for free.[78]

Bill and Cliff didn't publish "Emblems and Modes of Use" until September 1985, three years after Cliff received it and two months after McMurtry's death. This suggests that in some respects Cliff honored the restrictions on the document while McMurtry, someone whom both Bill and Cliff revered, was still alive and head of the California O.T.O. At any rate, there was no impulsive rush to print "Emblems and Modes of Use" as soon as it was obtained, as Miller's account might

---

72 A letter from James Wasserman was sent to Bill and Cliff dated November 17, 1985, ordering them to "cease and desist" distribution of the issue of *Mezla* containing "Emblems and Modes of Use."—Cliff Pollick to Don Karr, 7/13/2021.

73 *Secret Rituals of the O.T.O.* is a whole book of Crowley writings that, before this publication, had been restricted O.T.O. grade papers. The dust jacket of *The Secret Rituals...* states, "Now, at last, this volume makes available to the occult student not only the symbolic-masonic riches of the initiate on rituals of the O.T.O. but the secret magical instructions of the Order's seventh, eighth and ninth degrees, the full details of the techniques from which such occultists as Theodor Reuss and Aleister Crowley derived their mystic powers."

74 James Wasserman, founder of the Tahuti Lodge in New York City (1976), a branch of the California O.T.O.

75 William Breeze, McMurtry's successor.

76 Patrick King (1955-1997), O.T.O. XI°, one of the few openly gay members.

77 Bill's letter to Jim Wasserman, December 21, 1985, page 1.

In his book, *In the Center of the Fire: A Memoir of the Occult, 1966-1989* (Lake Worth: Ibis Press, 2012), pages 91-92, Wasserman reiterates the O.T.O. byline: "In order to have doctrinal coherence, we needed to have control of the message. It's not very complicated either to explain or understand. What religion or school of thought is not in a position to issue authorized editions of its own teachings?"

78 Jason Miller, "You are a Sovereign in the Chthonic Auranian Ordo Templi Orientis. What exactly is it, and how is it different from the OTO?" (Monday, June 14, 2010):
https://strategicsorcery.blogspot.com/2010/06/you-are-sovereign-in-chthonic-auranian.html

imply. In fact, Cliff was originally reluctant to accept "Emblems" from McMurtry. Cliff writes (Cliff Pollick's email to Don Karr, 7/12/2021):

> He [McMurtry] dug through his duffel bag and came up with two rather dog-eared pages. This was "Emblems," which he said was possibly the last unpublished document by A.C. specifically referring to the IX° secret. I remembered Heidrick mentioning this document in one of the old OTO newsletters. He offered it to me. I initially but reluctantly declined.
>
> I was very concerned as to the responsibility of having the documents. In no way did I wish to be an upper echelon officer in the order. I had already experienced the supposed statecraft of Jim Wasserman holding up my 3rd degree initiation, witnessed his angst and frustration with the politics of his position, and I didn't want any part of politics like that. I stated I was happy to leave that stuff to [Alan] Davis, Wasserman, Mike Ripple in Syracuse, Lon Duquette, *et al*. I reiterated my statements that I appreciated the opportunity of being a step away; the Merlin to the Leader rather than being Arthur on the throne. Grady then offered me the Status of Hermit. He said that he had given "Emblems" to several people already with the proviso of no official status in the order, but who were charged with protecting the secret through use.

Also, Bill and Cliff didn't give *Mezla* III away "for free." Complementary copies were sent out to HUMM supporters, and, in December, free copies were sent to ranking members of the California O.T.O. (as listed above, plus the IX° Council, the V° Senate, and the Board of Directors).[79] Otherwise, it cost $3.33. Bill could ill afford to squander a chance to make—or at least recoup—a little money.

J. Edward Cornelius' version, which doesn't mention Bill at all, cuts it a bit differently:

> ["Emblems and Modes of Use"] remained secret until after Bill Breeze's elevation to X°, which is when it was leaked by a disgruntled member of Tahuti Lodge OTO in New York named Cliff Pollick III° (who had taken his Minerval out of Thelema Lodge in Berkeley in November of 1977).[80] Pollick

---

[79] Bill's letter to Jim Wasserman, December 21, 1985, page 6.
[80] I was never a member, disgruntled or otherwise, of Tahuti Lodge. I received my III° from Wasserman at Tahuti Lodge. My minerval and II° were in Syracuse. Grady, Heidrick and Shirine Morton initiated me to I° in a tent in Grady's backyard September 1978.—C.Pollick

had somehow gotten a copy and published it in *Mezla* Vol. III No. 1, NY, 1985. Pollick was expelled on November 23rd, 1985 for acts "damaging to OTO proprietary interests." Its publishers threatened with a lawsuit, the issue was pulled before too many copies got out.[81]

Bill Breeze was elected as McMurtry's successor on September 21, 1985, just two days before *Mezla* III was released, September 23—the Autumn Equinox. But "Emblems and Modes of Use" had been "leaked"—to Cliff and others—well before that by McMurtry himself.

Inevitably, quite a few copies of *Mezla* III "got out," at least around Upstate New York and likely Cincinnati *via* the HUMM/Black Moon connection. It was some months after *Mezla* III was released that Bill and Cliff suspended its circulation.[82]

Cliff "took his Minerval" in October of 1977,[83] not November—a minor point.

Mezla III (pages 11-12) contains an essay that Cliff wrote, "A Memory: Maj. Grady Louis McMurtry, Hymenaeus Alpha—777," where he states, "My last personal contact with Grady was in 1981 when he visited Philadelphia and spent several days with my lady & I."[84] Cliff's journal records this encounter as occurring in June of 1982. Either way, this puts Cliff's reception of "Emblems…" some years before he and Bill published it.

As for Cliff's being "disgruntled," just about every O.T.O. member that I met (1984-1986), whether California or Typhonian, was disgruntled.[85] This greatly intensified for the California folks after McMurtry's death.

Given that Cliff was co-founder and Master of the Hadit Chapter in Philadelphia (as of 1984) and that his first impulse was to decline reception of documents beyond his grade, it would not appear that he plotted the exposure of "Emblems…" as part of any sort of cavalier agenda, as might be read into the brief accounts quoted above.

---

81   J. Edward Cornelius, *The Changing of the Guard: My Memoirs of being in Ordo Templi Orientis between 1989 and 1993* (Berkeley: [privately published], 2019), page 287, note 21.
82   Bill's letter to Jim Wasserman, December 21, 1985, page 1.
83   Cliff Pollick, "A Memory: Maj. Grady McMurtry, Hymenaeus Alpha—777," in *Mezla* III, page 11. This initiation took place is Syracuse, NY under the auspices of Alan Bennet Chapter with later became a lodge. Documentation indicated this occurred on November 19, 1977.
84   *ibid.*, page 12.
85   Both James Wasserman's *In the Center of the Fire* and J. Edward Cornelius' *Changing of the Guard* make it abundantly clear why California O.T.O. members were *disgruntled* around the time of Grady McMurtry's death and thereafter.

My conclusion: The primary fomenter of the whole "Emblems and Modes of Use"/*Mezla* III thing was Bill. This "heretical" action was fully in line with his *modus operandi*. Bill even says on page one of *Mezla* III, "As editor-in-chief & publisher, *Mezla* is issued solely upon my authority"—he doesn't say "our authority." Cliff, justifiably disgruntled with the state of the California O.T.O., especially after McMurtry's death, was easily, and perhaps a bit opportunistically, converted to *renegade*. Surely, Cliff's expulsion from the California O.T.O. in November 1985 sealed that.

C/A-OTO

Another example of Bill and Cliff's "rebellious" maneuvers was their co-founding, along with Sam Webster,[86] a *new* eclectic O.T.O. called the Chthonic Branch of the O.T.O. (later called the Chthonic Auranian O.T.O.), "a wholly new manifestation of the Order claiming no imprimatur from Crowley, and doing away (as much as possible) with hierarchy grades & restraint of individual enthusiasm."[87] Its manifestation coincided with and was announced in *Mezla* III (pages 8-10).

> The Chthonic-Auranian OTO is a branch of our illustrious Order founded on the premise that the OTO is not only a pyramid of Knight Monks (as emphasized by the Caliphate OTO), or a highly specialized Magical Engine (as emphasized by Grant's Typhonian OTO), but is also a family/tribe/fraternity of magickians who are each doing his/her Will as best as each of us is able, and who are each fully responsible for our actions/stillnesses, thoughts/trances/channelings, and speech/silence. We feel that each Thelemite by doing his/her will has access to the Fountainhead of the Order. It is from here that true initiation flows.[88]

Sam "designed the structure and the initiation method for the Chthonic-Auranian Order"[89] in which there were only three grades: (1) Hermit, (2) Lover, and (3) Sovereign, or Wo/Man of the Earth.[90]

---

86   Sam was then a II° member of the California O.T.O. He also had contributed an article, "Magical Personae & the Khu," to *Mezla* III.
87   *Some Brief Notes Regarding the On-Going Work of Our Miskatonic Alchemical Expedition*, (1994 preface, ¶ 4) (herein).
88   Bill Siebert, *The Chthonic-Auranian OTO: Origins, Purpose, & Structure*, (herein) https://www.angelfire.com/pa2/cthonicauranian/seibert.html
89   Sam Webster to Don Karr, email of 07/12/2020
90   See "The Chthonic-Auranian OTO..." for descriptions of the grades.

1986

After the *Mezla* dust up, Bill and I didn't see each other very much, but we stayed in touch by mail and infrequent phone calls for another year or so. I received announcements for HUMM events and a few modest publications.[91] There were no further Boleskine House catalogs and no more chapbooks from PVN.

Anne moved to Manhattan to work with the LRT (Loving Relationships Training). She and I continued to correspond for a few months after that.

LATE 1988-1990

"[Bill] left Math of the ChRySTAL HUMM in the hands of friends in 1988 to pursue the study of Megapolisomancy within dance clubs and dirty back streets of Buffalo New York. About 1989 or 1990 Math of the ChRySTAL HUMM reabsorbed itself back into the void from whence it came. The house/land which were the physical basis for this power-zone has been foreclosed upon by the banks."[92]

1991/2

The last time I saw Bill was in late 1991 or early 1992.[93] During that period, I was playing regularly at the now-defunct Rongo, or Rongovian Embassy (1973-2016), in Trumansburg, NY, with The Goods.[94] At one of those jobs, I suddenly noticed Bill in the crowd—unmistakably Bill, bemaned, wearing a cerulean blue warm-up suit, all sorts of things hung around his neck, dancing "hippie style" by himself. We exchanged warm greetings, but, alas, didn't have a chance to talk.

I remember asking Bill from the stage, "How are things at the HUMM?" In response he just shook his head.

Harry, the bass player, asked, "Who is *that*?" I answered, "It's a long story."

---

91   *e.g.*, *Arian*.
92   *Some Brief Notes Regarding the On-Going Work of Our Miskatonic Alchemical Expedition*, (1994 preface, ¶ 5) (herein)
93   This could have been as late as April 17, 1992. I have a Rongo board tape of The Goods for this date.
94   The Goods = the last incarnation of Moxie.

1994

"Currently, Bill is living amidst the social decadence, political corruption, and stagnant decay of New Orleans with his wife-&-Priestess Raven Greywalker. Together they are studying and learning arcane mysteries from diverse encounters with various megalomanic power-spots and with the plethora of individuals whose ancestry and magicks stem from an amalgamation of Haitian and African Voodoos, strange native American magicks, even-stranger heresies brought here from France and Spain by various prisoners of conscience fleeing from the long arm of Inquisition and Crown—as well as those not-quite human fringe-people whose swamp, bayou, & river ancestors possess a certain bactrian look analogous to their Innsmuthian kin, yet with an indolent balefulness not often found beyond the foetid nurturance of Louisiana's biological social spiritual and political backwater. Compounding this genetic, spiritual, and ethnic mire is an on-going influx of disaffected and disenfranchised persons from the world around, drawn to New Orleans by its astral and literary beacon proclaiming it to be a Mecca for the weird."[95]

2000's

"On the cosmic level, I am a theogenist who seeks to re-mythify that which is called reality, as well as that which has the potential of becoming reality. On the personal level, I am an alchemist, with a strong interest in entheogens, consciousness expansion, and indefinite prolongation of life, while maximizing the quality of life. The interplay between these two extremes manifests as a living mutable texture within which my life & philosophies evolve.

I am a Thelemite & co-founder of the Chthonic/Auranian-Templars of Thelema (C/A-ToT), which was once known as the Chthonic/Auranian Ordo Templi Orientis (C/A-OTO). While I certainly do enjoy creative dynamic ritual magick, I am far more shamanic in practice than a practitioner of the Rosicrucian/Masonic/Golden Dawn traditions.

---

[95] *Some Brief Notes Regarding the On-Going Work of Our Miskatonic Alchemical Expedition* (1994 preface, ¶ 7) (herein)

I have been involved in the 23 Current since before it had that name, and may possibly have been responsible for the 23 Current getting its name. I am a current member of & past lodgemaster of the Esoteric Order of Dagon, as well as the founder of the Miskatonic Alchemykal Expedition (which began as the Miskatonic Alchemical Expedition, back nearly 20 years ago).

As a pantheist, I feel everything is sacred, but I hold nothing sacrosanct. Like Crowley, I feel everything is questionable, and should be questioned assiduously on a regular basis. That said, over the decades I have found certain myths and techniques to be useful—whether they be in any sense ultimately true, or not.

I have been involved in the Horus/Maat Lodge nearly since its inception, and am most often a throneholder of the Sphere of Daäth. Although, it could truthfully be said that I work Chaos Magick, my grokking of that concept pre-dates my knowledge of Peter Carroll's work. My understanding of this field developed thru my work within the Typhonian OTO, my informal associations with various Discordian magickians, and various practical work with people from diverse backgrounds.

Since May of 1993, I have been a Tarot & Palmistry Counselor out on Jackson Square in the French Quarter of New Orleans. I am a past V° member of the Typhonian OTO. I was briefly a Minerval in the Caliphate OTO, and just as briefly a Neophyte in the Order of the Golden Dawn.

I am a II° in Coven Beth-Ra-Lune, a Thelemic-Gardnerian coven."[96]

"So I am famously idiosyncratic am I? I always consider myself first & foremost a Thelemite. I suppose in this day of OTO, inc. & the malignant travesties of the E[cclesia] G[nostica] C[atholica], actually living one's life as a Thelemite might be deemed idiosyncratic to some. Hopefully not to too many. I keep meeting interesting Thelemites as idiosyncratic as myself, so I know I am far from unique."
—*email to* thelema93-l@hollyfeld.org *from W. A. Greywalker,*
RE *"Grant and TOTO," June 5, 2000*

---

96 Alobar Greywalker, *Magickal Record,* January 30, 2002 > https://alobar.livejournal.com/profile

On Meeting and Knowing William Andrew David Siebert

A.K.A

Frater PVN
Master of Re-Creative Alchemies

OTz PTN-690
Initiate of Typhonian OTO (V°) and Caliphate OTO (O°)

La-Baj-AL
Mage and Watcher, Founding Sovereign of Chthonic/Auranian OTO

ASht Chozar SSaratu 1103
The Miskatonic Alchemical Expedition, Esoteric Order of Dagon

Alobar Greywalker

Born: MAY 27, 1945
Notification of Death by Wife
via Live journal note to community
JULY 9, 2020

By Cliff Pollick

I was sitting in my kitchen a week after Yule in 1981 when I got a call from Frater NOT[1] that he wanted to drop by with a few folks.

These folks turned out to be Sor. 0-Maku, Fra. Hegit, Ann and Victor of the Typhonian branch of the OTO. The details of Alan's meeting them initially are vague to me now, but my meeting was at my apartment in Philadelphia, which had also functioned as our OTO Temple for group rites and for the Gnostic Mass which we had been performing for some time.

Victor lived in South Philly, and he and Ann had a relationship dating to the famous "warrior lord working", a gathering of North

---

1 Fra NOT=129 was the Magical Motto of Alan Davis, II degree at the time. Together we had founded Hadit Camp, and then Chapter of the Caliphate branch of the Ordo Templi Orientis in Philadelphia.

American members of the Typhonian branch of the OTO at the Abbey of Thelma near Cincinnati Ohio hosted by Maggie Ingalls/ Soror Nema the Mage who brought forth *Liber Pennae Praenumbra*. Ann lived with Bill Siebert on a farm he called The Math of the Crystal Humm,[2] just outside Ithaca New York. This was their Power Zone, as a working unit or group was known in the Typhonian order as differentiated from the more Masonic type lodge structure used by the Caliphate branch of the OTO.[3] Ann travelled to Philly regularly to sell some organic produce they had grown on the farm, an aspect of Bill's Alchemical work, and to spend time with Victor. Bill's relationship with Ann was complex and complicated, as was Ann herself.

I was familiar with Bill's name as far back as 1977 from mention in copies of Mezla, the Typhonian Order's newsletter (of which he was the editor), in The Cincinnati journal of Ceremonial Magick, and the old *Gnostica News*—an early tabloid style advertising catalog of Llewellyn Books that carried many great articles by company authors and luminaries in the still new field of occult publishing.

Ann sold us some Psilocybin mushrooms, which was their income source, and gifted us with some of Bill's writings that I still have copies of, with the initials of group members whose hands copies had been through.

Bill's perspective on the effect of the Alchemy of Entheogenic substances, or, as defined by the Oxford online dictionary, "a chemical substance, typically of plant origin, that is ingested to produce a non-ordinary state of consciousness for religious or spiritual purposes" was fascinating. In this particular instance it was the Sacred Psilocybin Mushrooms used by indigenous people of the Americas, North and South, for untold centuries. Bill's formula as he would describe it to me at length later, was more than knowledge of mycological growth and optimization, but rather a relationship with the egregore of the fungi itself; not what might be termed a "servitor" so much

---

2 The title, *Math of the Crystal Humm* which Bill gave to their property/powerzone is derived from the work Bill was engaged with in working with quartz crystals as memory retainers for consciousness while dreaming. He told me once that he knew he had achieved his "contact' with the dream space via a sub-audible sound "something like humming". Math was his pronunciation of a Sanskrit word for a center of spiritual teaching. Famously there is the Ramakrishna Math (pronounced 'Mutt') in Hyderabad, India.

3 Please note that I refer to "branches" of the order. As an initiate of the Caliphate branch under the leadership of Grady McMurtry, and proud to be initiated by the man who had been so by Crowley, and the man I knew him to be, I still felt that the Typhonian, and yes, even the Motta branch, as well as any other groups working Crowley's Magick I might not have known were still "family" who I would gladly know and interact with.

as a "colleague" in a project with mutual benefit from a partnership. This was a eureka moment for me, as the greater part of my previous personal use of psychedelics since 1969 had been with laboratory derived substances. This was a completely new experience.

Bill's take altered forever my further interactions with subtle entities. I find the idea of all my interactions with nature spirits, sacred plants, genii loci, planetary, elemental, angelic and infernal entities seem to work significantly better when approached as enlisting a specialist in a particular field who will be respected as a partner in Magick rather than a servant or slave. I have never looked back on the concept of 'commanding spirits' the same, and my Magicks have been the better for it since.

One of Bill's writings spoke to entheogens themselves on the Alchemy of human sexual fluids through the tangible (neurochemical/biological) and intangible (chakras/meridian etc.) nervous systems. In his writings I saw syntony with my own researches and experiments on imbuing bodily fluids with intention that could be transferred to another nervous system via magical congress or to inanimate objects for talismanic purposes.

In addition to the Thelemic and Golden Dawn based technique and rituals I practiced, I had combined aspects of writings on Alchemy, Arthurian mythos correlative to the Gnostic Mass, meditative techniques of Kaula Shakti Tantra and the relatively new to me at the time, Taoist Esoteric Yoga tech of Mantak Chia, whose work completely opened the esoteric symbolism of so many traditional Taoist writings I had been previously exposed to in the way that Crowley's work elucidated the Western esoteric tradition. I attended classes by Chia in NYC even before making contact with Alan Davis of the Caliphate who had strong links to Tahuti Lodge OTO as he had received his Minerval, First and Second Degree initiations there. Through brief contact with the previous NYC group, Mobius Lodge and its Master Chris Dowling and attending what felt like an immature and clownish version of the Gnostic Mass, I had chosen to not be active with the NYC group. My later contacts with Tahuti Lodge through Alan, sadly reinforced my lack of desire to hang with the New York City OTO. Interestingly, both Mike Ripple of the Caliphate who hosted Grady's first ever initiations on the East coast, and Bill, who he physically resembled, were both upstate New York folk and were absent the city 'vibe" that only the Big Apple and intense sixty cycle hum seem to provide.

My first actual meeting with Bill was at Harriman State Park in New York. Hadit (then) Camp had been planning a camp out and were looking forward to doing Minerval initiations for a sister of our group, Denise and a close friend of Sam Webster, Diana, out in nature's splendor. We had invited Bill and Ann for a chance to meet them on common ground midway from Philadelphia and Ithaca.

Having met Ann several times by then, she introduced me to Bill. My first impression was of an obviously fit, pot bellied man with piercing eyes, a long grey beard and hair to match. Bill pinged my internalized image of Gandalf the Grey from The Hobbit (decades prior to any of the films), with a touch of Santa Claus due to Bill's ruddy cheeked smile. He was dressed in sweat pants and a colorful African daishiki; my first exposure to Bill's taste for bright colors.

Alan Davis had invited Jim Wasserman, the head of Tahuti Lodge in NYC and a member of the IX°, who brought along his wife Wileda and their young son, Satra and a few other NYC folks. Alan told me that this was a wonderful opportunity for Bill to meet Wasserman and hopefully forge some cross order connections. This seemed like a great idea. (At the time!)

Bill and Ann had arrived earlier than our group and established a campsite. Most of us pitched our tents a few hundred feet from each other in proximity to Ann and Bill's space. I planned some personal ritual for later, wanting to take advantage of the rare opportunity for a city boy of the woods and a fairly full moon, so I made my space a bit further out. This important for later. Part of our formal initiation prep was dying sheets red for what I thought would be the symbolic tent of the oasis; a necessary part of the "setting". This was foregone. I was told Wasserman instead wanted them, as well as any blankets or sleeping gear we could use to put up a "wall" so "they" couldn't see. This felt kind of strange, as Bill and Ann had attained V° in their own system.

In earlier discussions during a collective impromptu dinner, actual discussion of Francis King's book *The Secret Rituals of the OTO* came up, and it was obvious Bill had read it. He stated in conversation that there were no rituals of that nature used in the Typhonian branch of OTO and that he personally didn't see much to them from his reading of the book. He cited Freemasonry, on which much of the rituals were based, seemed an old Æonic order structure to him. Bill asked, though, if he and Ann might attend the initiations. They were politely declined and each agreed that they would keep space on their honor as Thelemites, if we wished. This made the "Walls" unnecessary and, well, rude.

Before sunset we had arranged a space to do the initiations and moved there after chilling for awhile.

The initiations were completed and beautifully so, as Wasserman was a fine ritualist who knew the material and the vibe. Sadly though, he seemed obsessive about the possibility of "the Typhonians" lurking nearby. He had the "Blackguard", an officer in the rite, frequently check the environs to insure no one was watching. No one was noted and the initiations took place without a hitch.

Bill had previously invited us to partake later of some of his personal Alchemy; a distillate of Psilocybin Fungi he had grown, nurtured and prepared. As folks wound down from the rite and de-robed we began to filter to Bill and Ann's campsite. We'd been sitting around for awhile when Bill produced a round glass flask. I recognized it as a Chambord Liqueur bottle. Bill began to explain the Alchemy of working with the mushrooms as a magical entity, and the process by which he extracted the viscous green liquid. He had another bottle of actual Chambord which he used to cut the strength of the Elixir. Bill warned that the Elixir has a strong and unpleasant taste, and this is one of the things he was currently experimenting with to make more palatable. He poured first the Elixir and then the Liqueur into a small wide mouthed silver bowl with a blue enamel coating. Bill advised that two tablespoons or a liquid ounce was approximate to 1,000 to 1,200 mcg of LSD, and that a mouthful of the Elixir was equivalent to two cups of dried shroom, so start gently, observe and feel free to take more later, as the cup would be available all night. Several of us were already familiar with Bill's dried mushrooms—I'd had them twice by myself prior to this meeting. I had a healthy respect.

As the night progressed, other sacraments of an herbal nature came out. Wasserman instead chose to drink liberally from a bottle of Jack Daniels Whiskey. Bill warned that there was already a lot of alcohol in the Elixir, which was then cut with Chambord and he advised taking it easy with more hard liquor. As with masks during Covid, good advice is often unheeded. Several hours in, Bill prepared another cup and when passed to Wasserman, he downed the cup.

His wife became noticeably upset, as his behavior had been escalating into loud proclamations of his authority, belligerent arguing and increasingly aggressive behavior toward most everyone. I came around to Alan at one point and said I had something other to do and excused myself from the group in general and thanked Bill for the experience but I would like to use some of this energy not for socializing but for the rite I had planned. Promising to return in a few hours with the caveat that "I AM tripping in the woods so time might be a little loose, and might if necessary find my way back by sunlight". I cannot say how long I'd been gone.

I know I built a fire in front of my tent, used my sleeping bag as a zafu and sat just inside and performed my personal ritual for healing of my back from an auto accident several months previous. I was hoping to tap into the Earth Mother's abundant growth and channel it into my spine. I am not sure how long I'd been finished, but I lay down in my tent and some time later heard footsteps. It was Mareena?? a young woman from Brazil, who had been associated with Marcello Motta's OTO group in South America. She was visiting NYC and drove up with the Wassermans. Due to Jim's bad blood with Motta, (having left Motta's group for the Caliphate) he had expressed that she might be a "spy". She had no gear, no tent, no food, and was wearing sandals and shorts in the woods. I invited her into my tent and gave her a sweatshirt to wear. I was in the midst of trying to explain—with my poor Spanish and her equally poor English—that the sweater was just offered to keep her warm and I wasn't trying to barter for sex, when David Borofsky came scratching on the side of the tent. He told me things had gotten out of hand back at the fireside. I told him "That's why I'm out here". He said, "Alan told me to specifically tell you that he needs you".

Alan and I had grown very close in a relatively short period of time and the urgency in David's words had me off with him immediately. When I came into the space, Wasserman was siting in front of the fire berating his 5-6 year old son, holding him up by the shoulders yelling "Listen to me, I am your father, Do what thou wilt"! When anyone tried to interject something to change the focus and thus the energy he would snap at them. When I came into his view, he came up to me inches from my face and shouted, "What ya want Buddy"? I replied in a whisper, "maybe a little quiet, I was trying to get some rest". Wasserman ran to Alan and said something I didn't hear and then burst out with a string of invective and insults aimed at various people assembled. He howled obscenities into the night at a number of names; some I knew from the NYC group and some I had never heard. He went on about "fake" OTOs "polluting" the 93 current and stealing Crowley libraries from the "real" OTO. (An accusation leveled at Wasserman himself by Motta) Voices came back from other distant campers in the park with Wasserman yelling back at them. At one point while stalking around, his son Satra came up to him and Jim shoved him aside, the child falling close to the fire and being pulled away by several folks while he ranted on apparently unaware of how his actions endangered his own child.

This continued on for the next several hours. At one point Wasserman picked up a machete and began swinging it near people. Requests to put it down elicited more belligerence. He yelled, "Don't tell ME what to do, I carry the Caliph's 45". This last statement made more ominous when his wife stated "He does have a gun back at the tent".

Following some serious threats Alan and I eventually tackled him and various folk essentially sat on him the remainder of the night. He was so adrenalized that it took 3-4 of us to keep him down, with him kicking and punching anyone he could and seeming to be able to tap into the psychological triggers of the assembled group (having landed more than one kick to my already aching back). With little resource of aid, proximity to emergency medical assistance with some antipsychotic meds to bring him down we were left to our resources. Folks did rituals, exorcisms, etc. that we had in our arsenals. One of us had some Ativan, a medication for anxiety. This was offered but Jim wasn't having any.

Inevitably, his screaming had brought other park campers to our site in response to his behaviors. Two people walked through the brush with flashlights to find, one of us doing a Star Ruby ritual with the machete, several of us holding Jim down, Sam sitting on his chest swishing Wasserman's face with a fan of feathers and plunging a Japanese sai into the ground above his head. One of the strangers - after realizing the guy being held down was the one yelling profanities into the night asked, "Are you going to kill him"? Bill looked at them and said rather matter of factly "We hope we don't have to"! They retreated into the dark quickly.

Bill, who had been very quiet, holding onto a piece of log protruding from the fire, turned to me at one point saying, "I'd like to help, but I'm not of your initiatic communion. Can you let me into your Kundalini and maybe my experience navigating the mushroom "space" can reach him through your connection. I was willing to try as I had seen

Bill operating nobly through this without judgment. Wasserman had accused Bill of "'dosing", or trying to poison him. It was perfectly clear WHO had done the dosing. I sat touching Jim while opening my aura and trying to let Bill in. I remember a rush of warmth. I mentally recited parts of the Priest's anthem from the Gnostic Mass as something I was aware Jim knew intimately, and it might function as a gateway in to help him find some equilibrium as his neurons were awash in the chemistry of the Elixir. For a few moments Jim seemed to calm down, then screamed "get out of my soul Choronzon" (The personification of the dread of the Abyss, when the personality dissolves in either, bliss or more frequently fear and paranoia.) Bill almost rolled over backward, sat up and said, "After several years, I'm familiar with the maelstrom of emotions and images this stuff elicits. The greater the control held onto, the greater the sense of being lost in it. That's why I cast a circle to focus energy, but NEVER banish. There are enough walls in my own Chapel Perilous, so I don't need to erect more of a fortress. Right now Jim is locked in his. Thanks for letting me try. I'm honored by your trust."

All survived the night, eventually retreating back to our tents with the sunlight for some much needed rest. Later that afternoon, Jim, after repeating the line, "Anyone get the number of the truck that hit me," several times, asked Bill to purchase some shroom or especially some Elixir. Bill in my hearing quoted him a price of $1,000 for an ounce of the shroom, and $3,000 for an ounce of Elixir. Wasserman taken aback said, "you won't sell much with prices like that". To which Bill replied, "That's the price TO YOU!" It was kind of sad to see Wasserman almost pleading with Bill for some shroom. He apologized for the accusations and derogatory things he'd said the night before saying "I wasn't really myself last night", but Bill was firm. I winked at Bill and stuck up my thumb. He later said, "I sell Shroom all over New York State, and I don't know or really care what folks choose to do with it. That is THEIR will. The Elixir is MY sacrament. I do NOT LIKE what he did with MY sacrament. He showed me who he truly was the first time".

He went on, "And speaking of that, you, Alan and your group showed me who YOU were. All of you looked out for him, no matter what he did or said to each of you. THAT really impressed me. My Magickal family is small and far flung. You guys are like close knit family, and I like that. I want to get to know you guys better"! As I came to know him, I realized that Bill was a hermit by nature, who loved to jump into the pool of community at times.

Bill and I exchanged contact info and began corresponding with long late night phone calls. Ann visited Philly multiple times over the next few months, and we started keeping company. On one visit I introduced her to the sensory isolation tank at a business called "Innervisions". She remarked after how well this tech would go with entheogenic exploration. I turned her on to the writings of Dr. John Lilly, who was working with both together in the 1960's using pharmaceutical grade LSD manufactured by Sandoz Laboratories, and wrote of his researches in three books: *The Center of the Cyclone, Programming and Meta Programming in the Human Biocomputer* and *The Deep Self*, the last of which was specifically written as a manual for using the tank for internal exploration and included reports by quite a few famous consciousness researchers on their experiences. I had all three of these and sent them home with her as a Thank You for Bill's writings. About a year later, Ann and Bill purchased one of the used tanks from the center, installed it in a bedroom at the Humm and began using it in conjunction with Shroom research. I used it myself fairly regularly after moving to the Humm. It was a very effective and safe tool to "turn off and park" the physical body while exalted via the Entheogens, and for just deep relaxation in general.

I began making a 14 hour Greyhound bus pilgrimage to Ithaca every few months. On my first visit, Bill, Ann and I spent a night with the Elixir in a teepee Ann had on the back land. We talked for hours about our individual takes on Magick, sexuality and tech we used. We covered so much ground and I had bonded so well with them that on my departure I impulsively said to Ann I would be honored to share seed with her, and turning to Bill that I would gladly receive his in any way he felt comfortable.

We continued speaking on the phone, and I began bringing books that had meant something to me to share with them and Bill was lending me rare Crowley books to copy. To this day, some of my most treasured possessions are the out of print Crowley books I copied from Bill's library. On one of her visits Ann and I became lovers. This ebbed and flowed for about a year with her splitting her time between Victor and myself when she came to Philly. This made visiting time at the Humm very busy. Bill slept a lot during the early part of the day so I'd spend time with Ann. Bill was a night owl and we'd sit up all night talking.

On April 2nd 1983 Ann and Bill travelled to Philly, and with Victor (who lived full time in the city) became the first cross initiates of the Typhonian as well as the Caliphate OTO. All involved in the rite had gotten to know Bill and Ann and they were welcomed warmly on a local level. I did not know at the time that Bill had corresponded fairly extensively with Bill Heidrick, the Grand treasurer general of the OTO and essentially Grady's right hand man. Much of their early correspondence was very cordial with intimations of cross recognition that devolved into offers to re-install Kenneth Grant to recognized membership if he would simply pay back dues to the Caliphate dating from the death of Crowley in 1947. I doubt Bill forwarded these to Grant for the obvious reasons.

I remember Bill saying that he was not only impressed with the small articles that Grady was writing for the 'Magical Link' (the Caliphate's newsletter) but also, the 'letters from home' that individual groups were writing in to report on their activities. There was a healthy respect for experimentation at the time, and a number of groups reported variants of classic Crowley and OTO rites.

Sadly, Bill's copies of the Magickal Link ceased after 3 issues and he had written Heidrick with no response. I had personally mailed his check for Minerval dues to Grand Lodge and after hearing from Bill that he was not getting the 'link' and he, Ann and Victor had not received their Minerval certificates, I had Alan make requests for some movement on this. Almost a year and a half later when I assumed leadership of the chapter I was still petitioning for the certs. Alan had sent second copies of the certificates to Grand Lodge for signing by Grady presuming them lost in the mail. Sadly both sets came to my address shortly before the closure of Hadit. Bill declined to accept his when I offered it to him and I have preserved it since then.

In 1984, after being to several Neo-Pagan gatherings, Bill wanted to host a small event at the Humm. I am to this day humbled that the day before the event he drove 11 hours each way to pick me up and drive back to Ithaca. This became the first Convocation of the Magi. On arriving at the Humm, I was met by Sam Webster who had arrived several days earlier. Sam had participated in several such gatherings and had some very necessary insights into how to make a success of the event. Never having been to a Pagan gathering or having been in the company of more than ten people into Magick at the same time I had no idea what to expect. It was an amazing experience! There were workshops where folks presented papers on Magical theory (with some controversies ensuing), and a presentation of art and artifacts of a Magical nature displayed. I remember Victor/Fra. Hegit's ritual tools displayed with the note, "Sacred but NOT sacrosanct—please feel free to handle". How refreshing in a world where I have seen people threatened with physical or Magical violence for inadvertently touching someone's stuff. There was also remarkable art by Nema and Don Karr displayed.

I took the West in the formal circle opening, with other directions being assumed by Louis Martinie and Nema, names I'd heard and whose writing I'd read. In the big time now! Alternity Elixir (as Bill was now calling it) was the sacrament and more than 25 people launched that night. Partly through the night I had an experience with, was totally overwhelmed by, and fell deeply for a friend of Ann and Bill who I had met a few months earlier. This was Maryann/Arian. This relationship brought me to Ithaca more frequently and I would stay at the Humm and visit Maryann in town.

At about this time, Alan Davis was gearing up to move to the San Francisco Bay Area to be closer to OTO Grand Lodge, a childhood friend also in the order who had moved there from NYC a year earlier, and to be closer to the people formulating the Eleventh Degree now within the order's structure. He left me with the leadership of Hadit which I assumed to maintain the group continuity. As I didn't have Alan's natural charisma or actually any interest in being the Master of an OTO body this was difficult.

Folks began to skip meetings and we trailed off doing the Gnostic Mass regularly. One of my difficulties was that new folks were presenting themselves for initiation and though I was the de facto Chapter Master, I could not get authorization to initiate people locally. Bill Heidrick told me personally on the phone that Grady would not issue the paperwork as Jim Wasserman specifically requested that I not be issued authorization to initiate, and that anyone in Philly wanting initiation should petition Tahuti Lodge in NYC. I followed this up with a call to Grady who told me he would not countermand Wasserman's request. He told me it was nothing personal with him (Grady) but was necessary politics. This was hurtful from the man I felt I had bonded with and received the document 'Emblems and Modes of Use' from. We talked a lot about changes within the order and whether the enactment of Crowley's 'Constitution of the OTO' was a truly good idea, as it was leading to this and that group claiming authority over another with a lot of NOT—"as brothers fight ye", but just petty mammalian ego based politics. He spoke of folks initiated into A.A. (Argentium Astrum or Argos Astron -depending on who initiated who) wearing "X-men" buttons or belt buckles to show their status as 'Inner Order members'. We also spoke of some of his concerns with certain bodies in the Caliphate who were trying to pack certain degrees, nominating multiple members for the 5th degree Senate, etc. (some of this was documented in the May and June 1984 issues of the Magickal Link) He pointedly mentioned he hoped it could be worked out before his 'greater feast'. This, sadly was my last conversation with Grady. Several months later I magically and formally closed down the remnants of Hadit Chapter with Grand Lodge as there was no-one of Third Degree to take the reigns and similarly no-one wanted to go to Tahuti to get their Third degree. Several months later I moved to the Humm to live and work the farm with Bill and Ann, and to pursue a relationship with Maryann.

I moved to Ithaca and lived at the Humm for just about nine months, I spent days and nights with Bill discussing so many different Magickal paradigms and the plasticity with which they can be adapted. We shared our different takes on body energy, spoke of entities we encountered on our entheogen and otherwise journeys, and how some of those beings would show up in more mundane circumstances. I remember how Bill walked up to a stranger in a bank one afternoon and said, "Didn't I see you on the astral last week"?. The man turned with a startled expression, looked deeply into Bill's eyes and replied, "Why yes, The Shadow Knights conference, really can't talk now, bye", and he was gone. I asked what the exchange was about and Bill just said, "I wouldn't have believed that he physically lived in Ithaca."

We worked together on renovating the barn on several of my earlier visits and completed a growing room with a sterile culturing setup when I moved to Ithaca in June 1985. Bill initiated me into working with the shroom and I came to enjoy my daily relationship with the mycelia and its children. They required watering every 12 hours and frequent harvesting. I would talk to "them" and came to a point of dialogue with the intelligence of the mycelia and was able to discover some internal pathways to more effective journeying in conjunction with the experience.

At this time, Bill was the owner of the first high powered home computer I had yet seen. Most of what was available to the public at the time was the Commodore 64. Bill's was an $8,000 IBM with a dot matrix printer. He would sit through the night corresponding with folks as far away as Japan, Australia, Germany, Britain, and multiple places in the U.S. Most had read some of his works produced on that computer. It never ceased to amaze me how far these writings he consigned to local bookshops, and mailed to friends in distant places would travel so widely and touch so many. However, just thinking how all of my associates in the Philly OTO had passed Bill's writings around and made copies for friends elsewhere was an indication of how hungry folk were for new Magical paradigms.

He would "power" himself in these sessions with a drink mix of flat Coca-Cola mixed with enormous amounts of table sugar. This was one of his many experiments with food as a consciousness alterant. Another was to simmer three pounds of espresso slowly for hours in milk, then add a twenty ounce can of dark unsweetened cocoa and lots of sugar. A tablespoon of this black sludge in a glass of milk was organic rocket fuel. This sadly may have contributed to his later life diabetes mellitus and serious dental problems. It was powerful Alchemy none the less.

Bill had a taste for spicy foods and created some hot sauces that could melt Pyrex. I remember one batch beginning with three quart bottles of different extreme hot sauces, which Bill called the "neutral base, NOW we begin to build" followed by ground dried Scotch Bonnet peppers, Habaneros, Cayenne, Sorrano peppers, Scorpion peppers, ginger, garlic, horseradish and then simmered on the stove for several hours. It was an olfactory Alchemy that could, and did bring well experienced hot sauce aficionados to choking tears. It truly did alter consciousness, and underscored it's historic use in ancient cultures.

One of my strongest impressions of Bill while living with him was his scrupulous sense of personal ethics. He was a devotee of the meme that when one lives outside the bounds of a societally imposed morality, one is even more responsible for maintaining a high level of personal ethics. One night in an all night supermarket I had pulled a small bag of cookies from a bulk bin. While wandering the market I ate one of the cookies from the bag. As we approached the checkout, Bill asked if I was going to tell them of the cookie I ate before the weighing charge. I said something to the effect it was a single cookie and the corporation could probably handle the loss. He then mentioned, without a sense of judgment of my actions, that the folks at the market never followed him through the market at weird hours even though his appearance might garner such attention. He appreciated that trust, which was now questionable due to MY actions. He also added that my own interactions with subtle entities on other planes was also one of trust, particularly if one did not use banishing rituals and other type of tech that treats entities as servitors to be commanded, rather than colleagues to be associated with. In the deep unconscious, the memories of less than honorable personal behaviors remain, and when we are declaring credentials in ritual, our innate sense of our ethical lapses are part of our 'record'. "Do you want to deal with the Gods or other entities with theft or dishonesty in your internal curriculum vitae"? I would conjecture this as one of the best pieces of Magical instruction I ever received and good advice to any treading similar paths.

Another aspect of Bill's repertoire was a sense of openness about who exactly was invited into circle when cast. It would unnerve some of the local Pagan or other more well-schooled Magical folk who would come out for circle to have Bill invoke Cthulhu, Belial (or the other Princes of Hell), Hagbard Celline, Jesus, James Bond or other literary characters or mythic entities of less than sterling reputation. He explained to me that those "entities" were all a part of our culture and memory, and that fear of them only gave our negative projections power. By inviting and "making friends" with the uncomfortable archetypes, we can assimilate the teaching or lessons such an entity could impart.

I will be the first to say that there is much in Bill's writings of that time that I did not get and to this day are a mystery to me. I found his take on a reconstruction of the Tree of Life to be interesting, but similar to Frater Achad's attempt at the same, there were parts that didn't make either rational or irrational sense to me and thus something I didn't pursue. Wonderfully, some of his writing being beyond the comprehension of even his close friends and colleagues was NOT a deterrent to him continuing his vision and his writings thereon.

During my time at the Humm Bill was reformulating ideas of the OTO in different contexts. He proposed an idea for an order called the "Thelemic OTO" as a point of connection for members of various branches to meet in collegial brotherhood, to interact and share personal and idiosyncratic researches inspired by Crowley and others of the Eastern and Western schools beyond what was currently available in print. It was a vision of Magick moving forward and reaching beyond the concepts and the few rituals Crowley, The Golden Dawn, etc. had left us. I remember Bill saying this was his take on Crowley's essence as a teacher and channel of the 93 current. "Crowley didn't say worship me or revere me, (except in his worst moments) so much as BE me. Be the original thinker and iconoclast. Take what you received from history and your mentors and go find your own path and do something unique with it." I would refer readers to the document "The Chthonic-Auranian OTO: Origin, Purpose and Structure", contained within this volume for his complete statement.

He also discussed a concept called the Chthonic OTO This later morphed into the Chthonic Auranian or Chthonic Ouranian OTO. In this context, the focus was on personal interaction, or as Bill referred to it "meat space" with accompanying entheogenic use and focused ritual. Over the next few months much of the ideation of the Thelemic OTO was absorbed into the C/A OTO.

The order was formally created in early fall 1985 at the Southern Pagan Renaissance Lunarfest or SPIRAL festival in Georgia. Bill, Sam Webster and I had all travelled there for the event and late one night in a cabin we brainstormed the idea. An order of Sovereigns, equals, with no hierarchy. No in group/out group secret signs, words, grips, etc. No restriction of tradition or individual paths, but generally focused on the Tantrick and Magical traditions of Self exploration and personal development. No restriction on the flow of information. Requirements? Participation! Recognition? A Sovereign is an individual that designates ONESELF as such! Similar to the "dreaded" Oath of the Abyss, The Oath of a Sovereign is an Individual declaring one's Self as responsible in the universe they inhabit or create.[4]

As an aside, during the SPIRAL festival three years later in 1988, Sam Webster, who by this time had accomplished Adeptus Minor in the Hermetic Order of the Golden Dawn, performed his first rite as Heirophant when he initiated Bill, myself and Sharon Raske as Neophytes. Sam went on to formulate the Open Source Order

---

4 It was always a point of interest though NOT contention, that Bill preferred "Auranian" as the Light (aur-Hebrew) or Gold (aureus-latin) which one excavates through one's deep digging of the psyche, where I have always preferred "Ouranian" (the heavens-Greek) aspect balancing the Chthonic or underworld elements. Quoting Crowley from Liber Tzaddi, "My adepts stand upright, their heads above the heavens, their feet below the hells". We enjoyed the double/triple entendre within the phonetic similarity.

of the Golden Dawn on more Thelemic lines with correction of the Egyptian and Greek forms, based on modern research which is light years beyond what the original founders had access to in the 1890's. Sharon was the High Priestess of Coven Lothlorien, a Gardnerian coven integrating Thelema. The following year Sharon initiated Bill into the coven. Sharon would be succeeded by my wife Micha as High Priestess and Bill continued active with the Coven which was now Beth Ra Lune. Both of these groups allowed Bill to play with different paradigms of Magick and work structured ritual in a way he had not previously known.

MEZLA: August 1985

It would not be possible to speak of the OTO as something we shared on several levels without speaking to the heretical Mezla Vol. 3:1. Bill had been the editor and publisher/printer of the original Mezla, the journal of the Typhonian branch of the OTO under the leadership of Kenneth Grant, one of Crowley's last students. Twelve issues were produced. When Bill parted ways with Grant he took Mezla with him.[5] Bill told me that Grant had once written him that "Magical orders are for those who have not yet reified their True Will". This was toward the end of their relationship as Bill was running foul of Grant for some of the chapbooks and other writings he sent him. It seems that someone who extrapolated on Crowley's work found someone else's extrapolations on HIS work unacceptable for a representative of his (Grant's) OTO. It also seems that the words Grant wrote Bill were true. He did not need the Typhonian OTO's (or the Caliphate, Motta, etc.) top down structure. What he did express wanting was a community of peers.

Bill approached me about working with him on producing a new version of Mezla. He had some theories on the OTO paradigm—specifically the Thelemic/Chthonic/Auranian OTO and wanted to get them down in print. Having heard several months earlier at the Starwood Pagan festival in Ohio (June 1985) that Grady McMurtry had passed, he asked me to write a reminiscence. There was also a tradition in previous issues of Mezla to print some previously unpublished writing by Crowley. While writing my memorial to Grady I

---

5 Sometime shortly after the Heretical Mezla 3:1 Grant released a Mezla #13 and quickly withdrew it for unknown reasons. Mezla was eventually handed off to Kenn Deigh and Keter Elan of Cincinnati, who published the Magazine MEZLIM for a number of years. It grew to a polished magazine with many known authors and wide distribution.

realized I HAD an unpublished writing of Crowley's that Grady had given me. This document was "Emblems and Modes of Use". It was recognized as the last unpublished piece of Crowley's instruction on the secret of the IX° since the publication of Francis King's Secret Rituals of the OTO and De Arte Magica.

Grady McMurtry had given this to me on June 15th, 1982 following a long night of talking when a guest in my home at the time. With it he offered advancement to a high degree in the order which I declined. I had no interest in being in the hierarchy of the order and did not feel I could work with several of the proclaimed members of that degree. I DID want to, and was attempting to work the tech of Crowley's Sex Magick. I was already using Hindu Tantric and Taoist Chi Gung techniques. It was the discussion and demonstration of these, plus artifacts in my Temple and a more personal point I will not mention, that generated the conversation which led Grady to offer me "Emblems".

I showed him my annotated copies of published Crowley writings on Sex Magick with my VIII° and IX° working journals, beside my magical diary of workings. Without too much story, Grady opined that no one he had given the IX° to had shown him any record of their work with the Theurgy and Thaumaturgy of the grade. He reiterated the offer and assured me that I could be free of the order's political structure and work as a "Hermit". He told me he had offered this to two other people like me with the aim of keeping the secret safe. Not through locking it away; but through USE. I accepted. Though we spoke on the phone a number of times, particularly after I assumed leadership of Hadit Chapter, I never saw him again.

Through early 1985 the Caliphate was in court trying to legally become "THE" OTO. Various folks we met at Neo-pagan festivals told of their experiences with the OTO, internally as members who left and externally as someone interested in Crowley but not liking what they found in the order. The impression I had, being out of touch for six months or so was that the Caliphate had become obsessed with lawsuits and was struggling as an order. Grady's words of infighting and power struggles within the order filled our final conversation. The caliphate had defeated Motta in court for his claim to heirship of Crowley's legacy AND lucrative publishing rights. It was now legally theirs in the eyes of U.S. law, but the thought of "you become what you eat…", well…!

We were attending numerous Neopagan festivals the summer of

1985 and sharing the Mezla 3:1 with folks. Word reached the Caliphate hierarchy and I received a call around November at the Humm from Jim Wasserman who then put someone he described as 'Baphomet' on the line. The person identified himself as Hymenaeus Beta, to which I responded "Hi Bill", having met him once as Bill breeze and being aware by that time of the succession. He 'corrected' me that his title was 'Baphomet'. I replied that I thought Baphomet was a magical name and not a title. He responded that it was HIS title as Outer Head of the order. This was a title even Grady had not assumed, to my knowledge. They, Wasserman and Breeze, were upset and demanded a cease and desist of our selling copies of Mezla. They also demanded all monies collected for publishing their legal material. The response to our telling them that we were giving away copies to interested folk upset them more.

I told Wasserman that Grady was the person who gave it to me at which point he called me a liar. He accused me of stealing it from Alan Davis who had a copy as a member of the eleventh degree. It was apparently OK for members who assumed the eleventh degree to have the document, whatever their initiated grade, but not for other members of the order, I informed him that I had viewed Alan's copy at my request, but only to compare it to the copy I had received from Grady. They were identical, Down to the typos and photo reproduction artifact. Wasserman followed up several days later with a registered letter reiterating the conversation. I know Alobar responded and sent copies for Wasserman, Beta, several copies for other ninth degree members and several for other bodies such as the fifth degree senate. He also responded with (I think) a masterful written response outlining the Old Æonic attitudes of hierarchy and secrecy. As I had written in the introduction to 'Emblems', quoting Crowley, "Mystery is the Enemy of Truth". With the information plain, one may attain…or not, but there is no question of "Am I following the correct procedure as explained by the giants on whose shoulders I wish to stand, and with that knowledge in hand where may I go with it"? All true science ("The method of Science, the aim of Religion") requires knowledge of the details of an experiment for reproducible results. How many OTO members have lived, worked and died with the question, that they have tried to put the picture together from Crowley's writings but never had access to 'the Secret'? The actual secret being SO SIMPLE in theory (however difficult to achieve without effort) it is a shame that the 'gem' of Crowley's teaching is reserved officially for less than twenty people worldwide, while the order consists of several thousands, and non-affiliated practitioners of Crowley's system in the tens of thousands worldwide.

After approximately nine months living at the Humm I moved into the town of Ithaca proper and got an apartment there, I still kept at least a weekly contact with Bill. I needed to be closer to the hospital I had taken work at as well as being closer to Maryann. My ability to get out to the Humm was decreased and there were many circles I had to miss due to professional responsibilities and scheduling. Still, we made time to get together almost weekly. Our relationship had moved beyond friends, housemates, shared ideals and ideas, shared lovers, to be brothers from different mothers.

Three years after moving to Ithaca, family responsibilities called me back to Philadelphia. Though involved in a relationship, I still made it back to Ithaca about every four to six months for a weekend. During my first year back in Philly, I took the bus to Ithaca and when Bill approached me at the bus depot I didn't recognize him at all. Gone was the long grey beard, hair and sweat pants. Bill was clean shaven, had a magenta Mohawk cut with the sides of his head shaved, had dropped about 30 pounds and was wearing day-glo spandex.

He had been hanging with friends from the Buffalo OTO group Pyramid Lodge, and had become involved with the club scene there and was out dancing 2-3 nights a week under the influence of an entheogen called MDMA (Methylene Dioxy Methamphetamine) and Ephedrine Hydrochloride This was a radical departure for Bill who had previously been judgmental of "canned" music for ritual. It was also a stretch for my hermit brother to go places with so many non-Magical humans packed so close.

Many of the Buffalo folks were fascinated by Bill, his writings and of course the Alternity elixir, but had reservations based on our publishing of Mezla 3:1 and the official Caliphate stance on apostates such as he and I. I am proud that most of the lodge members simply treated us as friends and brothers, while others were afraid of Bill, MA and myself calling negative attention to the Lodge and expressed their concern that we three were interacting sexually with members of the Lodge and felt uncomfortable about our potential "infecting" of the group proper with subversive/iconoclastic ideas or (gasp) physical disease. The more positive folk welcomed us while I lived in Ithaca and through the subsequent years. I have been happily married to a former lodge member for 30 years now.

Ann moved to NYC where she became a Massage Therapist and natural health practitioner. Bill moved to Buffalo around 1990 and bought a house, leaving the Humm in the hands of Maryann and her husband at the time. He became involved with one of the women in the community, Raven Greywalker and, after a few years together, they moved to New Orleans leaving their Buffalo home in the hands of my future wife Micha who had been their downstairs neighbor, and subsequently to another member of the Buffalo OTO community.

On a subsequent trip to Buffalo, Micha and I found that the house had been broken into and looted for the heating radiators, appliances and even holes broken through the walls for the copper piping. We picked through the rubble and found many of Alobar and Raven's personal magical implements, art, etc. I was able to recover some of his library but found almost all the Crowley books missing. I had lived with that library for some time and I knew it well. A couple of days later while visiting some of our friends in Buffalo, I noticed several of Alobar's more rare books on a shelf. Picking up one, sure enough, there was Bill Siebert's unique bookplate inside the front cover. Apparently the local OTO group had helped themselves to the library prior to the break-in. I am proud to possess a copy of the original 1939 edition of "The Equinox of the Gods" as a gift from Alobar for returning what I could of his library and possessions.

Bill and Raven began doing Tarot readings on Jackson Square in NOLA and apparently did quite well for a few years. Raven also worked as a Dominatrix for a time. It seems they found a home among the intense energies and community of New Orleans. They were legally married in, I recollect, 1992. This surprised me greatly as Bill (now going by the name Alobar Greywalker, having taken Raven's last name as his) had always ranted against formal pair-bonding as a "locking oneself up". Bill/Alobar was growing. Now, in his fifties, he was experiencing what most of us were feeling in our teens. At this time he became involved with Live Journal as a way to share his daily activities, but more importantly, to share his ideas to a wider audience. He grew a cadre of admirers and a few enemies. Nonetheless, his ideas now had a worldwide audience and his influence as a Magickal theorist grew.

Over the next few years, my wife Micha and I travelled to New

Orleans twice to visit them, once for Thanksgiving, and it was always a joyous time as Micha and Raven were like sisters and Alobar and I were always able to pick up like it hadn't been years since we'd last seen each other. Again, marathons of all night talking.

Another few years later, Alobar, Raven, and her new husband Patrick, another ex Typhonian member, travelled to Cincinnati for a deep rite for the benefit of Micha. It was early September of 2001. Micha had been living with Hepatitis C for a number of years from a blood transfusion during a surgery and had taken the allopathic route of chemotherapy with little success. Our intention was to, as a group, contact an entity we named "DRAN". This was a conjunction of DNA/RNA and a designation for the disease within her. We utilized intense entheogenic, ritual and sexual energy to scry the entity to presence. We asked that it not ravage her body as it would lose its "home". We initiated DRAN into the C/A OTO and shared with it as family. I have recently retired from 45 years in the medical field and know of no attempt to "make friends and family" with a disease in any literature. Part of the rite was for each of us to tell DRAN what Micha meant to each of us. Alobar's words of his respect and love for her was amazing. I will never forget the eloquence in that moment of a man who once told me years before that he really didn't know what "love" was. He was able to express it then![6]

The following Monday morning, we were at the airport seeing off Raven and Patrick to Austin Texas and Alobar to New Orleans. On returning home I switched on the tube to see what was going on the last 4 days, only to see one of the Twin Towers in NYC ablaze and immediately see the second plane crash. We had just seen some of our closest friends off on airplanes. In the next eight tense hours we found that Alobar was stranded in Chicago and that Raven and Patrick's plane returned to Cincinnati International and they stayed the next 5 days with us until able to make arrangements to return home. Alobar was a diabetic who was trying to handle the disease by diet and supplementation. Airport food was neither to his taste nor the appropriate fare for a brittle diabetic. As a man with a long grey beard, magenta hair, a wild African shirt and long multi colored fingernails he was easily <u>"overlooked"</u> by the social services at the airport. He was eventually

---

6   Micha went on with relatively low symptomatology of her failing liver till western medicine came up with a medication called Harvoni in 2017. Following a three month course she was able to eradicate it from her body completely and within the ethics of relationship. This medication does not kill anything. Viruses have a short lifespan and survive via rapid reproduction. Harvoni disables the virus ability to replicate itself.

invited to the home of a religious Christian couple as part of a church outreach to folk stranded due to the attack. I remember him saying these people were the closest thing to the Christian ideal of "Love thy neighbor" he had ever met. They provided the diet he needed and helped stabilize him prior to his returning to NOLA.

In the next few years, Alobar continued to live in NOLA and do divination on the square. As previously mentioned he had issues with traditional medical care, and did not want to pursue medications for his high blood sugars. Raven, Patrick, Micha and I combined resources to purchase a state of the art Glucose monitor that did not require sticking the fingers to draw blood. Frequent finger sticks made manipulating the Tarot cards Alobar used for a living very uncomfortable as he monitored 4-5 times a day. He spent enormous amounts of time researching natural supplementation and equally enormous amounts of his earnings on them to keep the damage of high blood sugar at bay. Alobar had no bank account and thus purchased online through Micha and I and reimbursed us. He sometimes took $600 to $800 per month of herbs and supplements. These were questionably helpful as he reported waking one morning with holes chewed in both his feet from rats, and that he was unaware of their chewing. This is known as diabetic neuropathy wherein the nerves, starved of appropriate circulation cease to transmit necessary information to the brain. I remember pleading with him once after hearing this to see a doctor and get on medication, that we would pay for it if he could not. He was adamant, and sadly mostly toothless. Those many nights of high sugar excess while writing had also taken their toll.

He was living in NOLA during hurricane Katrina in 2005; his apartment took on massive amounts of water, and he was forced to evacuate. He ended up living for a few weeks in a garage with a group of folk thrown together by the circumstances. It was reported that Alobar's unsympathetic, matter of fact approach was what helped his group survive in the Wild West environment and predation that was rampant there at the time. In the aftermath, a fellow from Cincinnati who went by the handle Ranger Rick and was a C/A OTO member came to NOLA and assisted Alobar with the recovery of his apartment.

After awhile the communication with Alobar became more infrequent. He stopped purchasing supplements and we heard less of him as time went on. Occasionally I would check into Live Journal to follow his uploads till they began to be more infrequent. I had no contact info and he went dark. I was first notified of Alobar's passing from Jason Miller, the occult author, then Al Basseti, an old member of Hadit chapter who had read it on the Horus Maat Lodge online site. His health had apparently declined so badly that NOLA social services had intervened and Alobar was sent to a nursing facility. Knowing those facilities intimately, and knowing Alobar, it was not an environment for someone like him. I would project he was not an easy client. It was confirmed by Raven, his ex-wife and listed legal "family" that Alobar died of the complications of Covid-19 in an upload to Live Journal July 9th, 2020

I found him a fascinating, yet at times, difficult man. I cannot say I have known a more dedicated person to the idea of personal integrity, self determination and advancement of the Thelemic ideal of DOING one's Will. Remembering the many conversations we had, the ideas shared and the man I admired and have been proud to call my Brother is hard. For all his knowledge and far out ideas, I am also proud to have known the hurt, lonely small child inside him that I was privileged to meet that once told me, "I don't really know what Love is".

During one of the last last conversations we had, I'll never forget his response to my saying "I love you." I have learned to do so to everyone that I do love when parting in person, online, or phone. With my experience of the ephemeral quality of incarnation, it is possible I truly MAY never see them again. Alobar responded "I love you, too, Cliff. Tell Micha I love her, too. Thank you guys for helping me understand what that really means. Talk to you later".

Maybe someday, I will.

Vale Frater!

About Concrescent Press

Concrescent Press is dedicated to publishing advanced magickal practice and Pagan scholarship. It takes advantage of the recent revolution in publishing technology and economics to bring forth works that, previously, might only have been circulated privately. Now, we are growing the future together.

Contact us at ConcrescentLLC@gmail.com

Colophon

This book is made of Minion Pro and 'A Charming Font Expanded' using Adobe InDesign, Illustrator and Photoshop. The sources were typescript or chapbooks printed in dot-matrix and justified, OCR'd and corrected before typesetting. The book was designed and typeset by Sam Webster, who drew all of the vector art from PVN's sketches. Some of those sketches are used herein. Don Karr drew the fine line art in the *Chalice of Ecstasy* and the *Rose of Charon*.

Visit our website at
www.Concrescent.net

www.ingramcontent.com/pod-product-compliance
Lightning Source LLC
Chambersburg PA
CBHW081754300426
44116CB00014B/2110